MARVEL .1

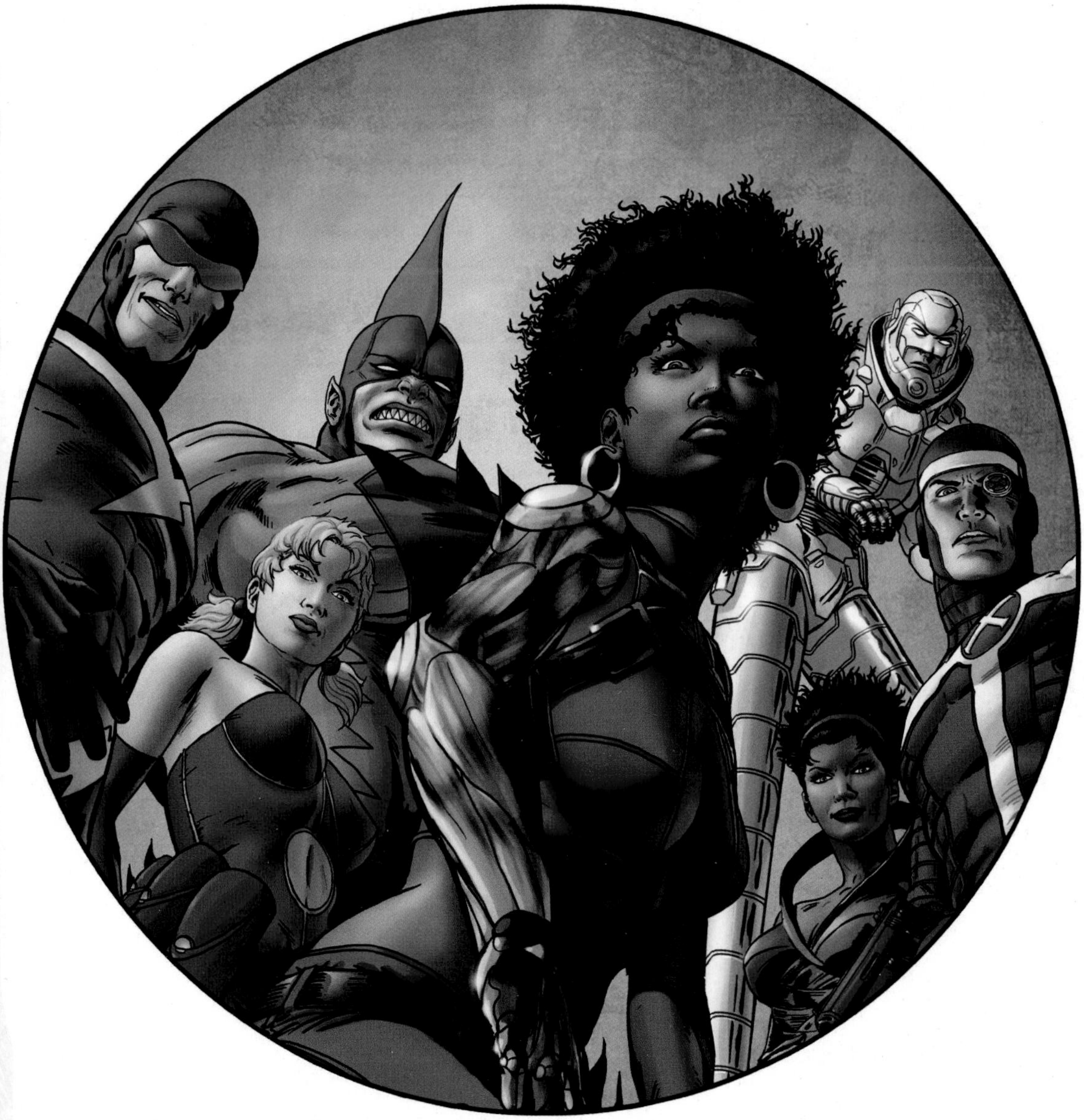

WRITERS

GREG PAK, FRED VAN LENTE, CHRISTOS GAGE, ROB WILLIAMS,
NICK SPENCER, ROB RODI, VICTOR GISCHLER, DAVID LISS,
BRIAN MICHAEL BENDIS, JEFF PARKER, PETER DAVID,
DAN ABNETT AND ANDY LANNING

ARTISTS

BEN OLIVER WITH DAN GREEN; SEAN CHEN & SCOTT HANNA;
MATTHEW CLARK & SEAN PARSONS; RON GARNEY; MIKE GRELL,
JASON PAZ & JEFF HUET; KANO; PASQUAL FERRY; WILL CONRAD;
JEFTE PALO; NEAL ADAMS & TOM PALMER; DECLAN SHALVEY;
VALENTINE DE LANDRO & PAT DAVIDSON; AND RENATO ARLEM

COLORISTS

FRANK MARTIN, JEROMY COX, ROBERT SCHWAGER,
JASON KEITH, JESUS ABURTOV, FRANK D'ARMATA, BRIAN REBER,
JEAN-FRANCOIS BEAULIEU, PAUL MOUNTS AND JAY DAVID RAMOS

LETTERERS

SIMON BOWLAND, VC'S JOE CARAMAGNA, VC'S CLAYTON COWLES
AND VC'S CORY PETIT

ASSISTANT EDITORS

JAKE THOMAS, JOHN DENNING, SEBASTIAN GIRNER, JODY LEHEUP,
JORDAN D. WHITE AND RACHEL PINNELAS

EDITORS

BILL ROSEMANN, JEANINE SCHAEFER, ALEJANDRO ARBONA,
TOM BRENNAN, LAUREN SANKOVITCH, DANIEL KETCHUM,
MARK PANICCIA, STEPHEN WACKER, NICK LOWE, RALPH MACCHIO
AND TOM BREVOORT

COVER ARTISTS

PHIL JIMENEZ & FRANK D'ARMATA; BILLY TAN & LEONARDO OLEA;
ARTURO LOZZI & MARTE GRACIA; GIUSEPPE CAMUNCOLI &
MARTE GRACIA; CARLO PAGULAYAN, JASON PAZ &
CHRIS SOTOMAYOR; SALVADOR LARROCA & FRANK D'ARMATA;
PASQUAL FERRY; JASON PEARSON; PATRICK ZIRCHER & ANDY TROY;
NEAL ADAMS & PAUL MOUNTS; ROBERTO DE LA TORRE
& DAN BROWN; AND DAVID YARDIN O

COLLECTION EDITOR: JENNIFER GRÜNWALD
ASSISTANT EDITORS: ALEX STARBUCK & NELSON RIBEIRO
EDITOR, SPECIAL PROJECTS: MARK D. BEAZLEY
SENIOR EDITOR, SPECIAL PROJECTS: JEFF YOUNGQUIST
SENIOR VICE PRESIDENT OF SALES: DAVID GABRIEL
SVP OF BRAND PLANNING & COMMUNICATIONS: MICHAEL PASCIULLO
BOOK DESIGN: JEFF POWELL

EDITOR IN CHIEF: AXEL ALONSO
CHIEF CREATIVE OFFICER: JOE QUESADA
PUBLISHER: DAN BUCKLEY
EXECUTIVE PRODUCER: ALAN FINE

CUP O' JOE

JOE QUESADA TALKS ABOUT THE MARVEL POINT ONE INITIATIVE!

If there was ever such a thing as a First Commandment of Comics, it would have to be Stan Lee's old adage that "every comic is someone's first."

Over the course of our history, we've always taken that rule very seriously and now we've decided to emphasize the point with our new Marvel: Point One initiative.

Okay, okay, I know what you're thinking, "Gee, JQ, what the heck is Marvel: Point One?" I'm so glad you asked! Each of our top titles will be getting a special, low-priced Point One issue that offers a chance for both longtime Marvelites to catch up on a book they may have overlooked, and a perfect jumping on point for readers just getting interested in Marvel Comics and our mind-blowing universe. These entirely self-contained stories are must-read road maps that'll be setting everyone from the Amazing Spider-Man to the Uncanny X-Force out on their next year's worth of adventures. And who better to tell these tales than some of the very best talents working in the world of comics today!

Now while it's almost impossible for me to imagine a world in which there are people who aren't familiar with the goings on in the Marvel Universe, each of these stories is one that any dedicated Marvel fan can hand to a friend, a relative, a colleague or even some stranger on the street, and all would enjoy the eye-popping action, explosive excitement and heartfelt tales of heroism with no need for explanations, footnotes or encyclopedic knowledge of the MU (that's Marvel Universe for you new kids — see, you already learned something). So whether you're a new fan to the fold, or a certified True Believer, there's never been a better chance to jump head first into the unexplored corners of the Marvel Universe — a place where, above all, anything is possible.

MARVEL POINT ONE II. Contains material originally published in magazine form as ALPHA FLIGHT #0.1, DAKEN: DARK WOLVERINE #9.1, AVENGERS ACADEMY #14.1, GHOST RIDER #0.1, IRON MAN 2.0 #7.1, X-MEN #15.1, HERC #6.1, JOURNEY INTO MYSTERY #626.1, X-FACTOR #224.1, VILLAINS FOR HIRE #0.1, THUNDERBOLTS #163.1, BLACK PANTHER: THE DEADLIEST MAN ALIVE #523.1 and NEW AVENGERS #16.1. First printing 2012. ISBN# 978-0-7851-6231-5. Published by MARVEL WORLDWIDE, INC., a subsidiary of MARVEL ENTERTAINMENT, LLC. OFFICE OF PUBLICATION: 135 West 50th Street, New York, NY 10020. Copyright © 2011 and 2012 Marvel Characters, Inc. All rights reserved. $24.99 per copy in the U.S. and $27.99 in Canada (GST #R127032852); Canadian Agreement #40668537. All characters featured in this issue and the distinctive names and likenesses thereof, and all related indicia are trademarks of Marvel Characters, Inc. No similarity between any of the names, characters, persons, and/or institutions in this magazine with those of any living or dead person or institution is intended, and any such similarity which may exist is purely coincidental. Printed in the U.S.A. ALAN FINE, EVP - Office of the President, Marvel Worldwide, Inc. and EVP & CMO Marvel Characters B.V.; DAN BUCKLEY, Publisher & President - Print, Animation & Digital Divisions; JOE QUESADA, Chief Creative Officer; DAVID BOGART, SVP of Business Affairs & Talent Management; TOM BREVOORT, SVP of Publishing; C.B. CEBULSKI, SVP of Creator & Content Development; DAVID GABRIEL, SVP of Publishing Sales & Circulation; MICHAEL PASCIULLO, SVP of Brand Planning & Communications; JIM O'KEEFE, VP of Operations & Logistics; DAN CARR, Executive Director of Publishing Technology; SUSAN CRESPI, Editorial Operations Manager; ALEX MORALES, Publishing Operations Manager; STAN LEE, Chairman Emeritus. For information regarding advertising in Marvel Comics or on Marvel.com, please contact John Dokes, SVP Integrated Sales and Marketing, at jdokes@marvel.com. For Marvel subscription inquiries, please call 800-217-9158. Manufactured between 12/15/2011 and 1/3/2012 by QUAD/GRAPHICS, DUBUQUE, IA, USA.

10 9 8 7 6 5 4 3 2 1

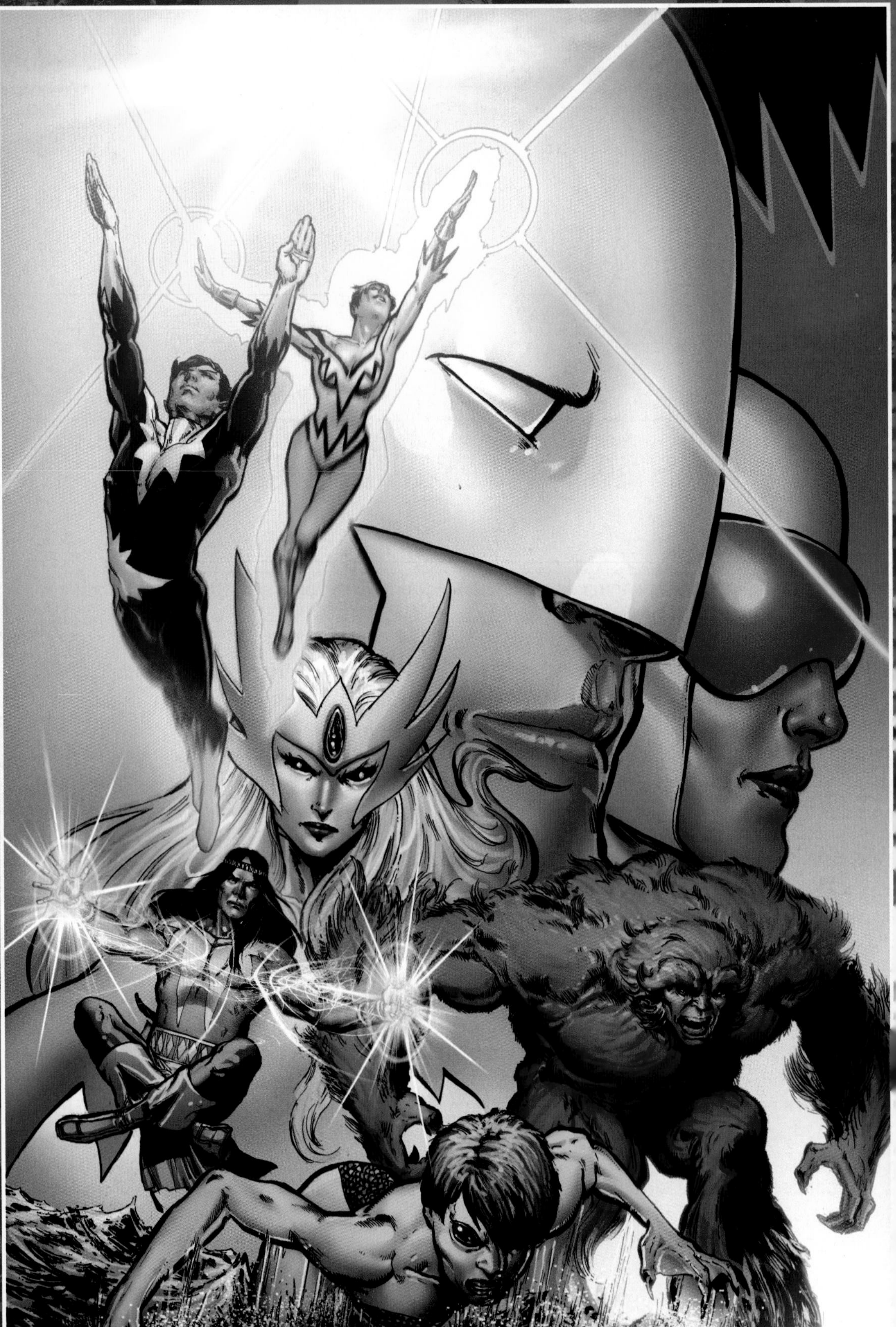

ALPHA FLIGHT #0.1

In the midst of the Chaos War some of the world's mightiest heroes were brought back from the dead. Amongst them were members of Canada's premier super hero group, Alpha Flight. Now reunited, original members Guardian, Vindicator, Sasquatch, Shaman, Snowbird, Northstar, Aurora and Marrina have once again taken up the call to protect their country against all enemies, foreign and domestic. They are strong. They are on guard. They are ...

ALPHA FLIGHT

Writers:
GREG PAK AND
FRED VAN LENTE

Artist:
BEN OLIVER
w/ DAN GREEN

Colorist:
FRANK MARTIN

Lettering:
SIMON BOWLAND

Cover:
PHIL JIMENEZ AND FRANK
D'ARMATA

Production:
TAYLOR ESPOSITO

Assistant Editor:
JAKE THOMAS

Editor:
MARK PANICCIA

Editor in Chief:
AXEL ALONSO

Chief Creative Officer:
JOE QUESADA

Publisher:
DAN BUCKLEY

Executive Producer:
ALAN FINE

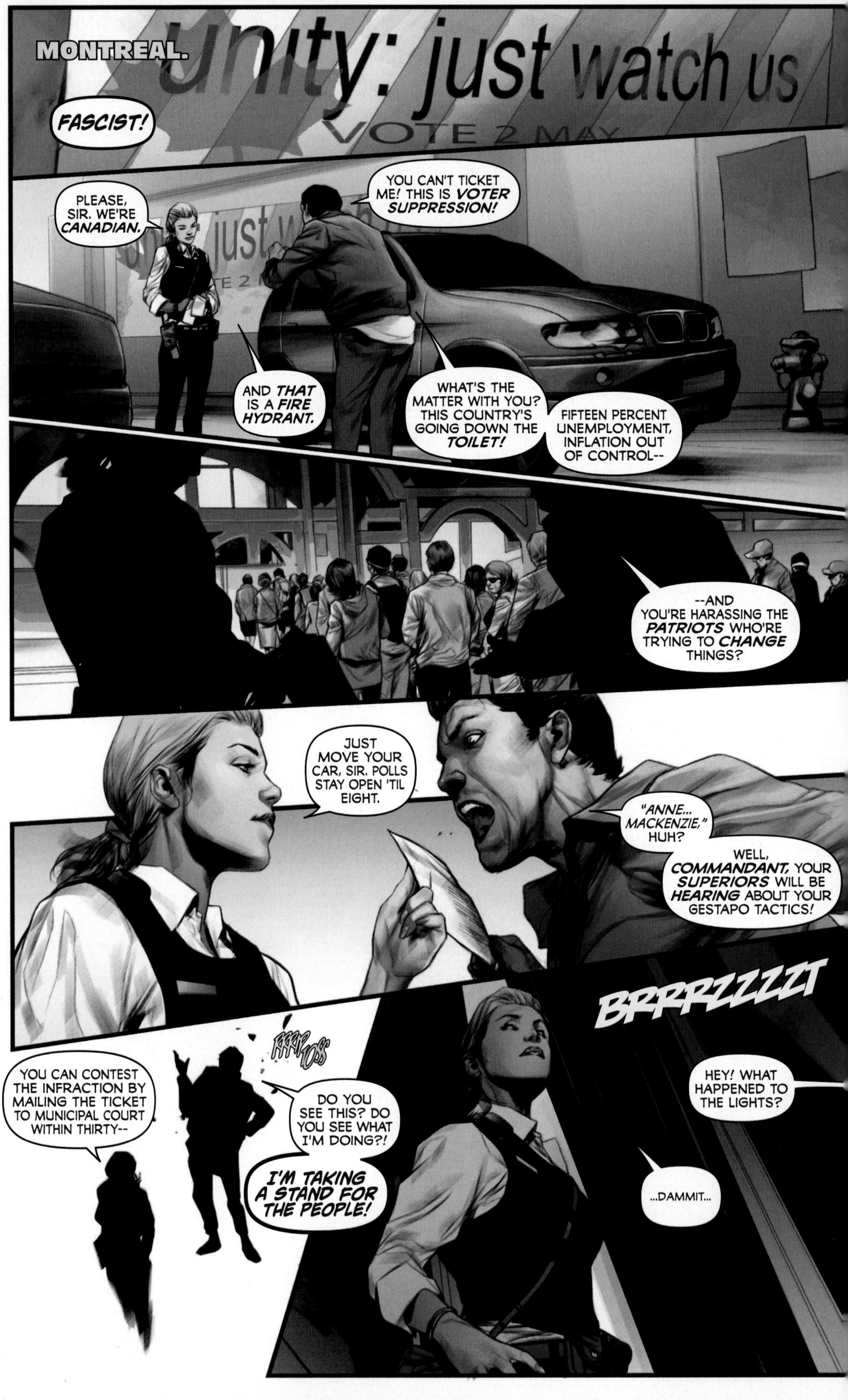
MONTREAL.
unity: just watch us
VOTE 2 MAY
FASCIST!
PLEASE, SIR. WE'RE CANADIAN.
YOU CAN'T TICKET ME! THIS IS VOTER SUPPRESSION!
AND THAT IS A FIRE HYDRANT.
WHAT'S THE MATTER WITH YOU? THIS COUNTRY'S GOING DOWN THE TOILET!
FIFTEEN PERCENT UNEMPLOYMENT, INFLATION OUT OF CONTROL--
--AND YOU'RE HARASSING THE PATRIOTS WHO'RE TRYING TO CHANGE THINGS?
JUST MOVE YOUR CAR, SIR. POLLS STAY OPEN 'TIL EIGHT.
"ANNE... MACKENZIE," HUH?
WELL, COMMANDANT, YOUR SUPERIORS WILL BE HEARING ABOUT YOUR GESTAPO TACTICS!
YOU CAN CONTEST THE INFRACTION BY MAILING THE TICKET TO MUNICIPAL COURT WITHIN THIRTY--
DO YOU SEE THIS? DO YOU SEE WHAT I'M DOING?!
I'M TAKING A STAND FOR THE PEOPLE!
BRRRZZZZZT
HEY! WHAT HAPPENED TO THE LIGHTS?
...DAMMIT...

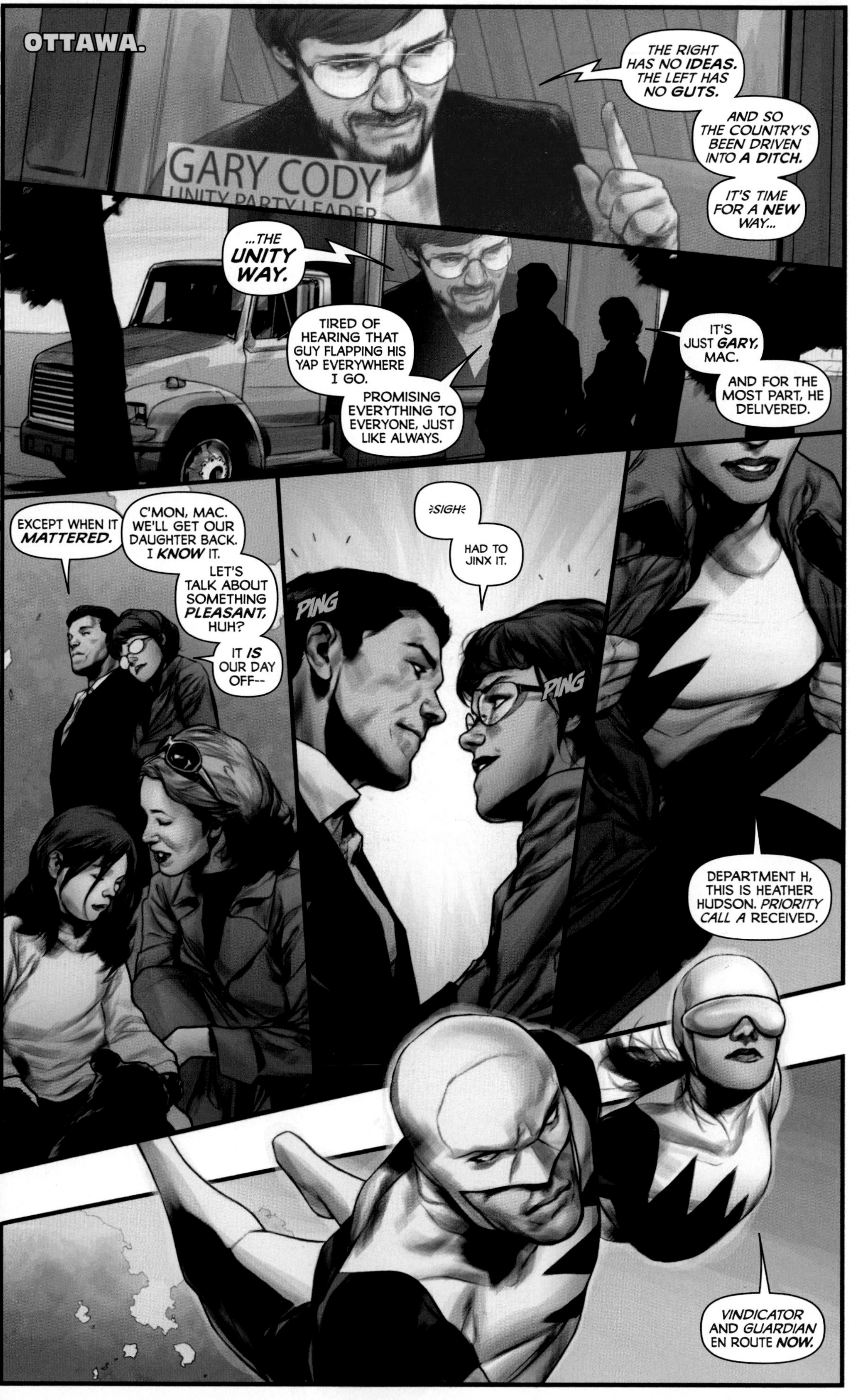
OTTAWA.
THE RIGHT HAS NO IDEAS. THE LEFT HAS NO GUTS.
AND SO THE COUNTRY'S BEEN DRIVEN INTO A DITCH.
IT'S TIME FOR A NEW WAY...
GARY CODY
...THE UNITY WAY.
TIRED OF HEARING THAT GUY FLAPPING HIS YAP EVERYWHERE I GO.
PROMISING EVERYTHING TO EVERYONE, JUST LIKE ALWAYS.
IT'S JUST GARY, MAC.
AND FOR THE MOST PART, HE DELIVERED.
EXCEPT WHEN IT MATTERED.
C'MON, MAC. WE'LL GET OUR DAUGHTER BACK. I KNOW IT.
LET'S TALK ABOUT SOMETHING PLEASANT, HUH?
IT IS OUR DAY OFF--
SIGH
HAD TO JINX IT.
PING
PING
DEPARTMENT H, THIS IS HEATHER HUDSON. PRIORITY CALL A RECEIVED.
VINDICATOR AND GUARDIAN EN ROUTE NOW.

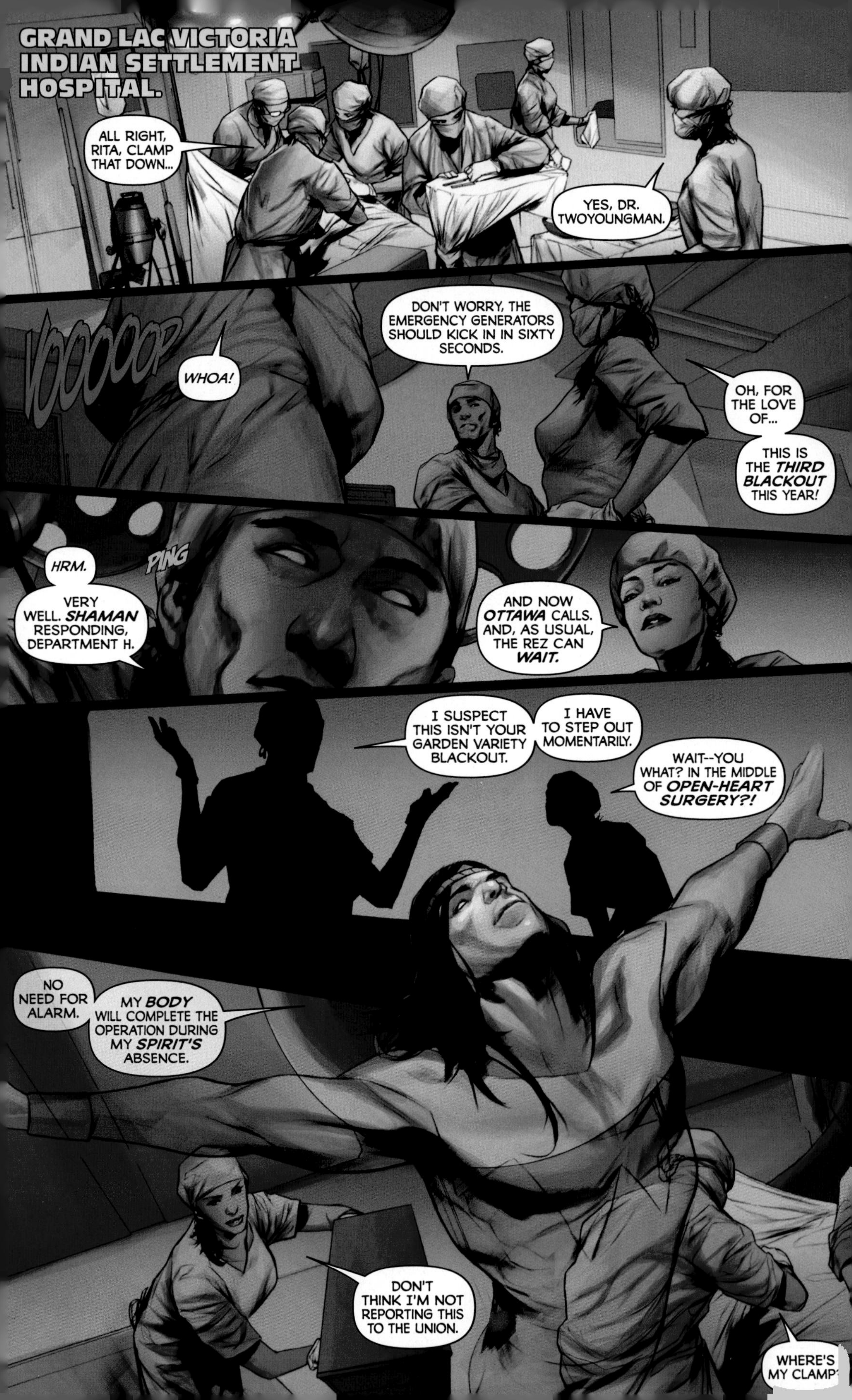
GRAND LAC VICTORIA INDIAN SETTLEMENT HOSPITAL.
ALL RIGHT, RITA, CLAMP THAT DOWN...
YES, DR. TWOYOUNGMAN.
VOOOOOP
WHOA!
DON'T WORRY, THE EMERGENCY GENERATORS SHOULD KICK IN IN SIXTY SECONDS.
OH, FOR THE LOVE OF...
THIS IS THE THIRD BLACKOUT THIS YEAR!
HRM.
PING
VERY WELL. SHAMAN RESPONDING, DEPARTMENT H.
AND NOW OTTAWA CALLS. AND, AS USUAL, THE REZ CAN WAIT.
I SUSPECT THIS ISN'T YOUR GARDEN VARIETY BLACKOUT.
I HAVE TO STEP OUT MOMENTARILY.
WAIT--YOU WHAT? IN THE MIDDLE OF OPEN-HEART SURGERY?!
NO NEED FOR ALARM.
MY BODY WILL COMPLETE THE OPERATION DURING MY SPIRIT'S ABSENCE.
DON'T THINK I'M NOT REPORTING THIS TO THE UNION.
WHERE'S MY CLAMP?

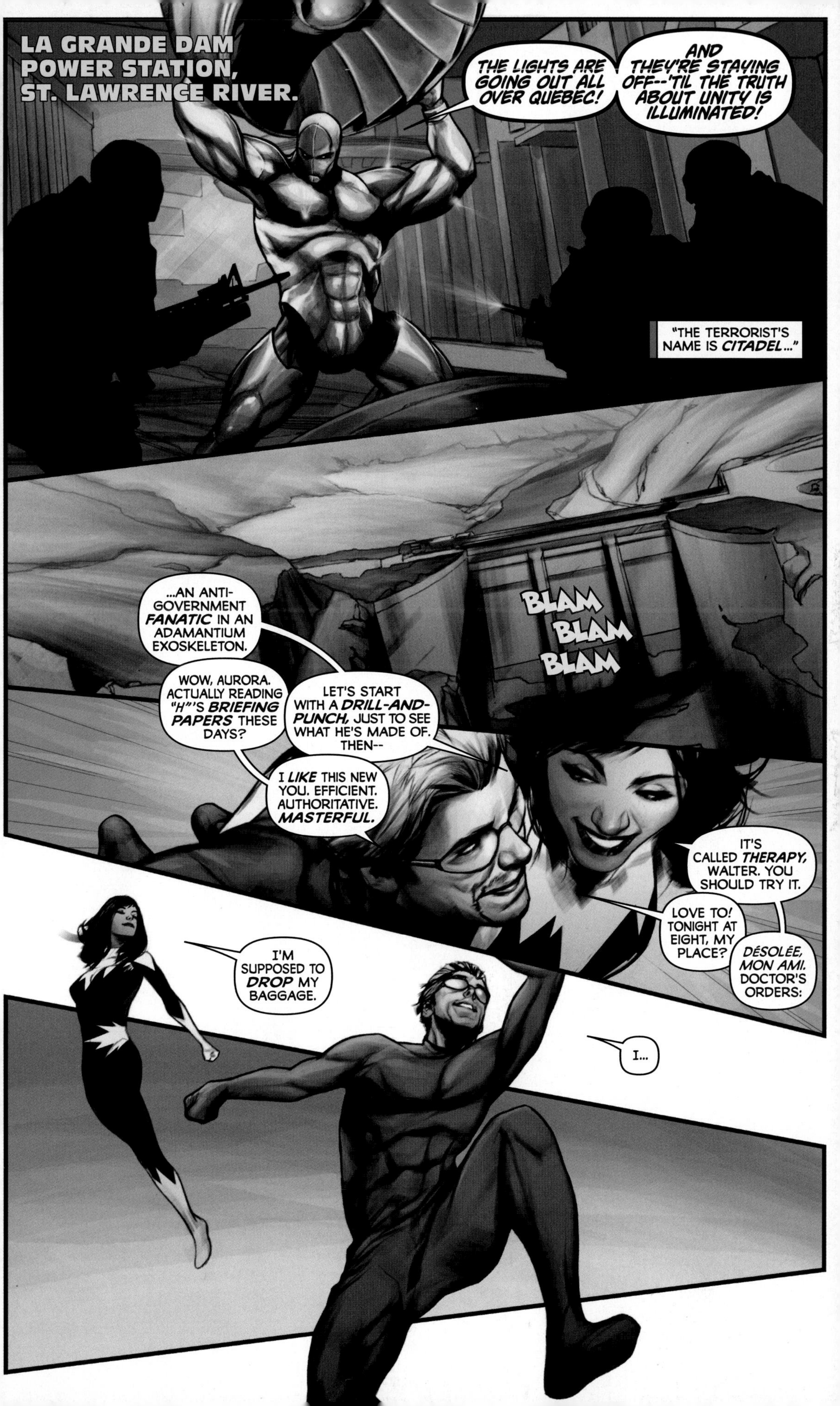
LA GRANDE DAM POWER STATION, ST. LAWRENCE RIVER.
THE LIGHTS ARE GOING OUT ALL OVER QUEBEC!
AND THEY'RE STAYING OFF--'TIL THE TRUTH ABOUT UNITY IS ILLUMINATED!
"THE TERRORIST'S NAME IS CITADEL..."
...AN ANTI-GOVERNMENT FANATIC IN AN ADAMANTIUM EXOSKELETON.
BLAM BLAM BLAM
WOW, AURORA. ACTUALLY READING "H"'S BRIEFING PAPERS THESE DAYS?
LET'S START WITH A DRILL-AND-PUNCH, JUST TO SEE WHAT HE'S MADE OF. THEN--
I LIKE THIS NEW YOU. EFFICIENT. AUTHORITATIVE. MASTERFUL.
IT'S CALLED THERAPY, WALTER. YOU SHOULD TRY IT.
LOVE TO! TONIGHT AT EIGHT, MY PLACE?
DÉSOLÉE, MON AMI. DOCTOR'S ORDERS:
I'M SUPPOSED TO DROP MY BAGGAGE.
I...

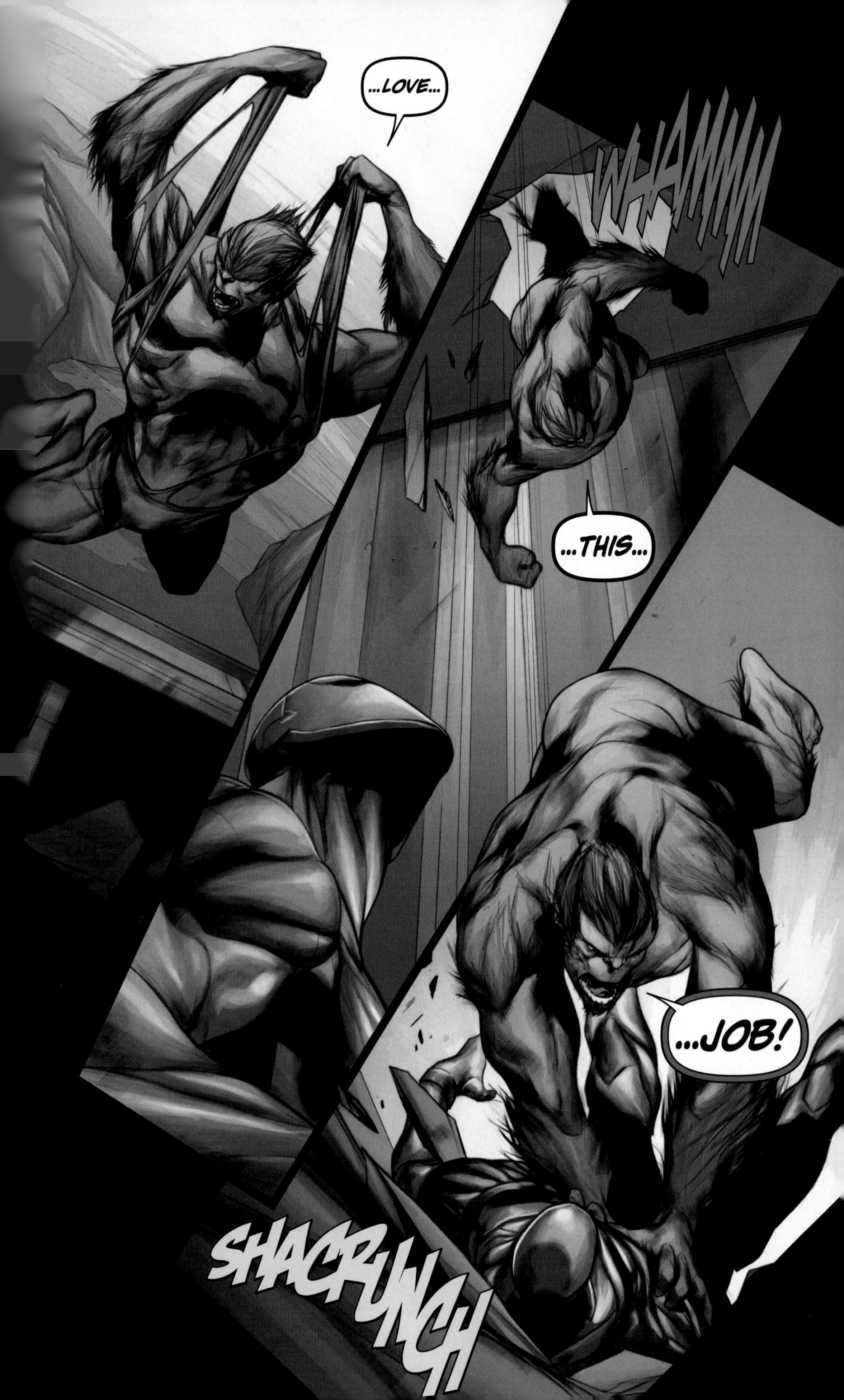
...LOVE...
WHAMMM
...THIS...
...JOB!
SHACRUNCH

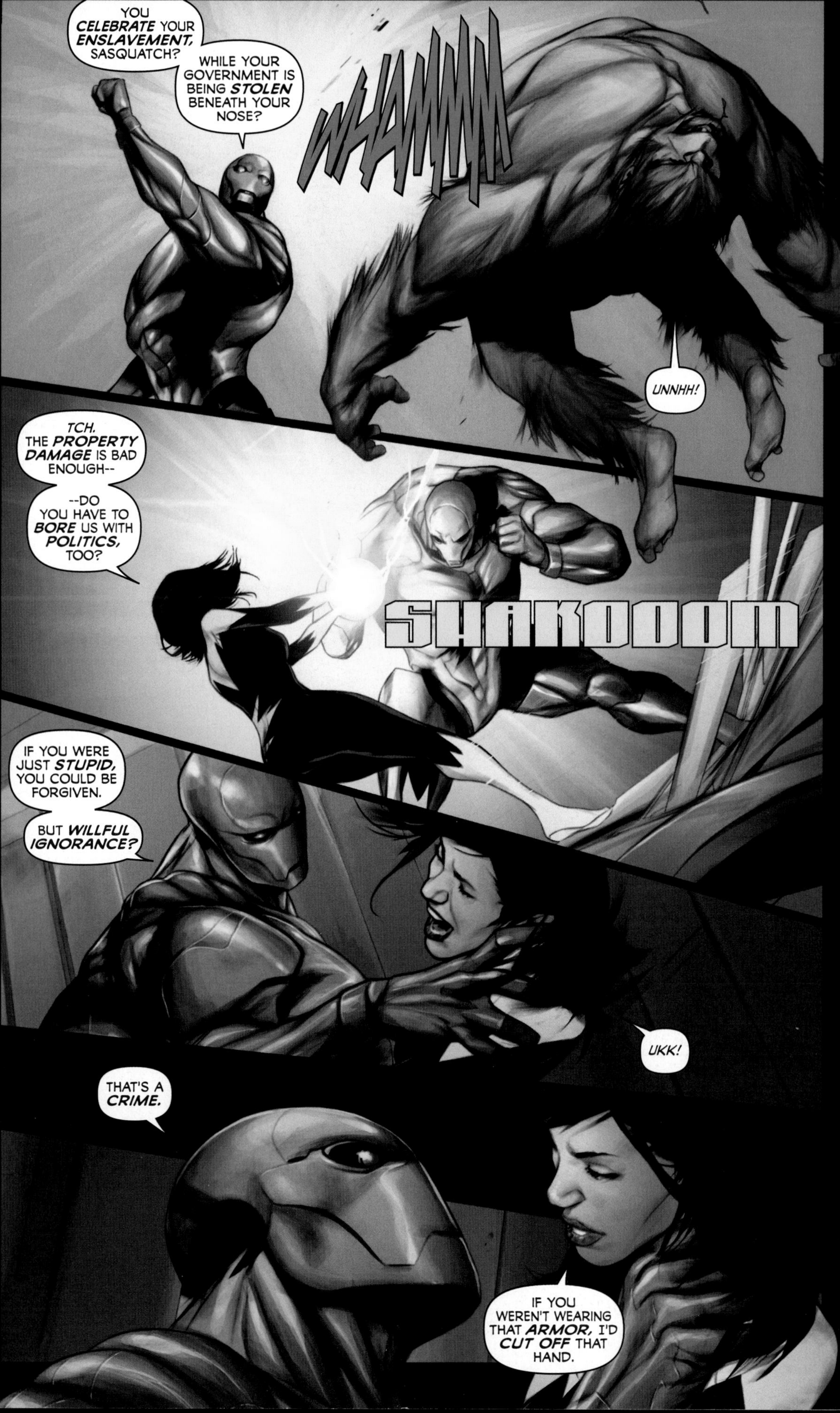
YOU CELEBRATE YOUR ENSLAVEMENT, SASQUATCH?
WHILE YOUR GOVERNMENT IS BEING STOLEN BENEATH YOUR NOSE?
WHAMMM
UNNHH!
TCH. THE PROPERTY DAMAGE IS BAD ENOUGH--
--DO YOU HAVE TO BORE US WITH POLITICS, TOO?
SHAKOOOM
IF YOU WERE JUST STUPID, YOU COULD BE FORGIVEN.
BUT WILLFUL IGNORANCE?
UKK!
THAT'S A CRIME.
IF YOU WEREN'T WEARING THAT ARMOR, I'D CUT OFF THAT HAND.

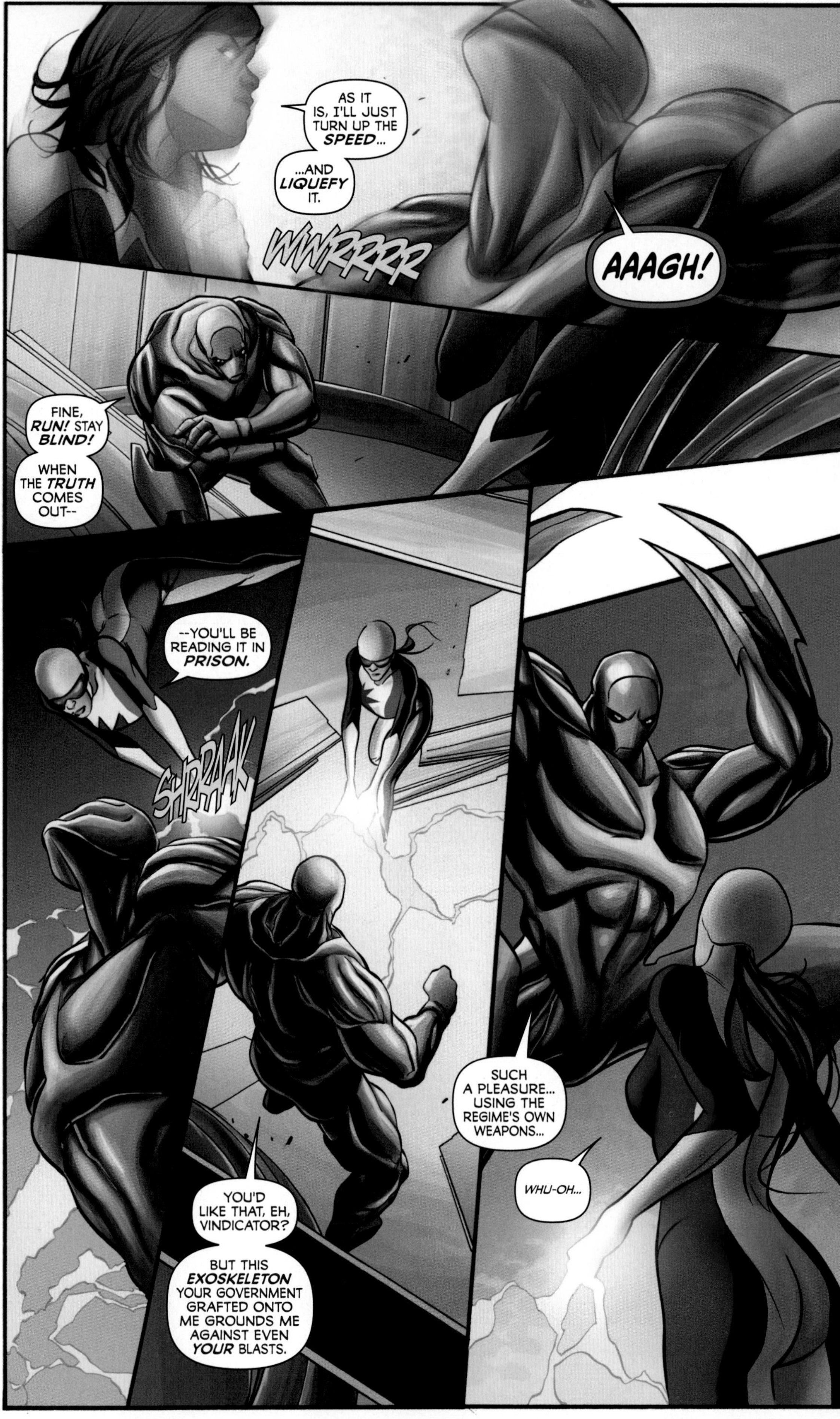
AS IT IS, I'LL JUST TURN UP THE SPEED...
...AND LIQUEFY IT.
WWRRRR
AAAGH!
FINE, RUN! STAY BLIND!
WHEN THE TRUTH COMES OUT--
--YOU'LL BE READING IT IN PRISON.
SHRAAK
YOU'D LIKE THAT, EH, VINDICATOR?
BUT THIS EXOSKELETON YOUR GOVERNMENT GRAFTED ONTO ME GROUNDS ME AGAINST EVEN YOUR BLASTS.
SUCH A PLEASURE... USING THE REGIME'S OWN WEAPONS...
WHU-OH...

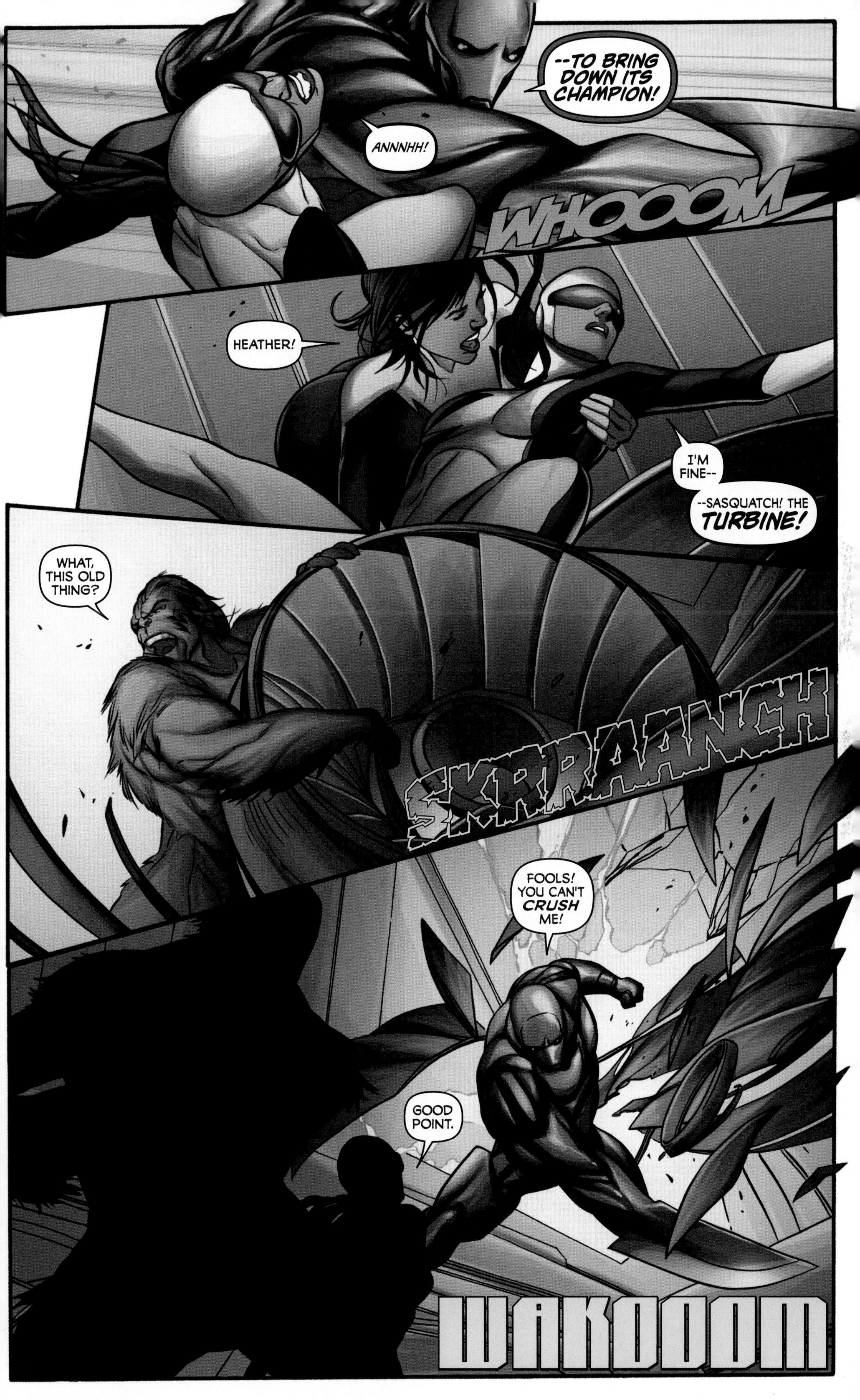
--TO BRING DOWN ITS CHAMPION!
ANNNHH!
WHOOOOM
HEATHER!
I'M FINE--
--SASQUATCH! THE TURBINE!
WHAT, THIS OLD THING?
SKRRAANCH
FOOLS! YOU CAN'T CRUSH ME!
GOOD POINT.
WAKOOOM

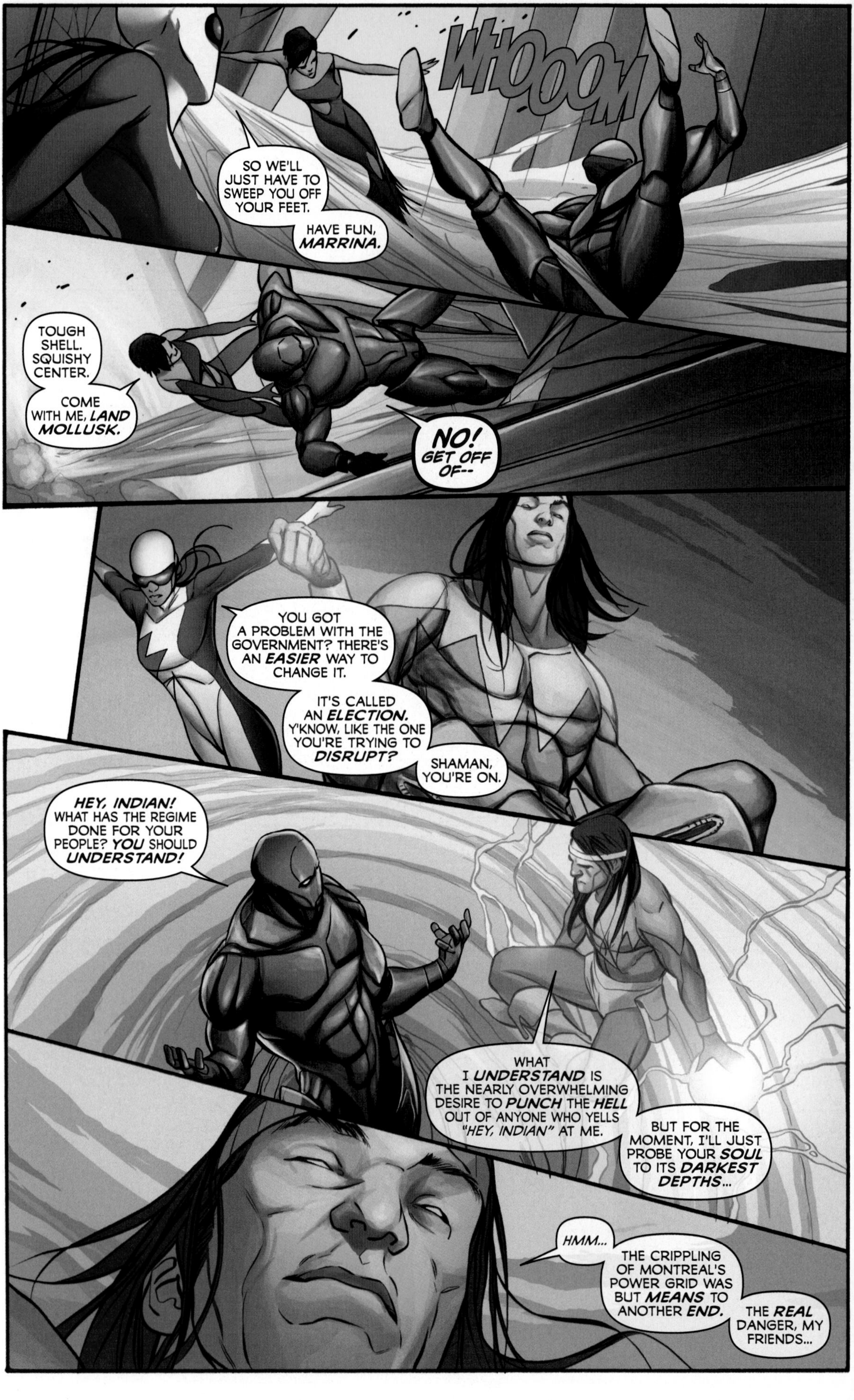
WHOOOM
SO WE'LL JUST HAVE TO SWEEP YOU OFF YOUR FEET.
HAVE FUN, MARRINA.
TOUGH SHELL. SQUISHY CENTER.
COME WITH ME, LAND MOLLUSK.
NO! GET OFF OF--
YOU GOT A PROBLEM WITH THE GOVERNMENT? THERE'S AN EASIER WAY TO CHANGE IT.
IT'S CALLED AN ELECTION. Y'KNOW, LIKE THE ONE YOU'RE TRYING TO DISRUPT?
SHAMAN, YOU'RE ON.
HEY, INDIAN! WHAT HAS THE REGIME DONE FOR YOUR PEOPLE? YOU SHOULD UNDERSTAND!
WHAT I UNDERSTAND IS THE NEARLY OVERWHELMING DESIRE TO PUNCH THE HELL OUT OF ANYONE WHO YELLS "HEY, INDIAN" AT ME.
BUT FOR THE MOMENT, I'LL JUST PROBE YOUR SOUL TO ITS DARKEST DEPTHS...
HMM...
THE CRIPPLING OF MONTREAL'S POWER GRID WAS BUT MEANS TO ANOTHER END.
THE REAL DANGER, MY FRIENDS...

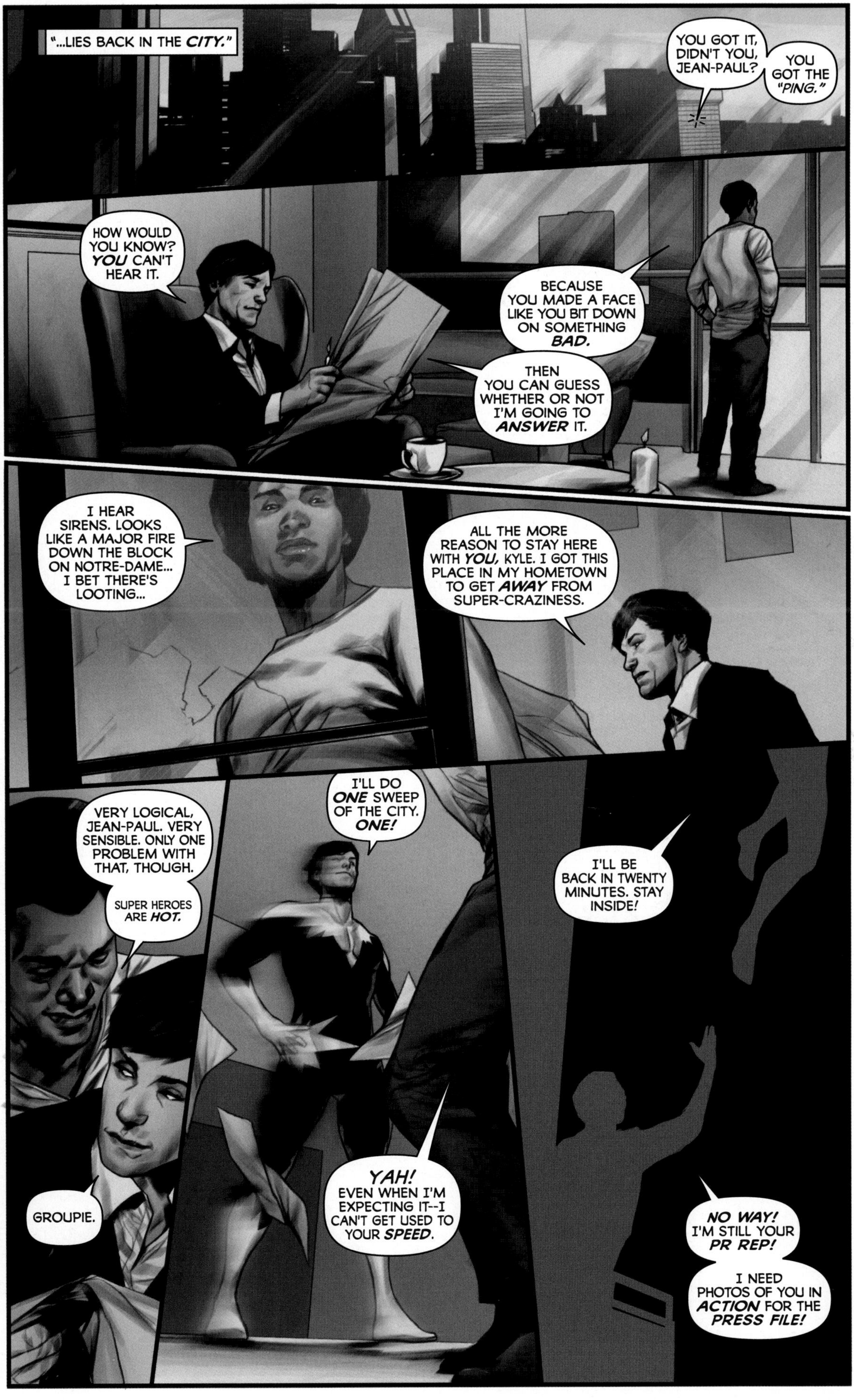
"...LIES BACK IN THE CITY."
YOU GOT IT, DIDN'T YOU, JEAN-PAUL?
YOU GOT THE "PING."
HOW WOULD YOU KNOW? YOU CAN'T HEAR IT.
BECAUSE YOU MADE A FACE LIKE YOU BIT DOWN ON SOMETHING BAD.
THEN YOU CAN GUESS WHETHER OR NOT I'M GOING TO ANSWER IT.
I HEAR SIRENS. LOOKS LIKE A MAJOR FIRE DOWN THE BLOCK ON NOTRE-DAME... I BET THERE'S LOOTING...
ALL THE MORE REASON TO STAY HERE WITH YOU, KYLE. I GOT THIS PLACE IN MY HOMETOWN TO GET AWAY FROM SUPER-CRAZINESS.
VERY LOGICAL, JEAN-PAUL. VERY SENSIBLE. ONLY ONE PROBLEM WITH THAT, THOUGH.
SUPER HEROES ARE HOT.
GROUPIE.
I'LL DO ONE SWEEP OF THE CITY. ONE!
YAH! EVEN WHEN I'M EXPECTING IT--I CAN'T GET USED TO YOUR SPEED.
I'LL BE BACK IN TWENTY MINUTES. STAY INSIDE!
NO WAY! I'M STILL YOUR PR REP!
I NEED PHOTOS OF YOU IN ACTION FOR THE PRESS FILE!

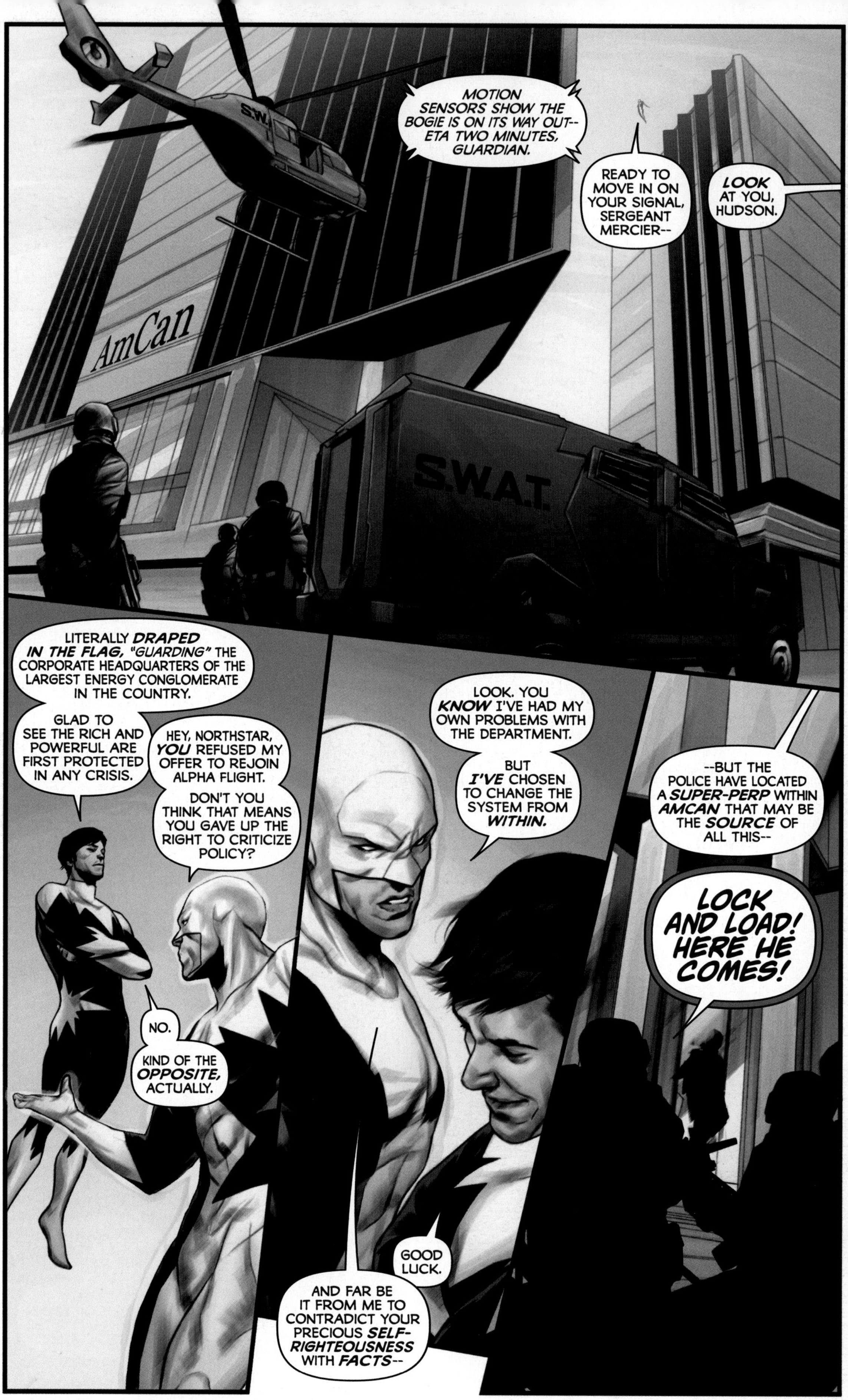
MOTION SENSORS SHOW THE BOGIE IS ON ITS WAY OUT--ETA TWO MINUTES, GUARDIAN.
READY TO MOVE IN ON YOUR SIGNAL, SERGEANT MERCIER--
LOOK AT YOU, HUDSON.
AmCan
S.W.A.T.
LITERALLY DRAPED IN THE FLAG, "GUARDING" THE CORPORATE HEADQUARTERS OF THE LARGEST ENERGY CONGLOMERATE IN THE COUNTRY.
GLAD TO SEE THE RICH AND POWERFUL ARE FIRST PROTECTED IN ANY CRISIS.
HEY, NORTHSTAR, YOU REFUSED MY OFFER TO REJOIN ALPHA FLIGHT.
DON'T YOU THINK THAT MEANS YOU GAVE UP THE RIGHT TO CRITICIZE POLICY?
NO.
KIND OF THE OPPOSITE, ACTUALLY.
LOOK. YOU KNOW I'VE HAD MY OWN PROBLEMS WITH THE DEPARTMENT.
BUT I'VE CHOSEN TO CHANGE THE SYSTEM FROM WITHIN.
AND FAR BE IT FROM ME TO CONTRADICT YOUR PRECIOUS SELF-RIGHTEOUSNESS WITH FACTS--
GOOD LUCK.
--BUT THE POLICE HAVE LOCATED A SUPER-PERP WITHIN AMCAN THAT MAY BE THE SOURCE OF ALL THIS--
LOCK AND LOAD! HERE HE COMES!

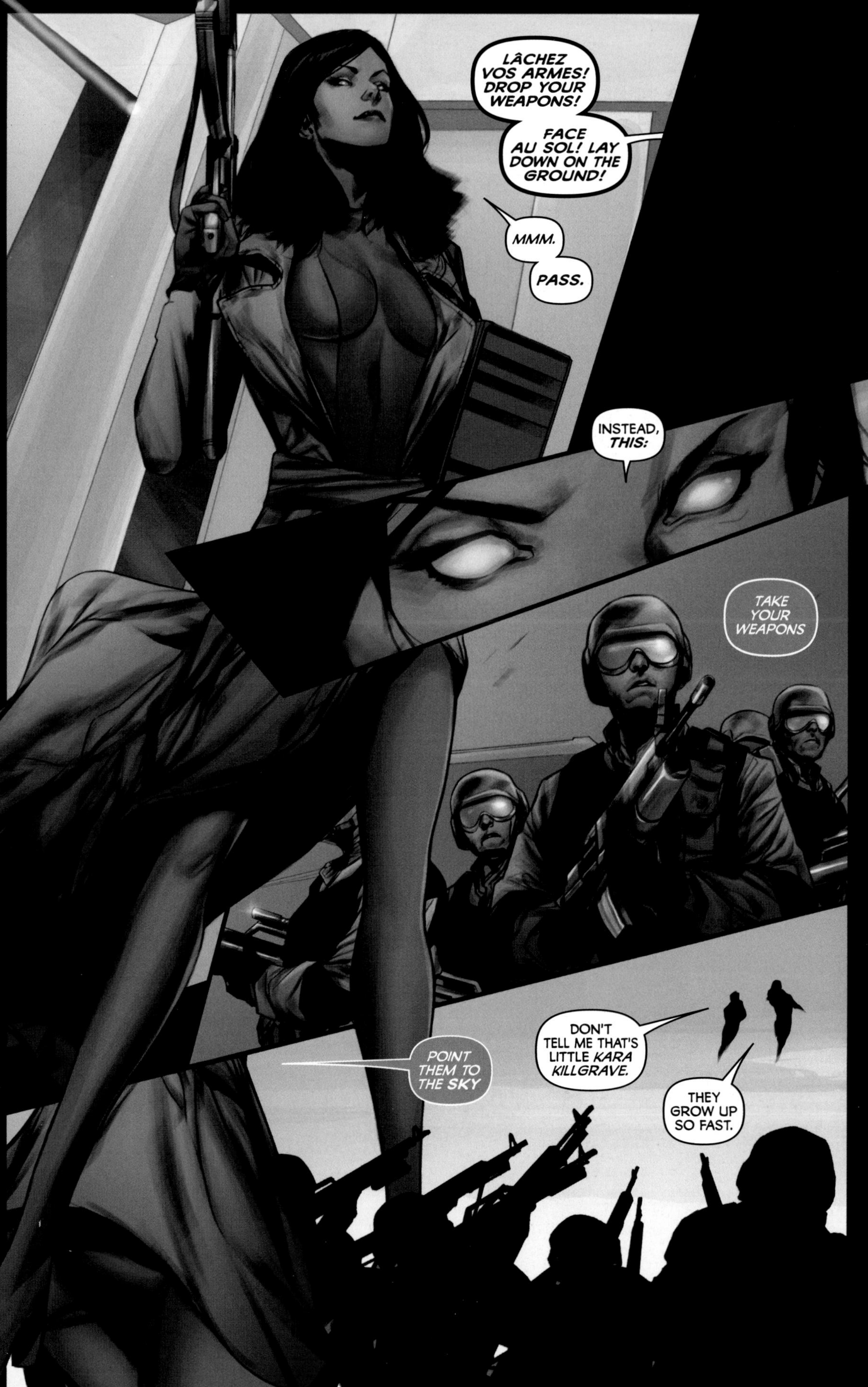
LÂCHEZ VOS ARMES! DROP YOUR WEAPONS!
FACE AU SOL! LAY DOWN ON THE GROUND!
MMM.
PASS.
INSTEAD, THIS:
TAKE YOUR WEAPONS
POINT THEM TO THE SKY
DON'T TELL ME THAT'S LITTLE KARA KILLGRAVE.
THEY GROW UP SO FAST.

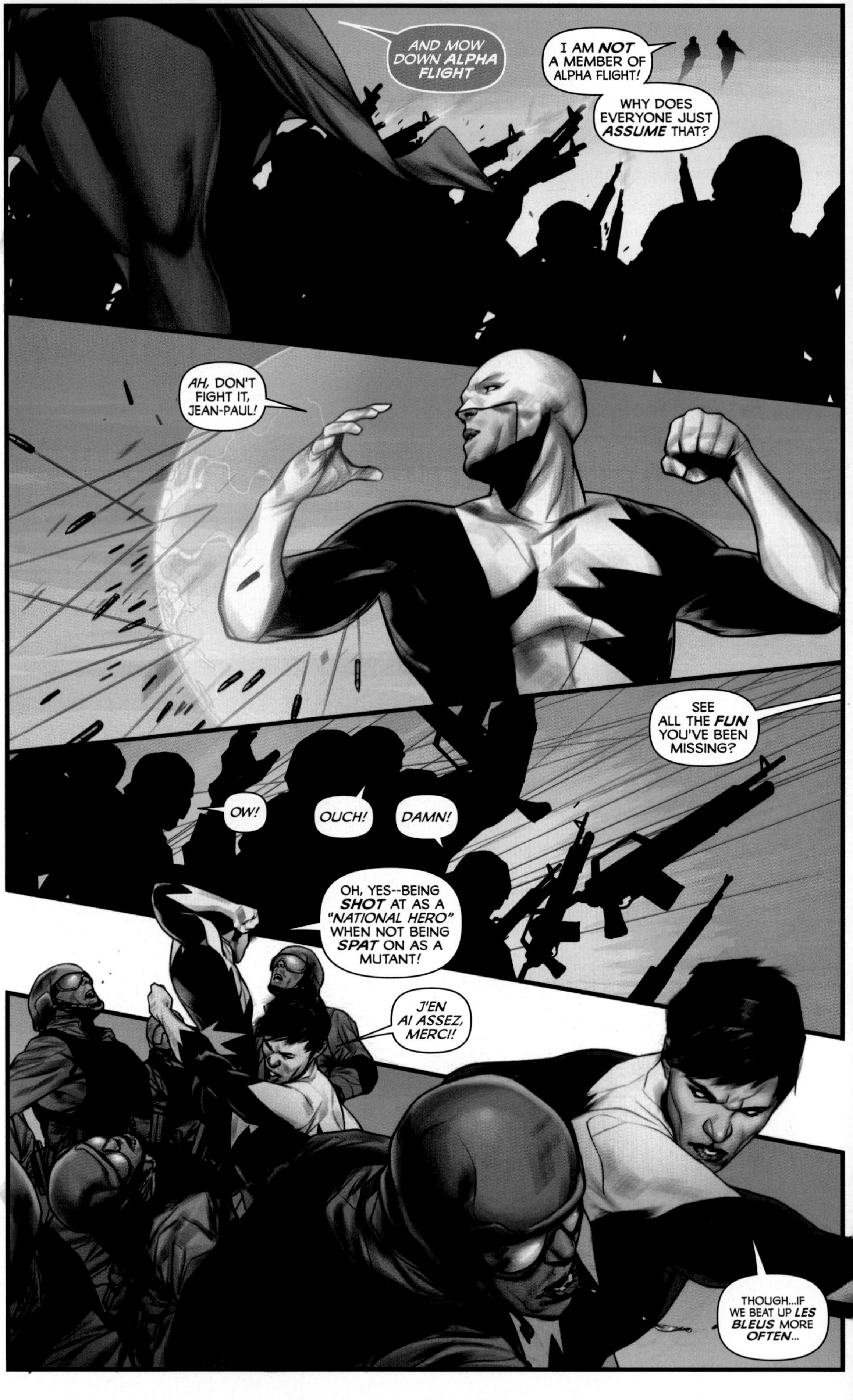
AND MOW DOWN ALPHA FLIGHT
I AM NOT A MEMBER OF ALPHA FLIGHT!
WHY DOES EVERYONE JUST ASSUME THAT?
AH, DON'T FIGHT IT, JEAN-PAUL!
SEE ALL THE FUN YOU'VE BEEN MISSING?
OW!
OUCH!
DAMN!
OH, YES--BEING SHOT AT AS A "NATIONAL HERO" WHEN NOT BEING SPAT ON AS A MUTANT!
J'EN AI ASSEZ, MERCI!
THOUGH...IF WE BEAT UP LES BLEUS MORE OFTEN...

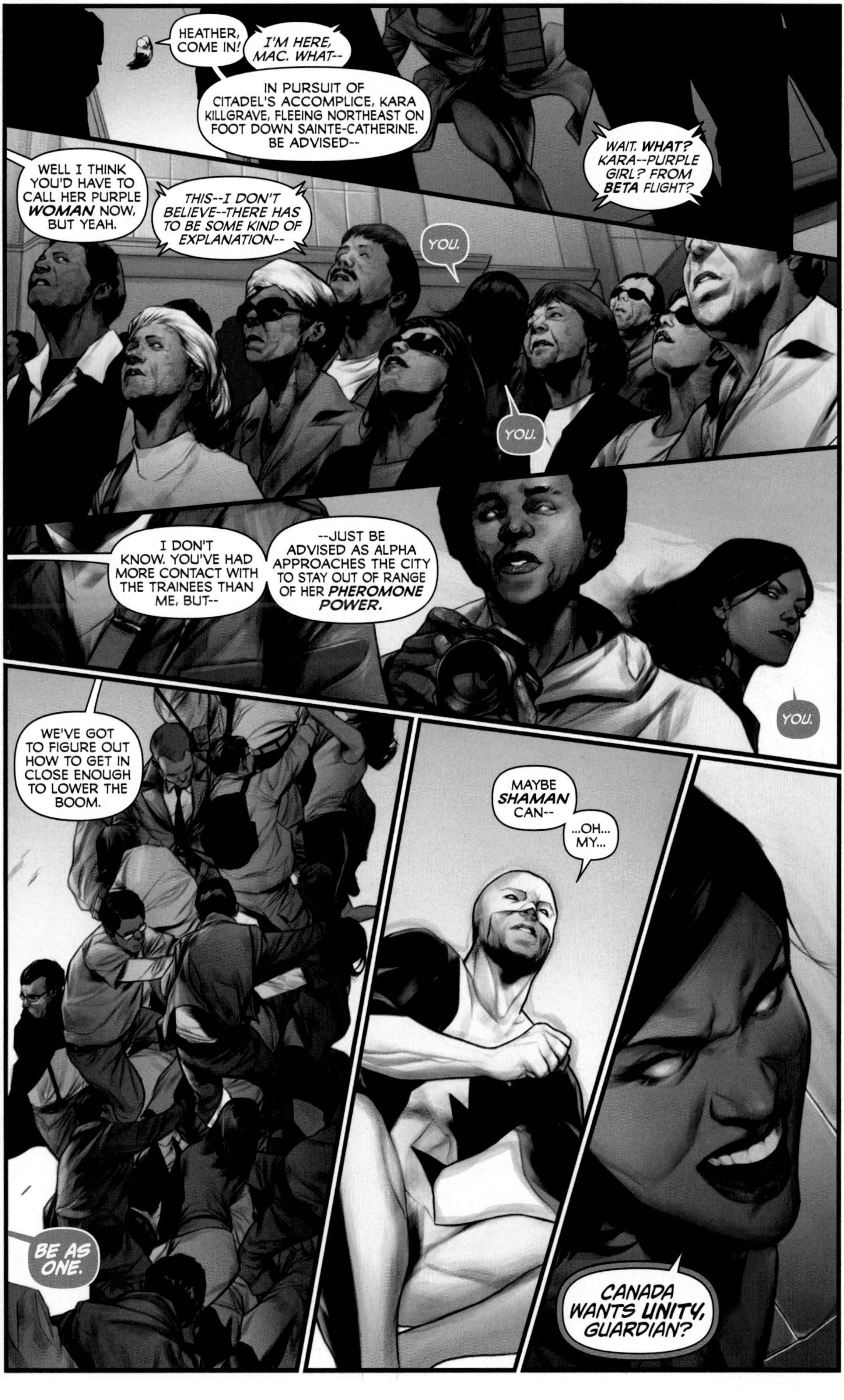
HEATHER, COME IN!
I'M HERE, MAC. WHAT--
IN PURSUIT OF CITADEL'S ACCOMPLICE, KARA KILLGRAVE, FLEEING NORTHEAST ON FOOT DOWN SAINTE-CATHERINE. BE ADVISED--
WAIT. WHAT? KARA--PURPLE GIRL? FROM BETA FLIGHT?
WELL I THINK YOU'D HAVE TO CALL HER PURPLE WOMAN NOW, BUT YEAH.
THIS--I DON'T BELIEVE--THERE HAS TO BE SOME KIND OF EXPLANATION--
YOU.
YOU.
I DON'T KNOW. YOU'VE HAD MORE CONTACT WITH THE TRAINEES THAN ME, BUT--
--JUST BE ADVISED AS ALPHA APPROACHES THE CITY TO STAY OUT OF RANGE OF HER PHEROMONE POWER.
YOU.
WE'VE GOT TO FIGURE OUT HOW TO GET IN CLOSE ENOUGH TO LOWER THE BOOM.
BE AS ONE.
MAYBE SHAMAN CAN--
...OH... MY...
CANADA WANTS UNITY, GUARDIAN?

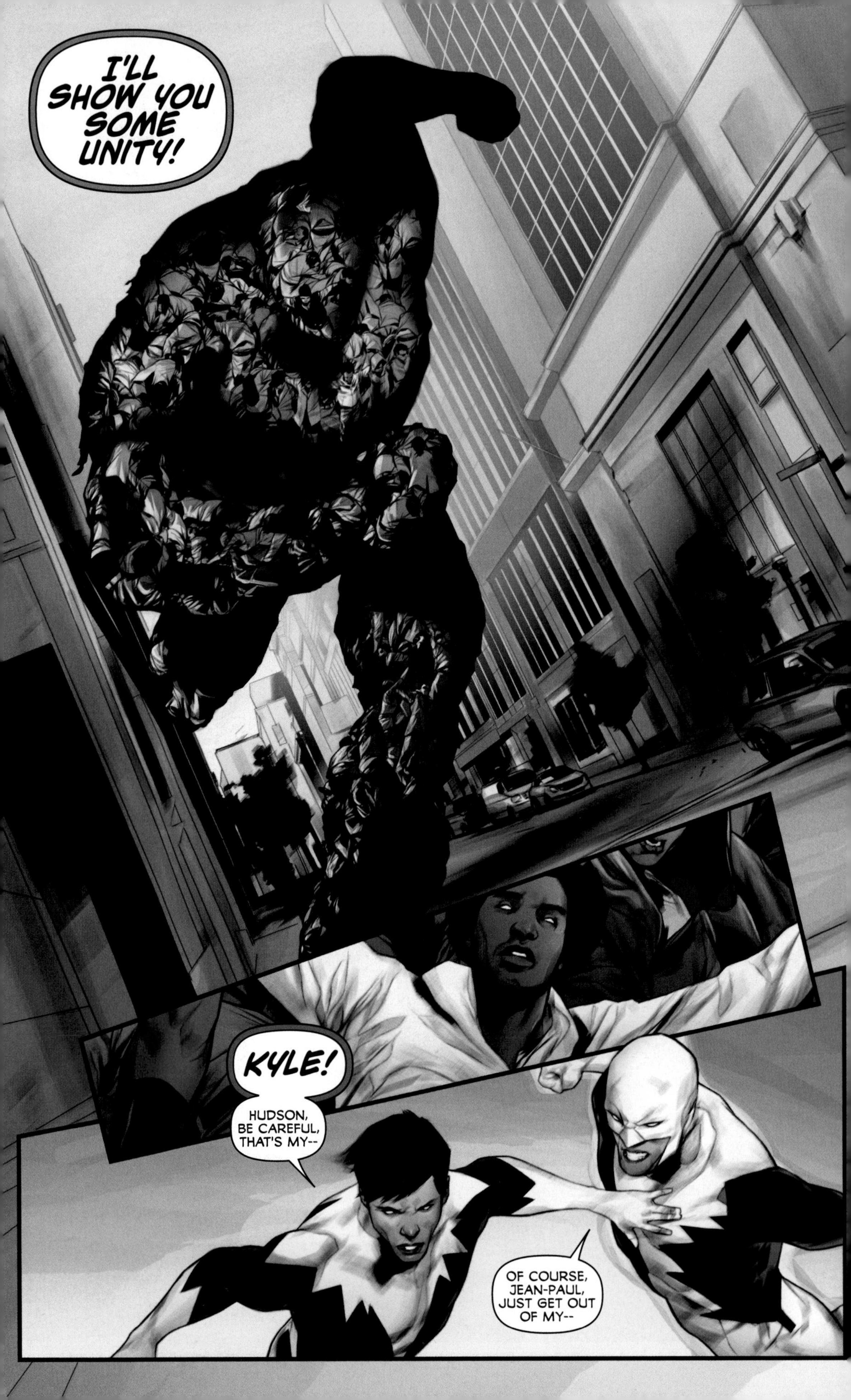
I'LL SHOW YOU SOME UNITY!
KYLE!
HUDSON, BE CAREFUL, THAT'S MY--
OF COURSE, JEAN-PAUL, JUST GET OUT OF MY--

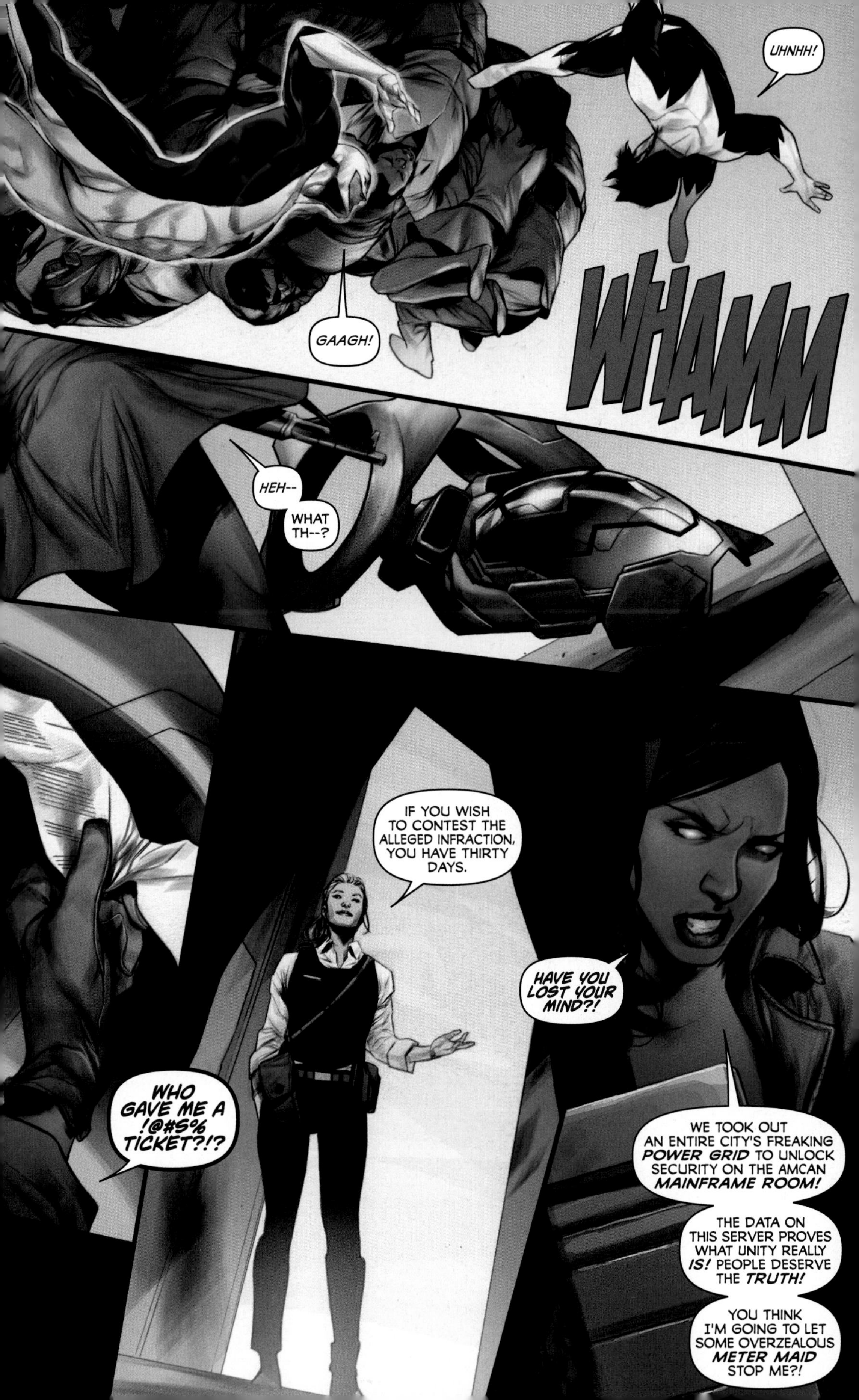
UHNHH!
GAAGH!
WHAMM
HEH--
WHAT TH--?
IF YOU WISH TO CONTEST THE ALLEGED INFRACTION, YOU HAVE THIRTY DAYS.
HAVE YOU LOST YOUR MIND?!
WHO GAVE ME A !@#$% TICKET?!?
WE TOOK OUT AN ENTIRE CITY'S FREAKING POWER GRID TO UNLOCK SECURITY ON THE AMCAN MAINFRAME ROOM!
THE DATA ON THIS SERVER PROVES WHAT UNITY REALLY IS! PEOPLE DESERVE THE TRUTH!
YOU THINK I'M GOING TO LET SOME OVERZEALOUS METER MAID STOP ME?!

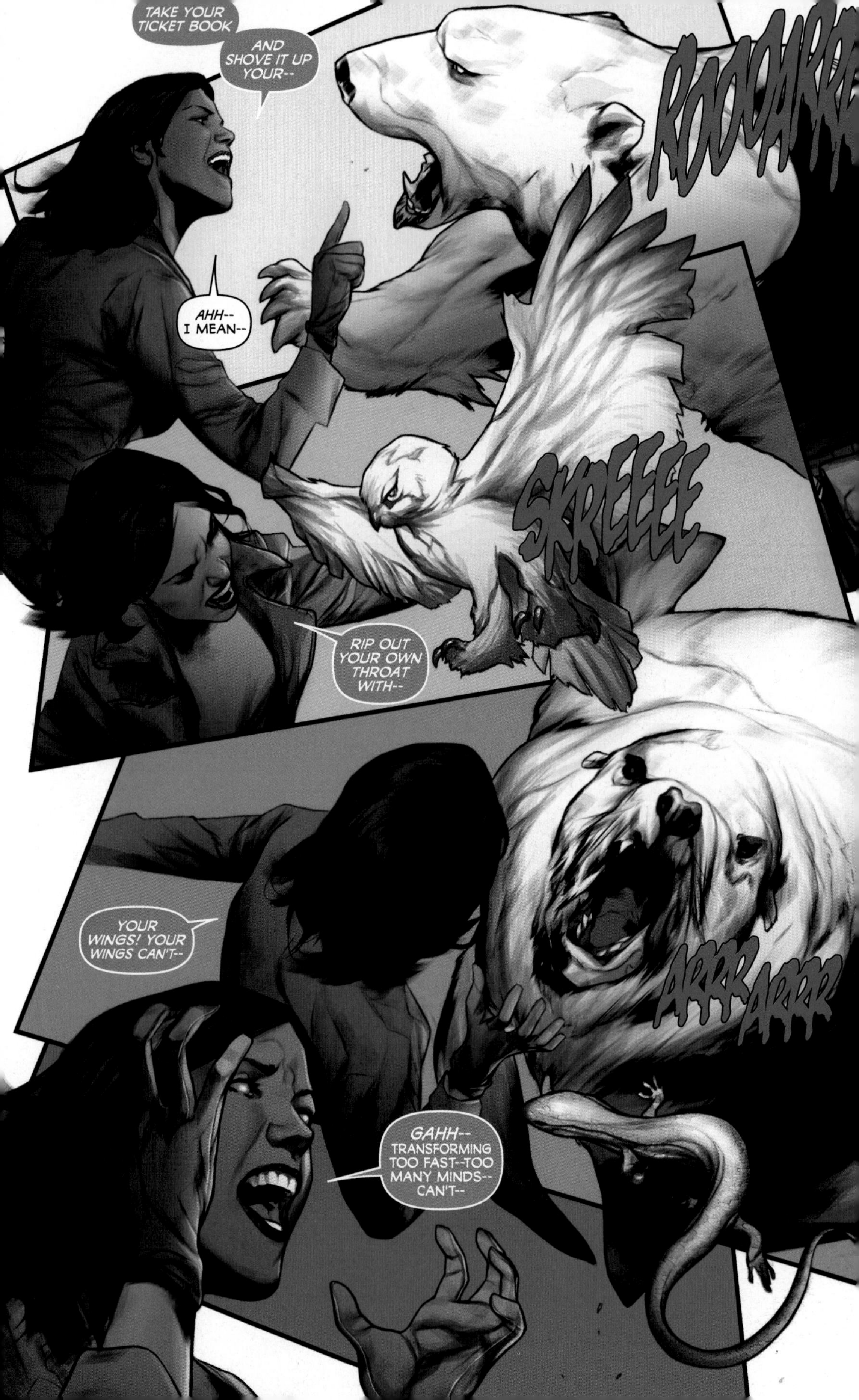
TAKE YOUR TICKET BOOK
AND SHOVE IT UP YOUR--
ROOOARRR
AHH-- I MEAN--
SKREEEEE
RIP OUT YOUR OWN THROAT WITH--
YOUR WINGS! YOUR WINGS CAN'T--
ARRRR ARRRR
GAHH-- TRANSFORMING TOO FAST--TOO MANY MINDS-- CAN'T--

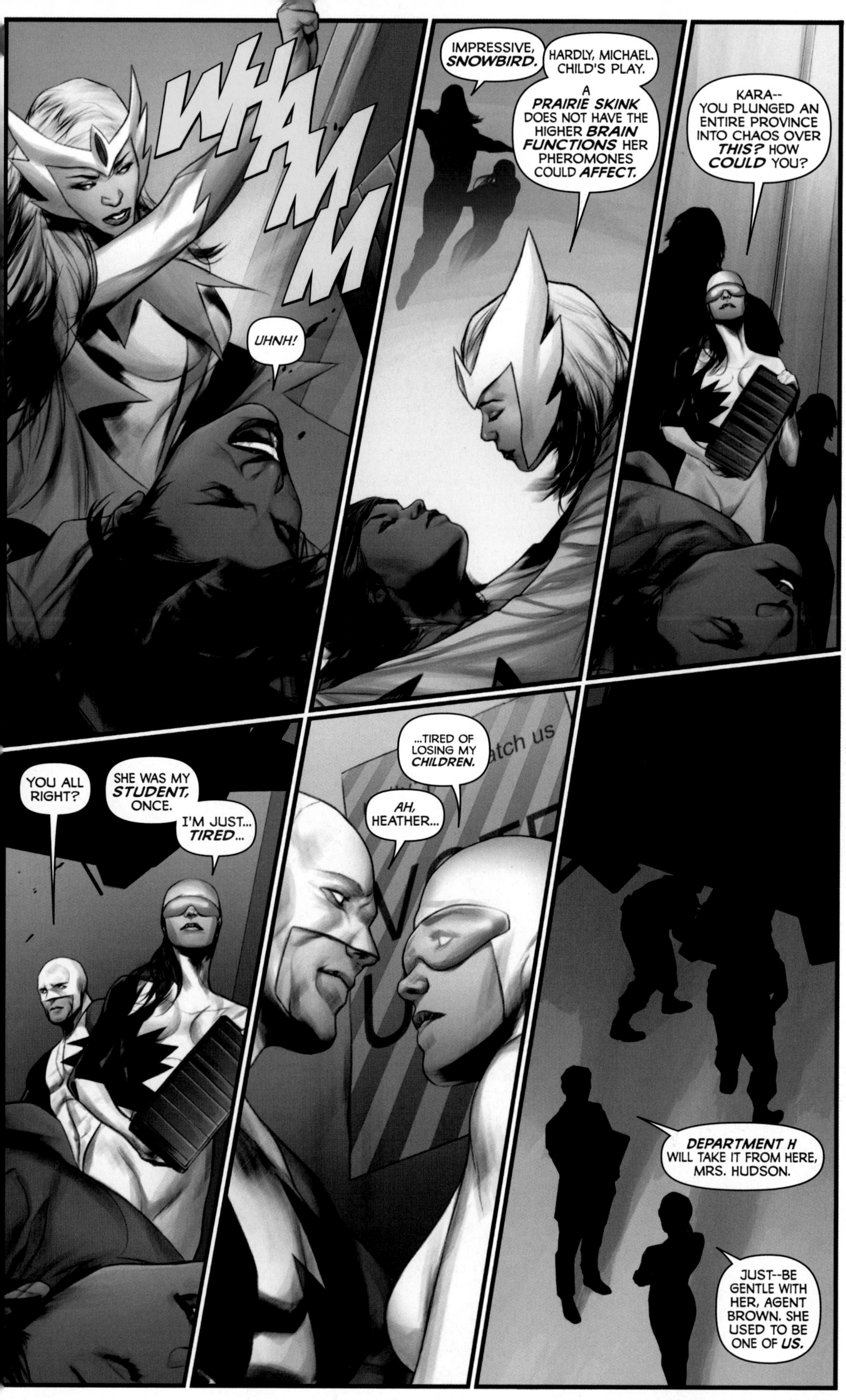
WHAMM
UHNH!
IMPRESSIVE, SNOWBIRD.
HARDLY, MICHAEL. CHILD'S PLAY.
A PRAIRIE SKINK DOES NOT HAVE THE HIGHER BRAIN FUNCTIONS HER PHEROMONES COULD AFFECT.
KARA-- YOU PLUNGED AN ENTIRE PROVINCE INTO CHAOS OVER THIS? HOW COULD YOU?
YOU ALL RIGHT?
SHE WAS MY STUDENT, ONCE.
I'M JUST... TIRED...
...TIRED OF LOSING MY CHILDREN.
AH, HEATHER...
DEPARTMENT H WILL TAKE IT FROM HERE, MRS. HUDSON.
JUST--BE GENTLE WITH HER, AGENT BROWN. SHE USED TO BE ONE OF US.

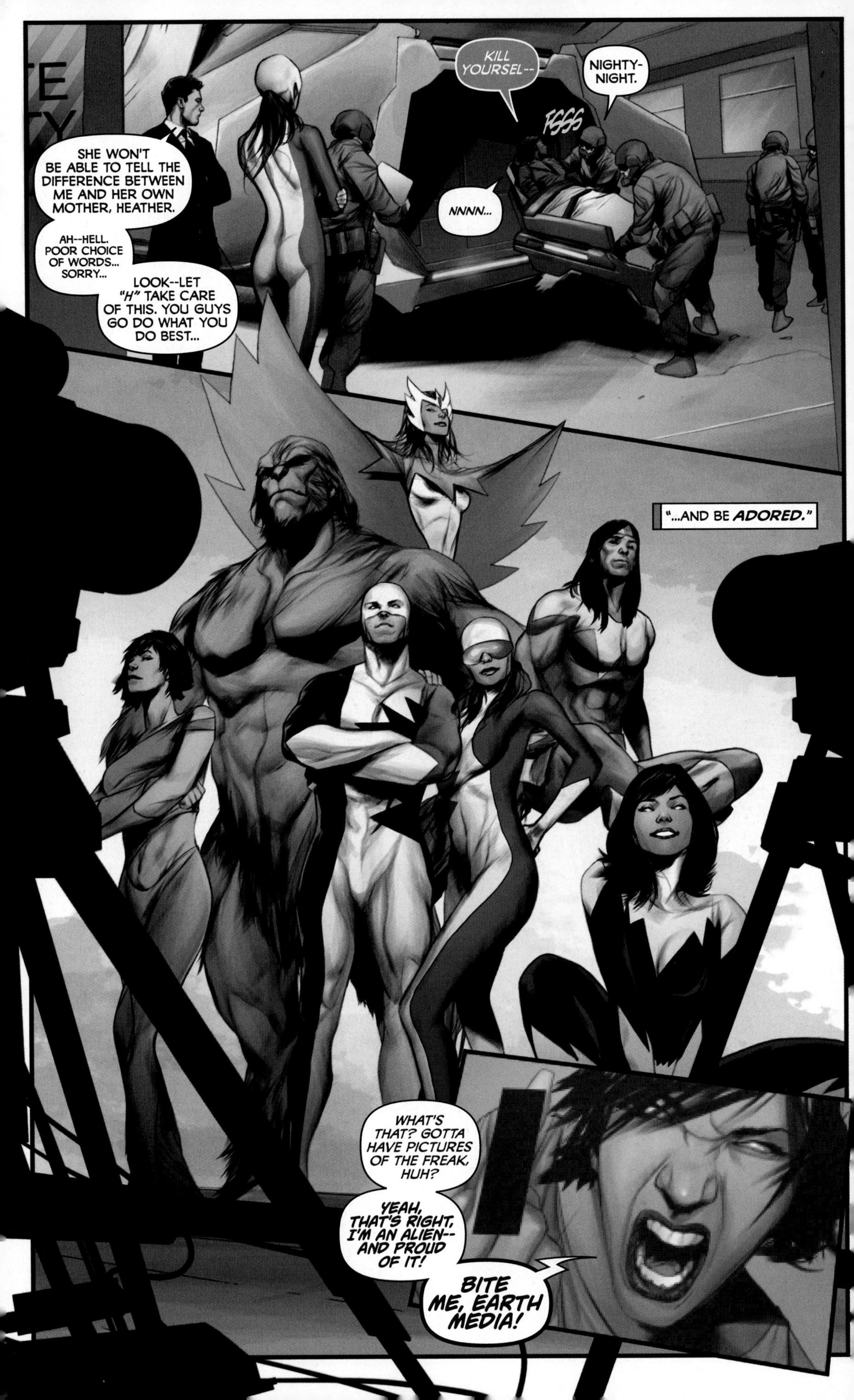
SHE WON'T BE ABLE TO TELL THE DIFFERENCE BETWEEN ME AND HER OWN MOTHER, HEATHER.
AH--HELL. POOR CHOICE OF WORDS... SORRY...
LOOK--LET "H" TAKE CARE OF THIS. YOU GUYS GO DO WHAT YOU DO BEST...
KILL YOURSEL--
FSSS
NIGHTY-NIGHT.
NNNN...
"...AND BE ADORED."
WHAT'S THAT? GOTTA HAVE PICTURES OF THE FREAK, HUH?
YEAH, THAT'S RIGHT, I'M AN ALIEN--AND PROUD OF IT!
BITE ME, EARTH MEDIA!

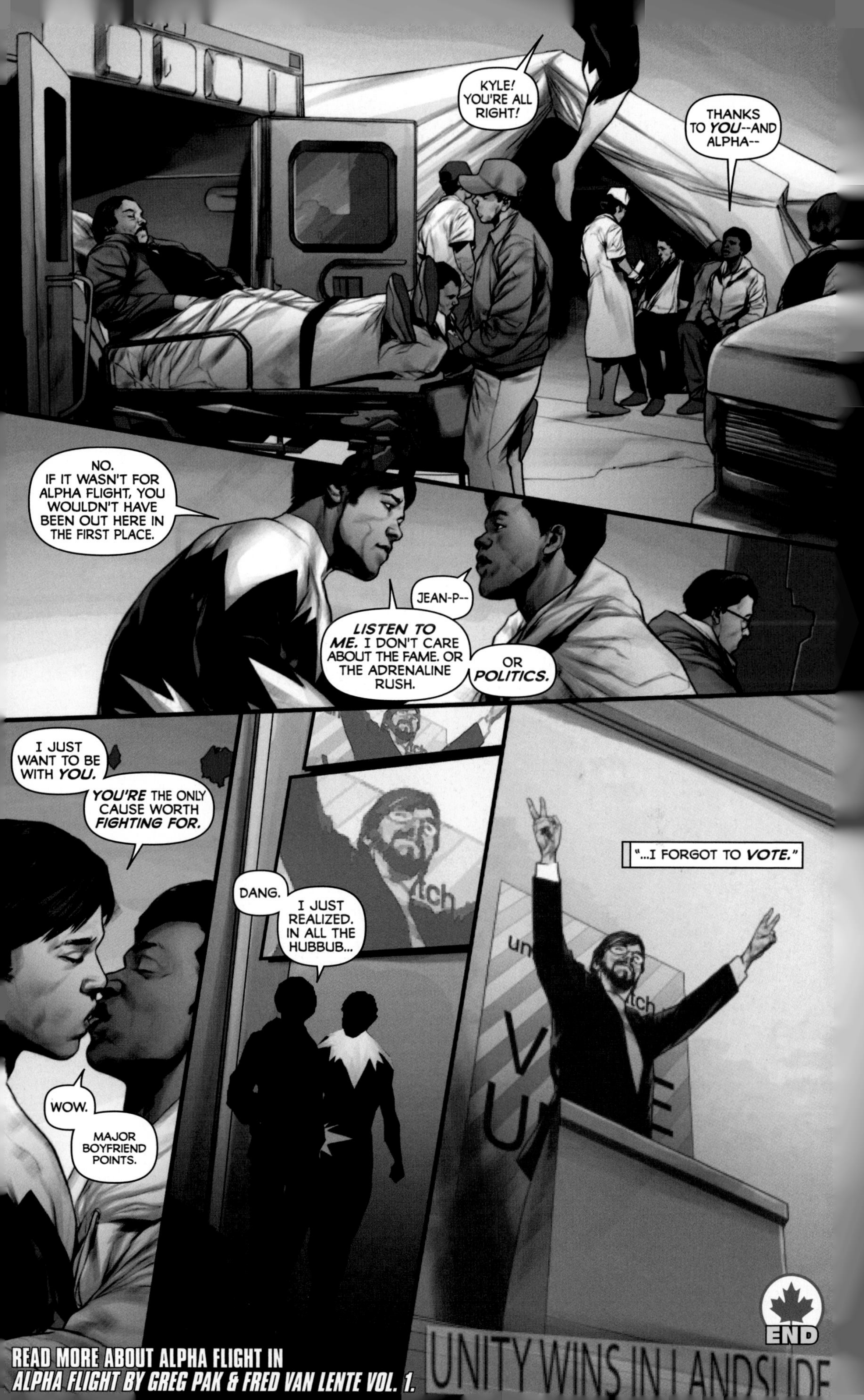
KYLE! YOU'RE ALL RIGHT!
THANKS TO YOU--AND ALPHA--
NO. IF IT WASN'T FOR ALPHA FLIGHT, YOU WOULDN'T HAVE BEEN OUT HERE IN THE FIRST PLACE.
JEAN-P--
LISTEN TO ME. I DON'T CARE ABOUT THE FAME. OR THE ADRENALINE RUSH.
OR POLITICS.
I JUST WANT TO BE WITH YOU.
YOU'RE THE ONLY CAUSE WORTH FIGHTING FOR.
WOW.
MAJOR BOYFRIEND POINTS.
DANG.
I JUST REALIZED. IN ALL THE HUBBUB...
"...I FORGOT TO VOTE."
UNITY WINS IN LANDSLIDE
END

READ MORE ABOUT ALPHA FLIGHT IN
ALPHA FLIGHT BY GREG PAK & FRED VAN LENTE VOL. 1.

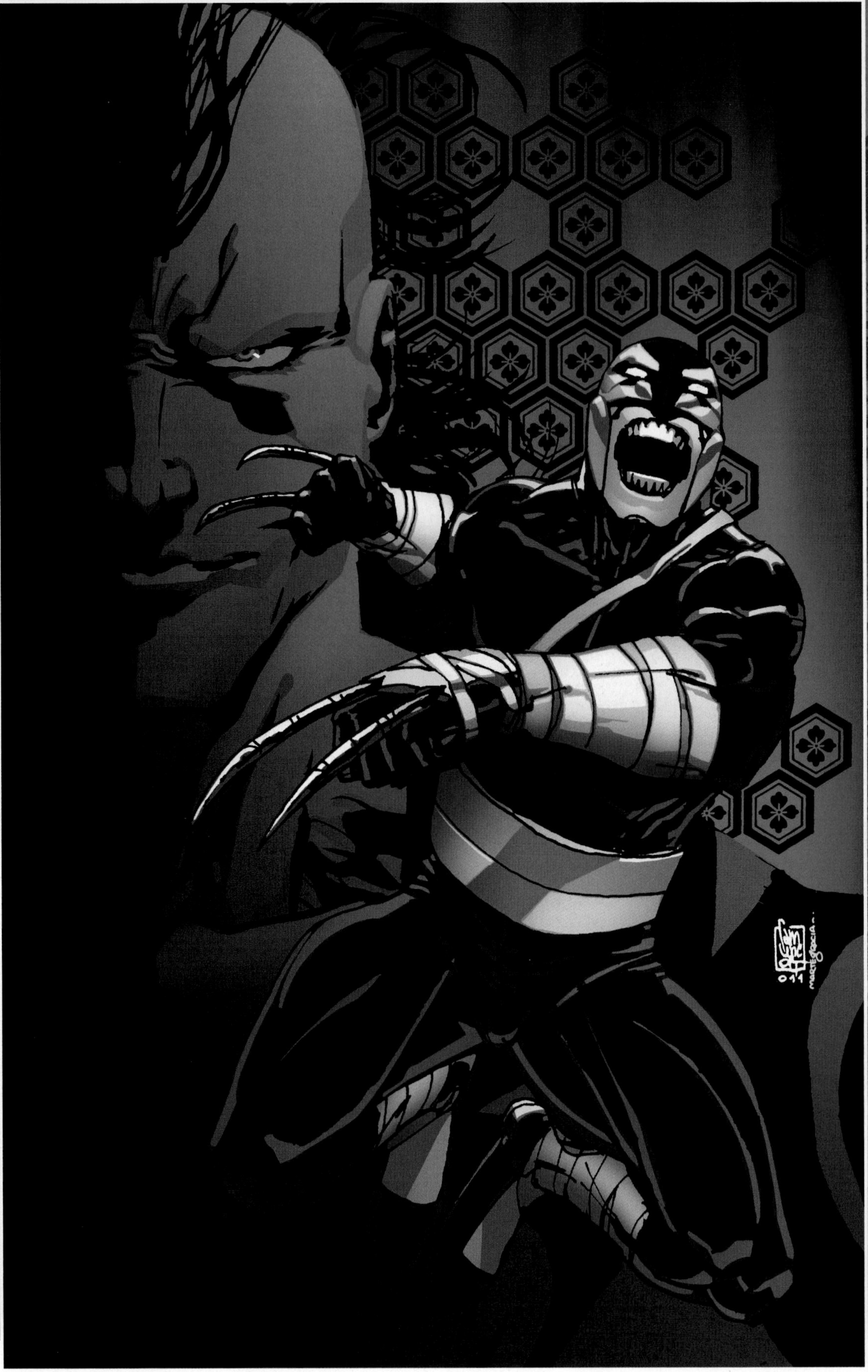

DAKEN #9.1

Years ago, the mutant known as Wolverine found peace in Japan and had a son with his wife, Itsu. The peace was short-lived--Itsu was murdered and Wolverine believed his son died with her...but the boy lived. The boy came to be known as Daken and grew up consumed with hatred for his father, wrongly blaming him for the death of his mother for much of his life. He discovered that he had the ability to manipulate the emotions of others, and like Wolverine, possessed a powerful healing factor and razor-sharp claws on each hand. But Daken walked a far different path than that of his father. Instead of righting the wrongs of the world, Daken wanted to set it on fire. He had become...

DAKEN DARK WOLVERINE

PREVIOUSLY...

Daken has set out on a quest to lie and murder his way to the top of the international criminal underworld and his first stop was the crime-infested island of Madripoor. Once there he plunged the city's infrastructure into a state of chaos and carefully manipulated the island's protector, Tyger Tiger, into working for him. Daken then challenged the crime lords of Madripoor, emerging with full control over the island and all of its wealth.

Now, with cash coming in, his enemies defeated and all of Madripoor at his feet, Daken must begin the next phase of his plan.

GONE

ROB WILLIAMS WRITER   **RON GARNEY** ART   **JASON KEITH** COLOR ART
VC's CORY PETIT LETTERER   **GIUSEPPE CAMUNCOLI** and **MARTE GRACIA** COVER ART   **JARED K. FLETCHER** DESIGNE
JODY LEHEUP ASST. EDITOR   **JEANINE SCHAEFER** EDITOR   **NICK LOWE** GROUP EDITOR
AXEL ALONSO EDITOR IN CHIEF   **JOE QUESADA** CHIEF CREATIVE OFFICER   **DAN BUCKLEY** PUBLISHER   **ALAN FINE** EXECUTIVE PRODUCE

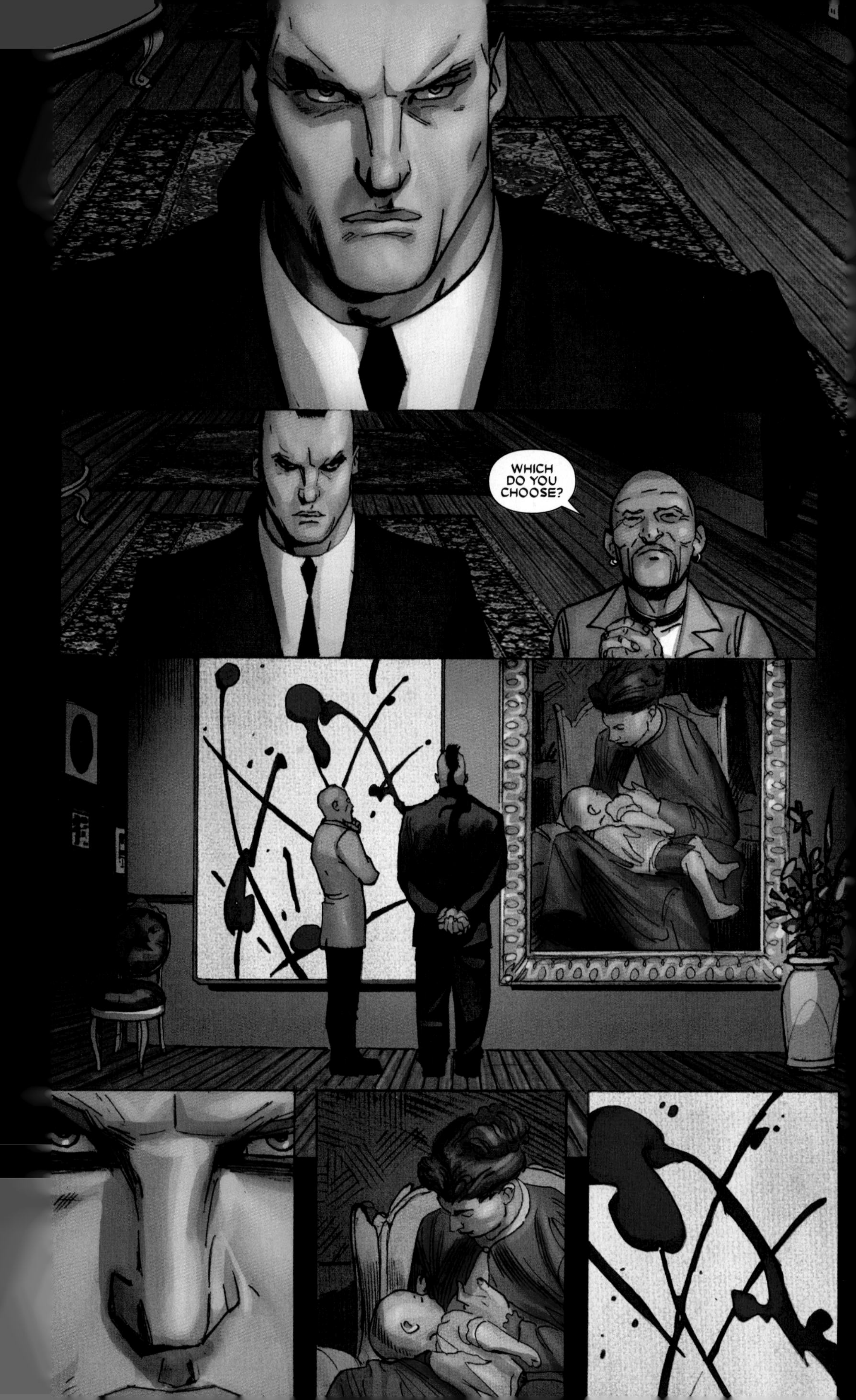
WHICH DO YOU CHOOSE?

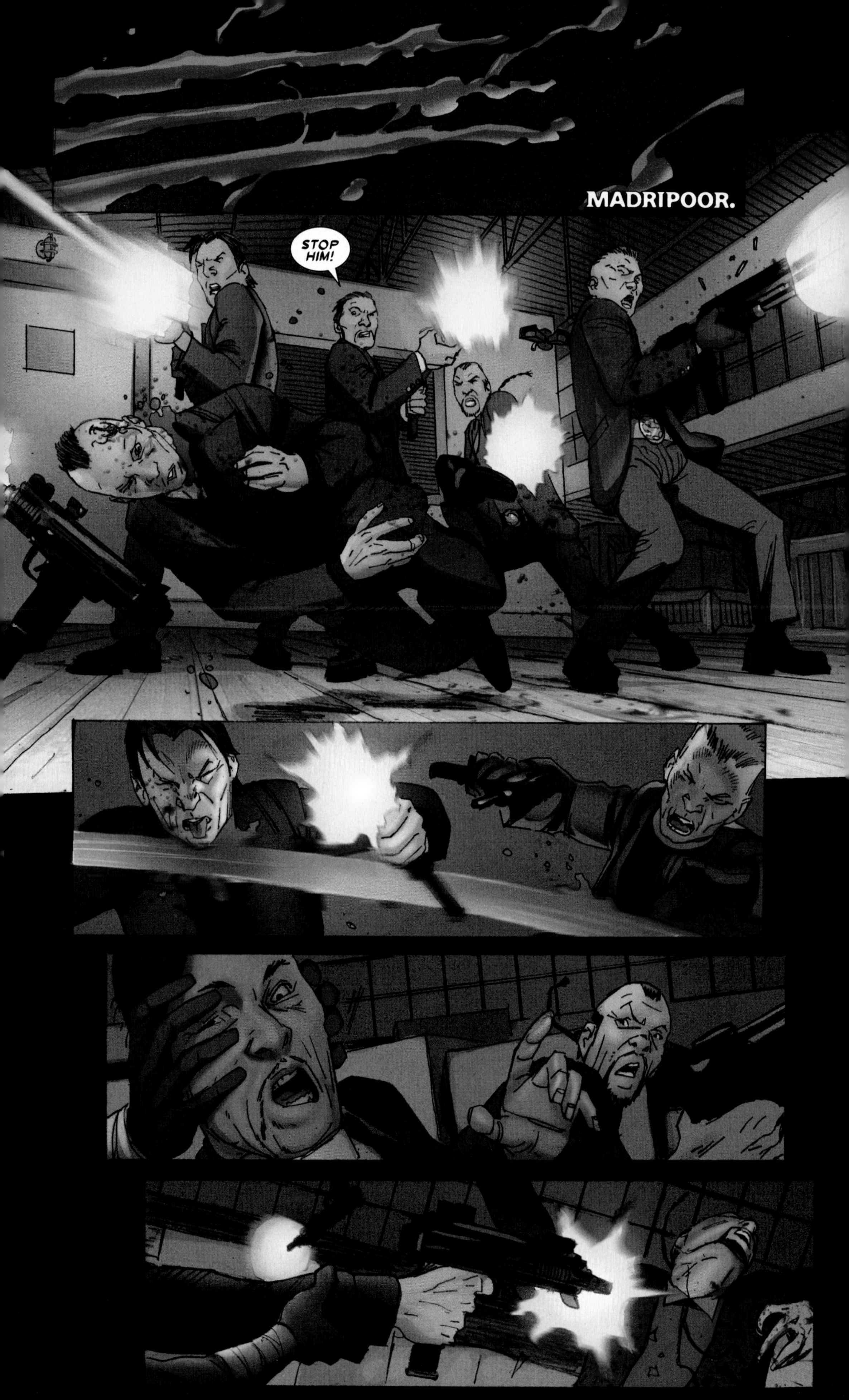
MADRIPOOR.
STOP HIM!

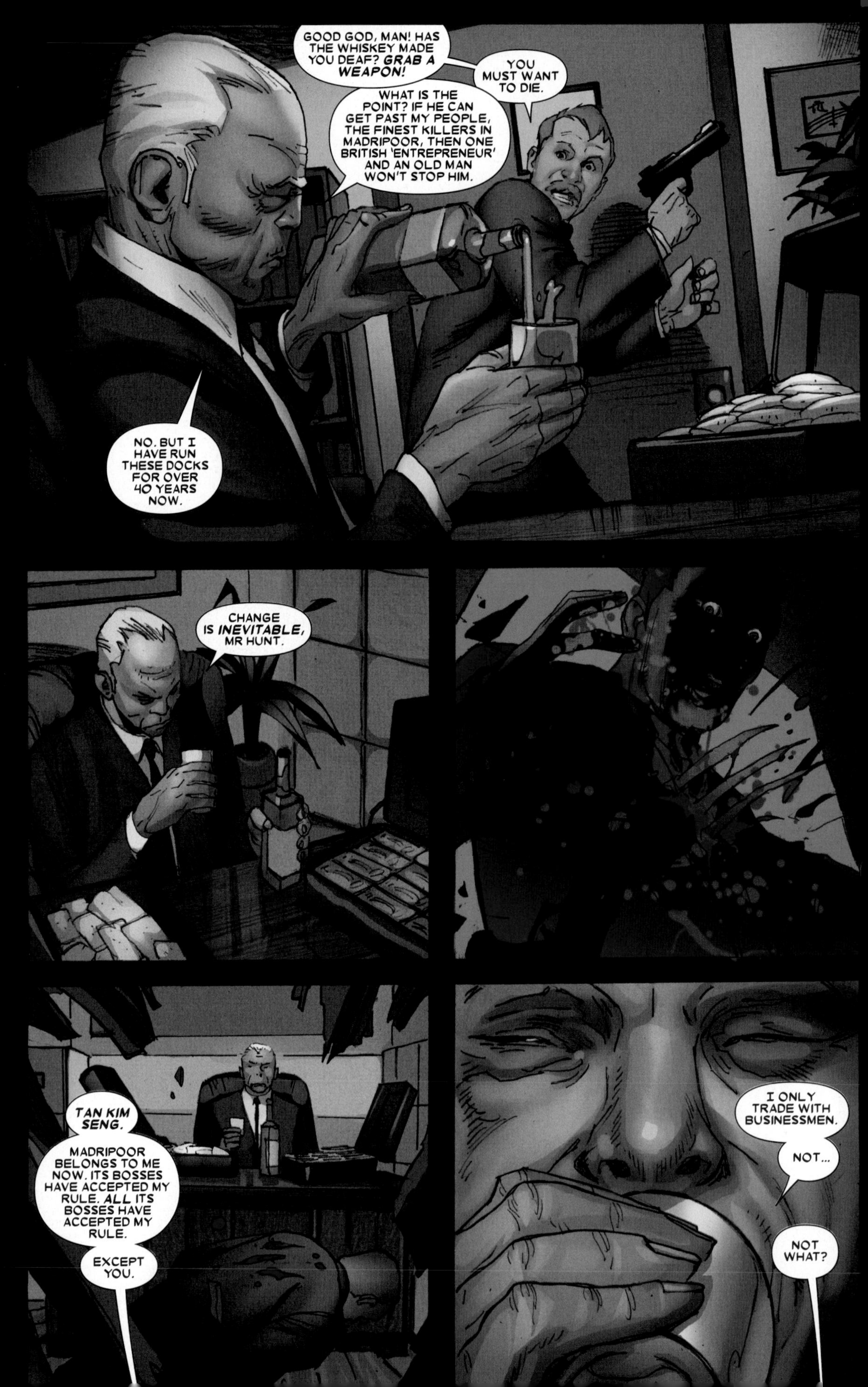

GOOD GOD, MAN! HAS THE WHISKEY MADE YOU DEAF? GRAB A WEAPON!
YOU MUST WANT TO DIE.
WHAT IS THE POINT? IF HE CAN GET PAST MY PEOPLE, THE FINEST KILLERS IN MADRIPOOR, THEN ONE BRITISH 'ENTREPRENEUR' AND AN OLD MAN WON'T STOP HIM.
NO. BUT I HAVE RUN THESE DOCKS FOR OVER 40 YEARS NOW.
CHANGE IS INEVITABLE, MR HUNT.
TAN KIM SENG.
MADRIPOOR BELONGS TO ME NOW. ITS BOSSES HAVE ACCEPTED MY RULE. ALL ITS BOSSES HAVE ACCEPTED MY RULE.
EXCEPT YOU.
I ONLY TRADE WITH BUSINESSMEN.
NOT...
NOT WHAT?

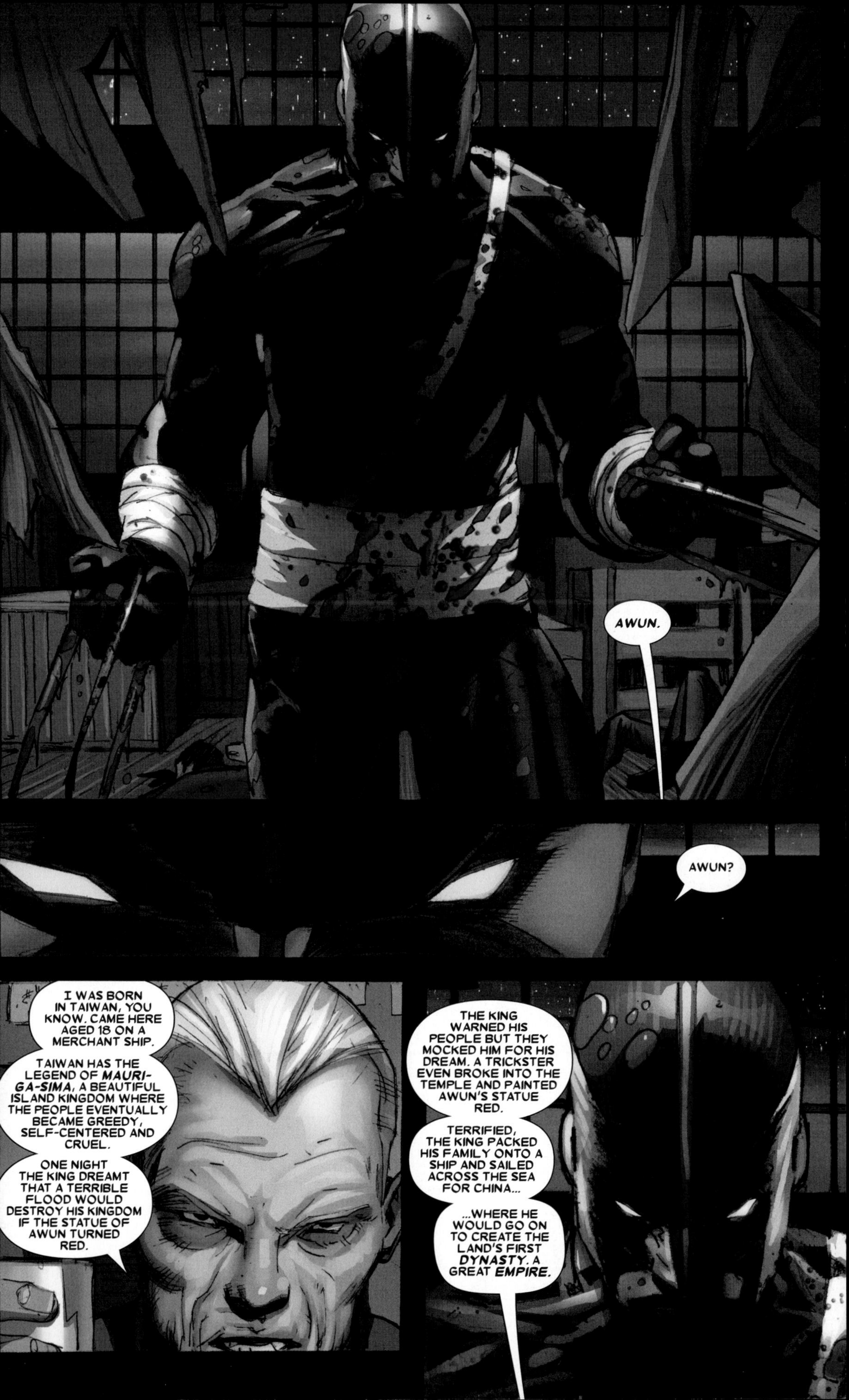
AWUN.
AWUN?
I WAS BORN IN TAIWAN, YOU KNOW. CAME HERE AGED 18 ON A MERCHANT SHIP.
TAIWAN HAS THE LEGEND OF MAURI-GA-SIMA, A BEAUTIFUL ISLAND KINGDOM WHERE THE PEOPLE EVENTUALLY BECAME GREEDY, SELF-CENTERED AND CRUEL.
ONE NIGHT THE KING DREAMT THAT A TERRIBLE FLOOD WOULD DESTROY HIS KINGDOM IF THE STATUE OF AWUN TURNED RED.
THE KING WARNED HIS PEOPLE BUT THEY MOCKED HIM FOR HIS DREAM. A TRICKSTER EVEN BROKE INTO THE TEMPLE AND PAINTED AWUN'S STATUE RED.
TERRIFIED, THE KING PACKED HIS FAMILY ONTO A SHIP AND SAILED ACROSS THE SEA FOR CHINA...
...WHERE HE WOULD GO ON TO CREATE THE LAND'S FIRST DYNASTY. A GREAT EMPIRE.

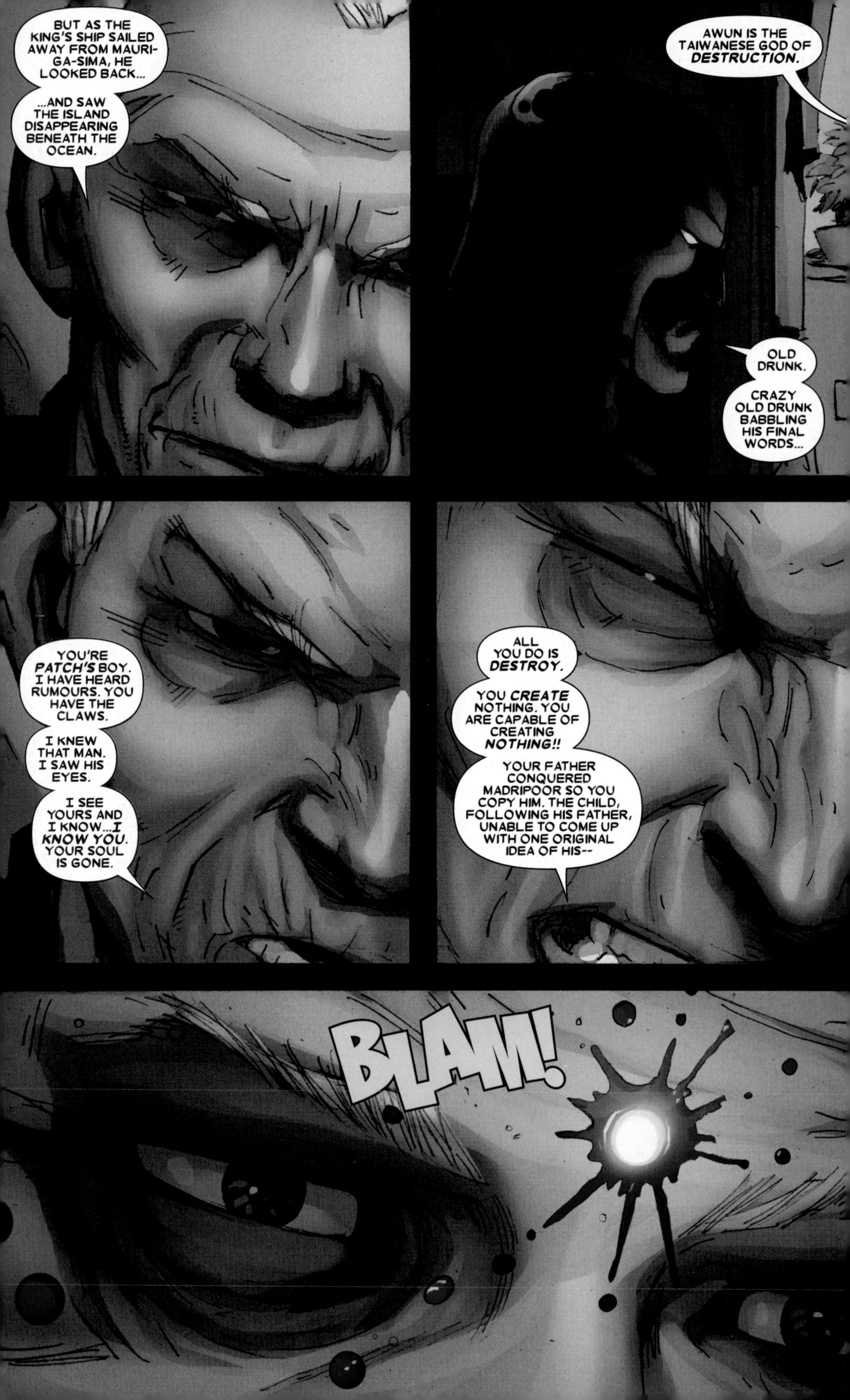
BUT AS THE KING'S SHIP SAILED AWAY FROM MAURI-GA-SIMA, HE LOOKED BACK...
...AND SAW THE ISLAND DISAPPEARING BENEATH THE OCEAN.
AWUN IS THE TAIWANESE GOD OF *DESTRUCTION.*
OLD DRUNK.
CRAZY OLD DRUNK BABBLING HIS FINAL WORDS...
YOU'RE *PATCH'S* BOY. I HAVE HEARD RUMOURS. YOU HAVE THE CLAWS.
I KNEW THAT MAN. I SAW HIS EYES.
I SEE YOURS AND I KNOW...*I KNOW YOU.* YOUR SOUL IS GONE.
ALL YOU DO IS *DESTROY.*
YOU *CREATE* NOTHING. YOU ARE CAPABLE OF CREATING *NOTHING!!*
YOUR FATHER CONQUERED MADRIPOOR SO YOU COPY HIM. THE CHILD, FOLLOWING HIS FATHER, UNABLE TO COME UP WITH ONE ORIGINAL IDEA OF HIS--
BLAM!

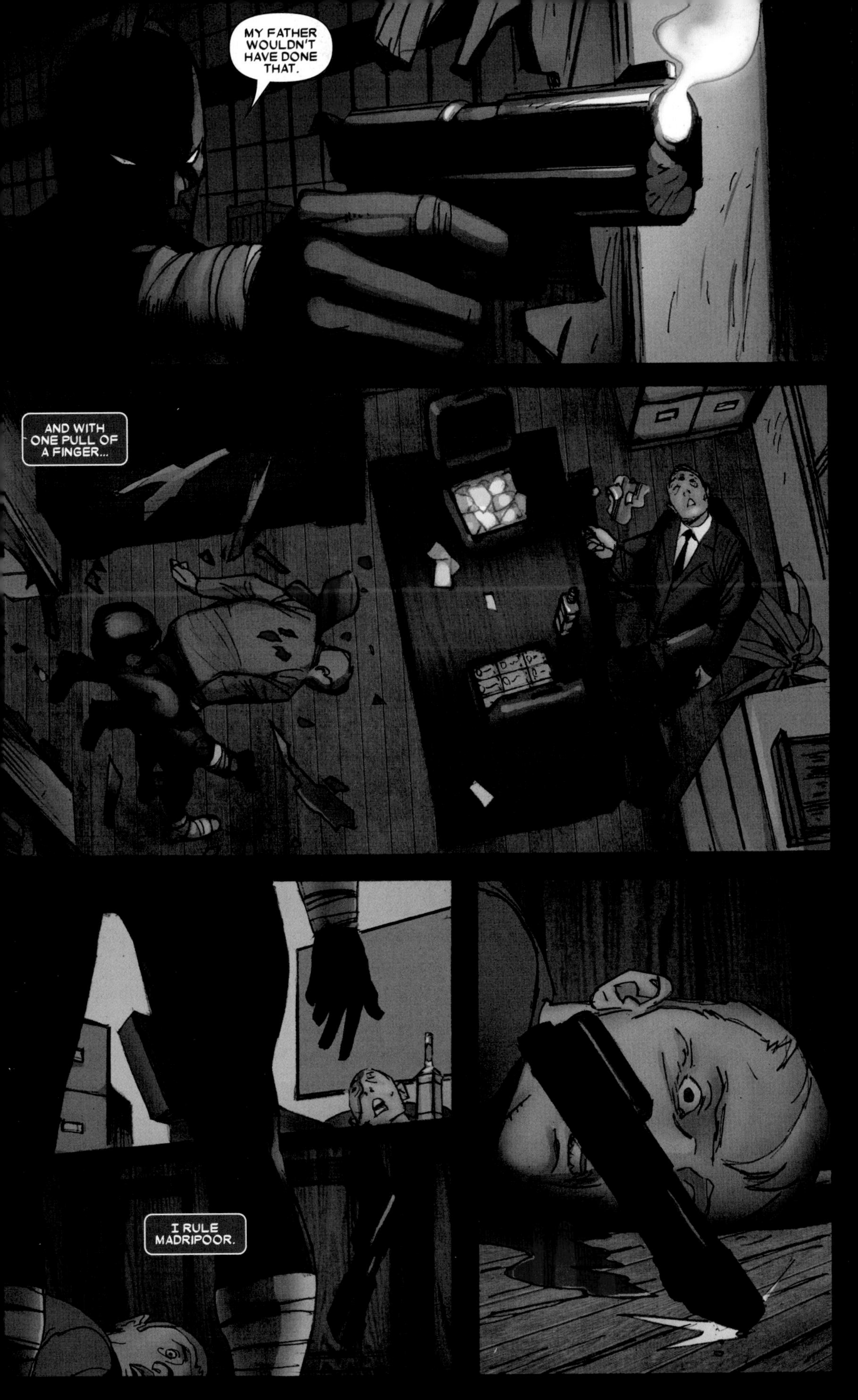
MY FATHER WOULDN'T HAVE DONE THAT.
AND WITH ONE PULL OF A FINGER...
I RULE MADRIPOOR.

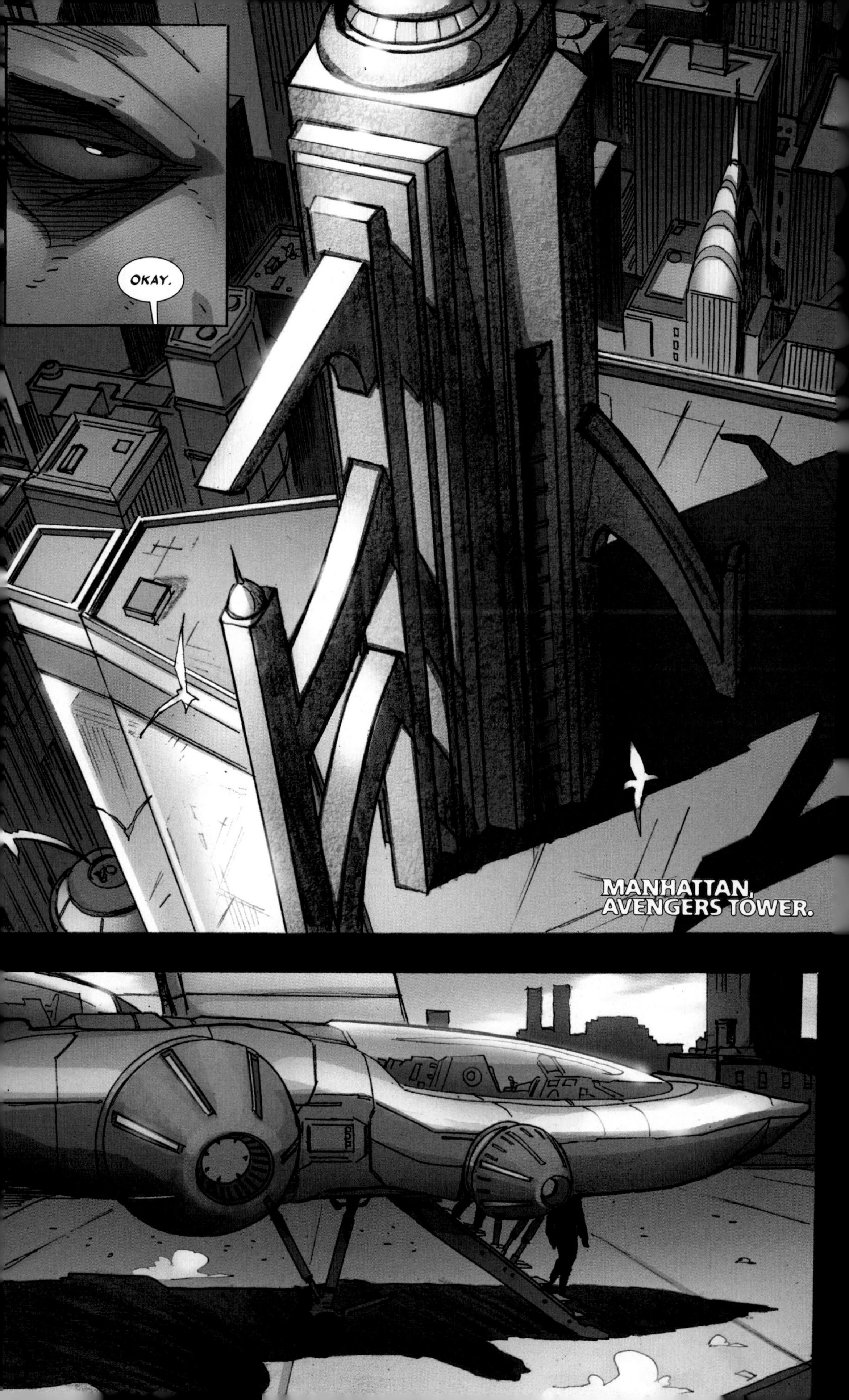
OKAY.
MANHATTAN, AVENGERS TOWER.

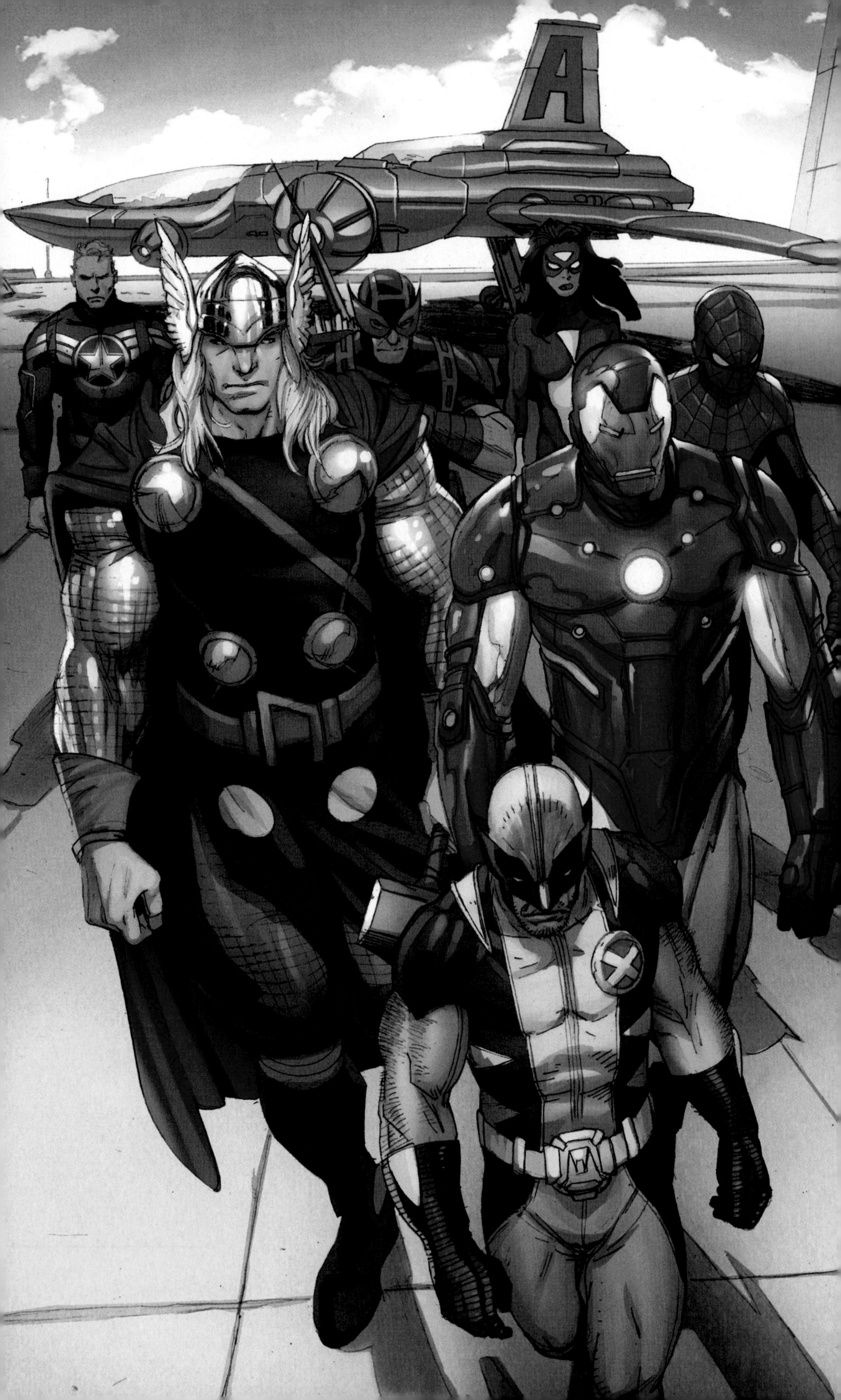

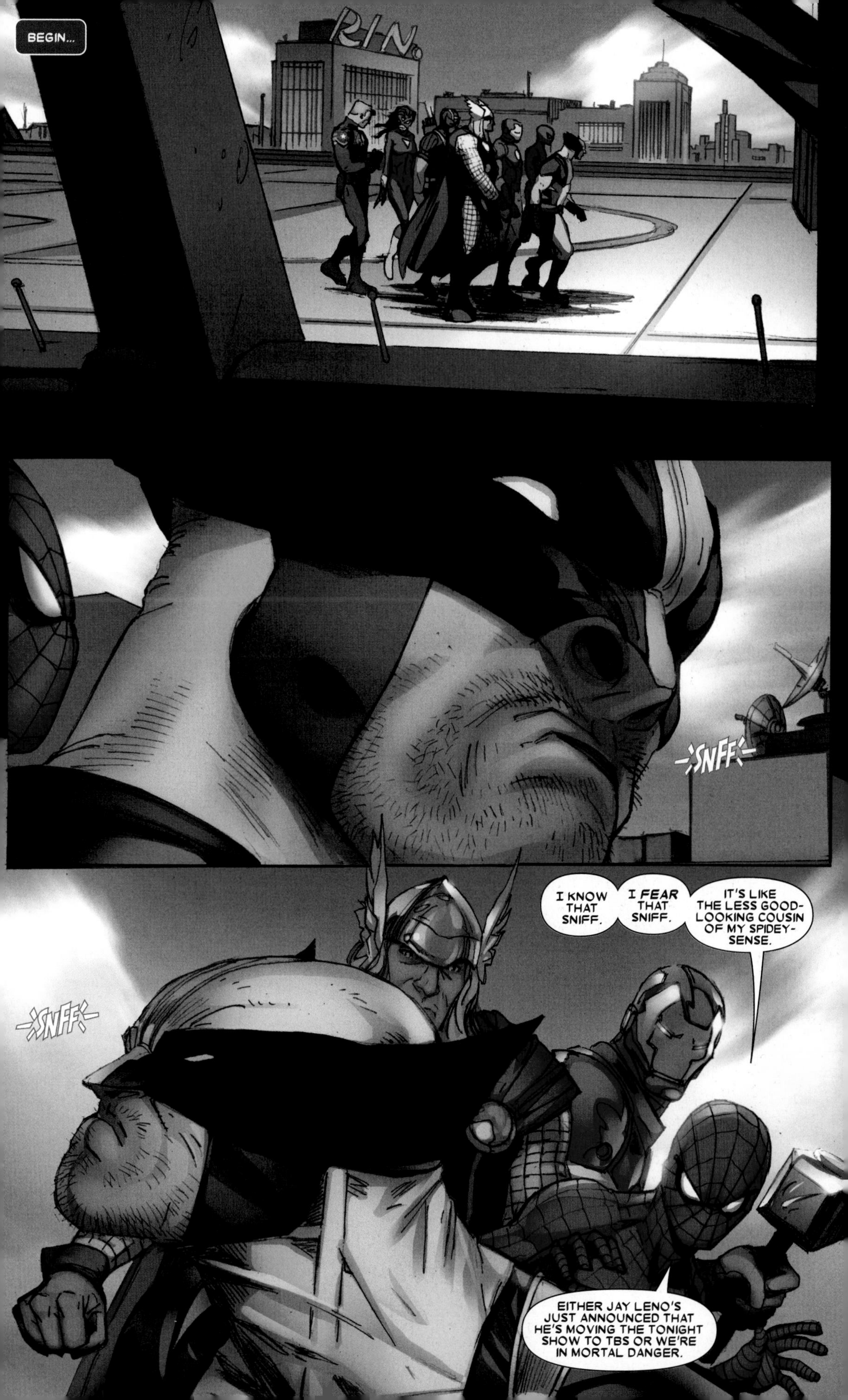
BEGIN...
RIN
SNFF
I KNOW THAT SNIFF.
I FEAR THAT SNIFF.
IT'S LIKE THE LESS GOOD-LOOKING COUSIN OF MY SPIDEY-SENSE.
SNFF
EITHER JAY LENO'S JUST ANNOUNCED THAT HE'S MOVING THE TONIGHT SHOW TO TBS OR WE'RE IN MORTAL DANGER.

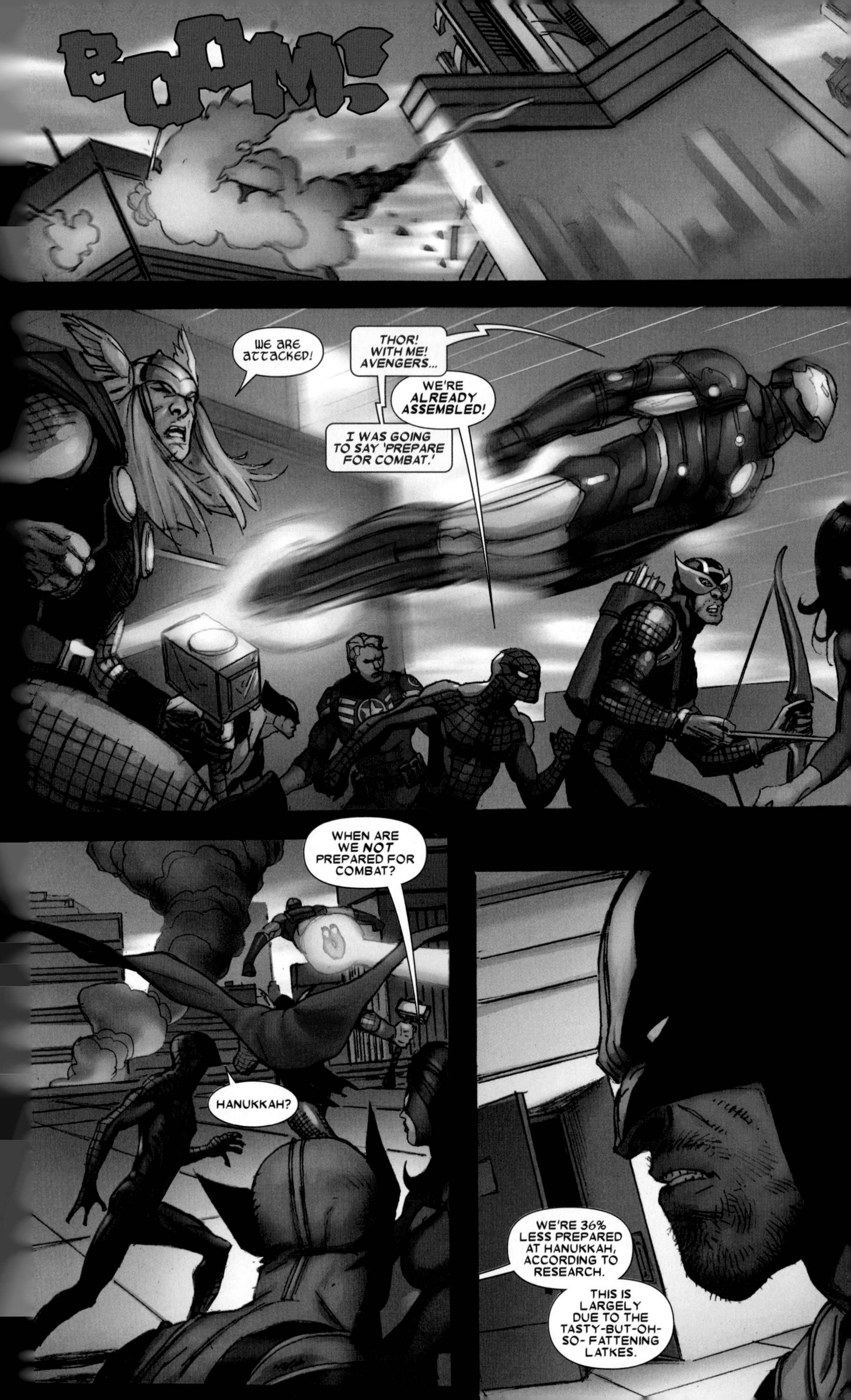
BOOM!
WE ARE ATTACKED!
THOR! WITH ME! AVENGERS...
WE'RE ALREADY ASSEMBLED!
I WAS GOING TO SAY 'PREPARE FOR COMBAT.'
WHEN ARE WE NOT PREPARED FOR COMBAT?
HANUKKAH?
WE'RE 36% LESS PREPARED AT HANUKKAH, ACCORDING TO RESEARCH.
THIS IS LARGELY DUE TO THE TASTY-BUT-OH-SO-FATTENING LATKES.

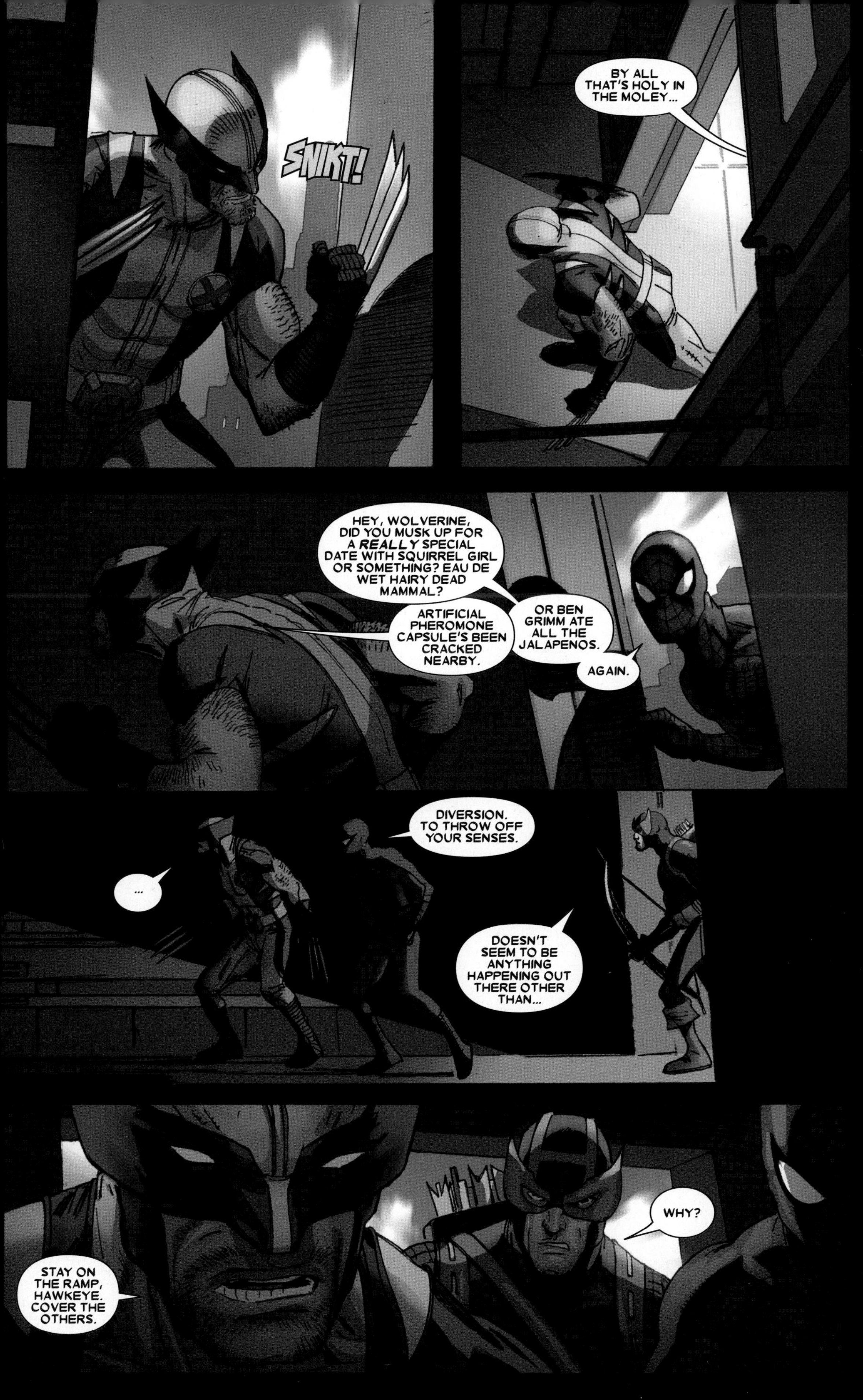
SNIKT!
BY ALL THAT'S HOLY IN THE MOLEY...
HEY, WOLVERINE, DID YOU MUSK UP FOR A REALLY SPECIAL DATE WITH SQUIRREL GIRL OR SOMETHING? EAU DE WET HAIRY DEAD MAMMAL?
ARTIFICIAL PHEROMONE CAPSULE'S BEEN CRACKED NEARBY.
OR BEN GRIMM ATE ALL THE JALAPENOS.
AGAIN.
DIVERSION. TO THROW OFF YOUR SENSES.
...
DOESN'T SEEM TO BE ANYTHING HAPPENING OUT THERE OTHER THAN...
STAY ON THE RAMP, HAWKEYE. COVER THE OTHERS.
WHY?

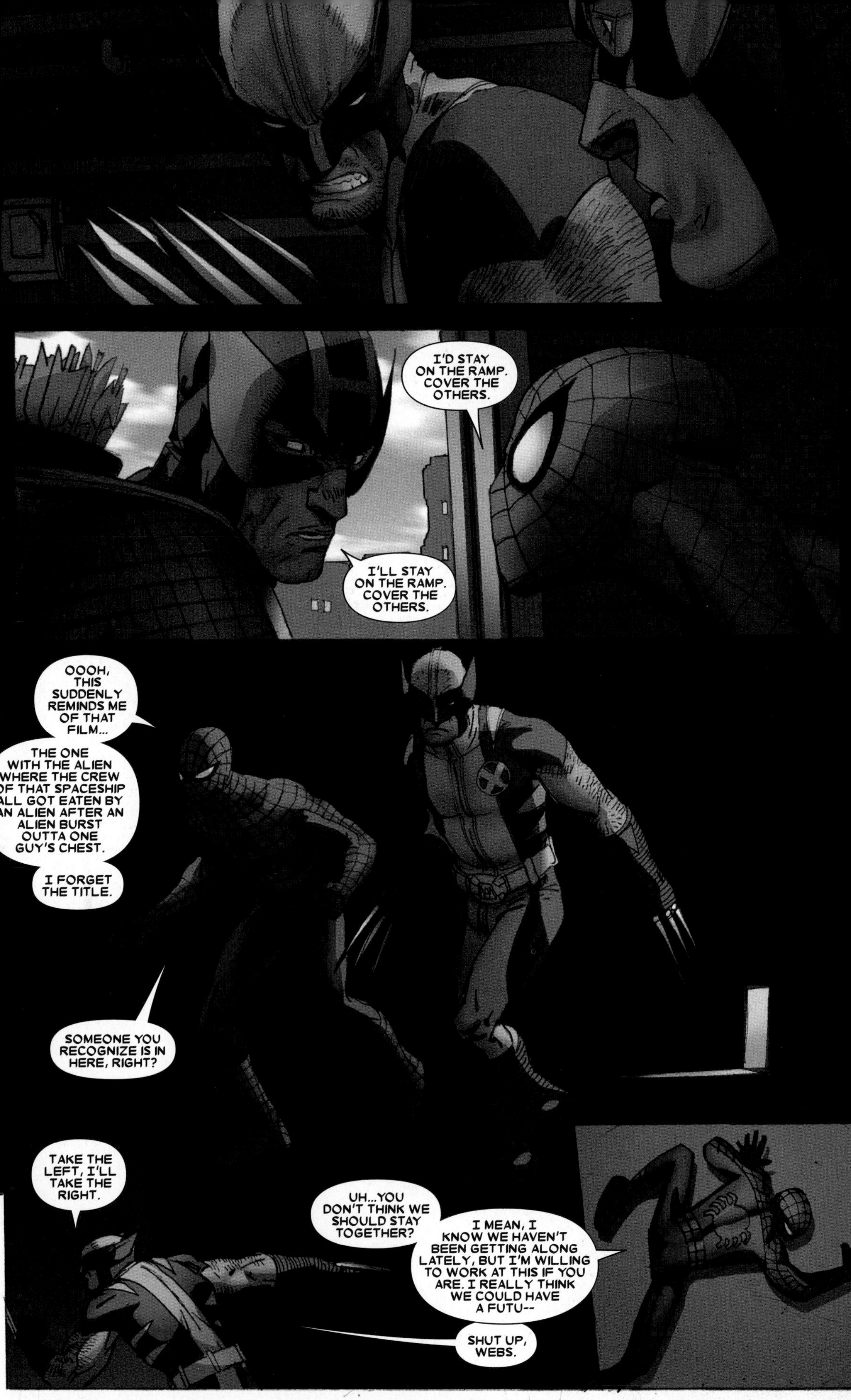
I'D STAY ON THE RAMP. COVER THE OTHERS.
I'LL STAY ON THE RAMP. COVER THE OTHERS.
OOOH, THIS SUDDENLY REMINDS ME OF THAT FILM...
THE ONE WITH THE ALIEN WHERE THE CREW OF THAT SPACESHIP ALL GOT EATEN BY AN ALIEN AFTER AN ALIEN BURST OUTTA ONE GUY'S CHEST.
I FORGET THE TITLE.
SOMEONE YOU RECOGNIZE IS IN HERE, RIGHT?
TAKE THE LEFT, I'LL TAKE THE RIGHT.
UH...YOU DON'T THINK WE SHOULD STAY TOGETHER?
I MEAN, I KNOW WE HAVEN'T BEEN GETTING ALONG LATELY, BUT I'M WILLING TO WORK AT THIS IF YOU ARE. I REALLY THINK WE COULD HAVE A FUTU--
SHUT UP, WEBS.

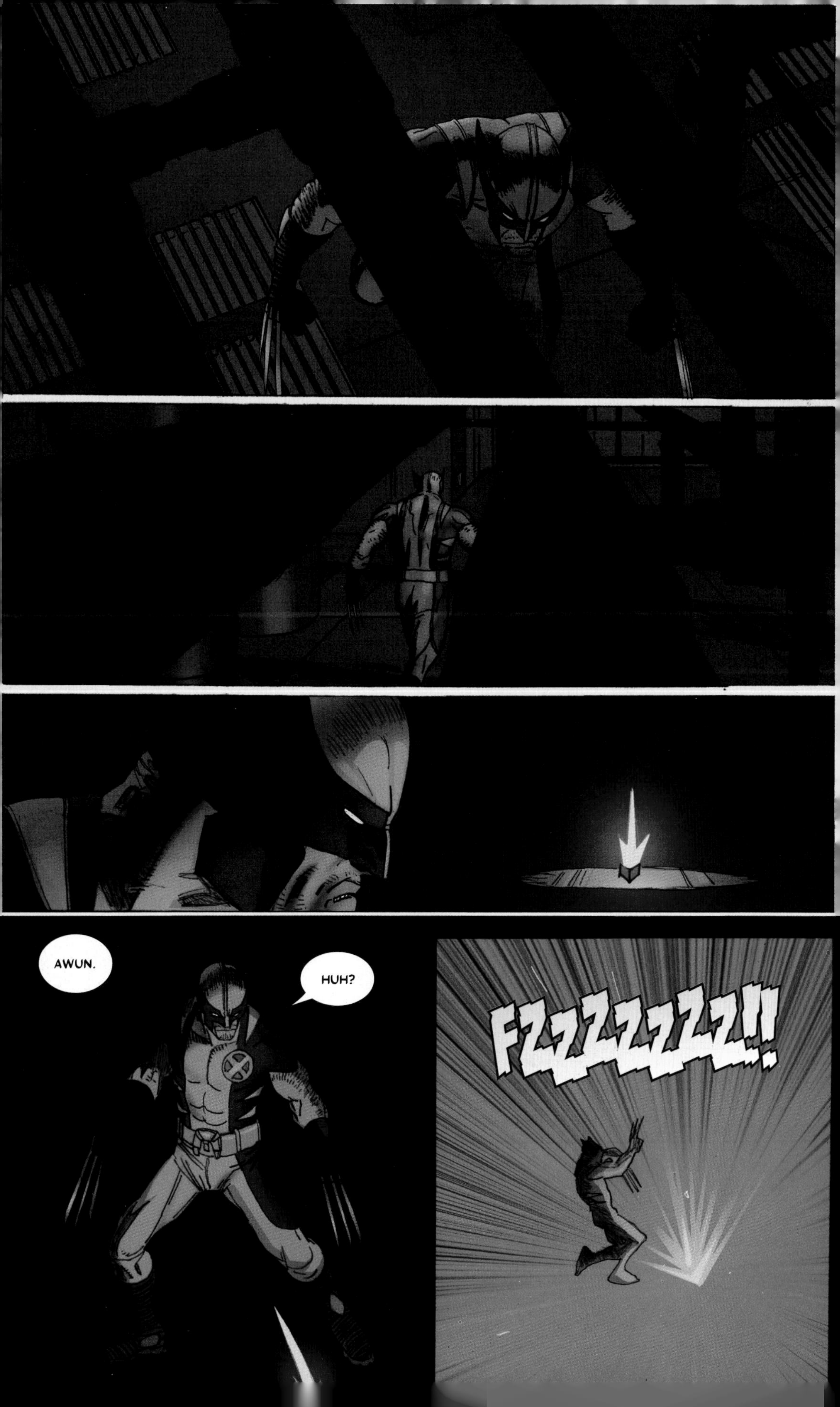
AWUN.
HUH?
FZZZZZZZZ!!

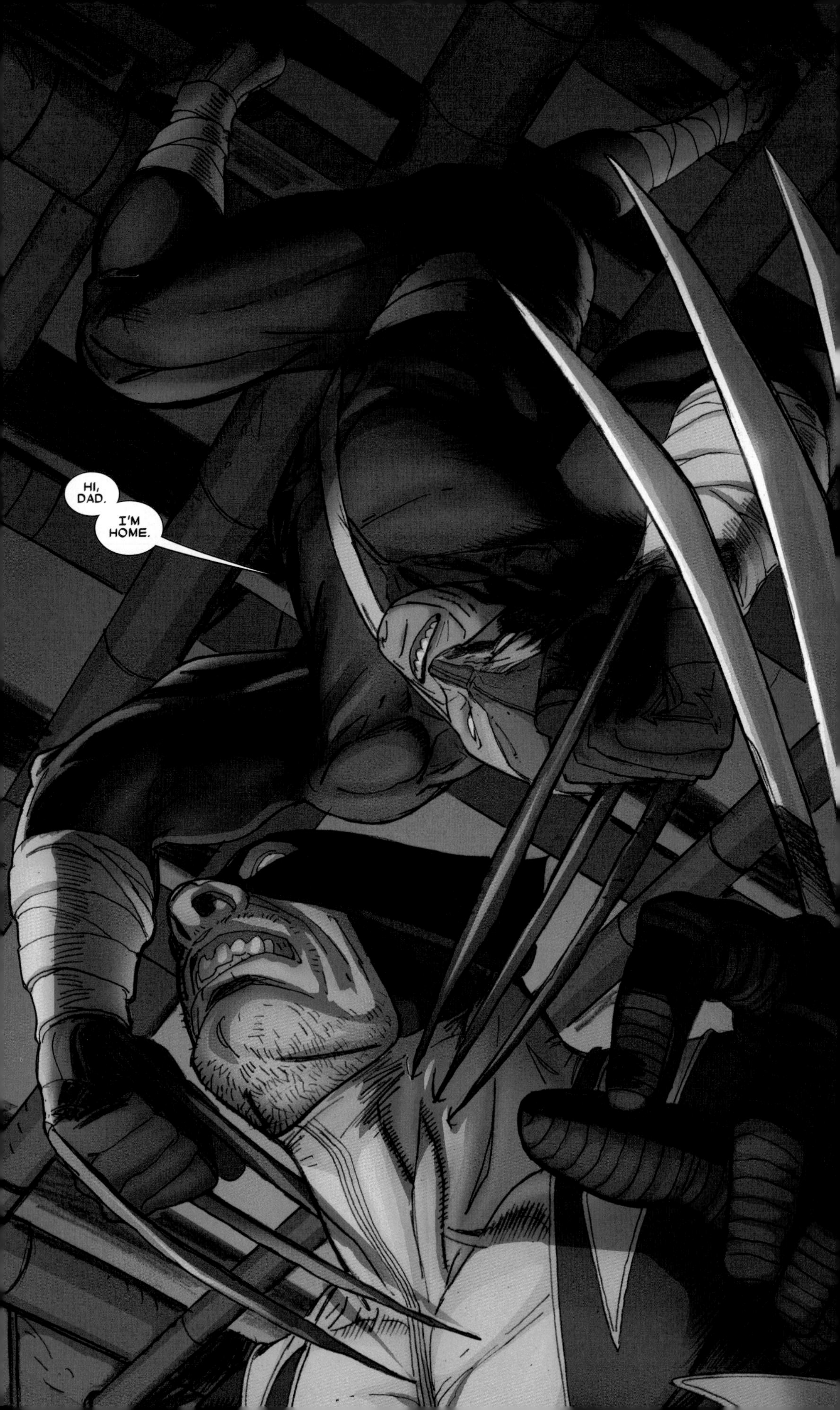
HI, DAD.
I'M HOME.

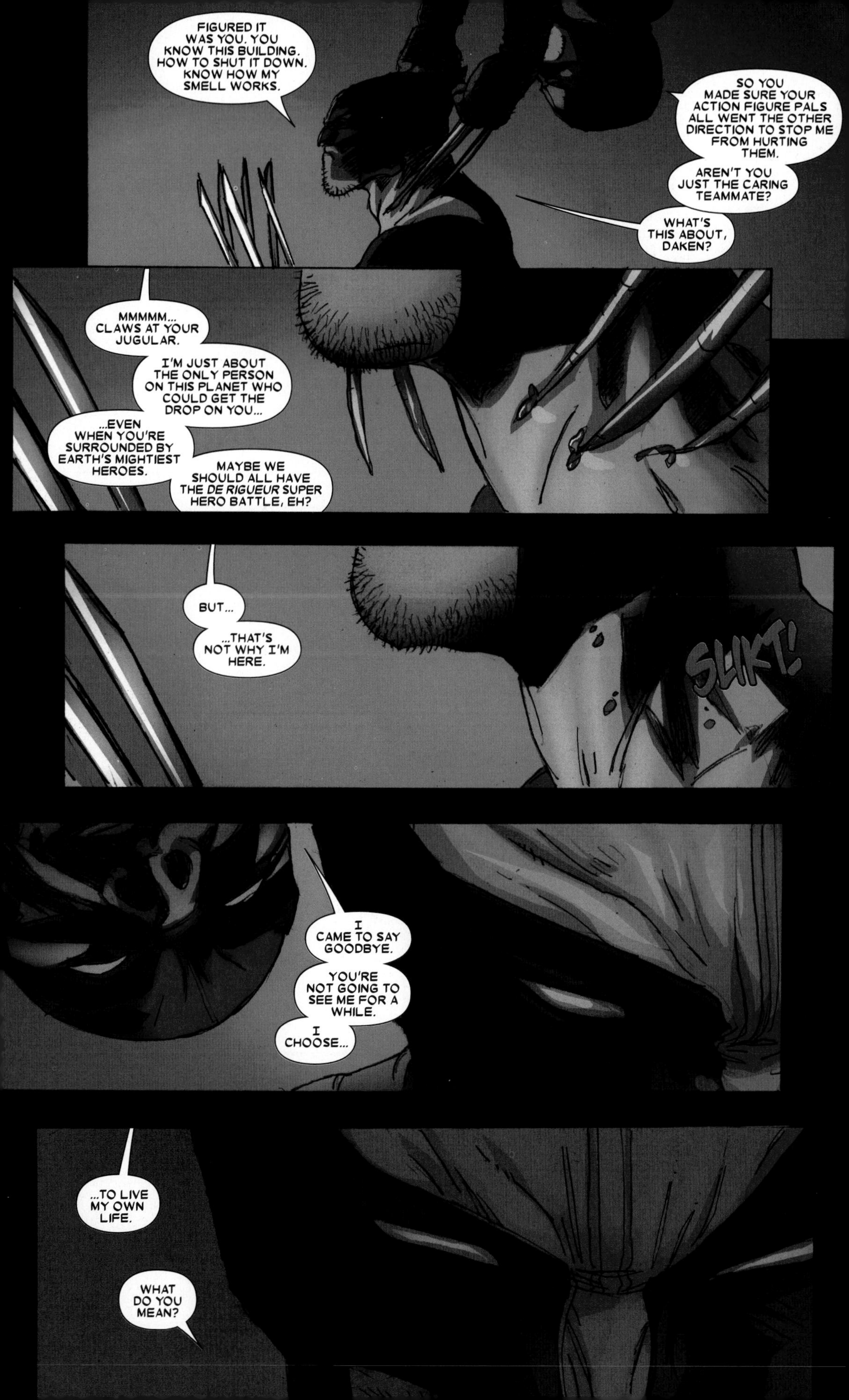
FIGURED IT WAS YOU. YOU KNOW THIS BUILDING. HOW TO SHUT IT DOWN. KNOW HOW MY SMELL WORKS.
SO YOU MADE SURE YOUR ACTION FIGURE PALS ALL WENT THE OTHER DIRECTION TO STOP ME FROM HURTING THEM.
AREN'T YOU JUST THE CARING TEAMMATE?
WHAT'S THIS ABOUT, DAKEN?
MMMMM... CLAWS AT YOUR JUGULAR.
I'M JUST ABOUT THE ONLY PERSON ON THIS PLANET WHO COULD GET THE DROP ON YOU...
...EVEN WHEN YOU'RE SURROUNDED BY EARTH'S MIGHTIEST HEROES.
MAYBE WE SHOULD ALL HAVE THE *DE RIGUEUR* SUPER HERO BATTLE, EH?
BUT...
...THAT'S NOT WHY I'M HERE.
SLIKT!
I CAME TO SAY GOODBYE.
YOU'RE NOT GOING TO SEE ME FOR A WHILE.
I CHOOSE...
...TO LIVE MY OWN LIFE.
WHAT DO YOU MEAN?

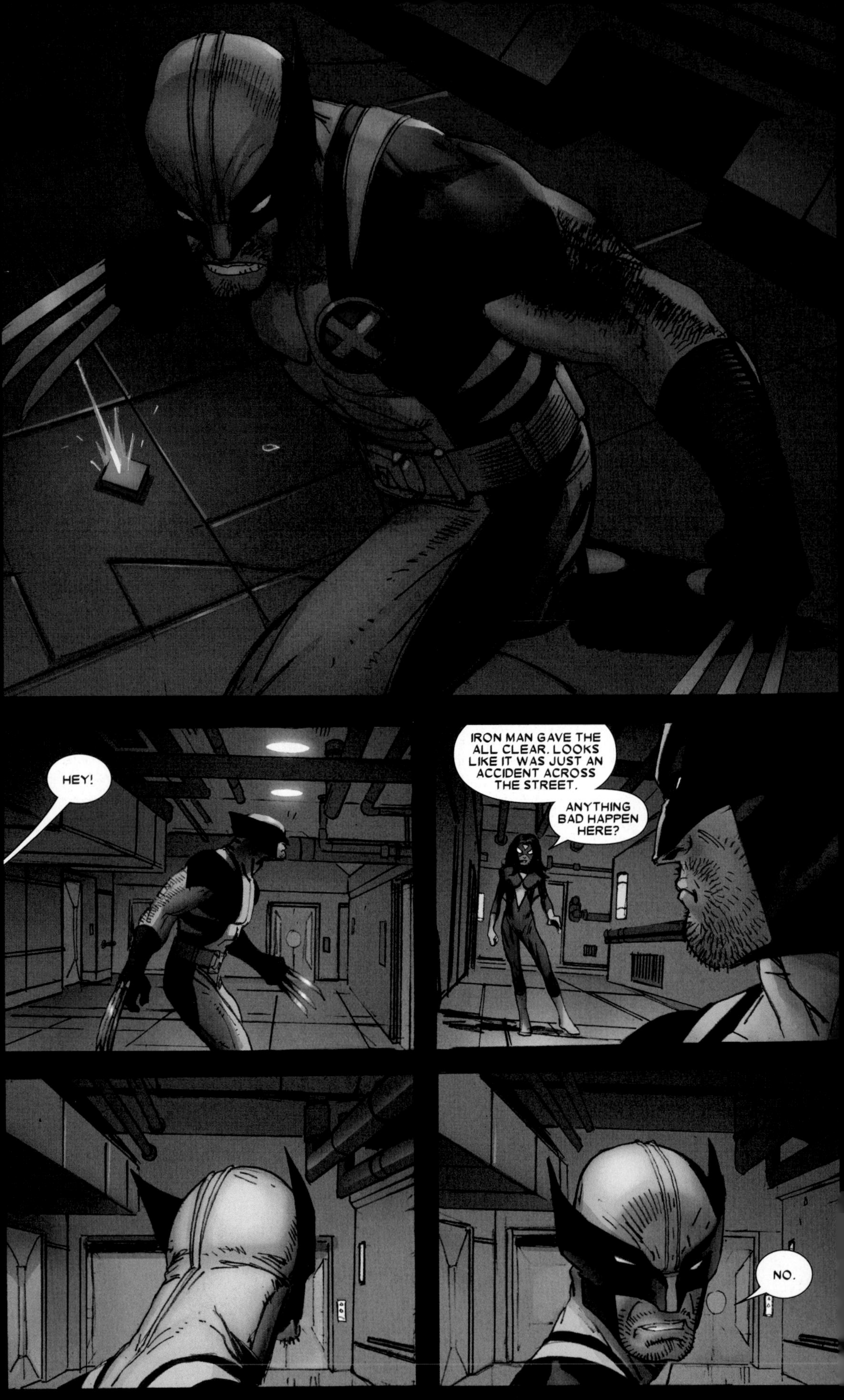
HEY!
IRON MAN GAVE THE ALL CLEAR. LOOKS LIKE IT WAS JUST AN ACCIDENT ACROSS THE STREET.
ANYTHING BAD HAPPEN HERE?
NO.

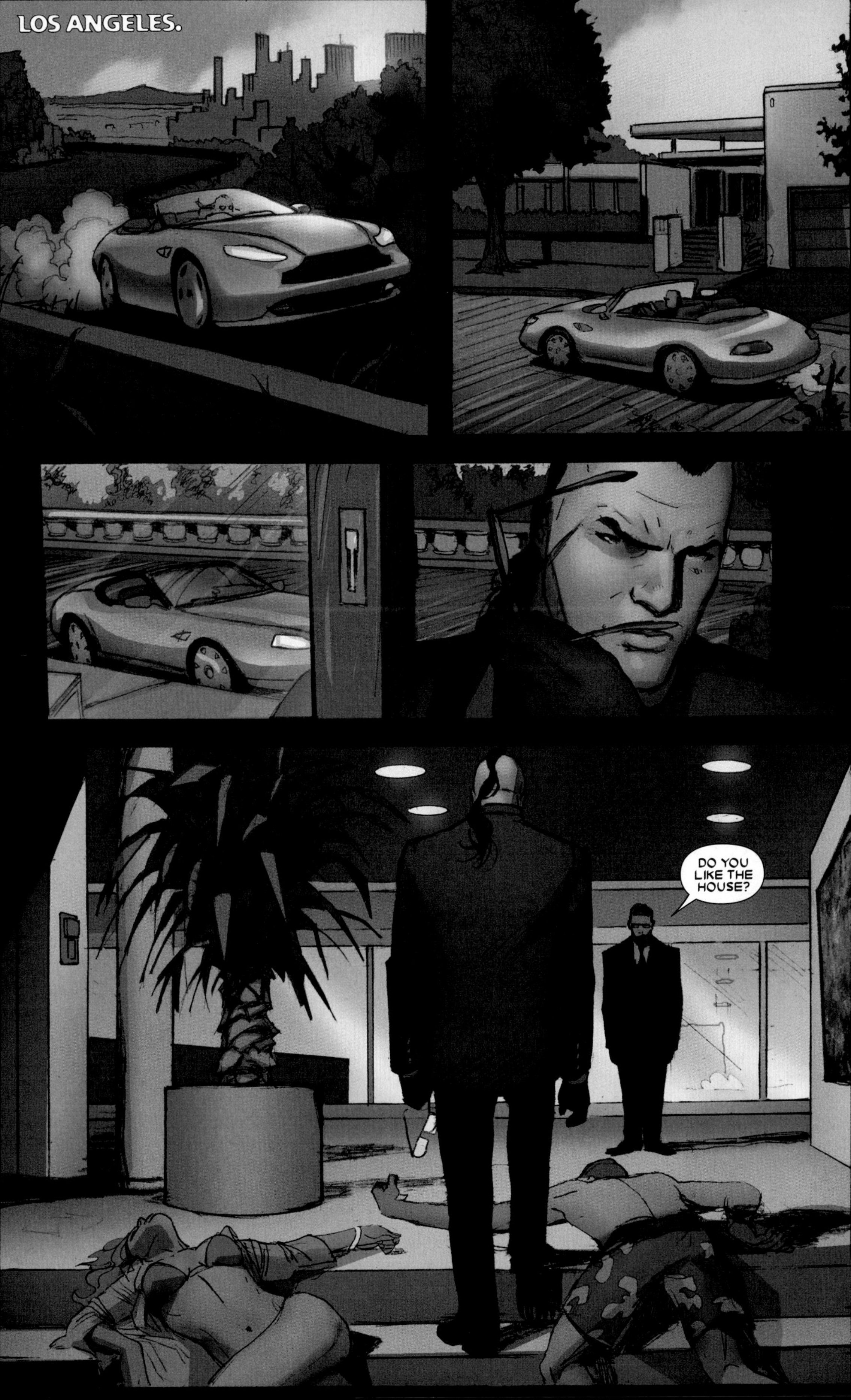
LOS ANGELES.
DO YOU LIKE THE HOUSE?

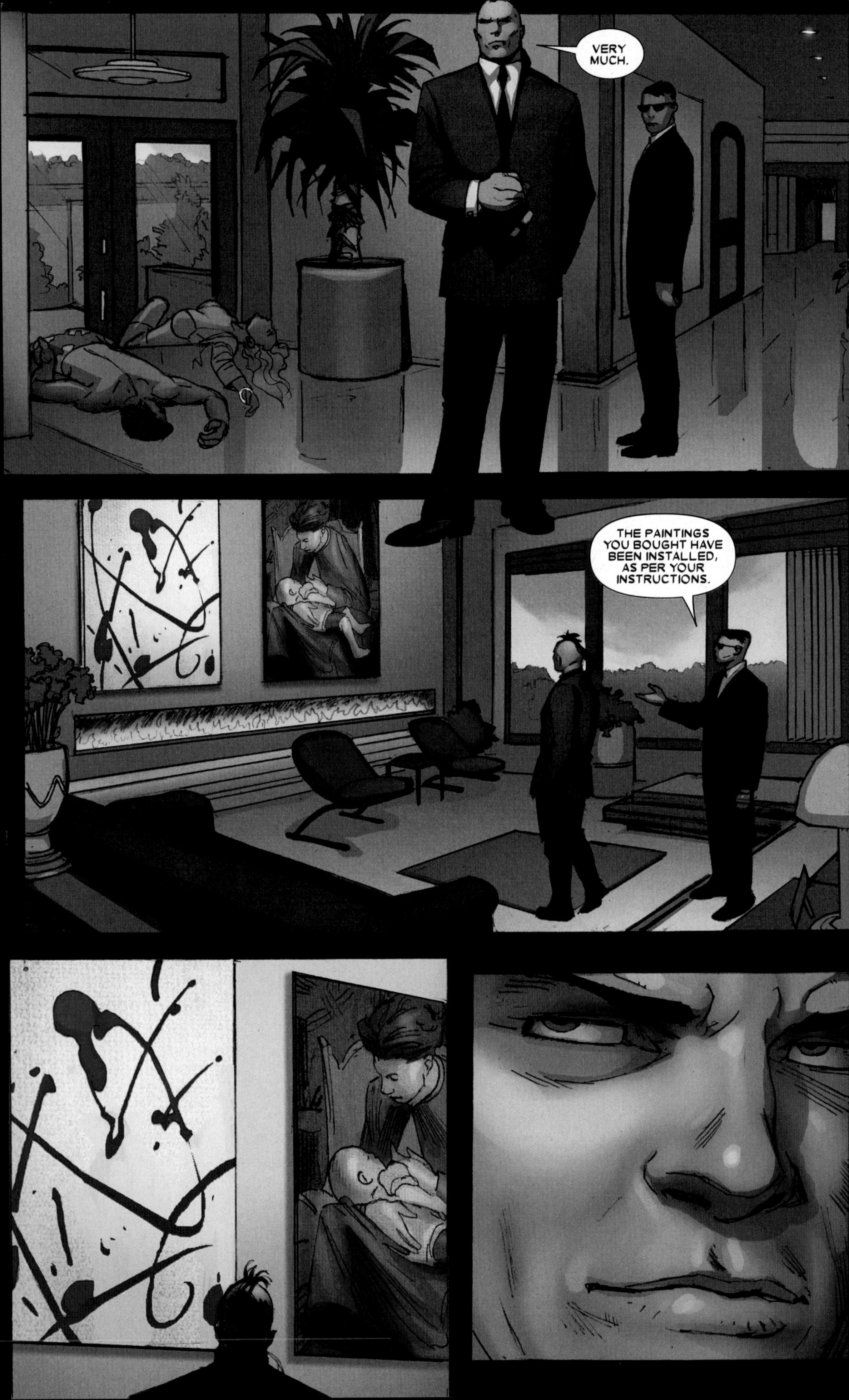
VERY MUCH.
THE PAINTINGS YOU BOUGHT HAVE BEEN INSTALLED, AS PER YOUR INSTRUCTIONS.

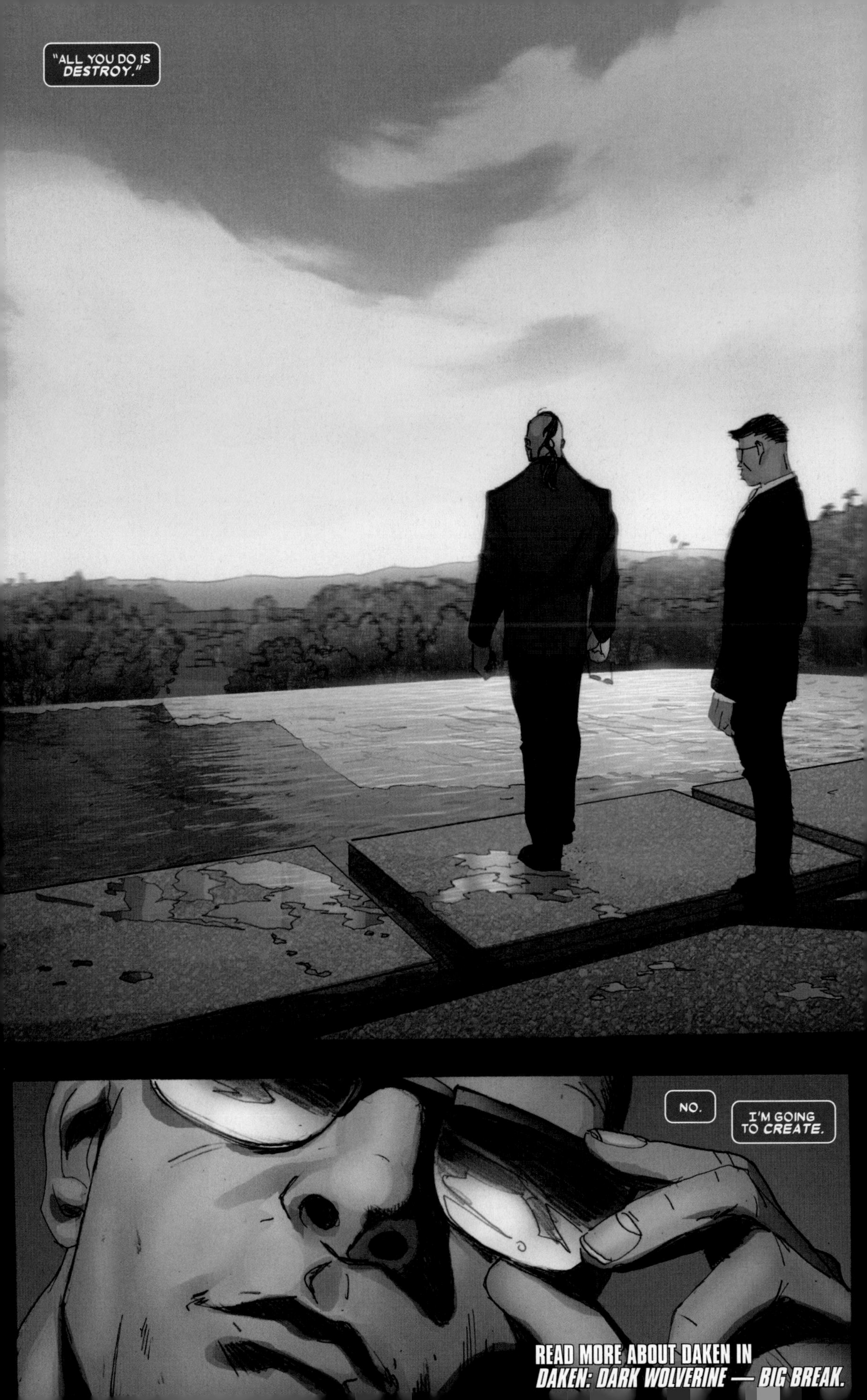
"ALL YOU DO IS DESTROY."
NO.
I'M GOING TO CREATE.
READ MORE ABOUT DAKEN IN DAKEN: DARK WOLVERINE — BIG BREAK.

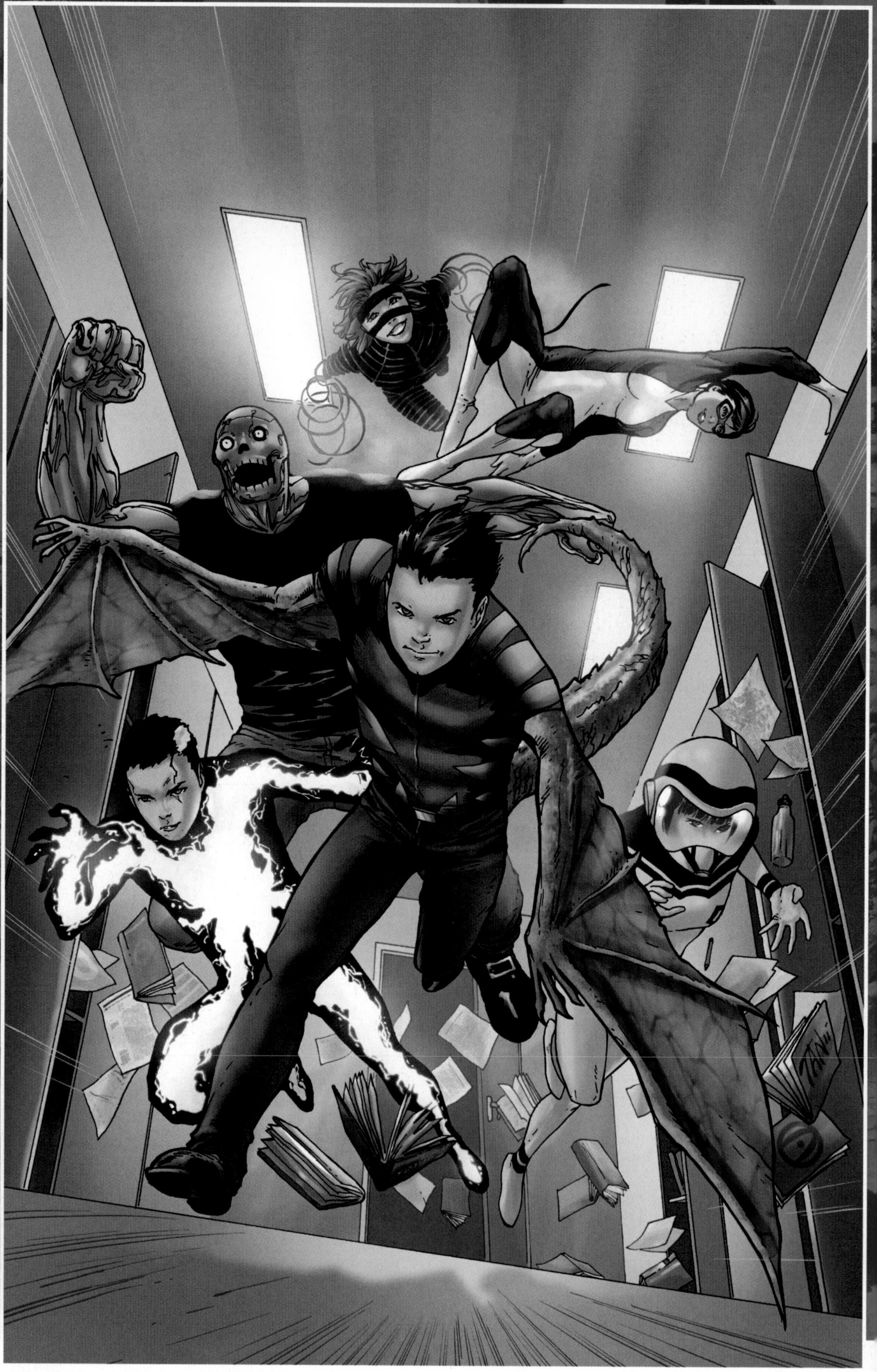

AVENGERS ACADEMY #14.1

AND THERE CAME A DAY, A DAY UNLIKE ANY OTHER, WHEN EARTH'S MIGHTIEST HEROES OPENED THEIR DOORS TO TEACH THE NEXT GENERATION! ON THAT DAY, THE AVENGERS ACADEMY WAS BORN, TO TRAIN YOUNG ADULTS TO FIGHT THE FOES NO SINGLE SUPER HERO COULD WITHSTAND!

AVENGERS ACADEMY

ORIGINAL AVENGER HANK PYM FOUNDED THE AVENGERS ACADEMY TO HELP GUIDE THE NEXT GENERATION OF SUPERHUMANS IN THE NOBLE TRADITION OF EARTH'S MIGHTIEST HEROES.

THE INAUGURAL CLASS IS COMPRISED OF YOUNG ADULTS PREVIOUSLY RECRUITED AND TORTURED BY THE VILLAIN NORMAN OSBORN, WHO, DURING HIS DARK REIGN OVER AMERICAN NATIONAL SECURITY, HOPED TO ASSEMBLE HIS OWN SUPER-POWERED ARMY.

NOT LONG AFTER THE ACADEMY OPENED, THE STUDENTS LEARNED THE SHOCKING TRUTH: THEY WERE SELECTED NOT BECAUSE OF THEIR POTENTIAL TO BECOME HEROES, BUT BECAUSE THEY WERE THE MOST AT RISK OF BECOMING VILLAINS...

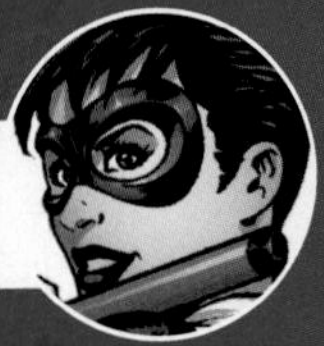

PHOTOGRAPHIC FIGHTER. ALL HEAD, NO HEART.

FINESSE

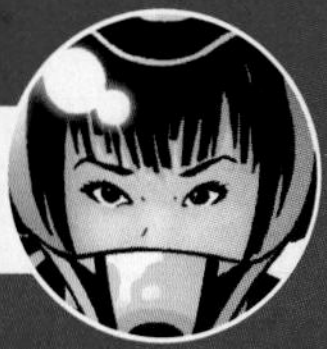

HUMAN TOXIC SPILL. CAUSTIC PERSONALITY.

HAZMAT

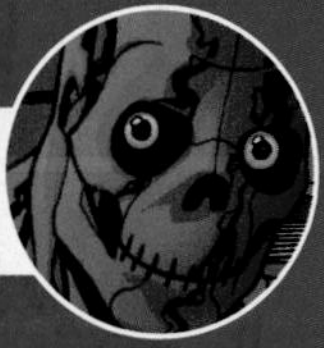

STEEL-SKINNED POWERHOUSE. ARMORED SHELL PROTECTING INNER FEELINGS.

METTLE

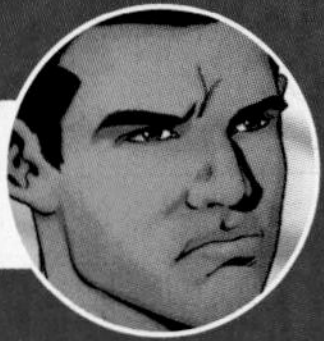

DINOSAUR MORPHER. FUTURE HERO OR NAIVE OPTIMIST?

REPTIL

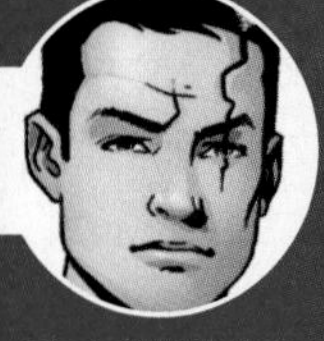

ELECTRIC DYNAMO. SELF-PROMOTES THROUGH SHOCK TACTICS.

STRIKER

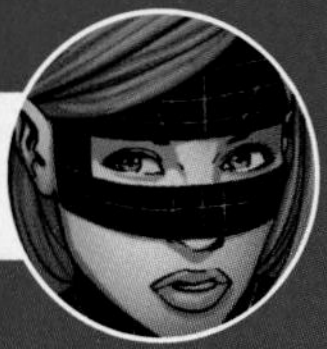

VARIABLE GAS GENERATOR. UNSEEN POTENTIAL... UNTIL SHE DISCORPORATES.

VEIL

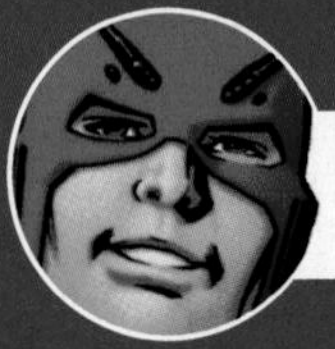

SIZE-CHANGING SCIENTIST SUPREME.

GIANT-MAN

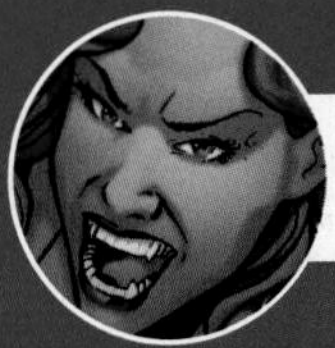

CAT WOMAN. ENHANCED STRENGTH, AGILITY AND ATTITUDE.

TIGRA

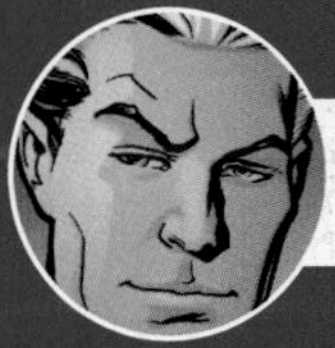

SURLY SPEEDSTER.

QUICKSILVER

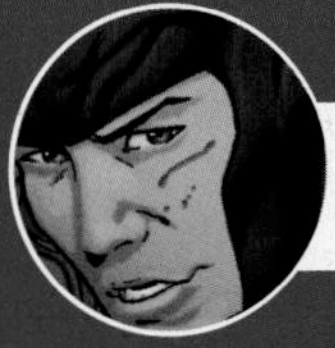

TELEKINETIC MORAL COMPASS.

JUSTICE

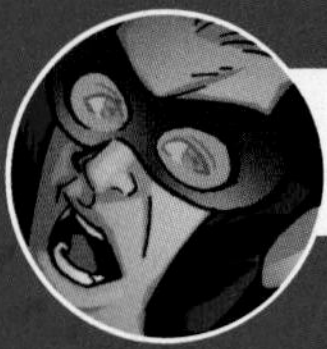

KINETIC ENERGY MANIPULATOR. TRYING TO BOUNCE BACK.

SPEEDBALL

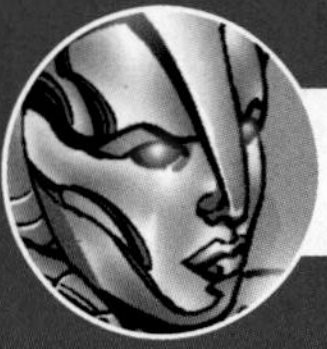

SYNTHETIC BEING. LOYAL TO GIANT-MAN... OR ULTRON?

JOCASTA

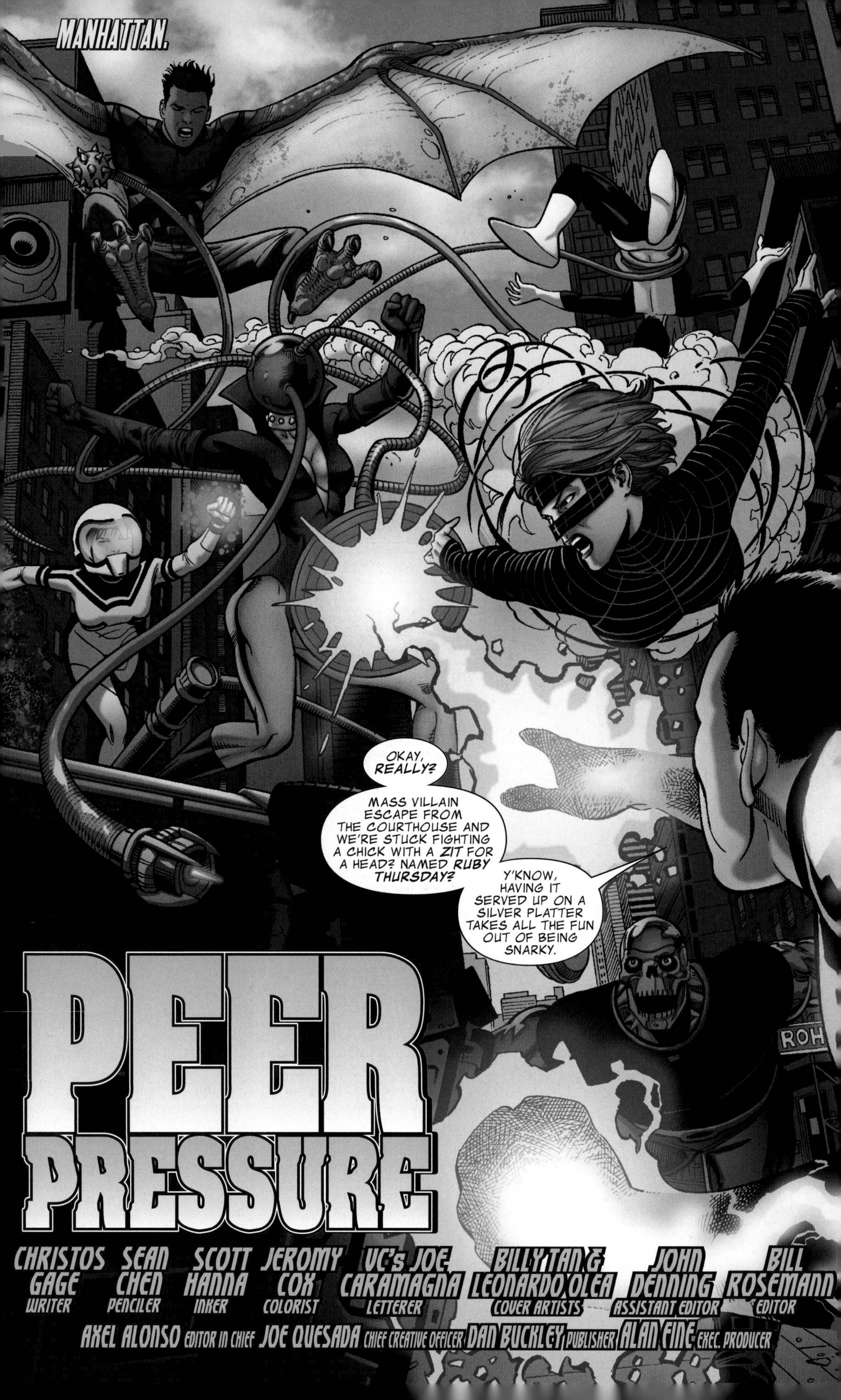
MANHATTAN.
OKAY, REALLY?
MASS VILLAIN ESCAPE FROM THE COURTHOUSE AND WE'RE STUCK FIGHTING A CHICK WITH A ZIT FOR A HEAD? NAMED RUBY THURSDAY?
Y'KNOW, HAVING IT SERVED UP ON A SILVER PLATTER TAKES ALL THE FUN OUT OF BEING SNARKY.
ROH
PEER PRESSURE
CHRISTOS GAGE WRITER
SEAN CHEN PENCILER
SCOTT HANNA INKER
JEROMY COX COLORIST
VC's JOE CARAMAGNA LETTERER
BILLY TAN & LEONARDO OLEA COVER ARTISTS
JOHN DENNING ASSISTANT EDITOR
BILL ROSEMANN EDITOR
AXEL ALONSO EDITOR IN CHIEF JOE QUESADA CHIEF CREATIVE OFFICER DAN BUCKLEY PUBLISHER ALAN FINE EXEC. PRODUCER

YOU'RE RIGHT. WHY WOULD ANYONE WALK AROUND LIKE THIS? SURELY I WOULDN'T WANT TO BE *UNDERESTIMATED* BY PEOPLE WHO'D NEVER DREAM I'M A Ph.D.

SMART ENOUGH TO FIGURE OUT THIS GIRL'S *SUIT* ISN'T MEANT TO KEEP HARMFUL MATERIALS *OUT*...BUT TO KEEP HER RADIATION *IN*.

HAZMAT!

BACK OFF, VEIL. I'M GONNA KNOCK THIS WITCH'S HEAD OFF AND USE IT FOR A CHRISTMAS ORNA--

RELAX, *METTLE*, YOUR SUGAR-BEAR'S FINE. WE'VE PRACTICED THIS. I'LL HAVE IT SEALED IN NO TIME.

OKAY...I TURNED INTO ETHER, BUT I'M HAVING TROUBLE KNOCKING HER OUT 'CAUSE OF THE, Y'KNOW, LACK OF A *NOSE*...

SKIZZ

K'UNG

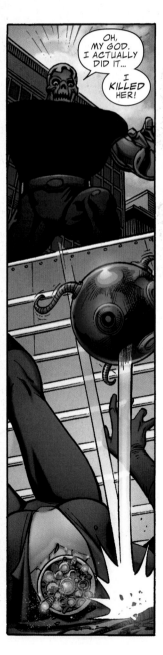

OH, MY GOD. I ACTUALLY DID IT... I *KILLED* HER!

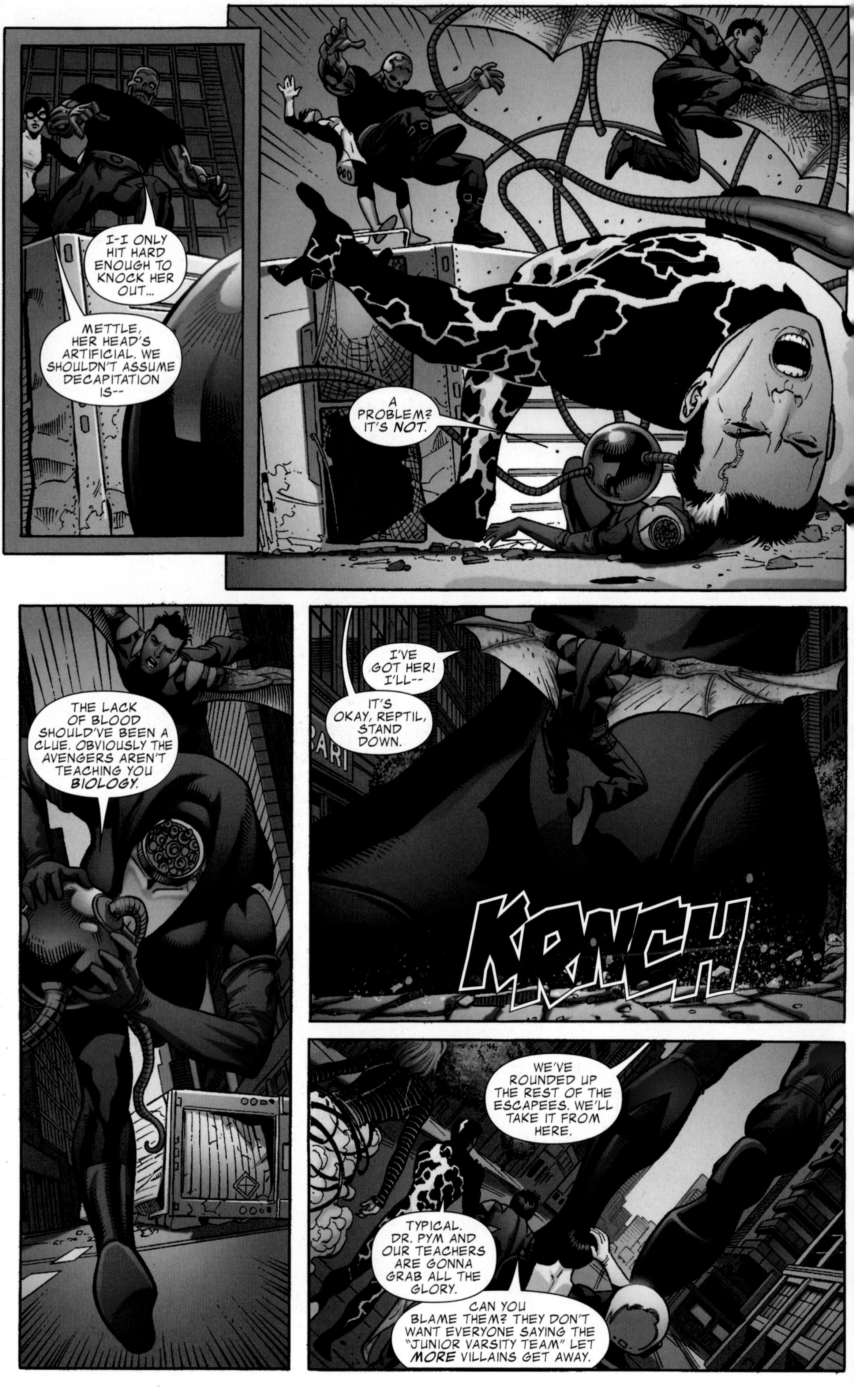
I-I ONLY HIT HARD ENOUGH TO KNOCK HER OUT...
METTLE, HER HEAD'S ARTIFICIAL. WE SHOULDN'T ASSUME DECAPITATION IS--
A PROBLEM? IT'S NOT.
THE LACK OF BLOOD SHOULD'VE BEEN A CLUE. OBVIOUSLY THE AVENGERS AREN'T TEACHING YOU BIOLOGY.
I'VE GOT HER! I'LL--
IT'S OKAY, REPTIL, STAND DOWN.
KRNCH
WE'VE ROUNDED UP THE REST OF THE ESCAPEES. WE'LL TAKE IT FROM HERE.
TYPICAL. DR. PYM AND OUR TEACHERS ARE GONNA GRAB ALL THE GLORY.
CAN YOU BLAME THEM? THEY DON'T WANT EVERYONE SAYING THE "JUNIOR VARSITY TEAM" LET MORE VILLAINS GET AWAY.

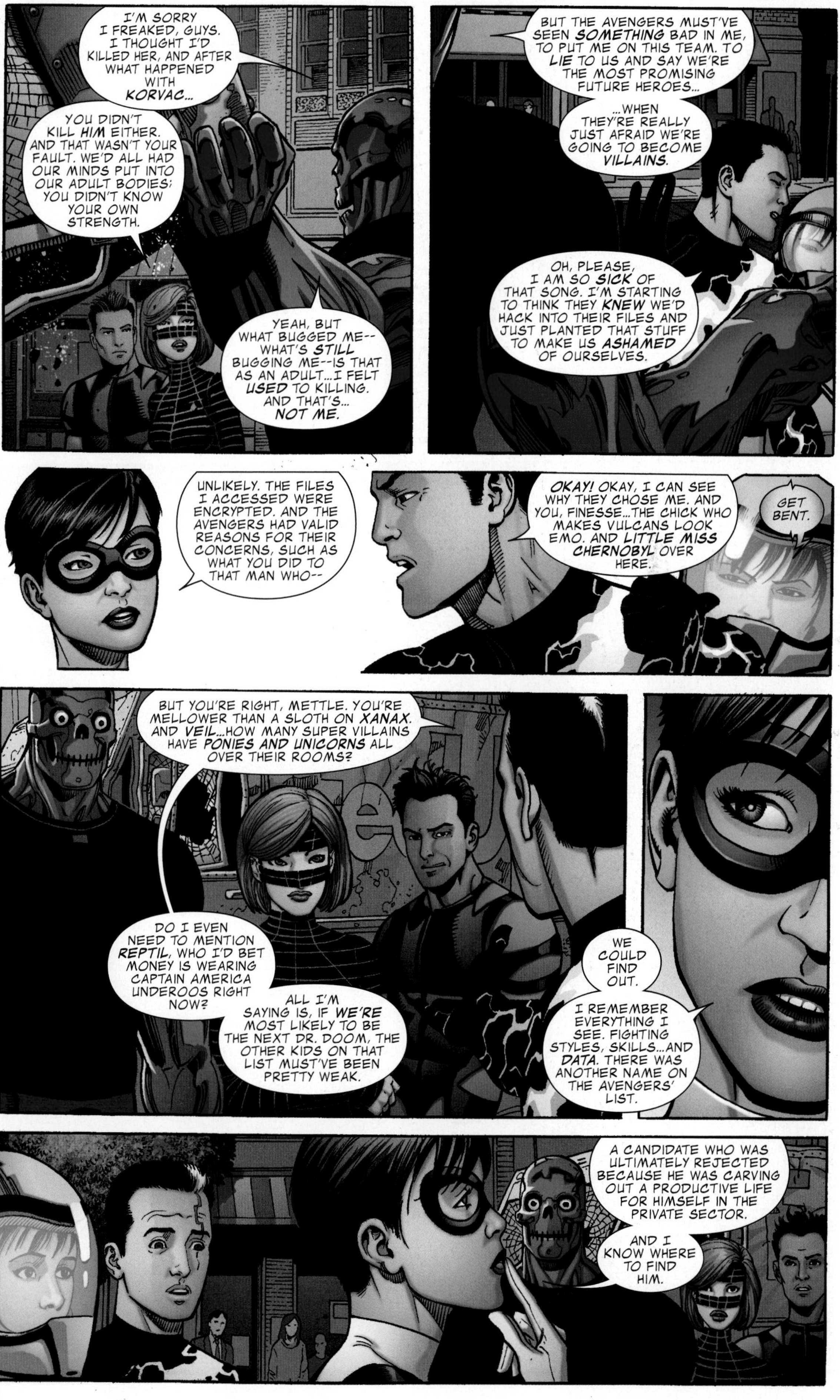

I'M SORRY I FREAKED, GUYS. I THOUGHT I'D KILLED HER, AND AFTER WHAT HAPPENED WITH KORVAC...
YOU DIDN'T KILL HIM EITHER. AND THAT WASN'T YOUR FAULT. WE'D ALL HAD OUR MINDS PUT INTO OUR ADULT BODIES; YOU DIDN'T KNOW YOUR OWN STRENGTH.
YEAH, BUT WHAT BUGGED ME-- WHAT'S STILL BUGGING ME--IS THAT AS AN ADULT...I FELT USED TO KILLING. AND THAT'S... NOT ME.
BUT THE AVENGERS MUST'VE SEEN SOMETHING BAD IN ME, TO PUT ME ON THIS TEAM. TO LIE TO US AND SAY WE'RE THE MOST PROMISING FUTURE HEROES...
...WHEN THEY'RE REALLY JUST AFRAID WE'RE GOING TO BECOME VILLAINS.
OH, PLEASE, I AM SO SICK OF THAT SONG. I'M STARTING TO THINK THEY KNEW WE'D HACK INTO THEIR FILES AND JUST PLANTED THAT STUFF TO MAKE US ASHAMED OF OURSELVES.
UNLIKELY. THE FILES I ACCESSED WERE ENCRYPTED. AND THE AVENGERS HAD VALID REASONS FOR THEIR CONCERNS, SUCH AS WHAT YOU DID TO THAT MAN WHO--
OKAY! OKAY, I CAN SEE WHY THEY CHOSE ME. AND YOU, FINESSE...THE CHICK WHO MAKES VULCANS LOOK EMO. AND LITTLE MISS CHERNOBYL OVER HERE.
GET BENT.
BUT YOU'RE RIGHT, METTLE. YOU'RE MELLOWER THAN A SLOTH ON XANAX. AND VEIL...HOW MANY SUPER VILLAINS HAVE PONIES AND UNICORNS ALL OVER THEIR ROOMS?
DO I EVEN NEED TO MENTION REPTIL, WHO I'D BET MONEY IS WEARING CAPTAIN AMERICA UNDEROOS RIGHT NOW?
ALL I'M SAYING IS, IF WE'RE MOST LIKELY TO BE THE NEXT DR. DOOM, THE OTHER KIDS ON THAT LIST MUST'VE BEEN PRETTY WEAK.
WE COULD FIND OUT.
I REMEMBER EVERYTHING I SEE. FIGHTING STYLES, SKILLS...AND DATA. THERE WAS ANOTHER NAME ON THE AVENGERS' LIST.
A CANDIDATE WHO WAS ULTIMATELY REJECTED BECAUSE HE WAS CARVING OUT A PRODUCTIVE LIFE FOR HIMSELF IN THE PRIVATE SECTOR.
AND I KNOW WHERE TO FIND HIM.

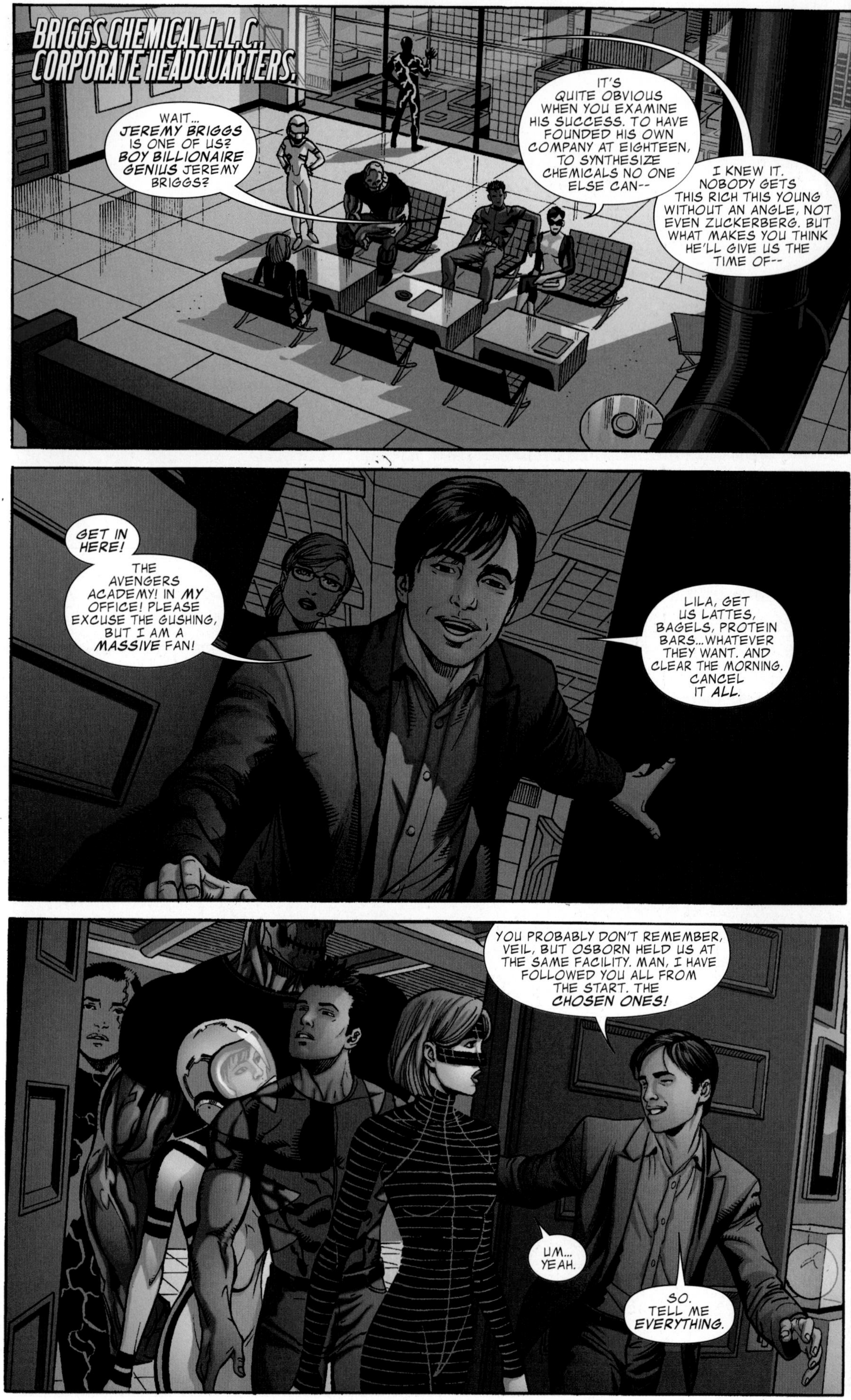
BRIGGS CHEMICAL L.L.C., CORPORATE HEADQUARTERS.
WAIT... JEREMY BRIGGS IS ONE OF US? BOY BILLIONAIRE GENIUS JEREMY BRIGGS?
IT'S QUITE OBVIOUS WHEN YOU EXAMINE HIS SUCCESS. TO HAVE FOUNDED HIS OWN COMPANY AT EIGHTEEN, TO SYNTHESIZE CHEMICALS NO ONE ELSE CAN--
I KNEW IT. NOBODY GETS THIS RICH THIS YOUNG WITHOUT AN ANGLE, NOT EVEN ZUCKERBERG. BUT WHAT MAKES YOU THINK HE'LL GIVE US THE TIME OF--
GET IN HERE!
THE AVENGERS ACADEMY! IN MY OFFICE! PLEASE EXCUSE THE GUSHING, BUT I AM A MASSIVE FAN!
LILA, GET US LATTES, BAGELS, PROTEIN BARS...WHATEVER THEY WANT. AND CLEAR THE MORNING. CANCEL IT ALL.
YOU PROBABLY DON'T REMEMBER, VEIL, BUT OSBORN HELD US AT THE SAME FACILITY. MAN, I HAVE FOLLOWED YOU ALL FROM THE START. THE CHOSEN ONES!
UM... YEAH.
SO. TELL ME EVERYTHING.

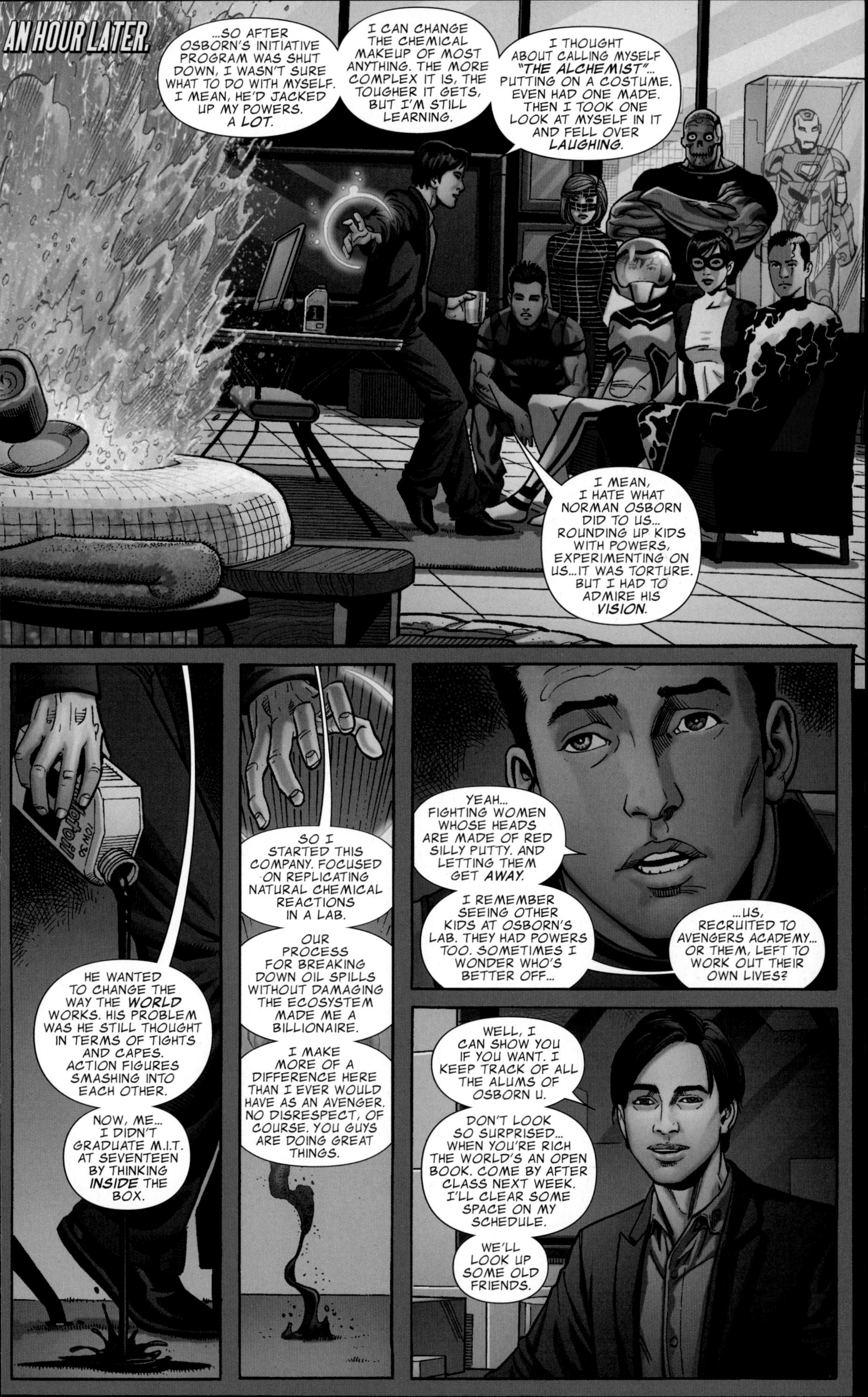
AN HOUR LATER.
...SO AFTER OSBORN'S INITIATIVE PROGRAM WAS SHUT DOWN, I WASN'T SURE WHAT TO DO WITH MYSELF. I MEAN, HE'D JACKED UP MY POWERS. A LOT.
I CAN CHANGE THE CHEMICAL MAKEUP OF MOST ANYTHING. THE MORE COMPLEX IT IS, THE TOUGHER IT GETS, BUT I'M STILL LEARNING.
I THOUGHT ABOUT CALLING MYSELF "THE ALCHEMIST"... PUTTING ON A COSTUME. EVEN HAD ONE MADE. THEN I TOOK ONE LOOK AT MYSELF IN IT AND FELL OVER LAUGHING.
I MEAN, I HATE WHAT NORMAN OSBORN DID TO US... ROUNDING UP KIDS WITH POWERS, EXPERIMENTING ON US...IT WAS TORTURE. BUT I HAD TO ADMIRE HIS VISION.
HE WANTED TO CHANGE THE WAY THE WORLD WORKS. HIS PROBLEM WAS HE STILL THOUGHT IN TERMS OF TIGHTS AND CAPES. ACTION FIGURES SMASHING INTO EACH OTHER.
NOW, ME... I DIDN'T GRADUATE M.I.T. AT SEVENTEEN BY THINKING INSIDE THE BOX.
SO I STARTED THIS COMPANY. FOCUSED ON REPLICATING NATURAL CHEMICAL REACTIONS IN A LAB.
OUR PROCESS FOR BREAKING DOWN OIL SPILLS WITHOUT DAMAGING THE ECOSYSTEM MADE ME A BILLIONAIRE.
I MAKE MORE OF A DIFFERENCE HERE THAN I EVER WOULD HAVE AS AN AVENGER. NO DISRESPECT, OF COURSE. YOU GUYS ARE DOING GREAT THINGS.
YEAH... FIGHTING WOMEN WHOSE HEADS ARE MADE OF RED SILLY PUTTY. AND LETTING THEM GET AWAY.
I REMEMBER SEEING OTHER KIDS AT OSBORN'S LAB. THEY HAD POWERS TOO. SOMETIMES I WONDER WHO'S BETTER OFF...
...US, RECRUITED TO AVENGERS ACADEMY... OR THEM, LEFT TO WORK OUT THEIR OWN LIVES?
WELL, I CAN SHOW YOU IF YOU WANT. I KEEP TRACK OF ALL THE ALUMS OF OSBORN U.
DON'T LOOK SO SURPRISED... WHEN YOU'RE RICH THE WORLD'S AN OPEN BOOK. COME BY AFTER CLASS NEXT WEEK. I'LL CLEAR SOME SPACE ON MY SCHEDULE.
WE'LL LOOK UP SOME OLD FRIENDS.

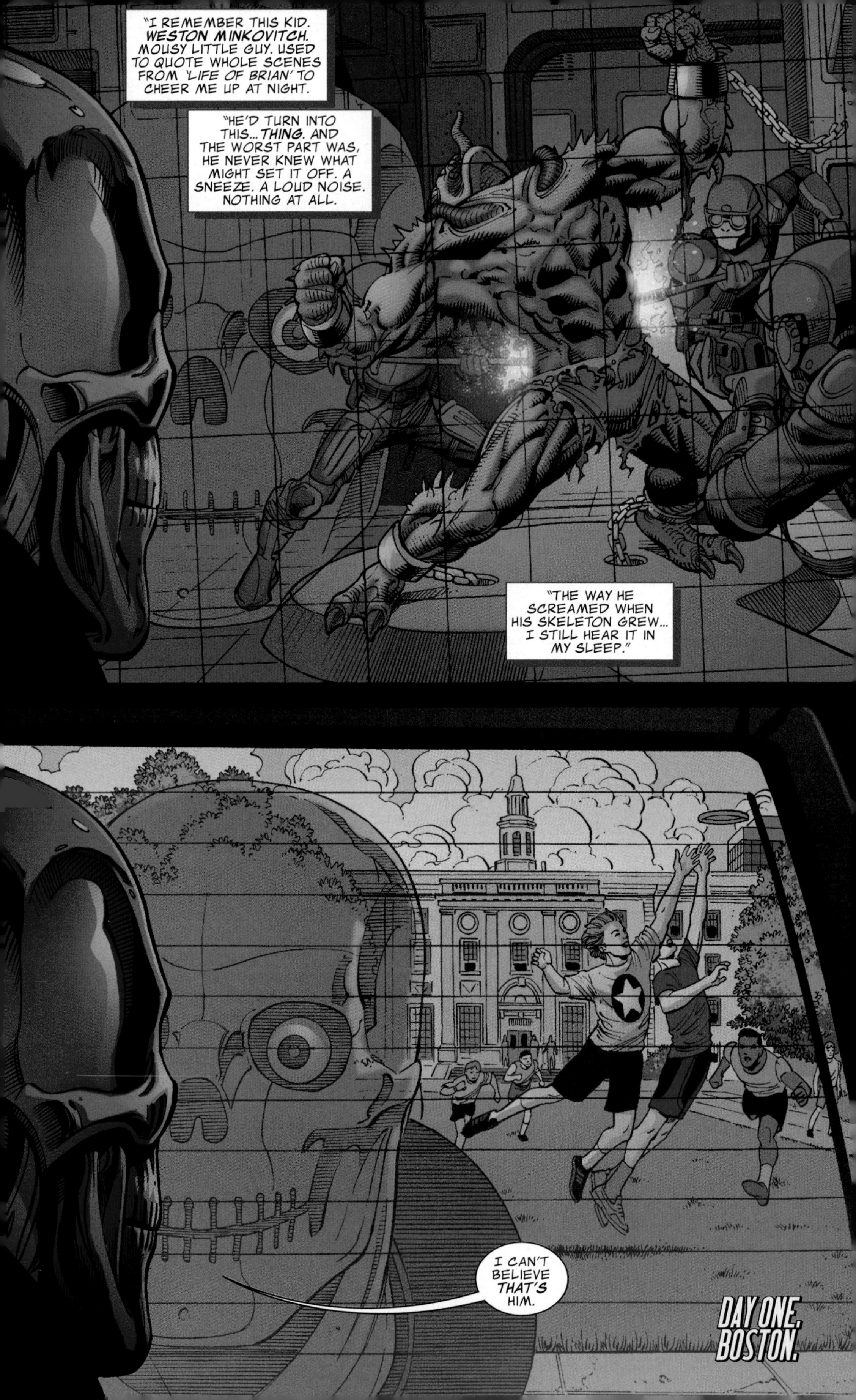
"I REMEMBER THIS KID. WESTON MINKOVITCH. MOUSY LITTLE GUY. USED TO QUOTE WHOLE SCENES FROM 'LIFE OF BRIAN' TO CHEER ME UP AT NIGHT.
"HE'D TURN INTO THIS... THING. AND THE WORST PART WAS, HE NEVER KNEW WHAT MIGHT SET IT OFF. A SNEEZE. A LOUD NOISE. NOTHING AT ALL.
"THE WAY HE SCREAMED WHEN HIS SKELETON GREW... I STILL HEAR IT IN MY SLEEP."
DAY ONE. BOSTON.
I CAN'T BELIEVE THAT'S HIM.

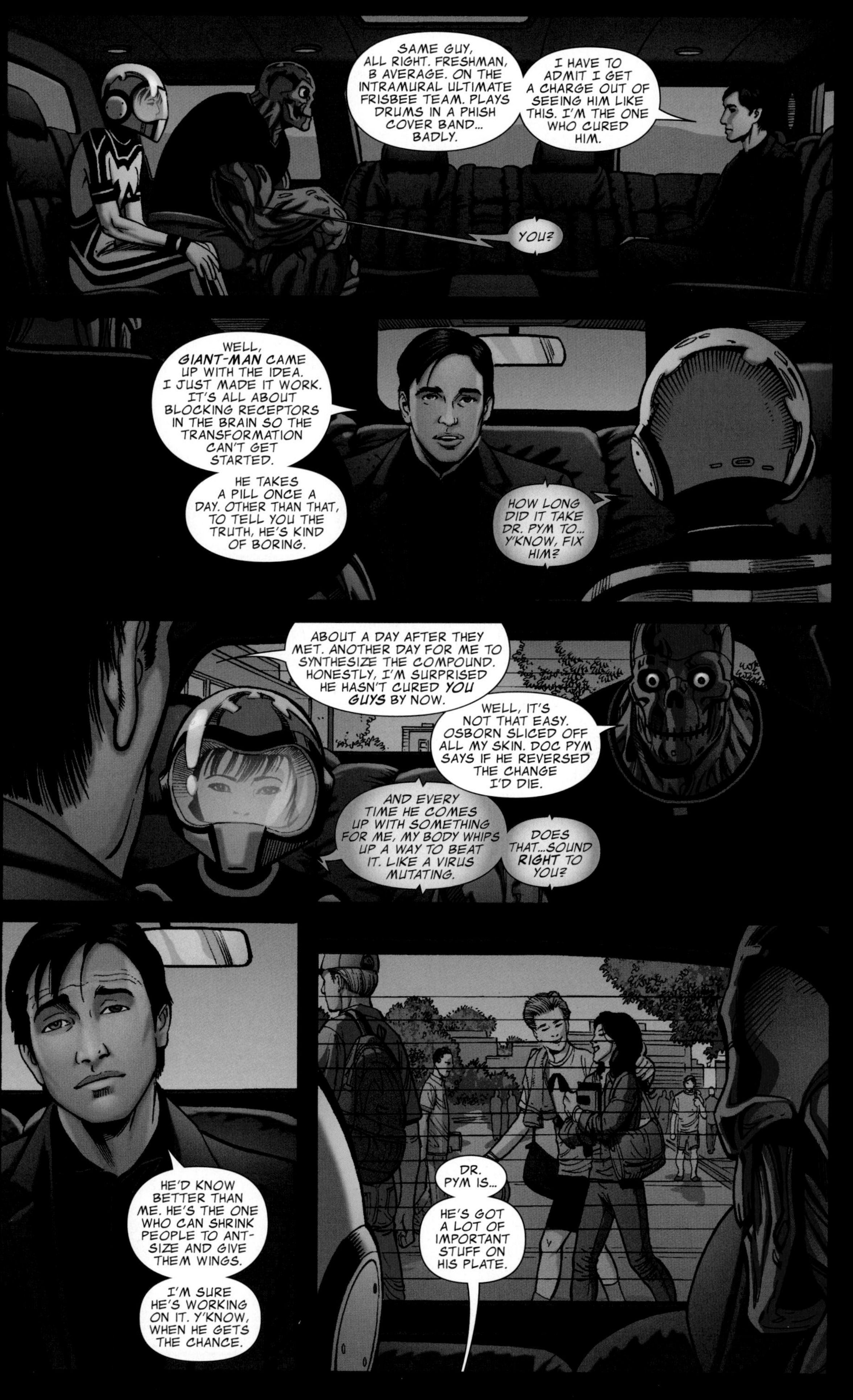
SAME GUY, ALL RIGHT. FRESHMAN, B AVERAGE. ON THE INTRAMURAL ULTIMATE FRISBEE TEAM. PLAYS DRUMS IN A PHISH COVER BAND... BADLY.
I HAVE TO ADMIT I GET A CHARGE OUT OF SEEING HIM LIKE THIS. I'M THE ONE WHO CURED HIM.
YOU?
WELL, GIANT-MAN CAME UP WITH THE IDEA. I JUST MADE IT WORK. IT'S ALL ABOUT BLOCKING RECEPTORS IN THE BRAIN SO THE TRANSFORMATION CAN'T GET STARTED.
HE TAKES A PILL ONCE A DAY. OTHER THAN THAT, TO TELL YOU THE TRUTH, HE'S KIND OF BORING.
HOW LONG DID IT TAKE DR. PYM TO... Y'KNOW, FIX HIM?
ABOUT A DAY AFTER THEY MET. ANOTHER DAY FOR ME TO SYNTHESIZE THE COMPOUND. HONESTLY, I'M SURPRISED HE HASN'T CURED YOU GUYS BY NOW.
WELL, IT'S NOT THAT EASY. OSBORN SLICED OFF ALL MY SKIN. DOC PYM SAYS IF HE REVERSED THE CHANGE I'D DIE.
AND EVERY TIME HE COMES UP WITH SOMETHING FOR ME, MY BODY WHIPS UP A WAY TO BEAT IT. LIKE A VIRUS MUTATING.
DOES THAT...SOUND RIGHT TO YOU?
HE'D KNOW BETTER THAN ME. HE'S THE ONE WHO CAN SHRINK PEOPLE TO ANT-SIZE AND GIVE THEM WINGS.
I'M SURE HE'S WORKING ON IT. Y'KNOW, WHEN HE GETS THE CHANCE.
DR. PYM IS...
HE'S GOT A LOT OF IMPORTANT STUFF ON HIS PLATE.

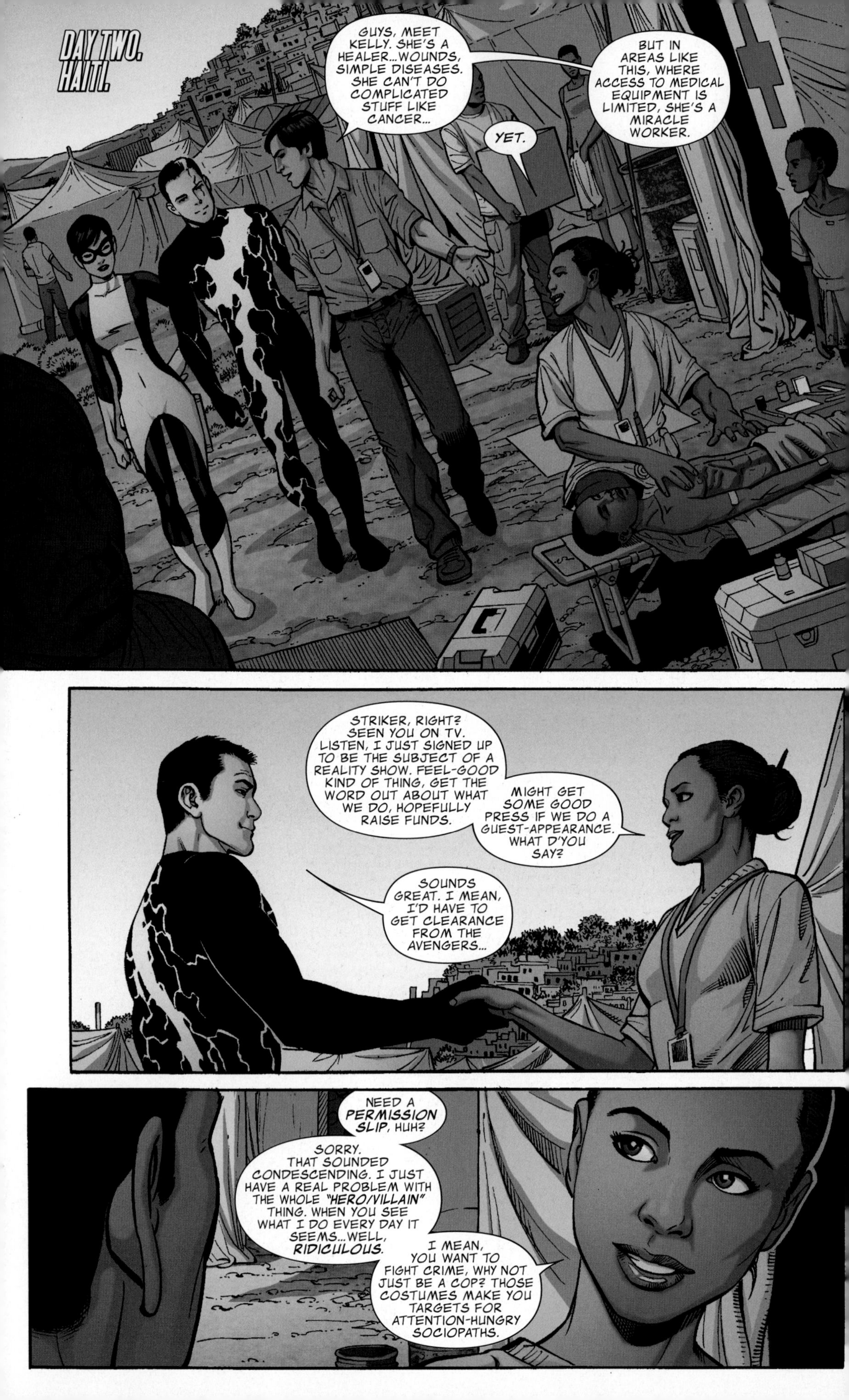
DAY TWO. HAITI.
GUYS, MEET KELLY. SHE'S A HEALER...WOUNDS, SIMPLE DISEASES. SHE CAN'T DO COMPLICATED STUFF LIKE CANCER...
YET.
BUT IN AREAS LIKE THIS, WHERE ACCESS TO MEDICAL EQUIPMENT IS LIMITED, SHE'S A MIRACLE WORKER.
STRIKER, RIGHT? SEEN YOU ON TV. LISTEN, I JUST SIGNED UP TO BE THE SUBJECT OF A REALITY SHOW. FEEL-GOOD KIND OF THING, GET THE WORD OUT ABOUT WHAT WE DO, HOPEFULLY RAISE FUNDS.
MIGHT GET SOME GOOD PRESS IF WE DO A GUEST-APPEARANCE. WHAT D'YOU SAY?
SOUNDS GREAT. I MEAN, I'D HAVE TO GET CLEARANCE FROM THE AVENGERS...
NEED A PERMISSION SLIP, HUH?
SORRY. THAT SOUNDED CONDESCENDING. I JUST HAVE A REAL PROBLEM WITH THE WHOLE "HERO/VILLAIN" THING. WHEN YOU SEE WHAT I DO EVERY DAY IT SEEMS...WELL, RIDICULOUS.
I MEAN, YOU WANT TO FIGHT CRIME, WHY NOT JUST BE A COP? THOSE COSTUMES MAKE YOU TARGETS FOR ATTENTION-HUNGRY SOCIOPATHS.

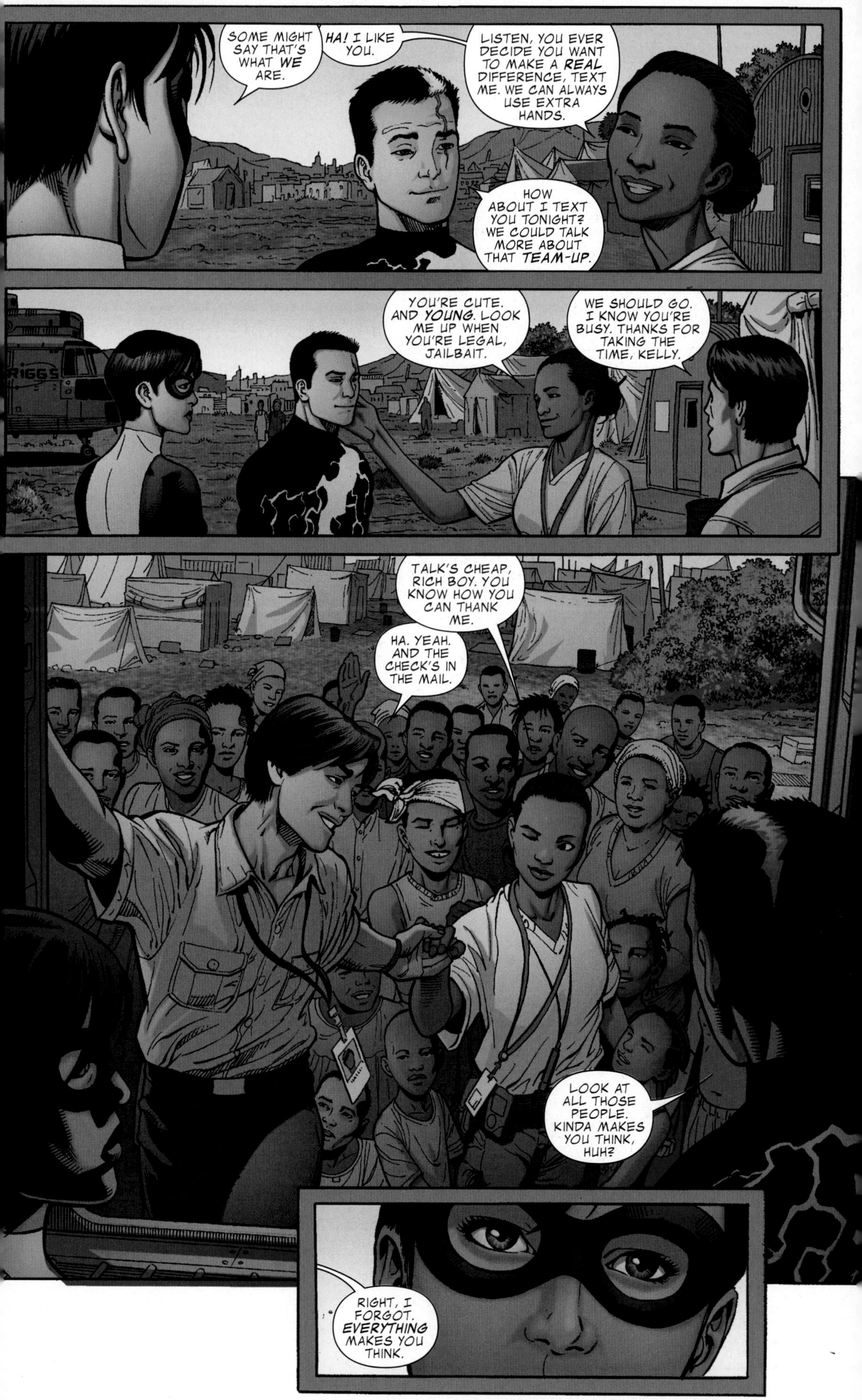

SOME MIGHT SAY THAT'S WHAT **WE** ARE.
HA! I LIKE YOU.
LISTEN, YOU EVER DECIDE YOU WANT TO MAKE A **REAL** DIFFERENCE, TEXT ME. WE CAN ALWAYS USE EXTRA HANDS.
HOW ABOUT I TEXT YOU TONIGHT? WE COULD TALK MORE ABOUT THAT ***TEAM-UP***.
RIGGS
YOU'RE CUTE. AND ***YOUNG***. LOOK ME UP WHEN YOU'RE LEGAL, JAILBAIT.
WE SHOULD GO. I KNOW YOU'RE BUSY. THANKS FOR TAKING THE TIME, KELLY.
TALK'S CHEAP, RICH BOY. YOU KNOW HOW YOU CAN THANK ME.
HA. YEAH. AND THE CHECK'S IN THE MAIL.
LOOK AT ALL THOSE PEOPLE. KINDA MAKES YOU THINK, HUH?
RIGHT, I FORGOT. ***EVERYTHING*** MAKES YOU THINK.

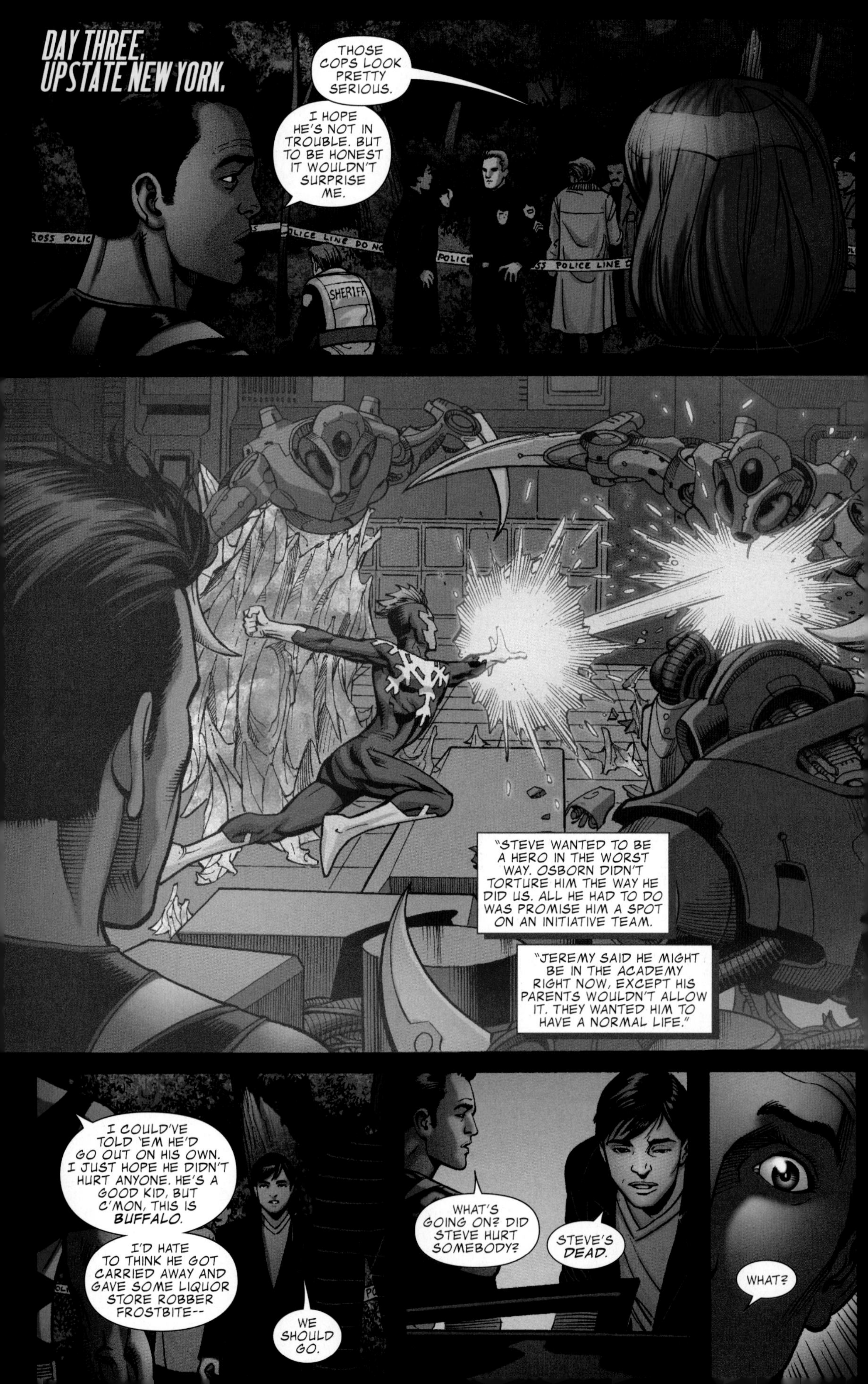
DAY THREE. UPSTATE NEW YORK.
THOSE COPS LOOK PRETTY SERIOUS.
I HOPE HE'S NOT IN TROUBLE. BUT TO BE HONEST IT WOULDN'T SURPRISE ME.
POLICE LINE DO NOT CROSS
SHERIFF
"STEVE WANTED TO BE A HERO IN THE WORST WAY. OSBORN DIDN'T TORTURE HIM THE WAY HE DID US. ALL HE HAD TO DO WAS PROMISE HIM A SPOT ON AN INITIATIVE TEAM.
"JEREMY SAID HE MIGHT BE IN THE ACADEMY RIGHT NOW, EXCEPT HIS PARENTS WOULDN'T ALLOW IT. THEY WANTED HIM TO HAVE A NORMAL LIFE."
I COULD'VE TOLD 'EM HE'D GO OUT ON HIS OWN. I JUST HOPE HE DIDN'T HURT ANYONE. HE'S A GOOD KID, BUT C'MON, THIS IS BUFFALO.
I'D HATE TO THINK HE GOT CARRIED AWAY AND GAVE SOME LIQUOR STORE ROBBER FROSTBITE--
WE SHOULD GO.
WHAT'S GOING ON? DID STEVE HURT SOMEBODY?
STEVE'S DEAD.
WHAT?

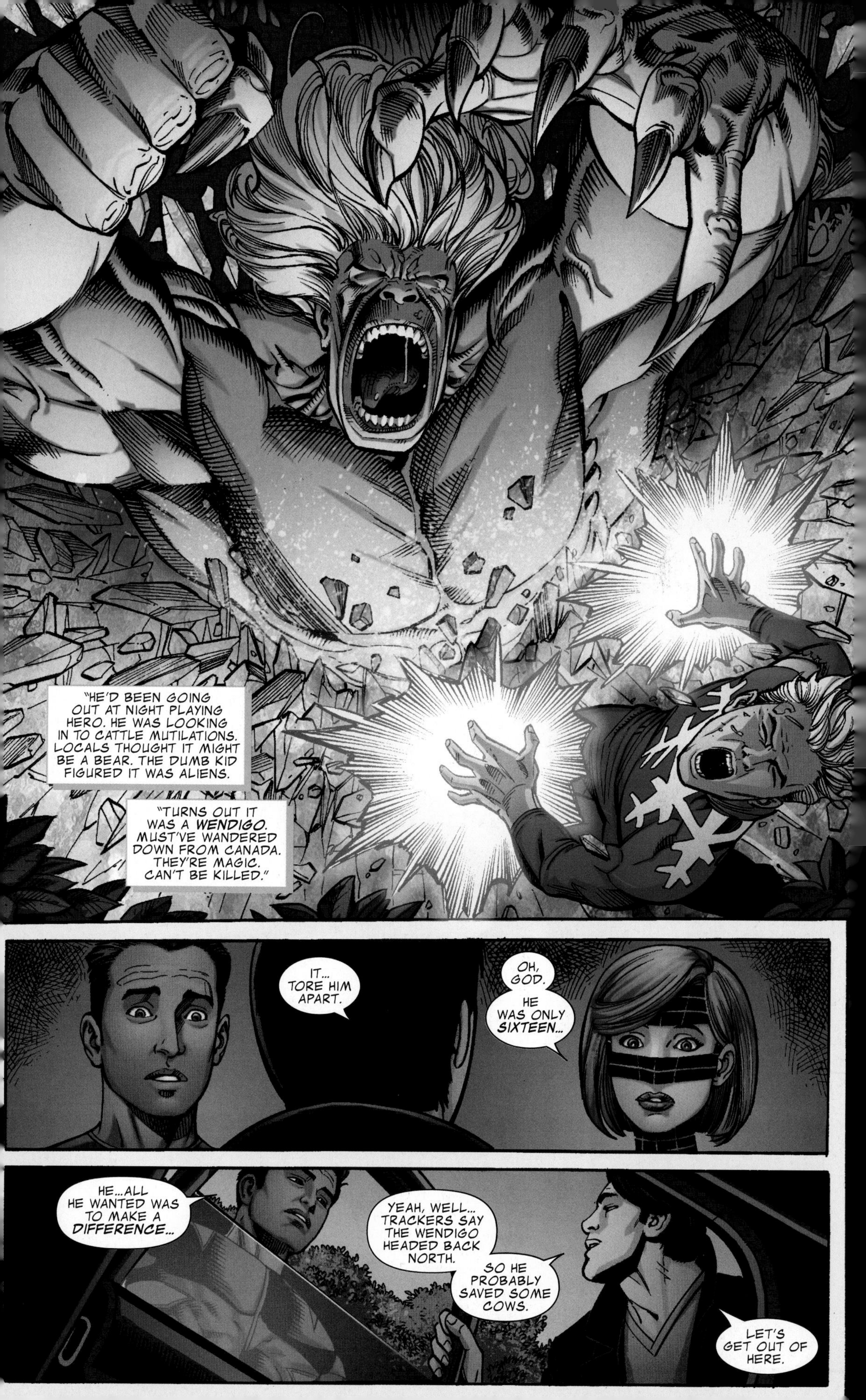
"HE'D BEEN GOING OUT AT NIGHT PLAYING HERO. HE WAS LOOKING IN TO CATTLE MUTILATIONS. LOCALS THOUGHT IT MIGHT BE A BEAR. THE DUMB KID FIGURED IT WAS ALIENS.
"TURNS OUT IT WAS A *WENDIGO*. MUST'VE WANDERED DOWN FROM CANADA. THEY'RE MAGIC. CAN'T BE KILLED."
IT... TORE HIM APART.
OH, GOD.
HE WAS ONLY *SIXTEEN*...
HE...ALL HE WANTED WAS TO MAKE A *DIFFERENCE*...
YEAH, WELL... TRACKERS SAY THE WENDIGO HEADED BACK NORTH.
SO HE PROBABLY SAVED SOME COWS.
LET'S GET OUT OF HERE.

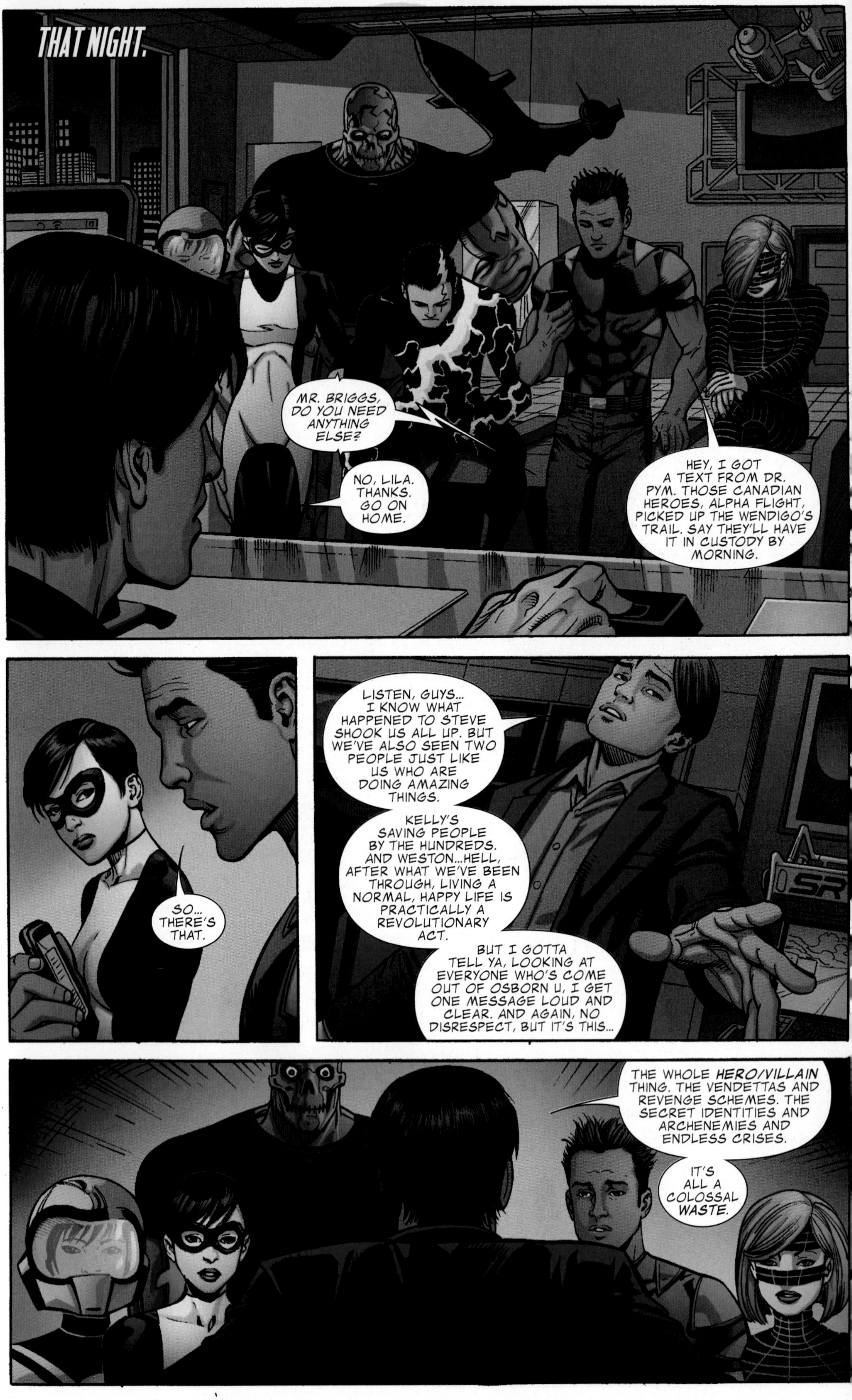
THAT NIGHT.
MR. BRIGGS, DO YOU NEED ANYTHING ELSE?
NO, LILA. THANKS. GO ON HOME.
HEY, I GOT A TEXT FROM DR. PYM. THOSE CANADIAN HEROES, ALPHA FLIGHT, PICKED UP THE WENDIGO'S TRAIL. SAY THEY'LL HAVE IT IN CUSTODY BY MORNING.
SO... THERE'S THAT.
LISTEN, GUYS... I KNOW WHAT HAPPENED TO STEVE SHOOK US ALL UP. BUT WE'VE ALSO SEEN TWO PEOPLE JUST LIKE US WHO ARE DOING AMAZING THINGS.
KELLY'S SAVING PEOPLE BY THE HUNDREDS. AND WESTON...HELL, AFTER WHAT WE'VE BEEN THROUGH, LIVING A NORMAL, HAPPY LIFE IS PRACTICALLY A REVOLUTIONARY ACT.
BUT I GOTTA TELL YA, LOOKING AT EVERYONE WHO'S COME OUT OF OSBORN U, I GET ONE MESSAGE LOUD AND CLEAR. AND AGAIN, NO DISRESPECT, BUT IT'S THIS...
THE WHOLE HERO/VILLAIN THING. THE VENDETTAS AND REVENGE SCHEMES. THE SECRET IDENTITIES AND ARCHENEMIES AND ENDLESS CRISES.
IT'S ALL A COLOSSAL WASTE.

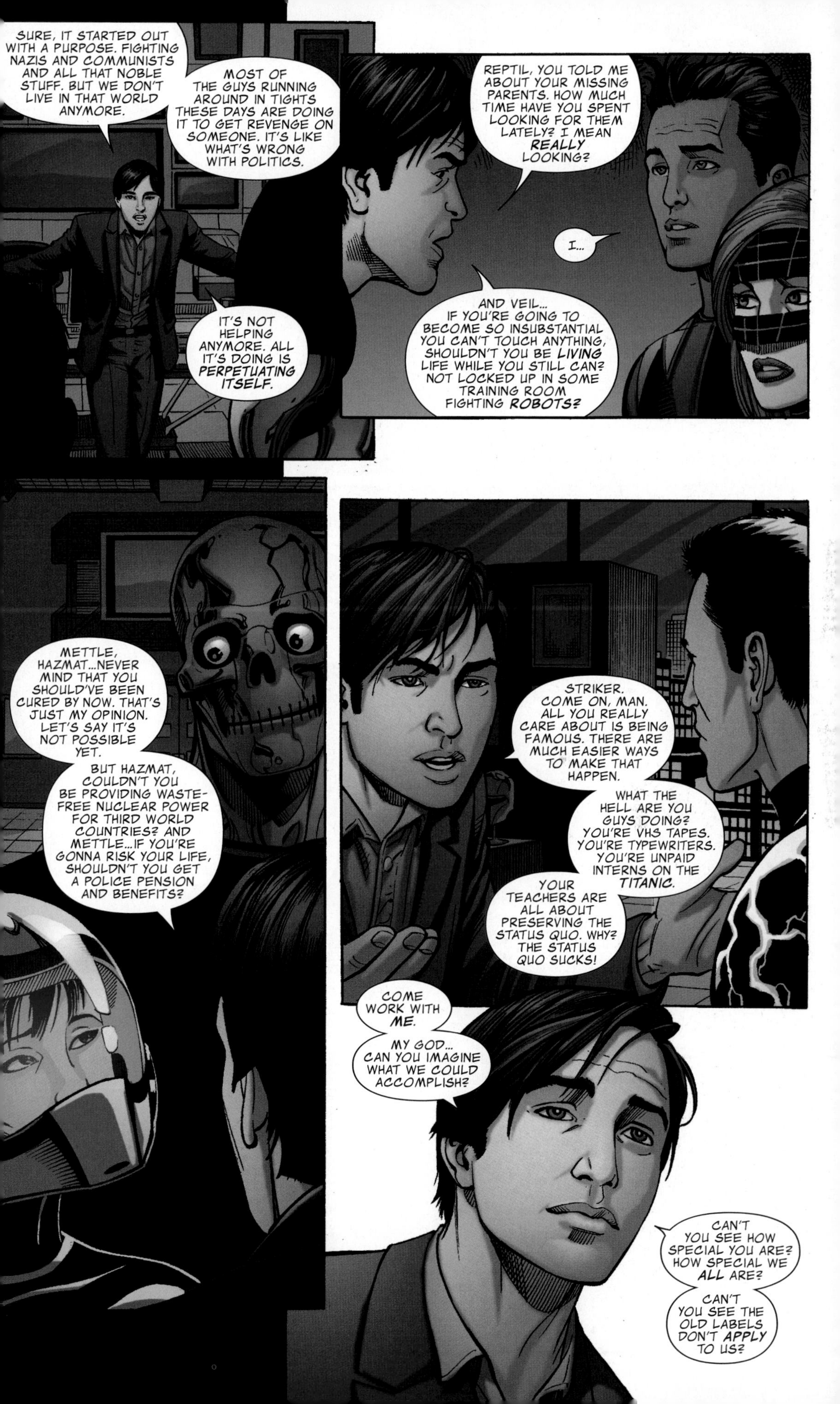
SURE, IT STARTED OUT WITH A PURPOSE. FIGHTING NAZIS AND COMMUNISTS AND ALL THAT NOBLE STUFF. BUT WE DON'T LIVE IN THAT WORLD ANYMORE.
MOST OF THE GUYS RUNNING AROUND IN TIGHTS THESE DAYS ARE DOING IT TO GET REVENGE ON SOMEONE. IT'S LIKE WHAT'S WRONG WITH POLITICS.
IT'S NOT HELPING ANYMORE. ALL IT'S DOING IS PERPETUATING ITSELF.
REPTIL, YOU TOLD ME ABOUT YOUR MISSING PARENTS. HOW MUCH TIME HAVE YOU SPENT LOOKING FOR THEM LATELY? I MEAN REALLY LOOKING?
I...
AND VEIL... IF YOU'RE GOING TO BECOME SO INSUBSTANTIAL YOU CAN'T TOUCH ANYTHING, SHOULDN'T YOU BE LIVING LIFE WHILE YOU STILL CAN? NOT LOCKED UP IN SOME TRAINING ROOM FIGHTING ROBOTS?
METTLE, HAZMAT...NEVER MIND THAT YOU SHOULD'VE BEEN CURED BY NOW. THAT'S JUST MY OPINION. LET'S SAY IT'S NOT POSSIBLE YET.
BUT HAZMAT, COULDN'T YOU BE PROVIDING WASTE-FREE NUCLEAR POWER FOR THIRD WORLD COUNTRIES? AND METTLE...IF YOU'RE GONNA RISK YOUR LIFE, SHOULDN'T YOU GET A POLICE PENSION AND BENEFITS?
STRIKER. COME ON, MAN. ALL YOU REALLY CARE ABOUT IS BEING FAMOUS. THERE ARE MUCH EASIER WAYS TO MAKE THAT HAPPEN.
WHAT THE HELL ARE YOU GUYS DOING? YOU'RE VHS TAPES. YOU'RE TYPEWRITERS. YOU'RE UNPAID INTERNS ON THE TITANIC.
YOUR TEACHERS ARE ALL ABOUT PRESERVING THE STATUS QUO. WHY? THE STATUS QUO SUCKS!
COME WORK WITH ME.
MY GOD... CAN YOU IMAGINE WHAT WE COULD ACCOMPLISH?
CAN'T YOU SEE HOW SPECIAL YOU ARE? HOW SPECIAL WE ALL ARE?
CAN'T YOU SEE THE OLD LABELS DON'T APPLY TO US?

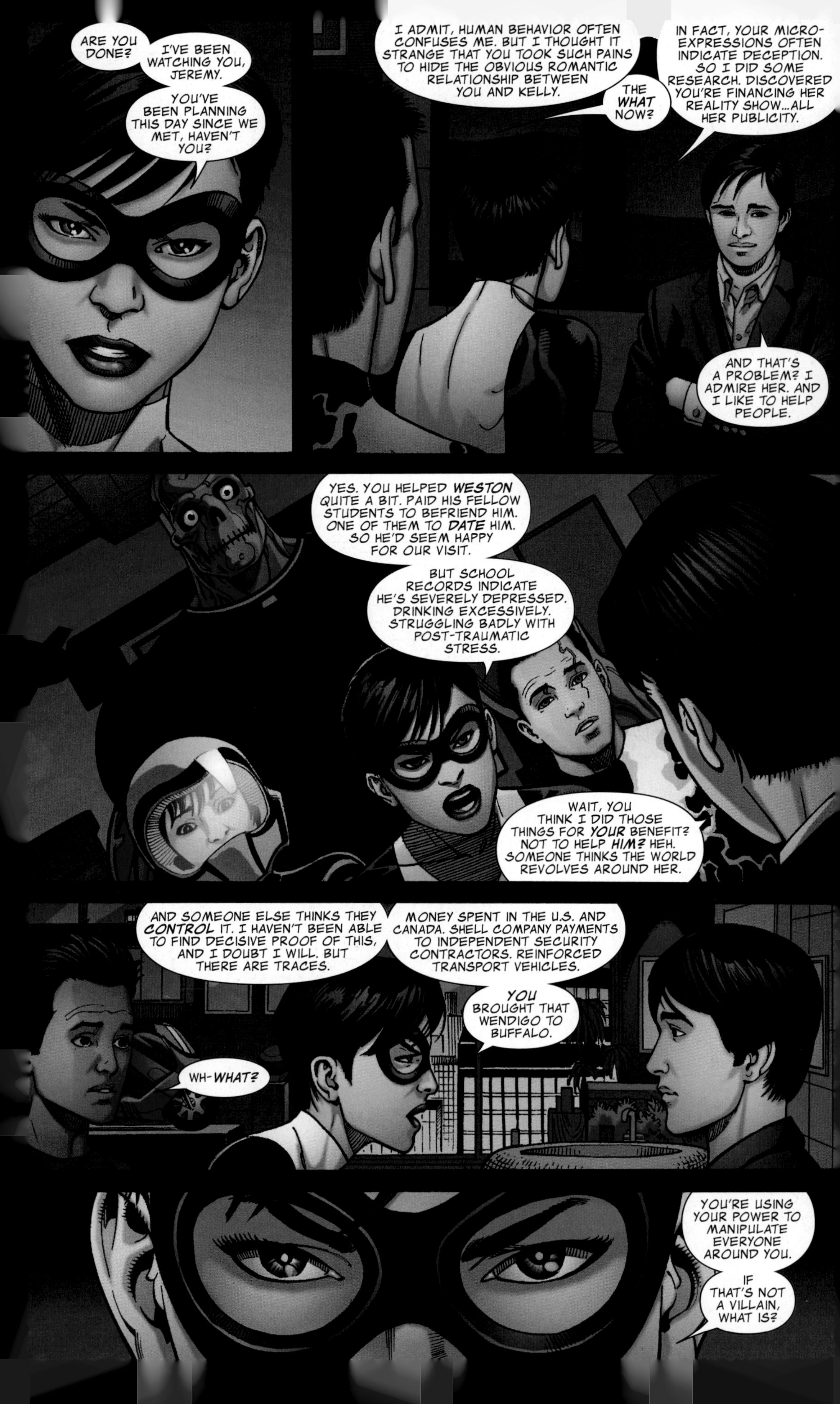
ARE YOU DONE?
I'VE BEEN WATCHING YOU, JEREMY.
YOU'VE BEEN PLANNING THIS DAY SINCE WE MET, HAVEN'T YOU?
I ADMIT, HUMAN BEHAVIOR OFTEN CONFUSES ME. BUT I THOUGHT IT STRANGE THAT YOU TOOK SUCH PAINS TO HIDE THE OBVIOUS ROMANTIC RELATIONSHIP BETWEEN YOU AND KELLY.
THE WHAT NOW?
IN FACT, YOUR MICRO-EXPRESSIONS OFTEN INDICATE DECEPTION. SO I DID SOME RESEARCH. DISCOVERED YOU'RE FINANCING HER REALITY SHOW...ALL HER PUBLICITY.
AND THAT'S A PROBLEM? I ADMIRE HER. AND I LIKE TO HELP PEOPLE.
YES. YOU HELPED WESTON QUITE A BIT. PAID HIS FELLOW STUDENTS TO BEFRIEND HIM. ONE OF THEM TO DATE HIM. SO HE'D SEEM HAPPY FOR OUR VISIT.
BUT SCHOOL RECORDS INDICATE HE'S SEVERELY DEPRESSED. DRINKING EXCESSIVELY. STRUGGLING BADLY WITH POST-TRAUMATIC STRESS.
WAIT, YOU THINK I DID THOSE THINGS FOR YOUR BENEFIT? NOT TO HELP HIM? HEH. SOMEONE THINKS THE WORLD REVOLVES AROUND HER.
AND SOMEONE ELSE THINKS THEY CONTROL IT. I HAVEN'T BEEN ABLE TO FIND DECISIVE PROOF OF THIS, AND I DOUBT I WILL. BUT THERE ARE TRACES.
MONEY SPENT IN THE U.S. AND CANADA. SHELL COMPANY PAYMENTS TO INDEPENDENT SECURITY CONTRACTORS. REINFORCED TRANSPORT VEHICLES.
YOU BROUGHT THAT WENDIGO TO BUFFALO.
WH-WHAT?
YOU'RE USING YOUR POWER TO MANIPULATE EVERYONE AROUND YOU.
IF THAT'S NOT A VILLAIN, WHAT IS?

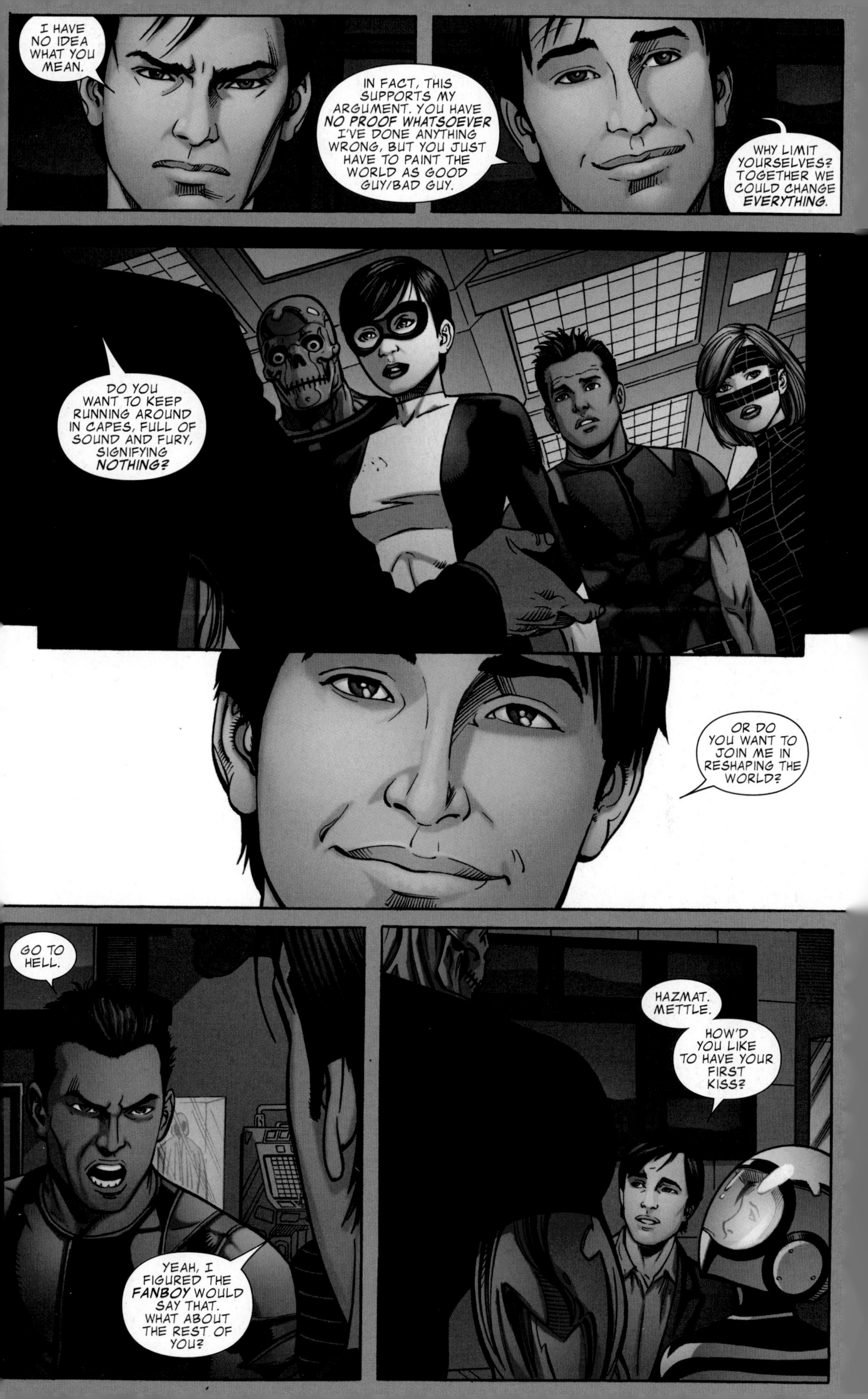

I HAVE NO IDEA WHAT YOU MEAN.
IN FACT, THIS SUPPORTS MY ARGUMENT. YOU HAVE NO PROOF WHATSOEVER I'VE DONE ANYTHING WRONG, BUT YOU JUST HAVE TO PAINT THE WORLD AS GOOD GUY/BAD GUY.
WHY LIMIT YOURSELVES? TOGETHER WE COULD CHANGE EVERYTHING.
DO YOU WANT TO KEEP RUNNING AROUND IN CAPES, FULL OF SOUND AND FURY, SIGNIFYING NOTHING?
OR DO YOU WANT TO JOIN ME IN RESHAPING THE WORLD?
GO TO HELL.
YEAH, I FIGURED THE FANBOY WOULD SAY THAT. WHAT ABOUT THE REST OF YOU?
HAZMAT. METTLE.
HOW'D YOU LIKE TO HAVE YOUR FIRST KISS?

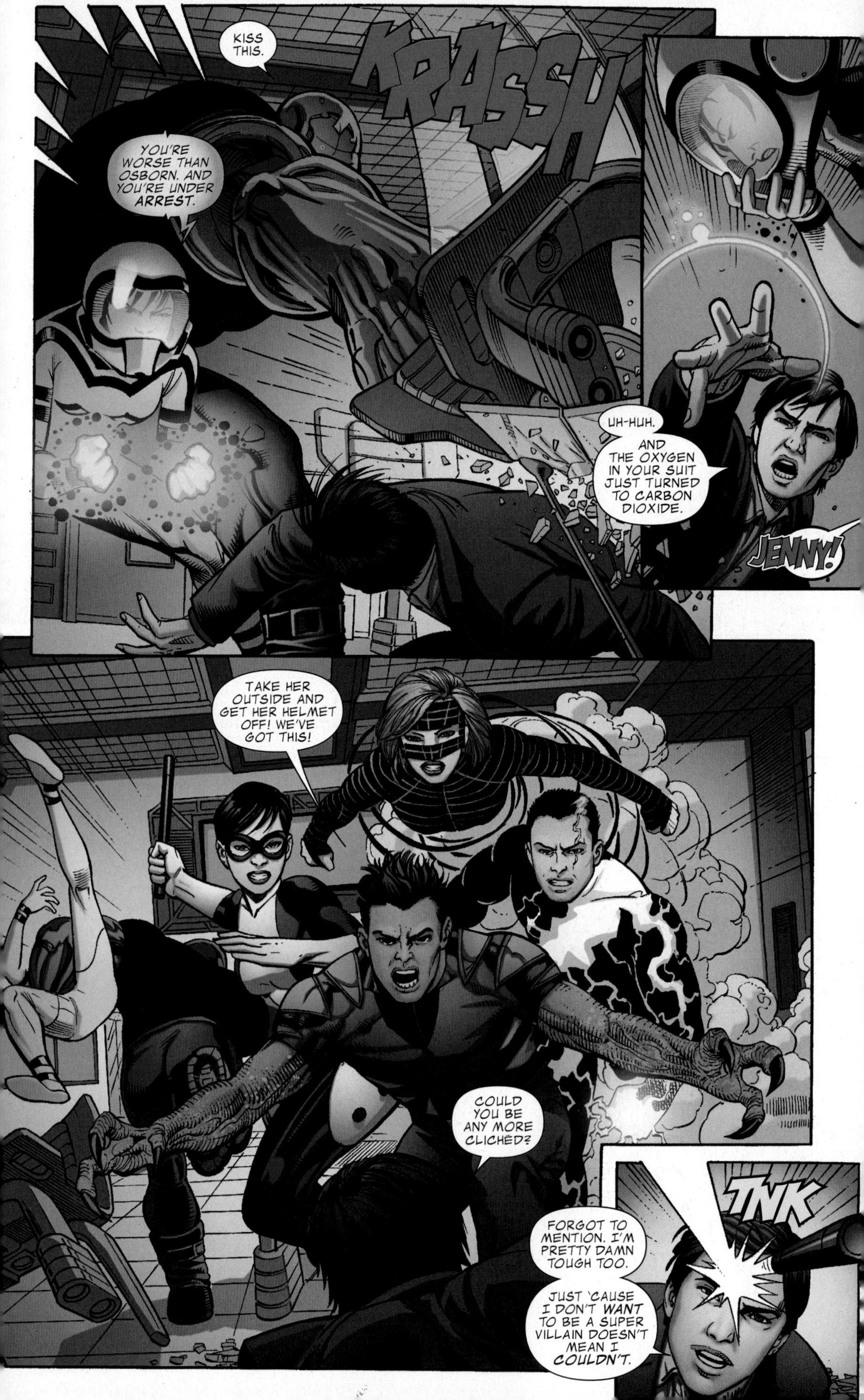

KISS THIS.
KRASSH
YOU'RE WORSE THAN OSBORN. AND YOU'RE UNDER ARREST.
UH-HUH.
AND THE OXYGEN IN YOUR SUIT JUST TURNED TO CARBON DIOXIDE.
JENNY!
TAKE HER OUTSIDE AND GET HER HELMET OFF! WE'VE GOT THIS!
COULD YOU BE ANY MORE CLICHÉD?
TNK
FORGOT TO MENTION. I'M PRETTY DAMN TOUGH TOO.
JUST 'CAUSE I DON'T WANT TO BE A SUPER VILLAIN DOESN'T MEAN I COULDN'T.

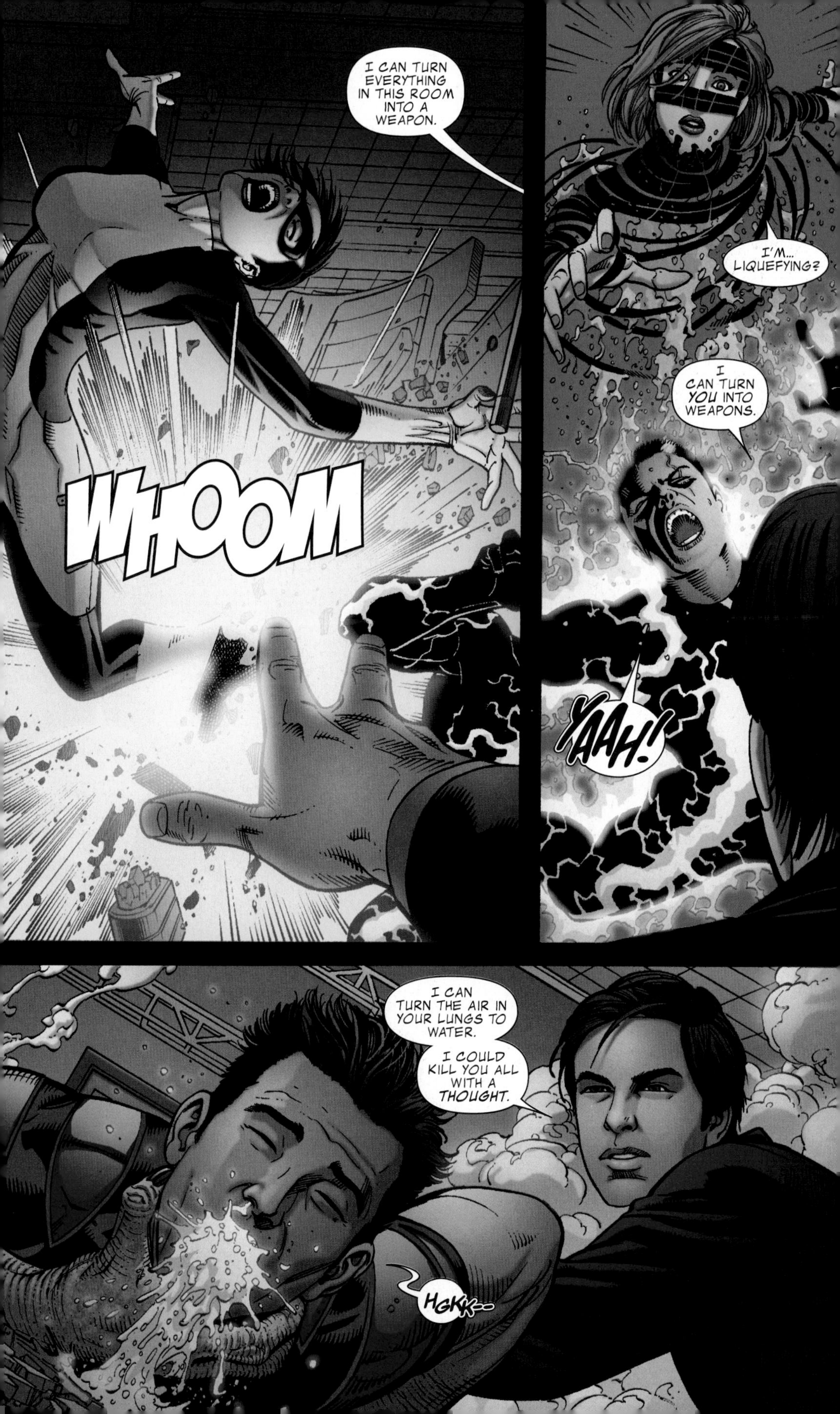
I CAN TURN EVERYTHING IN THIS ROOM INTO A WEAPON.
WHOOM
I'M... LIQUEFYING?
I CAN TURN YOU INTO WEAPONS.
YAAH!
I CAN TURN THE AIR IN YOUR LUNGS TO WATER.
I COULD KILL YOU ALL WITH A THOUGHT.
HGKK--

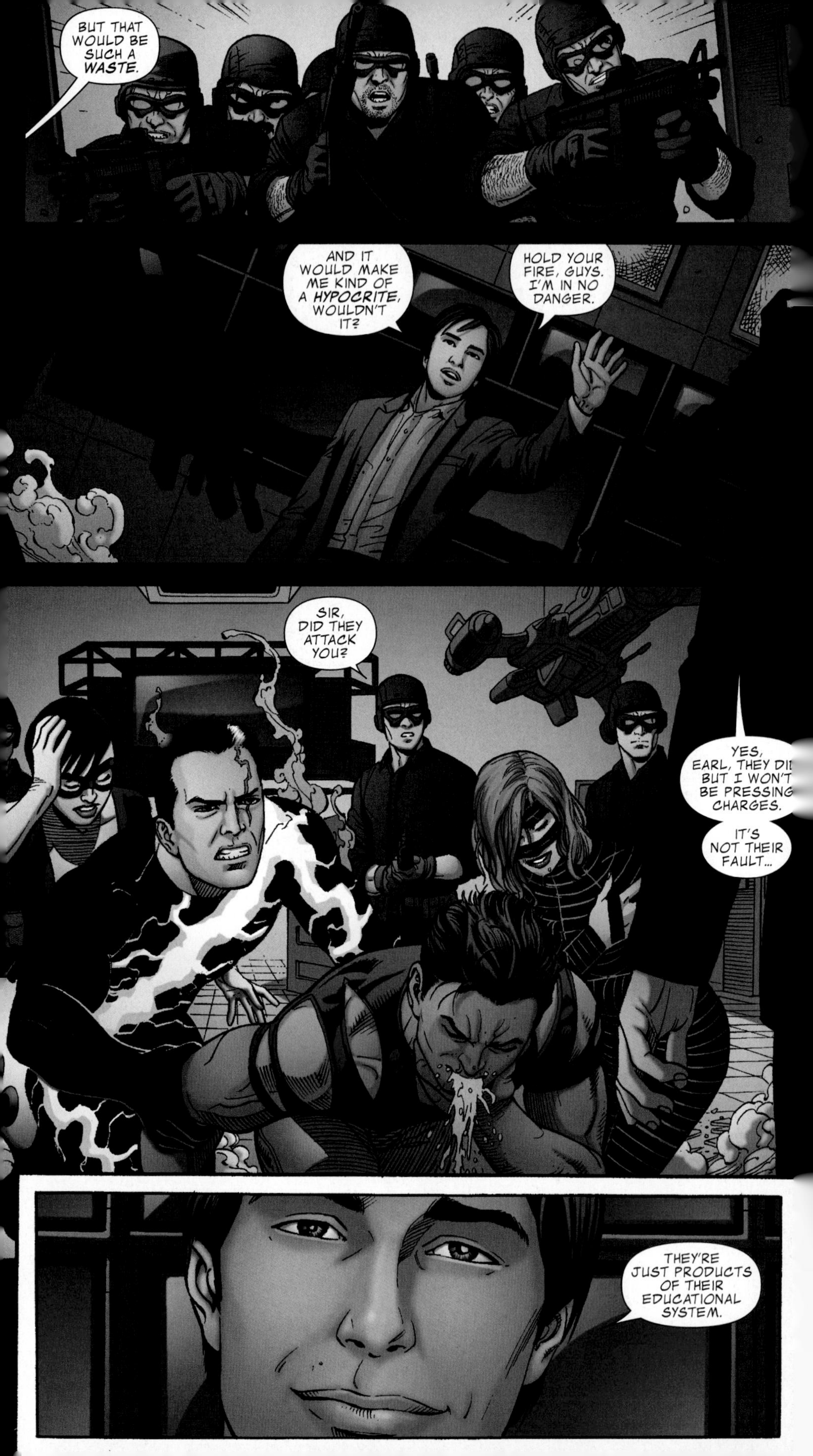
BUT THAT WOULD BE SUCH A WASTE.
AND IT WOULD MAKE ME KIND OF A HYPOCRITE, WOULDN'T IT?
HOLD YOUR FIRE, GUYS. I'M IN NO DANGER.
SIR, DID THEY ATTACK YOU?
YES, EARL, THEY DID BUT I WON'T BE PRESSING CHARGES.
IT'S NOT THEIR FAULT...
THEY'RE JUST PRODUCTS OF THEIR EDUCATIONAL SYSTEM.

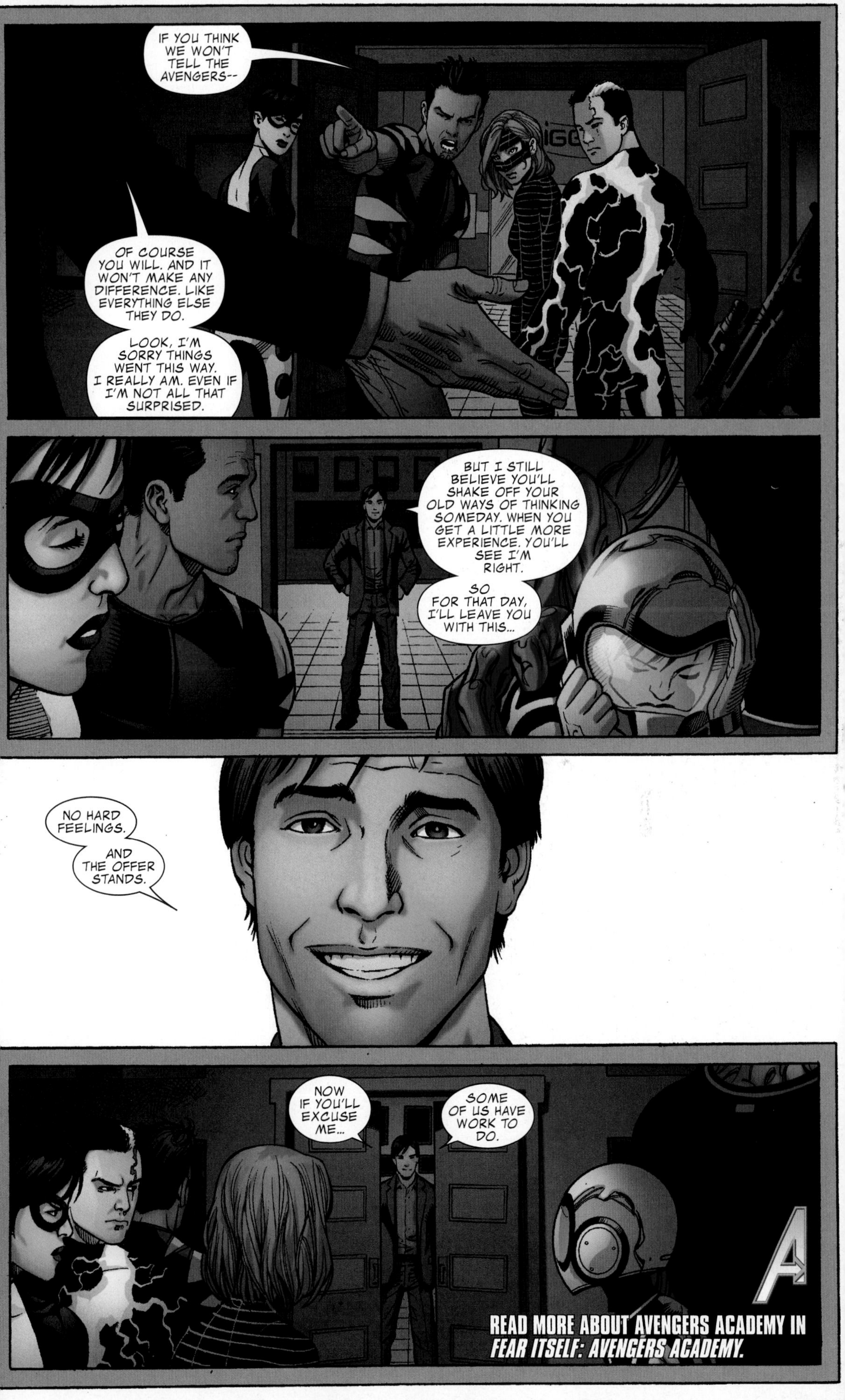
IF YOU THINK WE WON'T TELL THE AVENGERS--
OF COURSE YOU WILL. AND IT WON'T MAKE ANY DIFFERENCE. LIKE EVERYTHING ELSE THEY DO.
LOOK, I'M SORRY THINGS WENT THIS WAY. I REALLY AM. EVEN IF I'M NOT ALL THAT SURPRISED.
BUT I STILL BELIEVE YOU'LL SHAKE OFF YOUR OLD WAYS OF THINKING SOMEDAY. WHEN YOU GET A LITTLE MORE EXPERIENCE. YOU'LL SEE I'M RIGHT.
SO FOR THAT DAY, I'LL LEAVE YOU WITH THIS...
NO HARD FEELINGS.
AND THE OFFER STANDS.
NOW IF YOU'LL EXCUSE ME...
SOME OF US HAVE WORK TO DO.
READ MORE ABOUT AVENGERS ACADEMY IN
FEAR ITSELF: AVENGERS ACADEMY.

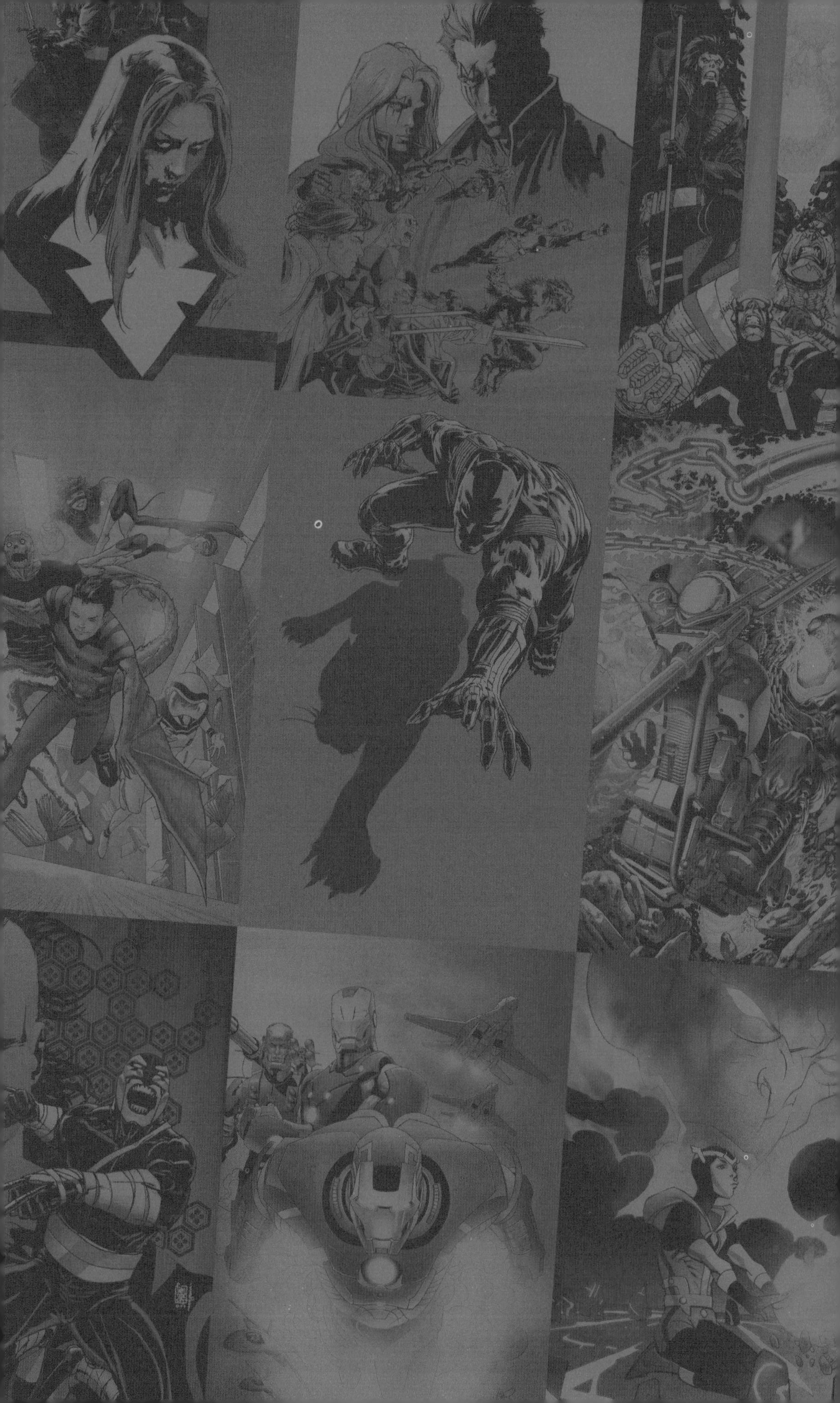

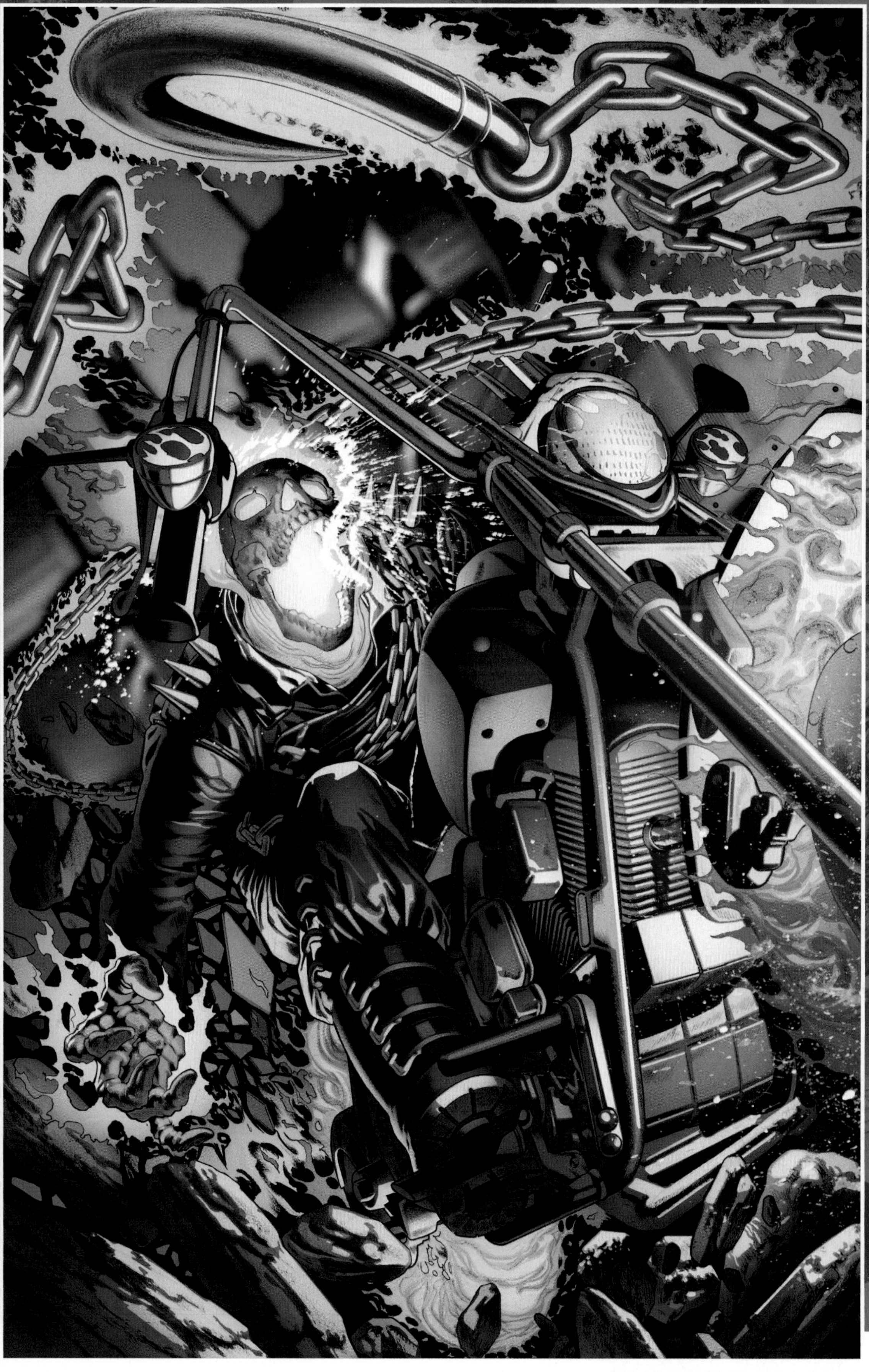

GHOST RIDER #0.1

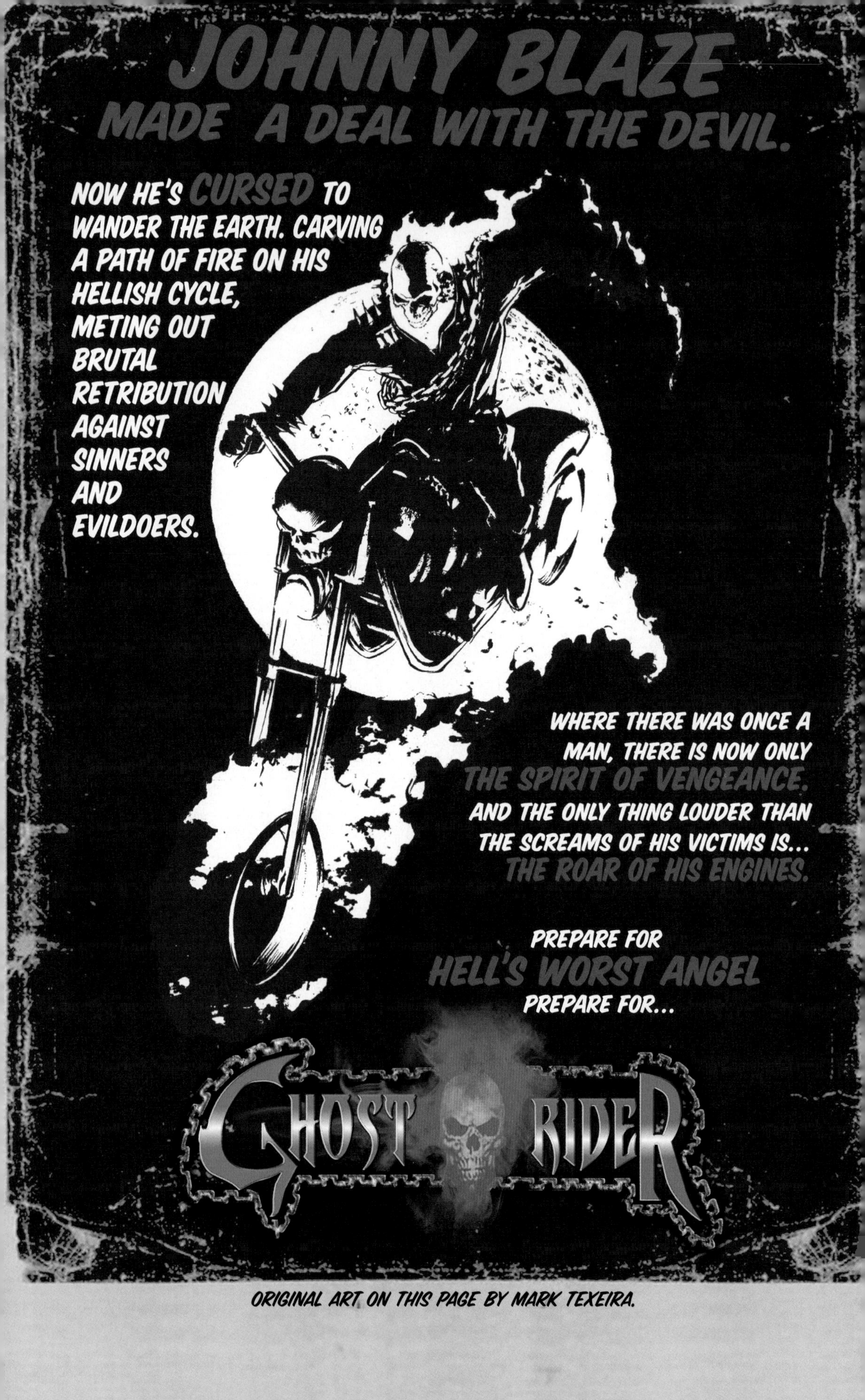
JOHNNY BLAZE
MADE A DEAL WITH THE DEVIL.
NOW HE'S CURSED TO WANDER THE EARTH. CARVING A PATH OF FIRE ON HIS HELLISH CYCLE, METING OUT BRUTAL RETRIBUTION AGAINST SINNERS AND EVILDOERS.
WHERE THERE WAS ONCE A MAN, THERE IS NOW ONLY THE SPIRIT OF VENGEANCE. AND THE ONLY THING LOUDER THAN THE SCREAMS OF HIS VICTIMS IS... THE ROAR OF HIS ENGINES.
PREPARE FOR
HELL'S WORST ANGEL
PREPARE FOR...
GHOST RIDER

ORIGINAL ART ON THIS PAGE BY MARK TEXEIRA.

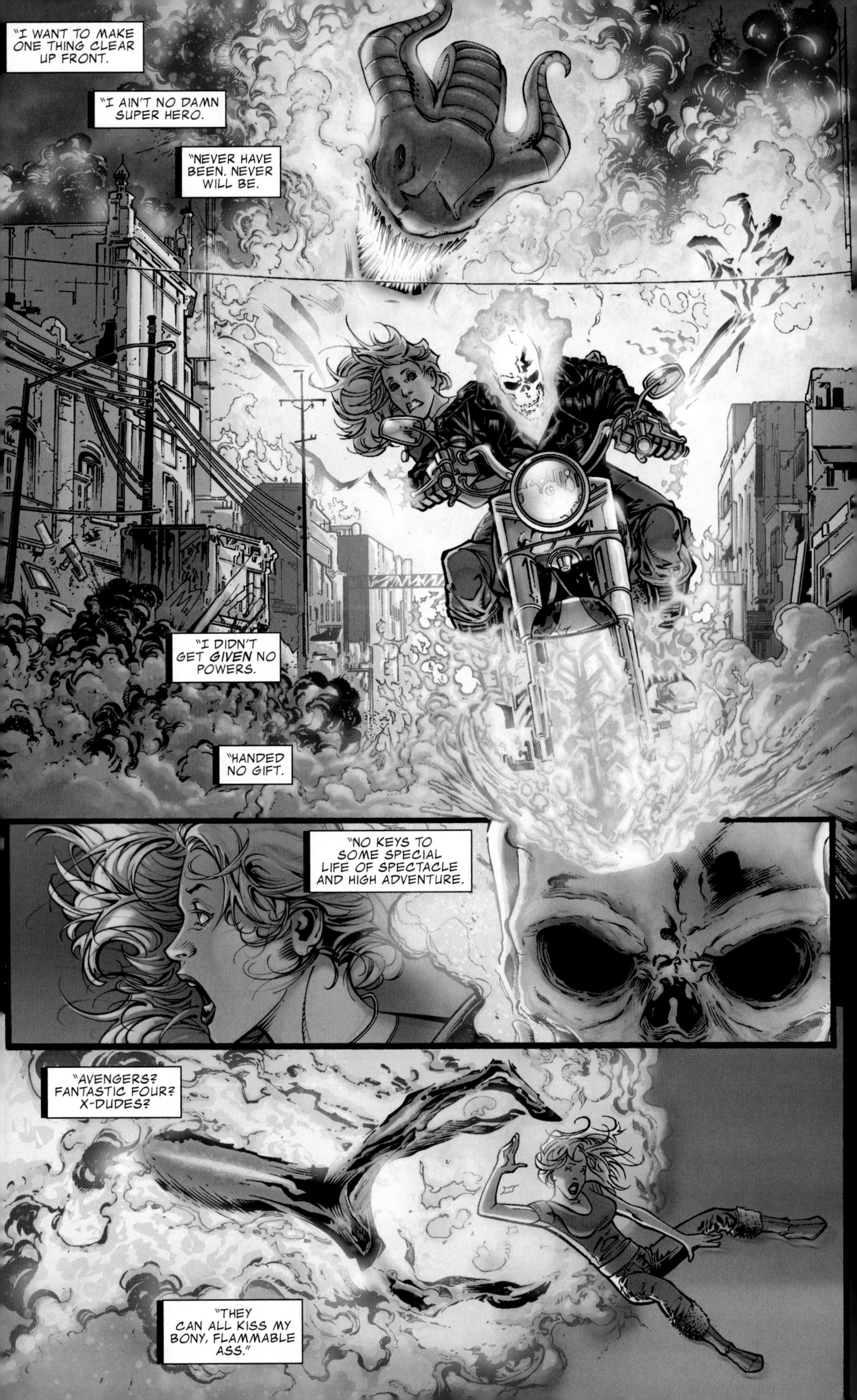
"I WANT TO MAKE ONE THING CLEAR UP FRONT.
"I AIN'T NO DAMN SUPER HERO.
"NEVER HAVE BEEN. NEVER WILL BE.
"I DIDN'T GET *GIVEN* NO POWERS.
"HANDED NO GIFT.
"NO KEYS TO SOME SPECIAL LIFE OF SPECTACLE AND HIGH ADVENTURE.
"AVENGERS? FANTASTIC FOUR? X-DUDES?
"THEY CAN ALL KISS MY BONY, FLAMMABLE ASS."

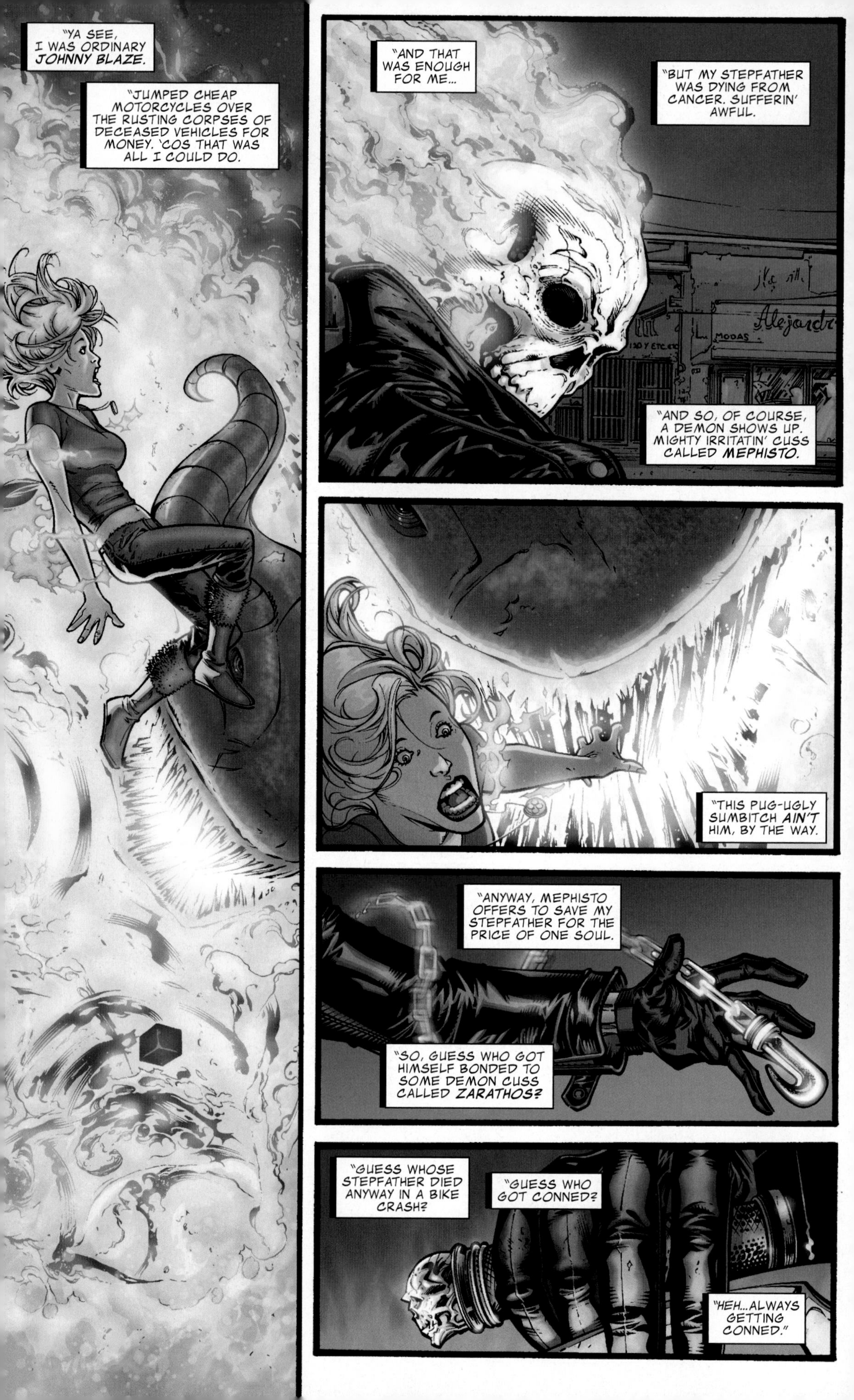
"YA SEE, I WAS ORDINARY JOHNNY BLAZE.
"JUMPED CHEAP MOTORCYCLES OVER THE RUSTING CORPSES OF DECEASED VEHICLES FOR MONEY. 'COS THAT WAS ALL I COULD DO.
"AND THAT WAS ENOUGH FOR ME...
"BUT MY STEPFATHER WAS DYING FROM CANCER. SUFFERIN' AWFUL.
"AND SO, OF COURSE, A DEMON SHOWS UP. MIGHTY IRRITATIN' CUSS CALLED MEPHISTO.
"THIS PUG-UGLY SUMBITCH AIN'T HIM, BY THE WAY.
"ANYWAY, MEPHISTO OFFERS TO SAVE MY STEPFATHER FOR THE PRICE OF ONE SOUL.
"SO, GUESS WHO GOT HIMSELF BONDED TO SOME DEMON CUSS CALLED ZARATHOS?
"GUESS WHOSE STEPFATHER DIED ANYWAY IN A BIKE CRASH?
"GUESS WHO GOT CONNED?
"HEH...ALWAYS GETTING CONNED."

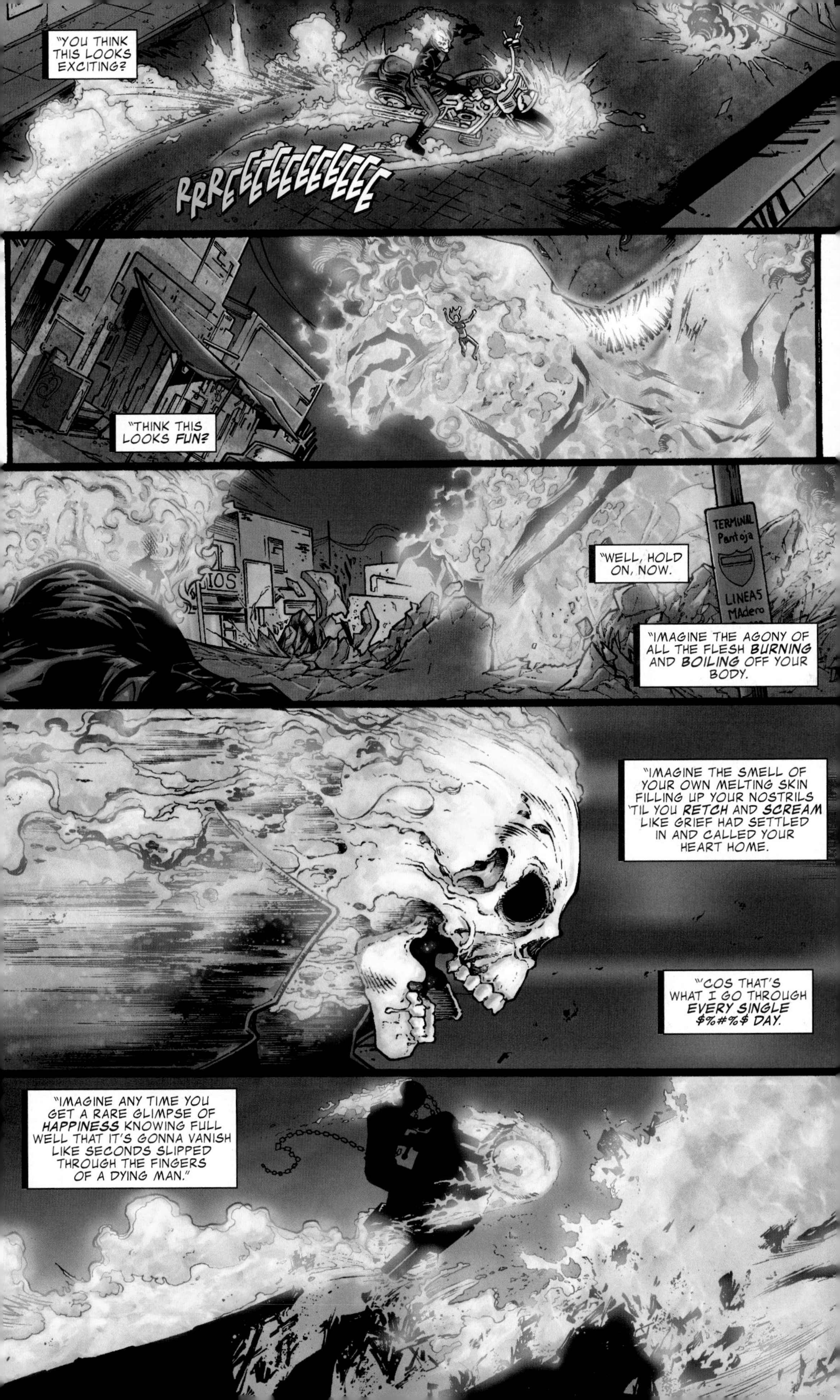
"YOU THINK THIS LOOKS EXCITING?
RRREEEEEEEEEEEEEE
"THINK THIS LOOKS FUN?
TERMINAL Pantoja
LINEAS Madero
"WELL, HOLD ON, NOW.
"IMAGINE THE AGONY OF ALL THE FLESH BURNING AND BOILING OFF YOUR BODY.
"IMAGINE THE SMELL OF YOUR OWN MELTING SKIN FILLING UP YOUR NOSTRILS 'TIL YOU RETCH AND SCREAM LIKE GRIEF HAD SETTLED IN AND CALLED YOUR HEART HOME.
"'COS THAT'S WHAT I GO THROUGH EVERY SINGLE $%#%$ DAY.
"IMAGINE ANY TIME YOU GET A RARE GLIMPSE OF HAPPINESS KNOWING FULL WELL THAT IT'S GONNA VANISH LIKE SECONDS SLIPPED THROUGH THE FINGERS OF A DYING MAN."

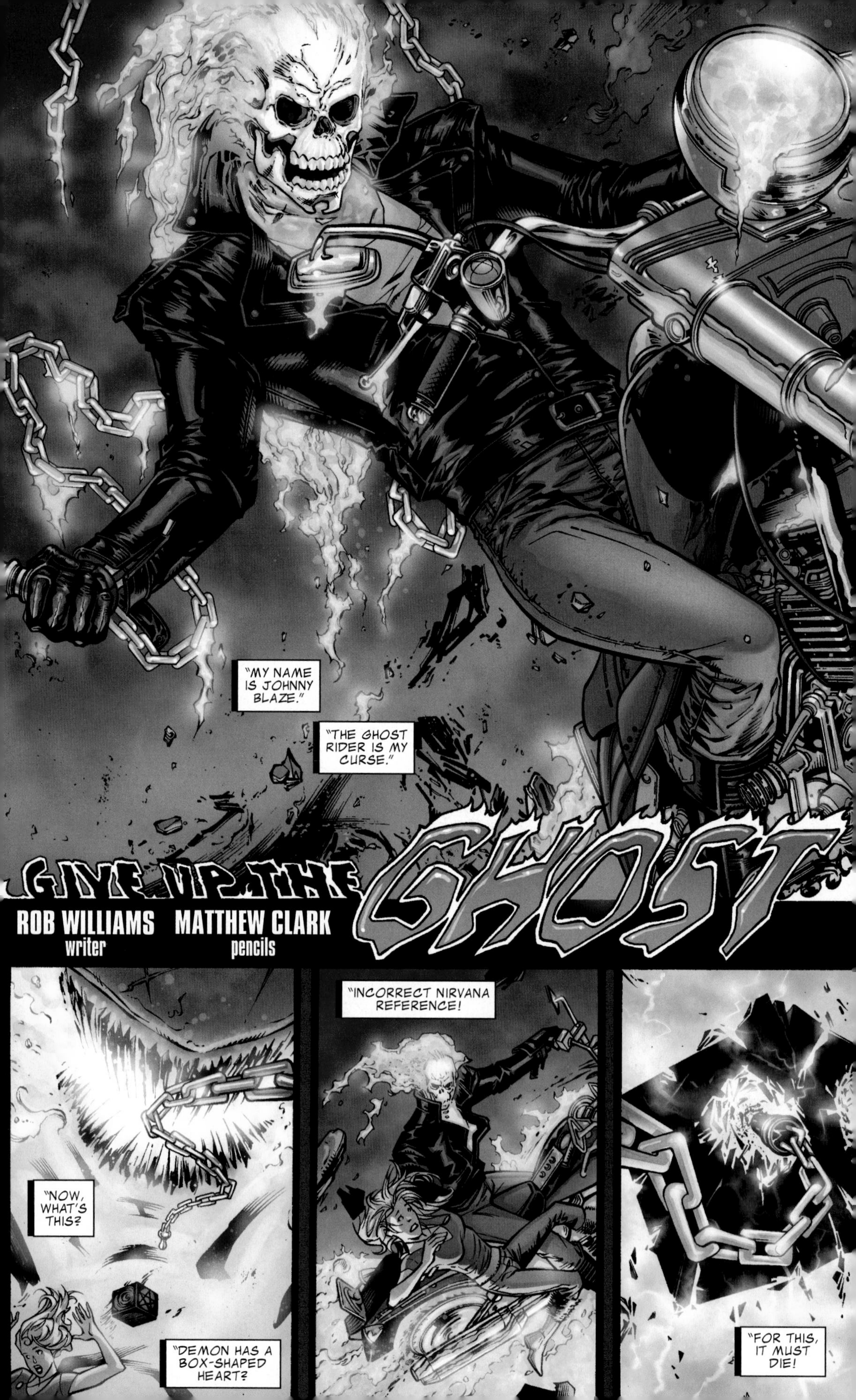
"MY NAME IS JOHNNY BLAZE."
"THE GHOST RIDER IS MY CURSE."
GIVE UP THE GHOST
ROB WILLIAMS writer
MATTHEW CLARK pencils
"NOW, WHAT'S THIS?
"DEMON HAS A BOX-SHAPED HEART?
"INCORRECT NIRVANA REFERENCE!
"FOR THIS, IT MUST DIE!

...EAN ...SONS ...ker | ROBERT SCHWAGER colorist | VC's CLAYTON COWLES letterer | SEBASTIAN GIRNER asst. editor | STEPHEN WACKER editor | AXEL ALONSO editor in chief | JOE QUESADA chief creative officer | DAN BUCKLEY publisher | ALAN FINE exec. producer

"ANYWAY, HERE WAS I?

"OH YEAH. SO IT'S THAT SAME OLD STORY WE'VE ALL HEARD, LIKE, A MILLION TIMES BEFORE.

"I KICKED THE DEMON DUDE'S ASS.

"SAVED THE OH-SO-GRATEFUL BEAUTIFUL LADY."

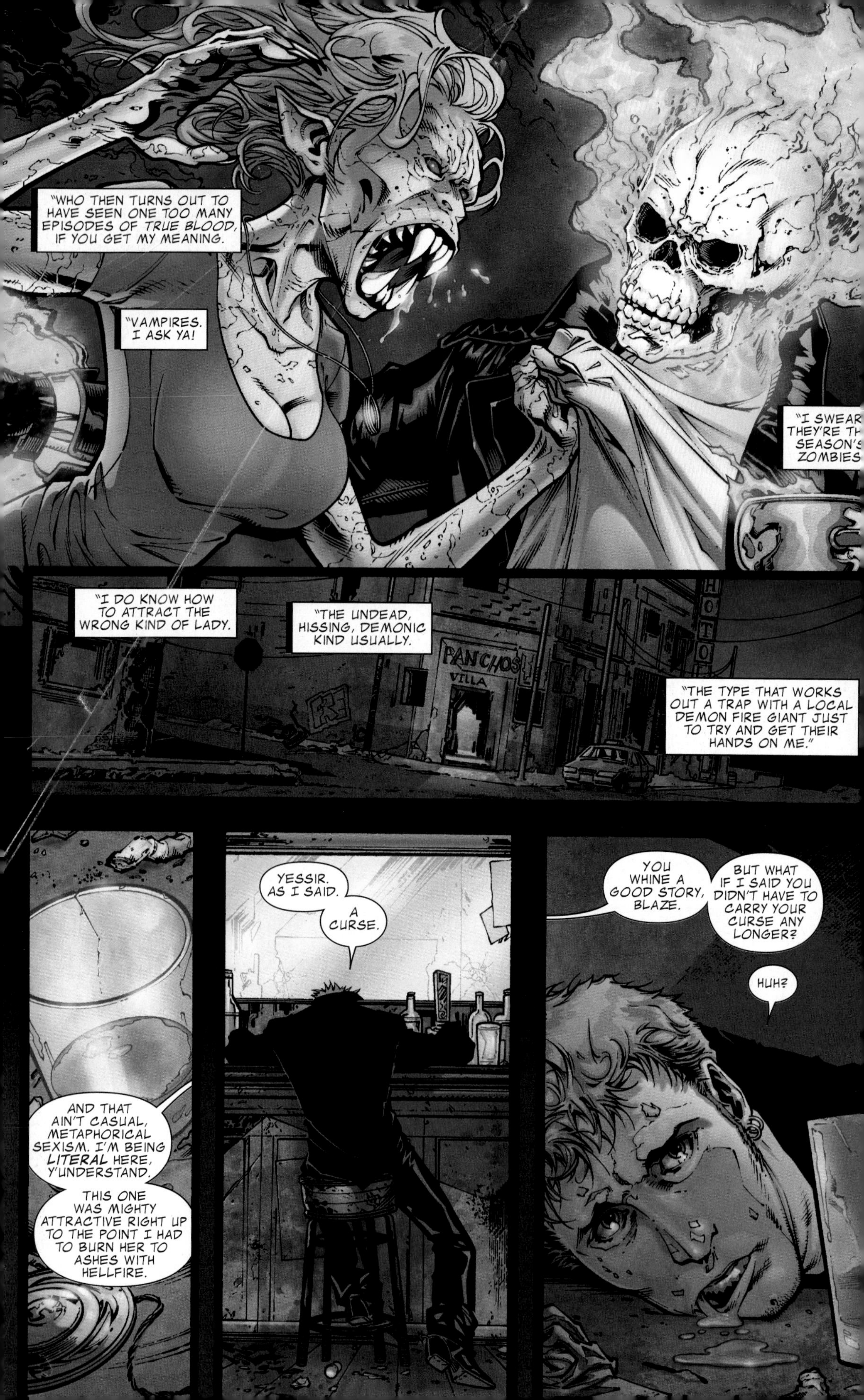
"WHO THEN TURNS OUT TO HAVE SEEN ONE TOO MANY EPISODES OF TRUE BLOOD, IF YOU GET MY MEANING.
"VAMPIRES. I ASK YA!
"I SWEAR THEY'RE TH SEASON'S ZOMBIES
"I DO KNOW HOW TO ATTRACT THE WRONG KIND OF LADY.
"THE UNDEAD, HISSING, DEMONIC KIND USUALLY.
PANCHOS VILLA
HOTO
"THE TYPE THAT WORKS OUT A TRAP WITH A LOCAL DEMON FIRE GIANT JUST TO TRY AND GET THEIR HANDS ON ME."
AND THAT AIN'T CASUAL, METAPHORICAL SEXISM. I'M BEING LITERAL HERE, Y'UNDERSTAND.
THIS ONE WAS MIGHTY ATTRACTIVE RIGHT UP TO THE POINT I HAD TO BURN HER TO ASHES WITH HELLFIRE.
YESSIR. AS I SAID.
A CURSE.
YOU WHINE A GOOD STORY, BLAZE.
BUT WHAT IF I SAID YOU DIDN'T HAVE TO CARRY YOUR CURSE ANY LONGER?
HUH?

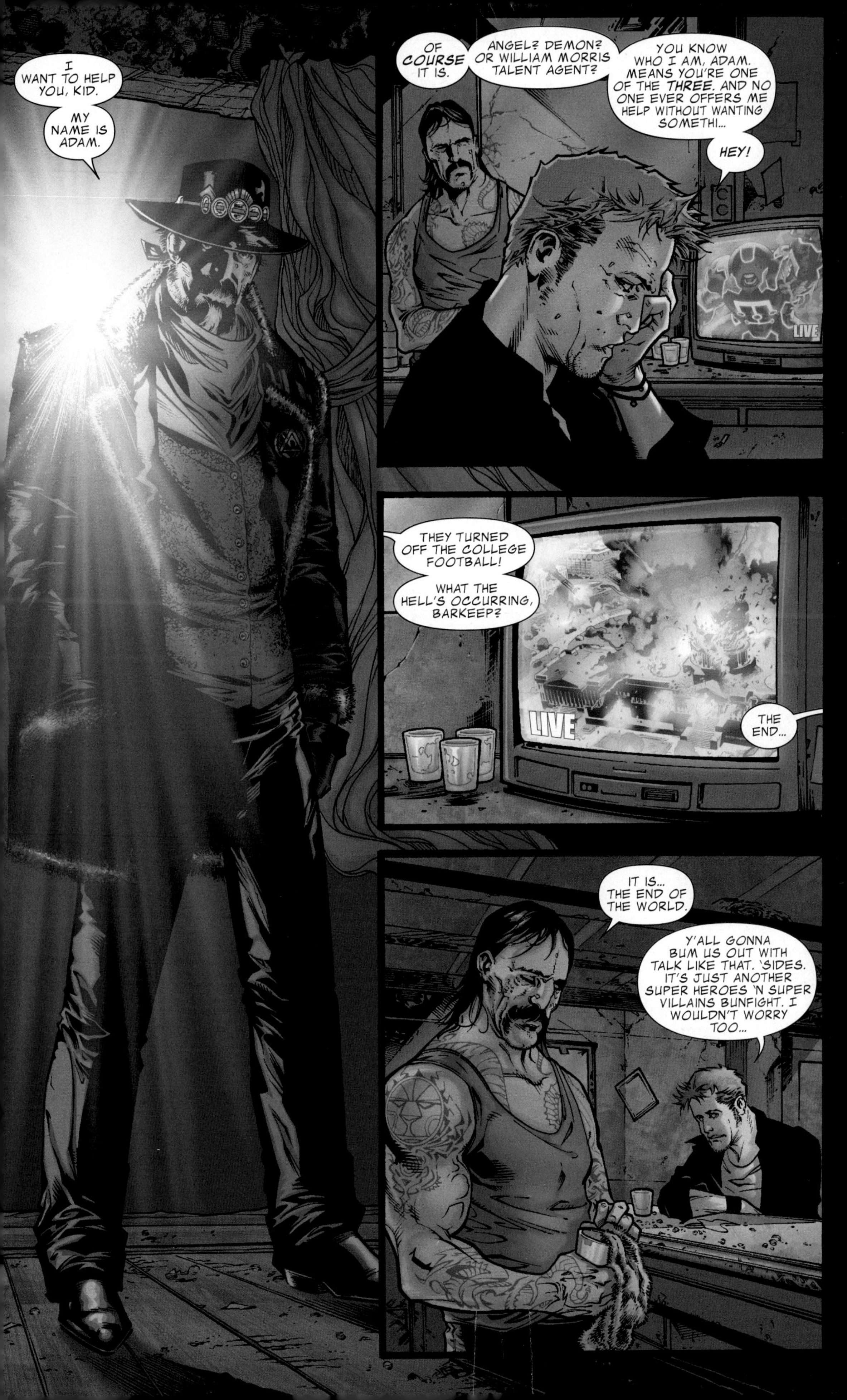
I WANT TO HELP YOU, KID.
MY NAME IS ADAM.
OF COURSE IT IS.
ANGEL? DEMON? OR WILLIAM MORRIS TALENT AGENT?
YOU KNOW WHO I AM, ADAM. MEANS YOU'RE ONE OF THE THREE. AND NO ONE EVER OFFERS ME HELP WITHOUT WANTING SOMETHI...
HEY!
LIVE
THEY TURNED OFF THE COLLEGE FOOTBALL!
WHAT THE HELL'S OCCURRING, BARKEEP?
LIVE
THE END...
IT IS... THE END OF THE WORLD.
Y'ALL GONNA BUM US OUT WITH TALK LIKE THAT. 'SIDES. IT'S JUST ANOTHER SUPER HEROES 'N SUPER VILLAINS BUNFIGHT. I WOULDN'T WORRY TOO...

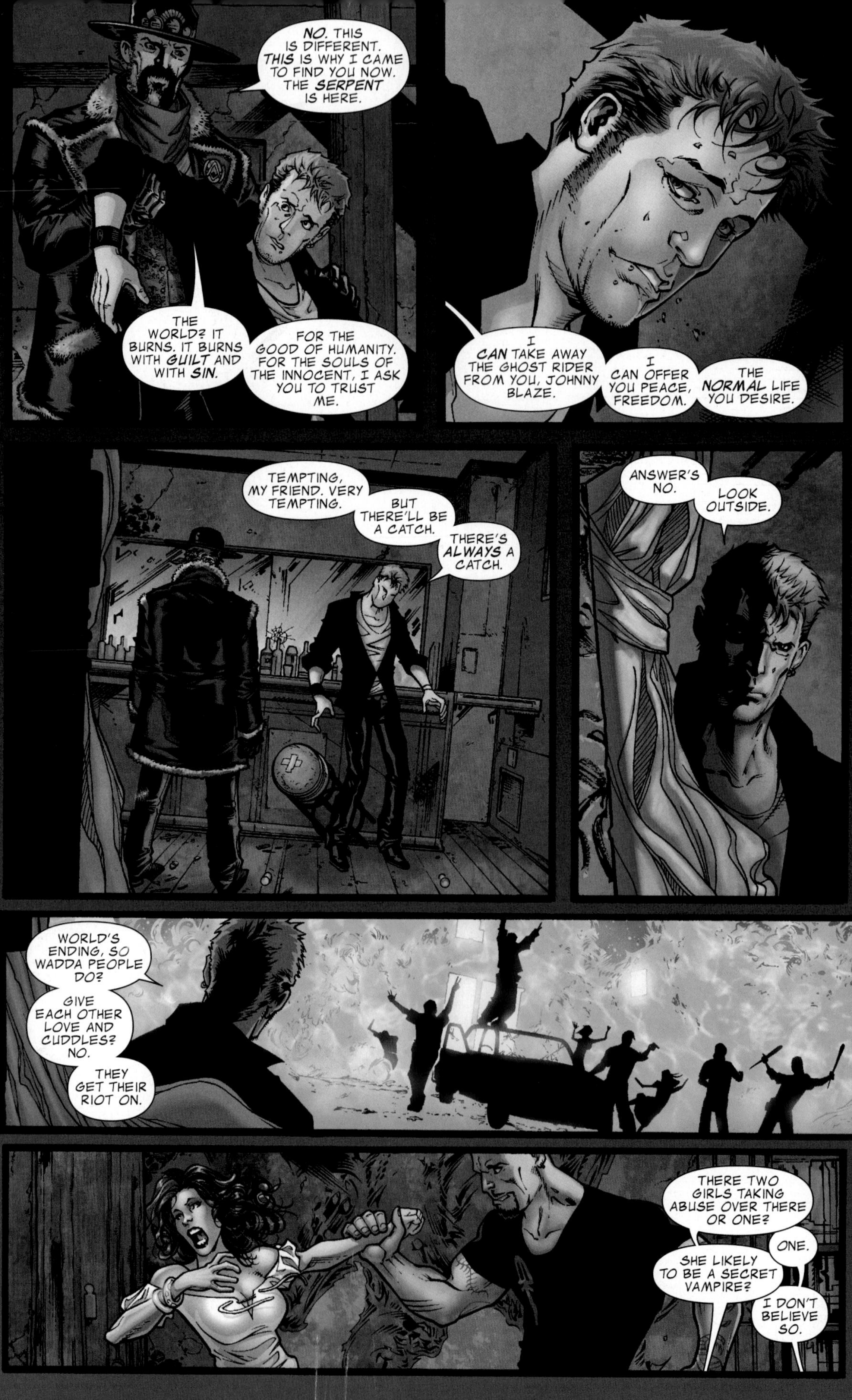
NO. THIS IS DIFFERENT. THIS IS WHY I CAME TO FIND YOU NOW. THE SERPENT IS HERE.
THE WORLD? IT BURNS. IT BURNS WITH GUILT AND WITH SIN.
FOR THE GOOD OF HUMANITY. FOR THE SOULS OF THE INNOCENT, I ASK YOU TO TRUST ME.
I CAN TAKE AWAY THE GHOST RIDER FROM YOU, JOHNNY BLAZE.
I CAN OFFER YOU PEACE, FREEDOM.
THE NORMAL LIFE YOU DESIRE.
TEMPTING, MY FRIEND. VERY TEMPTING.
BUT THERE'LL BE A CATCH.
THERE'S ALWAYS A CATCH.
ANSWER'S NO.
LOOK OUTSIDE.
WORLD'S ENDING, SO WADDA PEOPLE DO?
GIVE EACH OTHER LOVE AND CUDDLES? NO.
THEY GET THEIR RIOT ON.
THERE TWO GIRLS TAKING ABUSE OVER THERE OR ONE?
ONE.
SHE LIKELY TO BE A SECRET VAMPIRE?
I DON'T BELIEVE SO.

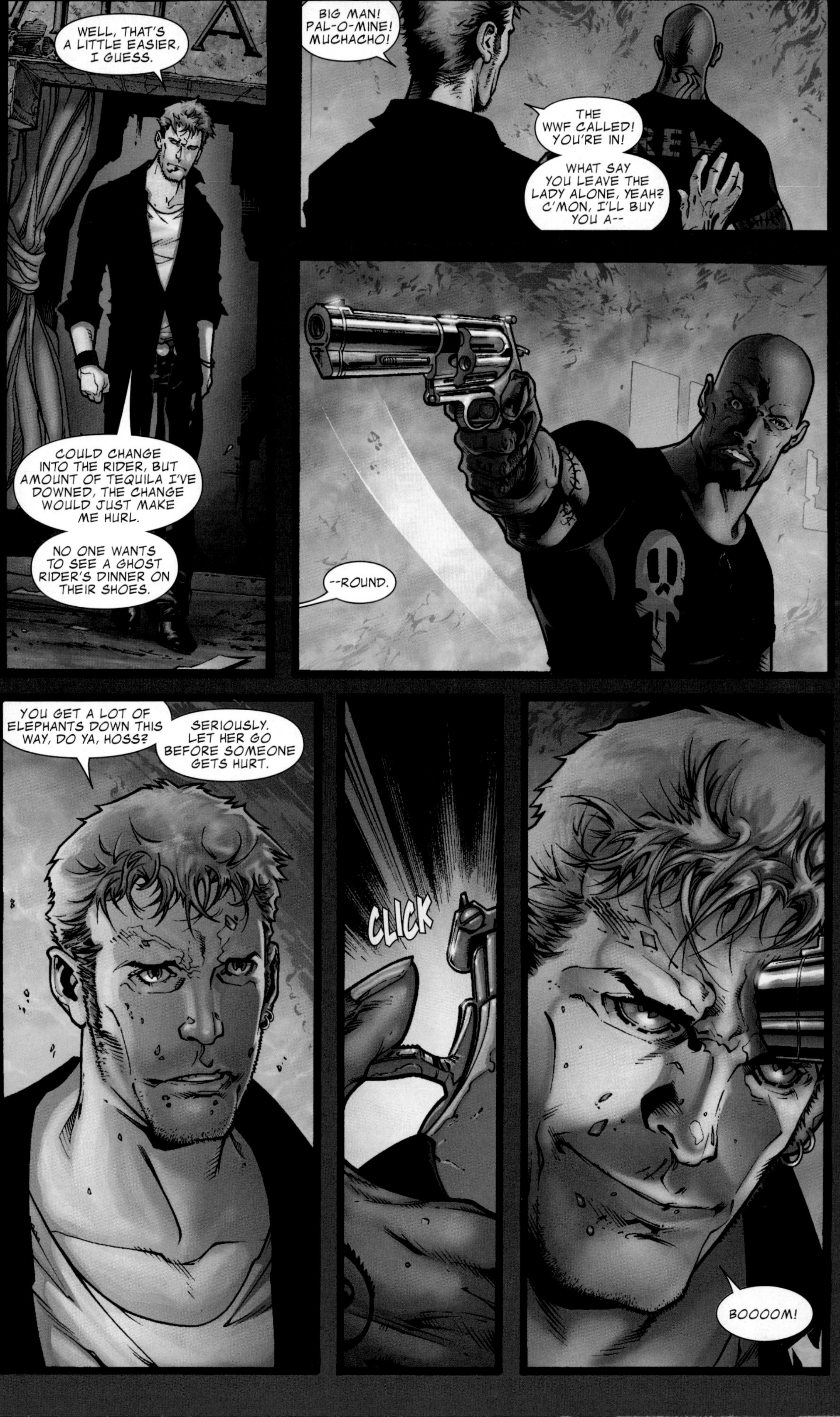
WELL, THAT'S A LITTLE EASIER, I GUESS.
COULD CHANGE INTO THE RIDER, BUT AMOUNT OF TEQUILA I'VE DOWNED, THE CHANGE WOULD JUST MAKE ME HURL.
NO ONE WANTS TO SEE A GHOST RIDER'S DINNER ON THEIR SHOES.
BIG MAN! PAL-O-MINE! MUCHACHO!
THE WWF CALLED! YOU'RE IN!
WHAT SAY YOU LEAVE THE LADY ALONE, YEAH? C'MON, I'LL BUY YOU A--
--ROUND.
YOU GET A LOT OF ELEPHANTS DOWN THIS WAY, DO YA, HOSS?
SERIOUSLY. LET HER GO BEFORE SOMEONE GETS HURT.
CLICK
BOOOOM!

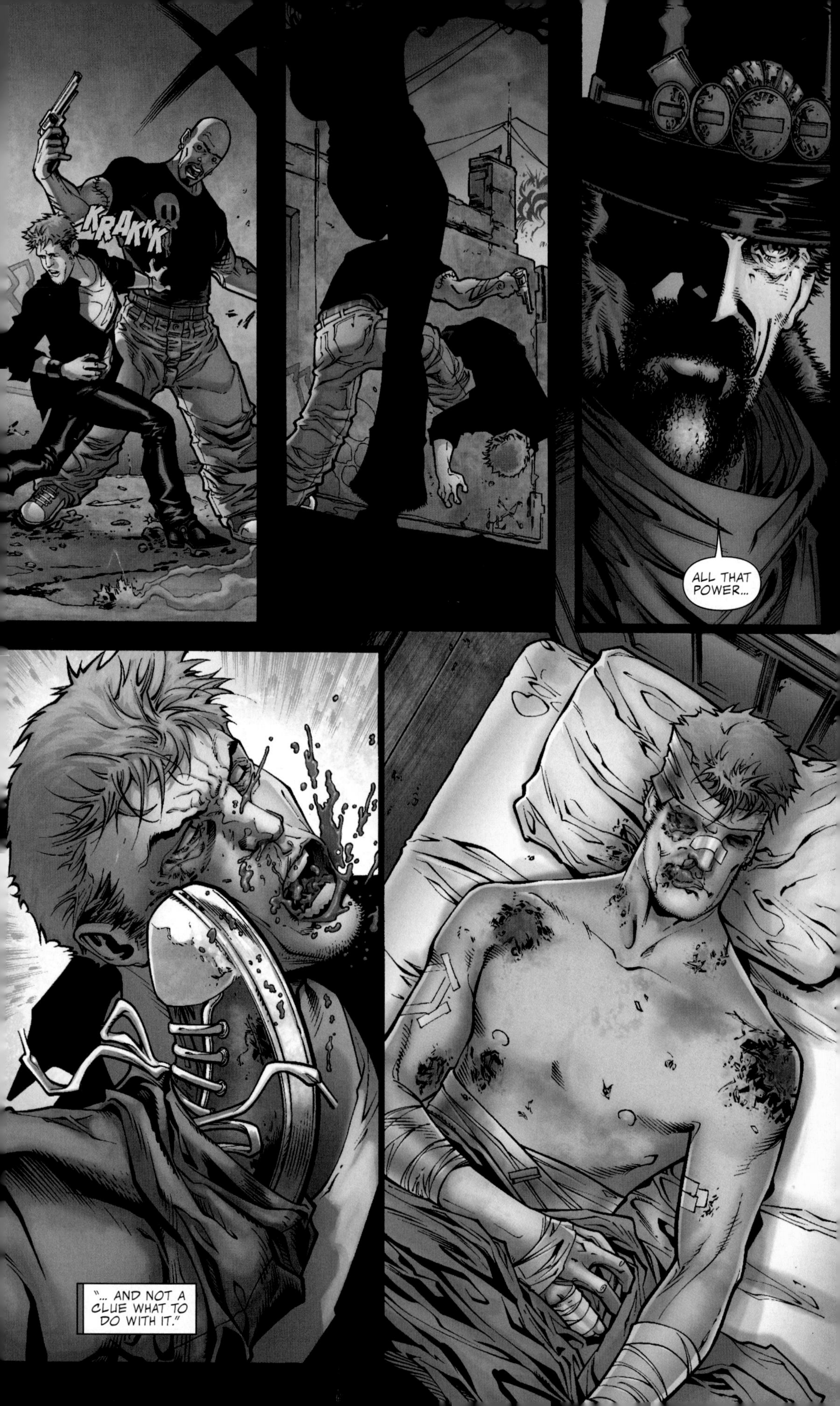
KRAKKK
ALL THAT POWER...
"... AND NOT A CLUE WHAT TO DO WITH IT."

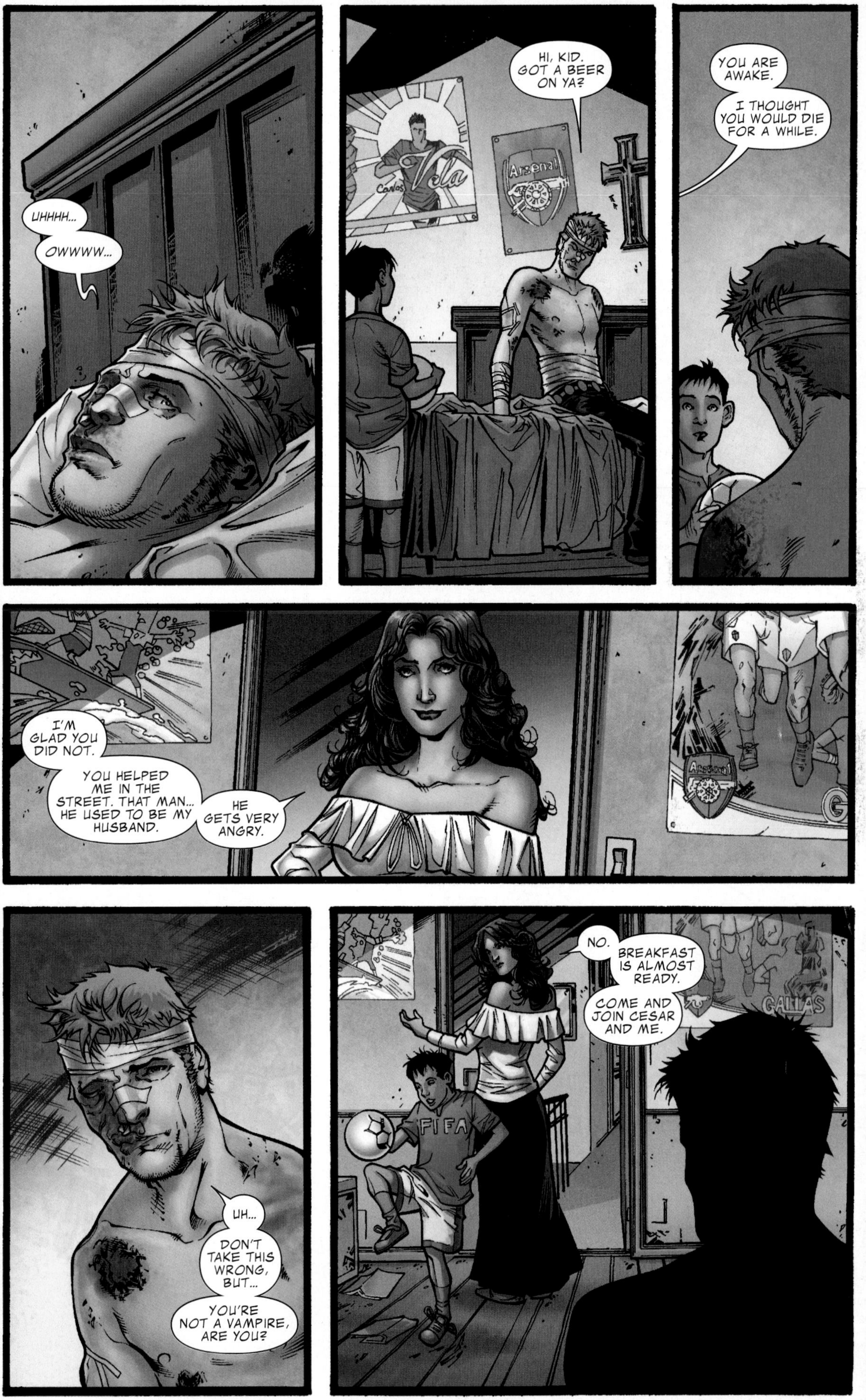
UHHHH...
OWWWW...
HI, KID. GOT A BEER ON YA?
Carlos Vela
Arsenal
YOU ARE AWAKE.
I THOUGHT YOU WOULD DIE FOR A WHILE.
I'M GLAD YOU DID NOT.
YOU HELPED ME IN THE STREET. THAT MAN... HE USED TO BE MY HUSBAND.
HE GETS VERY ANGRY.
Arsenal
UH...
DON'T TAKE THIS WRONG, BUT...
YOU'RE NOT A VAMPIRE, ARE YOU?
NO.
BREAKFAST IS ALMOST READY.
COME AND JOIN CESAR AND ME.
GALLAS
FIFA

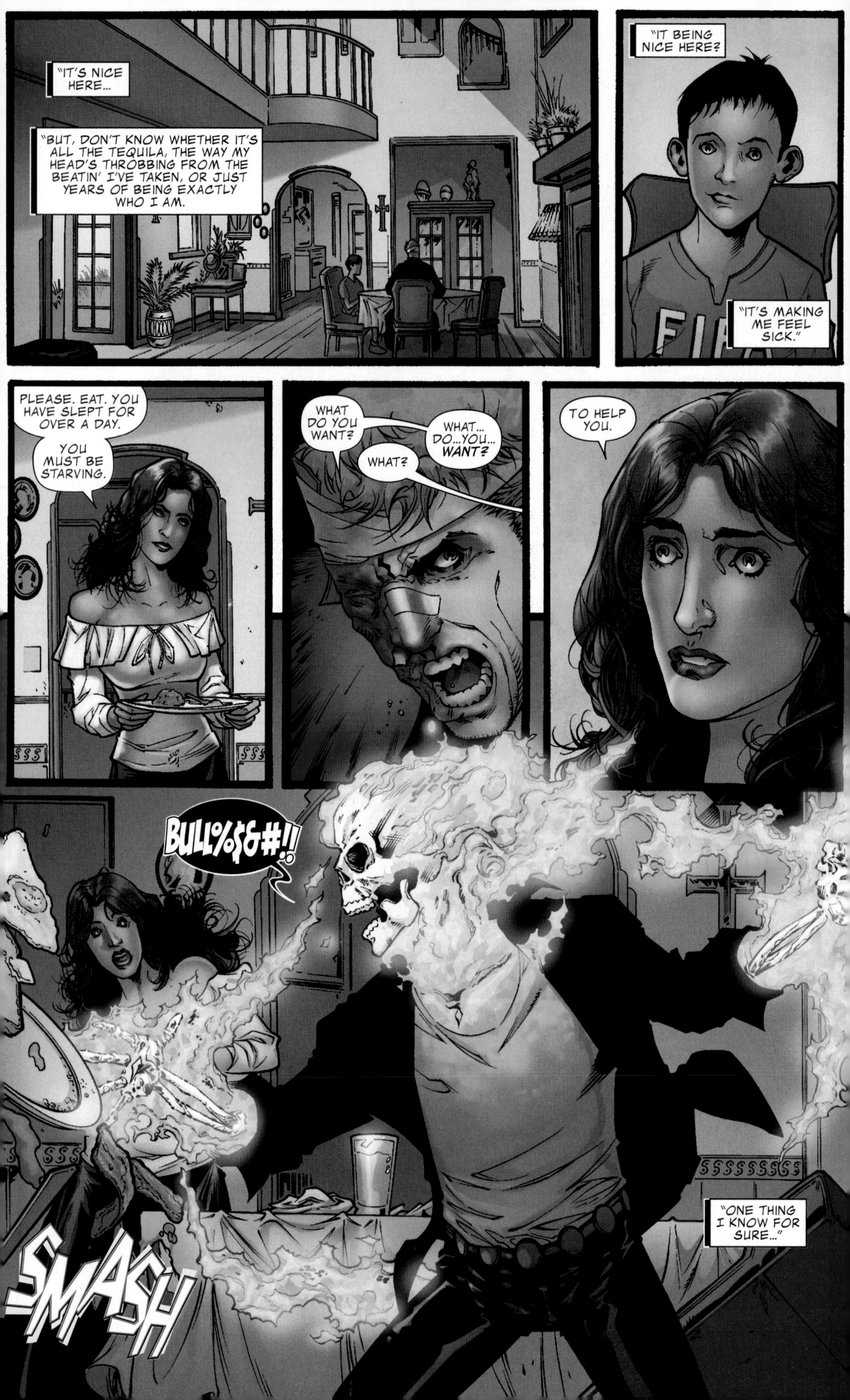
"IT'S NICE HERE...
"BUT, DON'T KNOW WHETHER IT'S ALL THE TEQUILA, THE WAY MY HEAD'S THROBBING FROM THE BEATIN' I'VE TAKEN, OR JUST YEARS OF BEING EXACTLY WHO I AM.
"IT BEING NICE HERE?
"IT'S MAKING ME FEEL SICK."
PLEASE. EAT. YOU HAVE SLEPT FOR OVER A DAY.
YOU MUST BE STARVING.
WHAT DO YOU WANT?
WHAT?
WHAT... DO...YOU... WANT?
TO HELP YOU.
BULL%$&#!!
"ONE THING I KNOW FOR SURE..."
SMASH

"...NO ONE EVER OFFERS ME HELP WITHOUT WANTING SOMETHING."

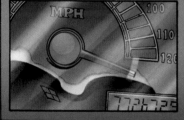

OKAY, ADAM. WHOEVER OR WHATEVER YOU ARE. IF YOU'RE LISTENING.

I'M IN.

SWEET.

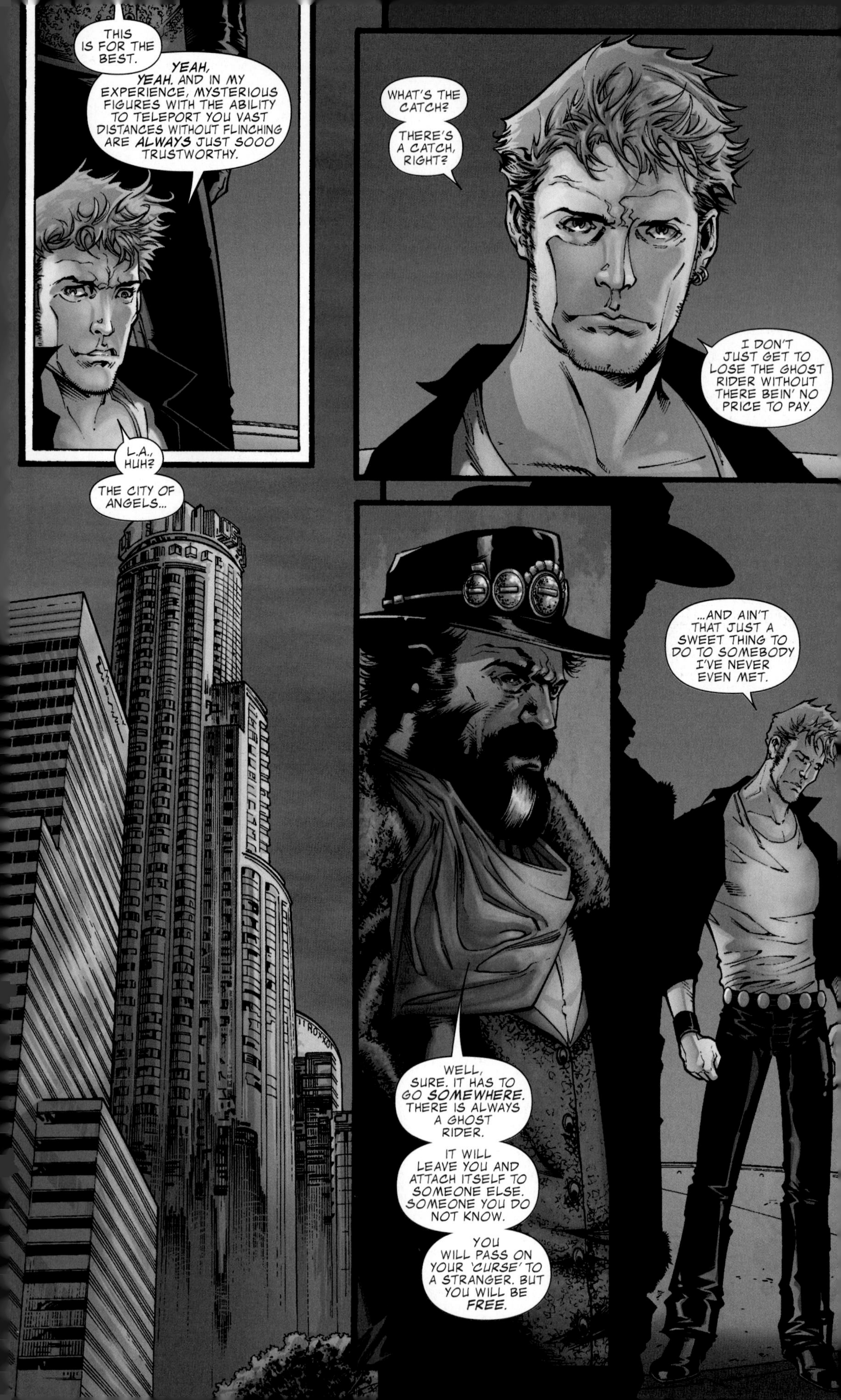

THIS IS FOR THE BEST.
YEAH, YEAH. AND IN MY EXPERIENCE, MYSTERIOUS FIGURES WITH THE ABILITY TO TELEPORT YOU VAST DISTANCES WITHOUT FLINCHING ARE ALWAYS JUST SOOO TRUSTWORTHY.
WHAT'S THE CATCH?
THERE'S A CATCH, RIGHT?
I DON'T JUST GET TO LOSE THE GHOST RIDER WITHOUT THERE BEIN' NO PRICE TO PAY.
L.A., HUH?
THE CITY OF ANGELS...
WELL, SURE. IT HAS TO GO SOMEWHERE. THERE IS ALWAYS A GHOST RIDER.
IT WILL LEAVE YOU AND ATTACH ITSELF TO SOMEONE ELSE. SOMEONE YOU DO NOT KNOW.
YOU WILL PASS ON YOUR 'CURSE' TO A STRANGER. BUT YOU WILL BE FREE.
...AND AIN'T THAT JUST A SWEET THING TO DO TO SOMEBODY I'VE NEVER EVEN MET.

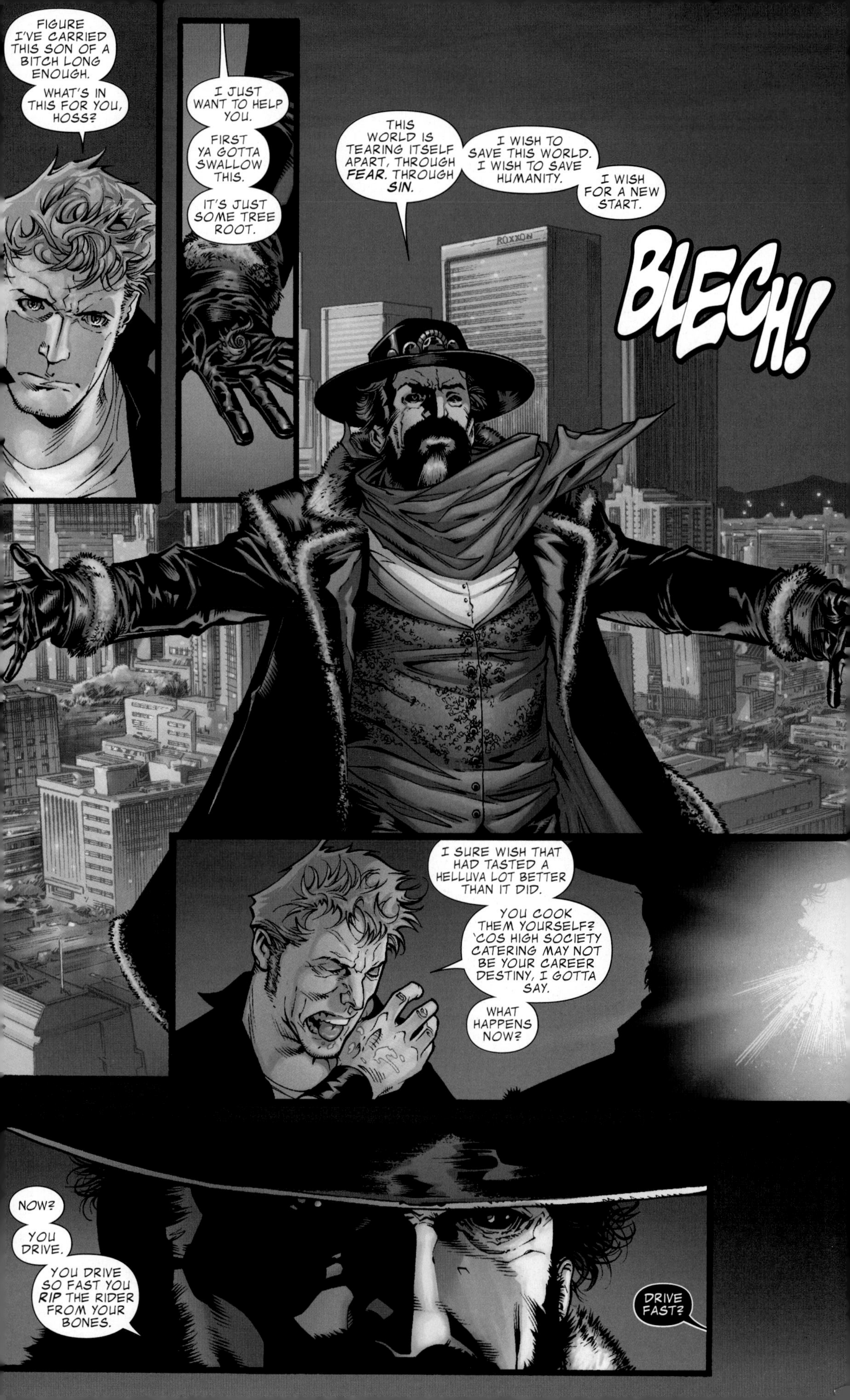

FIGURE I'VE CARRIED THIS SON OF A BITCH LONG ENOUGH.
WHAT'S IN THIS FOR YOU, HOSS?
I JUST WANT TO HELP YOU.
FIRST YA GOTTA SWALLOW THIS.
IT'S JUST SOME TREE ROOT.
THIS WORLD IS TEARING ITSELF APART, THROUGH FEAR. THROUGH SIN.
I WISH TO SAVE THIS WORLD. I WISH TO SAVE HUMANITY.
I WISH FOR A NEW START.
ROXXON
BLECH!
I SURE WISH THAT HAD TASTED A HELLUVA LOT BETTER THAN IT DID.
YOU COOK THEM YOURSELF? 'COS HIGH SOCIETY CATERING MAY NOT BE YOUR CAREER DESTINY, I GOTTA SAY.
WHAT HAPPENS NOW?
NOW?
YOU DRIVE.
YOU DRIVE SO FAST YOU RIP THE RIDER FROM YOUR BONES.
DRIVE FAST?

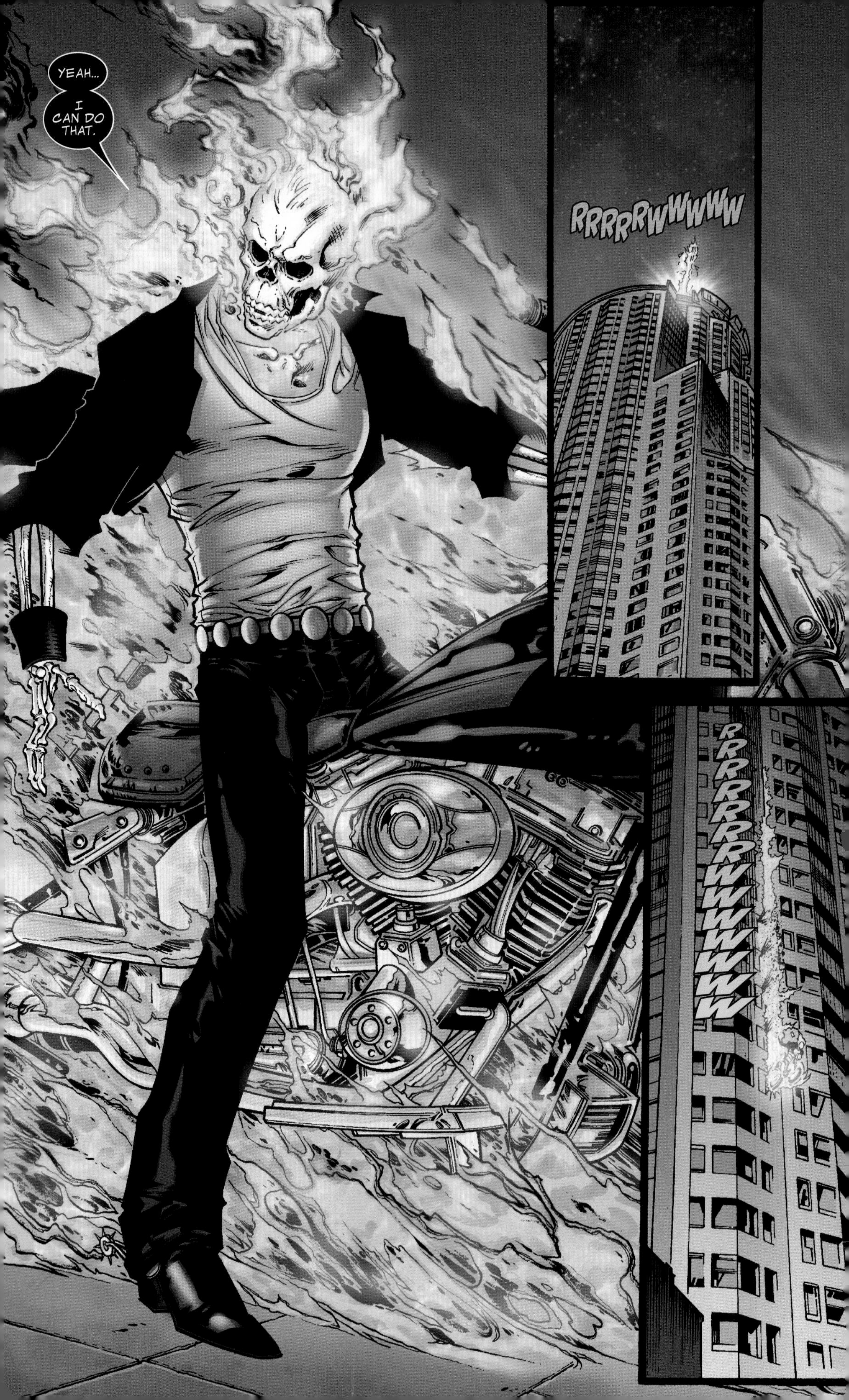
YEAH...
I CAN DO THAT.
RRRRRWWWWW
RRRRRRRRWWWWWWWW

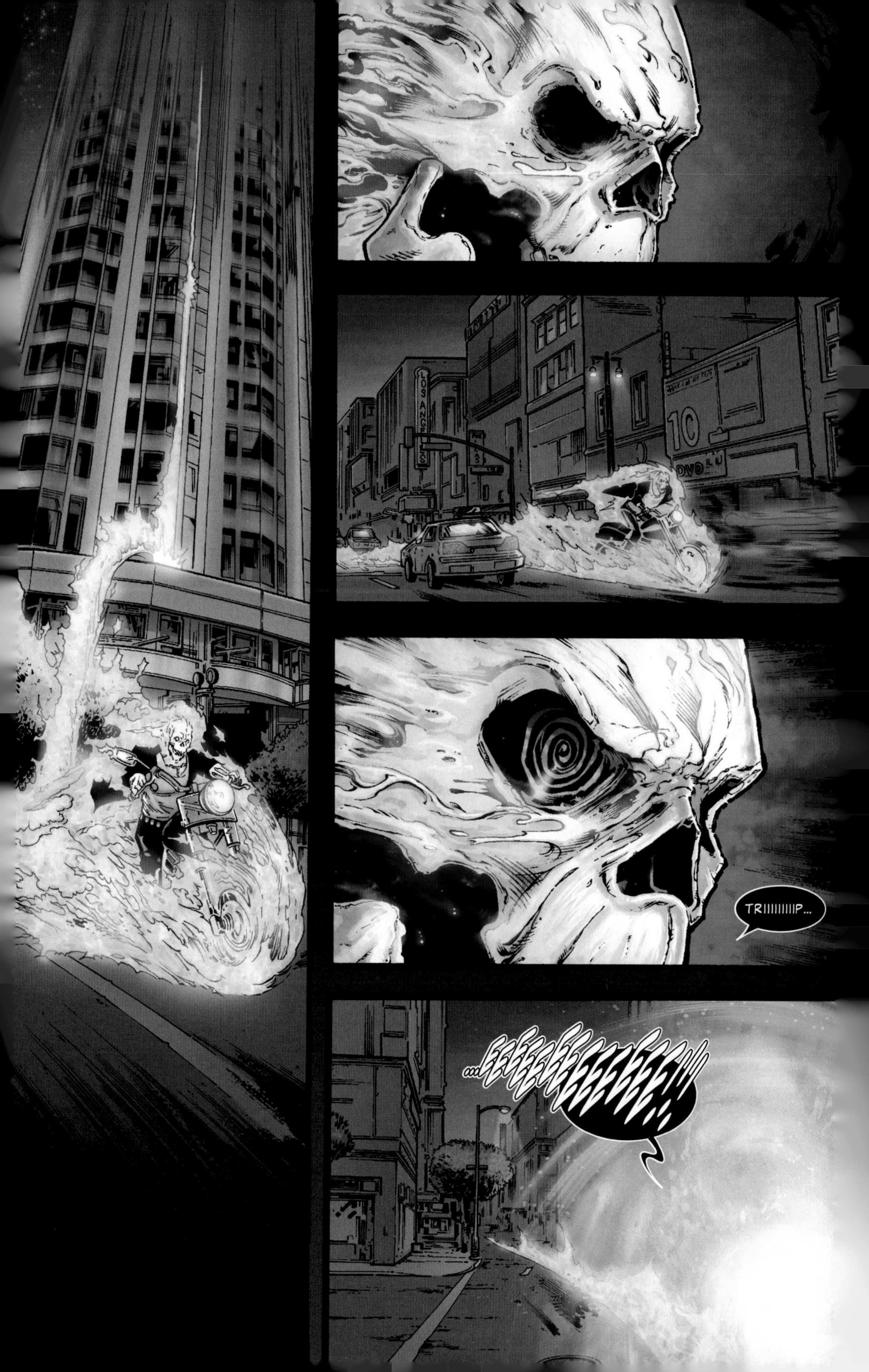
TRIIIIIIIIIP...
...EEEEEEEEEEEEEE!!!

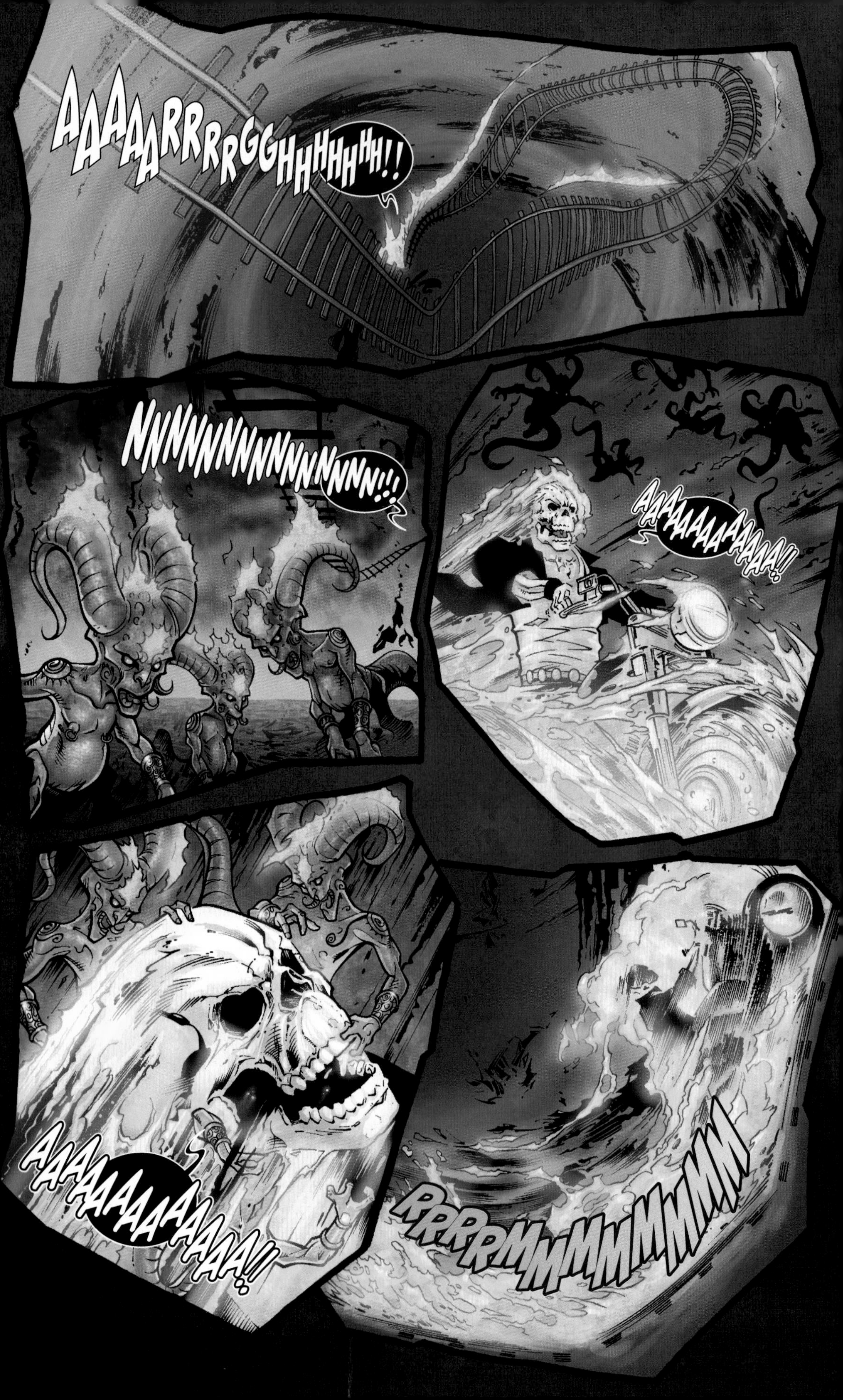
AAAAARRRRGGHHHHHH!!
NNNNNNNNNNNNNNNNN!!!
AAAAAAAAAAAA!!
AAAAAAAAAAAAA!!
RRRRMMMMMMMMMM

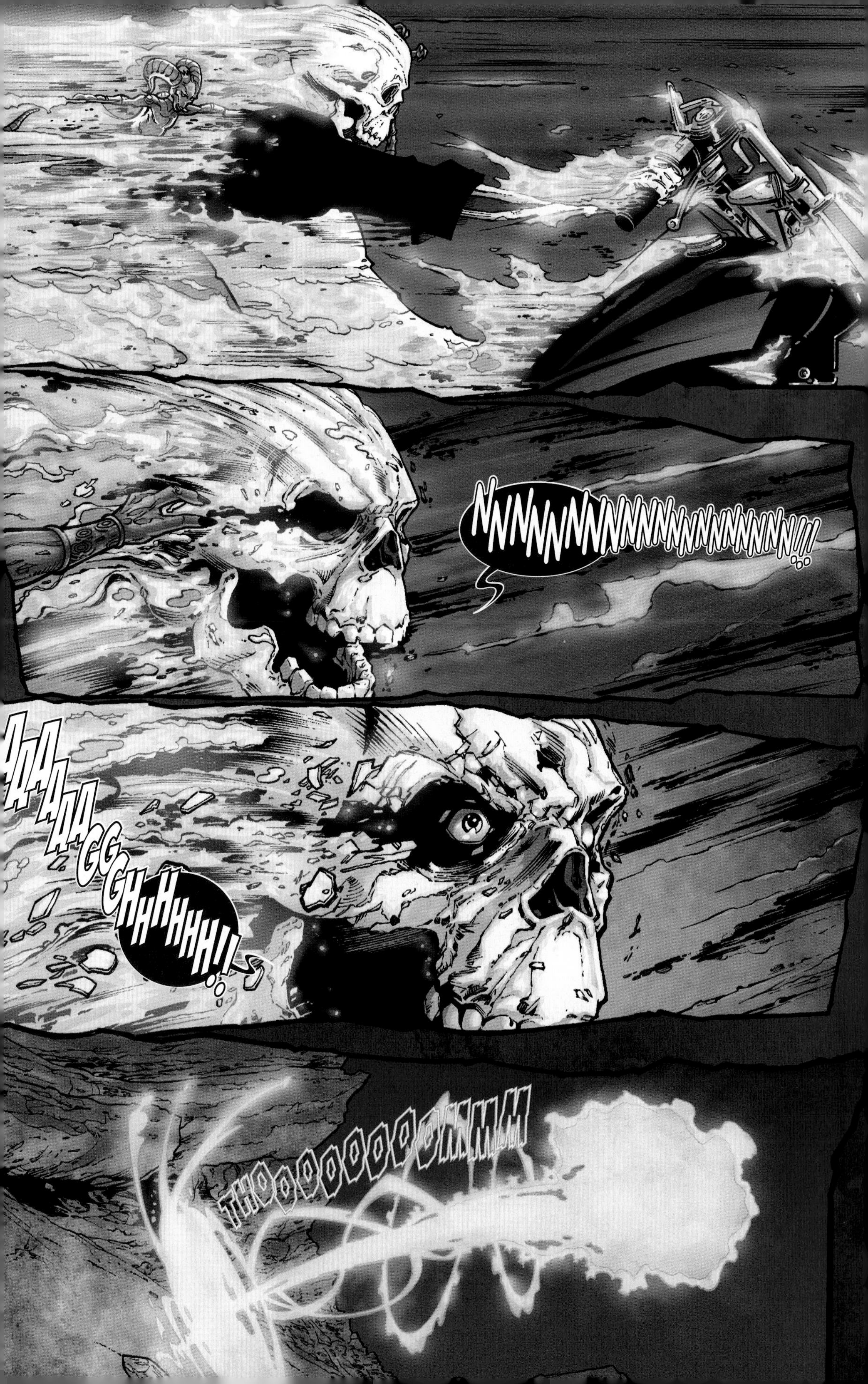
NNNNNNNNNNNNNNNNNNNNNNNNNNN!!!
AAAAAAAGGGHHHHHH!!
THOOOOOOOOMMMM

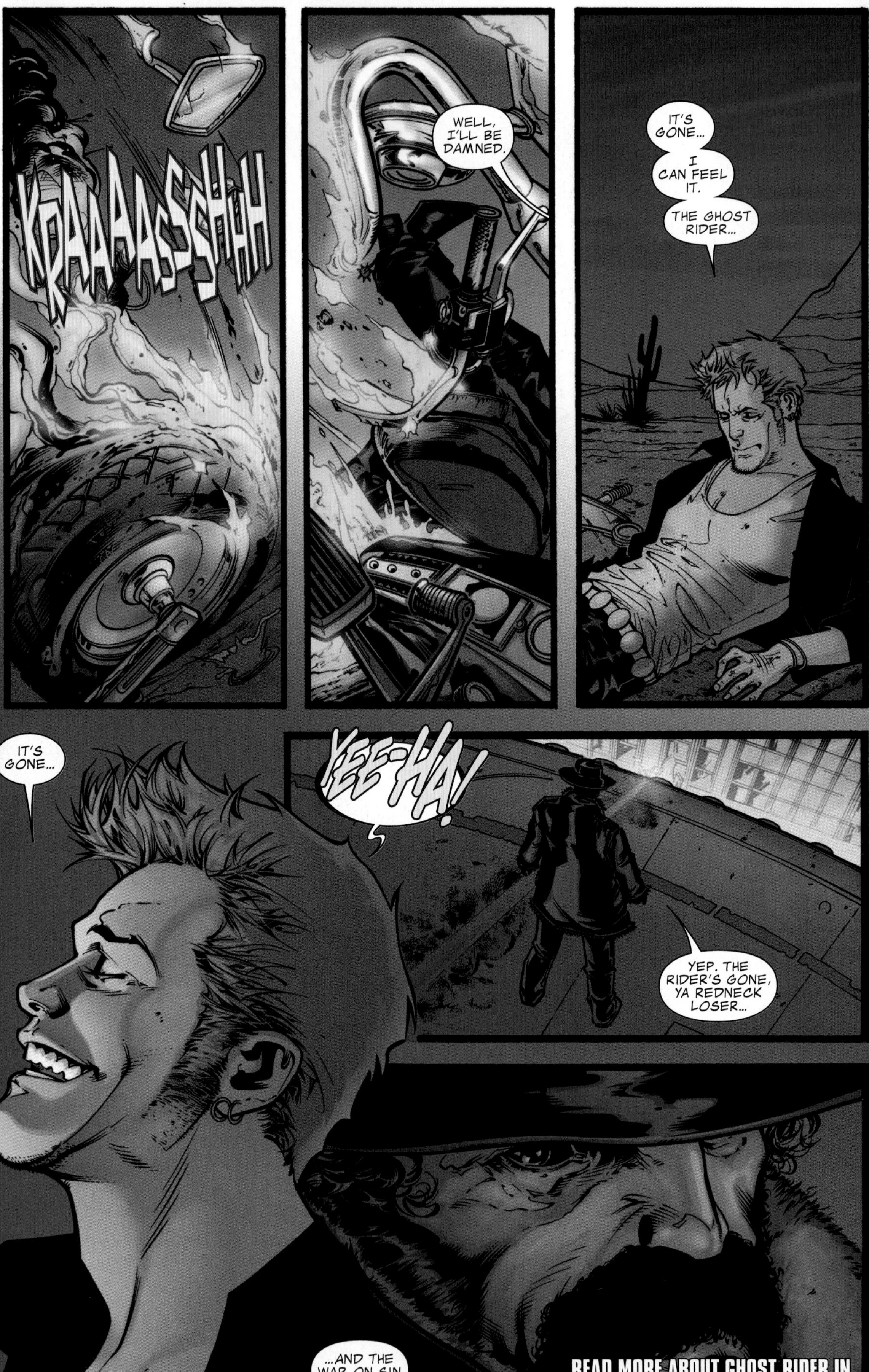
KRAAAASSHHH
WELL, I'LL BE DAMNED.
IT'S GONE...
I CAN FEEL IT.
THE GHOST RIDER...
IT'S GONE...
YEE-HA!
YEP. THE RIDER'S GONE, YA REDNECK LOSER...
...AND THE WAR ON SIN BEGINS.
READ MORE ABOUT GHOST RIDER IN
FEAR ITSELF: GHOST RIDER.

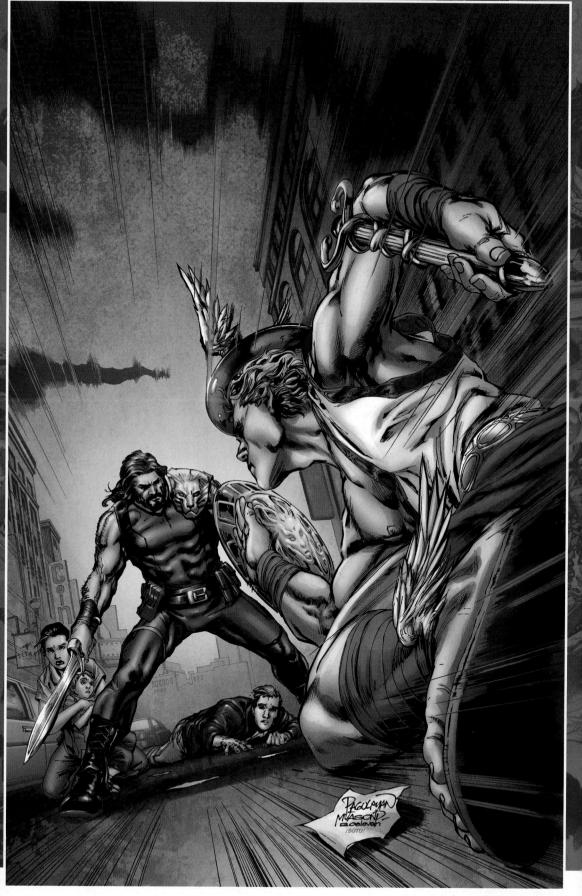

HERC #6.1

AT THE END OF THE GREAT CHAOS WAR THE DEMI-GOD HERCULES GAVE UP HIS POWERS TO BECOME A MERE MORTAL, BUT HE DIDN'T LET THIS STOP HIM FROM BEING A SUPER HERO. PROCLAIMING HIMSELF THE PROTECTOR OF BROOKLYN, THERE IS NO BATTLE HE WON'T FIGHT! NO ENEMY HE WON'T VANQUISH! NO BEER HE WON'T DRINK!

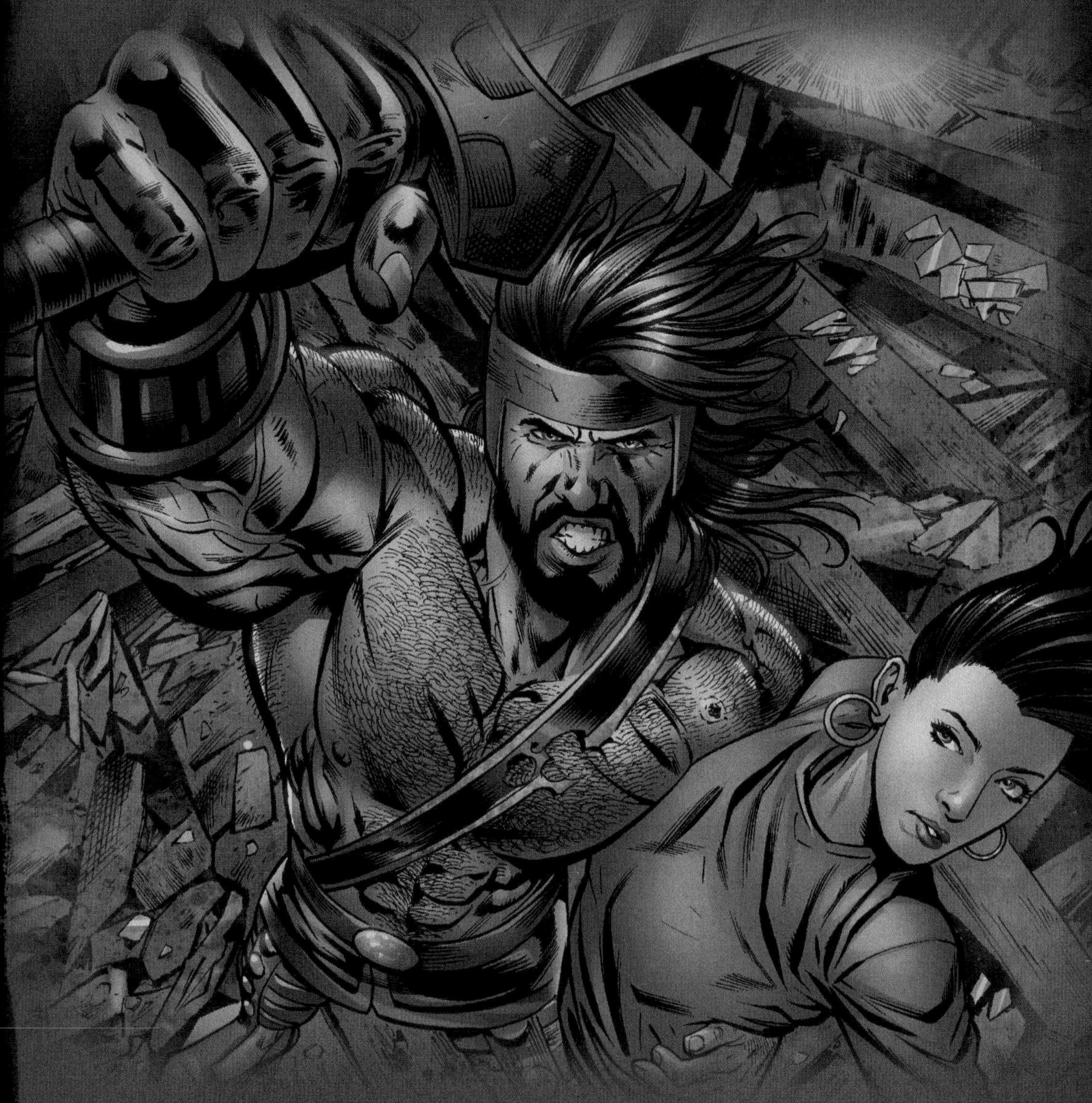

HE'S GOT A JOB AS A BARTENDER, A BRASSY BROOKLYN GIRLFRIEND AND AN ARSENAL OF GODLY WEAPONS... WHO COULD POSSIBLY STOP HIM?

OH. RIGHT. **GODS.**

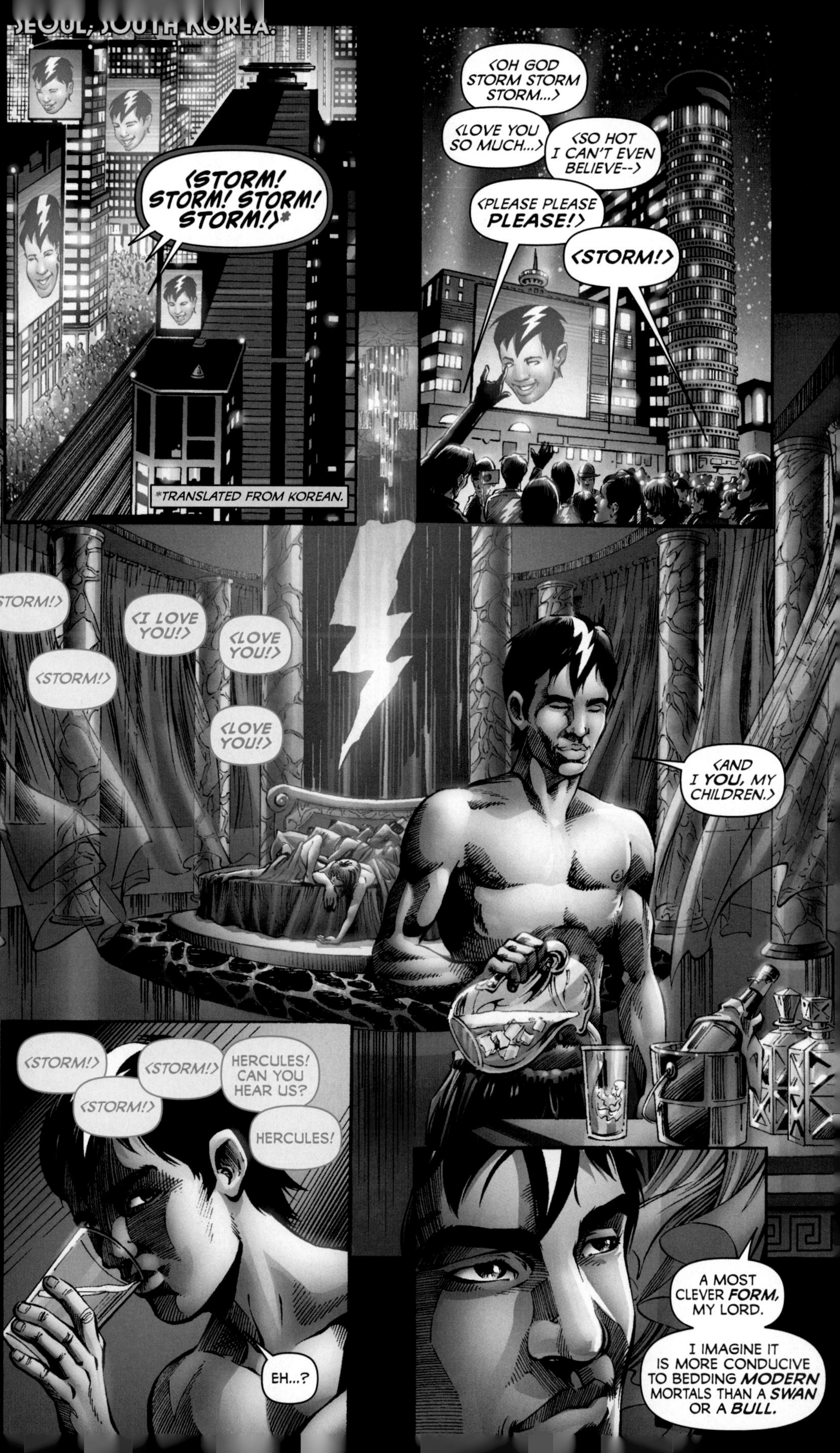
SEOUL, SOUTH KOREA.
<STORM! STORM! STORM! STORM!>*
*TRANSLATED FROM KOREAN.
<OH GOD STORM STORM STORM...>
<LOVE YOU SO MUCH...>
<SO HOT I CAN'T EVEN BELIEVE-->
<PLEASE PLEASE PLEASE!>
<STORM!>
<STORM!>
<STORM!>
<I LOVE YOU!>
<LOVE YOU!>
<LOVE YOU!>
<AND I YOU, MY CHILDREN.>
<STORM!>
<STORM!>
<STORM!>
HERCULES! CAN YOU HEAR US?
HERCULES!
EH...?
A MOST CLEVER FORM, MY LORD.
I IMAGINE IT IS MORE CONDUCIVE TO BEDDING MODERN MORTALS THAN A SWAN OR A BULL.

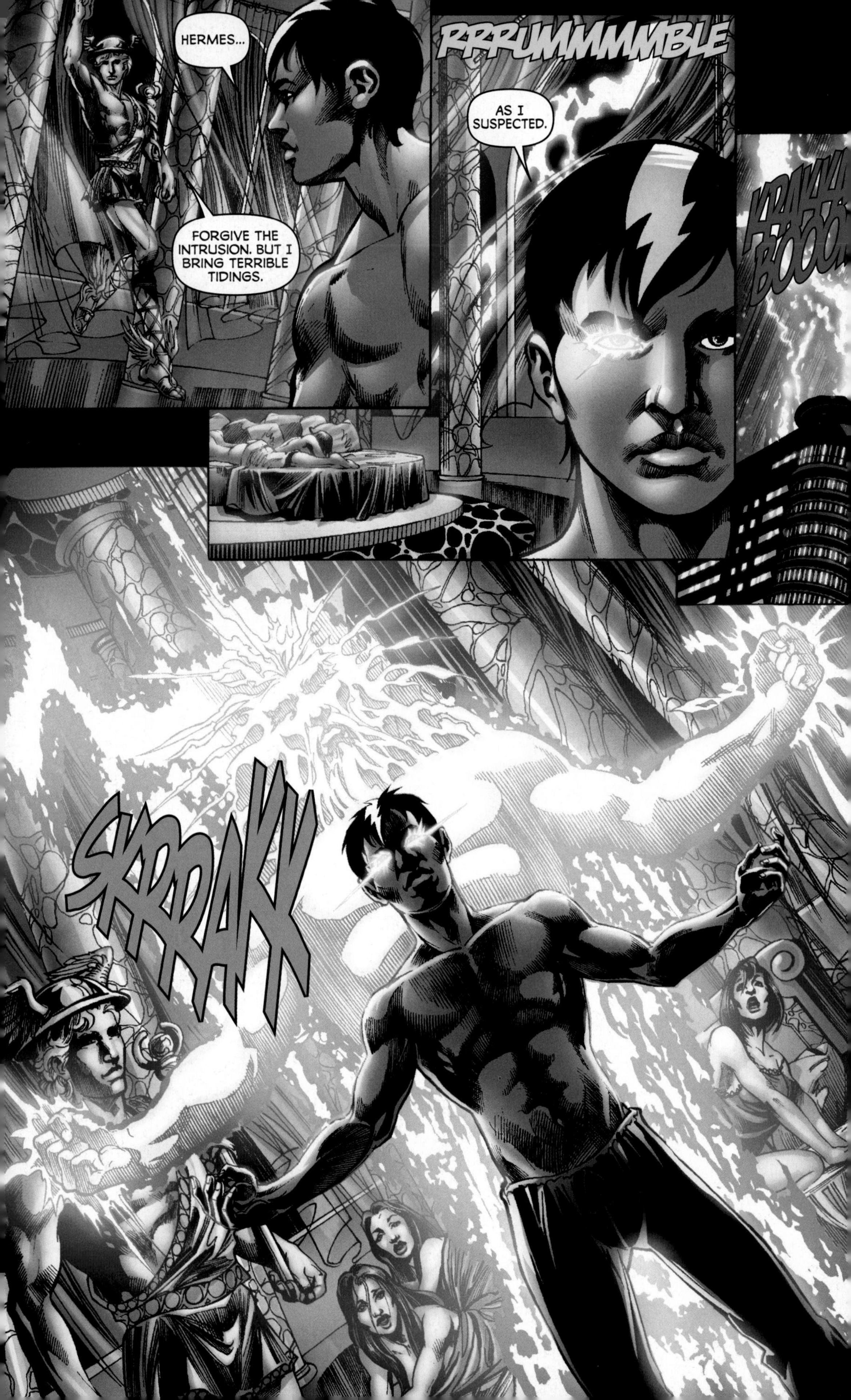
HERMES...
FORGIVE THE INTRUSION. BUT I BRING TERRIBLE TIDINGS.
RRRUMMMMMBLE
AS I SUSPECTED.
SKRRAKK

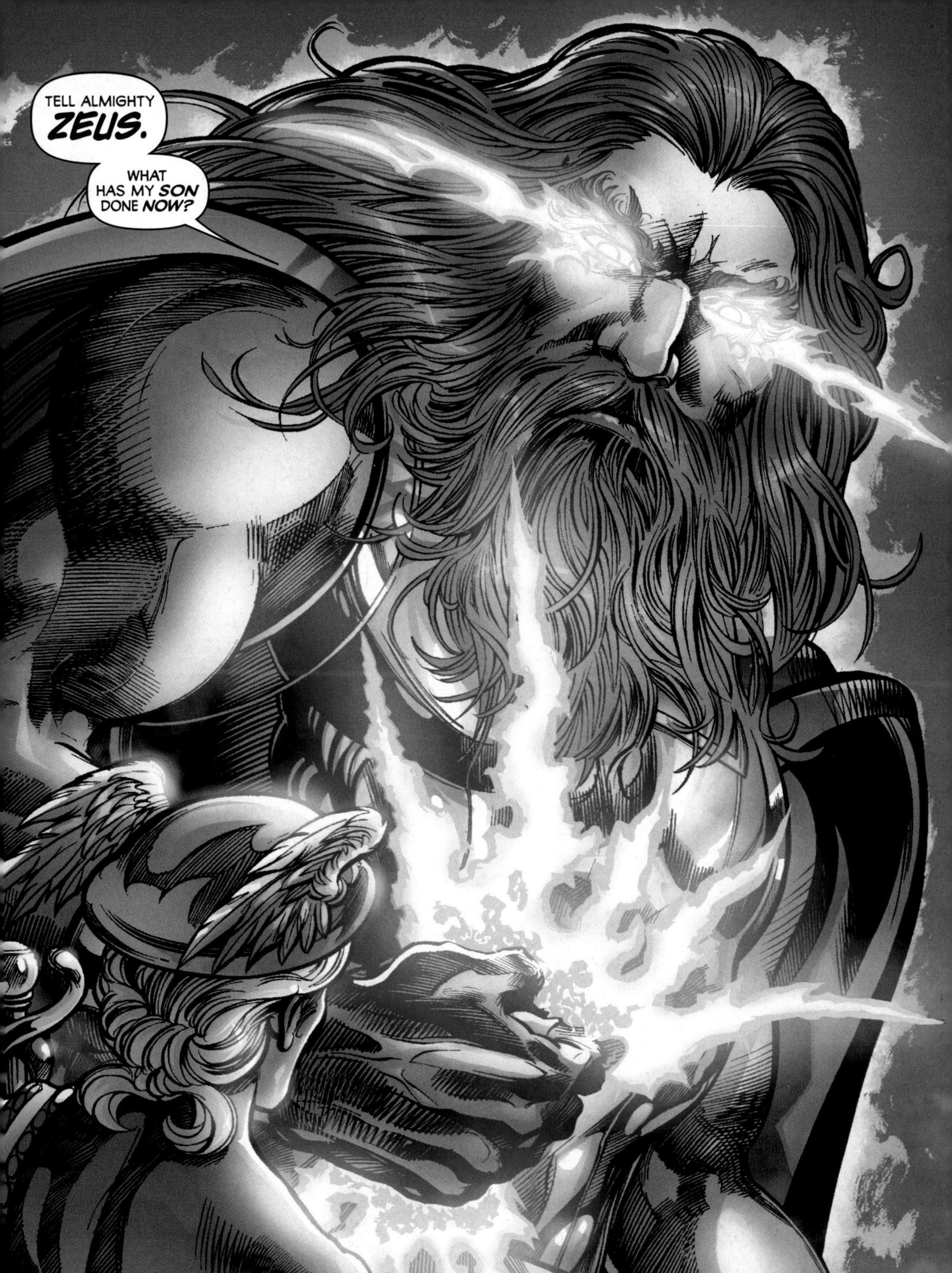
TELL ALMIGHTY ZEUS.
WHAT HAS MY SON DONE NOW?

THE MYSTERIES

GREG PAK & FRED VAN LENTE WRITERS | MIKE GRELL PENCILLER | JASON PAZ INKS PGS 3, 4, 14, 15, 18-24 | JEFF HUET INKS PGS 2, 6-13 | JESUS ABURTOV COLORIST | SIMON BOWLAND LETTERING | CARLO PAGULAYAN, JASON PAZ & CHRIS SOTOMAYOR COVER

TAYLOR ESPOSITO PRODUCTION   JAKE THOMAS ASSISTANT EDITOR   MARK PANICCIA EDITOR

AXEL ALONSO EDITOR IN CHIEF   JOE QUESADA CHIEF CREATIVE OFFICER   DAN BUCKLEY PUBLISHER   ALAN FINE EXEC. PRODUCER

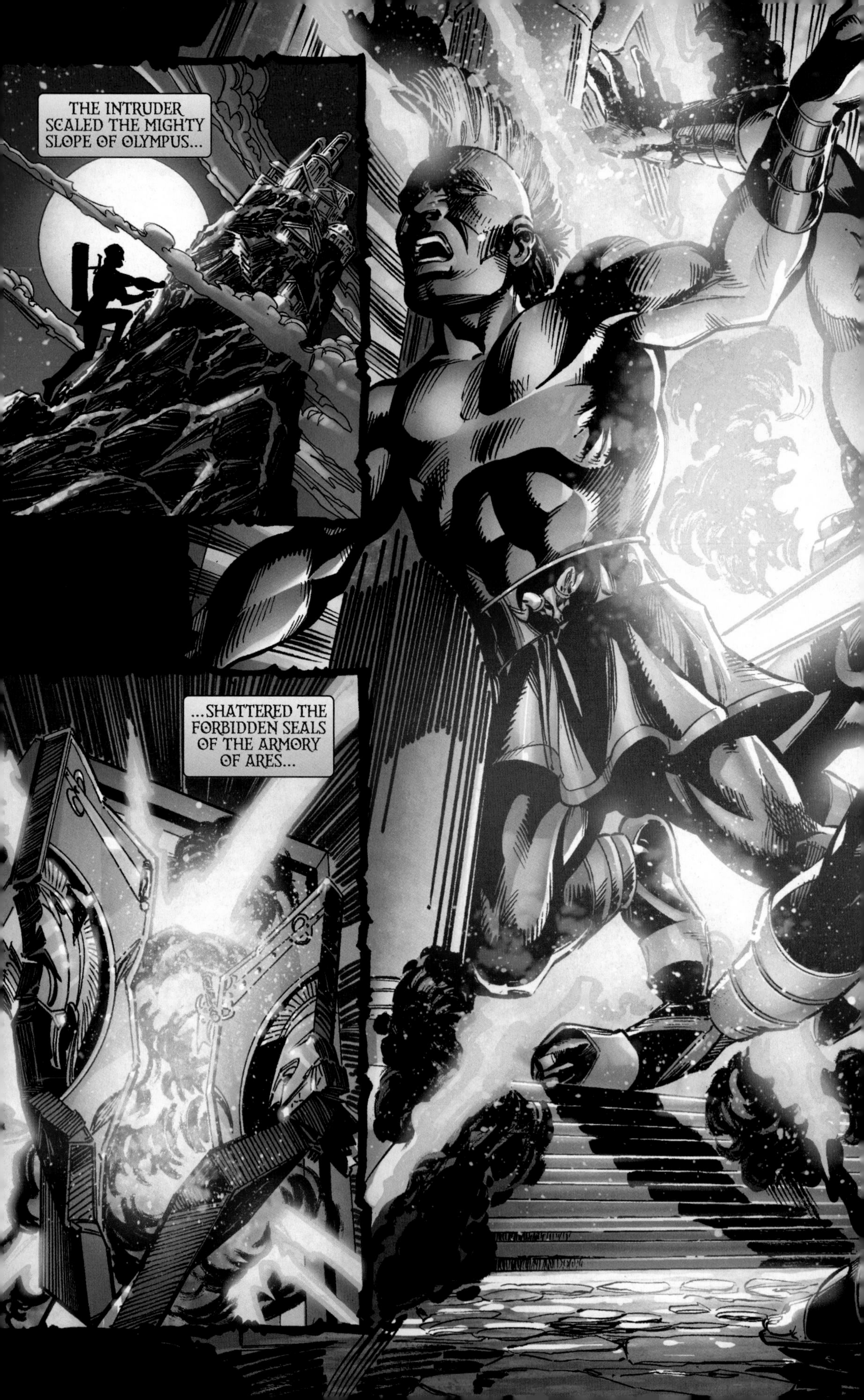
THE INTRUDER SCALED THE MIGHTY SLOPE OF OLYMPUS...
...SHATTERED THE FORBIDDEN SEALS OF THE ARMORY OF ARES...

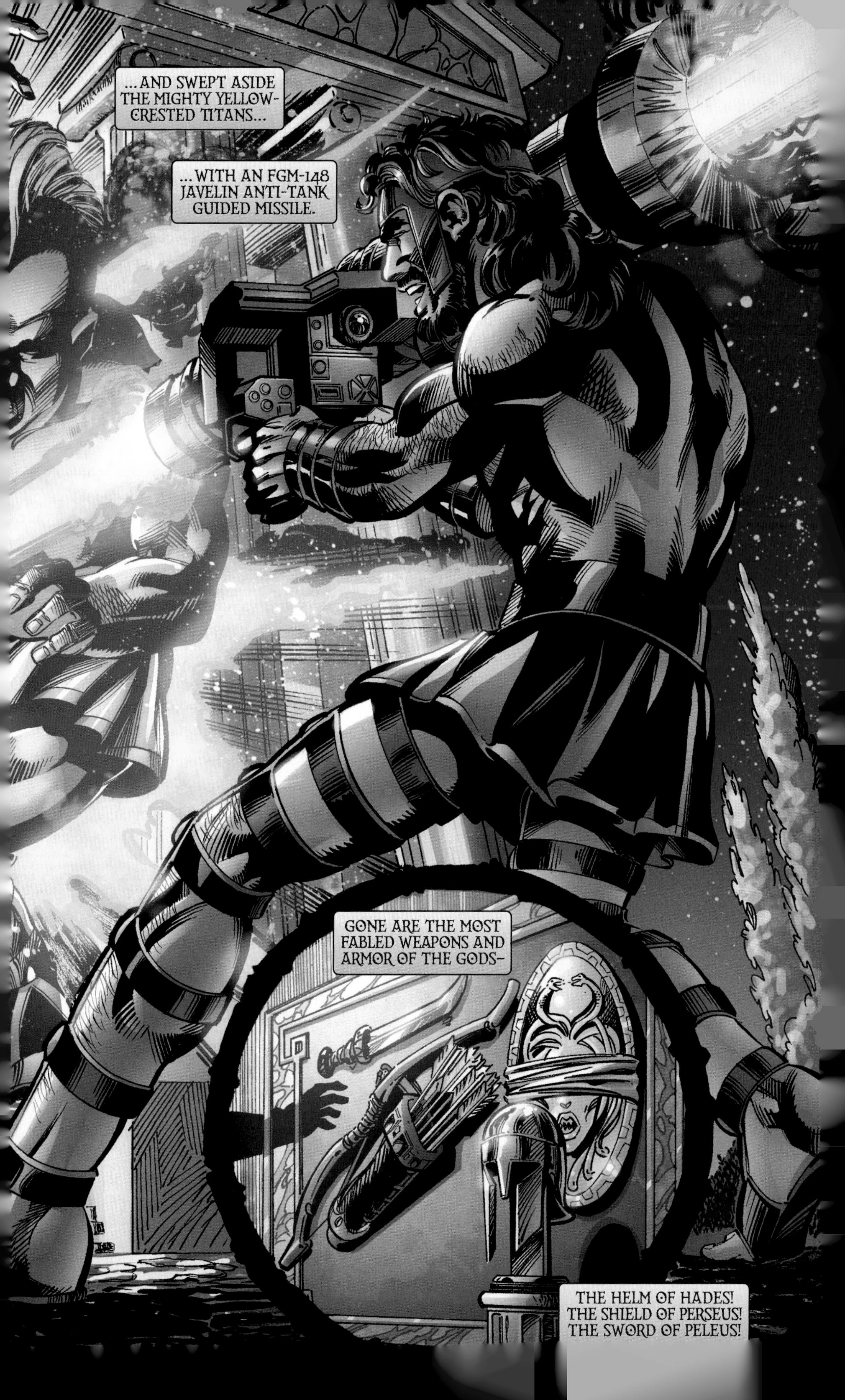
...AND SWEPT ASIDE THE MIGHTY YELLOW-CRESTED TITANS...
...WITH AN FGM-148 JAVELIN ANTI-TANK GUIDED MISSILE.
GONE ARE THE MOST FABLED WEAPONS AND ARMOR OF THE GODS-
THE HELM OF HADES! THE SHIELD OF PERSEUS! THE SWORD OF PELEUS!

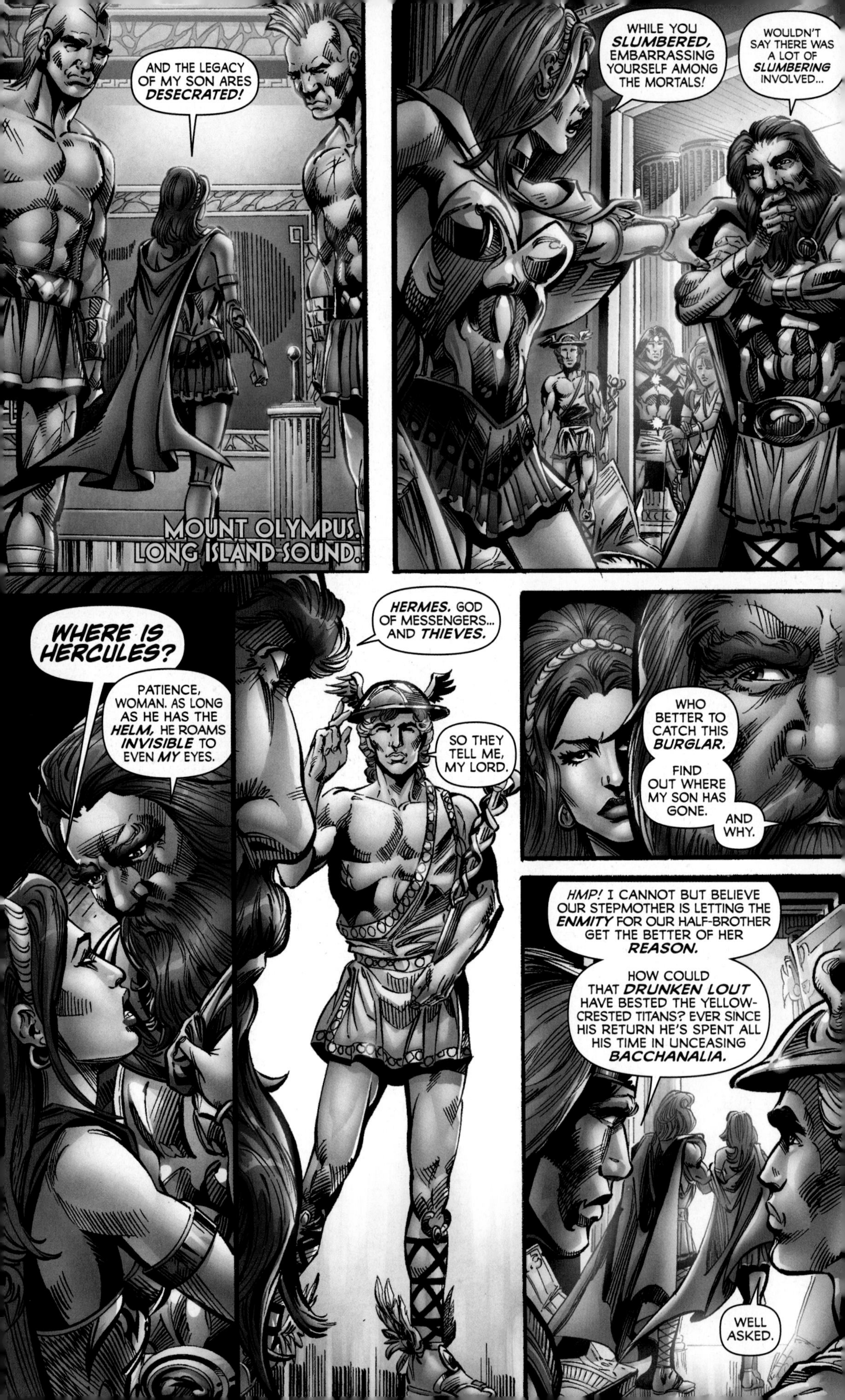
AND THE LEGACY OF MY SON ARES DESECRATED!
MOUNT OLYMPUS. LONG ISLAND SOUND.
WHILE YOU SLUMBERED, EMBARRASSING YOURSELF AMONG THE MORTALS!
WOULDN'T SAY THERE WAS A LOT OF SLUMBERING INVOLVED...
WHERE IS HERCULES?
PATIENCE, WOMAN. AS LONG AS HE HAS THE HELM, HE ROAMS INVISIBLE TO EVEN MY EYES.
HERMES. GOD OF MESSENGERS... AND THIEVES.
SO THEY TELL ME, MY LORD.
WHO BETTER TO CATCH THIS BURGLAR.
FIND OUT WHERE MY SON HAS GONE.
AND WHY.
HMP! I CANNOT BUT BELIEVE OUR STEPMOTHER IS LETTING THE ENMITY FOR OUR HALF-BROTHER GET THE BETTER OF HER REASON.
HOW COULD THAT DRUNKEN LOUT HAVE BESTED THE YELLOW-CRESTED TITANS? EVER SINCE HIS RETURN HE'S SPENT ALL HIS TIME IN UNCEASING BACCHANALIA.
WELL ASKED.

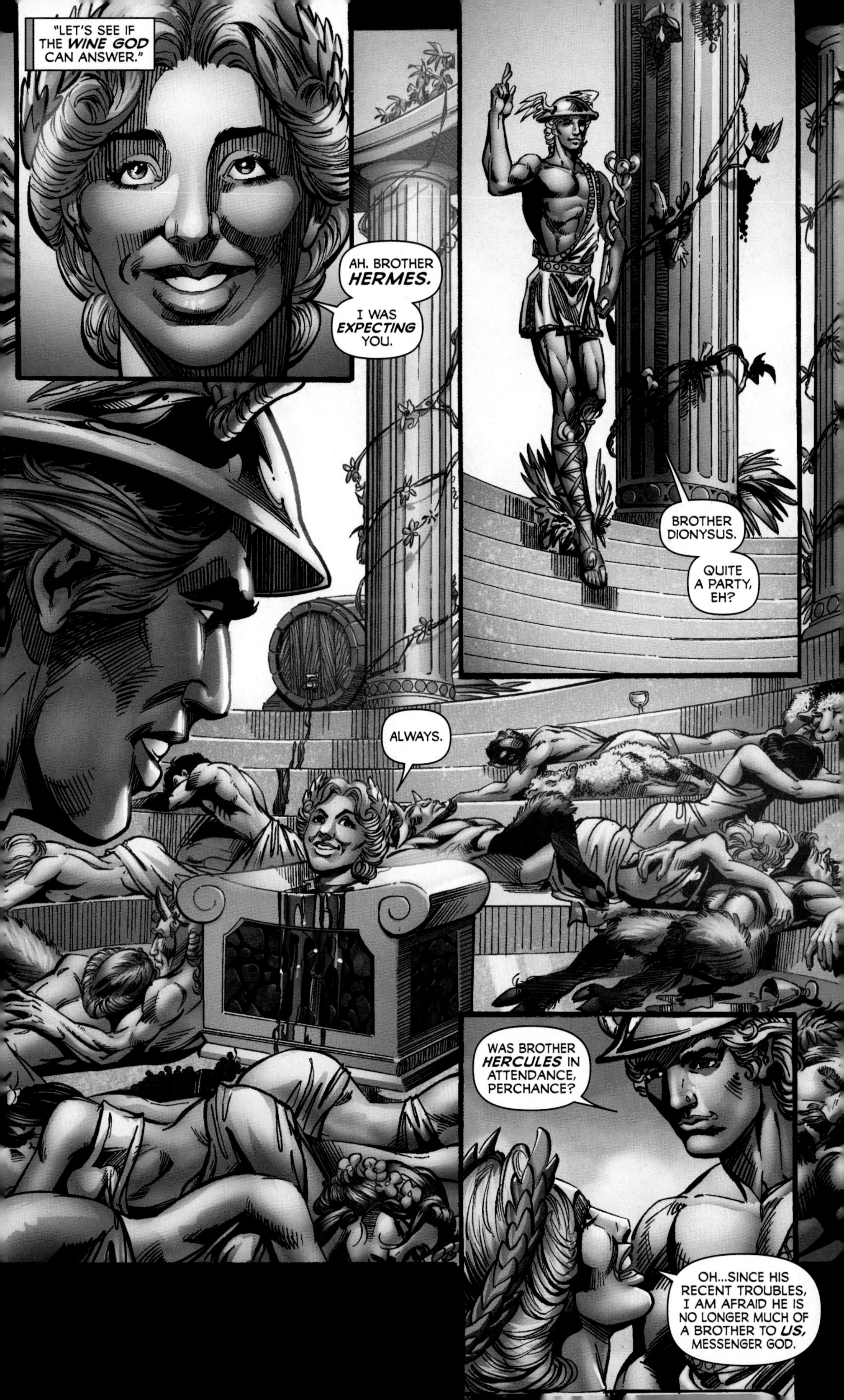
"LET'S SEE IF THE WINE GOD CAN ANSWER."
AH. BROTHER HERMES.
I WAS EXPECTING YOU.
BROTHER DIONYSUS.
QUITE A PARTY, EH?
ALWAYS.
WAS BROTHER HERCULES IN ATTENDANCE, PERCHANCE?
OH...SINCE HIS RECENT TROUBLES, I AM AFRAID HE IS NO LONGER MUCH OF A BROTHER TO US, MESSENGER GOD.

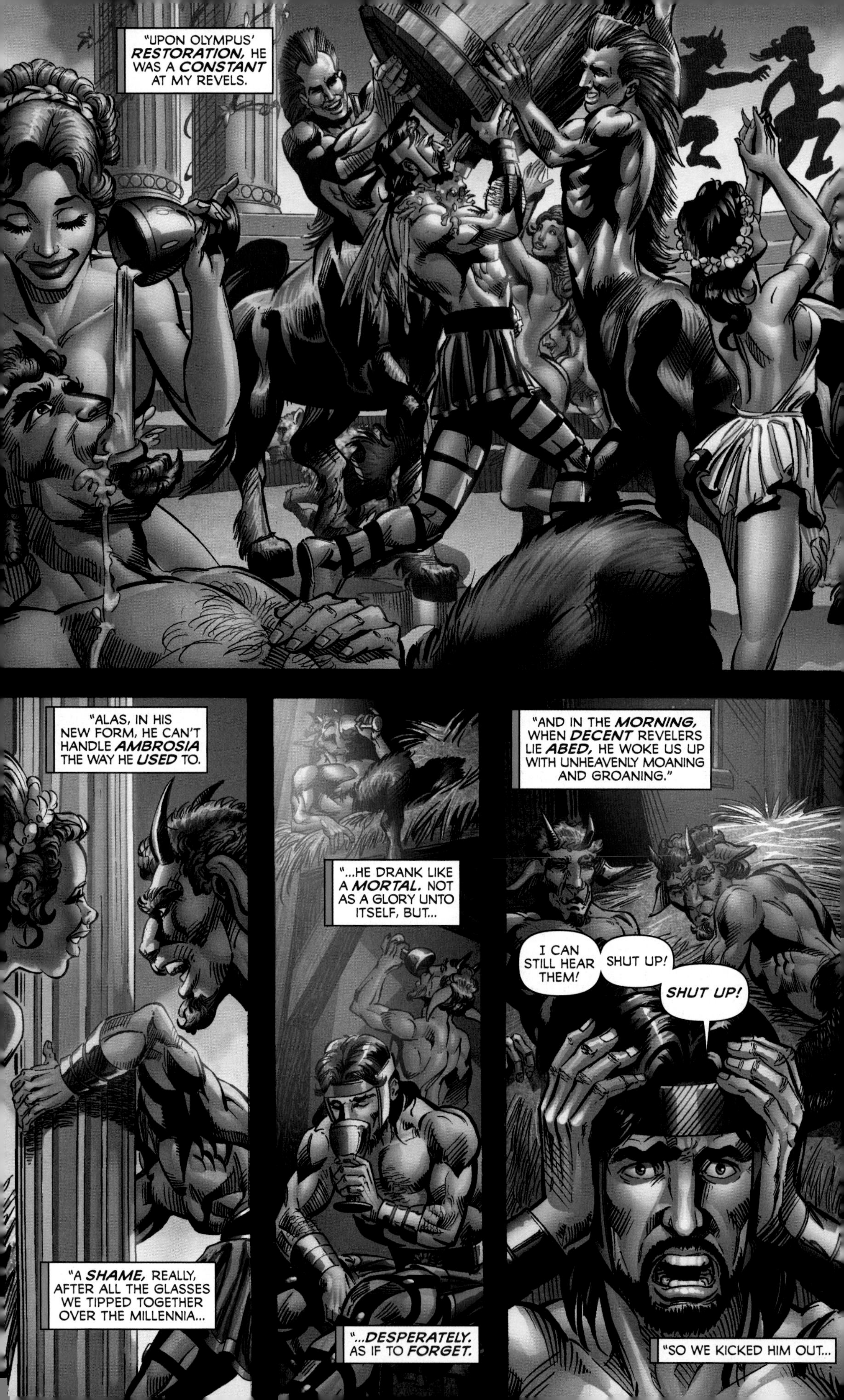
"UPON OLYMPUS' RESTORATION, HE WAS A CONSTANT AT MY REVELS.
"ALAS, IN HIS NEW FORM, HE CAN'T HANDLE AMBROSIA THE WAY HE USED TO.
"A SHAME, REALLY, AFTER ALL THE GLASSES WE TIPPED TOGETHER OVER THE MILLENNIA...
"...HE DRANK LIKE A MORTAL. NOT AS A GLORY UNTO ITSELF, BUT...
"...DESPERATELY. AS IF TO FORGET.
"AND IN THE MORNING, WHEN DECENT REVELERS LIE ABED, HE WOKE US UP WITH UNHEAVENLY MOANING AND GROANING."
I CAN STILL HEAR THEM!
SHUT UP!
SHUT UP!
"SO WE KICKED HIM OUT...

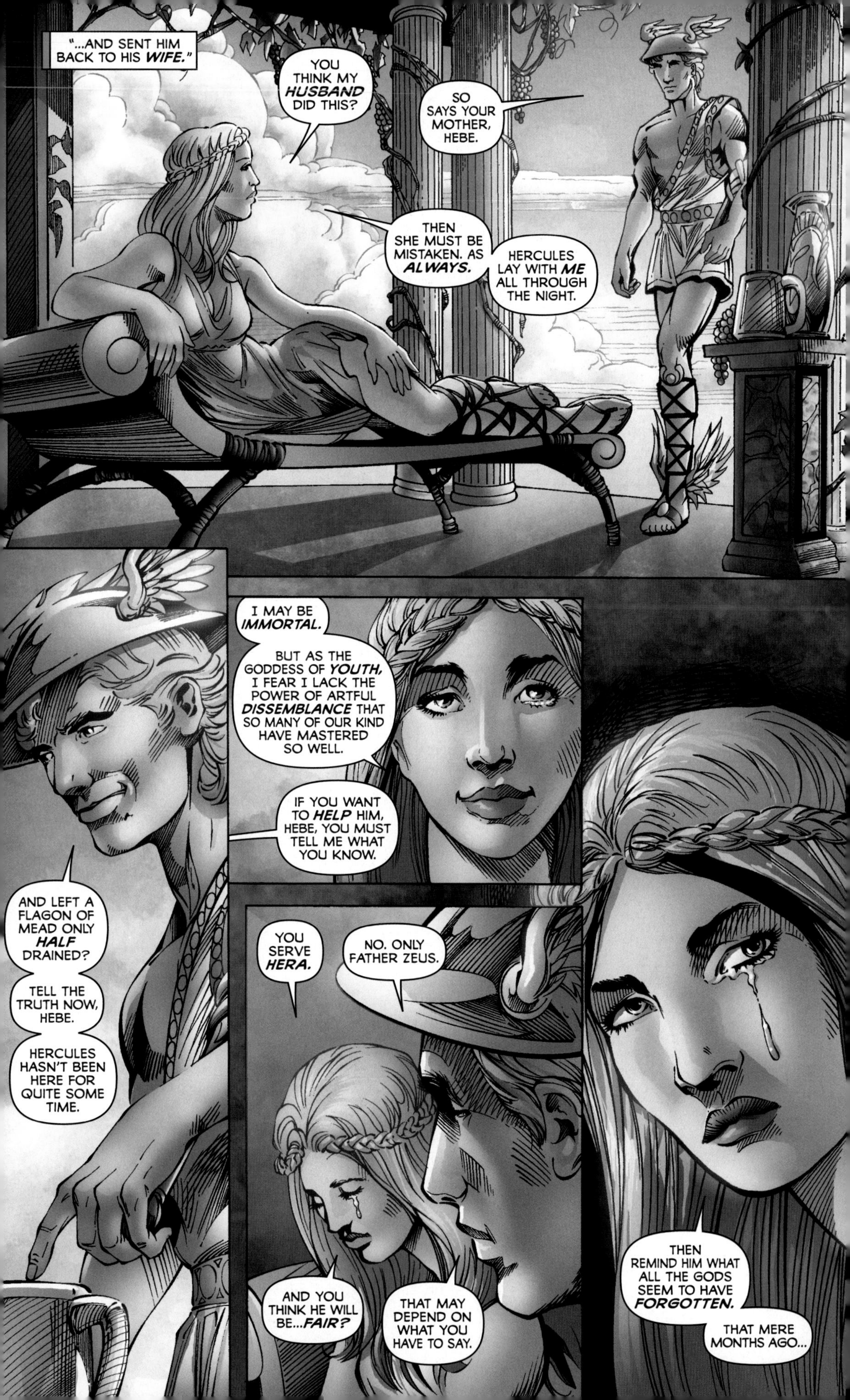
"...AND SENT HIM BACK TO HIS *WIFE.*"
YOU THINK MY *HUSBAND* DID THIS?
SO SAYS YOUR MOTHER, HEBE.
THEN SHE MUST BE MISTAKEN. AS *ALWAYS.*
HERCULES LAY WITH *ME* ALL THROUGH THE NIGHT.
AND LEFT A FLAGON OF MEAD ONLY *HALF* DRAINED?
TELL THE TRUTH NOW, HEBE.
HERCULES HASN'T BEEN HERE FOR QUITE SOME TIME.
I MAY BE *IMMORTAL.*
BUT AS THE GODDESS OF *YOUTH,* I FEAR I LACK THE POWER OF ARTFUL *DISSEMBLANCE* THAT SO MANY OF OUR KIND HAVE MASTERED SO WELL.
IF YOU WANT TO *HELP* HIM, HEBE, YOU MUST TELL ME WHAT YOU KNOW.
YOU SERVE *HERA.*
NO. ONLY FATHER ZEUS.
AND YOU THINK HE WILL BE...*FAIR?*
THAT MAY DEPEND ON WHAT YOU HAVE TO SAY.
THEN REMIND HIM WHAT ALL THE GODS SEEM TO HAVE *FORGOTTEN.*
THAT MERE MONTHS AGO...

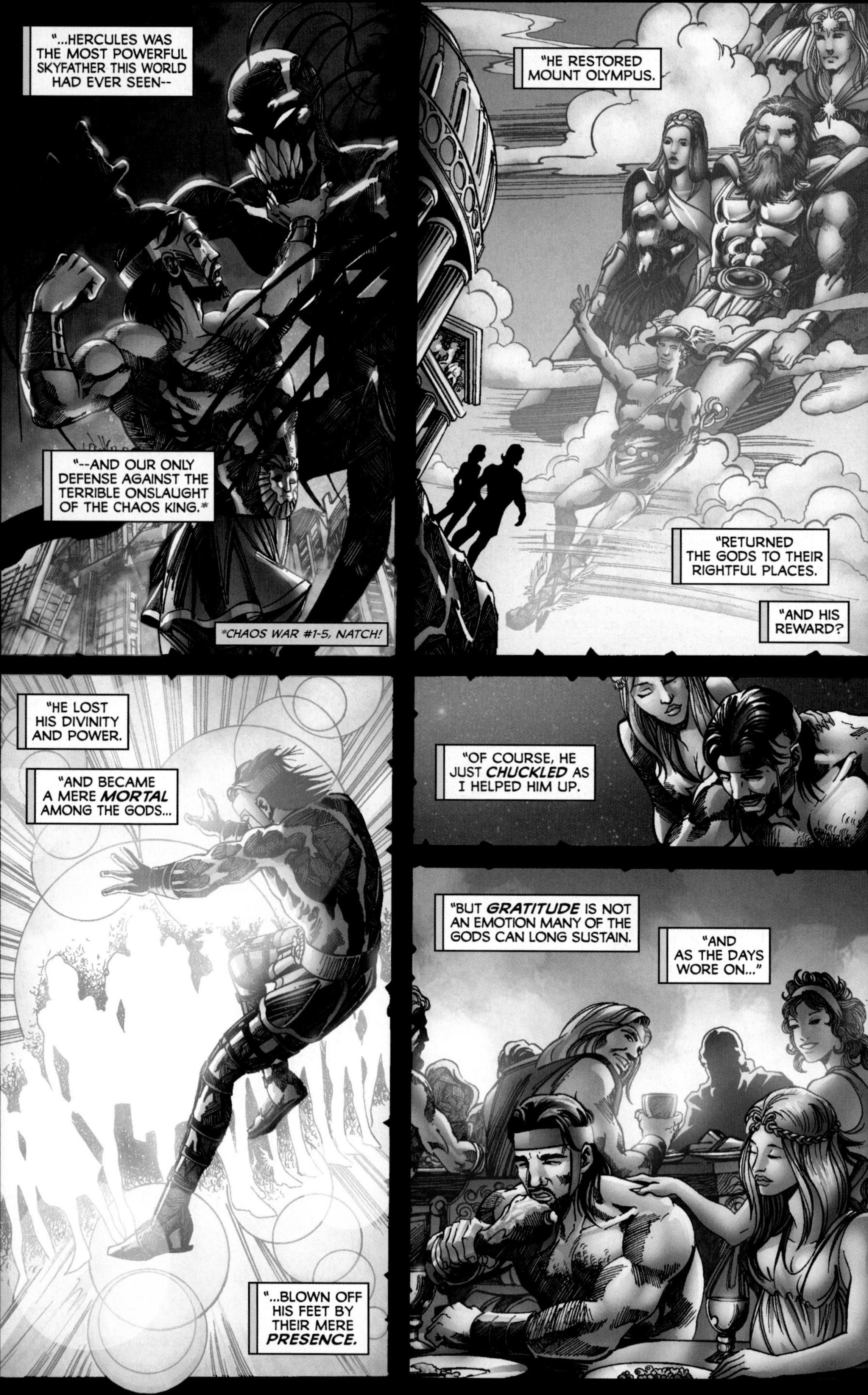
"...HERCULES WAS THE MOST POWERFUL SKYFATHER THIS WORLD HAD EVER SEEN--
"--AND OUR ONLY DEFENSE AGAINST THE TERRIBLE ONSLAUGHT OF THE CHAOS KING.*
*CHAOS WAR #1-5, NATCH!
"HE RESTORED MOUNT OLYMPUS.
"RETURNED THE GODS TO THEIR RIGHTFUL PLACES.
"AND HIS REWARD?
"HE LOST HIS DIVINITY AND POWER.
"AND BECAME A MERE *MORTAL* AMONG THE GODS...
"...BLOWN OFF HIS FEET BY THEIR MERE *PRESENCE.*
"OF COURSE, HE JUST *CHUCKLED* AS I HELPED HIM UP.
"BUT *GRATITUDE* IS NOT AN EMOTION MANY OF THE GODS CAN LONG SUSTAIN.
"AND AS THE DAYS WORE ON..."

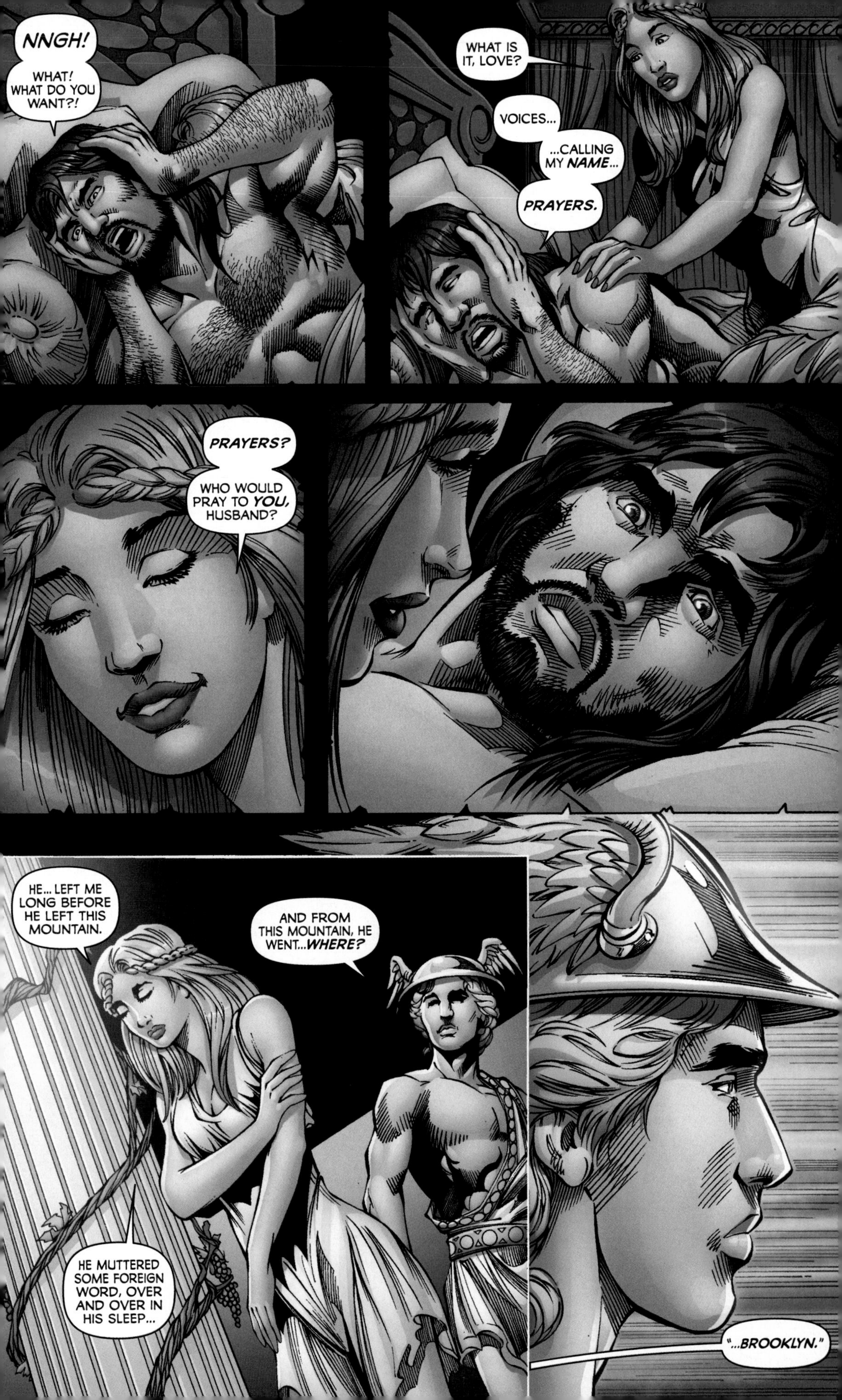
NNGH!
WHAT! WHAT DO YOU WANT?!
WHAT IS IT, LOVE?
VOICES...
...CALLING MY NAME...
PRAYERS.
PRAYERS?
WHO WOULD PRAY TO YOU, HUSBAND?
HE... LEFT ME LONG BEFORE HE LEFT THIS MOUNTAIN.
AND FROM THIS MOUNTAIN, HE WENT... WHERE?
HE MUTTERED SOME FOREIGN WORD, OVER AND OVER IN HIS SLEEP...
"...BROOKLYN."

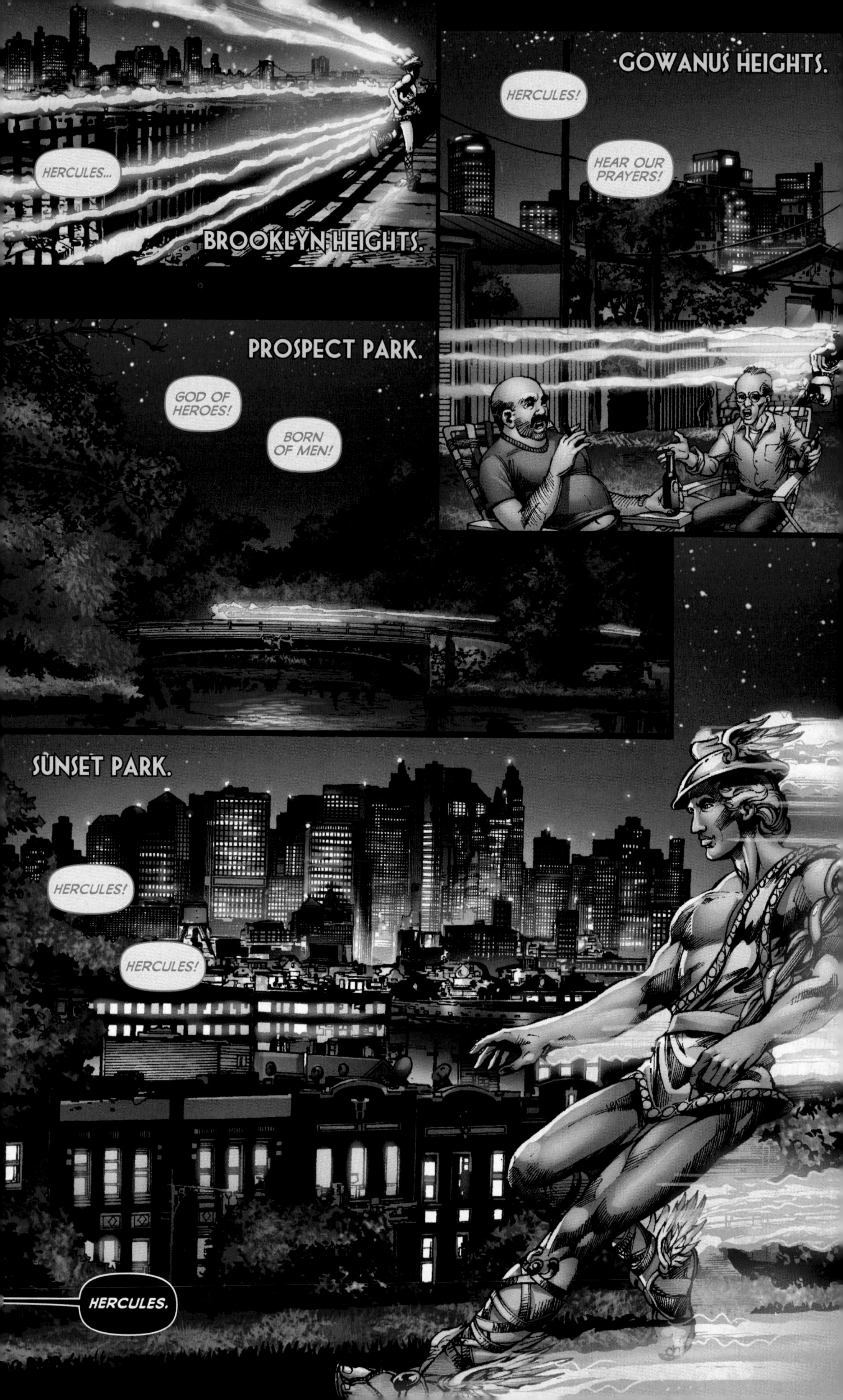
HERCULES...
BROOKLYN HEIGHTS.
GOWANUS HEIGHTS.
HERCULES!
HEAR OUR PRAYERS!
PROSPECT PARK.
GOD OF HEROES!
BORN OF MEN!
SUNSET PARK.
HERCULES!
HERCULES!
HERCULES.

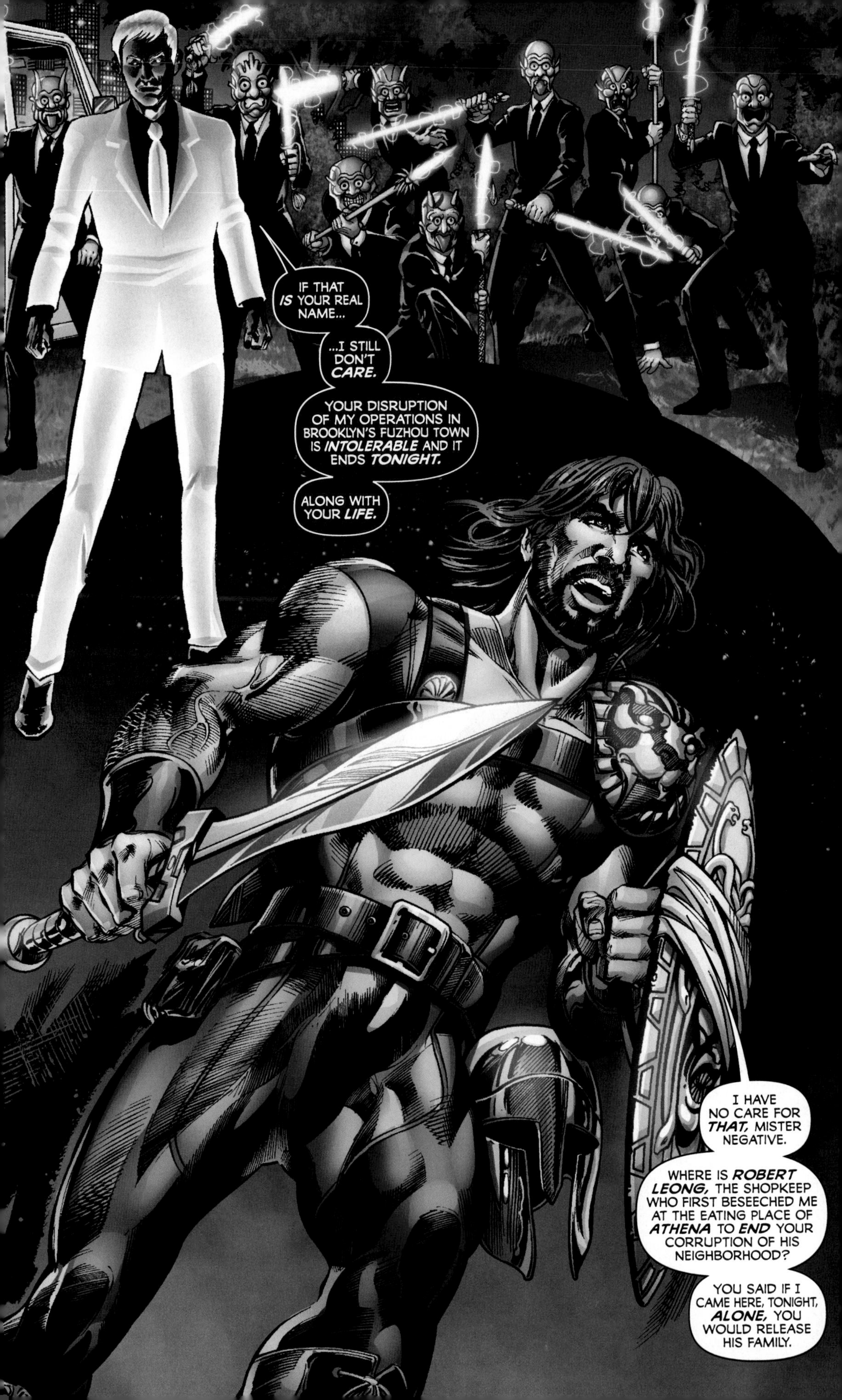

IF THAT *IS* YOUR REAL NAME...
...I STILL DON'T *CARE.*
YOUR DISRUPTION OF MY OPERATIONS IN BROOKLYN'S FUZHOU TOWN IS *INTOLERABLE* AND IT ENDS *TONIGHT.*
ALONG WITH YOUR *LIFE.*
I HAVE NO CARE FOR *THAT,* MISTER NEGATIVE.
WHERE IS *ROBERT LEONG,* THE SHOPKEEP WHO FIRST BESEECHED ME AT THE EATING PLACE OF *ATHENA* TO *END* YOUR CORRUPTION OF HIS NEIGHBORHOOD?
YOU SAID IF I CAME HERE, TONIGHT, *ALONE,* YOU WOULD RELEASE HIS FAMILY.

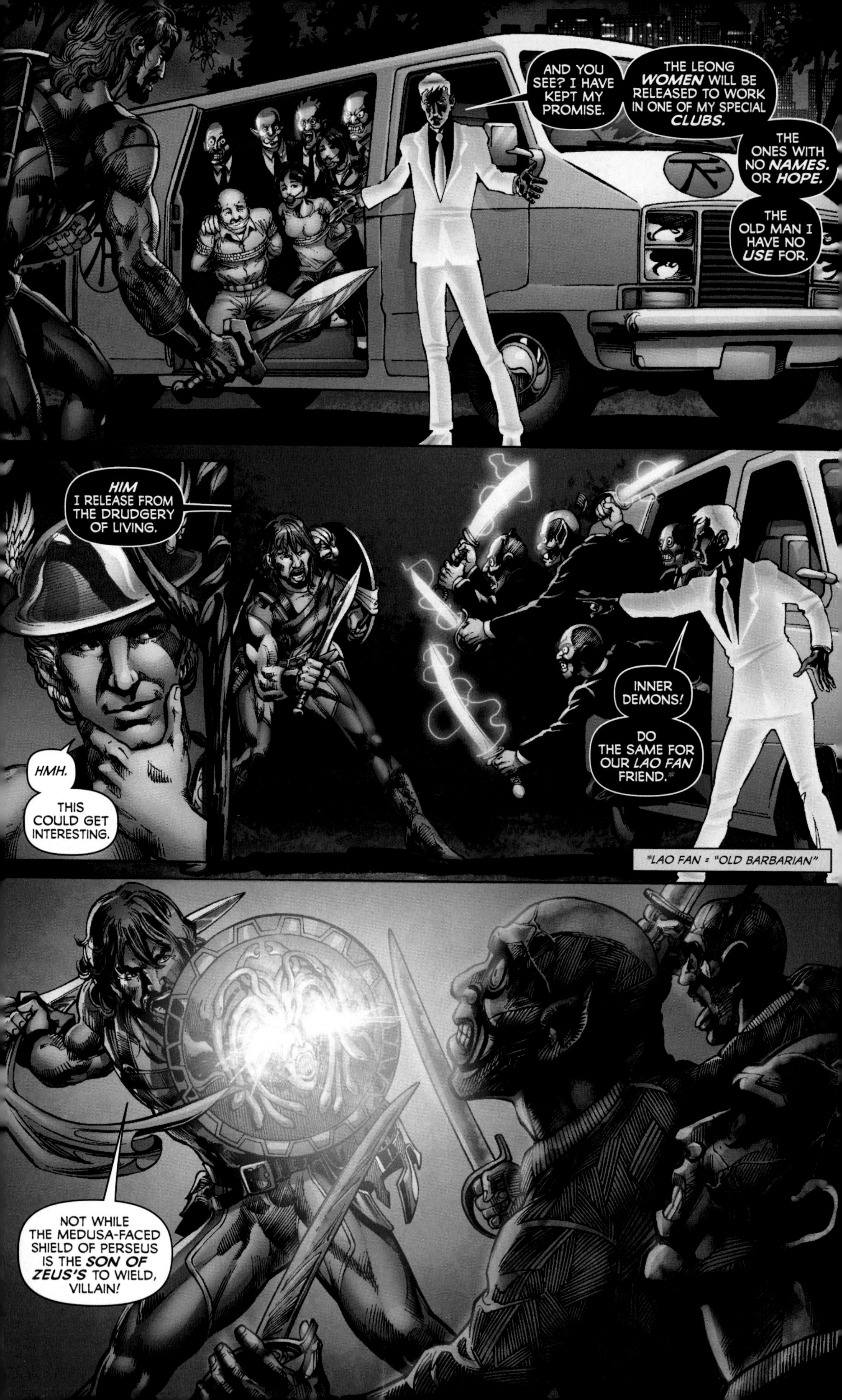
AND YOU SEE? I HAVE KEPT MY PROMISE.
THE LEONG WOMEN WILL BE RELEASED TO WORK IN ONE OF MY SPECIAL CLUBS.
THE ONES WITH NO NAMES. OR HOPE.
THE OLD MAN I HAVE NO USE FOR.
HIM I RELEASE FROM THE DRUDGERY OF LIVING.
HMH.
THIS COULD GET INTERESTING.
INNER DEMONS!
DO THE SAME FOR OUR LAO FAN FRIEND.*
*LAO FAN = "OLD BARBARIAN"
NOT WHILE THE MEDUSA-FACED SHIELD OF PERSEUS IS THE SON OF ZEUS'S TO WIELD, VILLAIN!

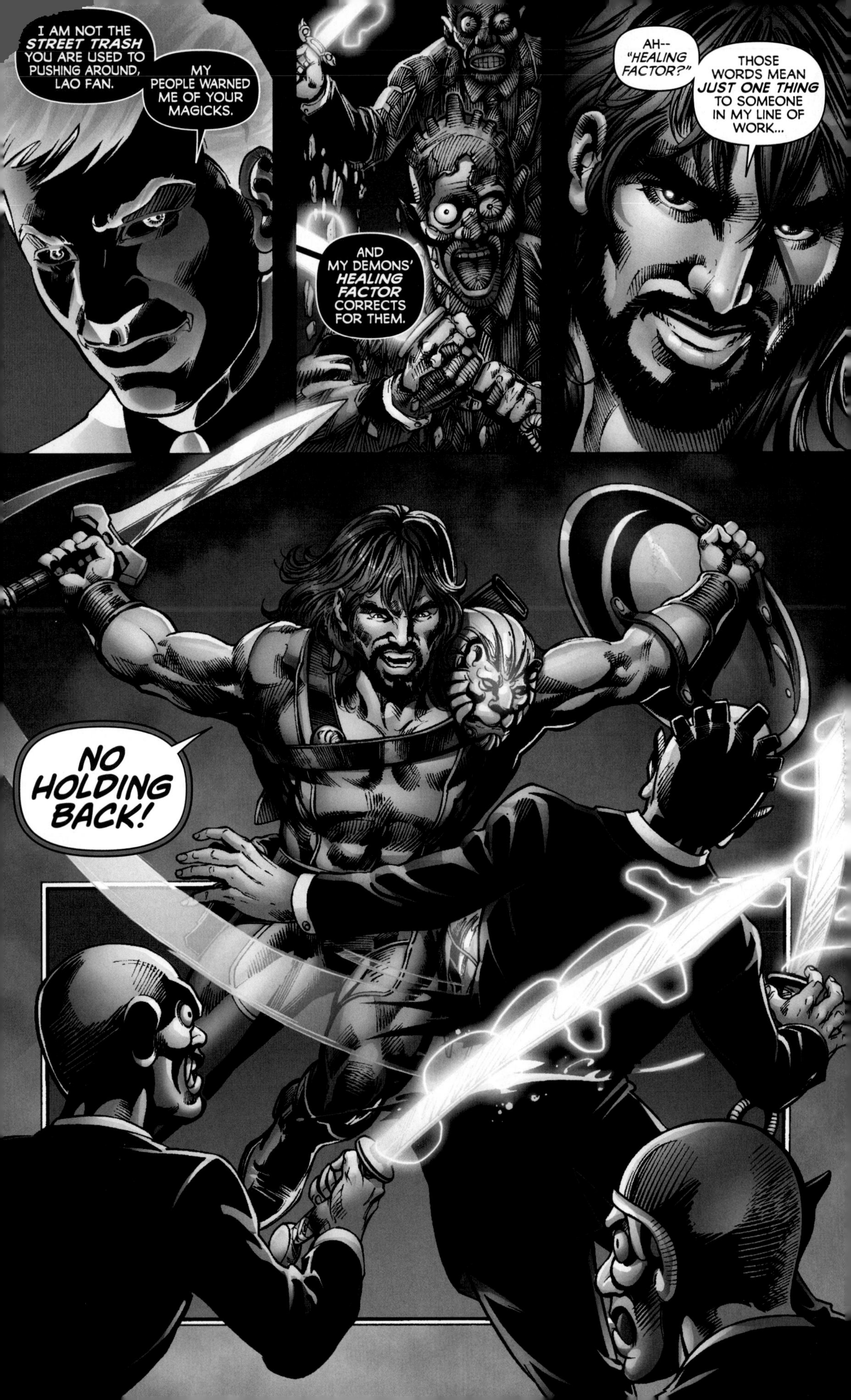

I AM NOT THE STREET TRASH YOU ARE USED TO PUSHING AROUND, LAO FAN.
MY PEOPLE WARNED ME OF YOUR MAGICKS.
AND MY DEMONS' HEALING FACTOR CORRECTS FOR THEM.
AH-- "HEALING FACTOR?"
THOSE WORDS MEAN JUST ONE THING TO SOMEONE IN MY LINE OF WORK...
NO HOLDING BACK!

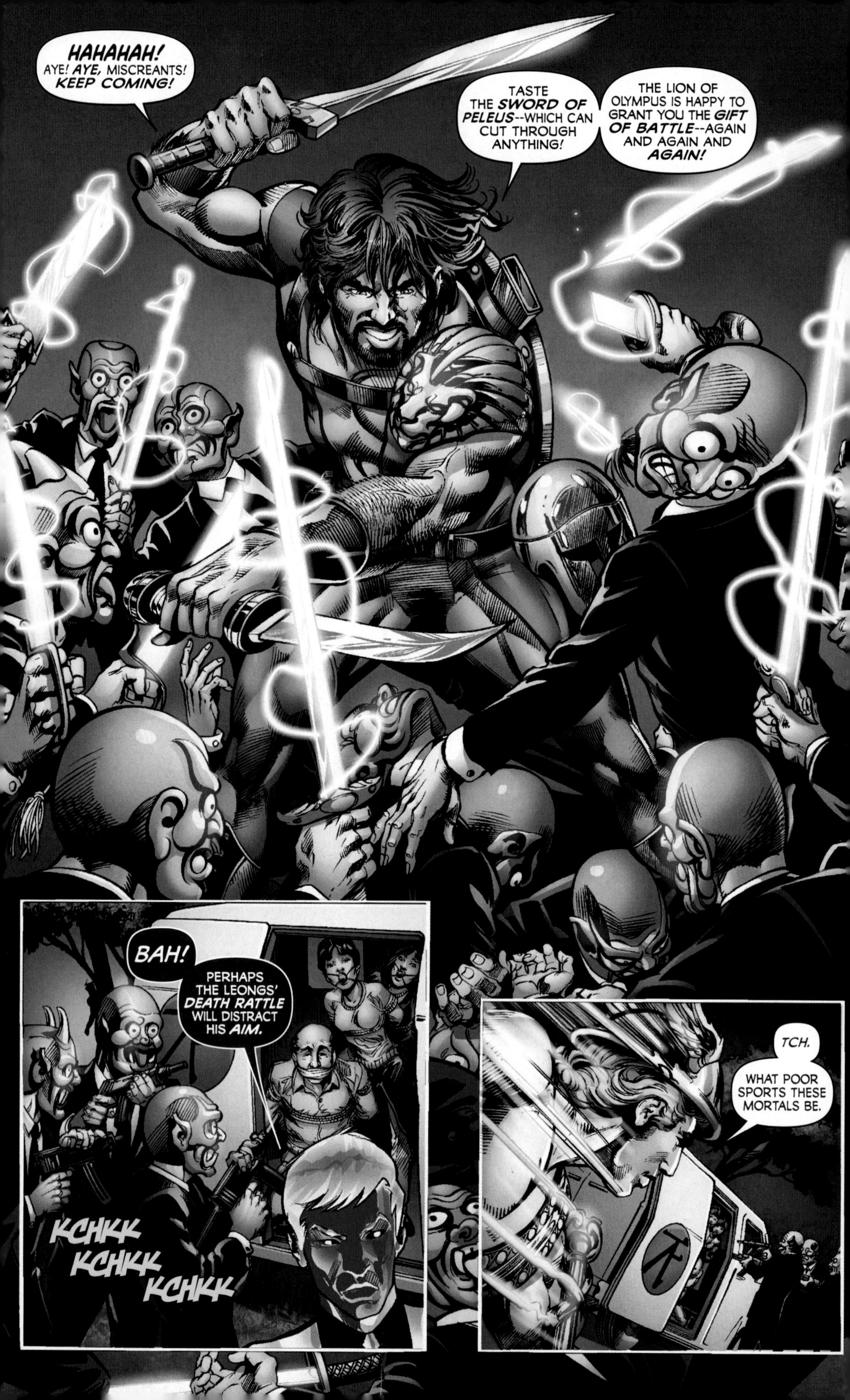

HAHAHAH! AYE! AYE, MISCREANTS! KEEP COMING!
TASTE THE SWORD OF PELEUS--WHICH CAN CUT THROUGH ANYTHING!
THE LION OF OLYMPUS IS HAPPY TO GRANT YOU THE GIFT OF BATTLE--AGAIN AND AGAIN AND AGAIN!
BAH!
PERHAPS THE LEONGS' DEATH RATTLE WILL DISTRACT HIS AIM.
KCHKK KCHKK KCHKK
TCH.
WHAT POOR SPORTS THESE MORTALS BE.

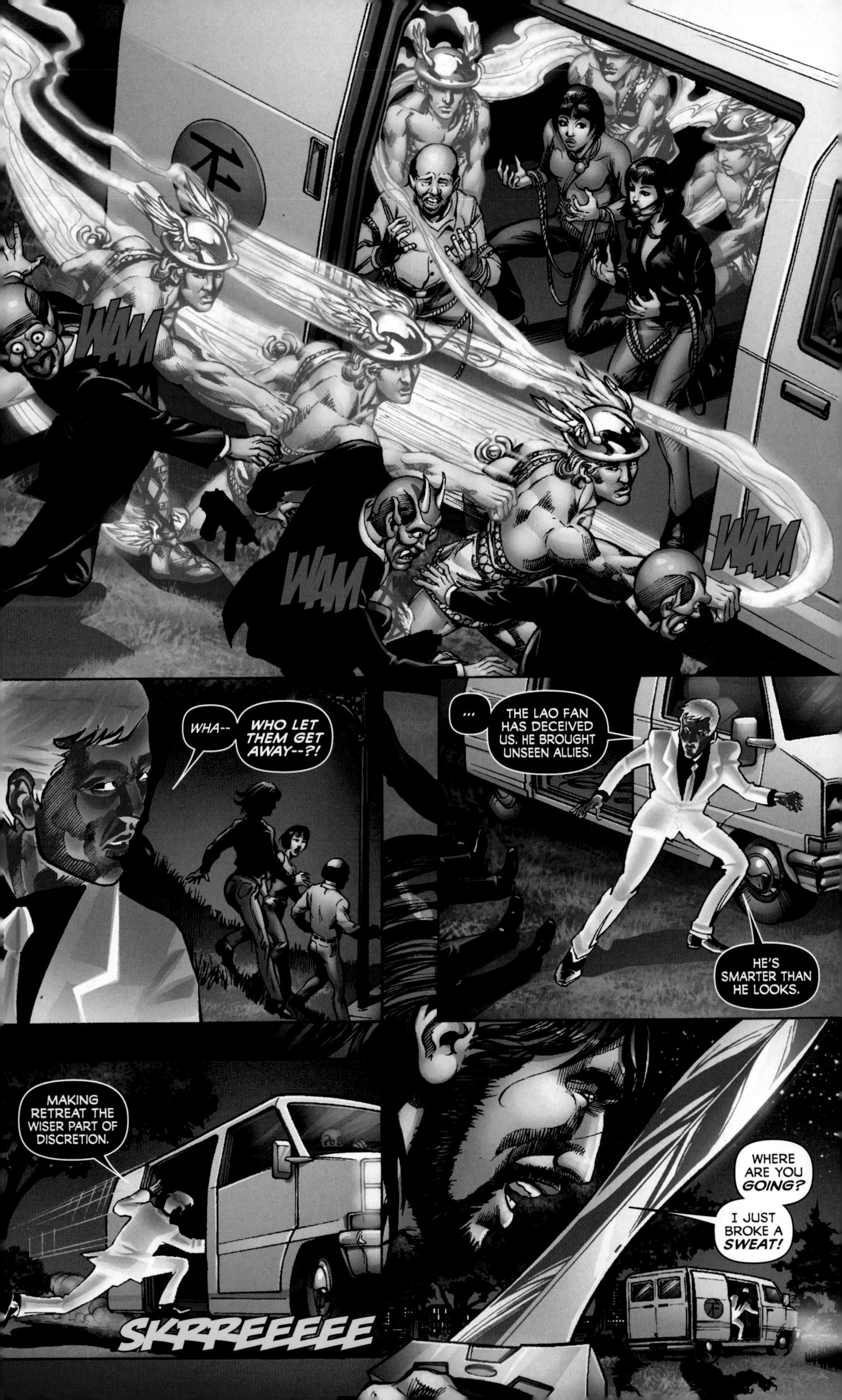
WAM
WAM
WAM
WHA--
WHO LET THEM GET AWAY--?!
...
THE LAO FAN HAS DECEIVED US. HE BROUGHT UNSEEN ALLIES.
HE'S SMARTER THAN HE LOOKS.
MAKING RETREAT THE WISER PART OF DISCRETION.
SKRREEEEEE
WHERE ARE YOU GOING?
I JUST BROKE A SWEAT!

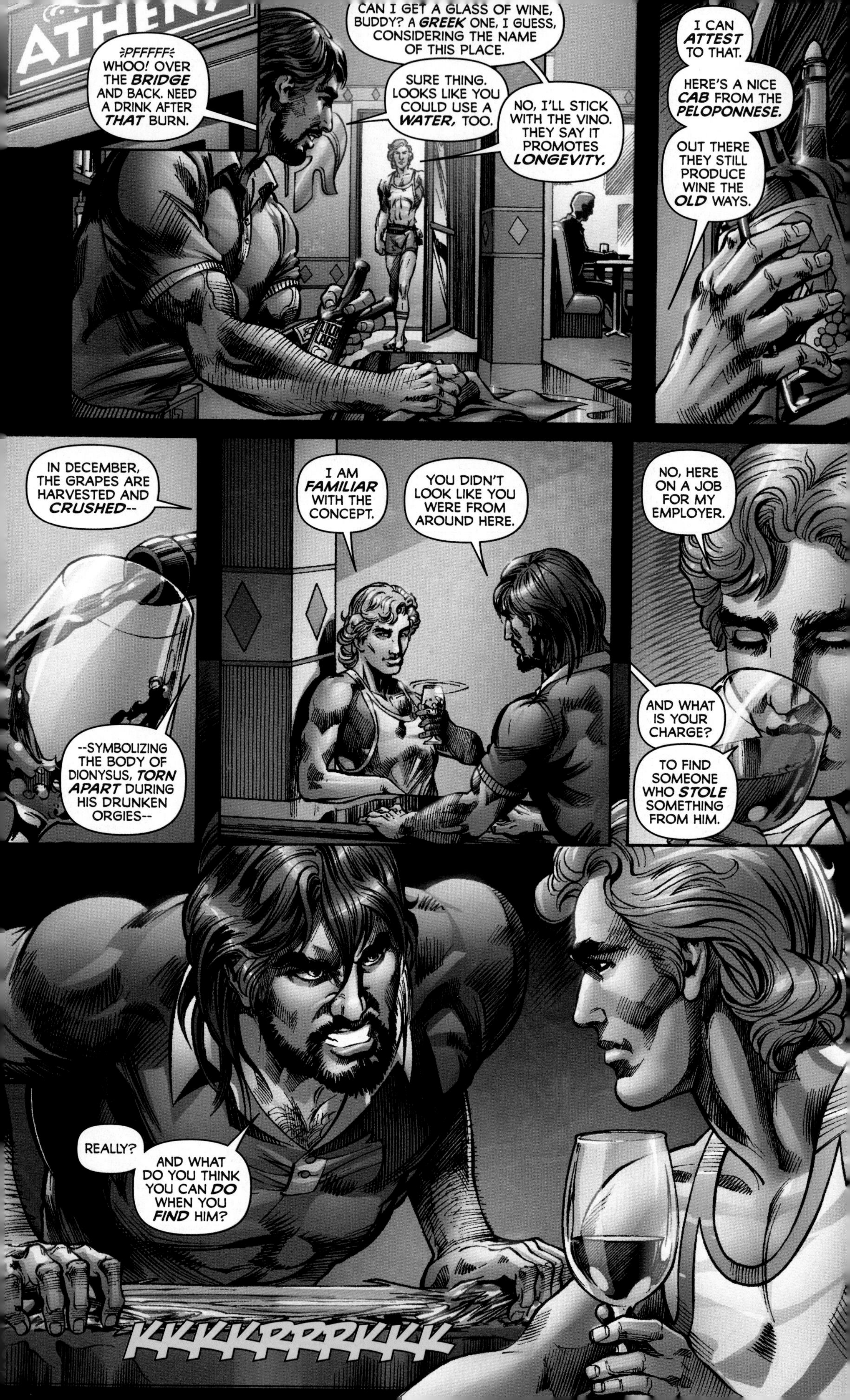
ATHEN
≈PFFFFF≈ WHOO! OVER THE BRIDGE AND BACK. NEED A DRINK AFTER THAT BURN.
SURE THING. LOOKS LIKE YOU COULD USE A WATER, TOO.
CAN I GET A GLASS OF WINE, BUDDY? A GREEK ONE, I GUESS, CONSIDERING THE NAME OF THIS PLACE.
NO, I'LL STICK WITH THE VINO. THEY SAY IT PROMOTES LONGEVITY.
I CAN ATTEST TO THAT.
HERE'S A NICE CAB FROM THE PELOPONNESE.
OUT THERE THEY STILL PRODUCE WINE THE OLD WAYS.
IN DECEMBER, THE GRAPES ARE HARVESTED AND CRUSHED--
--SYMBOLIZING THE BODY OF DIONYSUS, TORN APART DURING HIS DRUNKEN ORGIES--
I AM FAMILIAR WITH THE CONCEPT.
YOU DIDN'T LOOK LIKE YOU WERE FROM AROUND HERE.
NO, HERE ON A JOB FOR MY EMPLOYER.
AND WHAT IS YOUR CHARGE?
TO FIND SOMEONE WHO STOLE SOMETHING FROM HIM.
REALLY?
AND WHAT DO YOU THINK YOU CAN DO WHEN YOU FIND HIM?
KKKKKRRRKKKK

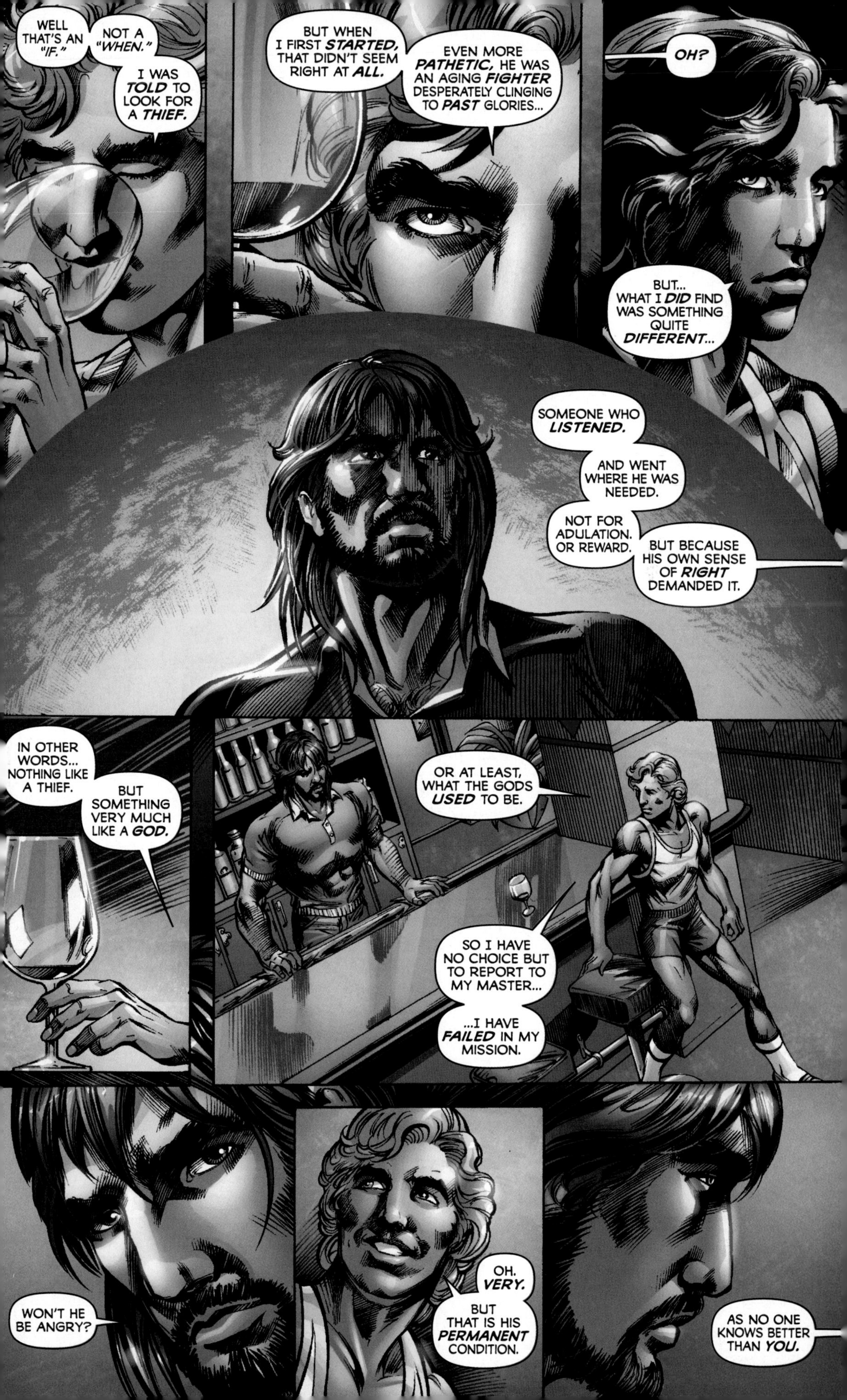

WELL THAT'S AN "IF."
NOT A "WHEN."
I WAS TOLD TO LOOK FOR A THIEF.
BUT WHEN I FIRST STARTED, THAT DIDN'T SEEM RIGHT AT ALL.
EVEN MORE PATHETIC, HE WAS AN AGING FIGHTER DESPERATELY CLINGING TO PAST GLORIES...
OH?
BUT... WHAT I DID FIND WAS SOMETHING QUITE DIFFERENT...
SOMEONE WHO LISTENED.
AND WENT WHERE HE WAS NEEDED.
NOT FOR ADULATION. OR REWARD.
BUT BECAUSE HIS OWN SENSE OF RIGHT DEMANDED IT.
IN OTHER WORDS... NOTHING LIKE A THIEF.
BUT SOMETHING VERY MUCH LIKE A GOD.
OR AT LEAST, WHAT THE GODS USED TO BE.
SO I HAVE NO CHOICE BUT TO REPORT TO MY MASTER...
...I HAVE FAILED IN MY MISSION.
WON'T HE BE ANGRY?
OH. VERY.
BUT THAT IS HIS PERMANENT CONDITION.
AS NO ONE KNOWS BETTER THAN YOU.

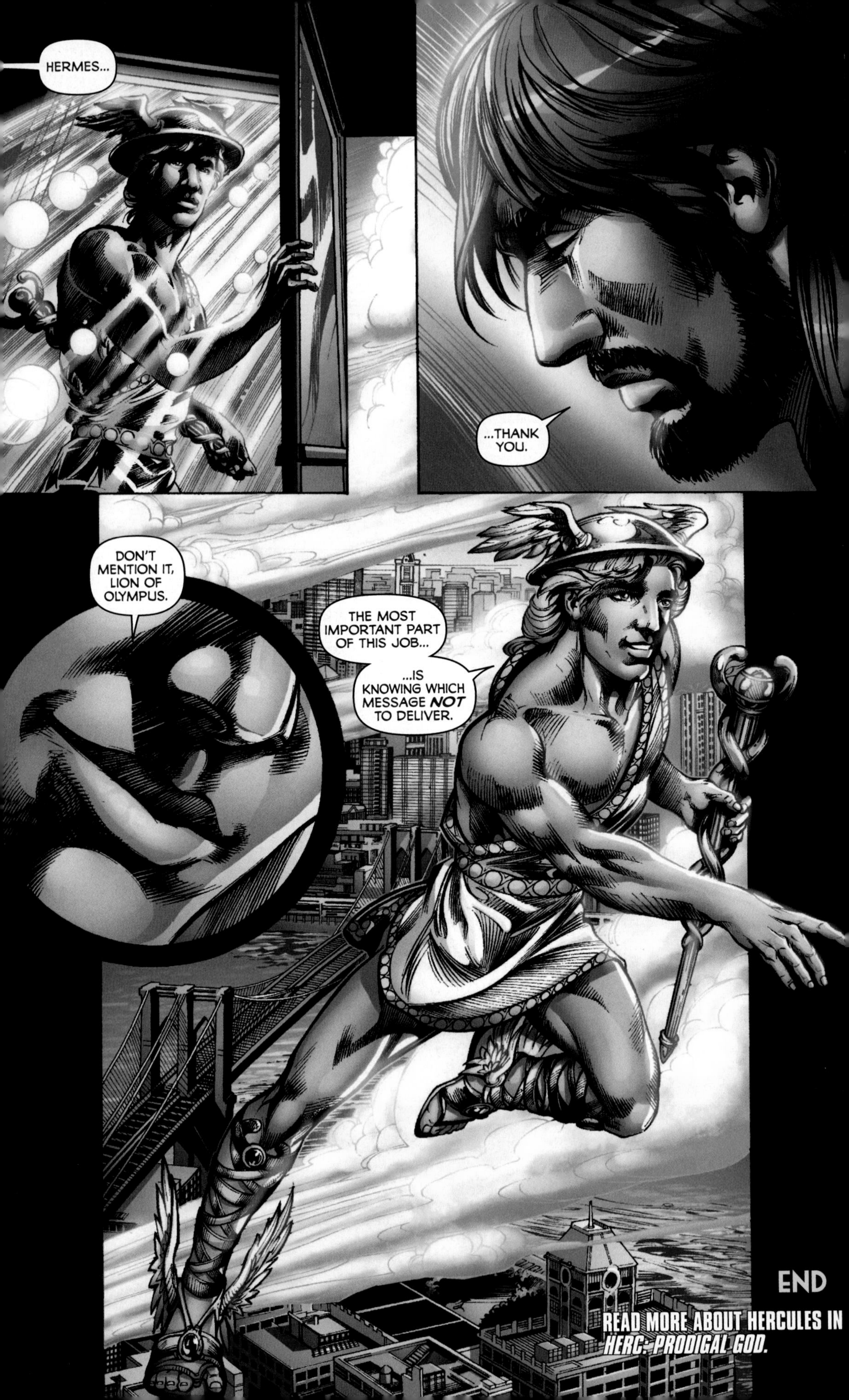
HERMES...
...THANK YOU.
DON'T MENTION IT, LION OF OLYMPUS.
THE MOST IMPORTANT PART OF THIS JOB...
...IS KNOWING WHICH MESSAGE NOT TO DELIVER.
END
READ MORE ABOUT HERCULES IN HERC: PRODIGAL GOD.

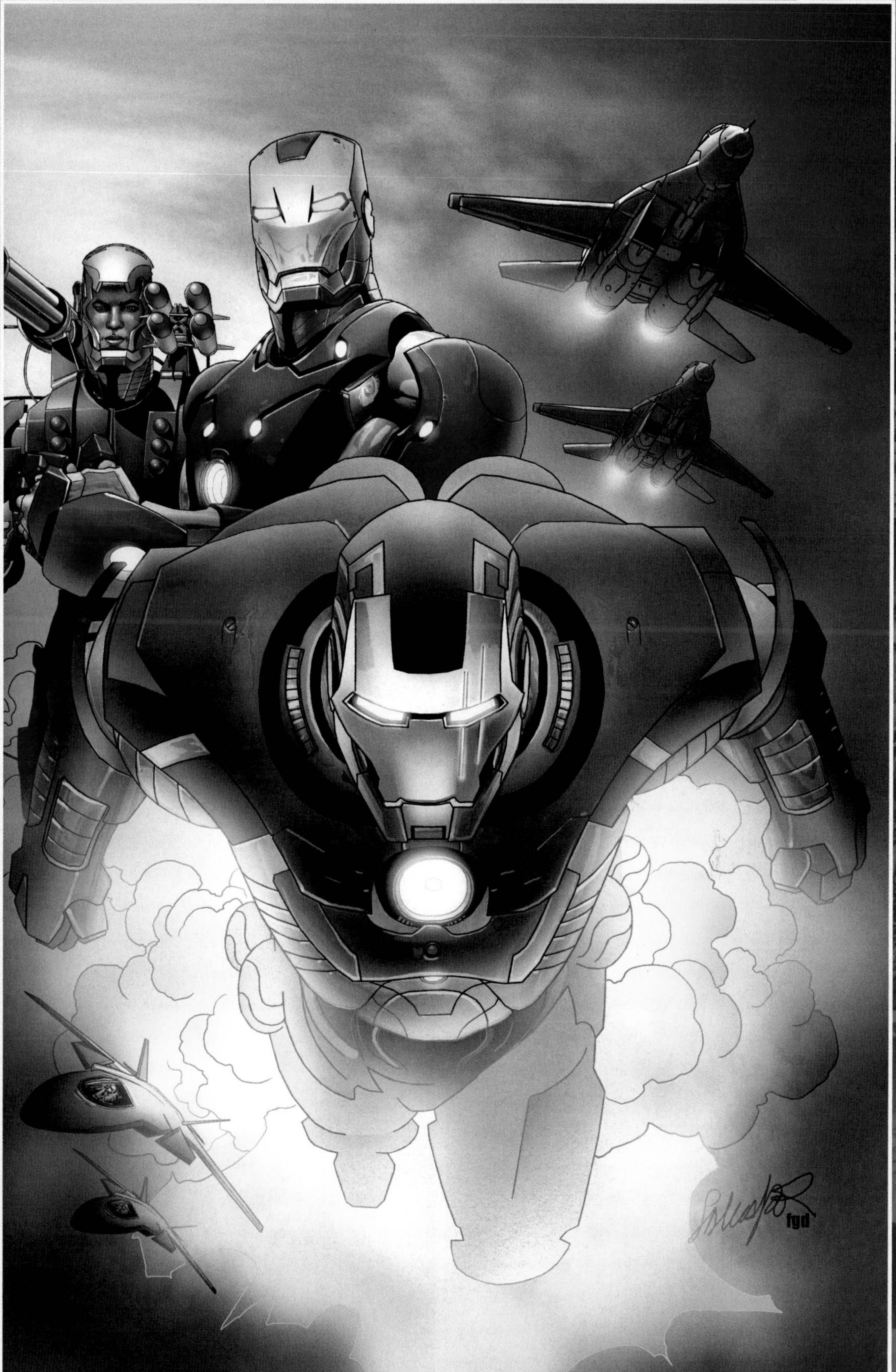

IRON MAN 2.0 #7.1

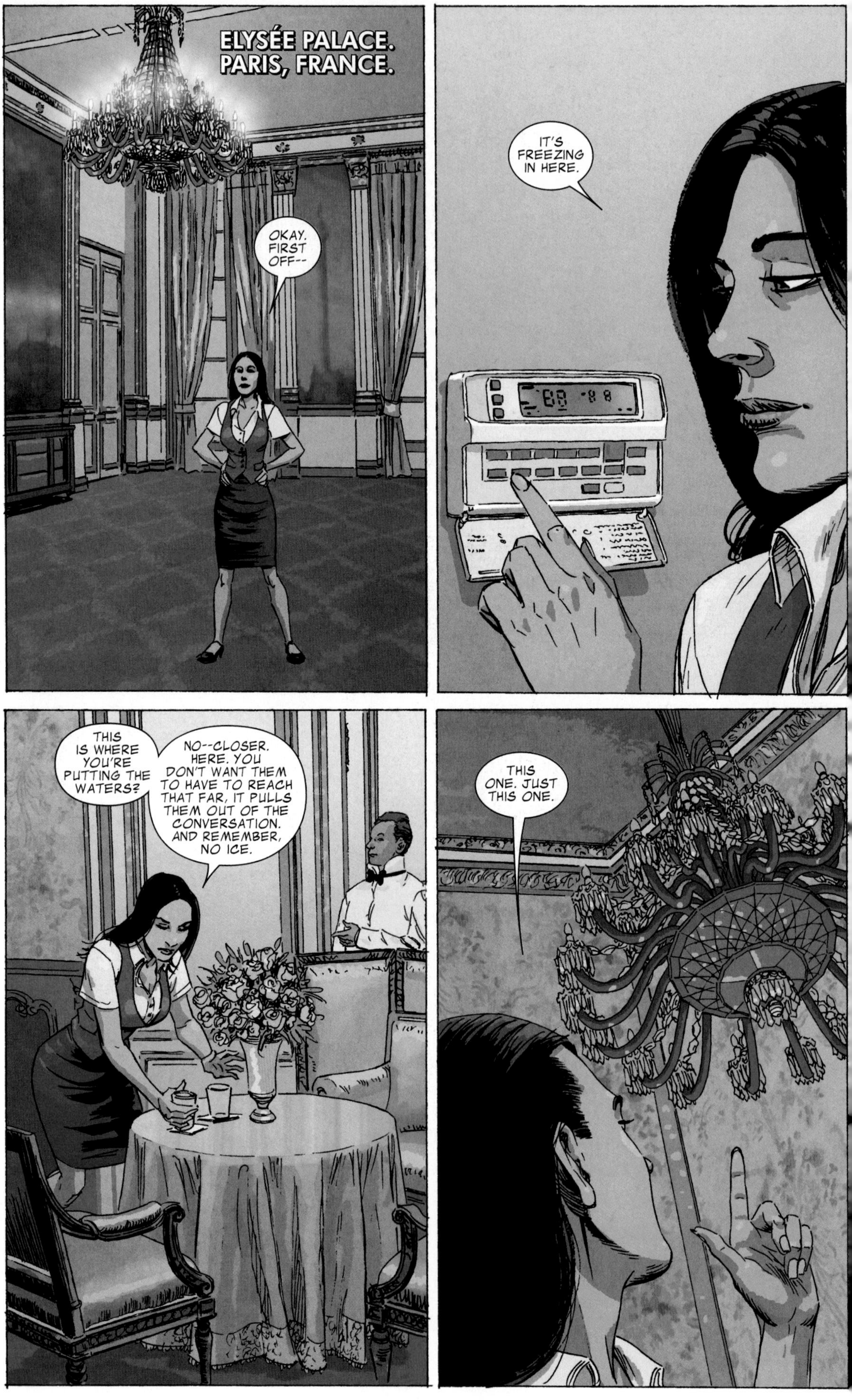
ELYSÉE PALACE. PARIS, FRANCE.
OKAY. FIRST OFF--
IT'S FREEZING IN HERE.
THIS IS WHERE YOU'RE PUTTING THE WATERS?
NO--CLOSER. HERE. YOU DON'T WANT THEM TO HAVE TO REACH THAT FAR, IT PULLS THEM OUT OF THE CONVERSATION. AND REMEMBER, NO ICE.
THIS ONE. JUST THIS ONE.

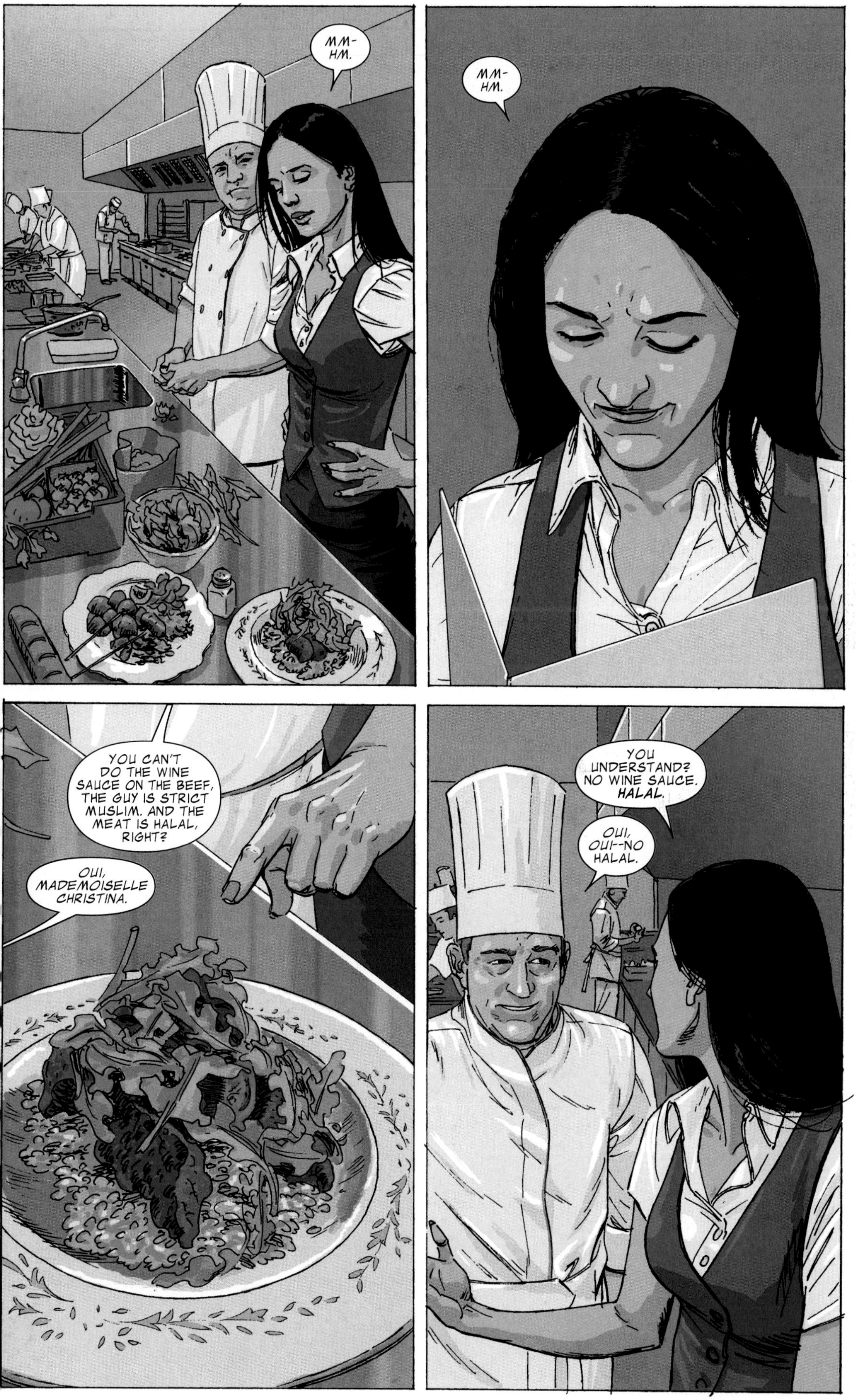
MM-HM.
MM-HM.
YOU CAN'T DO THE WINE SAUCE ON THE BEEF, THE GUY IS STRICT MUSLIM. AND THE MEAT IS HALAL, RIGHT?
OUI, MADEMOISELLE CHRISTINA.
YOU UNDERSTAND? NO WINE SAUCE. HALAL.
OUI, OUI--NO HALAL.

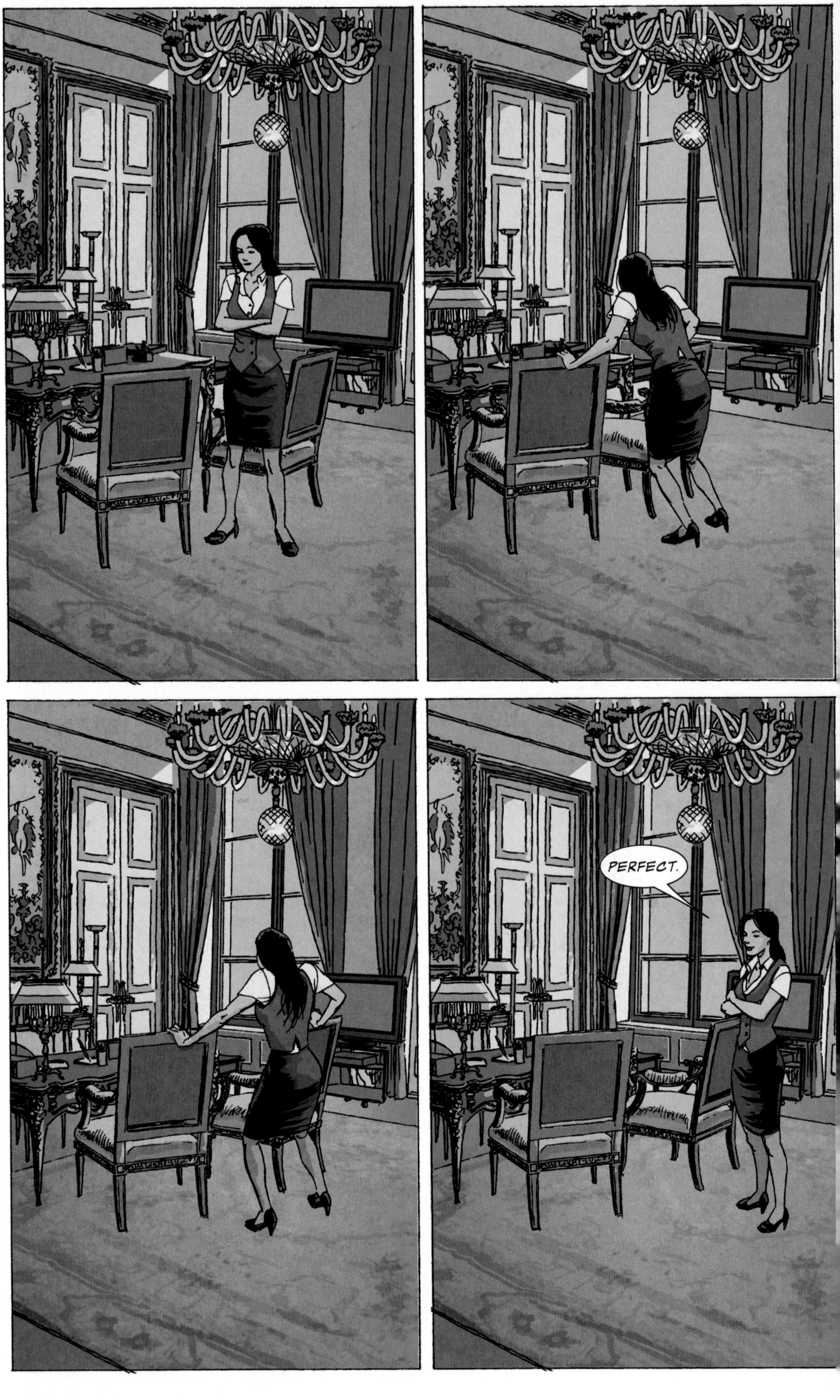
PERFECT.

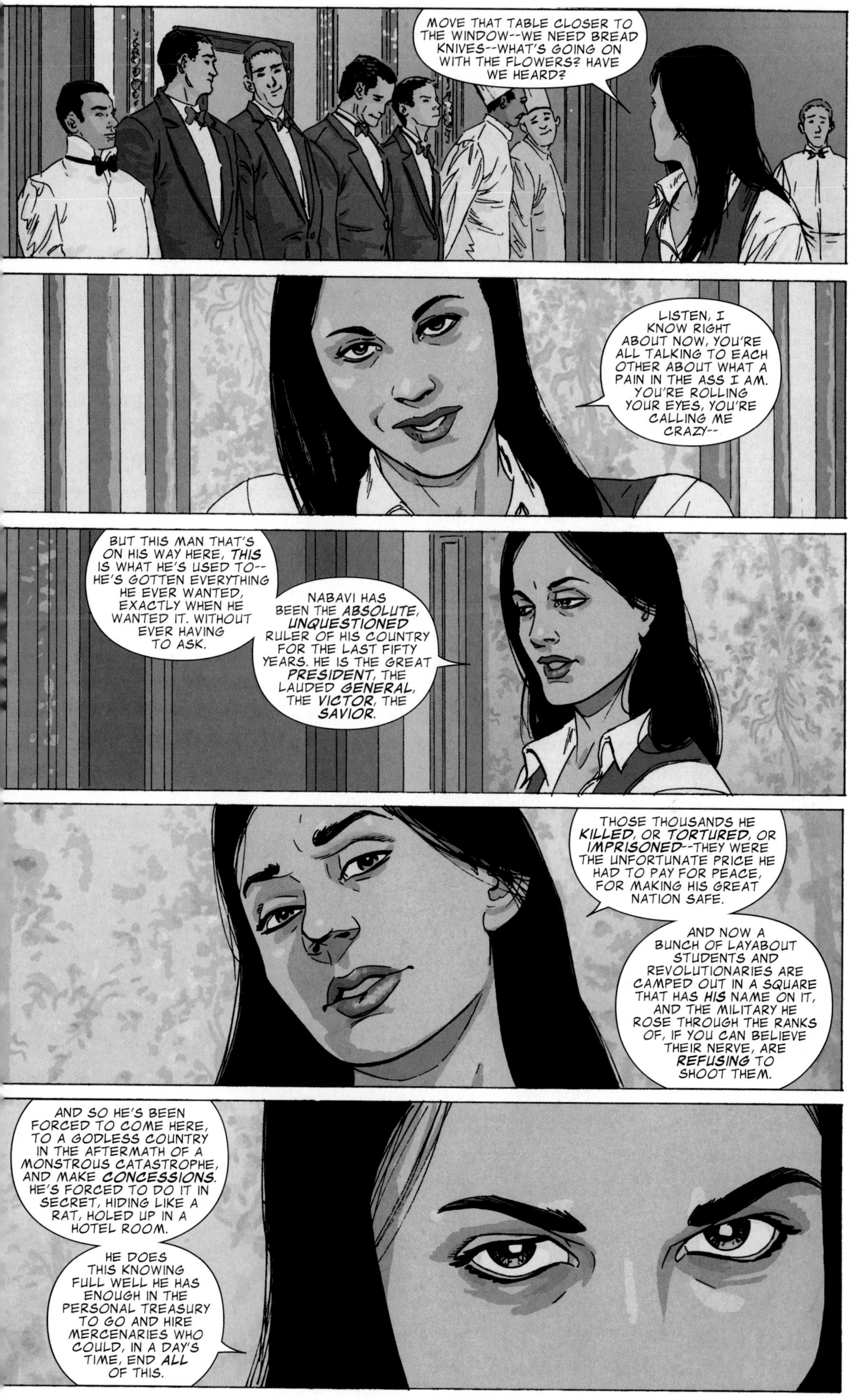
MOVE THAT TABLE CLOSER TO THE WINDOW--WE NEED BREAD KNIVES--WHAT'S GOING ON WITH THE FLOWERS? HAVE WE HEARD?
LISTEN, I KNOW RIGHT ABOUT NOW, YOU'RE ALL TALKING TO EACH OTHER ABOUT WHAT A PAIN IN THE ASS I AM. YOU'RE ROLLING YOUR EYES, YOU'RE CALLING ME CRAZY--
BUT THIS MAN THAT'S ON HIS WAY HERE, THIS IS WHAT HE'S USED TO--HE'S GOTTEN EVERYTHING HE EVER WANTED, EXACTLY WHEN HE WANTED IT. WITHOUT EVER HAVING TO ASK.
NABAVI HAS BEEN THE ABSOLUTE, UNQUESTIONED RULER OF HIS COUNTRY FOR THE LAST FIFTY YEARS. HE IS THE GREAT PRESIDENT, THE LAUDED GENERAL, THE VICTOR, THE SAVIOR.
THOSE THOUSANDS HE KILLED, OR TORTURED, OR IMPRISONED--THEY WERE THE UNFORTUNATE PRICE HE HAD TO PAY FOR PEACE, FOR MAKING HIS GREAT NATION SAFE.
AND NOW A BUNCH OF LAYABOUT STUDENTS AND REVOLUTIONARIES ARE CAMPED OUT IN A SQUARE THAT HAS HIS NAME ON IT, AND THE MILITARY HE ROSE THROUGH THE RANKS OF, IF YOU CAN BELIEVE THEIR NERVE, ARE REFUSING TO SHOOT THEM.
AND SO HE'S BEEN FORCED TO COME HERE, TO A GODLESS COUNTRY IN THE AFTERMATH OF A MONSTROUS CATASTROPHE, AND MAKE CONCESSIONS. HE'S FORCED TO DO IT IN SECRET, HIDING LIKE A RAT, HOLED UP IN A HOTEL ROOM.
HE DOES THIS KNOWING FULL WELL HE HAS ENOUGH IN THE PERSONAL TREASURY TO GO AND HIRE MERCENARIES WHO COULD, IN A DAY'S TIME, END ALL OF THIS.

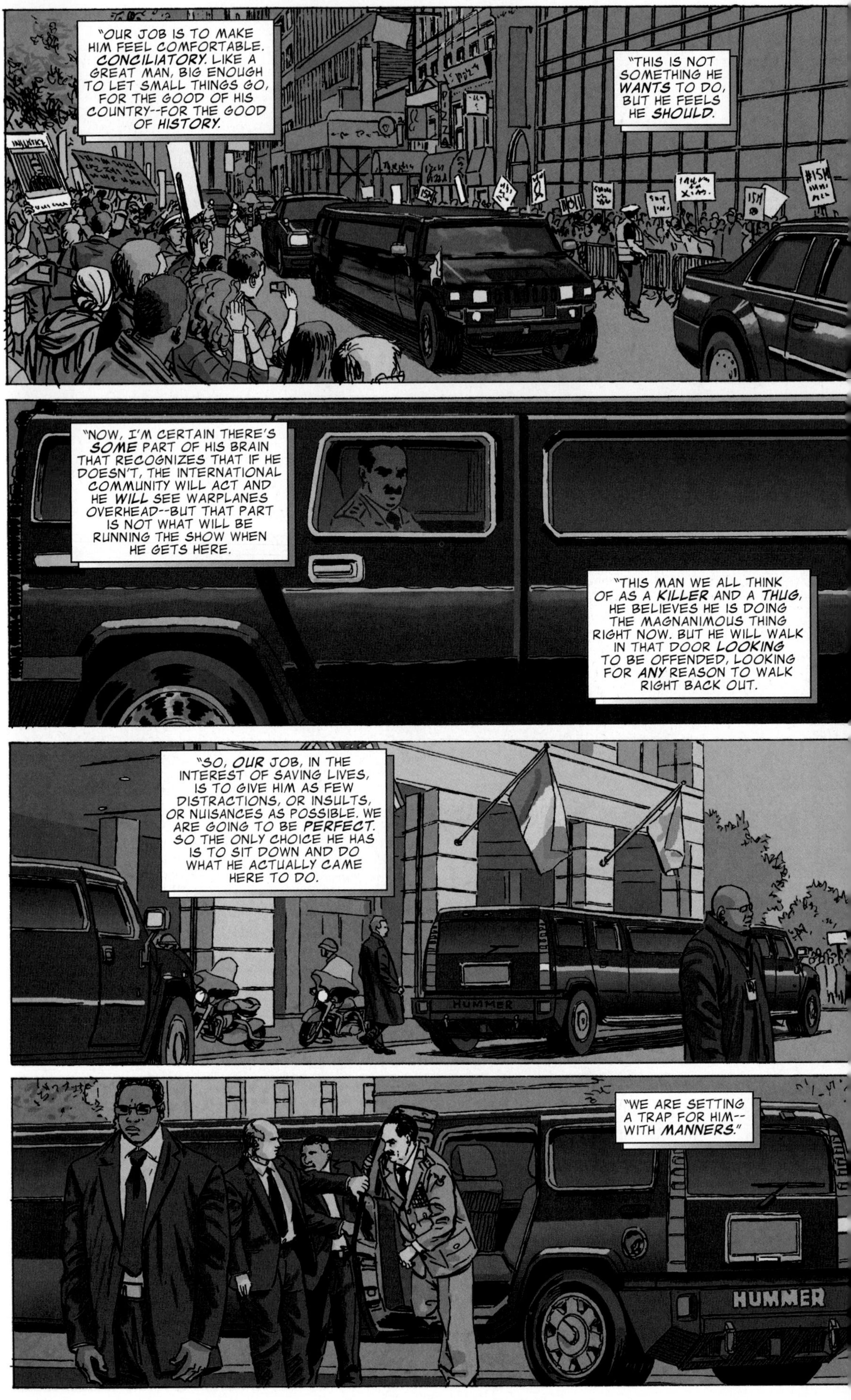
"OUR JOB IS TO MAKE HIM FEEL COMFORTABLE. CONCILIATORY. LIKE A GREAT MAN, BIG ENOUGH TO LET SMALL THINGS GO, FOR THE GOOD OF HIS COUNTRY--FOR THE GOOD OF HISTORY.
"THIS IS NOT SOMETHING HE WANTS TO DO, BUT HE FEELS HE SHOULD.
"NOW, I'M CERTAIN THERE'S SOME PART OF HIS BRAIN THAT RECOGNIZES THAT IF HE DOESN'T, THE INTERNATIONAL COMMUNITY WILL ACT AND HE WILL SEE WARPLANES OVERHEAD--BUT THAT PART IS NOT WHAT WILL BE RUNNING THE SHOW WHEN HE GETS HERE.
"THIS MAN WE ALL THINK OF AS A KILLER AND A THUG, HE BELIEVES HE IS DOING THE MAGNANIMOUS THING RIGHT NOW. BUT HE WILL WALK IN THAT DOOR LOOKING TO BE OFFENDED, LOOKING FOR ANY REASON TO WALK RIGHT BACK OUT.
"SO, OUR JOB, IN THE INTEREST OF SAVING LIVES, IS TO GIVE HIM AS FEW DISTRACTIONS, OR INSULTS, OR NUISANCES AS POSSIBLE. WE ARE GOING TO BE PERFECT. SO THE ONLY CHOICE HE HAS IS TO SIT DOWN AND DO WHAT HE ACTUALLY CAME HERE TO DO.
HUMMER
"WE ARE SETTING A TRAP FOR HIM--WITH MANNERS."
HUMMER

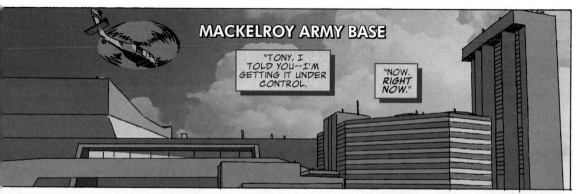

MACKELROY ARMY BASE

"TONY, I TOLD YOU--I'M GETTING IT UNDER CONTROL."

"NOW. RIGHT NOW."

I ALREADY **SAID** THANK YOU FOR THE NEW ARMOR, DIDN'T I? WHY DO WE NEED SO MUCH REASSURANCE TODAY? IS CAPTAIN AMERICA MAD AT YOU AGAIN?

UH-HUH. RIGHT. I GOTTA GO.

WELL, YOU TELL GENERAL BABBAGE IF HE'S **THAT** UPSET WITH ME, THE PENTAGON CAN FIND A NEW LIAISON TO STARK RESILIENT. GET SOMEBODY **ELSE** TO CLEAN UP THIS PALMER ADDLEY MESS FOR THEM.

HE DID?

OKAY, WELL, NO, THEN. DO **NOT** FOLLOW HIS ADVICE AND FIRE ME.

OKAY, FELLAS-- THANKS FOR GETTING HERE SO FAST. LET'S TAKE IT FROM THE TOP, YEAH?

PALMER ADDLEY, A TO Z.

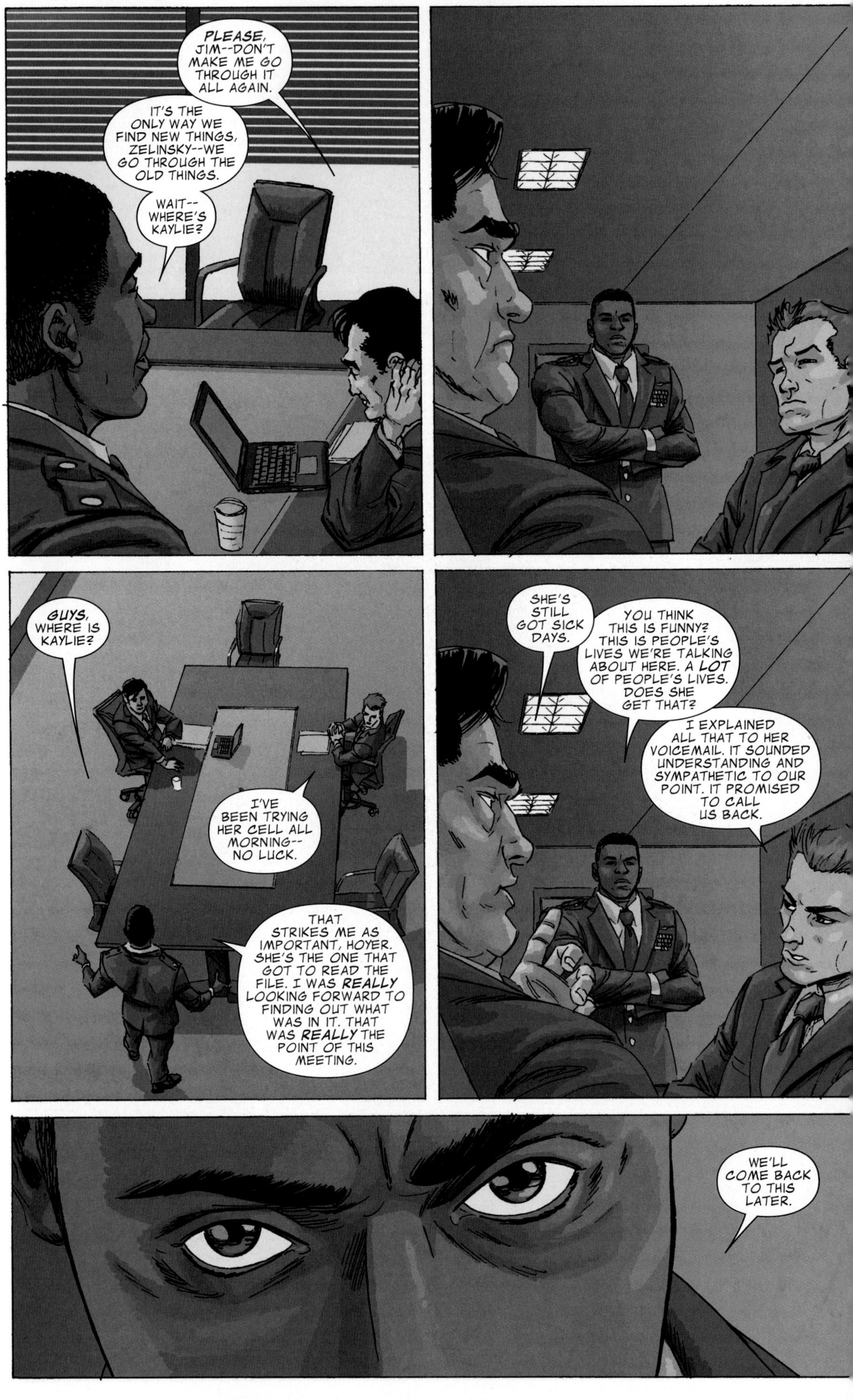
PLEASE, JIM--DON'T MAKE ME GO THROUGH IT ALL AGAIN.
IT'S THE ONLY WAY WE FIND NEW THINGS, ZELINSKY--WE GO THROUGH THE OLD THINGS.
WAIT-- WHERE'S KAYLIE?
GUYS, WHERE IS KAYLIE?
I'VE BEEN TRYING HER CELL ALL MORNING-- NO LUCK.
THAT STRIKES ME AS IMPORTANT, HOYER. SHE'S THE ONE THAT GOT TO READ THE FILE. I WAS REALLY LOOKING FORWARD TO FINDING OUT WHAT WAS IN IT. THAT WAS REALLY THE POINT OF THIS MEETING.
SHE'S STILL GOT SICK DAYS.
YOU THINK THIS IS FUNNY? THIS IS PEOPLE'S LIVES WE'RE TALKING ABOUT HERE. A LOT OF PEOPLE'S LIVES. DOES SHE GET THAT?
I EXPLAINED ALL THAT TO HER VOICEMAIL. IT SOUNDED UNDERSTANDING AND SYMPATHETIC TO OUR POINT. IT PROMISED TO CALL US BACK.
WE'LL COME BACK TO THIS LATER.

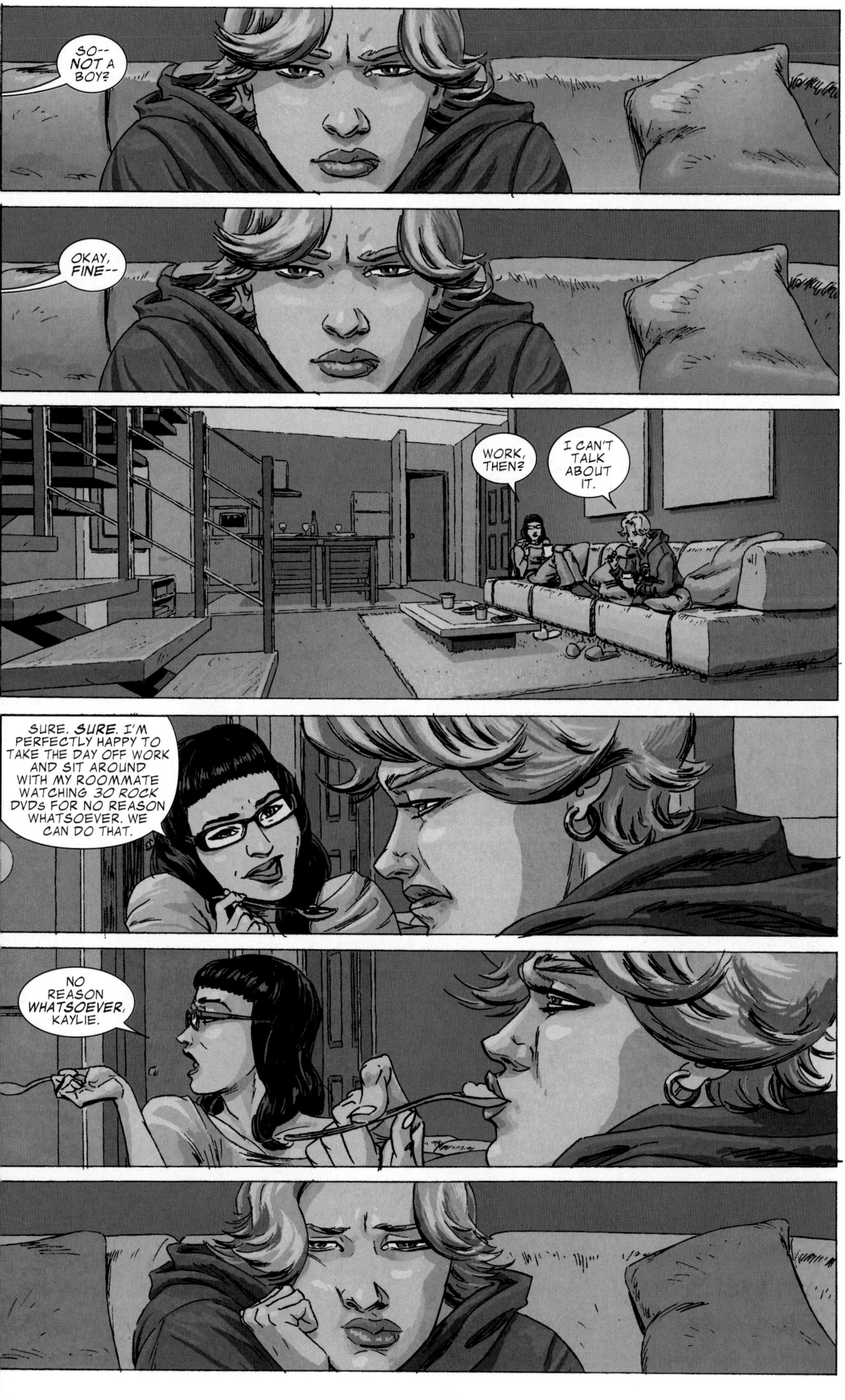
SO--
NOT A BOY?
OKAY, FINE--
WORK, THEN?
I CAN'T TALK ABOUT IT.
SURE. SURE. I'M PERFECTLY HAPPY TO TAKE THE DAY OFF WORK AND SIT AROUND WITH MY ROOMMATE WATCHING 30 ROCK DVDs FOR NO REASON WHATSOEVER. WE CAN DO THAT.
NO REASON WHATSOEVER, KAYLIE.

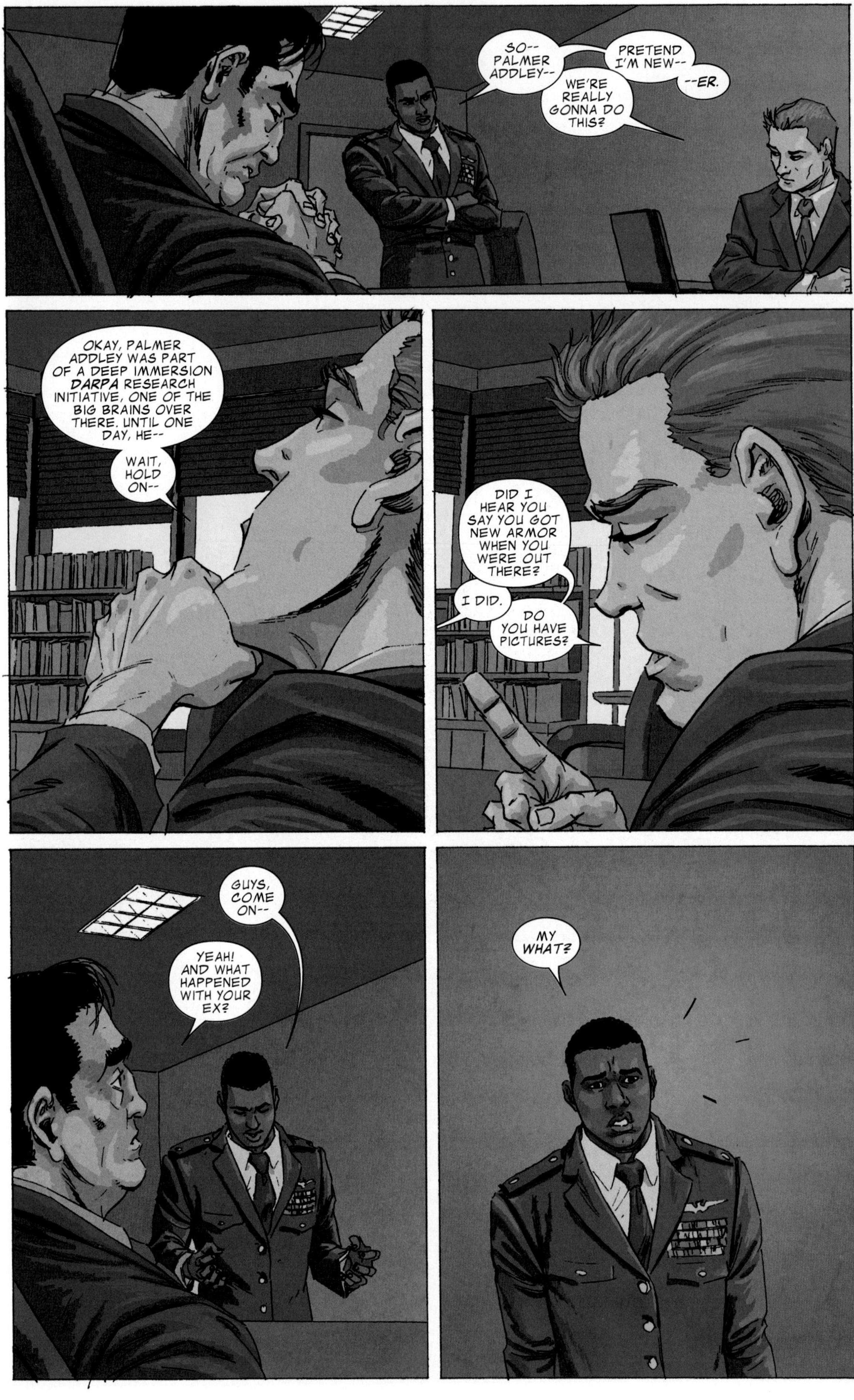
SO-- PALMER ADDLEY--
PRETEND I'M NEW--
--ER.
WE'RE REALLY GONNA DO THIS?
OKAY, PALMER ADDLEY WAS PART OF A DEEP IMMERSION *DARPA* RESEARCH INITIATIVE, ONE OF THE BIG BRAINS OVER THERE. UNTIL ONE DAY, HE--
WAIT, HOLD ON--
DID I HEAR YOU SAY YOU GOT NEW ARMOR WHEN YOU WERE OUT THERE?
I DID.
DO YOU HAVE PICTURES?
GUYS, COME ON--
YEAH! AND WHAT HAPPENED WITH YOUR EX?
MY *WHAT?*

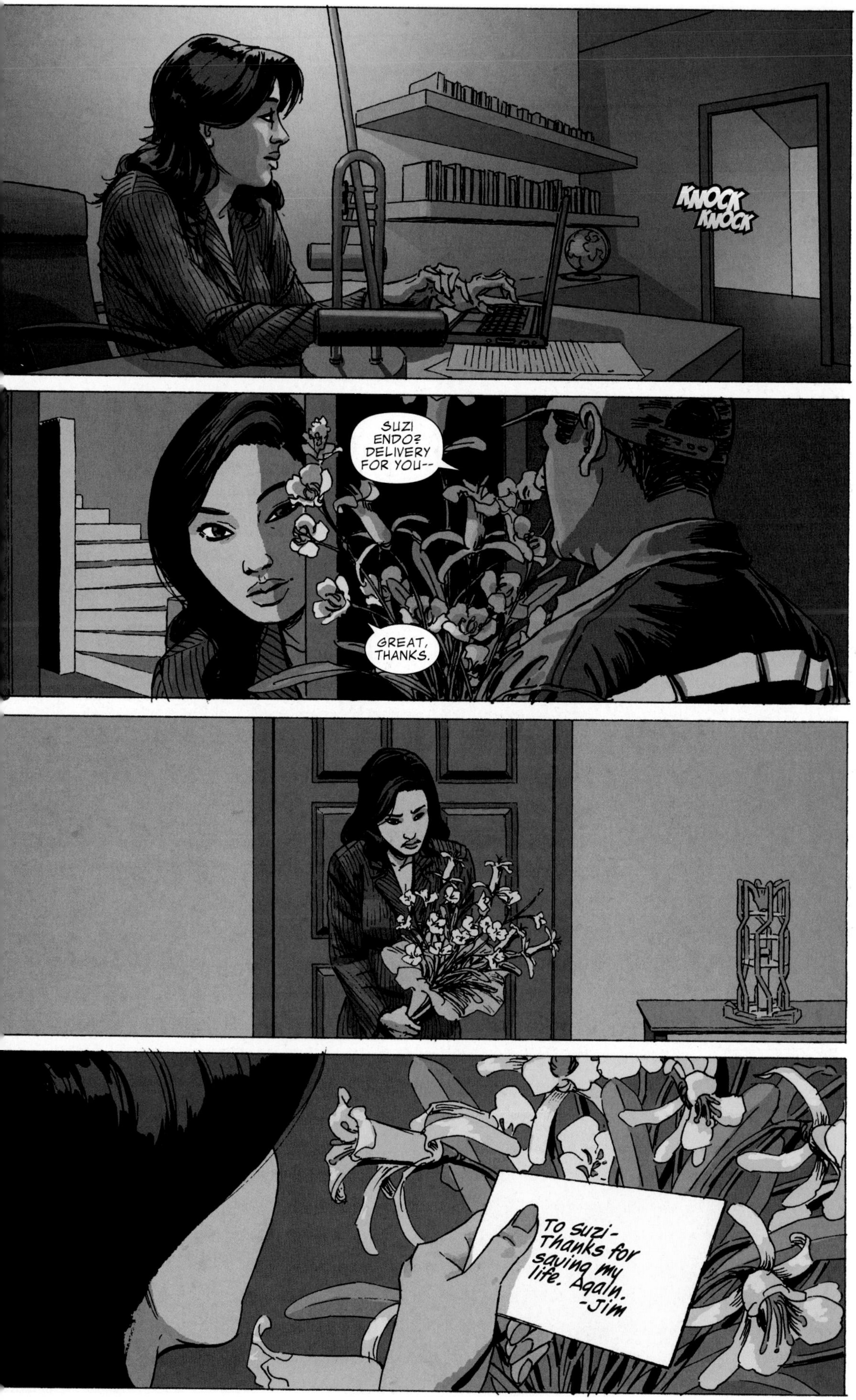
KNOCK KNOCK
SUZI ENDO? DELIVERY FOR YOU--
GREAT, THANKS.
To Suzi-
Thanks for saving my life. Again.
-Jim

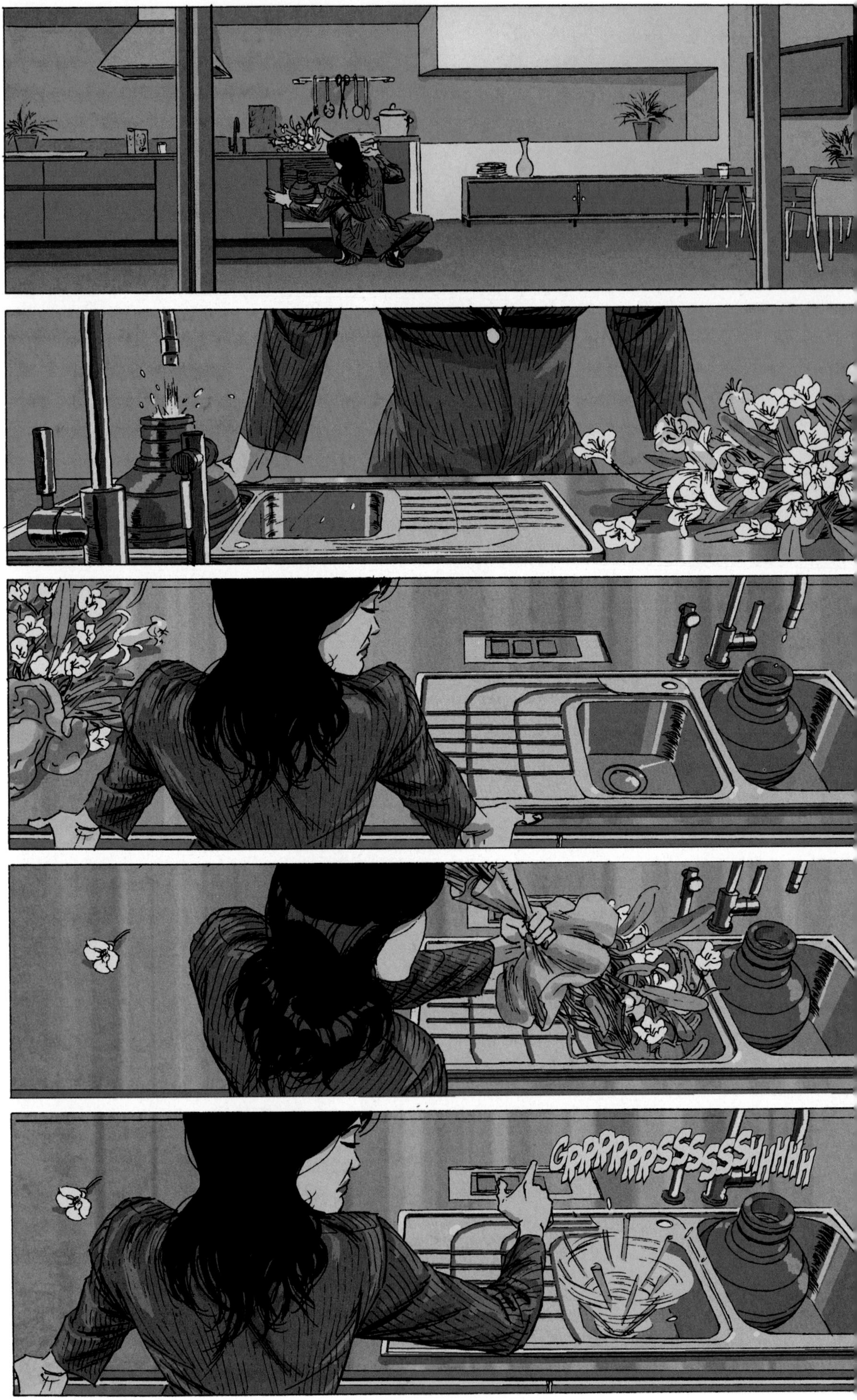
GRRRRRSSSSSSHHHHH

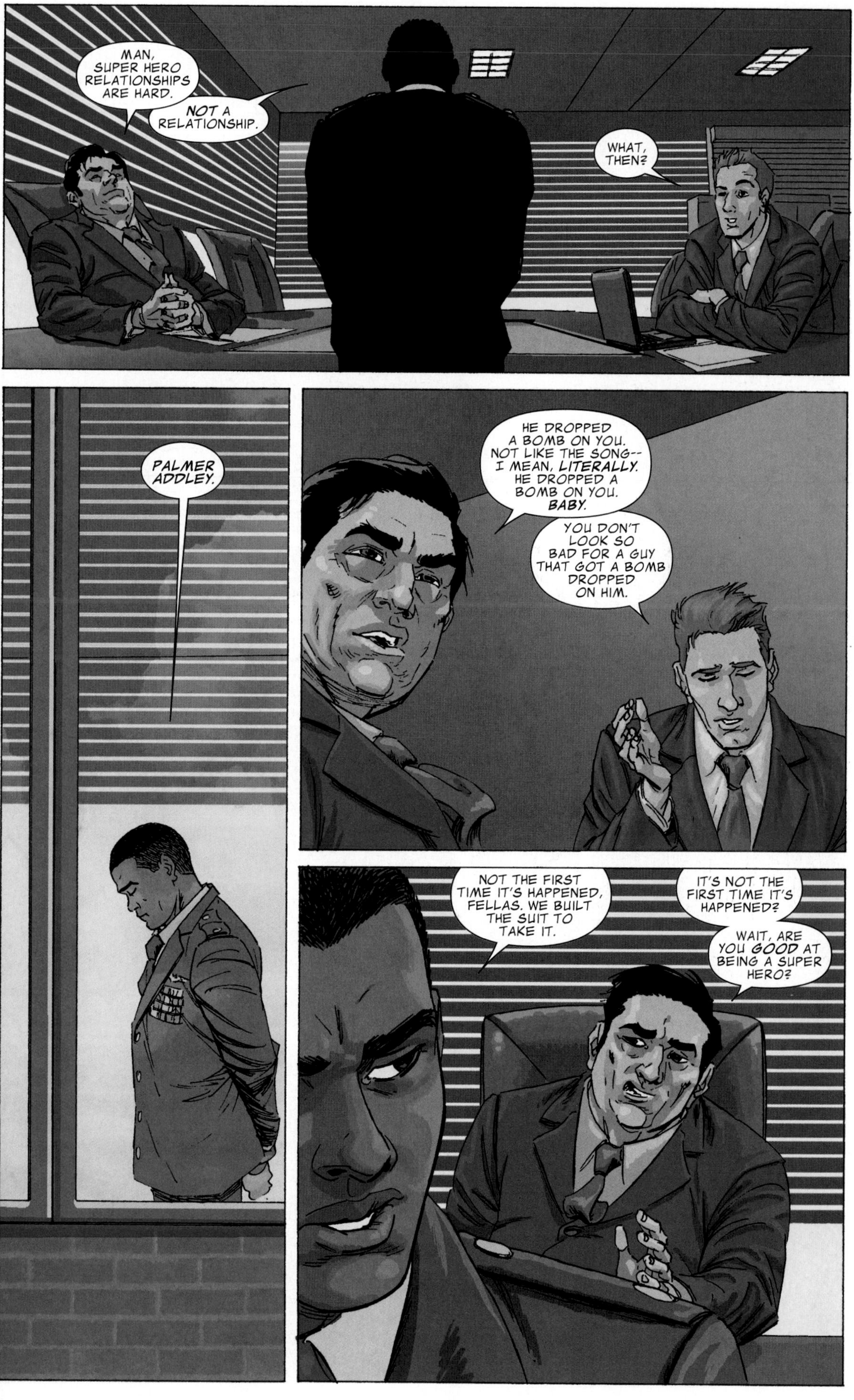
MAN, SUPER HERO RELATIONSHIPS ARE HARD.
NOT A RELATIONSHIP.
WHAT, THEN?
PALMER ADDLEY.
HE DROPPED A BOMB ON YOU. NOT LIKE THE SONG-- I MEAN, LITERALLY. HE DROPPED A BOMB ON YOU. BABY.
YOU DON'T LOOK SO BAD FOR A GUY THAT GOT A BOMB DROPPED ON HIM.
NOT THE FIRST TIME IT'S HAPPENED, FELLAS. WE BUILT THE SUIT TO TAKE IT.
IT'S NOT THE FIRST TIME IT'S HAPPENED?
WAIT, ARE YOU GOOD AT BEING A SUPER HERO?

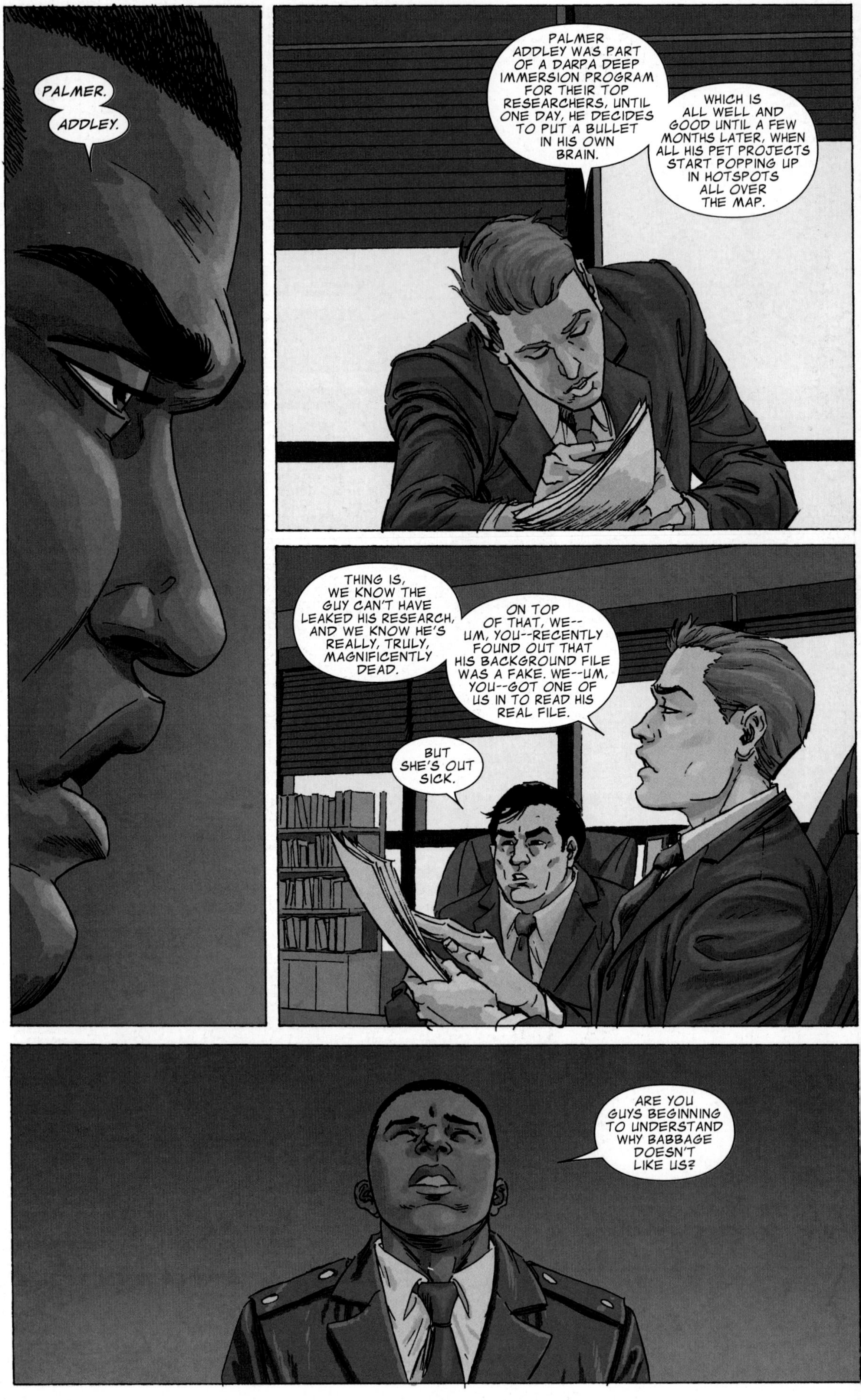
PALMER.
ADDLEY.
PALMER ADDLEY WAS PART OF A DARPA DEEP IMMERSION PROGRAM FOR THEIR TOP RESEARCHERS, UNTIL ONE DAY, HE DECIDES TO PUT A BULLET IN HIS OWN BRAIN.
WHICH IS ALL WELL AND GOOD UNTIL A FEW MONTHS LATER, WHEN ALL HIS PET PROJECTS START POPPING UP IN HOTSPOTS ALL OVER THE MAP.
THING IS, WE KNOW THE GUY CAN'T HAVE LEAKED HIS RESEARCH, AND WE KNOW HE'S REALLY, TRULY, MAGNIFICENTLY DEAD.
ON TOP OF THAT, WE-- UM, YOU--RECENTLY FOUND OUT THAT HIS BACKGROUND FILE WAS A FAKE. WE--UM, YOU--GOT ONE OF US IN TO READ HIS REAL FILE.
BUT SHE'S OUT SICK.
ARE YOU GUYS BEGINNING TO UNDERSTAND WHY BABBAGE DOESN'T LIKE US?

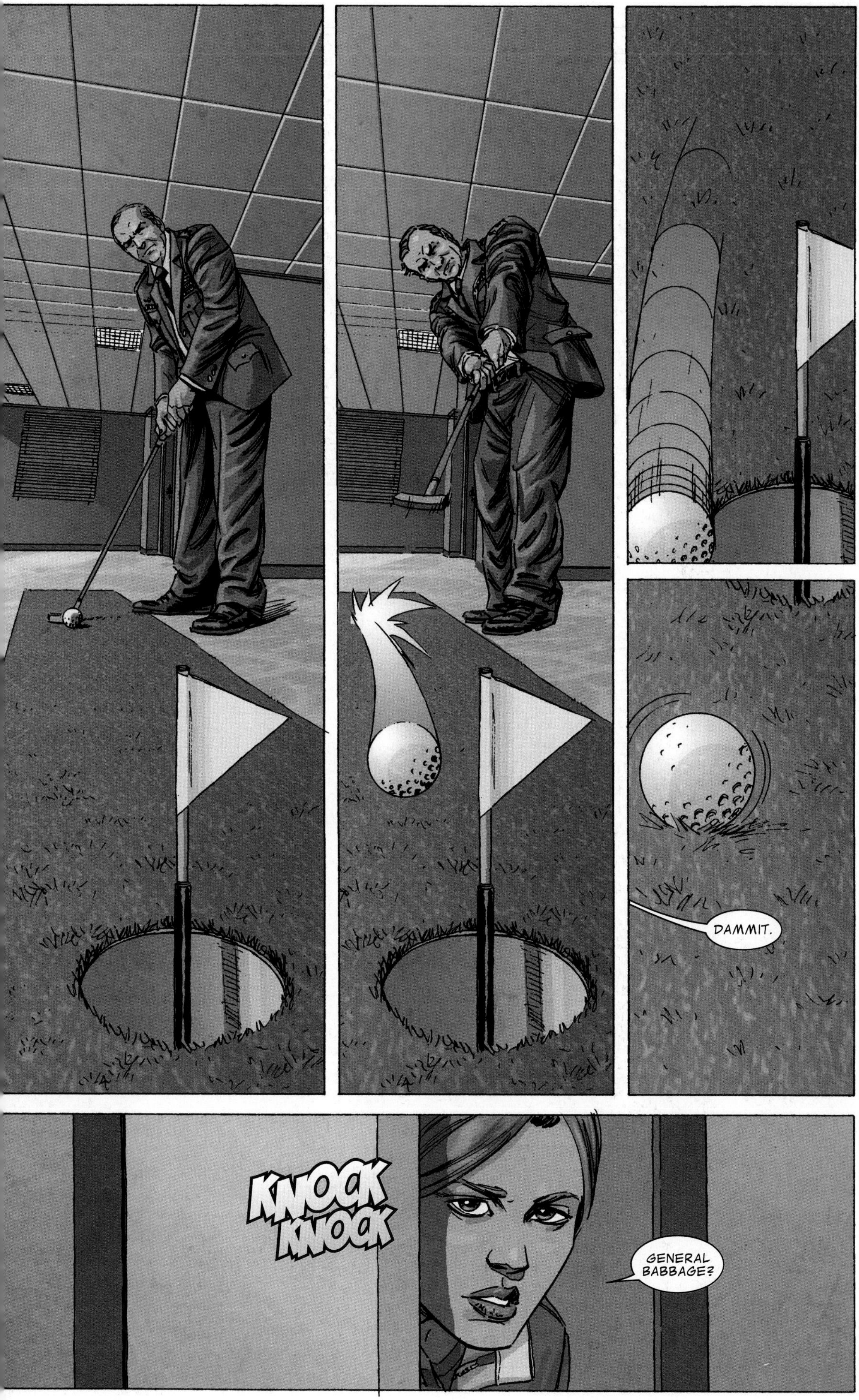
DAMMIT.
KNOCK KNOCK
GENERAL BABBAGE?

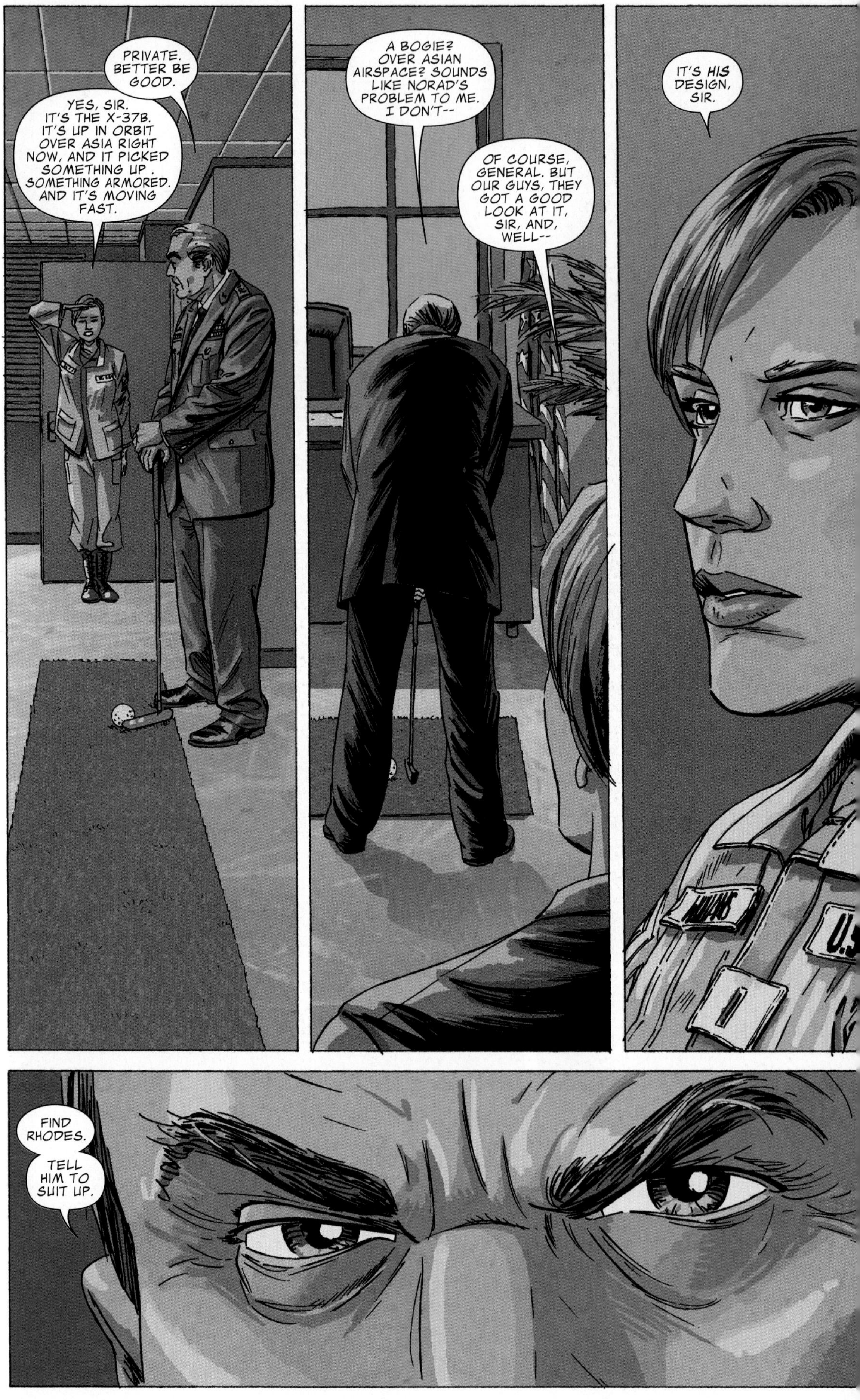
PRIVATE. BETTER BE GOOD.
YES, SIR. IT'S THE X-37B. IT'S UP IN ORBIT OVER ASIA RIGHT NOW, AND IT PICKED SOMETHING UP . SOMETHING ARMORED. AND IT'S MOVING FAST.
A BOGIE? OVER ASIAN AIRSPACE? SOUNDS LIKE NORAD'S PROBLEM TO ME. I DON'T--
OF COURSE, GENERAL. BUT OUR GUYS, THEY GOT A GOOD LOOK AT IT, SIR, AND, WELL--
IT'S HIS DESIGN, SIR.
FIND RHODES.
TELL HIM TO SUIT UP.

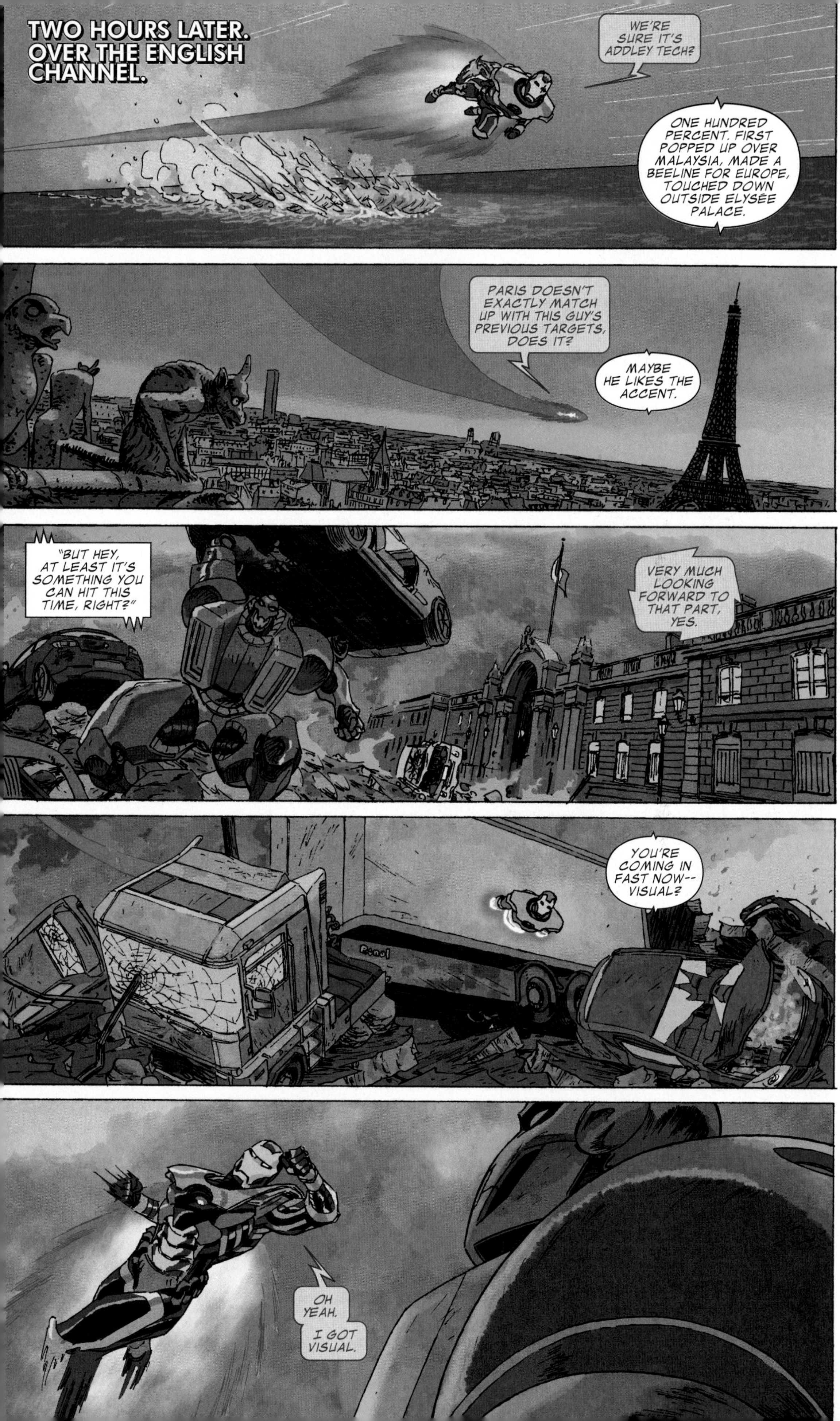

TWO HOURS LATER. OVER THE ENGLISH CHANNEL.
WE'RE SURE IT'S ADDLEY TECH?
ONE HUNDRED PERCENT. FIRST POPPED UP OVER MALAYSIA, MADE A BEELINE FOR EUROPE, TOUCHED DOWN OUTSIDE ELYSÉE PALACE.
PARIS DOESN'T EXACTLY MATCH UP WITH THIS GUY'S PREVIOUS TARGETS, DOES IT?
MAYBE HE LIKES THE ACCENT.
"BUT HEY, AT LEAST IT'S SOMETHING YOU CAN HIT THIS TIME, RIGHT?"
VERY MUCH LOOKING FORWARD TO THAT PART, YES.
YOU'RE COMING IN FAST NOW-- VISUAL?
OH YEAH.
I GOT VISUAL.

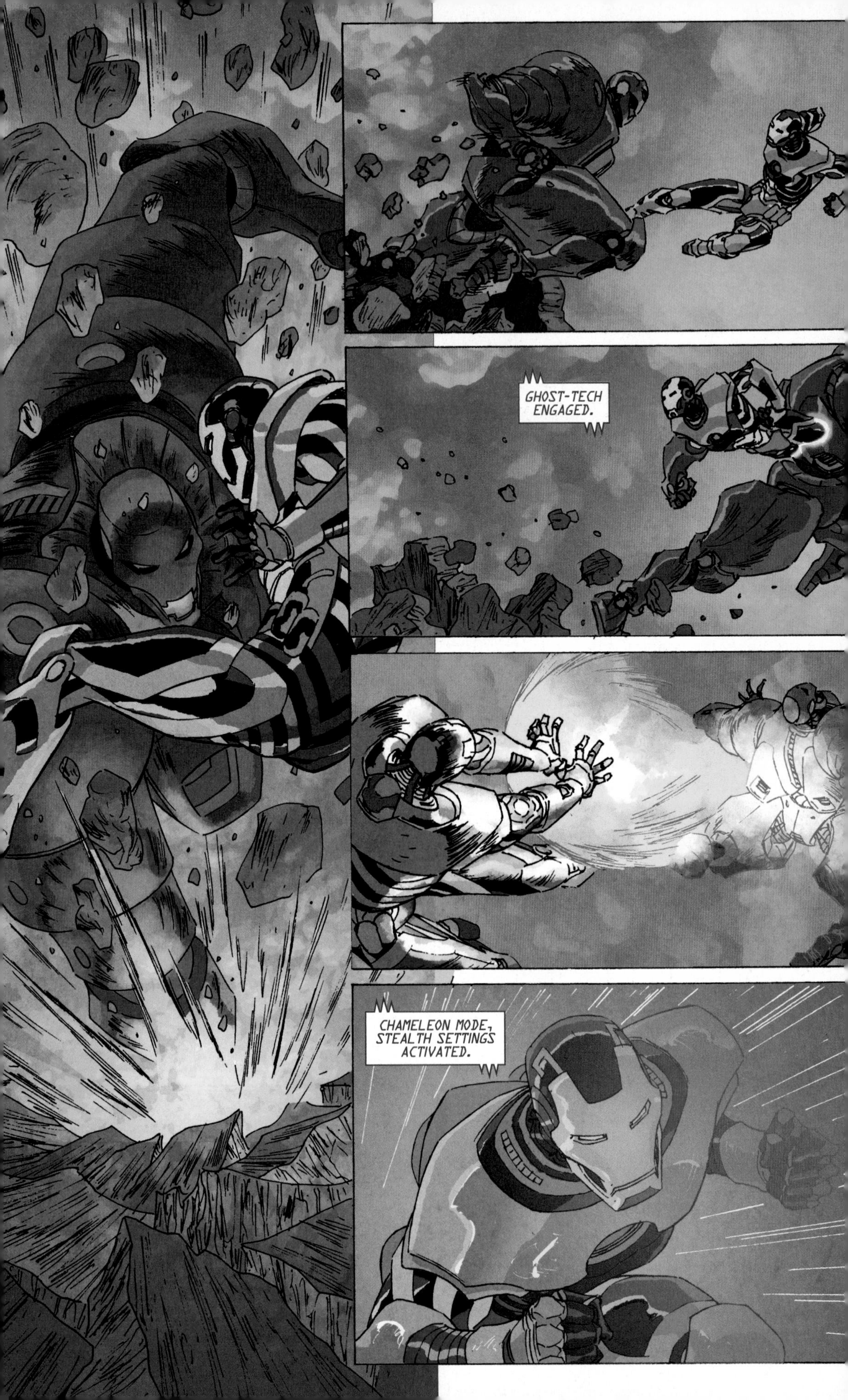
GHOST-TECH ENGAGED.
CHAMELEON MODE, STEALTH SETTINGS ACTIVATED.

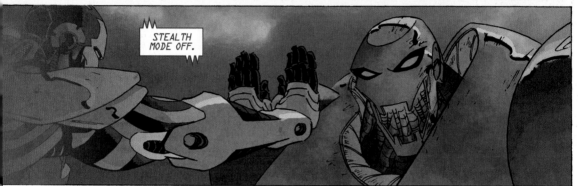

STEALTH MODE OFF.

REPULSOR POWER, 92 PERCENT.

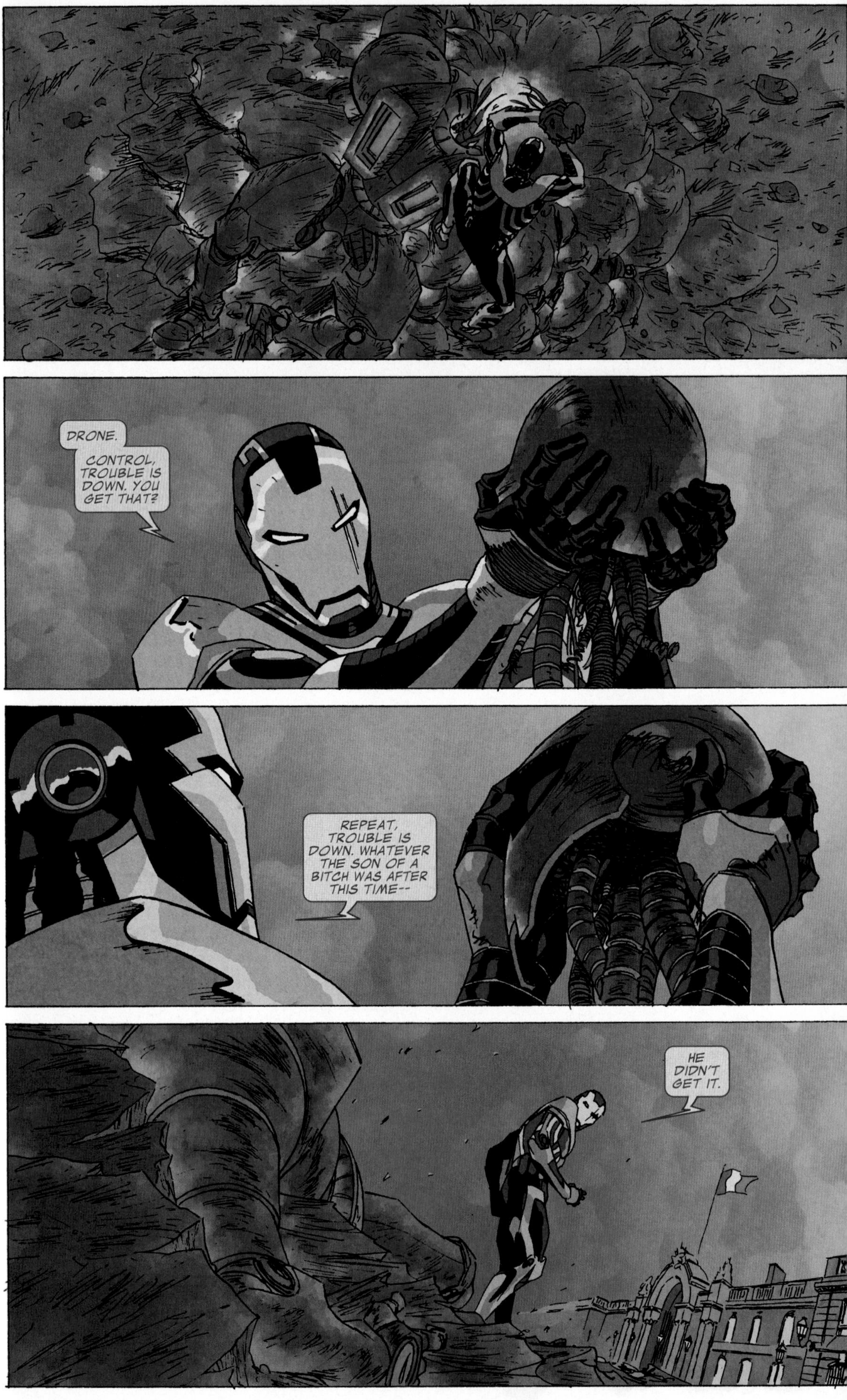
DRONE.
CONTROL, TROUBLE IS DOWN. YOU GET THAT?
REPEAT, TROUBLE IS DOWN. WHATEVER THE SON OF A BITCH WAS AFTER THIS TIME--
HE DIDN'T GET IT.

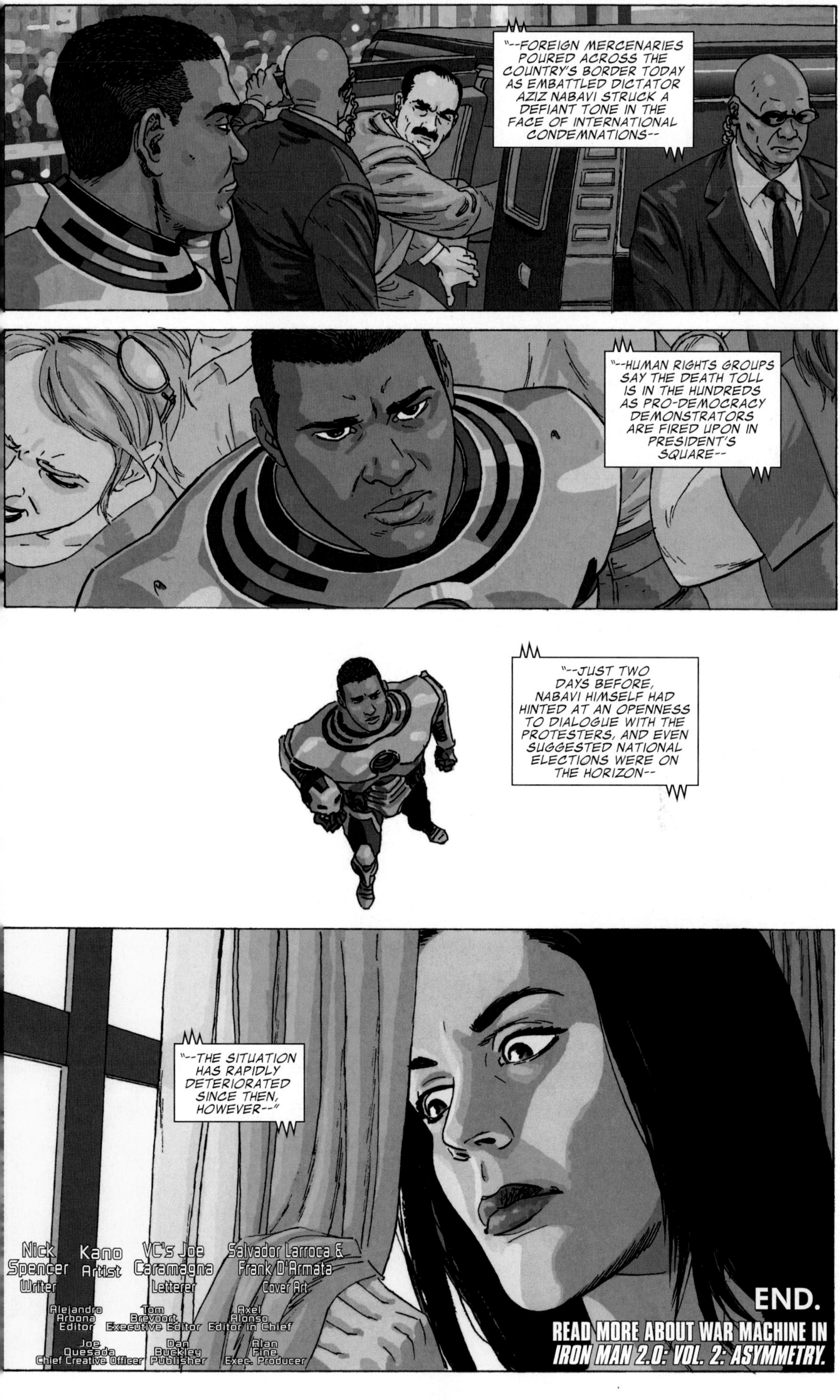
"--FOREIGN MERCENARIES POURED ACROSS THE COUNTRY'S BORDER TODAY AS EMBATTLED DICTATOR AZIZ NABAVI STRUCK A DEFIANT TONE IN THE FACE OF INTERNATIONAL CONDEMNATIONS--
"--HUMAN RIGHTS GROUPS SAY THE DEATH TOLL IS IN THE HUNDREDS AS PRO-DEMOCRACY DEMONSTRATORS ARE FIRED UPON IN PRESIDENT'S SQUARE--
"--JUST TWO DAYS BEFORE, NABAVI HIMSELF HAD HINTED AT AN OPENNESS TO DIALOGUE WITH THE PROTESTERS, AND EVEN SUGGESTED NATIONAL ELECTIONS WERE ON THE HORIZON--
"--THE SITUATION HAS RAPIDLY DETERIORATED SINCE THEN, HOWEVER--"
Nick Spencer Writer
Kano Artist
VC's Joe Caramagna Letterer
Salvador Larroca & Frank D'Armata Cover Art
Alejandro Arbona Editor
Tom Brevoort Executive Editor
Axel Alonso Editor in Chief
Joe Quesada Chief Creative Officer
Dan Buckley Publisher
Alan Fine Exec. Producer
END.
READ MORE ABOUT WAR MACHINE IN IRON MAN 2.0: VOL. 2: ASYMMETRY.

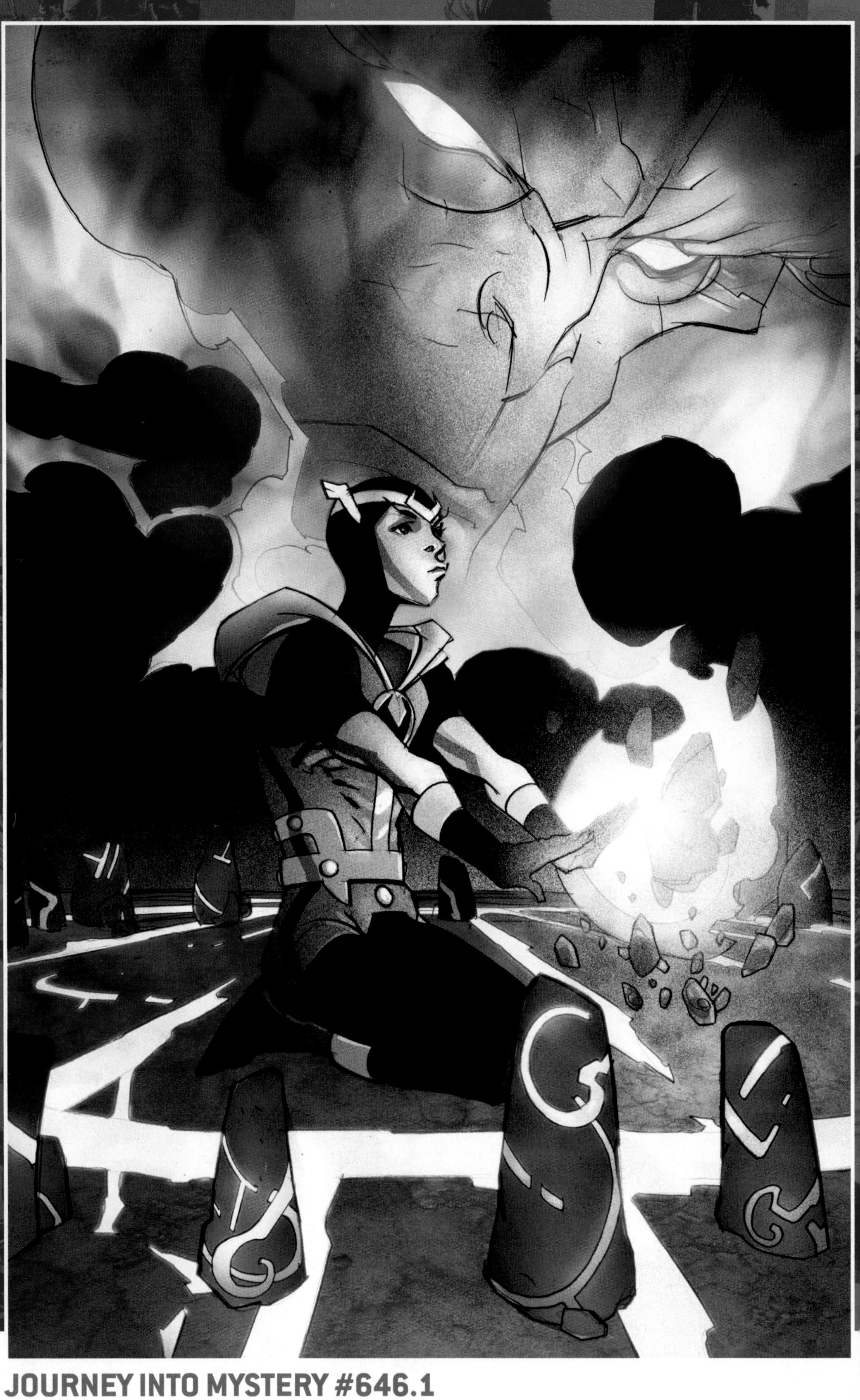

JOURNEY INTO MYSTERY #646.1

CULMINATION OF HIS GREATEST SCHEME, LOKI, GOD OF TRICKERY, GOT HIMSELF KI

EFENDING ASGARD FROM A THREAT THAT HE HIMSELF HAD ARRANGED. NOT LO
E MADE AN AGREEMENT WITH HELA, GODDESS OF HEL, TO WRITE HIM OUT OF TH
IS SOUL HAD ESCAPED THE CYCLE OF DEATH AND REBIRTH THAT DICTATES THE FA
DIANS. WHEN THOR FOUND HIS SPIRIT AND RETURNED HIM TO THE LAND OF THE LI
LOKI WAS A NEW MAN. WELL, A NEW BOY.

DID IT ALL TO MAKE HIMSELF A BETTER PERSON. REALLY. HONEST TO ODIN. WE PRO

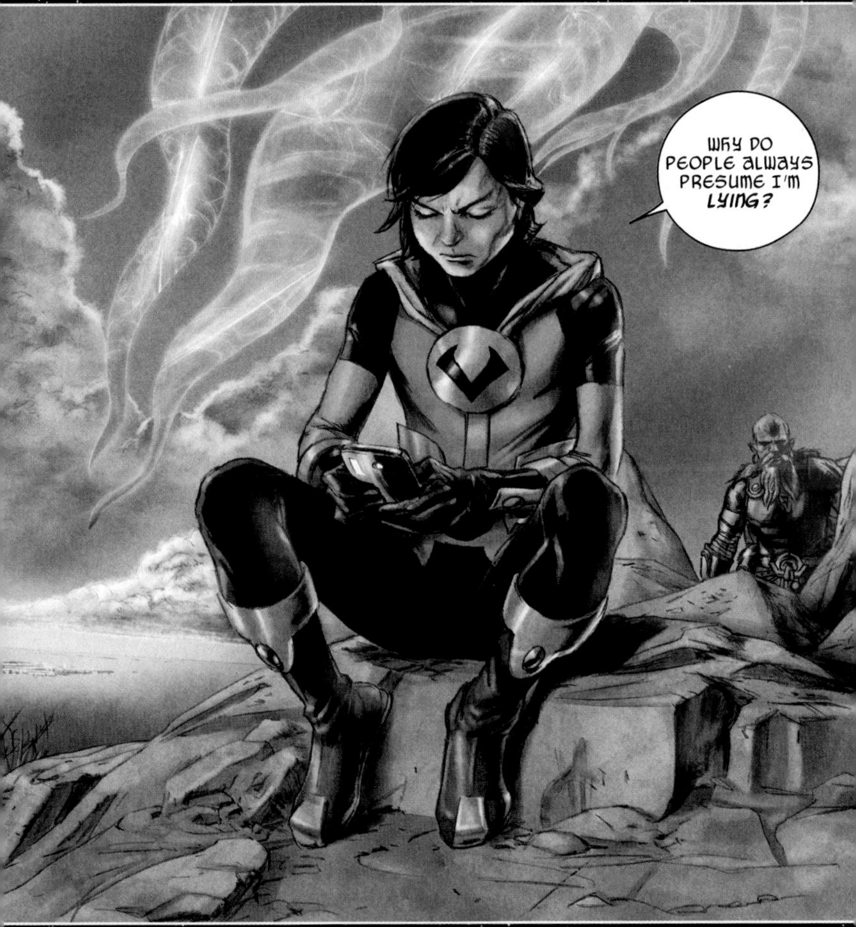
WHY DO PEOPLE ALWAYS PRESUME I'M *LYING?*

HIS ISSUE TAKES PLACE BETWEEN PANELS 4 & 5 ON PAGE 21 OF JOURNEY INTO MYSTERY #622. IN CASE YOU WE

URNEY INTO MYSTE

PASQUAL FERRY
ARTIST

FRANK D'ARMATA
COLORIST

VC'S CLA COWL
LETTERS & PRO

PASQUAL FERRY
COVER ART

JOHN DENNING
ASST. EDITOR

RALPH MACCHIO
SENIOR EDITOR

O
CHIEF

JOE QUESADA
CHIEF CREATIVE OFFICER

DAN BUCKLEY
PUBLISHER

ALA FIN
EXECUTIVE P

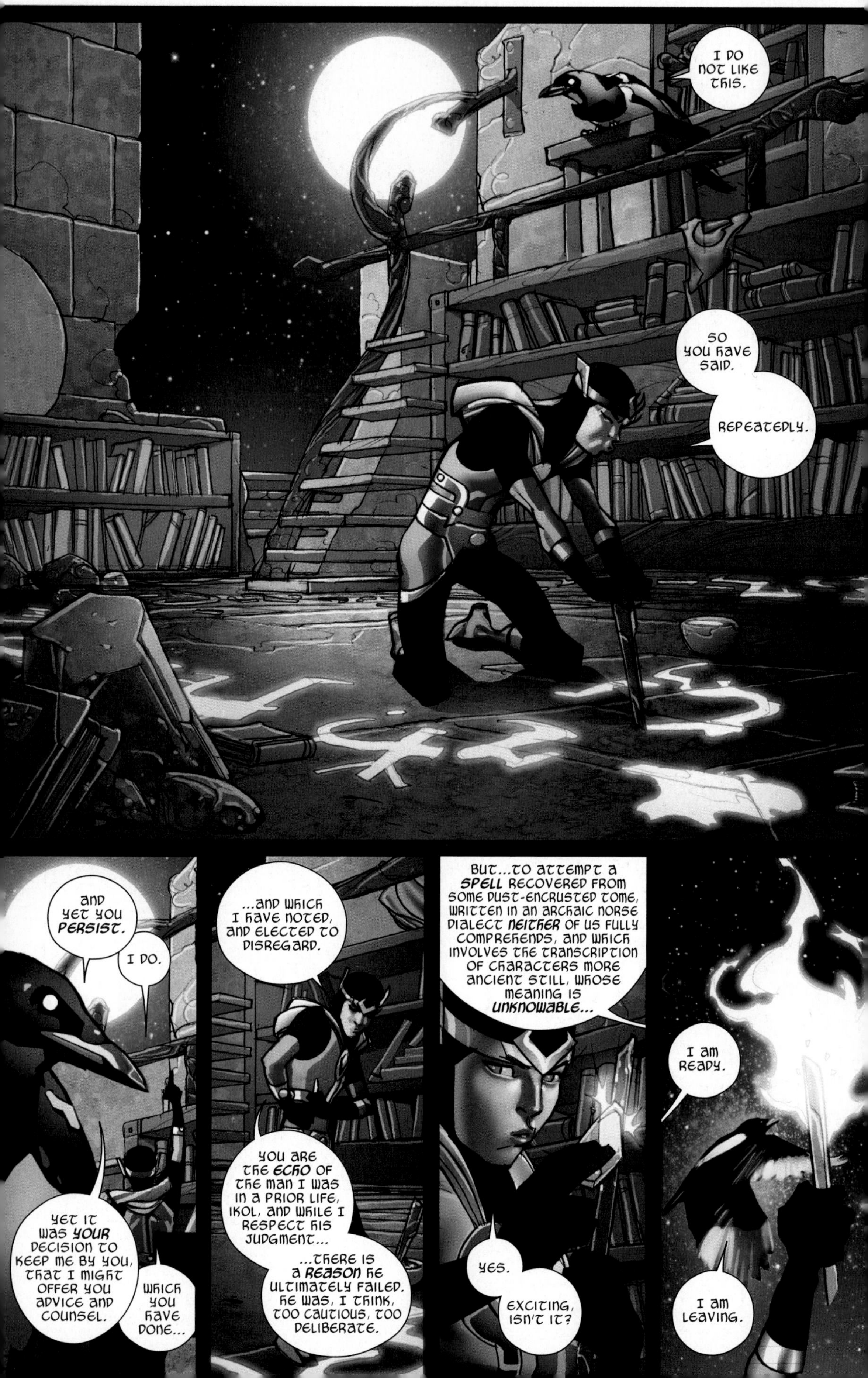

I DO NOT LIKE THIS.
SO YOU HAVE SAID.
REPEATEDLY.
AND YET YOU **PERSIST**.
I DO.
YET IT WAS **YOUR** DECISION TO KEEP ME BY YOU, THAT I MIGHT OFFER YOU ADVICE AND COUNSEL.
WHICH YOU HAVE DONE...
...AND WHICH I HAVE NOTED, AND ELECTED TO DISREGARD.
YOU ARE THE **ECHO** OF THE MAN I WAS IN A PRIOR LIFE, IKOL, AND WHILE I RESPECT HIS JUDGMENT...
...THERE IS A **REASON** HE ULTIMATELY FAILED. HE WAS, I THINK, TOO CAUTIOUS, TOO DELIBERATE.
BUT...TO ATTEMPT A **SPELL** RECOVERED FROM SOME DUST-ENCRUSTED TOME, WRITTEN IN AN ARCHAIC NORSE DIALECT **NEITHER** OF US FULLY COMPREHENDS, AND WHICH INVOLVES THE TRANSCRIPTION OF CHARACTERS MORE ANCIENT STILL, WHOSE MEANING IS **UNKNOWABLE...**
YES.
EXCITING, ISN'T IT?
I AM READY.
I AM LEAVING.

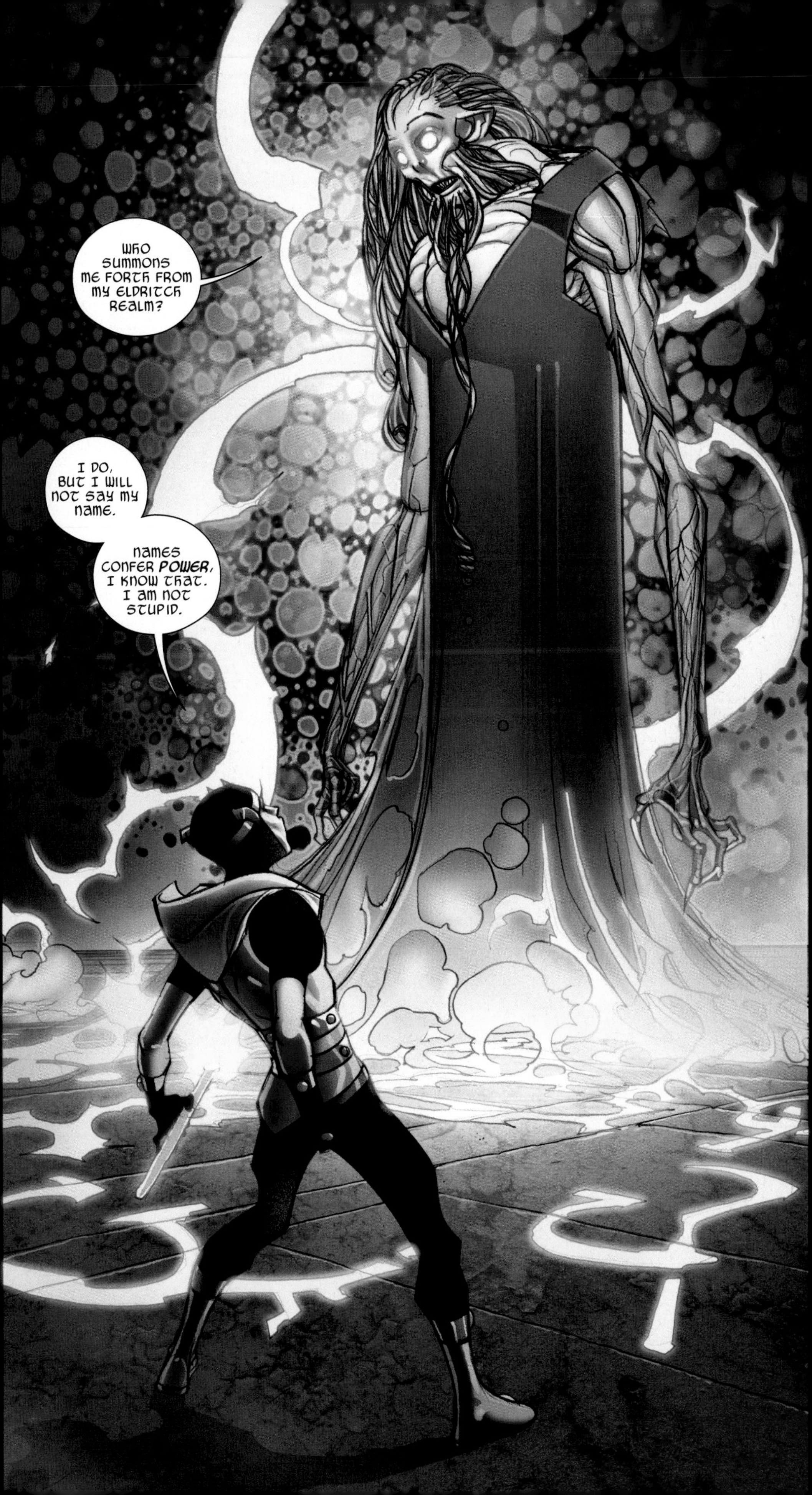
WHO SUMMONS ME FORTH FROM MY ELDRITCH REALM?
I DO, BUT I WILL NOT SAY MY NAME.
NAMES CONFER **POWER**, I KNOW THAT. I AM NOT STUPID.

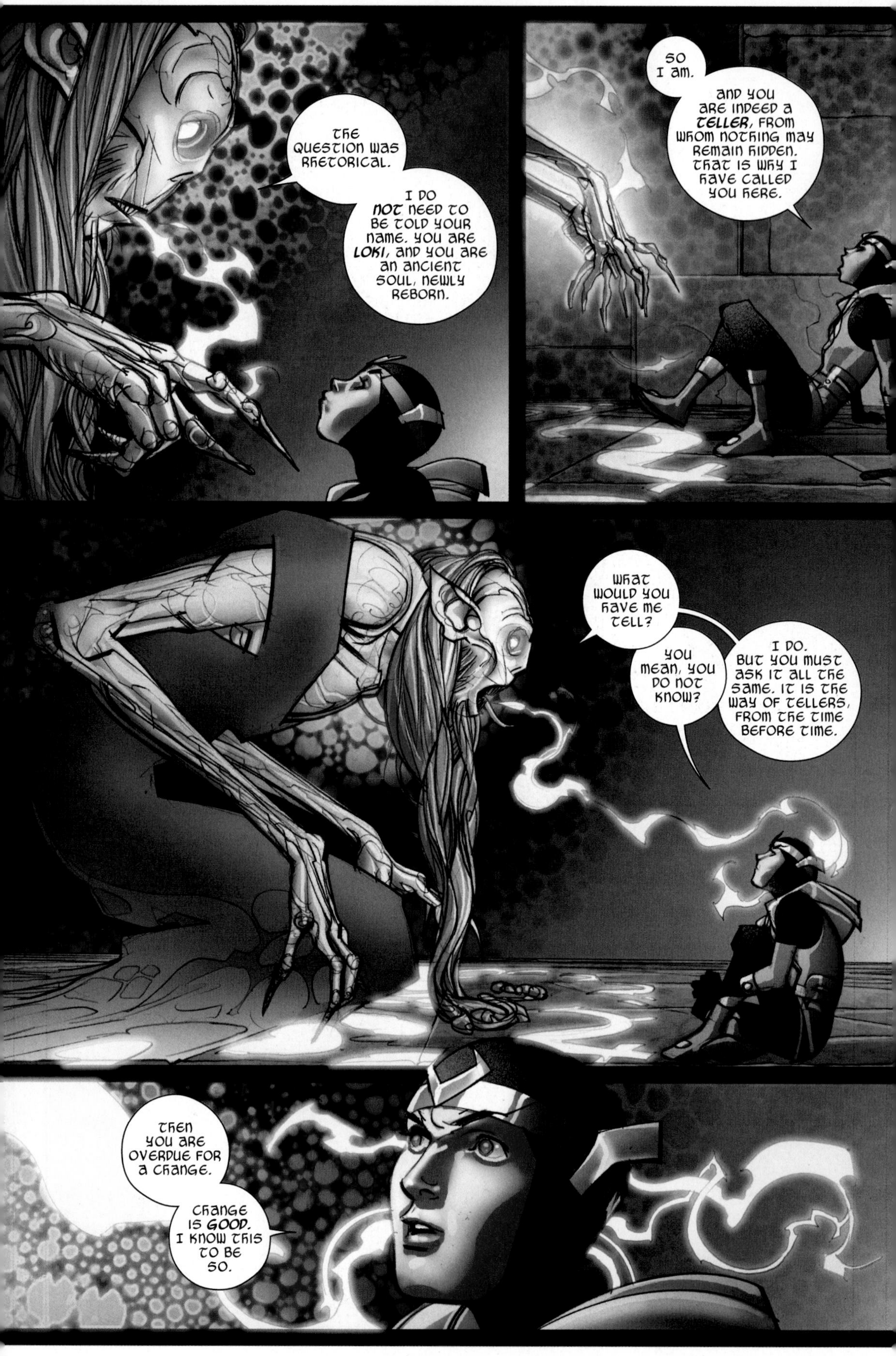
THE QUESTION WAS RHETORICAL.
I DO NOT NEED TO BE TOLD YOUR NAME. YOU ARE LOKI, AND YOU ARE AN ANCIENT SOUL, NEWLY REBORN.
SO I AM.
AND YOU ARE INDEED A TELLER, FROM WHOM NOTHING MAY REMAIN HIDDEN. THAT IS WHY I HAVE CALLED YOU HERE.
WHAT WOULD YOU HAVE ME TELL?
YOU MEAN, YOU DO NOT KNOW?
I DO. BUT YOU MUST ASK IT ALL THE SAME. IT IS THE WAY OF TELLERS, FROM THE TIME BEFORE TIME.
THEN YOU ARE OVERDUE FOR A CHANGE.
CHANGE IS GOOD. I KNOW THIS TO BE SO.

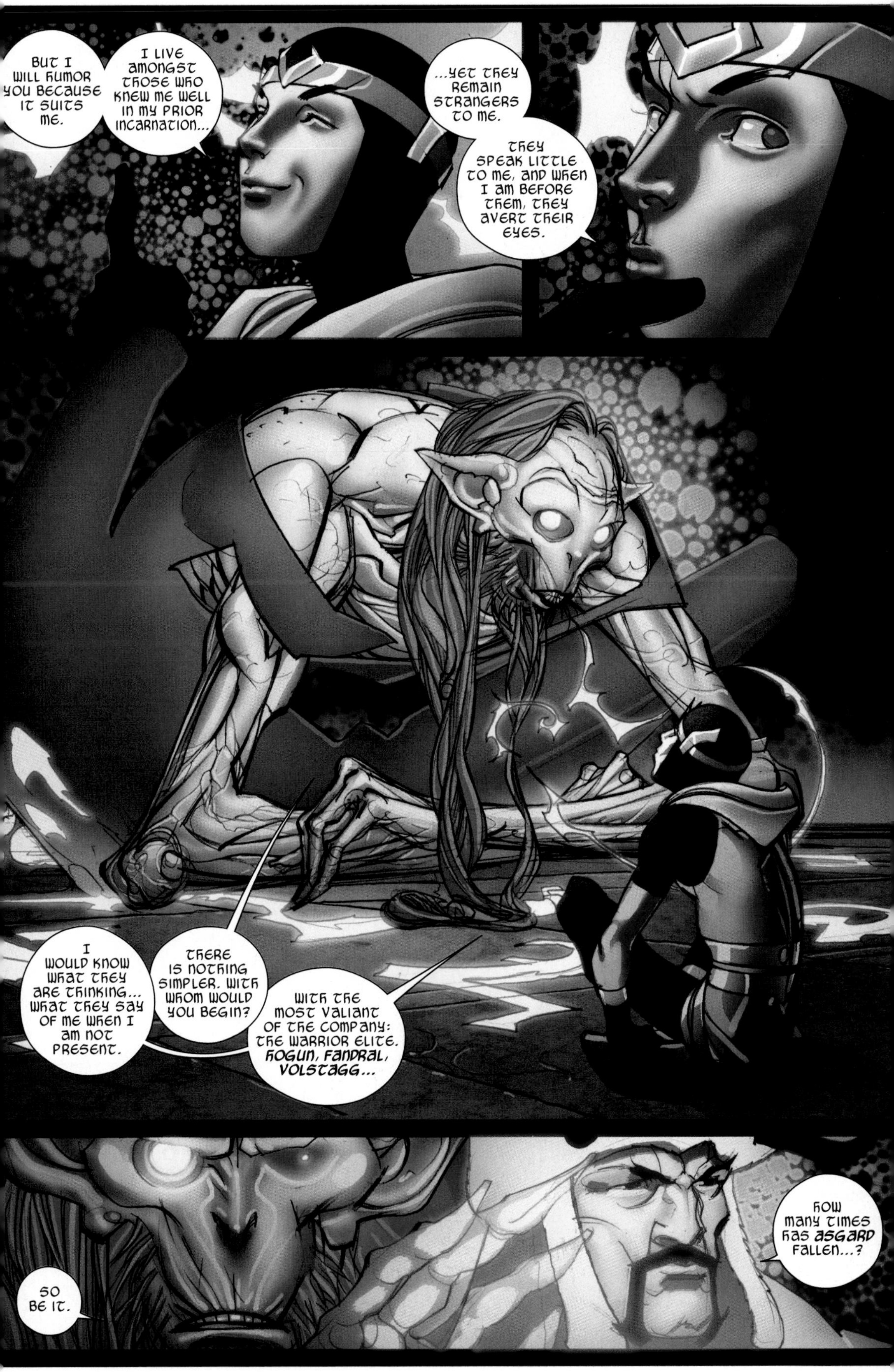
BUT I WILL HUMOR YOU BECAUSE IT SUITS ME.
I LIVE AMONGST THOSE WHO KNEW ME WELL IN MY PRIOR INCARNATION...
...YET THEY REMAIN STRANGERS TO ME.
THEY SPEAK LITTLE TO ME, AND WHEN I AM BEFORE THEM, THEY AVERT THEIR EYES.
I WOULD KNOW WHAT THEY ARE THINKING... WHAT THEY SAY OF ME WHEN I AM NOT PRESENT.
THERE IS NOTHING SIMPLER. WITH WHOM WOULD YOU BEGIN?
WITH THE MOST VALIANT OF THE COMPANY: THE WARRIOR ELITE. HOGUN, FANDRAL, VOLSTAGG...
HOW MANY TIMES HAS ASGARD FALLEN...?
SO BE IT.

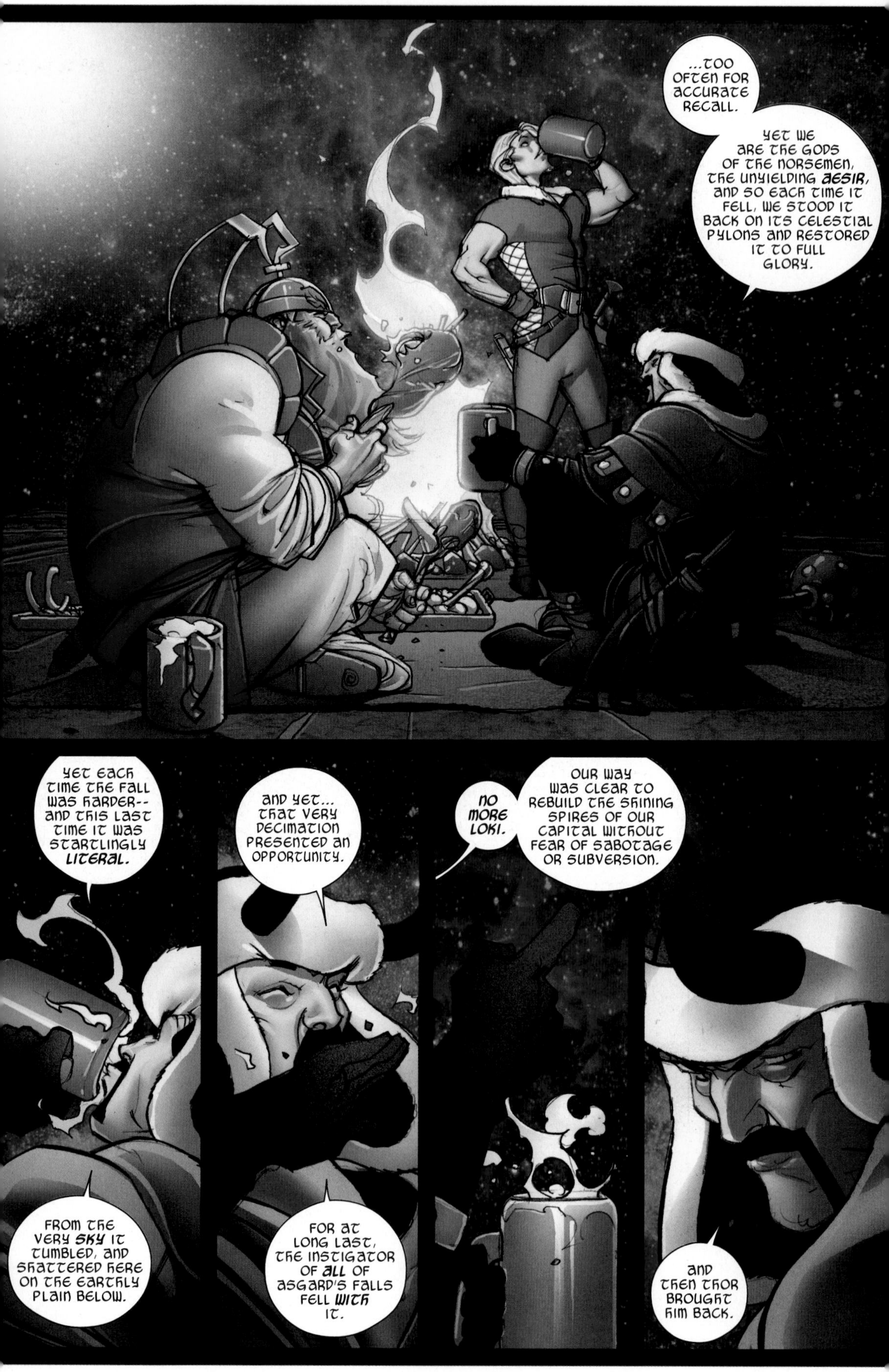
...TOO OFTEN FOR ACCURATE RECALL.
YET WE ARE THE GODS OF THE NORSEMEN, THE UNYIELDING AESIR, AND SO EACH TIME IT FELL, WE STOOD IT BACK ON ITS CELESTIAL PYLONS AND RESTORED IT TO FULL GLORY.
YET EACH TIME THE FALL WAS HARDER-- AND THIS LAST TIME IT WAS STARTLINGLY LITERAL.
FROM THE VERY SKY IT TUMBLED, AND SHATTERED HERE ON THE EARTHLY PLAIN BELOW.
AND YET... THAT VERY DECIMATION PRESENTED AN OPPORTUNITY.
FOR AT LONG LAST, THE INSTIGATOR OF ALL OF ASGARD'S FALLS FELL WITH IT.
NO MORE LOKI.
OUR WAY WAS CLEAR TO REBUILD THE SHINING SPIRES OF OUR CAPITAL WITHOUT FEAR OF SABOTAGE OR SUBVERSION.
AND THEN THOR BROUGHT HIM BACK.

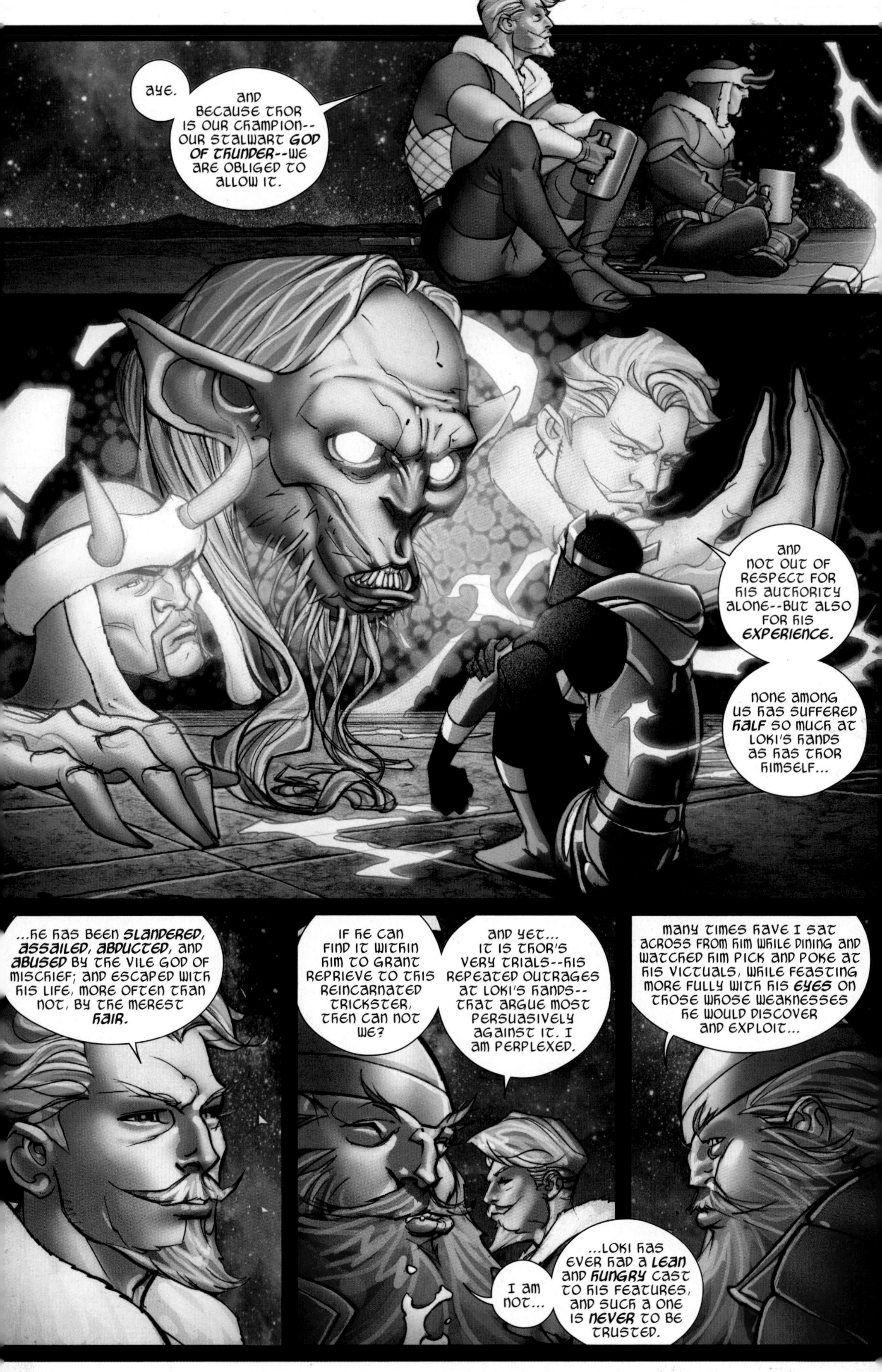
AYE.
AND BECAUSE THOR IS OUR CHAMPION-- OUR STALWART GOD OF THUNDER--WE ARE OBLIGED TO ALLOW IT.
AND NOT OUT OF RESPECT FOR HIS AUTHORITY ALONE--BUT ALSO FOR HIS EXPERIENCE.
NONE AMONG US HAS SUFFERED HALF SO MUCH AT LOKI'S HANDS AS HAS THOR HIMSELF...
...HE HAS BEEN SLANDERED, ASSAILED, ABDUCTED, AND ABUSED BY THE VILE GOD OF MISCHIEF; AND ESCAPED WITH HIS LIFE, MORE OFTEN THAN NOT, BY THE MEREST HAIR.
IF HE CAN FIND IT WITHIN HIM TO GRANT REPRIEVE TO THIS REINCARNATED TRICKSTER, THEN CAN NOT WE?
AND YET... IT IS THOR'S VERY TRIALS--HIS REPEATED OUTRAGES AT LOKI'S HANDS-- THAT ARGUE MOST PERSUASIVELY AGAINST IT. I AM PERPLEXED.
I AM NOT...
MANY TIMES HAVE I SAT ACROSS FROM HIM WHILE DINING AND WATCHED HIM PICK AND POKE AT HIS VICTUALS, WHILE FEASTING MORE FULLY WITH HIS EYES ON THOSE WHOSE WEAKNESSES HE WOULD DISCOVER AND EXPLOIT...
...LOKI HAS EVER HAD A LEAN AND HUNGRY CAST TO HIS FEATURES, AND SUCH A ONE IS NEVER TO BE TRUSTED.

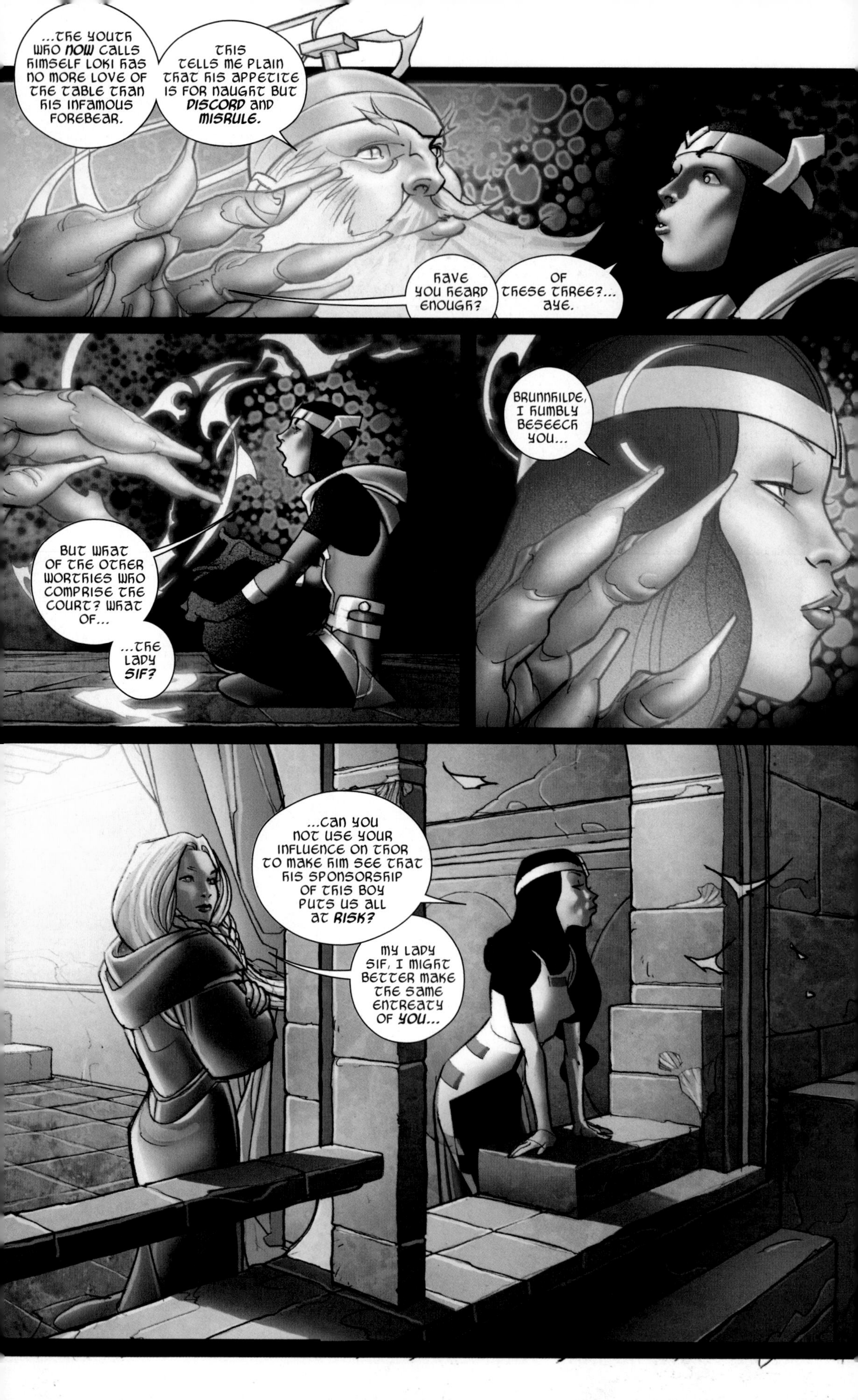
...THE YOUTH WHO NOW CALLS HIMSELF LOKI HAS NO MORE LOVE OF THE TABLE THAN HIS INFAMOUS FOREBEAR.
THIS TELLS ME PLAIN THAT HIS APPETITE IS FOR NAUGHT BUT DISCORD AND MISRULE.
HAVE YOU HEARD ENOUGH?
OF THESE THREE?... AYE.
BUT WHAT OF THE OTHER WORTHIES WHO COMPRISE THE COURT? WHAT OF...
...THE LADY SIF?
BRUNNHILDE, I HUMBLY BESEECH YOU...
...CAN YOU NOT USE YOUR INFLUENCE ON THOR TO MAKE HIM SEE THAT HIS SPONSORSHIP OF THIS BOY PUTS US ALL AT RISK?
MY LADY SIF, I MIGHT BETTER MAKE THE SAME ENTREATY OF YOU...

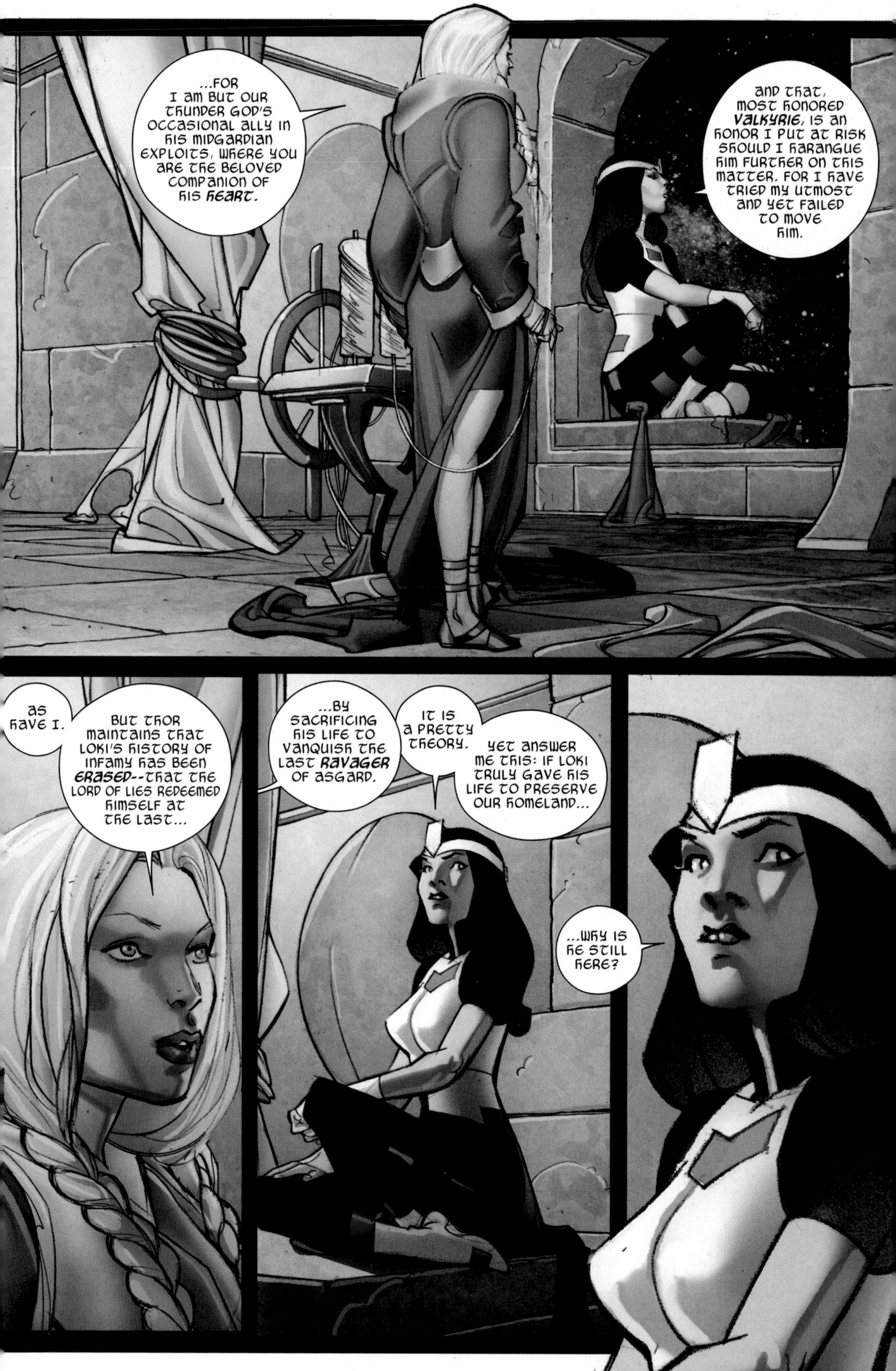
...FOR I AM BUT OUR THUNDER GOD'S OCCASIONAL ALLY IN HIS MIDGARDIAN EXPLOITS, WHERE YOU ARE THE BELOVED COMPANION OF HIS HEART.
AND THAT, MOST HONORED VALKYRIE, IS AN HONOR I PUT AT RISK SHOULD I HARANGUE HIM FURTHER ON THIS MATTER. FOR I HAVE TRIED MY UTMOST AND YET FAILED TO MOVE HIM.
AS HAVE I.
BUT THOR MAINTAINS THAT LOKI'S HISTORY OF INFAMY HAS BEEN ERASED--THAT THE LORD OF LIES REDEEMED HIMSELF AT THE LAST...
...BY SACRIFICING HIS LIFE TO VANQUISH THE LAST RAVAGER OF ASGARD.
IT IS A PRETTY THEORY.
YET ANSWER ME THIS: IF LOKI TRULY GAVE HIS LIFE TO PRESERVE OUR HOMELAND...
...WHY IS HE STILL HERE?

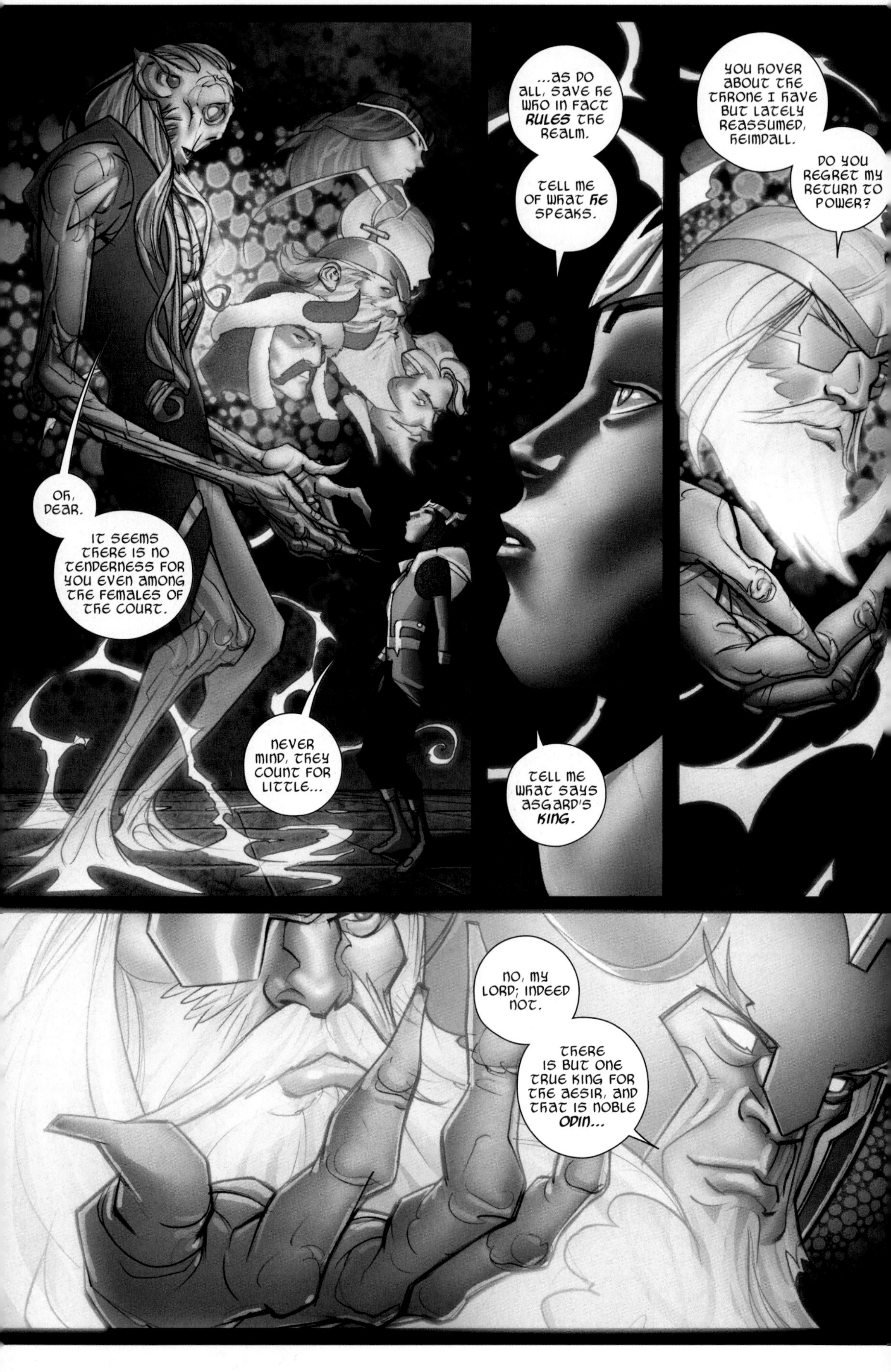
OH, DEAR.
IT SEEMS THERE IS NO TENDERNESS FOR YOU EVEN AMONG THE FEMALES OF THE COURT.
NEVER MIND, THEY COUNT FOR LITTLE...
...AS DO ALL, SAVE HE WHO IN FACT RULES THE REALM.
TELL ME OF WHAT HE SPEAKS.
TELL ME WHAT SAYS ASGARD'S KING.
YOU HOVER ABOUT THE THRONE I HAVE BUT LATELY REASSUMED, HEIMDALL.
DO YOU REGRET MY RETURN TO POWER?
NO, MY LORD; INDEED NOT.
THERE IS BUT ONE TRUE KING FOR THE AESIR, AND THAT IS NOBLE ODIN...

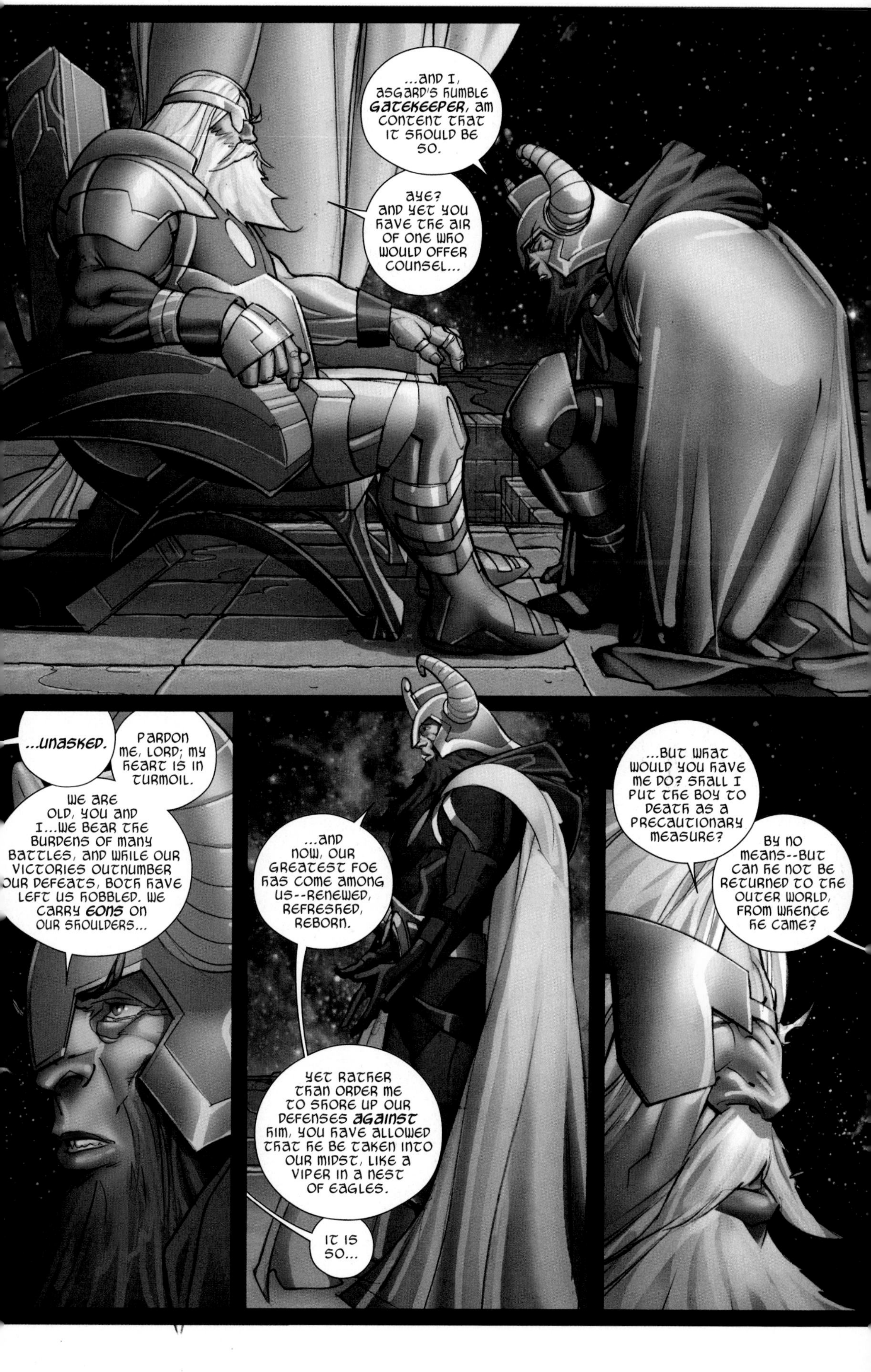
...AND I, ASGARD'S HUMBLE GATEKEEPER, AM CONTENT THAT IT SHOULD BE SO.
AYE? AND YET YOU HAVE THE AIR OF ONE WHO WOULD OFFER COUNSEL...
...UNASKED.
PARDON ME, LORD; MY HEART IS IN TURMOIL.
WE ARE OLD, YOU AND I...WE BEAR THE BURDENS OF MANY BATTLES, AND WHILE OUR VICTORIES OUTNUMBER OUR DEFEATS, BOTH HAVE LEFT US HOBBLED. WE CARRY EONS ON OUR SHOULDERS...
...AND NOW, OUR GREATEST FOE HAS COME AMONG US--RENEWED, REFRESHED, REBORN.
YET RATHER THAN ORDER ME TO SHORE UP OUR DEFENSES AGAINST HIM, YOU HAVE ALLOWED THAT HE BE TAKEN INTO OUR MIDST, LIKE A VIPER IN A NEST OF EAGLES.
IT IS SO...
...BUT WHAT WOULD YOU HAVE ME DO? SHALL I PUT THE BOY TO DEATH AS A PRECAUTIONARY MEASURE?
BY NO MEANS--BUT CAN HE NOT BE RETURNED TO THE OUTER WORLD, FROM WHENCE HE CAME?

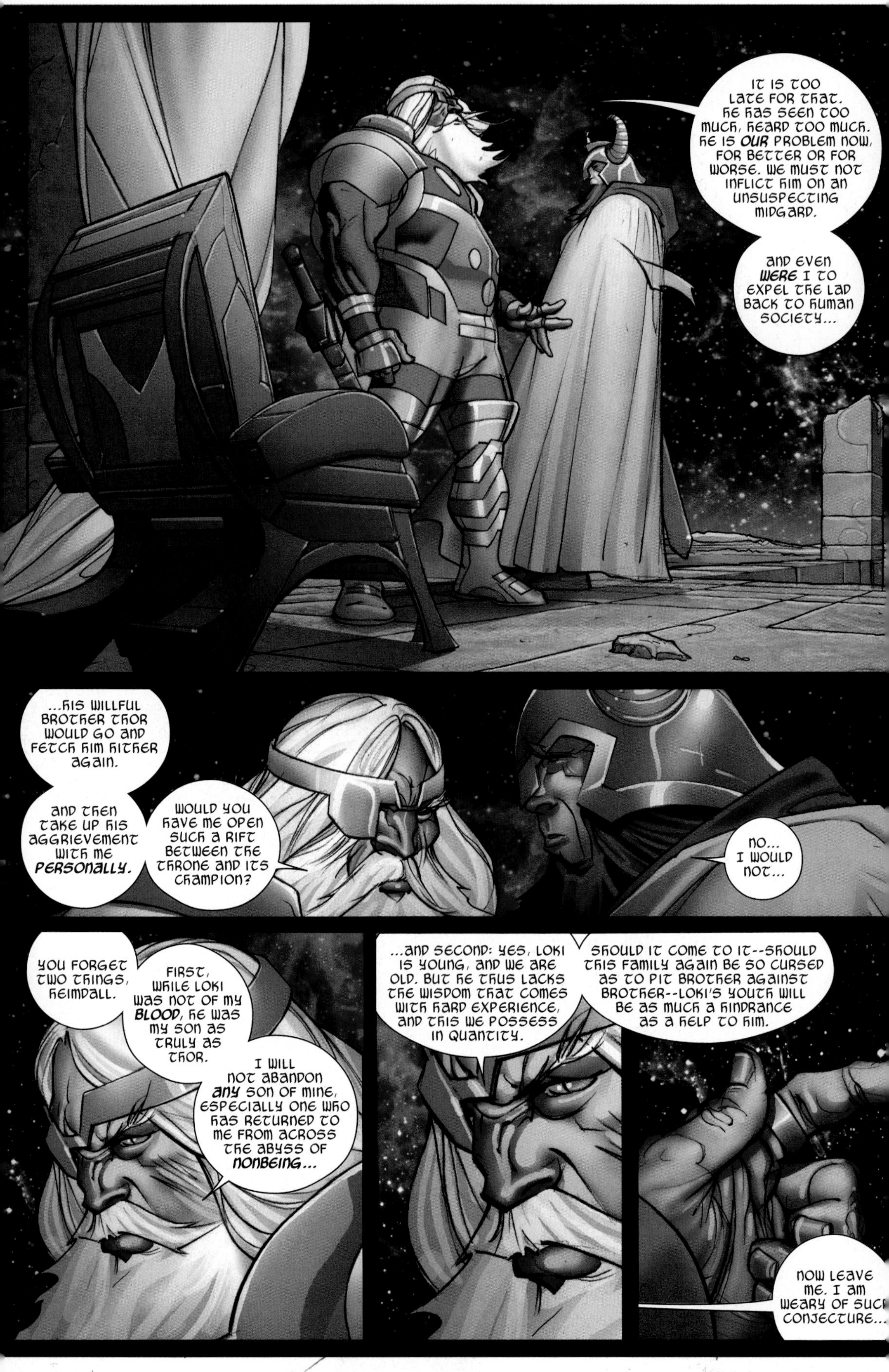

IT IS TOO LATE FOR THAT. HE HAS SEEN TOO MUCH, HEARD TOO MUCH. HE IS OUR PROBLEM NOW, FOR BETTER OR FOR WORSE. WE MUST NOT INFLICT HIM ON AN UNSUSPECTING MIDGARD.
AND EVEN WERE I TO EXPEL THE LAD BACK TO HUMAN SOCIETY...
...HIS WILLFUL BROTHER THOR WOULD GO AND FETCH HIM HITHER AGAIN.
AND THEN TAKE UP HIS AGGRIEVEMENT WITH ME PERSONALLY.
WOULD YOU HAVE ME OPEN SUCH A RIFT BETWEEN THE THRONE AND ITS CHAMPION?
NO... I WOULD NOT...
YOU FORGET TWO THINGS, HEIMDALL.
FIRST, WHILE LOKI WAS NOT OF MY BLOOD, HE WAS MY SON AS TRULY AS THOR.
I WILL NOT ABANDON ANY SON OF MINE, ESPECIALLY ONE WHO HAS RETURNED TO ME FROM ACROSS THE ABYSS OF NONBEING...
...AND SECOND: YES, LOKI IS YOUNG, AND WE ARE OLD. BUT HE THUS LACKS THE WISDOM THAT COMES WITH HARD EXPERIENCE, AND THIS WE POSSESS IN QUANTITY.
SHOULD IT COME TO IT--SHOULD THIS FAMILY AGAIN BE SO CURSED AS TO PIT BROTHER AGAINST BROTHER--LOKI'S YOUTH WILL BE AS MUCH A HINDRANCE AS A HELP TO HIM.
NOW LEAVE ME. I AM WEARY OF SUCH CONJECTURE...

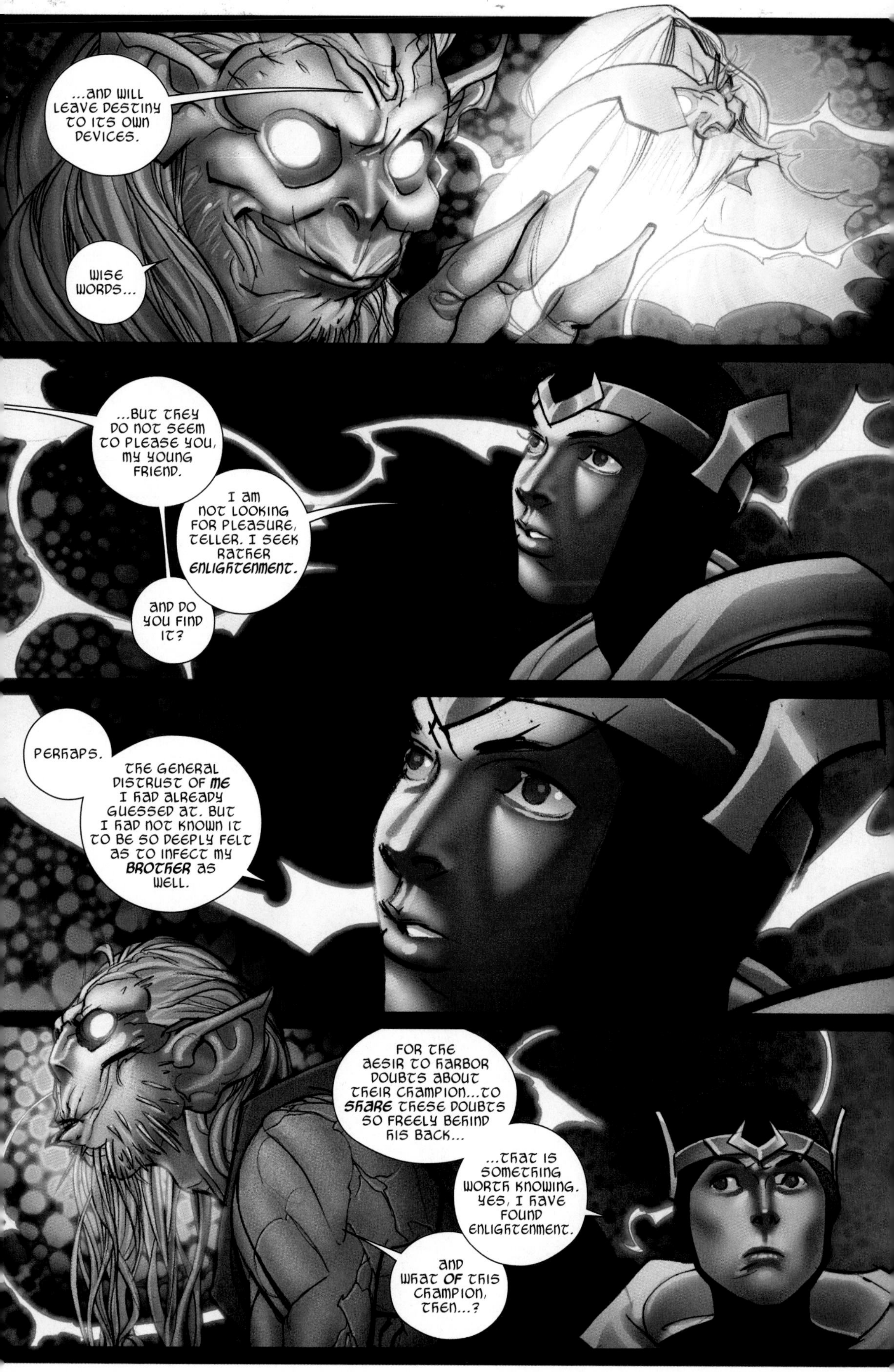

...AND WILL LEAVE DESTINY TO ITS OWN DEVICES.
WISE WORDS...
...BUT THEY DO NOT SEEM TO PLEASE YOU, MY YOUNG FRIEND.
I AM NOT LOOKING FOR PLEASURE, TELLER. I SEEK RATHER ENLIGHTENMENT.
AND DO YOU FIND IT?
PERHAPS.
THE GENERAL DISTRUST OF ME I HAD ALREADY GUESSED AT. BUT I HAD NOT KNOWN IT TO BE SO DEEPLY FELT AS TO INFECT MY BROTHER AS WELL.
FOR THE AESIR TO HARBOR DOUBTS ABOUT THEIR CHAMPION...TO SHARE THESE DOUBTS SO FREELY BEHIND HIS BACK...
...THAT IS SOMETHING WORTH KNOWING. YES, I HAVE FOUND ENLIGHTENMENT.
AND WHAT OF THIS CHAMPION, THEN...?

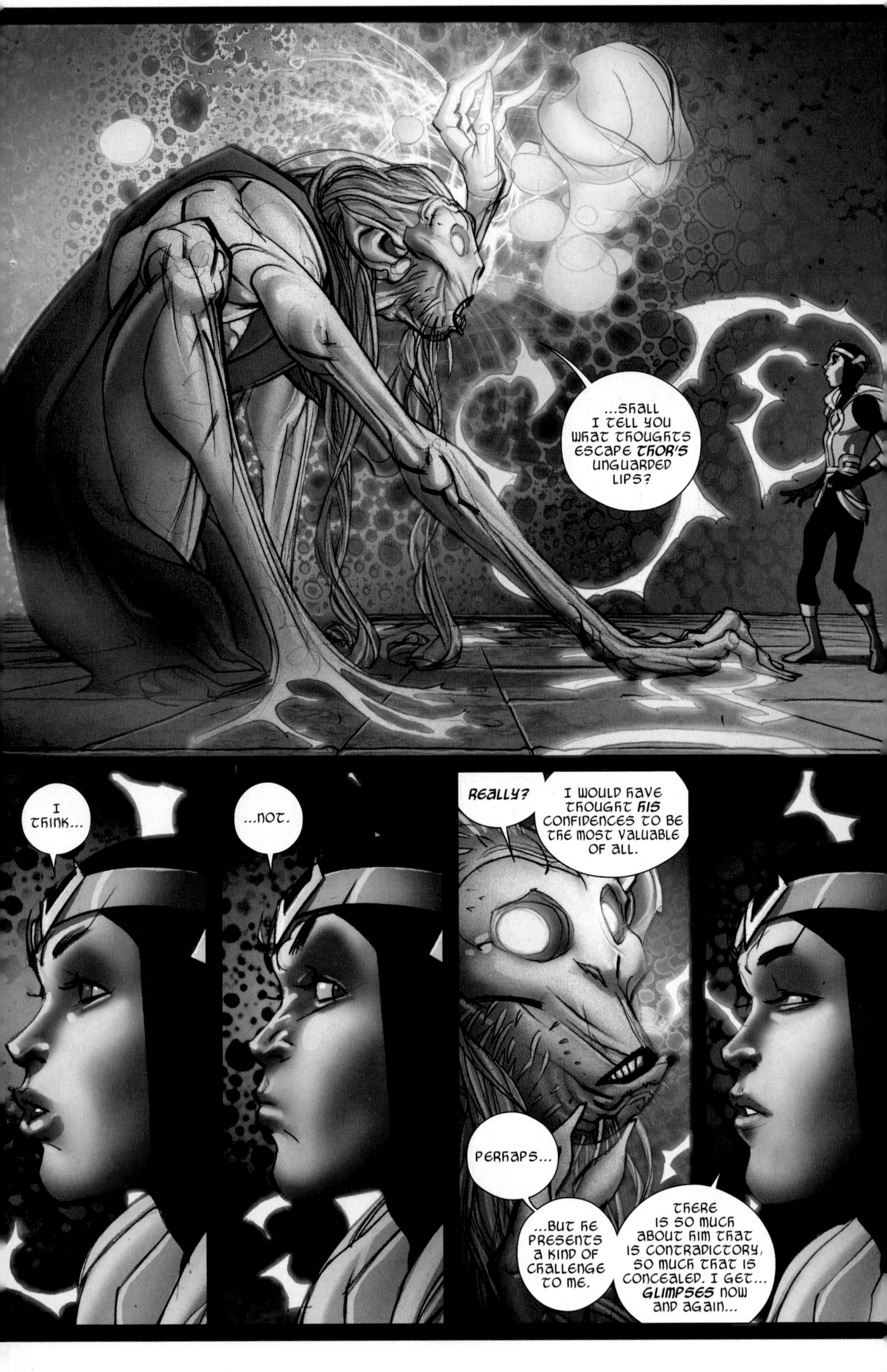
...SHALL I TELL YOU WHAT THOUGHTS ESCAPE **THOR'S** UNGUARDED LIPS?
I THINK...
...NOT.
REALLY?
I WOULD HAVE THOUGHT **HIS** CONFIDENCES TO BE THE MOST VALUABLE OF ALL.
PERHAPS...
...BUT HE PRESENTS A KIND OF CHALLENGE TO ME.
THERE IS SO MUCH ABOUT HIM THAT IS CONTRADICTORY, SO MUCH THAT IS CONCEALED. I GET... **GLIMPSES** NOW AND AGAIN...

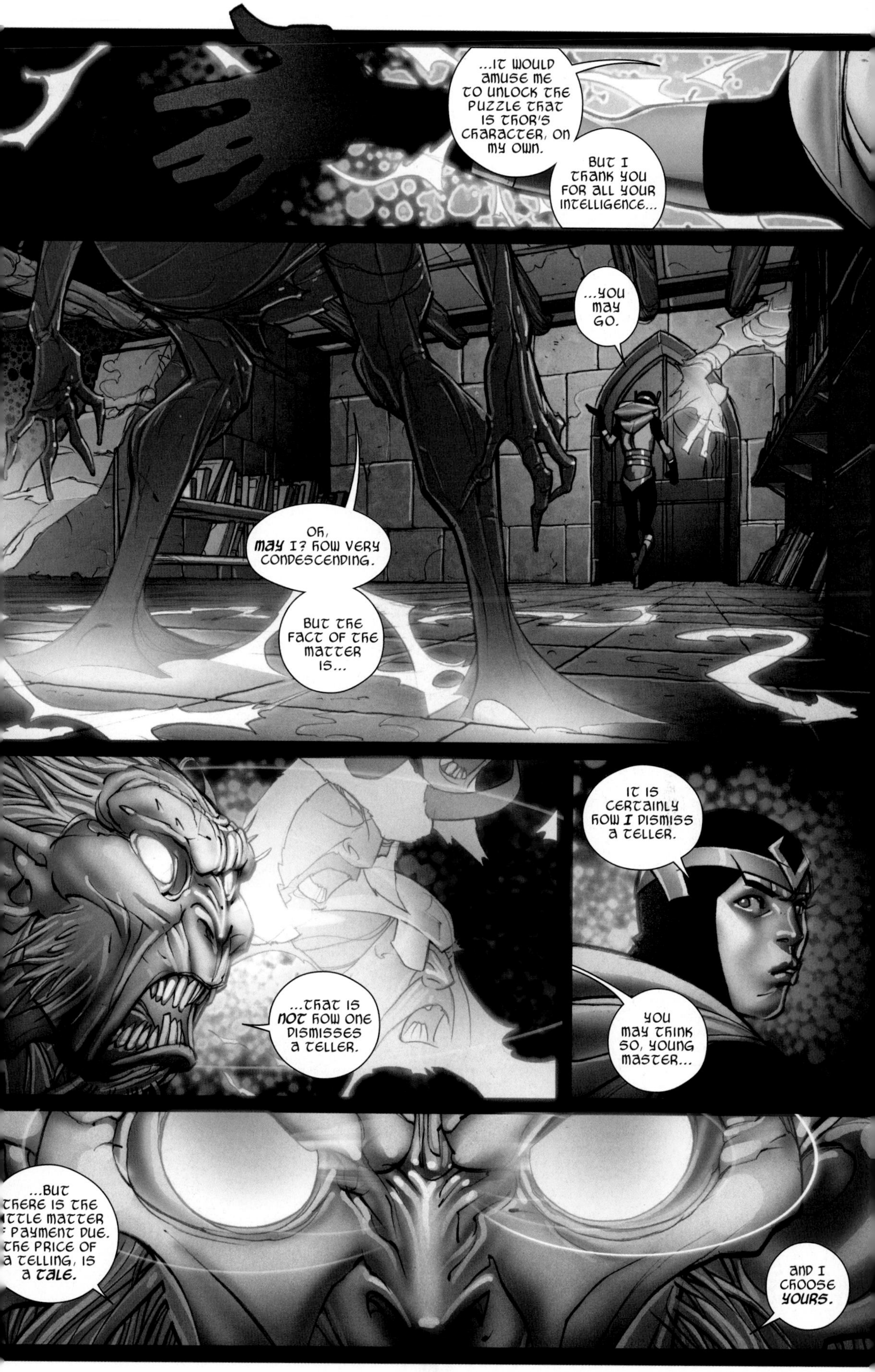
...IT WOULD AMUSE ME TO UNLOCK THE PUZZLE THAT IS THOR'S CHARACTER, ON MY OWN.
BUT I THANK YOU FOR ALL YOUR INTELLIGENCE...
...YOU MAY GO.
OH, MAY I? HOW VERY CONDESCENDING.
BUT THE FACT OF THE MATTER IS...
...THAT IS NOT HOW ONE DISMISSES A TELLER.
IT IS CERTAINLY HOW I DISMISS A TELLER.
YOU MAY THINK SO, YOUNG MASTER...
...BUT THERE IS THE TTLE MATTER F PAYMENT DUE. THE PRICE OF A TELLING, IS A TALE.
AND I CHOOSE YOURS.

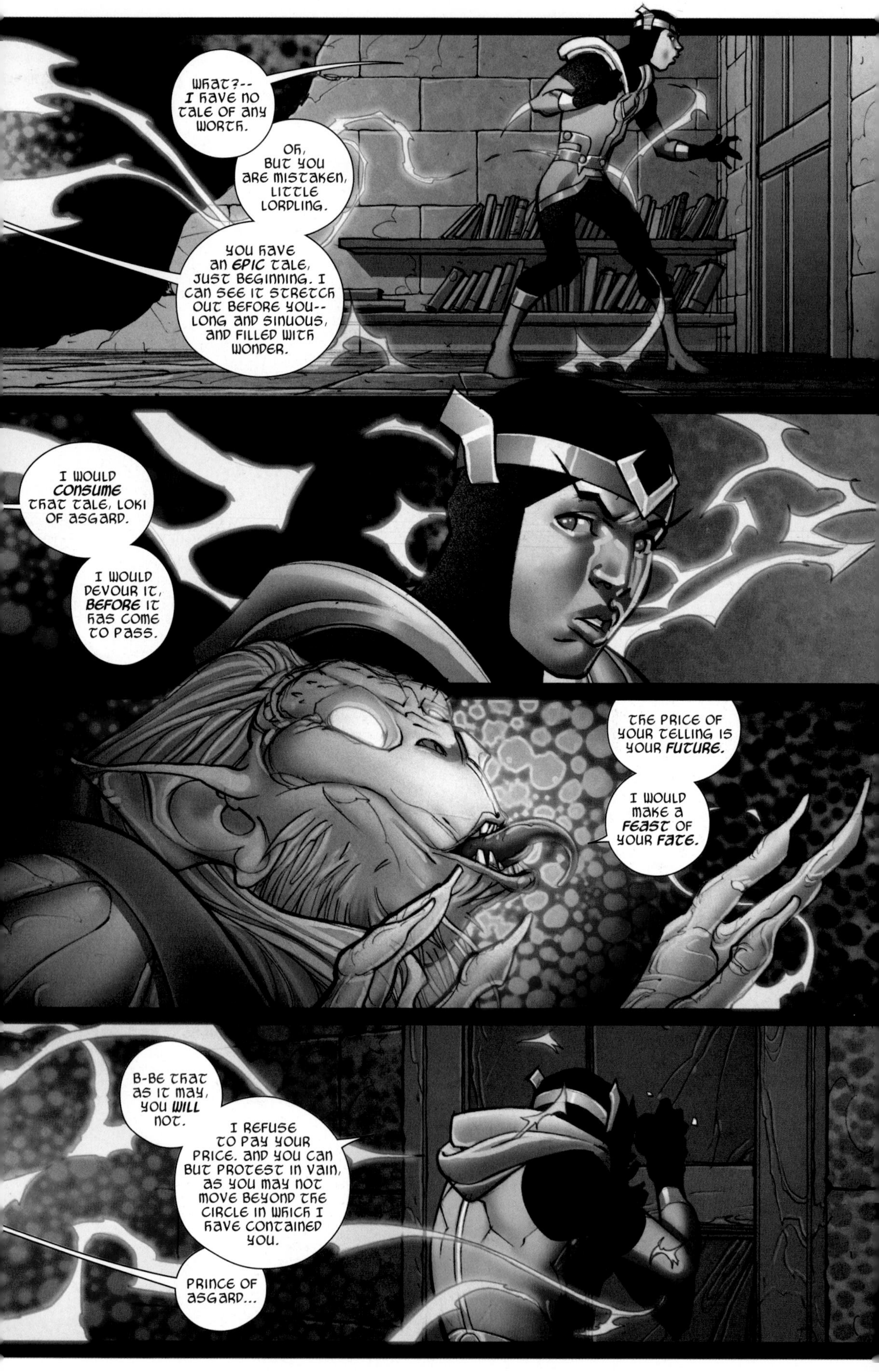
WHAT?--
I HAVE NO TALE OF ANY WORTH.
OH, BUT YOU ARE MISTAKEN, LITTLE LORDLING.
YOU HAVE AN EPIC TALE, JUST BEGINNING. I CAN SEE IT STRETCH OUT BEFORE YOU-- LONG AND SINUOUS, AND FILLED WITH WONDER.
I WOULD CONSUME THAT TALE, LOKI OF ASGARD.
I WOULD DEVOUR IT, BEFORE IT HAS COME TO PASS.
THE PRICE OF YOUR TELLING IS YOUR FUTURE.
I WOULD MAKE A FEAST OF YOUR FATE.
B-BE THAT AS IT MAY, YOU WILL NOT.
I REFUSE TO PAY YOUR PRICE. AND YOU CAN BUT PROTEST IN VAIN, AS YOU MAY NOT MOVE BEYOND THE CIRCLE IN WHICH I HAVE CONTAINED YOU.
PRINCE OF ASGARD...

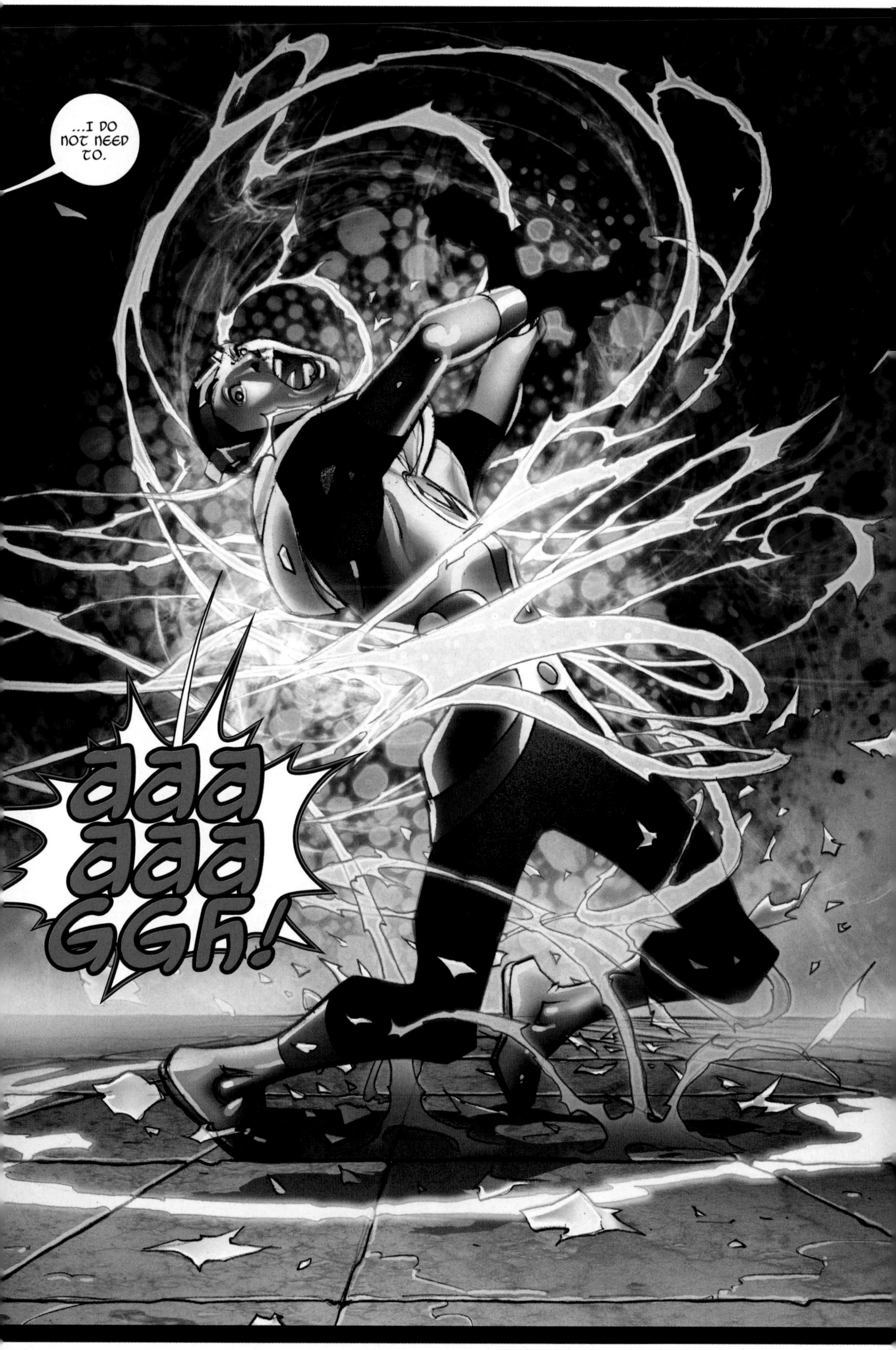
...I DO NOT NEED TO.
AAAAAAGGH!

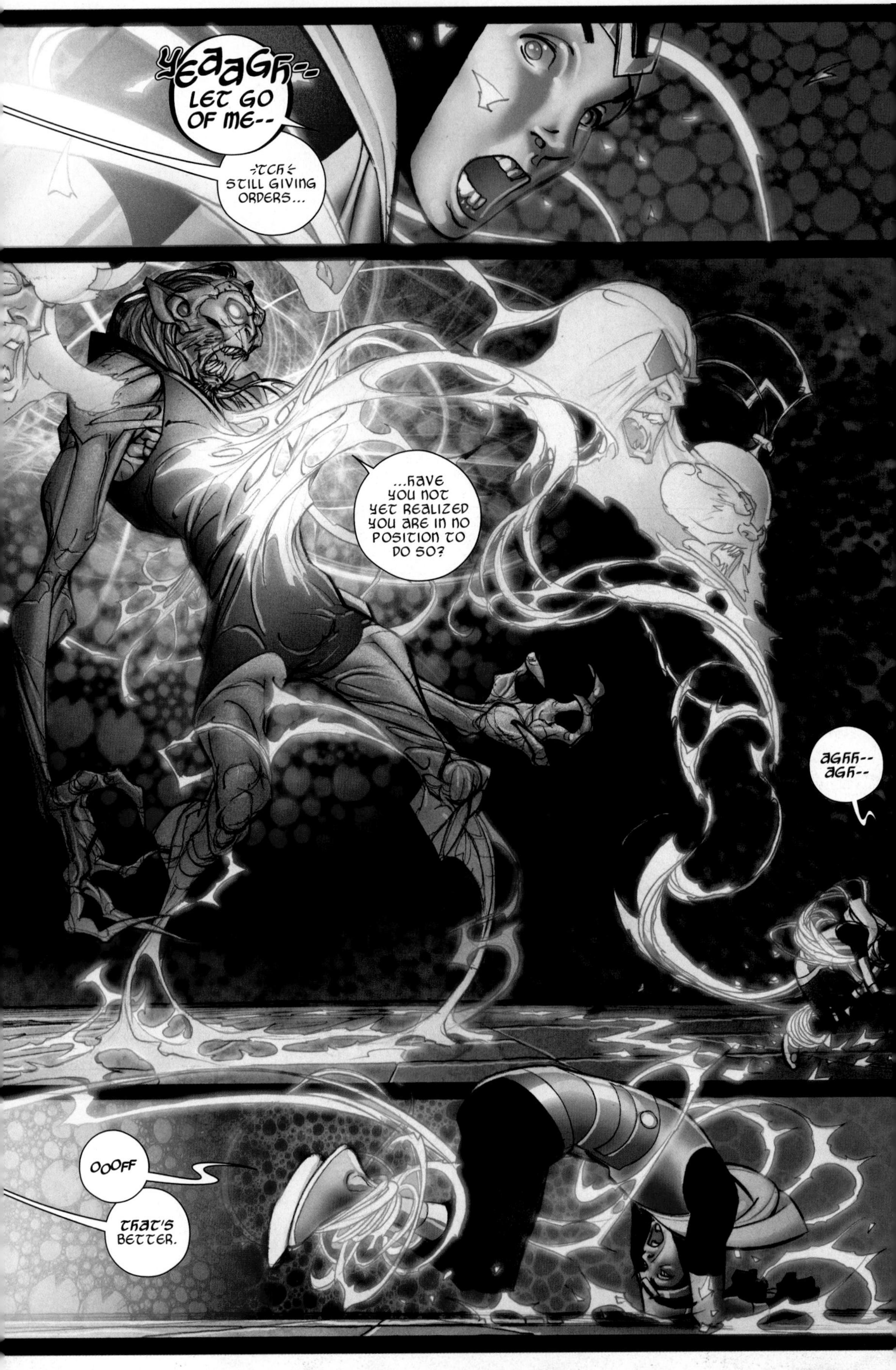
YEAAGH--
LET GO OF ME--
-TCH- STILL GIVING ORDERS...
...HAVE YOU NOT YET REALIZED YOU ARE IN NO POSITION TO DO SO?
AGHH-- AGH--
OOOFF
THAT'S BETTER.

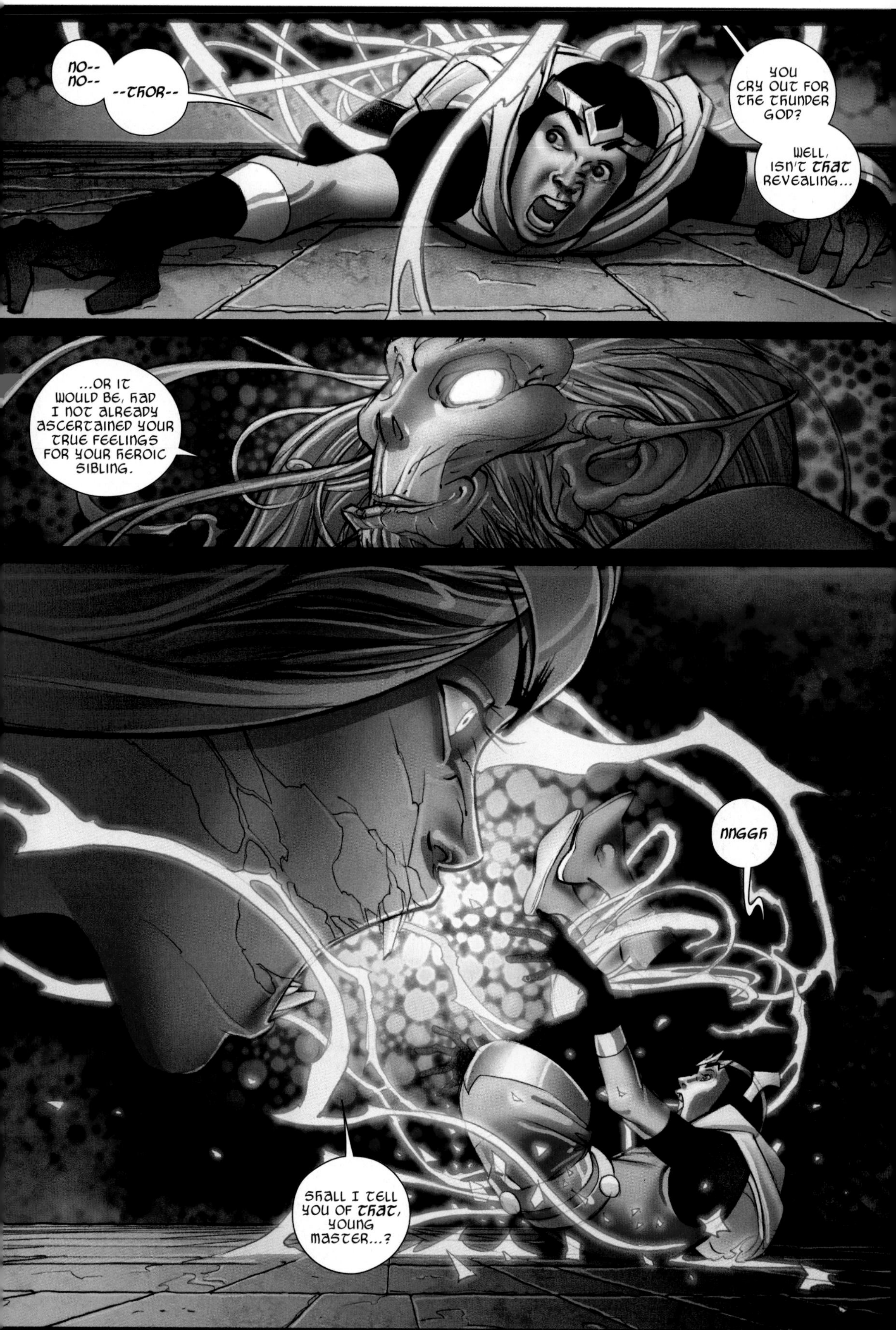
NO-- NO--
--THOR--
YOU CRY OUT FOR THE THUNDER GOD?
WELL, ISN'T THAT REVEALING...
...OR IT WOULD BE, HAD I NOT ALREADY ASCERTAINED YOUR TRUE FEELINGS FOR YOUR HEROIC SIBLING.
NNGGH
SHALL I TELL YOU OF THAT, YOUNG MASTER...?

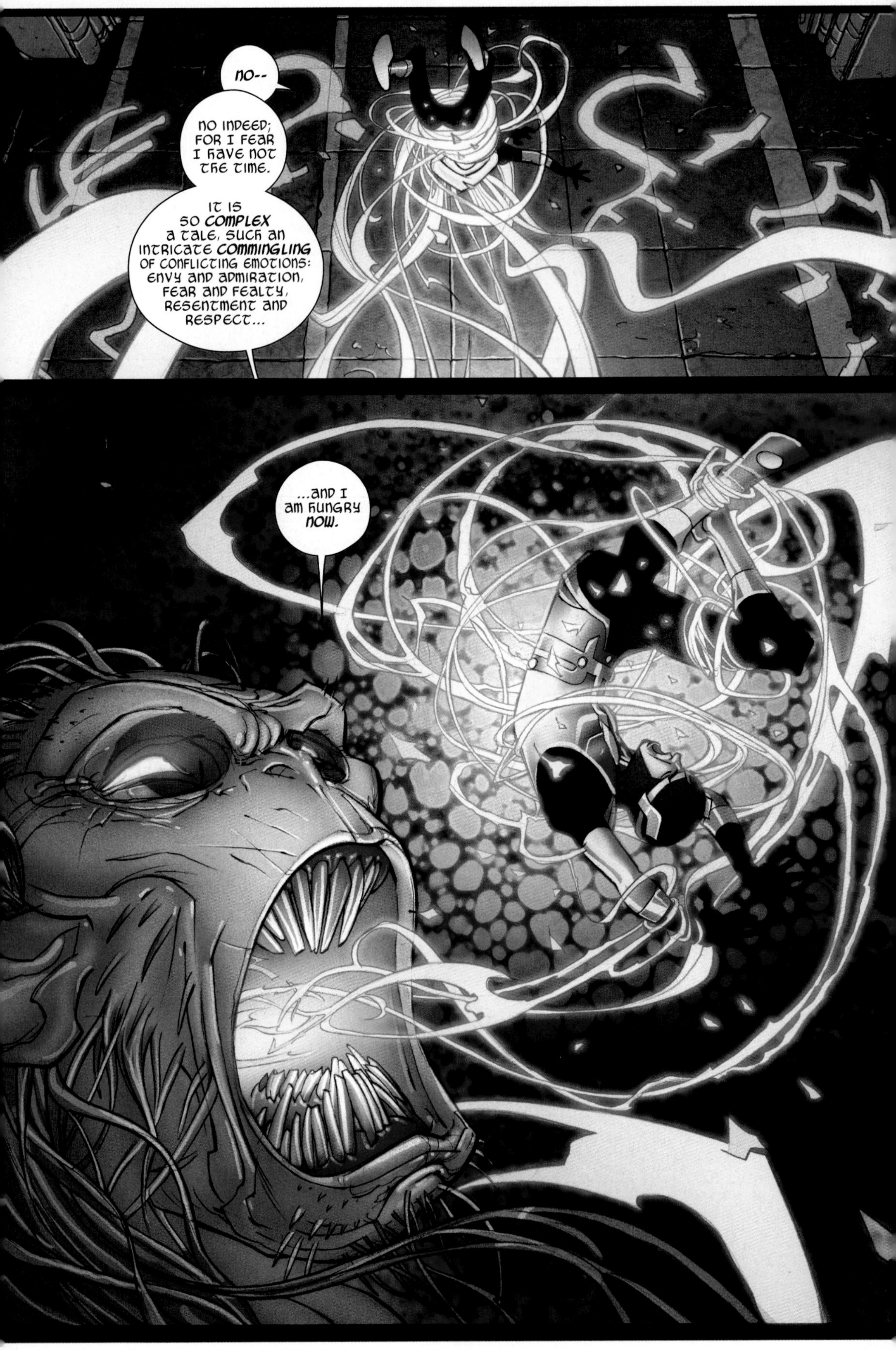
NO--
NO INDEED; FOR I FEAR I HAVE NOT THE TIME.
IT IS SO COMPLEX A TALE, SUCH AN INTRICATE COMMINGLING OF CONFLICTING EMOTIONS: ENVY AND ADMIRATION, FEAR AND FEALTY, RESENTMENT AND RESPECT...
...AND I AM HUNGRY NOW.

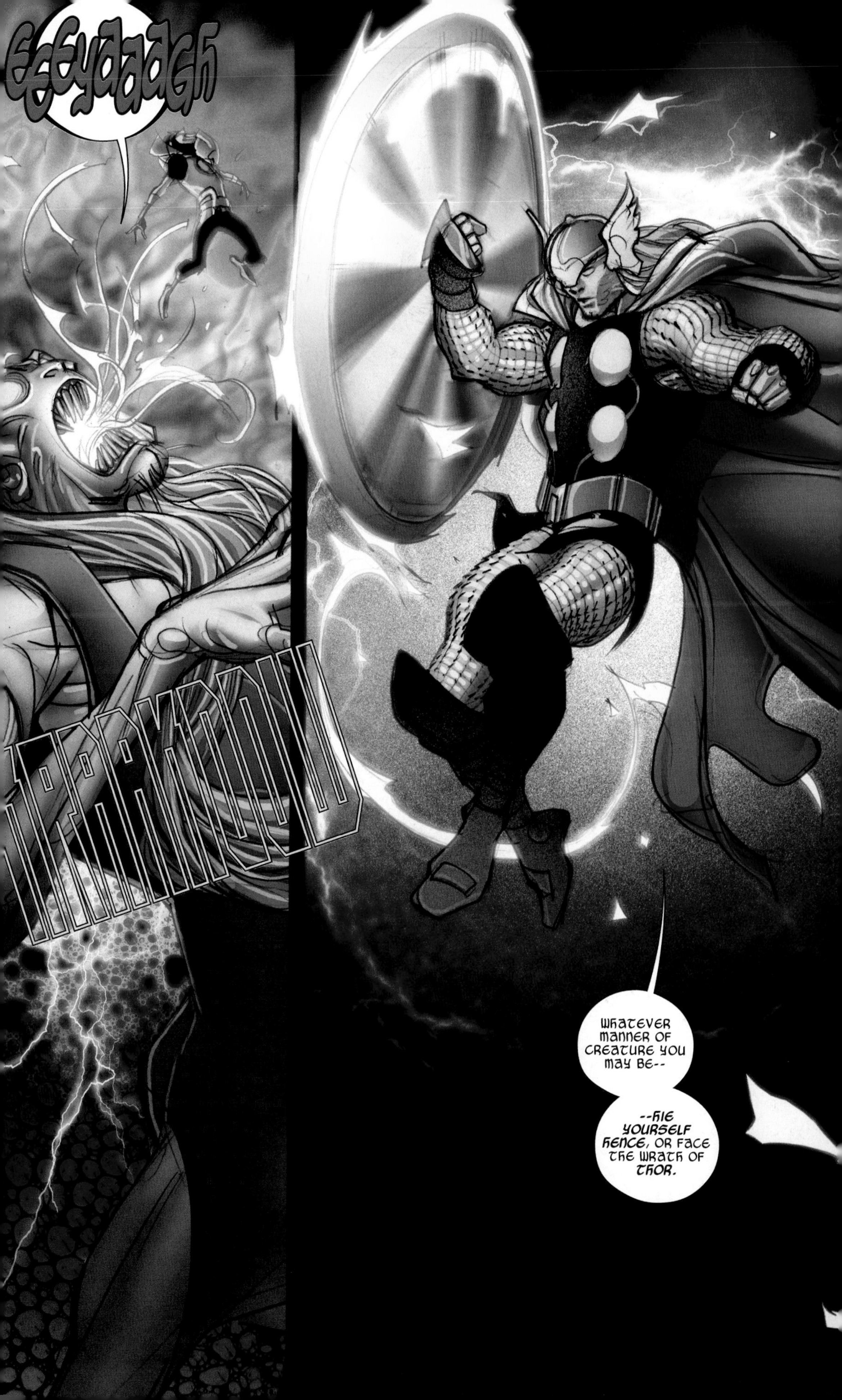

EEEYAAAAGH
KRRAKKOOM
WHATEVER MANNER OF CREATURE YOU MAY BE--
--HIE YOURSELF HENCE, OR FACE THE WRATH OF THOR.

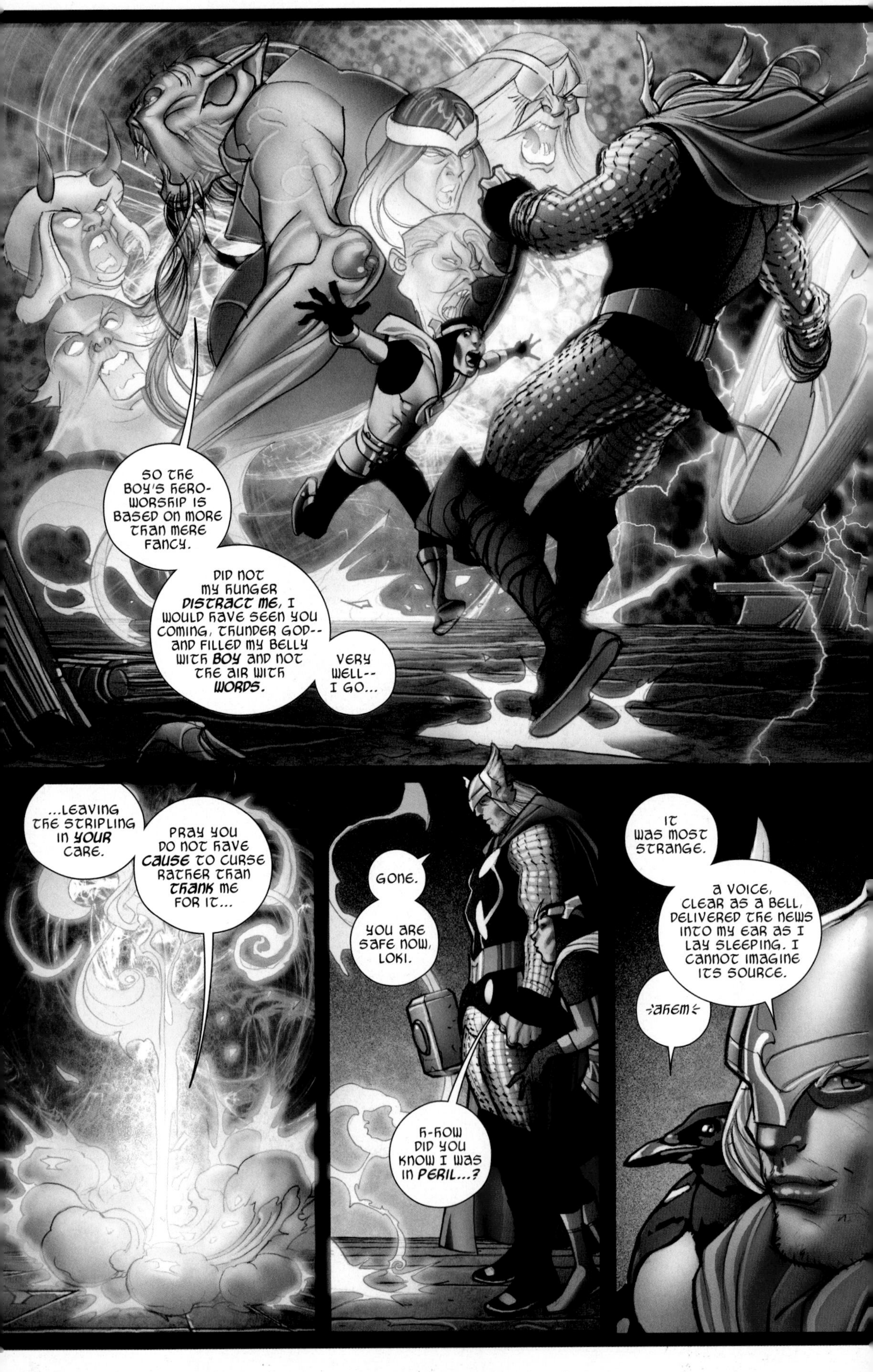
SO THE BOY'S HERO-WORSHIP IS BASED ON MORE THAN MERE FANCY.
DID NOT MY HUNGER DISTRACT ME, I WOULD HAVE SEEN YOU COMING, THUNDER GOD-- AND FILLED MY BELLY WITH BOY AND NOT THE AIR WITH WORDS.
VERY WELL-- I GO...
...LEAVING THE STRIPLING IN YOUR CARE.
PRAY YOU DO NOT HAVE CAUSE TO CURSE RATHER THAN THANK ME FOR IT...
GONE.
YOU ARE SAFE NOW, LOKI.
H-HOW DID YOU KNOW I WAS IN PERIL...?
IT WAS MOST STRANGE.
A VOICE, CLEAR AS A BELL, DELIVERED THE NEWS INTO MY EAR AS I LAY SLEEPING. I CANNOT IMAGINE ITS SOURCE.
-AHEM-

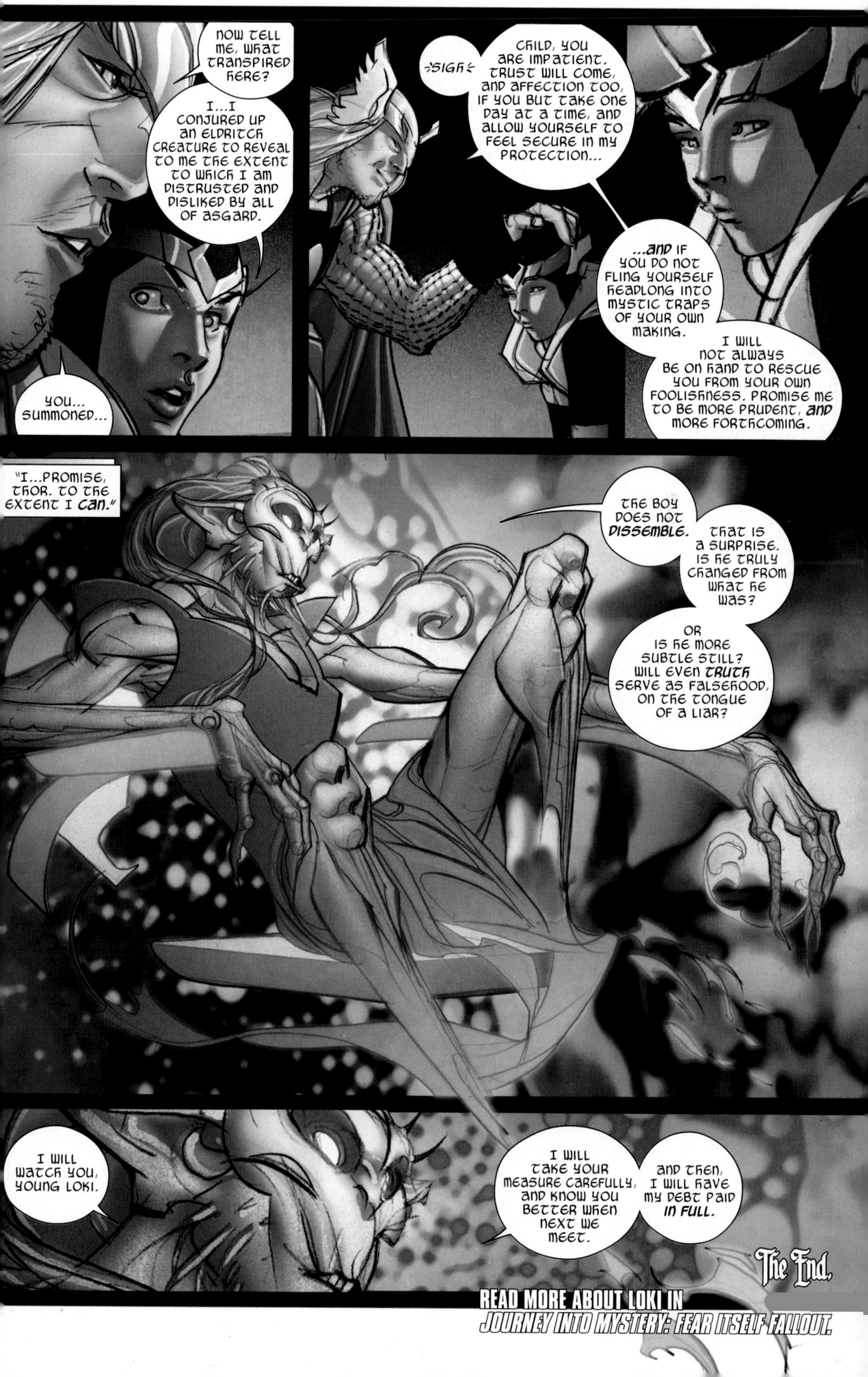
NOW TELL ME, WHAT TRANSPIRED HERE?
I...I CONJURED UP AN ELDRITCH CREATURE TO REVEAL TO ME THE EXTENT TO WHICH I AM DISTRUSTED AND DISLIKED BY ALL OF ASGARD.
YOU... SUMMONED...
⇒SIGH⇐
CHILD, YOU ARE IMPATIENT. TRUST WILL COME, AND AFFECTION TOO, IF YOU BUT TAKE ONE DAY AT A TIME, AND ALLOW YOURSELF TO FEEL SECURE IN MY PROTECTION...
...AND IF YOU DO NOT FLING YOURSELF HEADLONG INTO MYSTIC TRAPS OF YOUR OWN MAKING.
I WILL NOT ALWAYS BE ON HAND TO RESCUE YOU FROM YOUR OWN FOOLISHNESS. PROMISE ME TO BE MORE PRUDENT, AND MORE FORTHCOMING.
"I...PROMISE, THOR. TO THE EXTENT I CAN."
THE BOY DOES NOT DISSEMBLE.
THAT IS A SURPRISE. IS HE TRULY CHANGED FROM WHAT HE WAS?
OR IS HE MORE SUBTLE STILL? WILL EVEN TRUTH SERVE AS FALSEHOOD, ON THE TONGUE OF A LIAR?
I WILL WATCH YOU, YOUNG LOKI.
I WILL TAKE YOUR MEASURE CAREFULLY, AND KNOW YOU BETTER WHEN NEXT WE MEET.
AND THEN, I WILL HAVE MY DEBT PAID IN FULL.
The End.
READ MORE ABOUT LOKI IN
JOURNEY INTO MYSTERY: FEAR ITSELF FALLOUT.

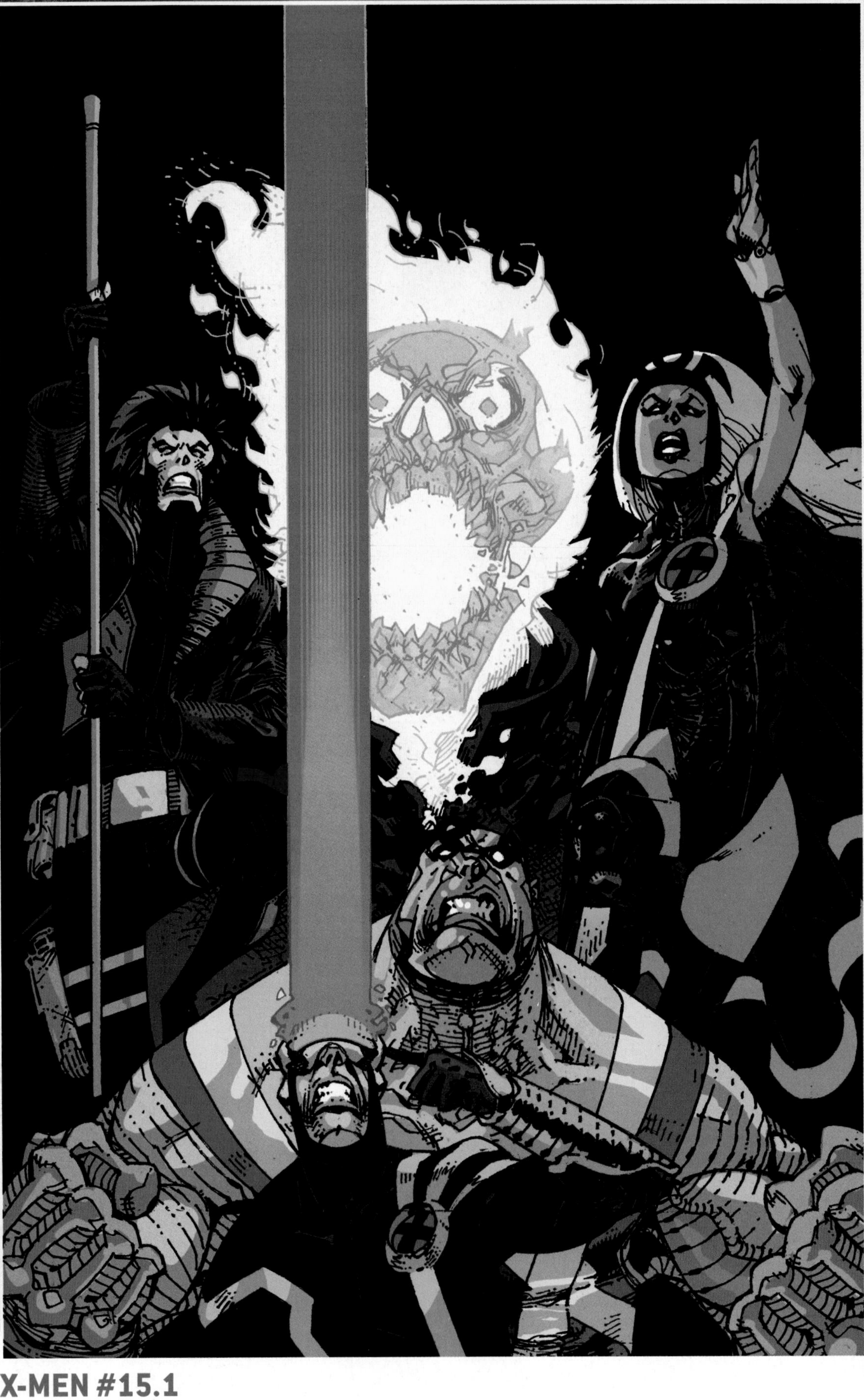

X-MEN #15.1

PREVIOUSLY IN

Born with special abilities beyond those of normal men, but hated and feared by the masses of humanity, the mutant species has long been put upon. The X-Men are looking to change that. Banded together to fight for the good of both mutants and humans, the X-Men seek to change the world's view of mutantkind.

They have a rocky road ahead.

"HELL TO PAY"

Written by Victor Gischler
Art by Will Conrad
Colored by Brian Reber
Lettered by VC's Joe Caramagna
Cover by Jason Pearson
Assistant Editor: Jordan D. White
Associate Editor: Daniel Ketchum
Editor: Nick Lowe
Editor in Chief: Axel Alonso
Chief Creative Officer: Joe Quesada
Publisher: Dan Buckley
Executive Producer: Alan Fine

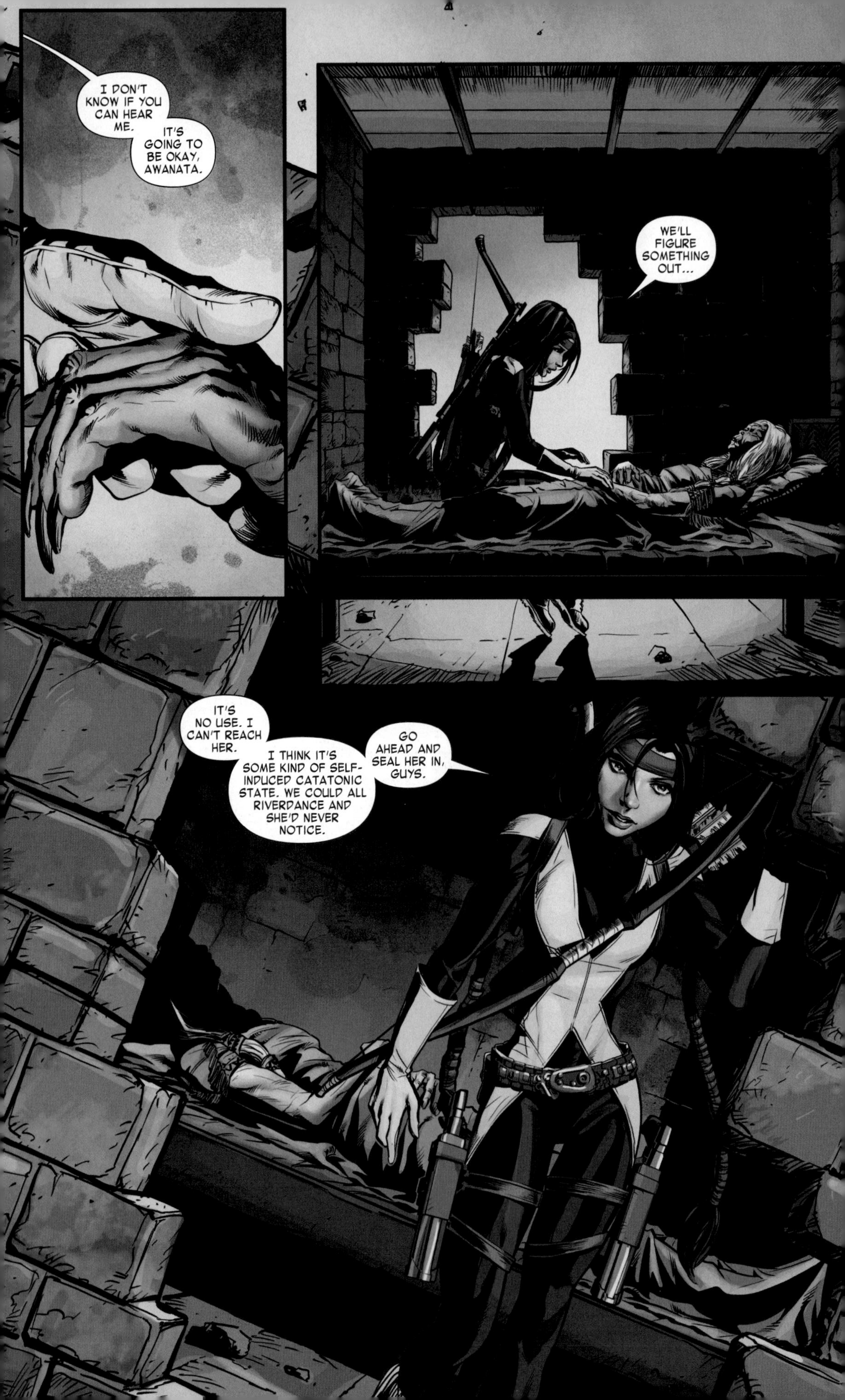
I DON'T KNOW IF YOU CAN HEAR ME.
IT'S GOING TO BE OKAY, AWANATA.
WE'LL FIGURE SOMETHING OUT...
IT'S NO USE. I CAN'T REACH HER.
I THINK IT'S SOME KIND OF SELF-INDUCED CATATONIC STATE. WE COULD ALL RIVERDANCE AND SHE'D NEVER NOTICE.
GO AHEAD AND SEAL HER IN, GUYS.

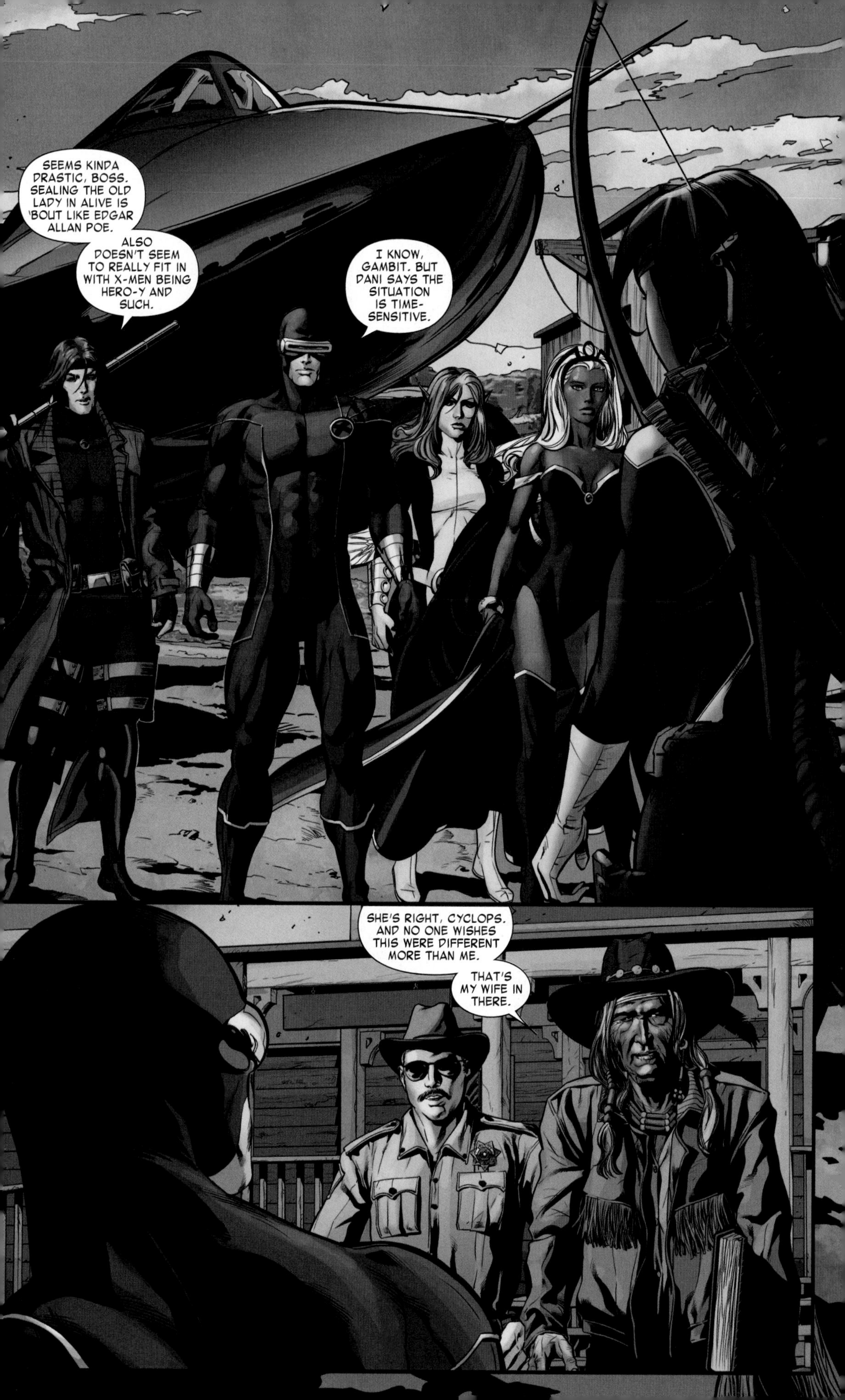
SEEMS KINDA DRASTIC, BOSS. SEALING THE OLD LADY IN ALIVE IS 'BOUT LIKE EDGAR ALLAN POE.
ALSO DOESN'T SEEM TO REALLY FIT IN WITH X-MEN BEING HERO-Y AND SUCH.
I KNOW, GAMBIT. BUT DANI SAYS THE SITUATION IS TIME-SENSITIVE.
SHE'S RIGHT, CYCLOPS. AND NO ONE WISHES THIS WERE DIFFERENT MORE THAN ME.
THAT'S MY WIFE IN THERE.

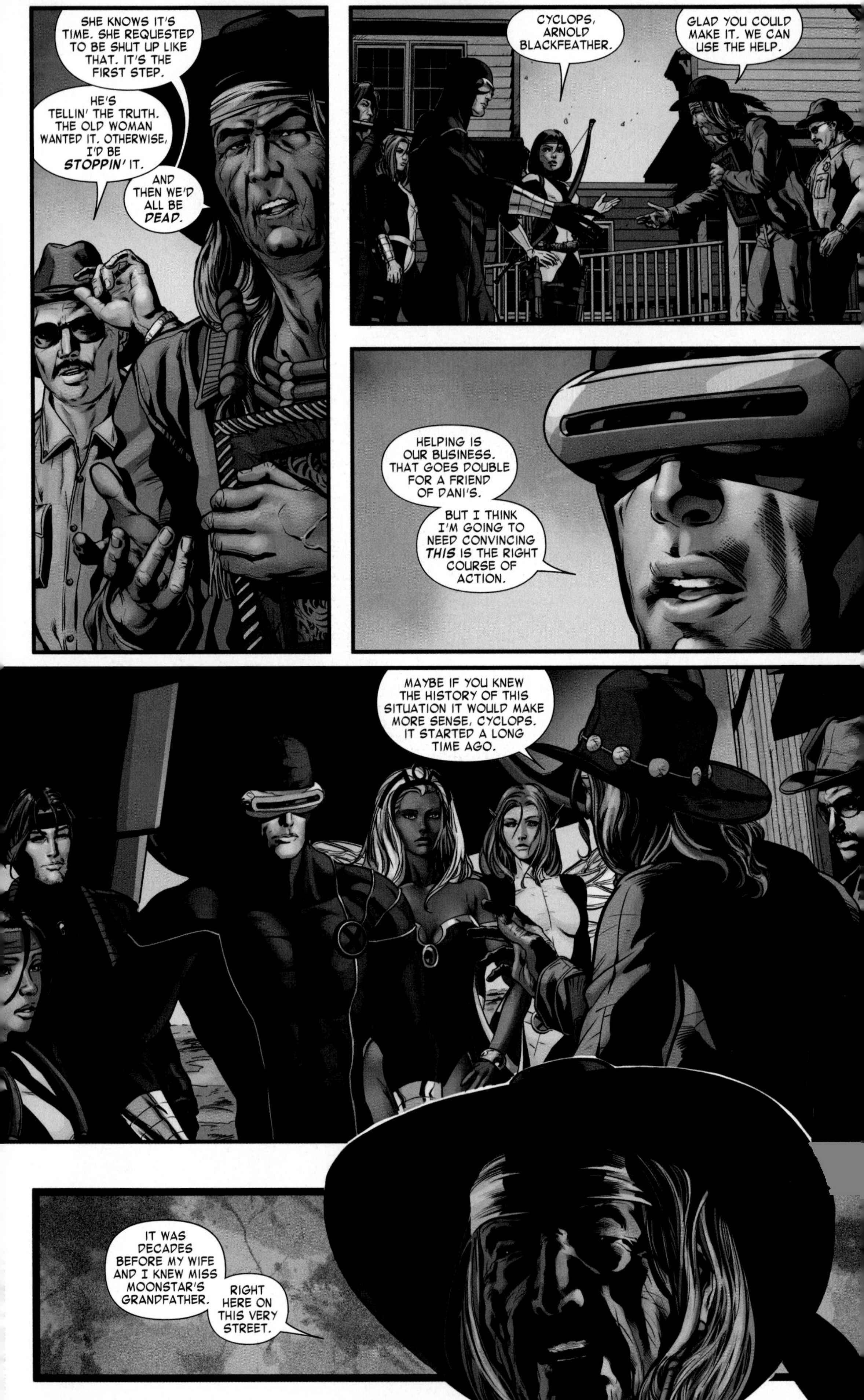
SHE KNOWS IT'S TIME. SHE REQUESTED TO BE SHUT UP LIKE THAT. IT'S THE FIRST STEP.
HE'S TELLIN' THE TRUTH. THE OLD WOMAN WANTED IT. OTHERWISE, I'D BE STOPPIN' IT.
AND THEN WE'D ALL BE DEAD.
CYCLOPS, ARNOLD BLACKFEATHER.
GLAD YOU COULD MAKE IT. WE CAN USE THE HELP.
HELPING IS OUR BUSINESS. THAT GOES DOUBLE FOR A FRIEND OF DANI'S.
BUT I THINK I'M GOING TO NEED CONVINCING THIS IS THE RIGHT COURSE OF ACTION.
MAYBE IF YOU KNEW THE HISTORY OF THIS SITUATION IT WOULD MAKE MORE SENSE, CYCLOPS. IT STARTED A LONG TIME AGO.
IT WAS DECADES BEFORE MY WIFE AND I KNEW MISS MOONSTAR'S GRANDFATHER.
RIGHT HERE ON THIS VERY STREET.

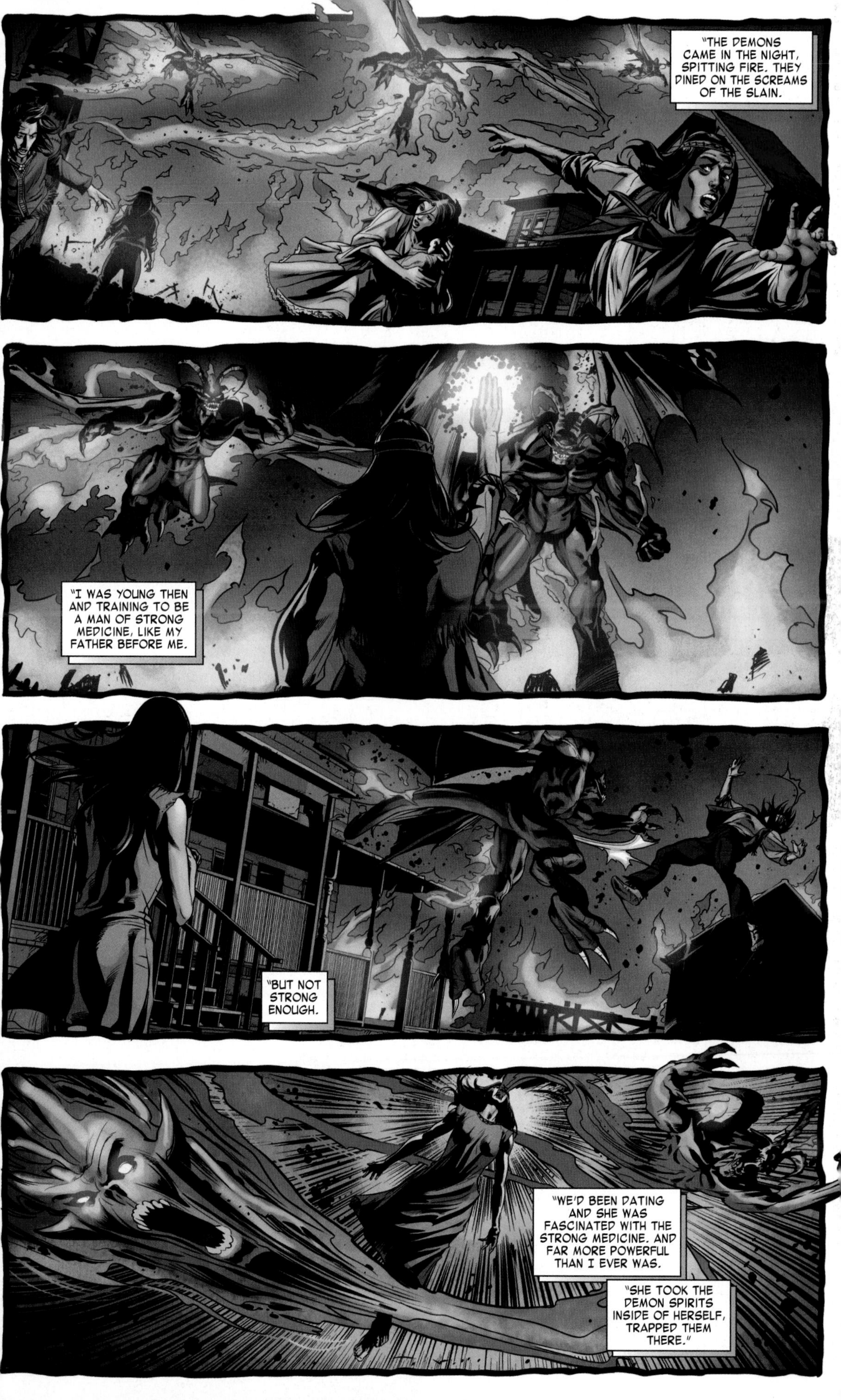
"THE DEMONS CAME IN THE NIGHT, SPITTING FIRE. THEY DINED ON THE SCREAMS OF THE SLAIN.
"I WAS YOUNG THEN AND TRAINING TO BE A MAN OF STRONG MEDICINE, LIKE MY FATHER BEFORE ME.
"BUT NOT STRONG ENOUGH.
"WE'D BEEN DATING AND SHE WAS FASCINATED WITH THE STRONG MEDICINE. AND FAR MORE POWERFUL THAN I EVER WAS.
"SHE TOOK THE DEMON SPIRITS INSIDE OF HERSELF, TRAPPED THEM THERE."

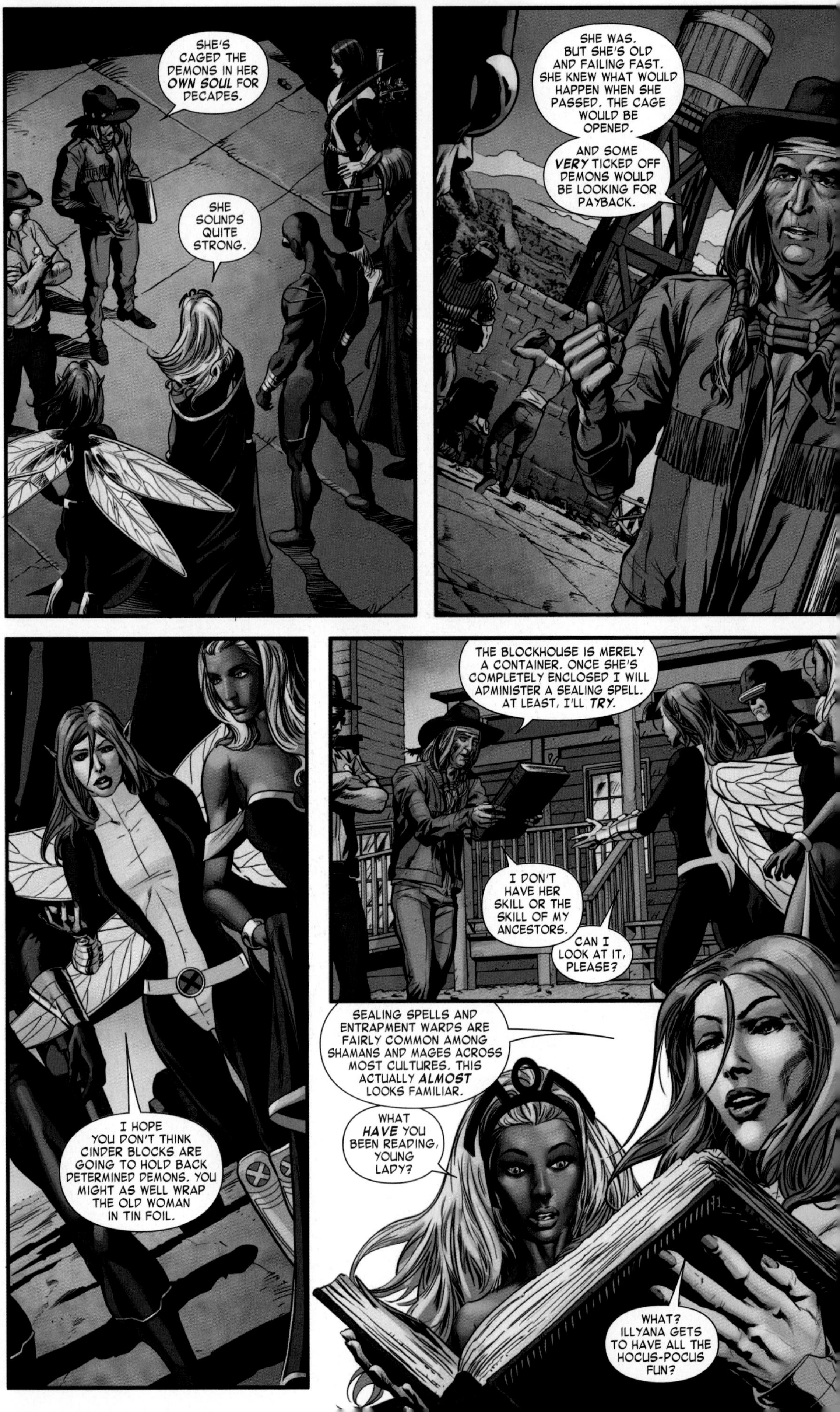
SHE'S CAGED THE DEMONS IN HER OWN SOUL FOR DECADES.
SHE SOUNDS QUITE STRONG.
SHE WAS. BUT SHE'S OLD AND FAILING FAST. SHE KNEW WHAT WOULD HAPPEN WHEN SHE PASSED. THE CAGE WOULD BE OPENED.
AND SOME VERY TICKED OFF DEMONS WOULD BE LOOKING FOR PAYBACK.
I HOPE YOU DON'T THINK CINDER BLOCKS ARE GOING TO HOLD BACK DETERMINED DEMONS. YOU MIGHT AS WELL WRAP THE OLD WOMAN IN TIN FOIL.
THE BLOCKHOUSE IS MERELY A CONTAINER. ONCE SHE'S COMPLETELY ENCLOSED I WILL ADMINISTER A SEALING SPELL. AT LEAST, I'LL TRY.
I DON'T HAVE HER SKILL OR THE SKILL OF MY ANCESTORS.
CAN I LOOK AT IT, PLEASE?
SEALING SPELLS AND ENTRAPMENT WARDS ARE FAIRLY COMMON AMONG SHAMANS AND MAGES ACROSS MOST CULTURES. THIS ACTUALLY ALMOST LOOKS FAMILIAR.
WHAT HAVE YOU BEEN READING, YOUNG LADY?
WHAT? ILLYANA GETS TO HAVE ALL THE HOCUS-POCUS FUN?

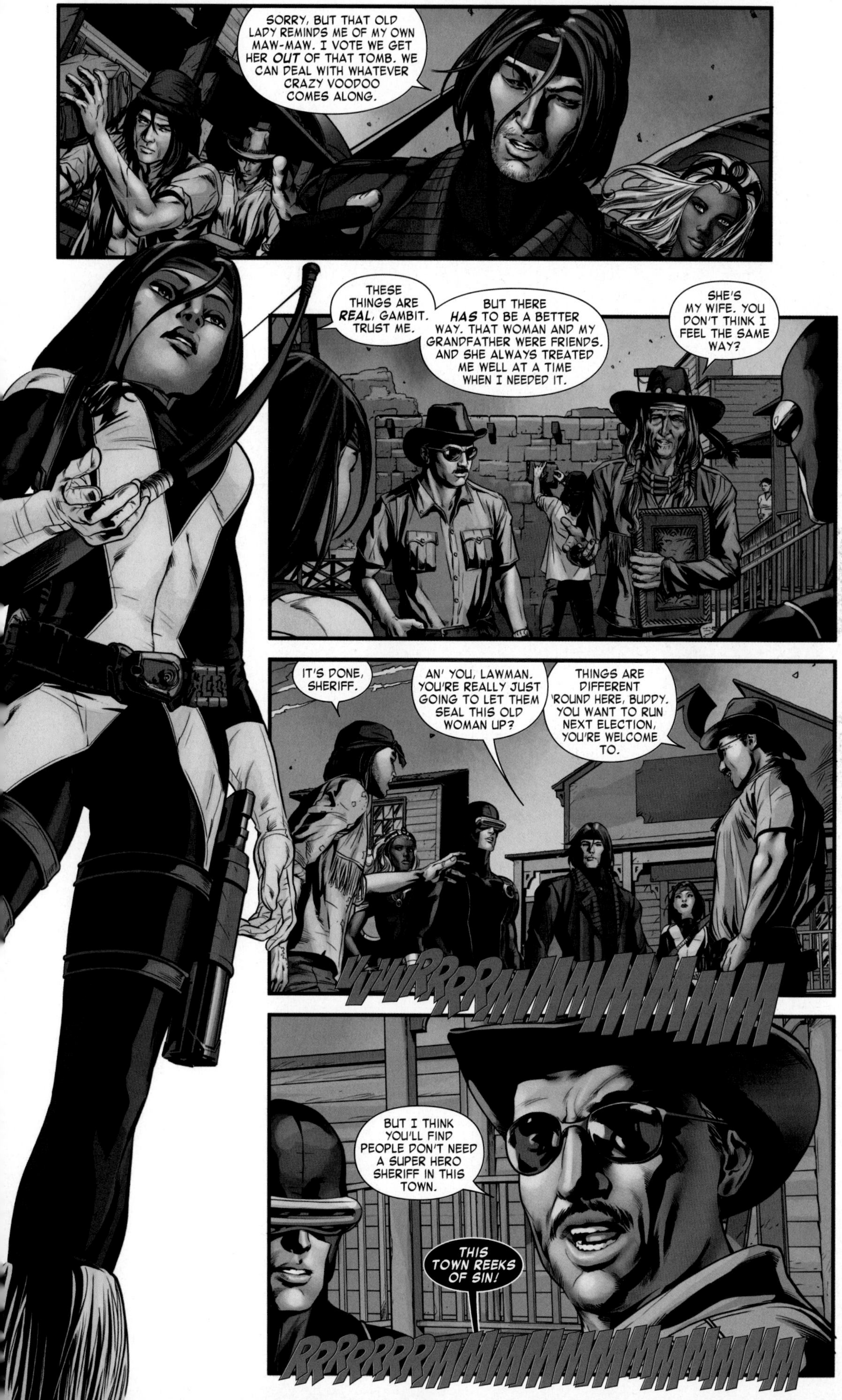
SORRY, BUT THAT OLD LADY REMINDS ME OF MY OWN MAW-MAW. I VOTE WE GET HER OUT OF THAT TOMB. WE CAN DEAL WITH WHATEVER CRAZY VOODOO COMES ALONG.
THESE THINGS ARE REAL, GAMBIT. TRUST ME.
BUT THERE HAS TO BE A BETTER WAY. THAT WOMAN AND MY GRANDFATHER WERE FRIENDS. AND SHE ALWAYS TREATED ME WELL AT A TIME WHEN I NEEDED IT.
SHE'S MY WIFE. YOU DON'T THINK I FEEL THE SAME WAY?
IT'S DONE, SHERIFF.
AN' YOU, LAWMAN. YOU'RE REALLY JUST GOING TO LET THEM SEAL THIS OLD WOMAN UP?
THINGS ARE DIFFERENT 'ROUND HERE, BUDDY. YOU WANT TO RUN NEXT ELECTION, YOU'RE WELCOME TO.
VVVVRRRRRMMMMMMMMMM
BUT I THINK YOU'LL FIND PEOPLE DON'T NEED A SUPER HERO SHERIFF IN THIS TOWN.
THIS TOWN REEKS OF SIN!
RRRRRRMMMMMMMMMMMMMM

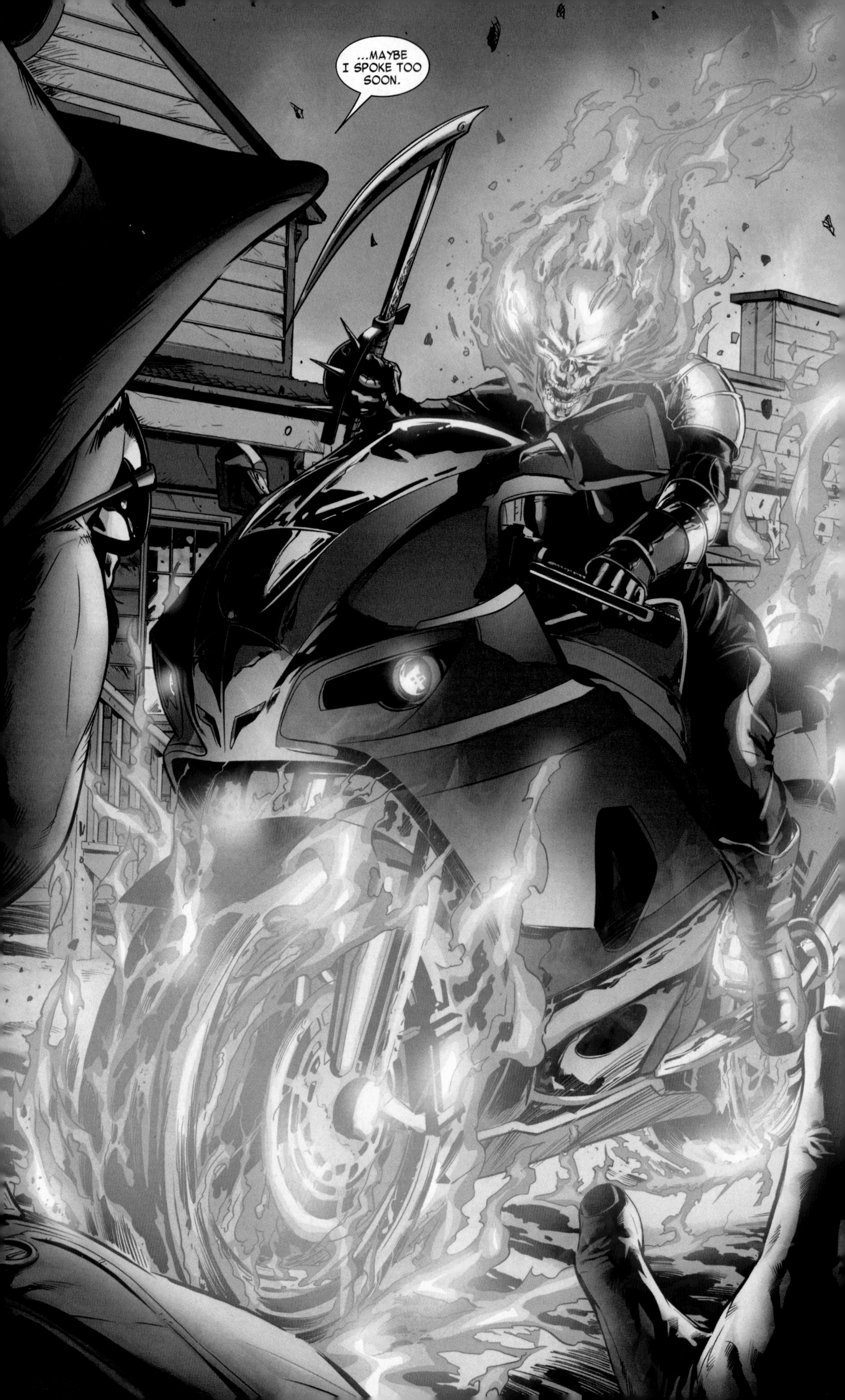
...MAYBE I SPOKE TOO SOON.

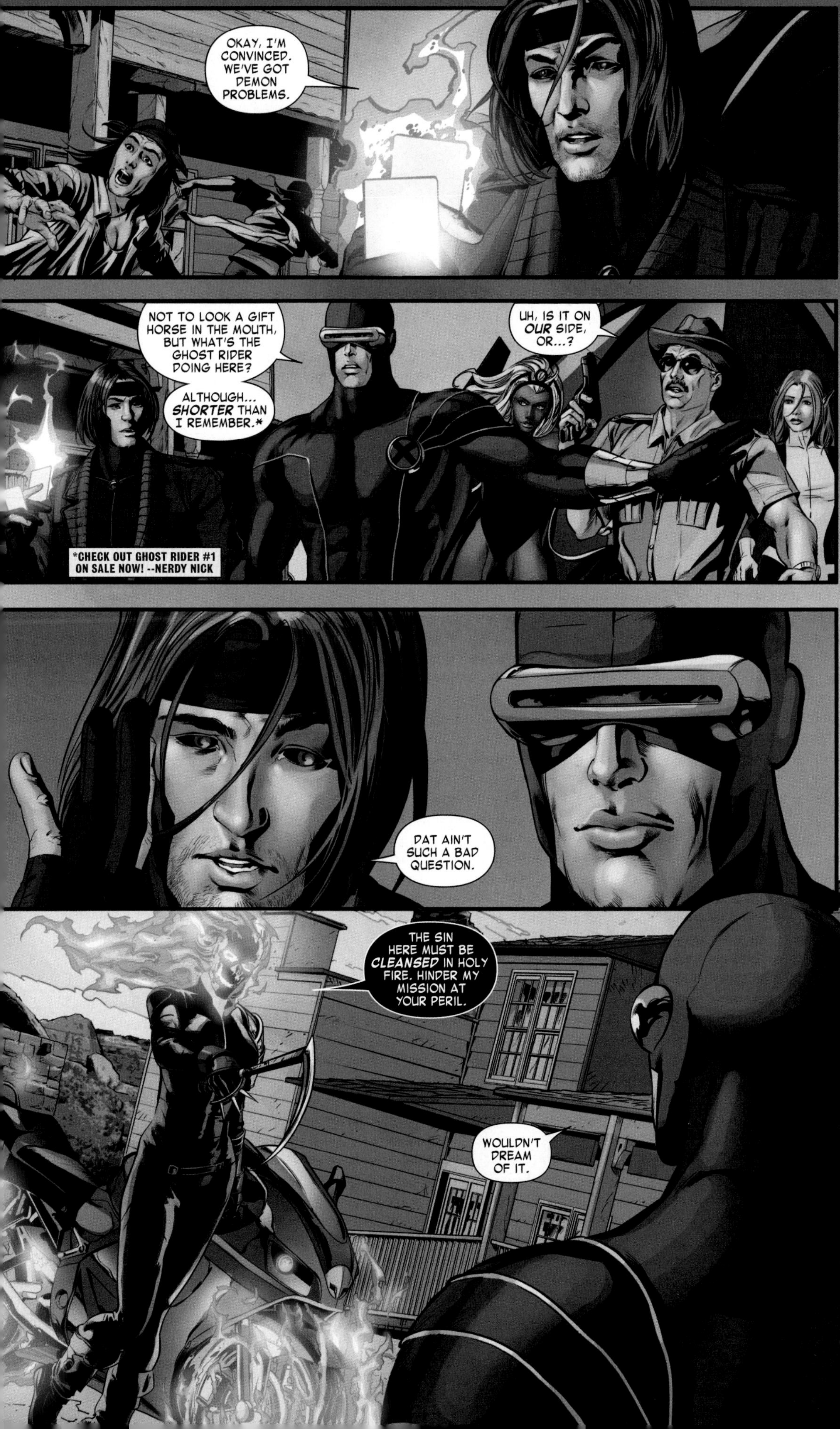

OKAY, I'M CONVINCED. WE'VE GOT DEMON PROBLEMS.
NOT TO LOOK A GIFT HORSE IN THE MOUTH, BUT WHAT'S THE GHOST RIDER DOING HERE?
ALTHOUGH... SHORTER THAN I REMEMBER.*
UH, IS IT ON OUR SIDE, OR...?
*CHECK OUT GHOST RIDER #1 ON SALE NOW! --NERDY NICK
DAT AIN'T SUCH A BAD QUESTION.
THE SIN HERE MUST BE CLEANSED IN HOLY FIRE. HINDER MY MISSION AT YOUR PERIL.
WOULDN'T DREAM OF IT.

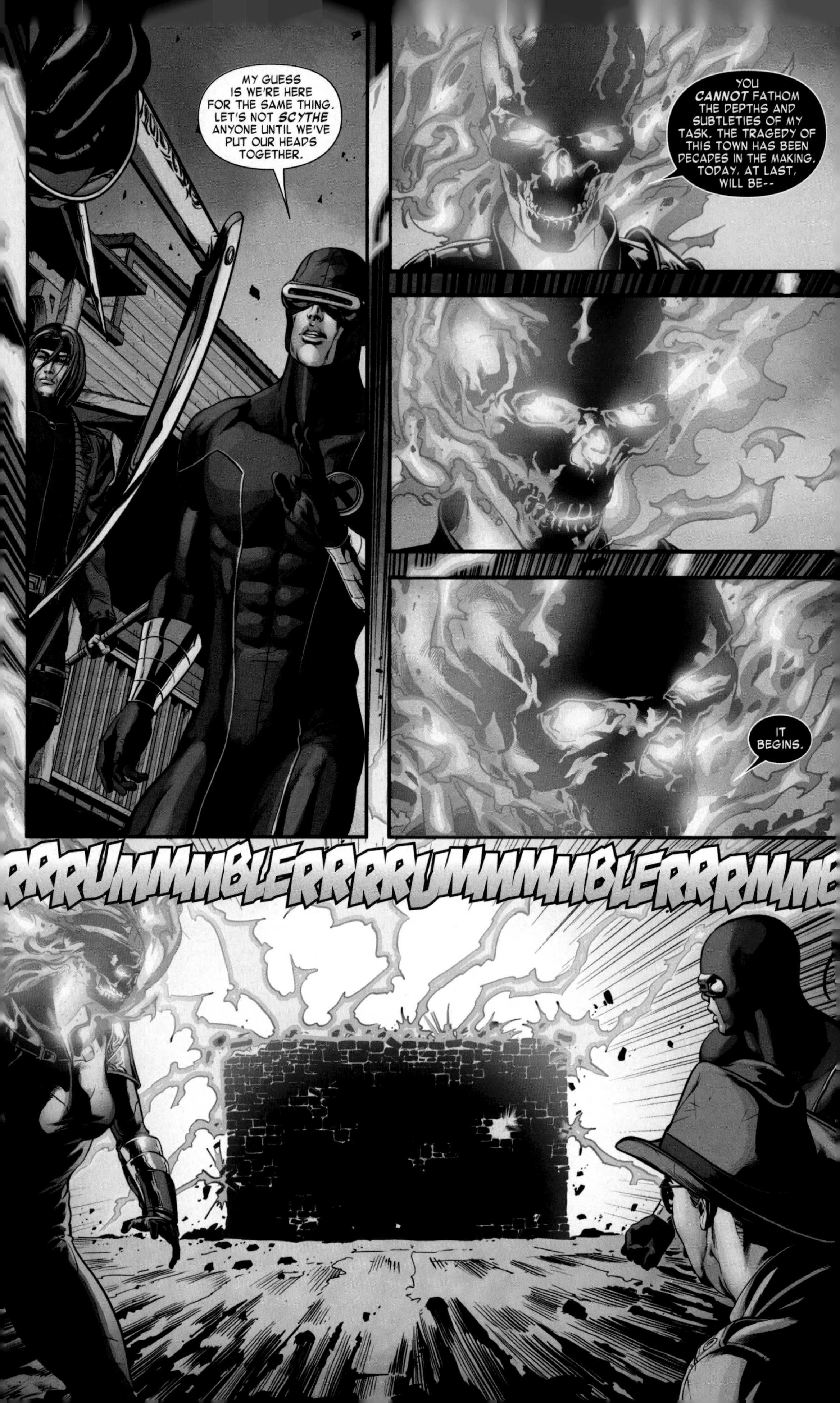
MY GUESS IS WE'RE HERE FOR THE SAME THING. LET'S NOT SCYTHE ANYONE UNTIL WE'VE PUT OUR HEADS TOGETHER.
YOU CANNOT FATHOM THE DEPTHS AND SUBTLETIES OF MY TASK. THE TRAGEDY OF THIS TOWN HAS BEEN DECADES IN THE MAKING. TODAY, AT LAST, WILL BE--
IT BEGINS.
RRRUMMMMBLERRRRUMMMMMBLERRRMMM

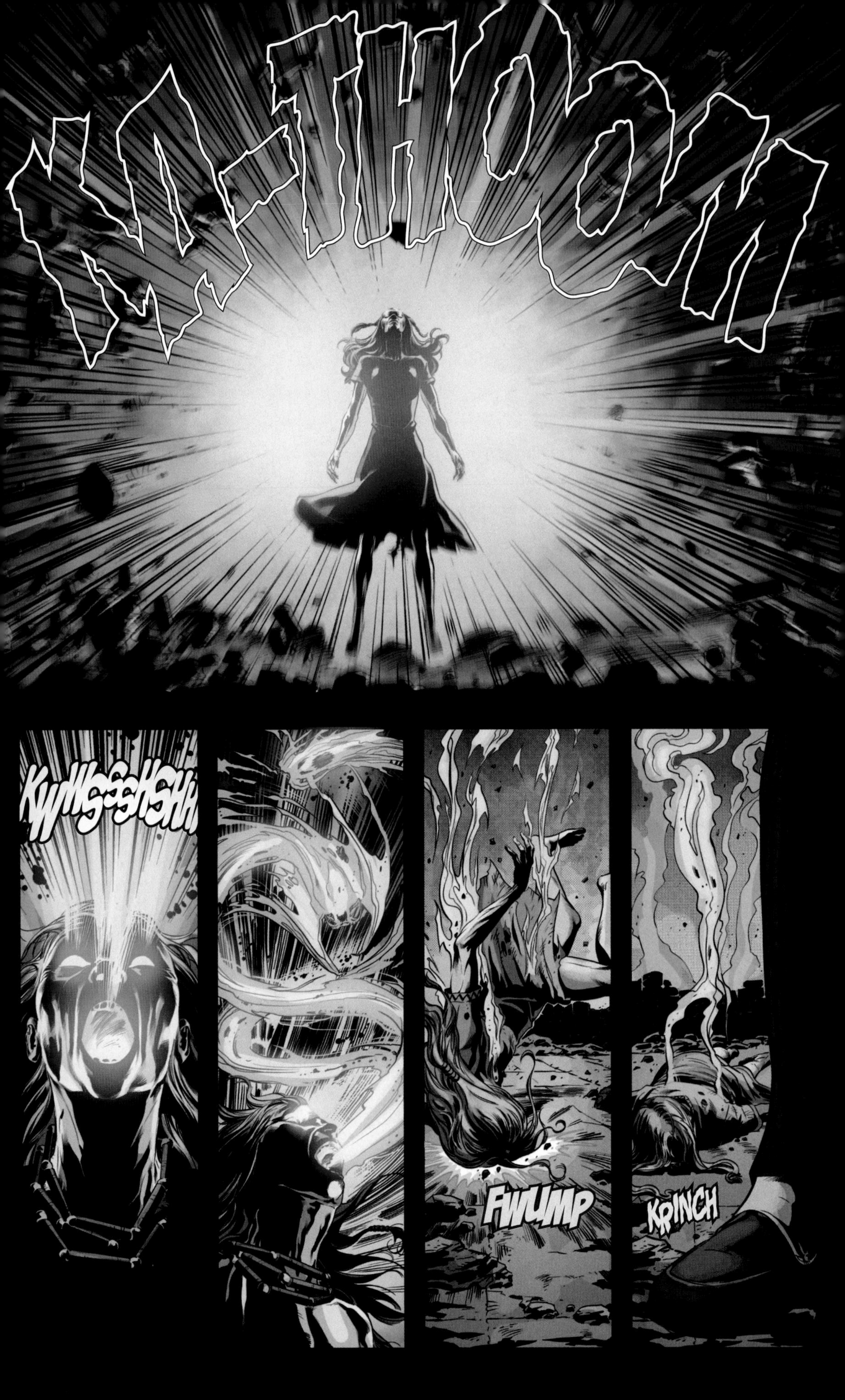
KA-THOOM
FWUMP
KRINCH

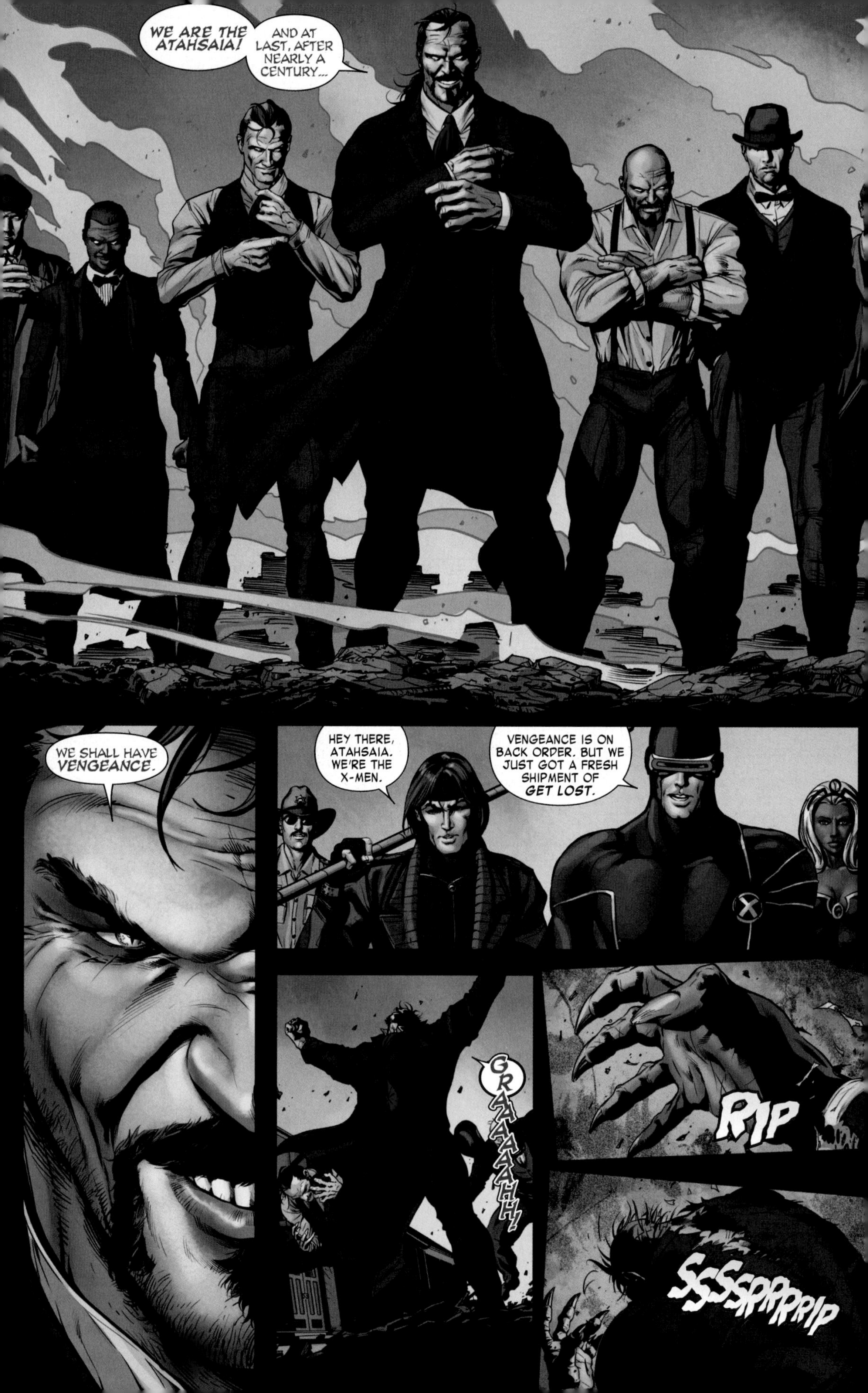
WE ARE THE ATAHSAIA!
AND AT LAST, AFTER NEARLY A CENTURY...
WE SHALL HAVE VENGEANCE.
HEY THERE, ATAHSAIA. WE'RE THE X-MEN.
VENGEANCE IS ON BACK ORDER. BUT WE JUST GOT A FRESH SHIPMENT OF GET LOST.
GRAAAAAHH!
RIP
SSSSPRRRRIP

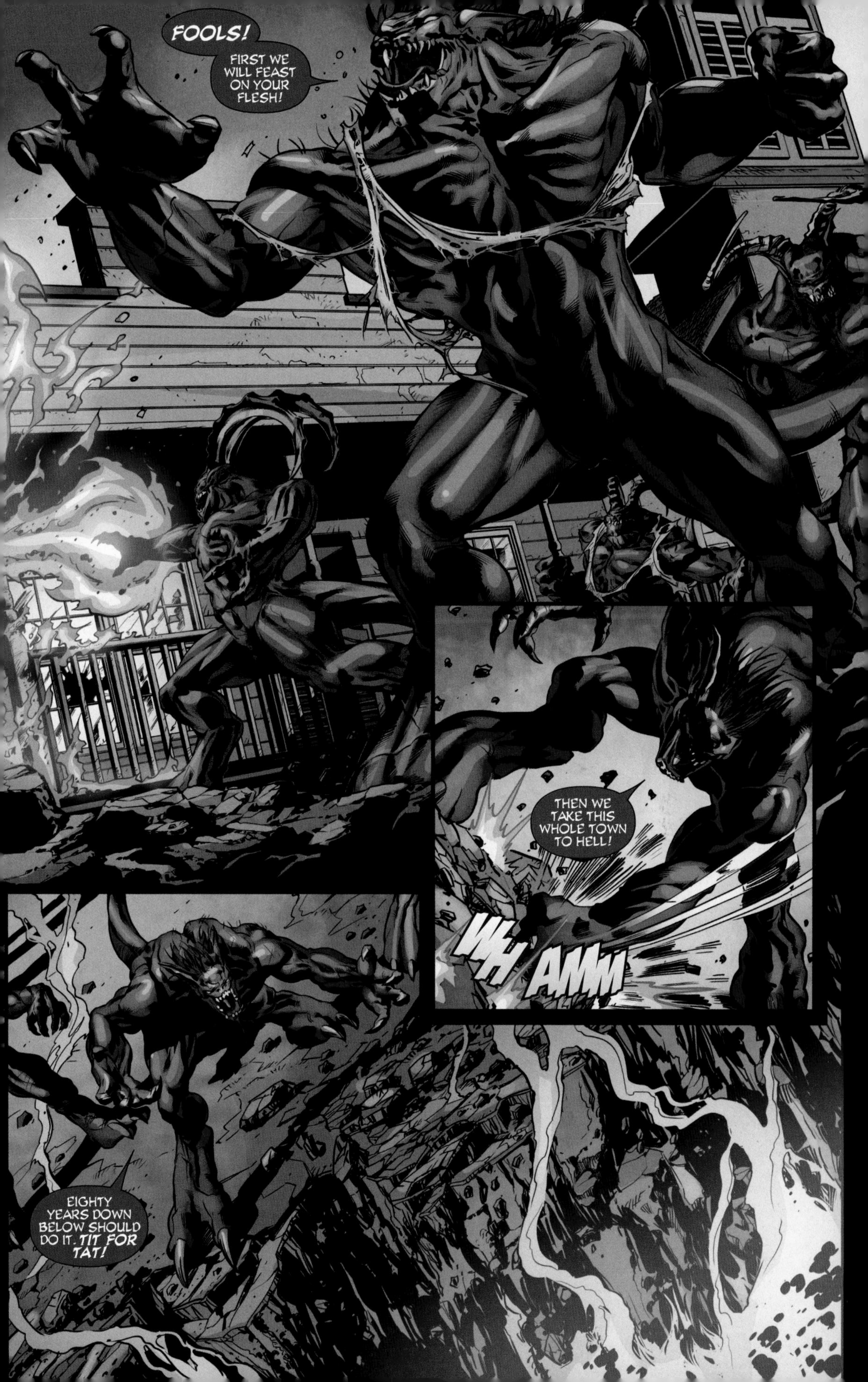
FOOLS!
FIRST WE WILL FEAST ON YOUR FLESH!
THEN WE TAKE THIS WHOLE TOWN TO HELL!
WHAMM
EIGHTY YEARS DOWN BELOW SHOULD DO IT. TIT FOR TAT!

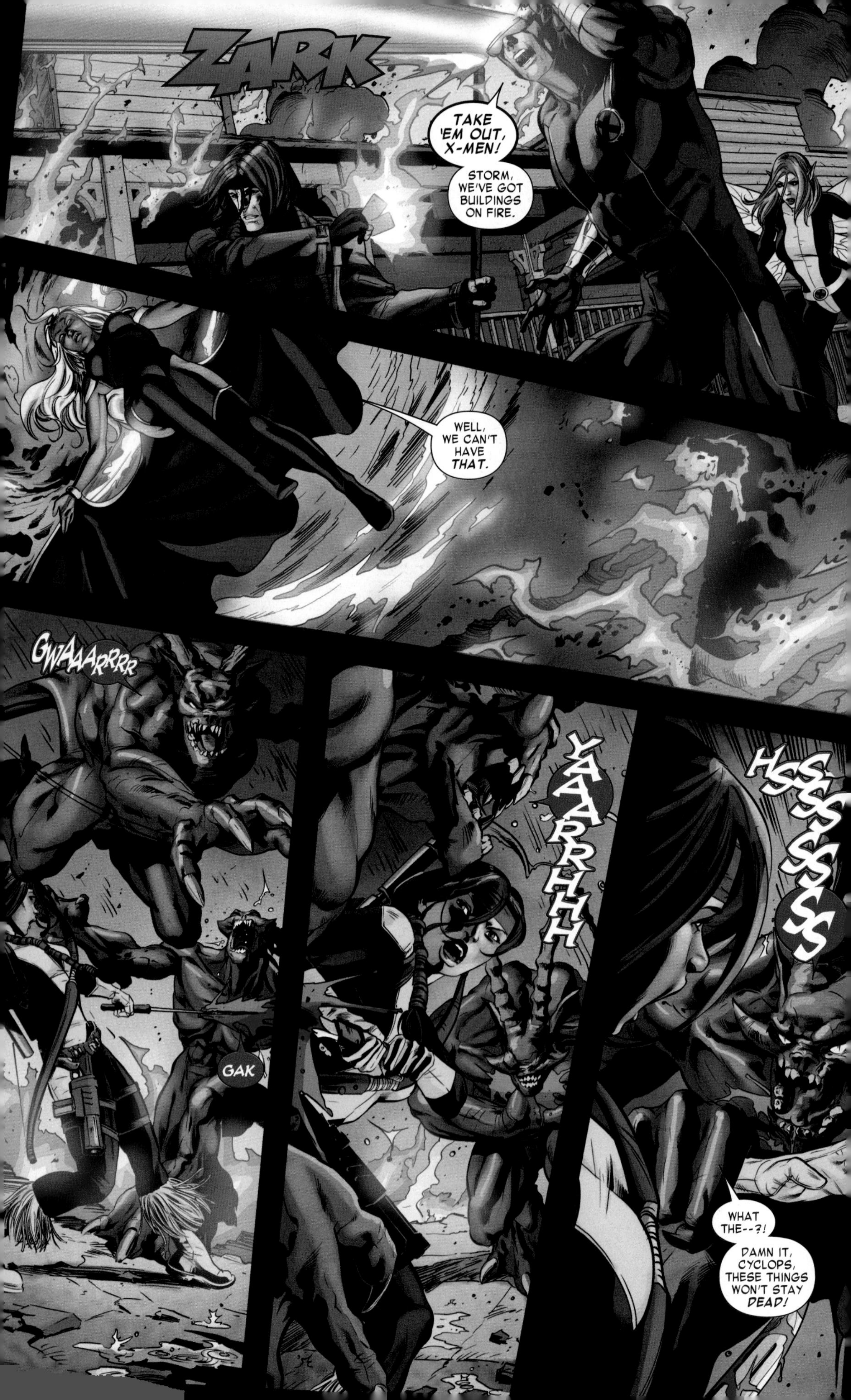
ZARK
TAKE 'EM OUT, X-MEN!
STORM, WE'VE GOT BUILDINGS ON FIRE.
WELL, WE CAN'T HAVE THAT.
GWAAARRRR
GAK
YAAARRHHH
HSSSSSSSS
WHAT THE--?!
DAMN IT, CYCLOPS, THESE THINGS WON'T STAY DEAD!

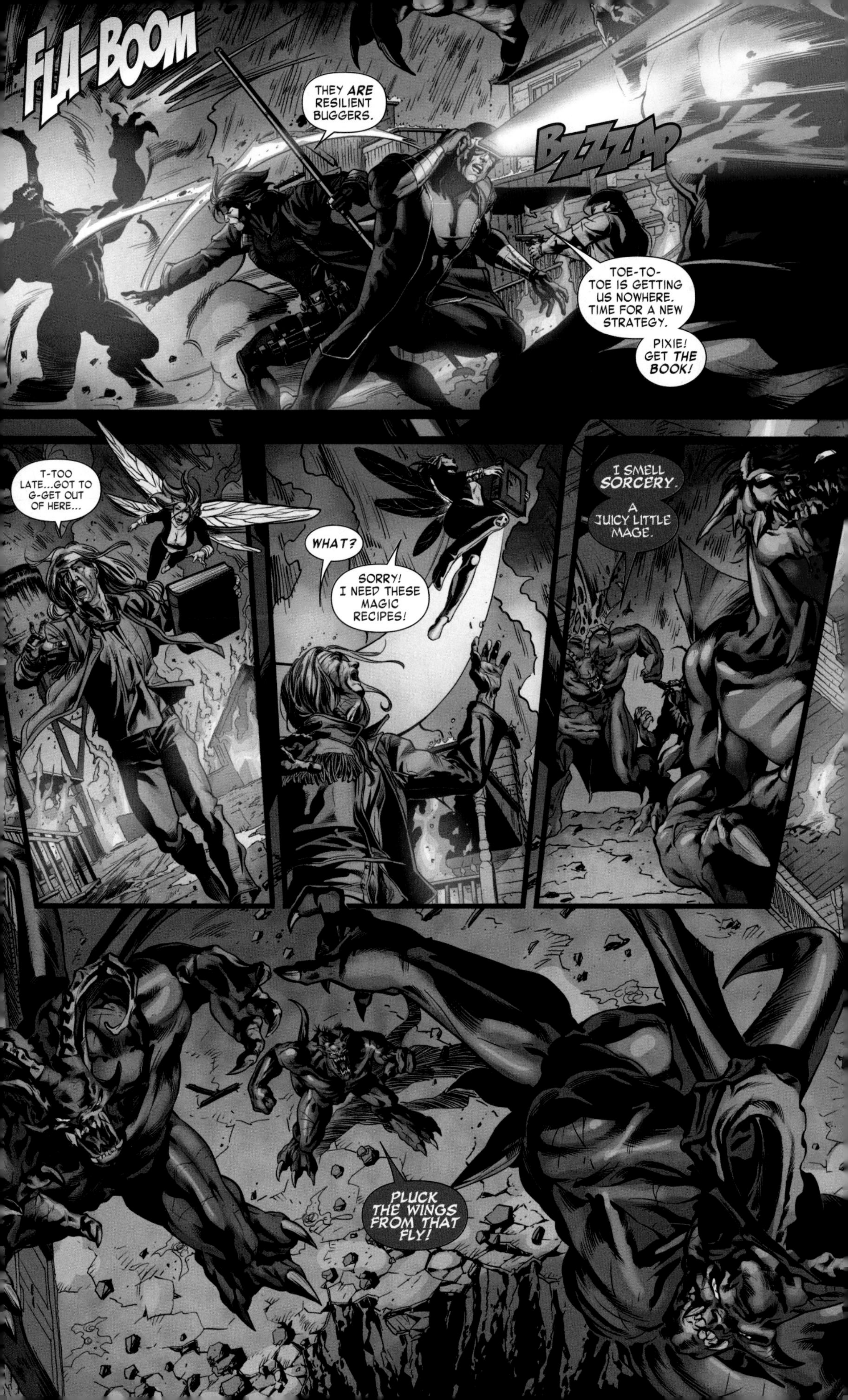
FLA-BOOM
THEY ARE RESILIENT BUGGERS.
BZZZAP
TOE-TO-TOE IS GETTING US NOWHERE. TIME FOR A NEW STRATEGY.
PIXIE! GET THE BOOK!
T-TOO LATE...GOT TO G-GET OUT OF HERE...
WHAT?
SORRY! I NEED THESE MAGIC RECIPES!
I SMELL SORCERY.
A JUICY LITTLE MAGE.
PLUCK THE WINGS FROM THAT FLY!

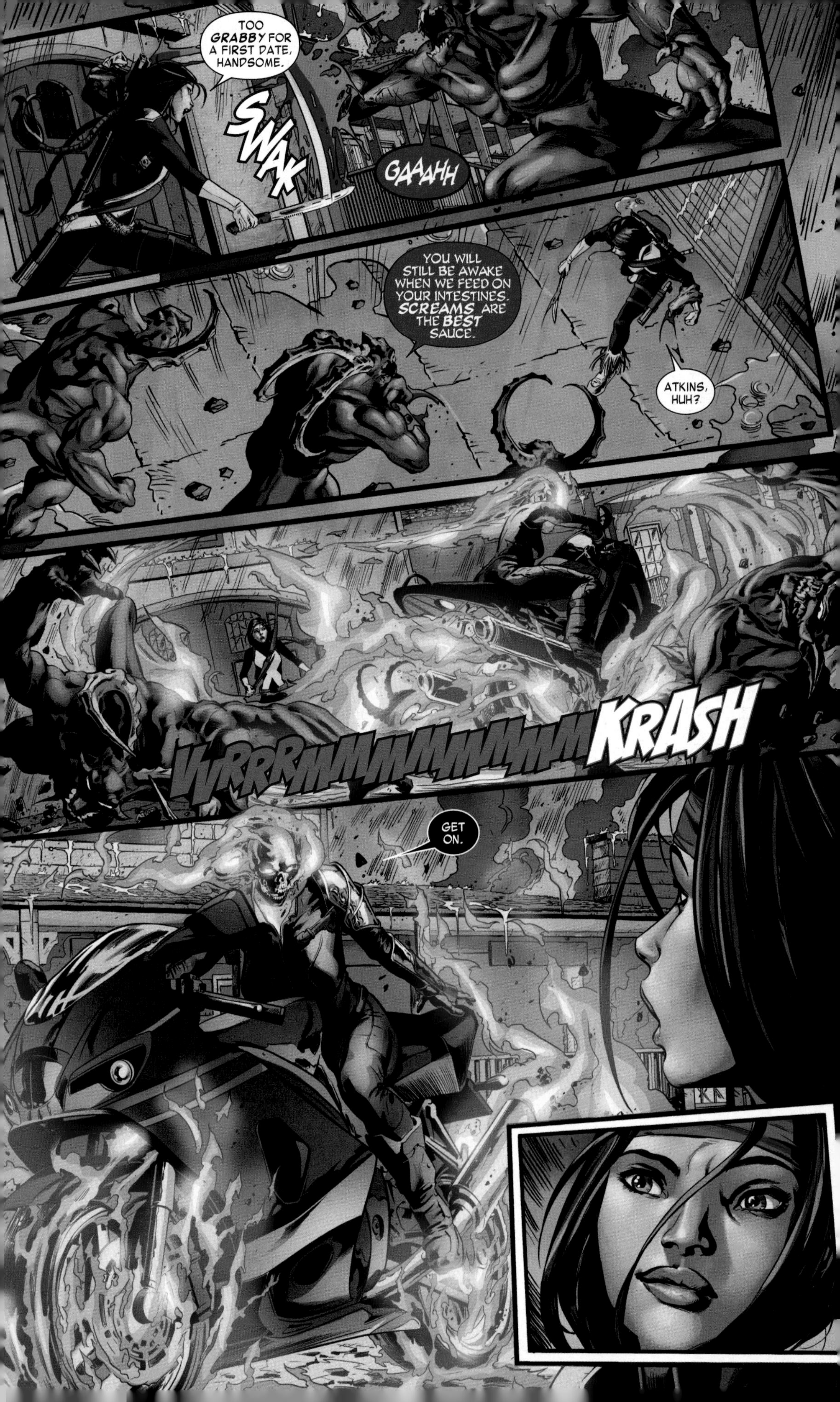
TOO GRABBY FOR A FIRST DATE, HANDSOME.
SWAK
GAAAHH
YOU WILL STILL BE AWAKE WHEN WE FEED ON YOUR INTESTINES. SCREAMS ARE THE BEST SAUCE.
ATKINS, HUH?
VRRRMMMMMMMMMM
KRASH
GET ON.

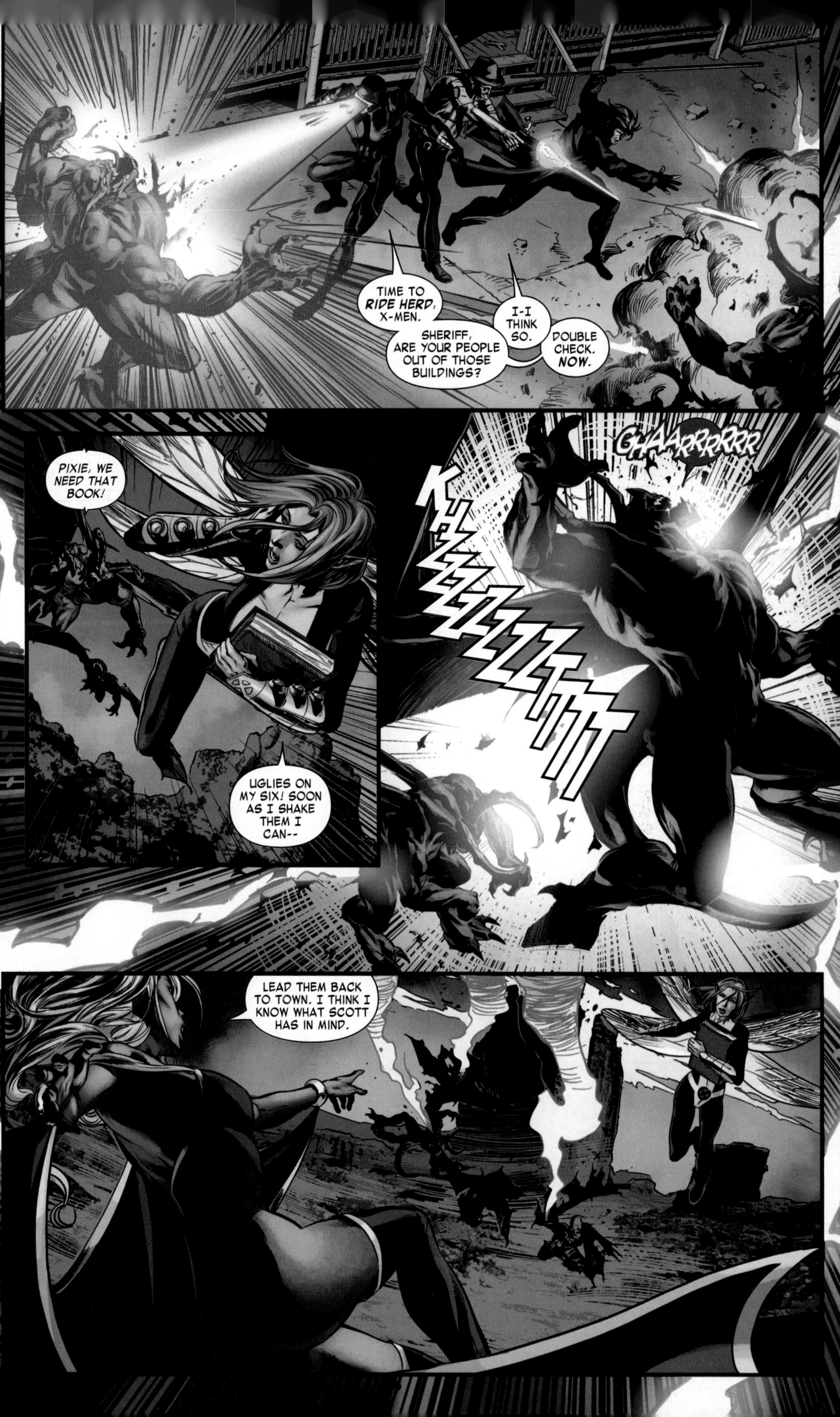

TIME TO RIDE HERD, X-MEN.
SHERIFF, ARE YOUR PEOPLE OUT OF THOSE BUILDINGS?
I-I THINK SO.
DOUBLE CHECK. NOW.
PIXIE, WE NEED THAT BOOK!
UGLIES ON MY SIX! SOON AS I SHAKE THEM I CAN--
KZZZZZZZTTTT
GHAARRRRRR
LEAD THEM BACK TO TOWN. I THINK I KNOW WHAT SCOTT HAS IN MIND.

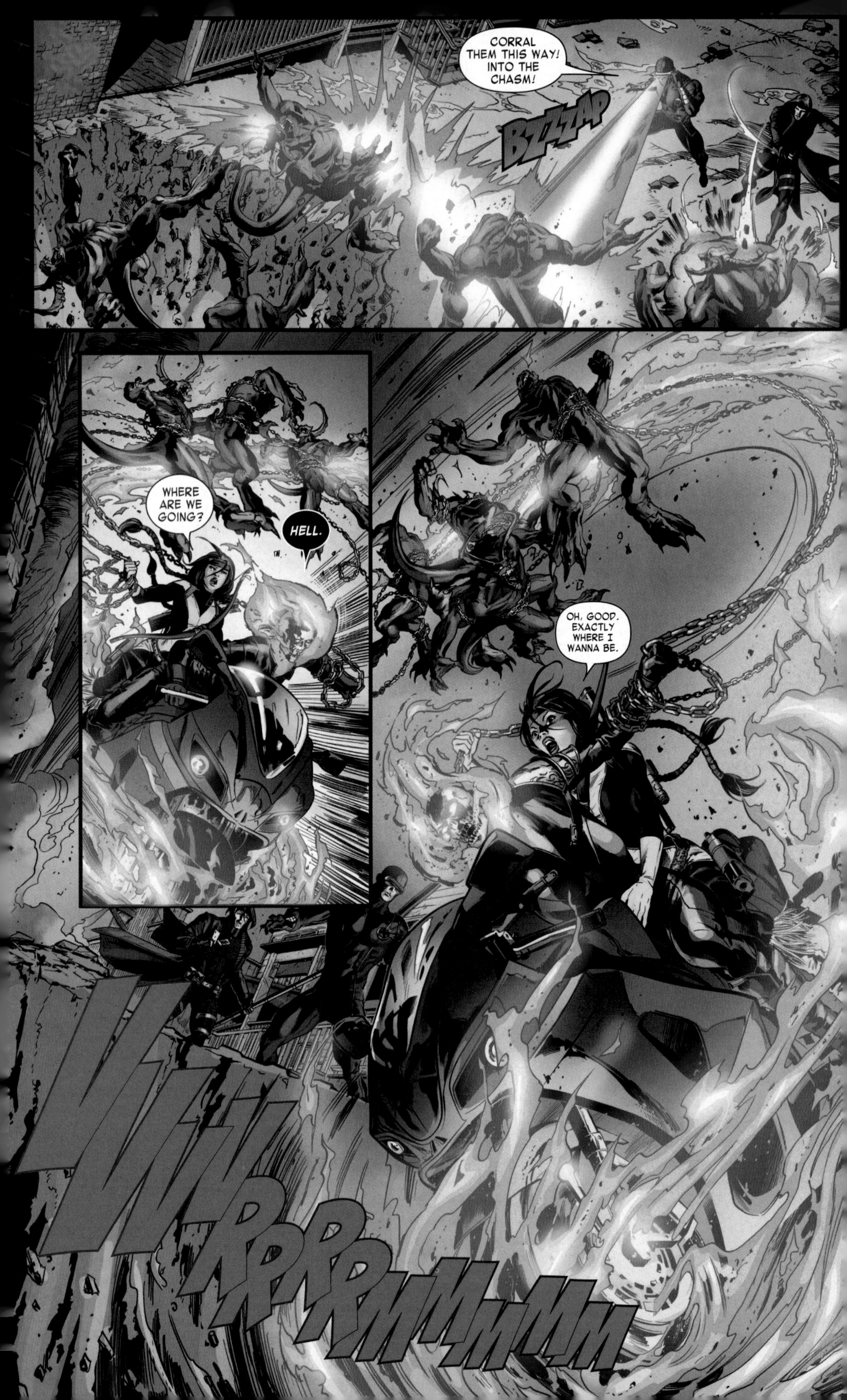
CORRAL THEM THIS WAY! INTO THE CHASM!
BZZZZAP
WHERE ARE WE GOING?
HELL.
OH, GOOD. EXACTLY WHERE I WANNA BE.
VVVRRRRRMMMMMMMM

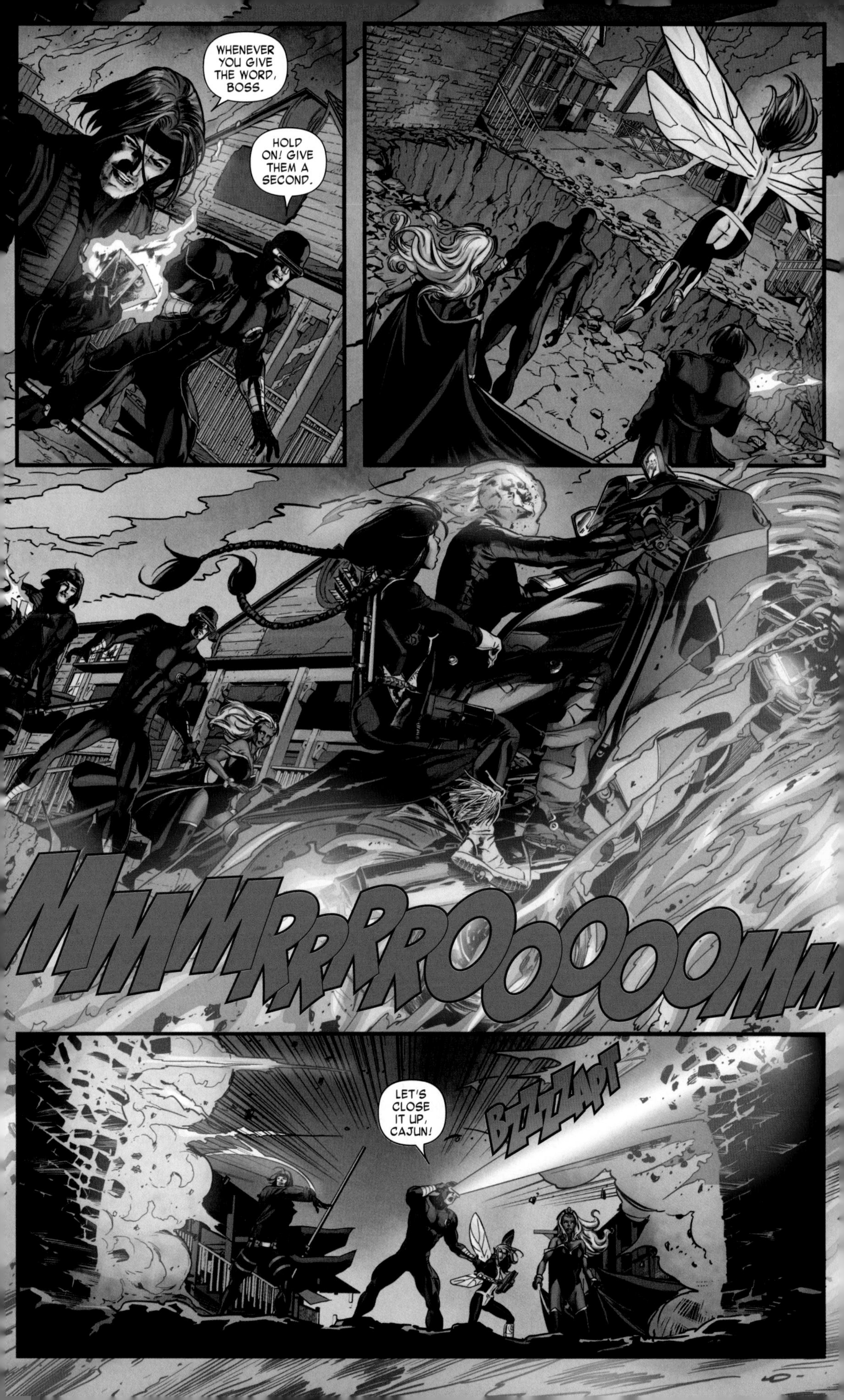
WHENEVER YOU GIVE THE WORD, BOSS.
HOLD ON! GIVE THEM A SECOND.
MMMRRRROOOOOOMM
LET'S CLOSE IT UP, CAJUN!
BZZZZAPT

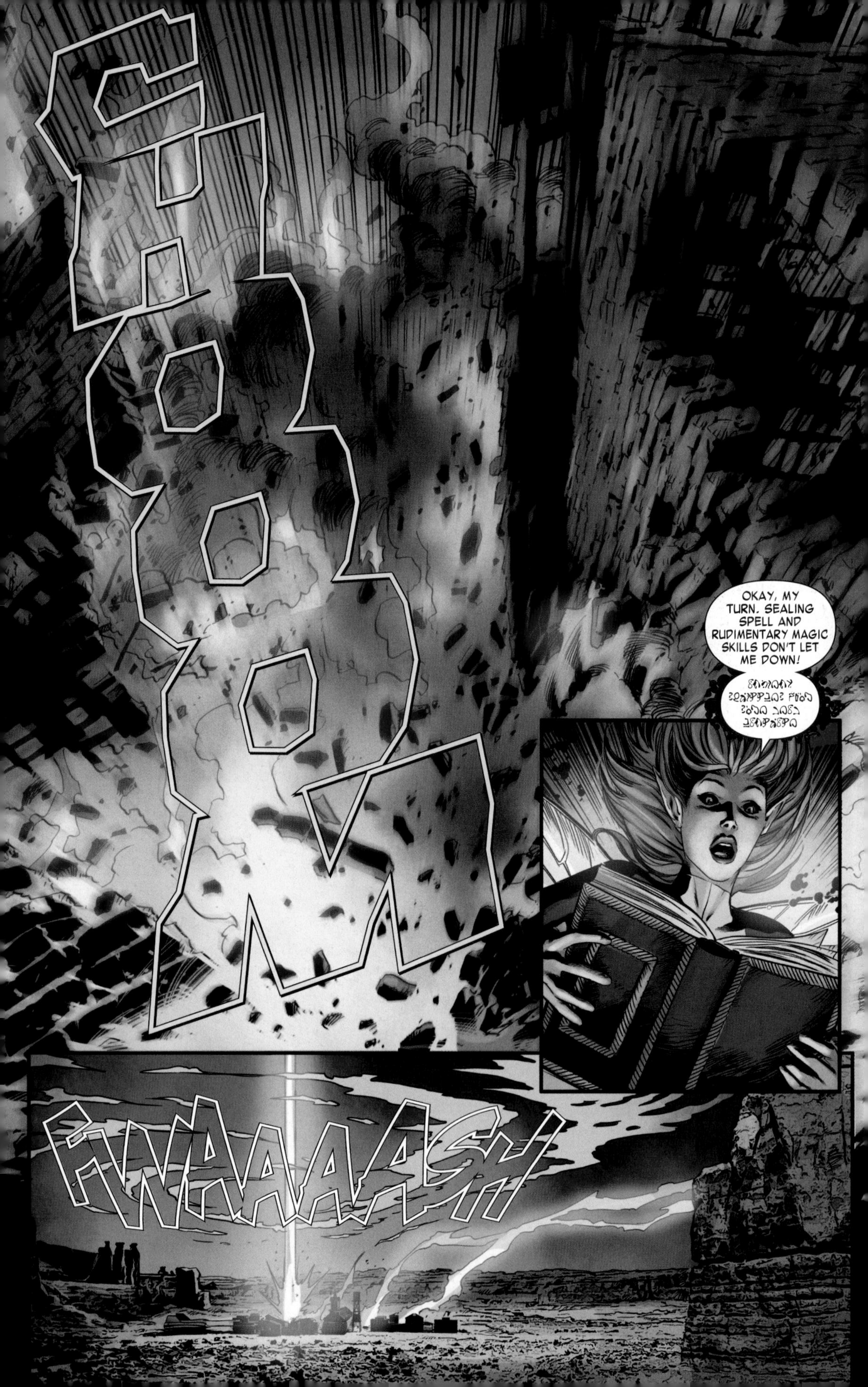

CHOOOM
OKAY, MY TURN. SEALING SPELL AND RUDIMENTARY MAGIC SKILLS DON'T LET ME DOWN!
FWAAAASH

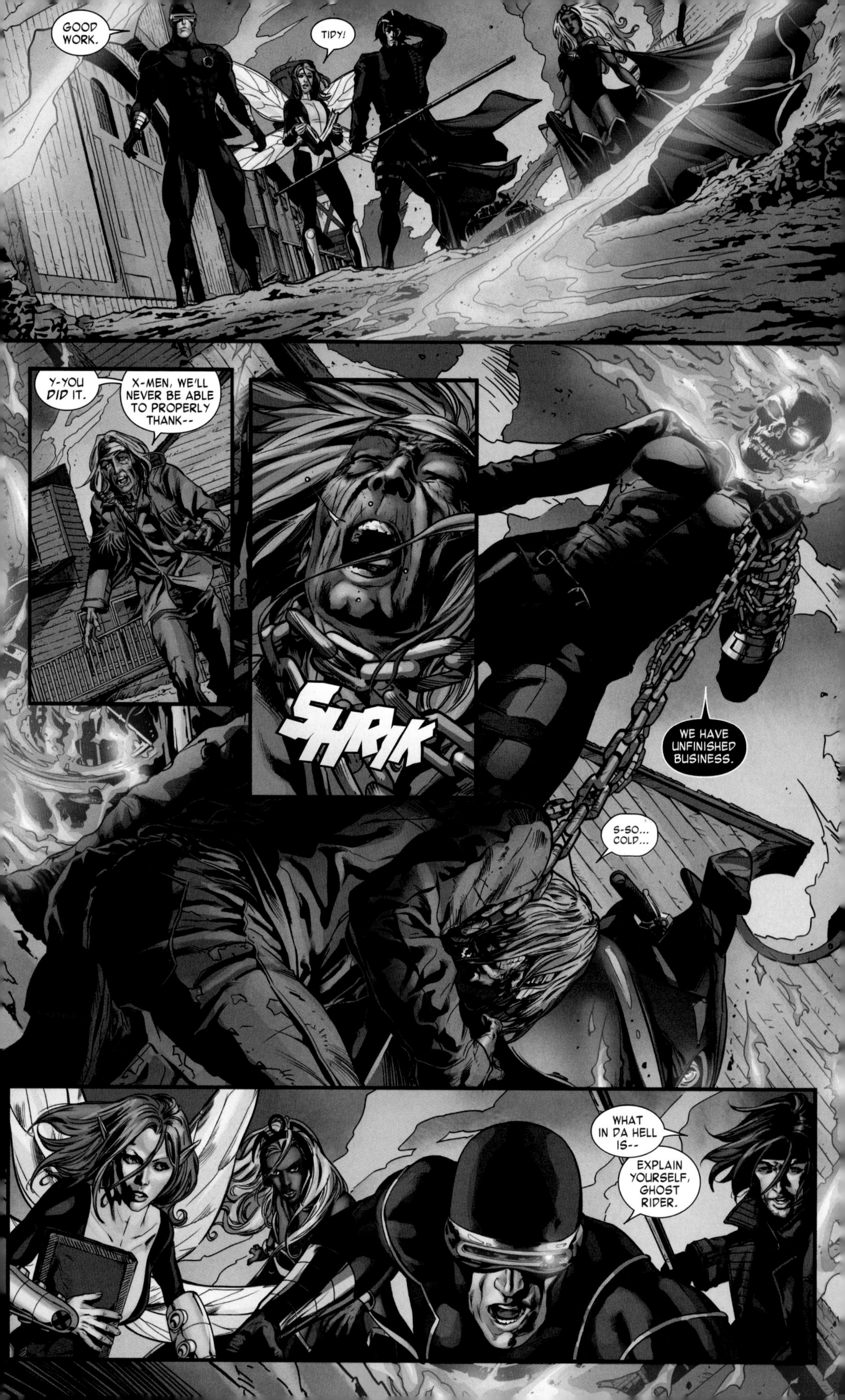
GOOD WORK.
TIDY!
Y-YOU DID IT.
X-MEN, WE'LL NEVER BE ABLE TO PROPERLY THANK--
SHRIK
WE HAVE UNFINISHED BUSINESS.
S-SO... COLD...
WHAT IN DA HELL IS--
EXPLAIN YOURSELF, GHOST RIDER.

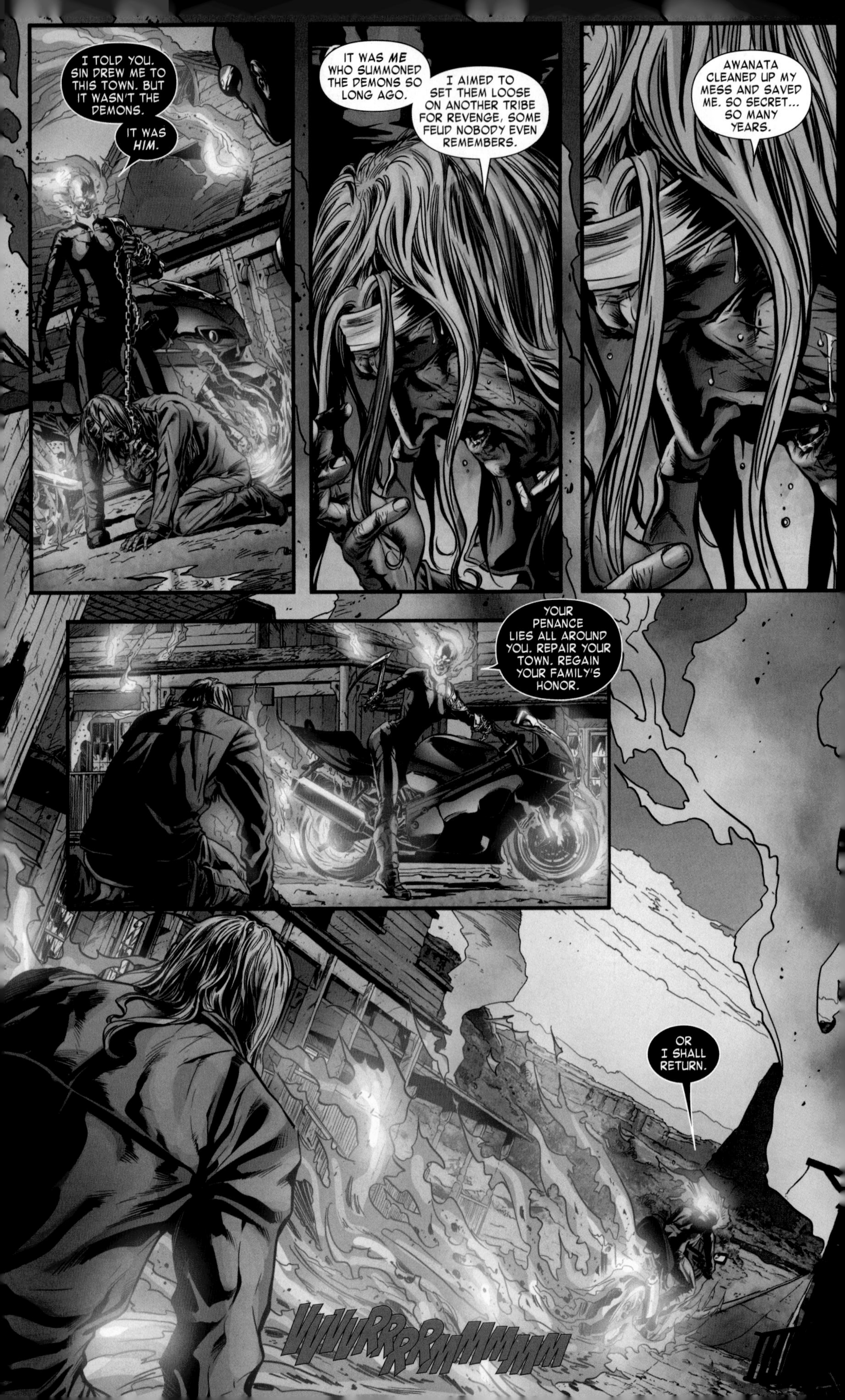
I TOLD YOU. SIN DREW ME TO THIS TOWN. BUT IT WASN'T THE DEMONS.
IT WAS HIM.
IT WAS ME WHO SUMMONED THE DEMONS SO LONG AGO.
I AIMED TO SET THEM LOOSE ON ANOTHER TRIBE FOR REVENGE, SOME FEUD NOBODY EVEN REMEMBERS.
AWANATA CLEANED UP MY MESS AND SAVED ME. SO SECRET... SO MANY YEARS.
YOUR PENANCE LIES ALL AROUND YOU. REPAIR YOUR TOWN. REGAIN YOUR FAMILY'S HONOR.
OR I SHALL RETURN.
VVVVRRRRRMMMMMM

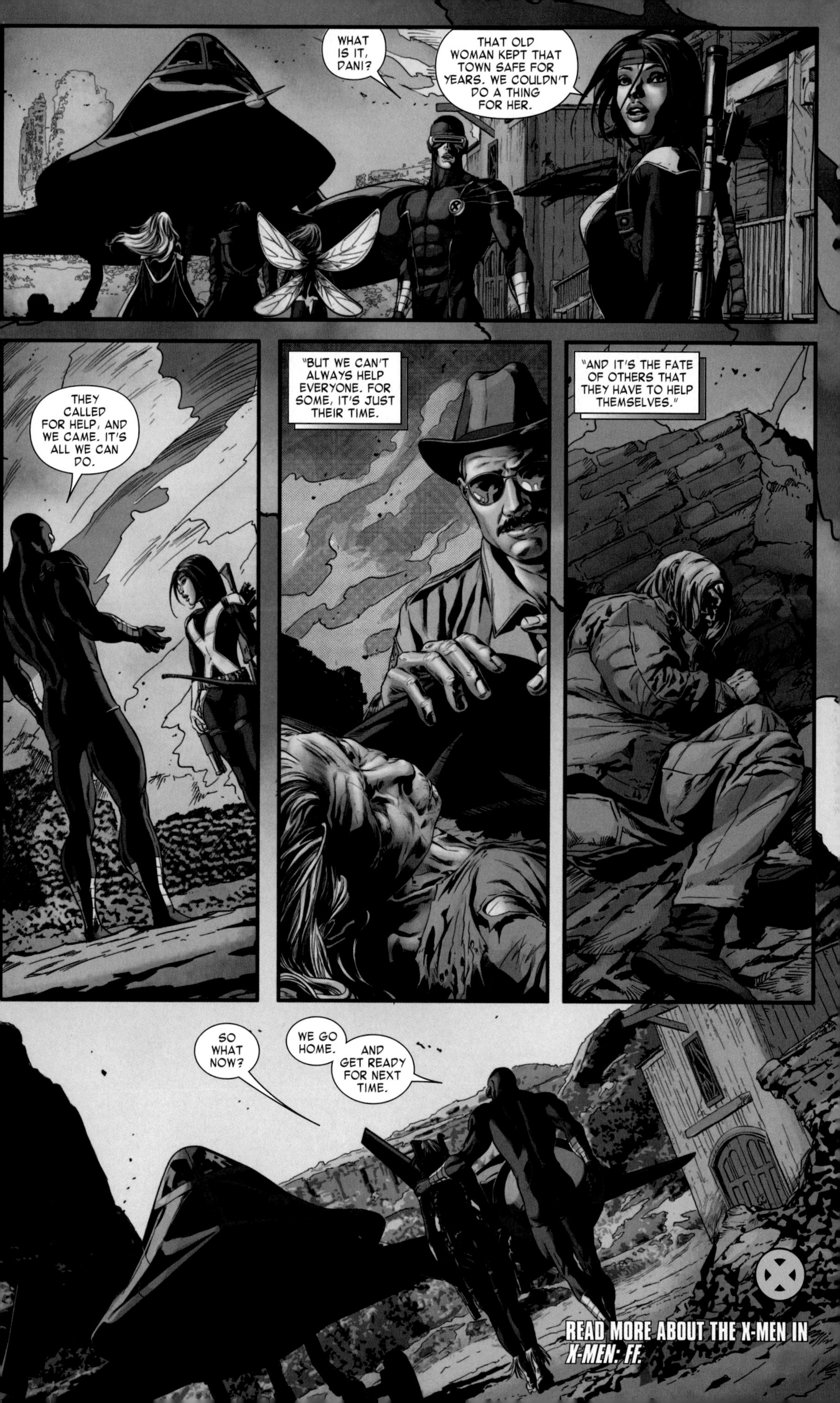

WHAT IS IT, DANI?
THAT OLD WOMAN KEPT THAT TOWN SAFE FOR YEARS. WE COULDN'T DO A THING FOR HER.
THEY CALLED FOR HELP, AND WE CAME. IT'S ALL WE CAN DO.
"BUT WE CAN'T ALWAYS HELP EVERYONE. FOR SOME, IT'S JUST THEIR TIME.
"AND IT'S THE FATE OF OTHERS THAT THEY HAVE TO HELP THEMSELVES."
SO WHAT NOW?
WE GO HOME.
AND GET READY FOR NEXT TIME.
READ MORE ABOUT THE X-MEN IN *X-MEN: FF.*

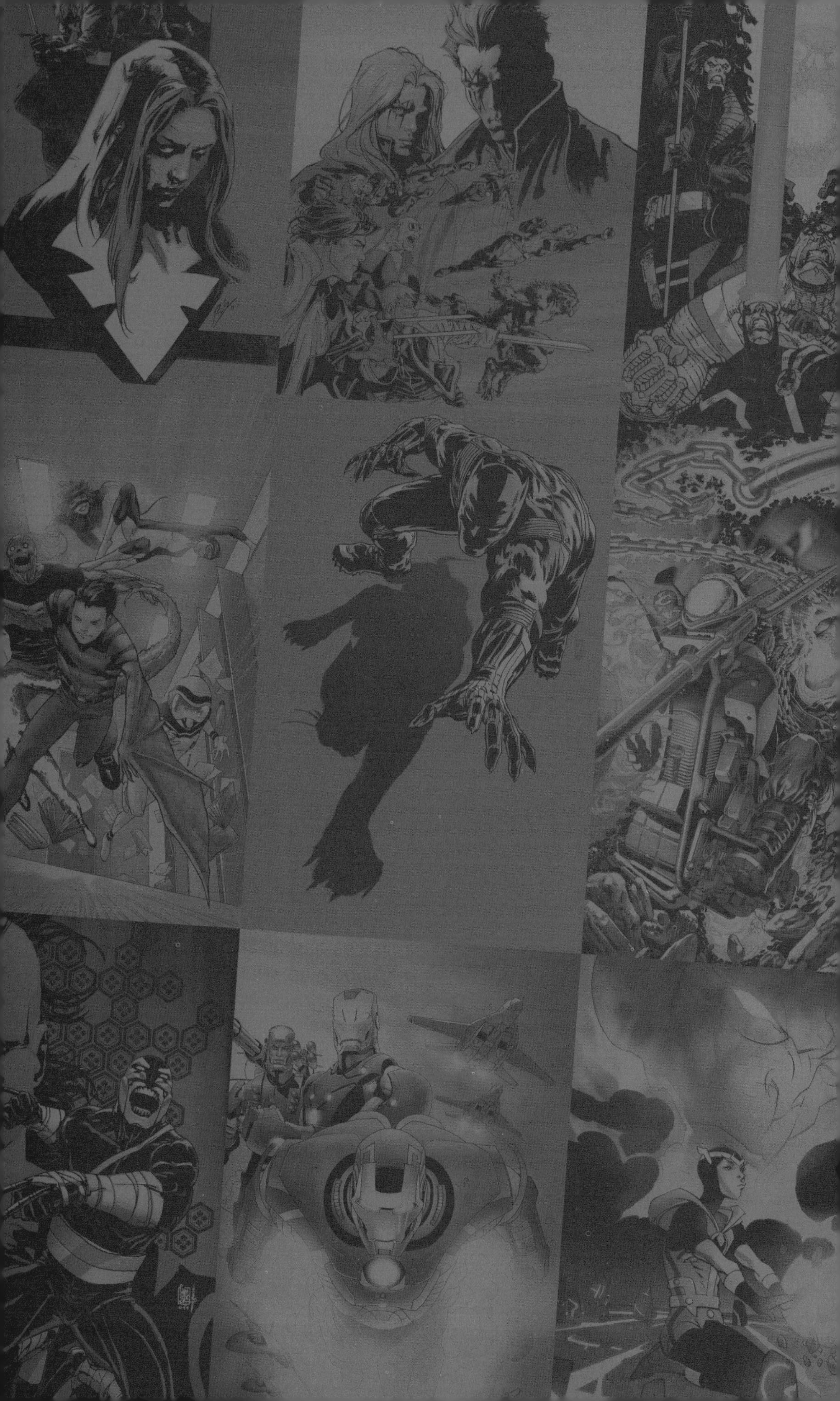

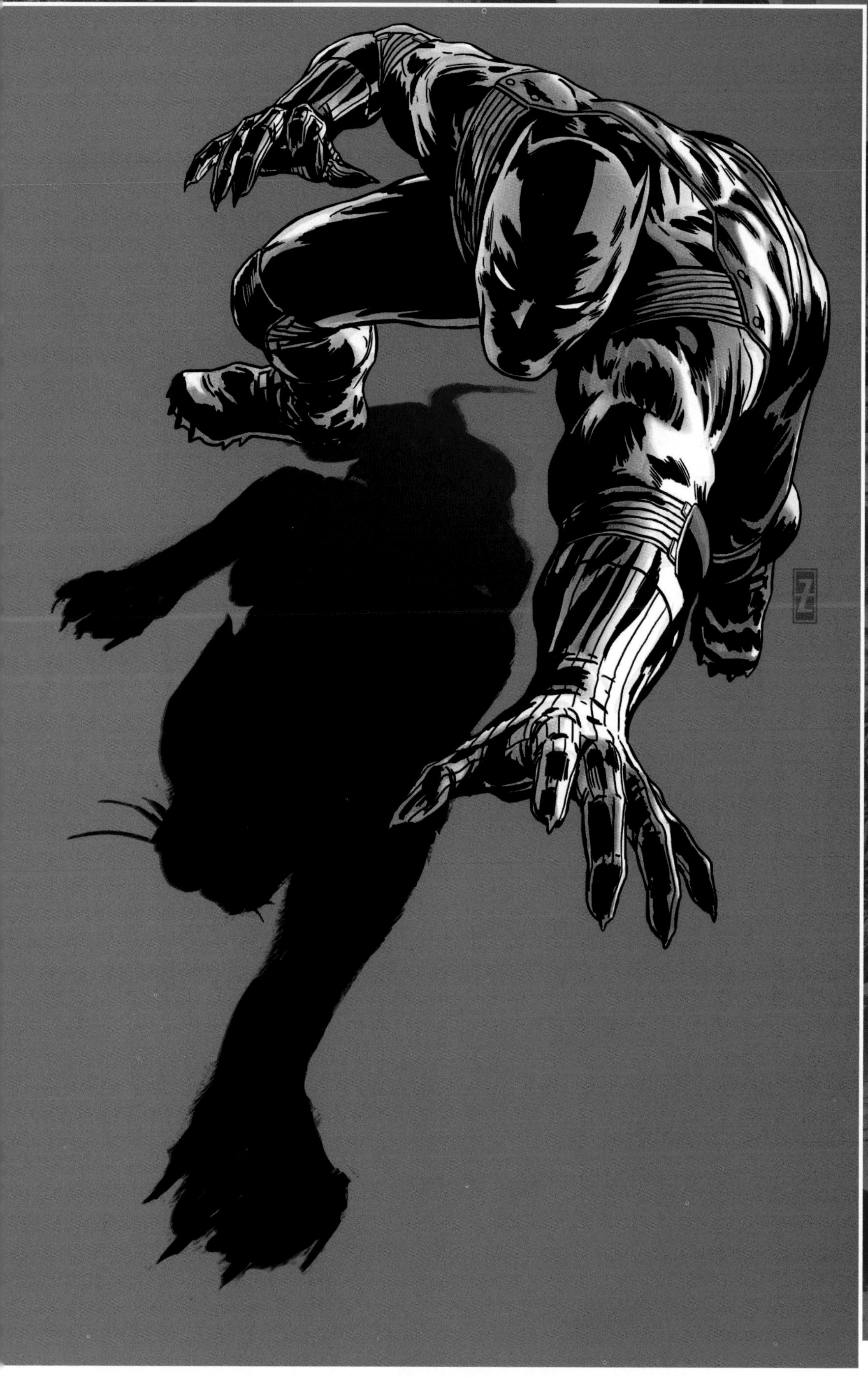

BLACK PANTHER: THE MOST DANGEROUS MAN ALIVE #523.1

PREVIOUSLY IN...

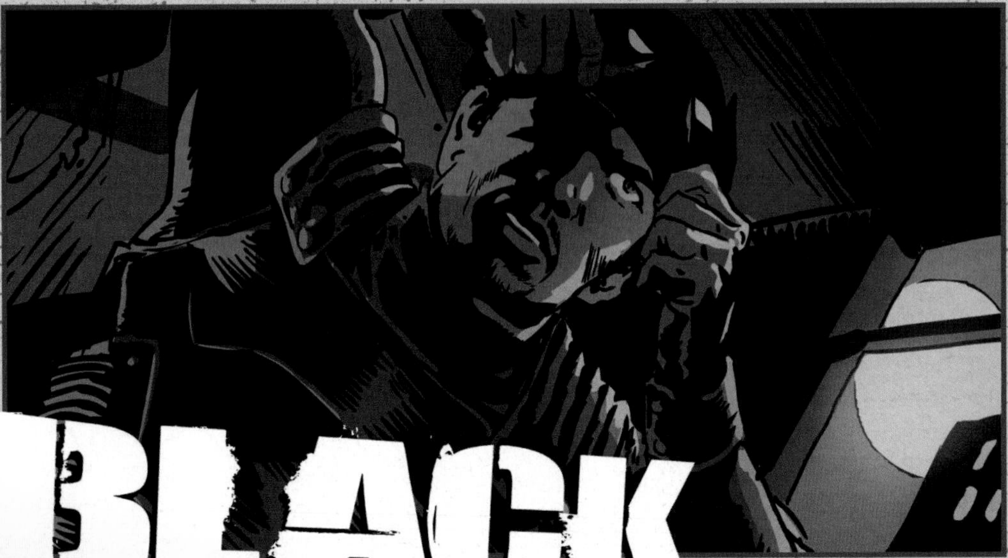

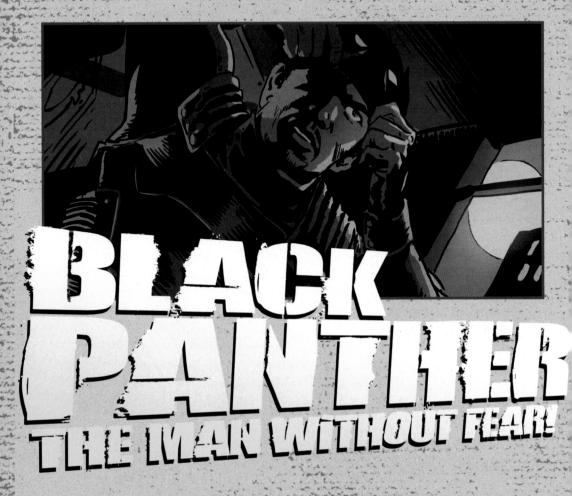

BLACK PANTHER
THE MAN WITHOUT FEAR!

T'CHALLA, THE FORMER BLACK PANTHER AND KING OF THE AFRICAN NATION WAKANDA, HAS ABDICATED HIS THRONE AND LEFT HIS HOMELAND. NOW STRIPPED OF HIS POWERS AND WEALTH, HE SEEKS TO PROVE HIS WORTH ON HIS OWN TERMS AS THE GUARDIAN OF THE MEAN STREETS OF THE MANHATTAN NEIGHBORHOOD KNOWN AS HELL'S KITCHEN.

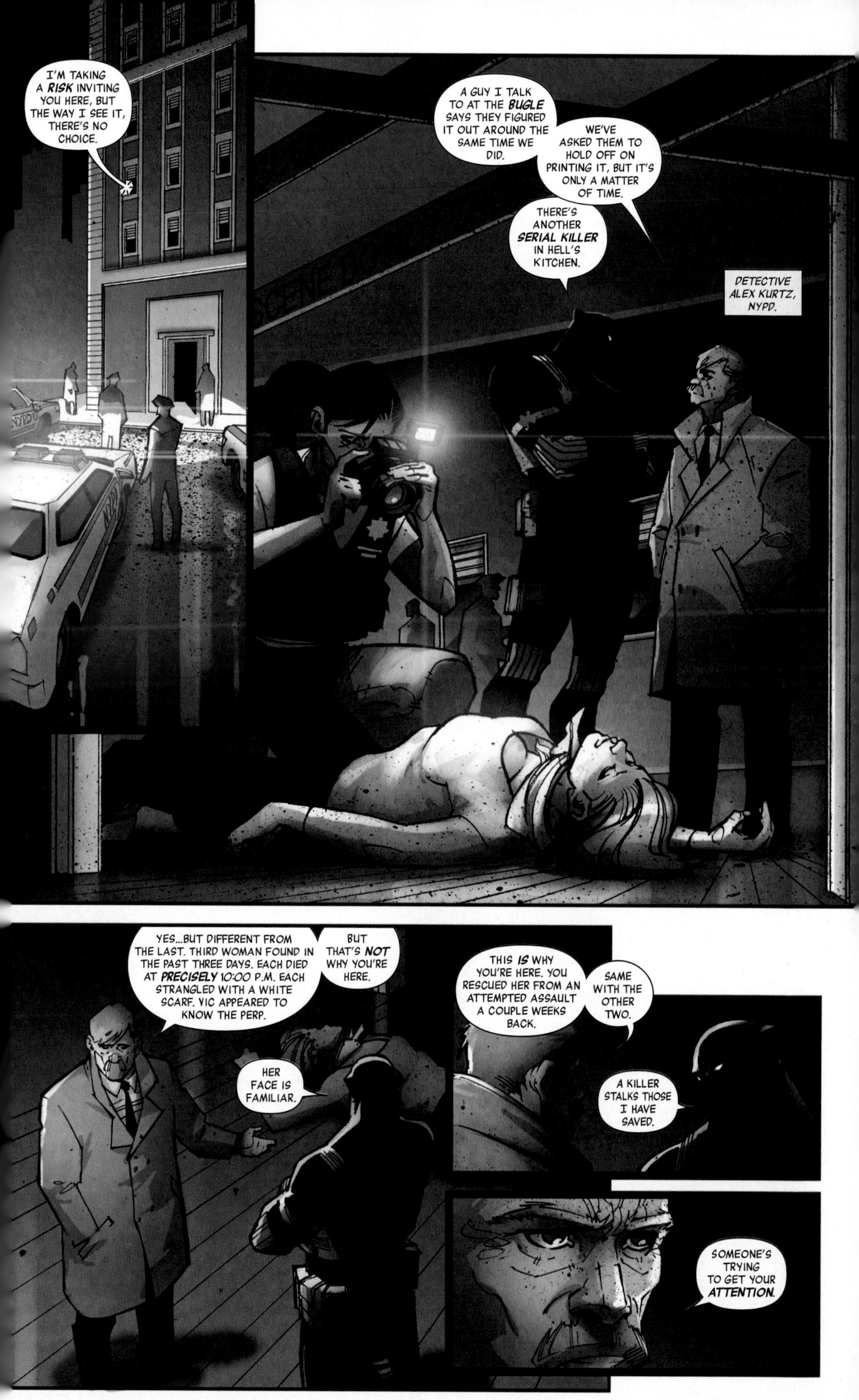
I'M TAKING A RISK INVITING YOU HERE, BUT THE WAY I SEE IT, THERE'S NO CHOICE.
A GUY I TALK TO AT THE BUGLE SAYS THEY FIGURED IT OUT AROUND THE SAME TIME WE DID.
WE'VE ASKED THEM TO HOLD OFF ON PRINTING IT, BUT IT'S ONLY A MATTER OF TIME.
THERE'S ANOTHER SERIAL KILLER IN HELL'S KITCHEN.
DETECTIVE ALEX KURTZ, NYPD.
YES...BUT DIFFERENT FROM THE LAST. THIRD WOMAN FOUND IN THE PAST THREE DAYS. EACH DIED AT PRECISELY 10:00 P.M. EACH STRANGLED WITH A WHITE SCARF. VIC APPEARED TO KNOW THE PERP.
BUT THAT'S NOT WHY YOU'RE HERE.
HER FACE IS FAMILIAR.
THIS IS WHY YOU'RE HERE. YOU RESCUED HER FROM AN ATTEMPTED ASSAULT A COUPLE WEEKS BACK.
SAME WITH THE OTHER TWO.
A KILLER STALKS THOSE I HAVE SAVED.
SOMEONE'S TRYING TO GET YOUR ATTENTION.

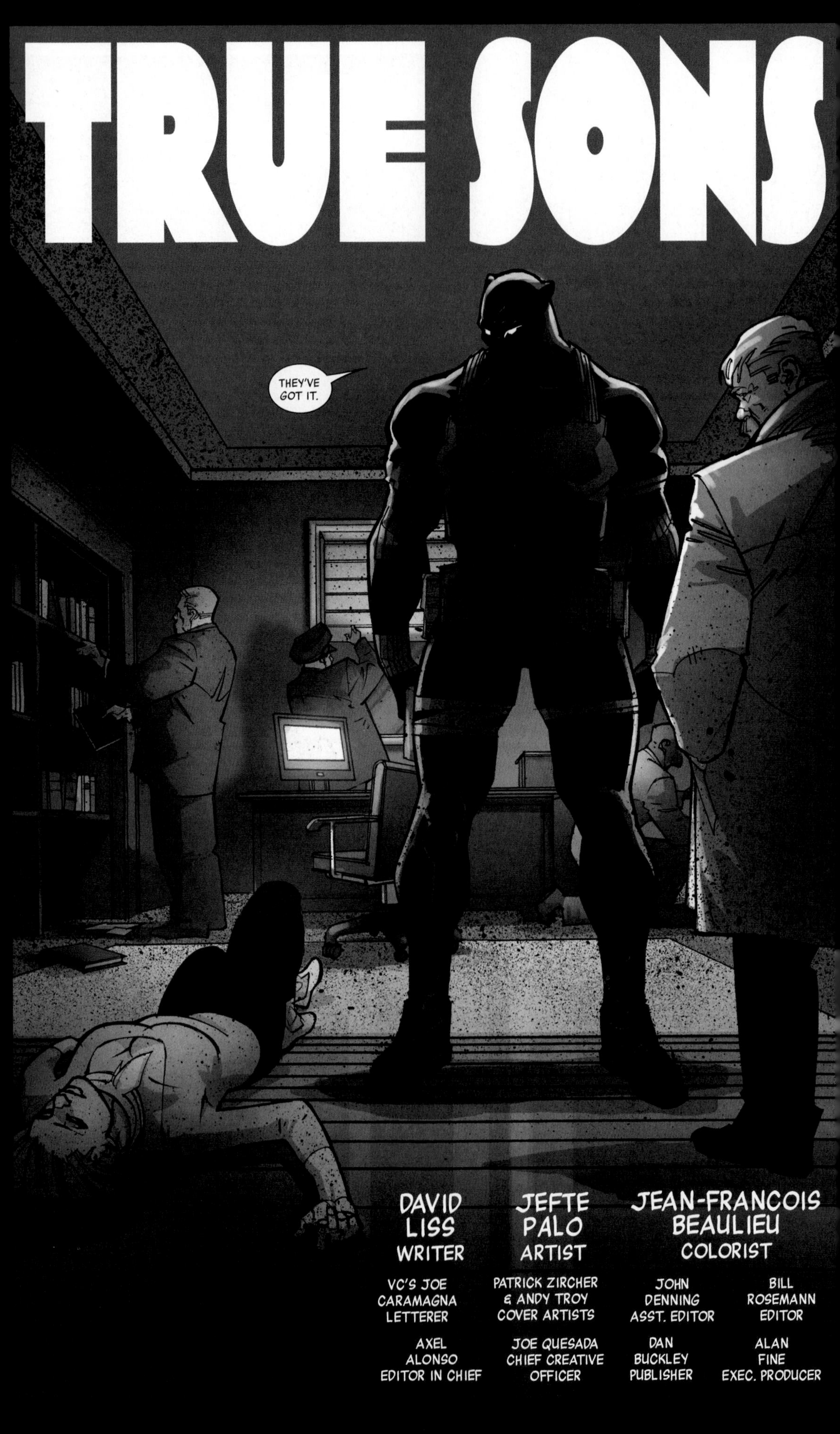

TRUE SONS
THEY'VE GOT IT.
DAVID LISS WRITER
JEFTE PALO ARTIST
JEAN-FRANCOIS BEAULIEU COLORIST
VC'S JOE CARAMAGNA LETTERER
PATRICK ZIRCHER & ANDY TROY COVER ARTISTS
JOHN DENNING ASST. EDITOR
BILL ROSEMANN EDITOR
AXEL ALONSO EDITOR IN CHIEF
JOE QUESADA CHIEF CREATIVE OFFICER
DAN BUCKLEY PUBLISHER
ALAN FINE EXEC. PRODUCER

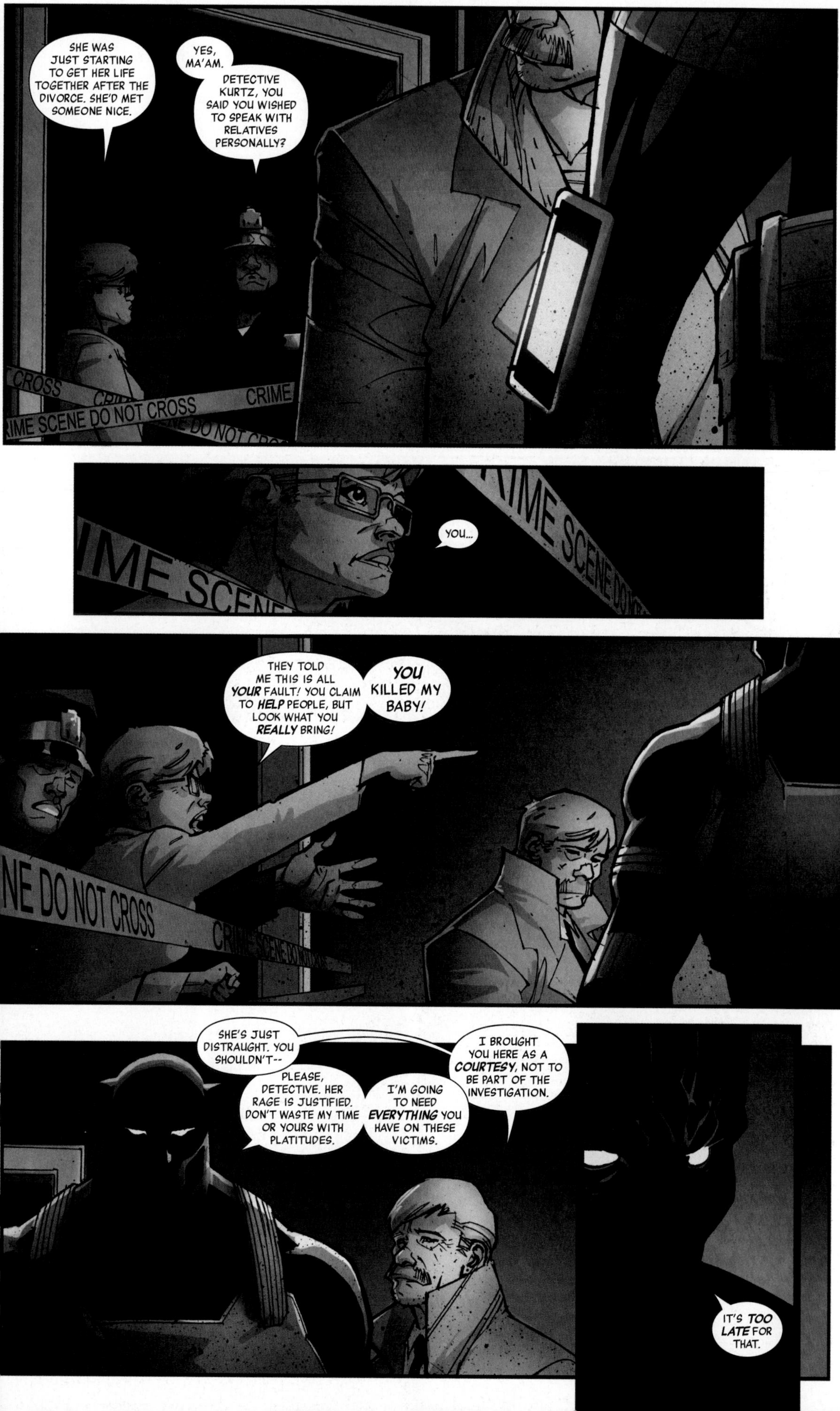
SHE WAS JUST STARTING TO GET HER LIFE TOGETHER AFTER THE DIVORCE. SHE'D MET SOMEONE NICE.
YES, MA'AM.
DETECTIVE KURTZ, YOU SAID YOU WISHED TO SPEAK WITH RELATIVES PERSONALLY?
CRIME SCENE DO NOT CROSS
YOU...
THEY TOLD ME THIS IS ALL *YOUR* FAULT! YOU CLAIM TO *HELP* PEOPLE, BUT LOOK WHAT YOU *REALLY* BRING!
YOU KILLED MY BABY!
NE DO NOT CROSS
SHE'S JUST DISTRAUGHT. YOU SHOULDN'T--
PLEASE, DETECTIVE. HER RAGE IS JUSTIFIED. DON'T WASTE MY TIME OR YOURS WITH PLATITUDES.
I'M GOING TO NEED *EVERYTHING* YOU HAVE ON THESE VICTIMS.
I BROUGHT YOU HERE AS A *COURTESY*, NOT TO BE PART OF THE INVESTIGATION.
IT'S *TOO LATE* FOR THAT.

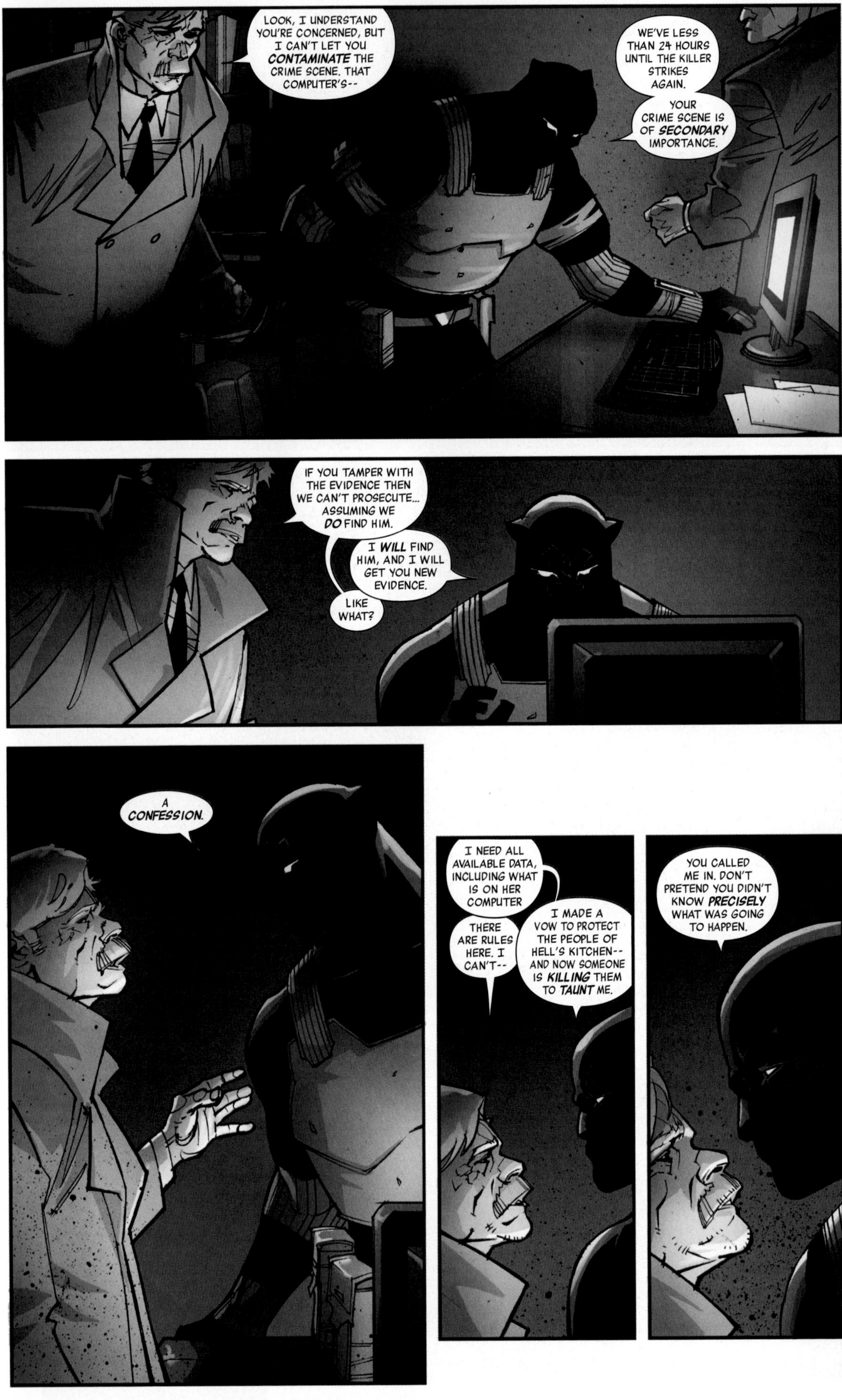
LOOK, I UNDERSTAND YOU'RE CONCERNED, BUT I CAN'T LET YOU CONTAMINATE THE CRIME SCENE. THAT COMPUTER'S--
WE'VE LESS THAN 24 HOURS UNTIL THE KILLER STRIKES AGAIN.
YOUR CRIME SCENE IS OF SECONDARY IMPORTANCE.
IF YOU TAMPER WITH THE EVIDENCE THEN WE CAN'T PROSECUTE... ASSUMING WE DO FIND HIM.
I WILL FIND HIM, AND I WILL GET YOU NEW EVIDENCE.
LIKE WHAT?
A CONFESSION.
I NEED ALL AVAILABLE DATA, INCLUDING WHAT IS ON HER COMPUTER
THERE ARE RULES HERE. I CAN'T--
I MADE A VOW TO PROTECT THE PEOPLE OF HELL'S KITCHEN--AND NOW SOMEONE IS KILLING THEM TO TAUNT ME.
YOU CALLED ME IN. DON'T PRETEND YOU DIDN'T KNOW PRECISELY WHAT WAS GOING TO HAPPEN.

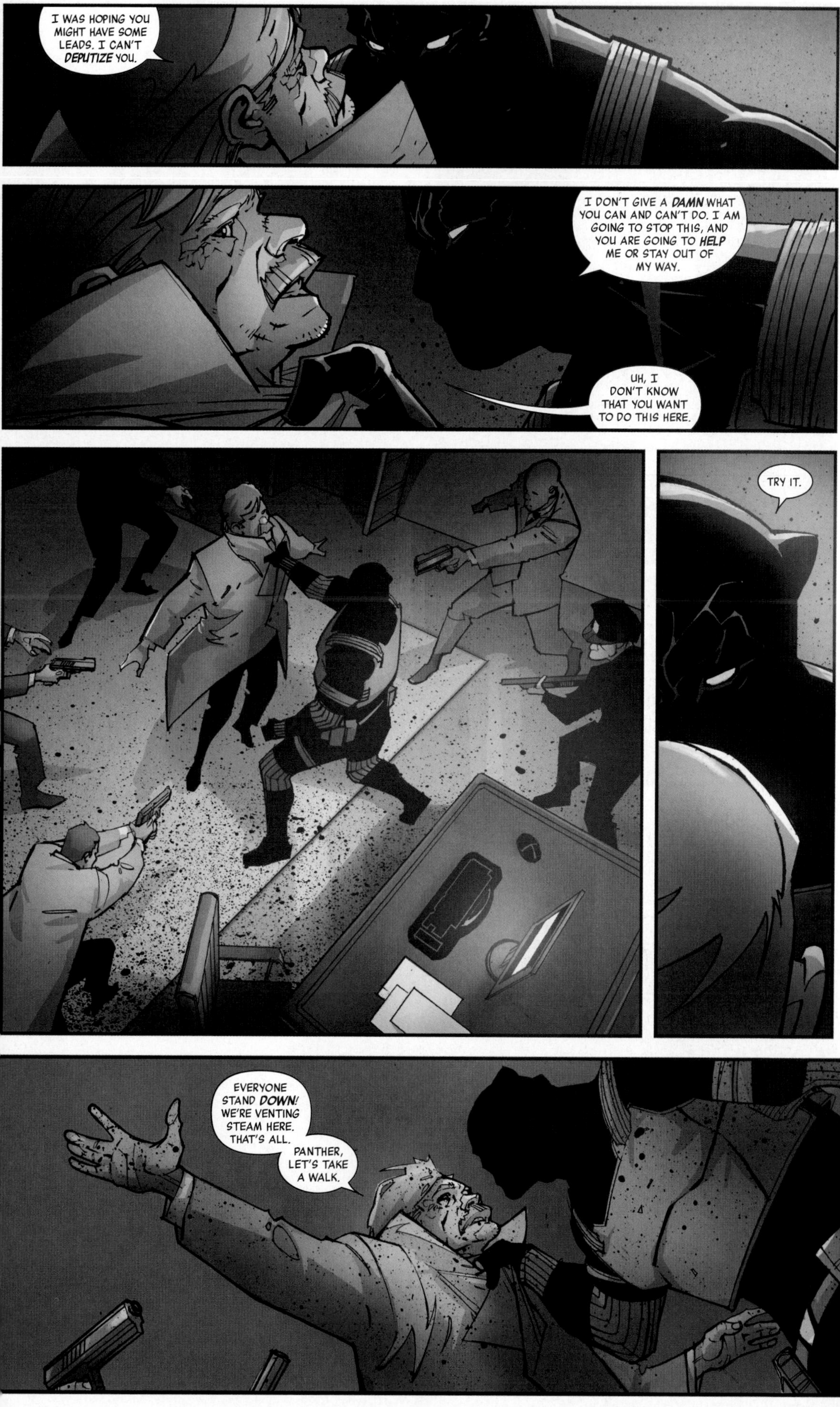
I WAS HOPING YOU MIGHT HAVE SOME LEADS. I CAN'T DEPUTIZE YOU.
I DON'T GIVE A DAMN WHAT YOU CAN AND CAN'T DO. I AM GOING TO STOP THIS, AND YOU ARE GOING TO HELP ME OR STAY OUT OF MY WAY.
UH, I DON'T KNOW THAT YOU WANT TO DO THIS HERE.
TRY IT.
EVERYONE STAND DOWN! WE'RE VENTING STEAM HERE. THAT'S ALL.
PANTHER, LET'S TAKE A WALK.

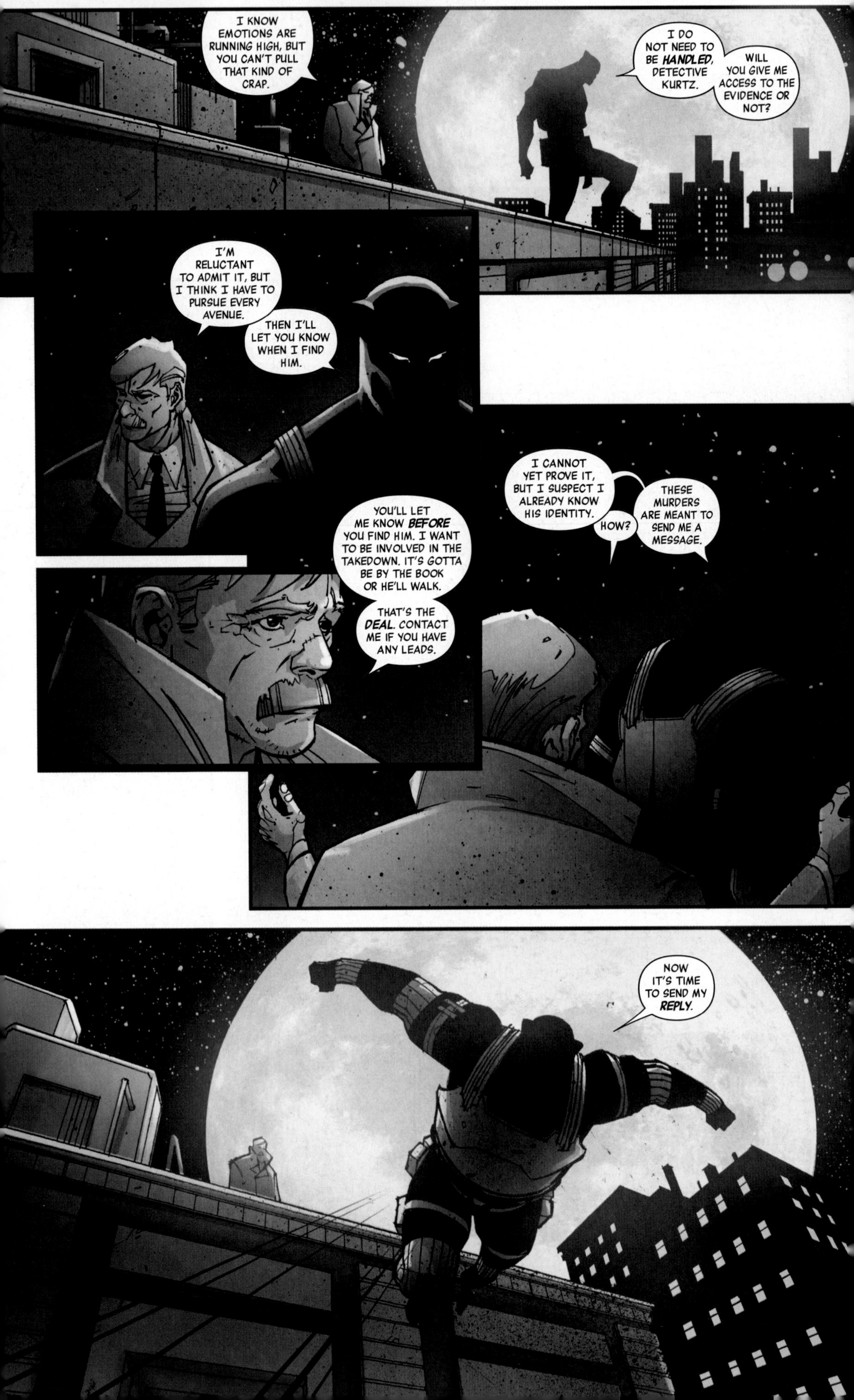
I KNOW EMOTIONS ARE RUNNING HIGH, BUT YOU CAN'T PULL THAT KIND OF CRAP.
I DO NOT NEED TO BE HANDLED, DETECTIVE KURTZ.
WILL YOU GIVE ME ACCESS TO THE EVIDENCE OR NOT?
I'M RELUCTANT TO ADMIT IT, BUT I THINK I HAVE TO PURSUE EVERY AVENUE.
THEN I'LL LET YOU KNOW WHEN I FIND HIM.
YOU'LL LET ME KNOW BEFORE YOU FIND HIM. I WANT TO BE INVOLVED IN THE TAKEDOWN. IT'S GOTTA BE BY THE BOOK OR HE'LL WALK.
THAT'S THE DEAL. CONTACT ME IF YOU HAVE ANY LEADS.
I CANNOT YET PROVE IT, BUT I SUSPECT I ALREADY KNOW HIS IDENTITY.
HOW?
THESE MURDERS ARE MEANT TO SEND ME A MESSAGE.
NOW IT'S TIME TO SEND MY REPLY.

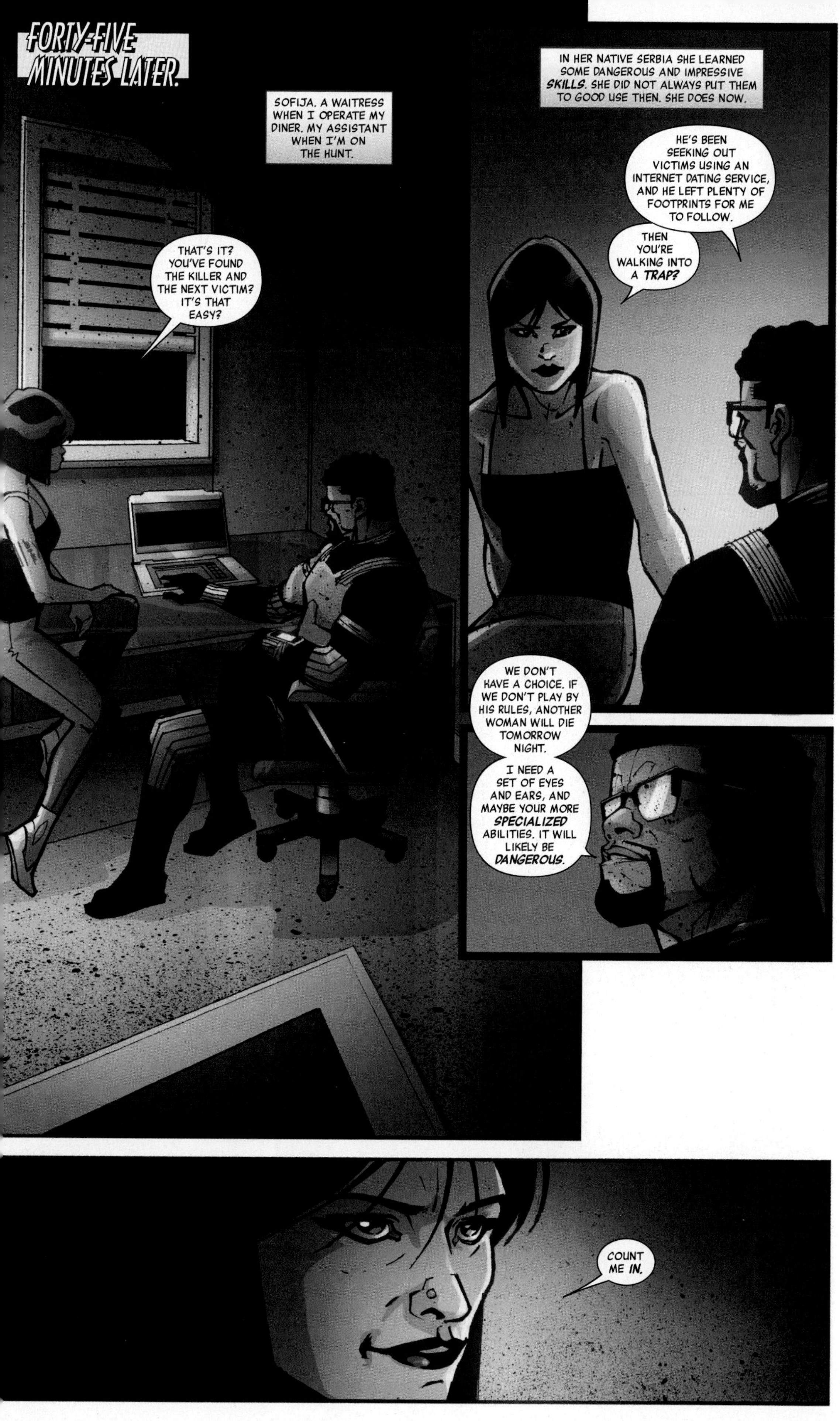

FORTY-FIVE MINUTES LATER.
SOFIJA. A WAITRESS WHEN I OPERATE MY DINER. MY ASSISTANT WHEN I'M ON THE HUNT.
THAT'S IT? YOU'VE FOUND THE KILLER AND THE NEXT VICTIM? IT'S THAT EASY?
IN HER NATIVE SERBIA SHE LEARNED SOME DANGEROUS AND IMPRESSIVE SKILLS. SHE DID NOT ALWAYS PUT THEM TO GOOD USE THEN. SHE DOES NOW.
HE'S BEEN SEEKING OUT VICTIMS USING AN INTERNET DATING SERVICE, AND HE LEFT PLENTY OF FOOTPRINTS FOR ME TO FOLLOW.
THEN YOU'RE WALKING INTO A TRAP?
WE DON'T HAVE A CHOICE. IF WE DON'T PLAY BY HIS RULES, ANOTHER WOMAN WILL DIE TOMORROW NIGHT.
I NEED A SET OF EYES AND EARS, AND MAYBE YOUR MORE SPECIALIZED ABILITIES. IT WILL LIKELY BE DANGEROUS.
COUNT ME IN.

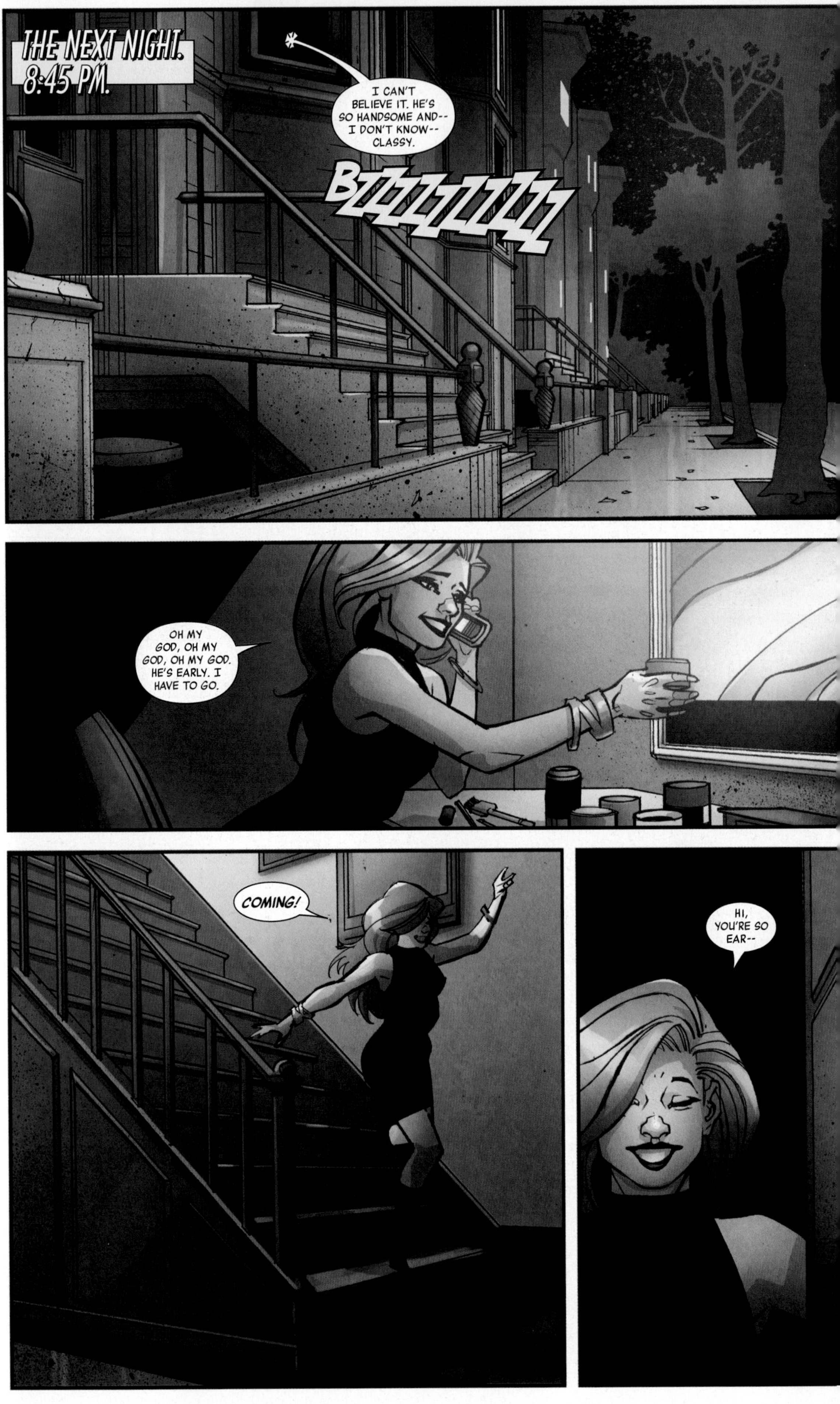
THE NEXT NIGHT. 8:45 PM.
I CAN'T BELIEVE IT. HE'S SO HANDSOME AND-- I DON'T KNOW-- CLASSY.
BZZZZZZZZZZ
OH MY GOD, OH MY GOD, OH MY GOD. HE'S EARLY. I HAVE TO GO.
COMING!
HI, YOU'RE SO EAR--

MEGAN JEDA? YOU REMEMBER THE PANTHER. THAT BANK ROBBERY HOSTAGE SITUATION HE SAVED YOU FROM A FEW WEEKS BACK?

I'M SOFIJA, BY THE WAY. GIRL WONDER.

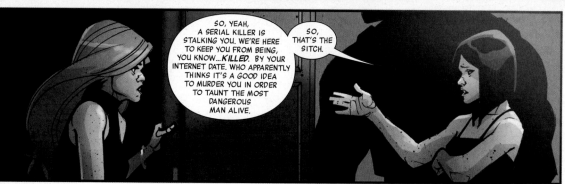

SO, YEAH, A SERIAL KILLER IS STALKING YOU. WE'RE HERE TO KEEP YOU FROM BEING, YOU KNOW...*KILLED*. BY YOUR INTERNET DATE. WHO APPARENTLY THINKS IT'S A GOOD IDEA TO MURDER YOU IN ORDER TO TAUNT THE MOST DANGEROUS MAN ALIVE.

SO, THAT'S THE SITCH.

BUT I...HE... UNHH...

WELL, THAT MAKES THINGS MORE COMPLICATED.

OR EASIER.

OR EASIER.

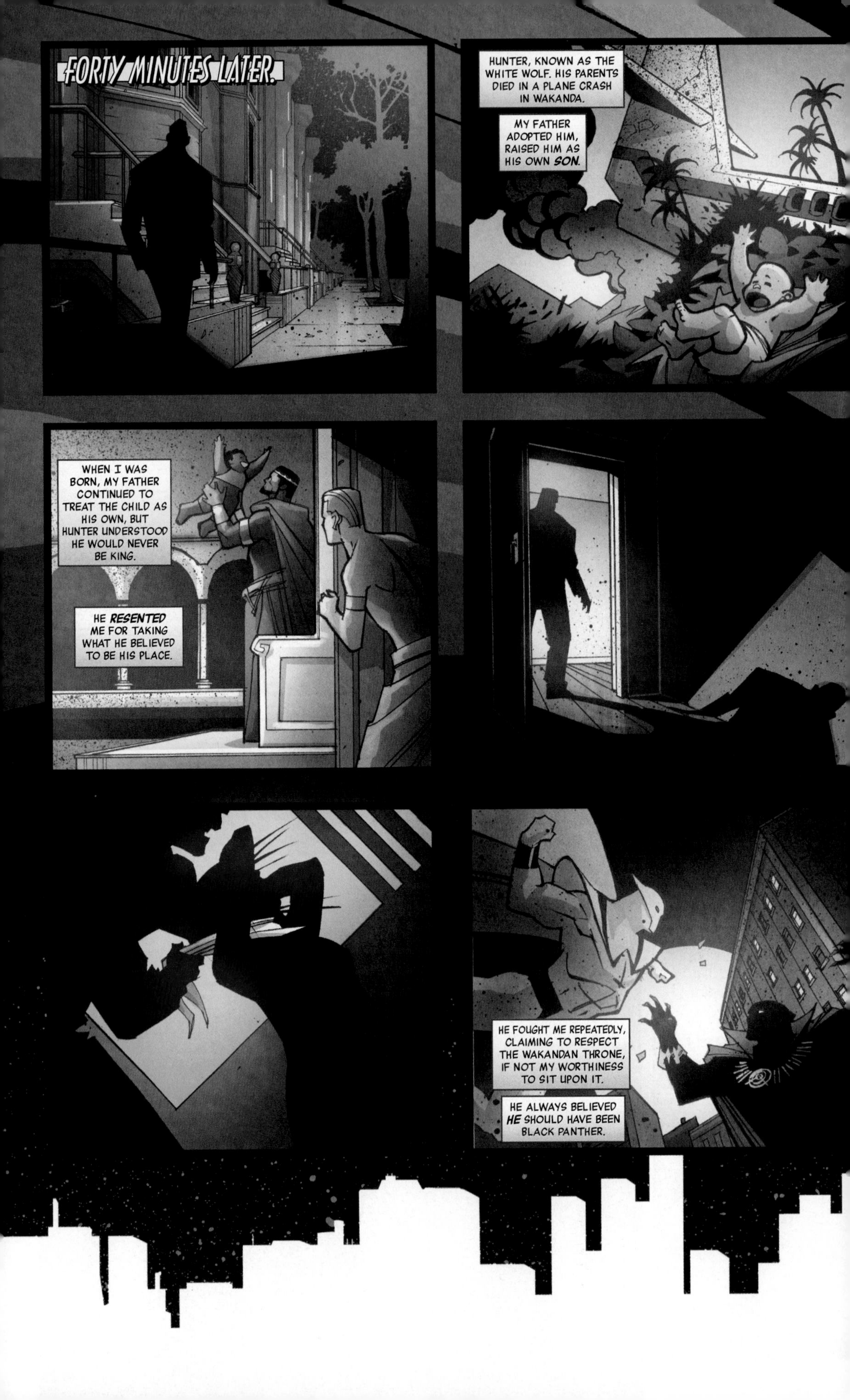
FORTY MINUTES LATER.
HUNTER, KNOWN AS THE WHITE WOLF. HIS PARENTS DIED IN A PLANE CRASH IN WAKANDA.
MY FATHER ADOPTED HIM, RAISED HIM AS HIS OWN SON.
WHEN I WAS BORN, MY FATHER CONTINUED TO TREAT THE CHILD AS HIS OWN, BUT HUNTER UNDERSTOOD HE WOULD NEVER BE KING.
HE RESENTED ME FOR TAKING WHAT HE BELIEVED TO BE HIS PLACE.
HE FOUGHT ME REPEATEDLY, CLAIMING TO RESPECT THE WAKANDAN THRONE, IF NOT MY WORTHINESS TO SIT UPON IT.
HE ALWAYS BELIEVED HE SHOULD HAVE BEEN BLACK PANTHER.

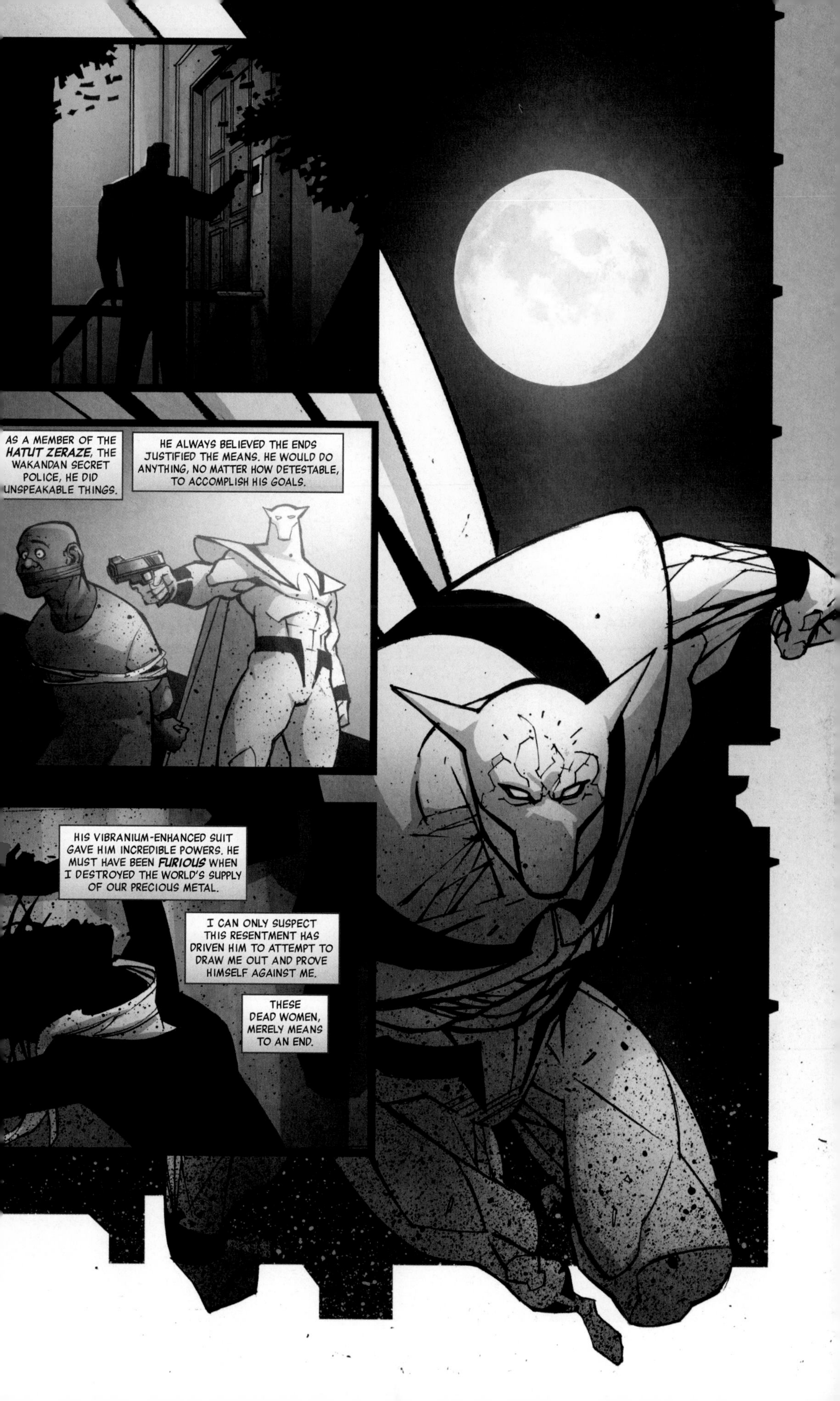
AS A MEMBER OF THE HATUT ZERAZE, THE WAKANDAN SECRET POLICE, HE DID UNSPEAKABLE THINGS.
HE ALWAYS BELIEVED THE ENDS JUSTIFIED THE MEANS. HE WOULD DO ANYTHING, NO MATTER HOW DETESTABLE, TO ACCOMPLISH HIS GOALS.
HIS VIBRANIUM-ENHANCED SUIT GAVE HIM INCREDIBLE POWERS. HE MUST HAVE BEEN FURIOUS WHEN I DESTROYED THE WORLD'S SUPPLY OF OUR PRECIOUS METAL.
I CAN ONLY SUSPECT THIS RESENTMENT HAS DRIVEN HIM TO ATTEMPT TO DRAW ME OUT AND PROVE HIMSELF AGAINST ME.
THESE DEAD WOMEN, MERELY MEANS TO AN END.

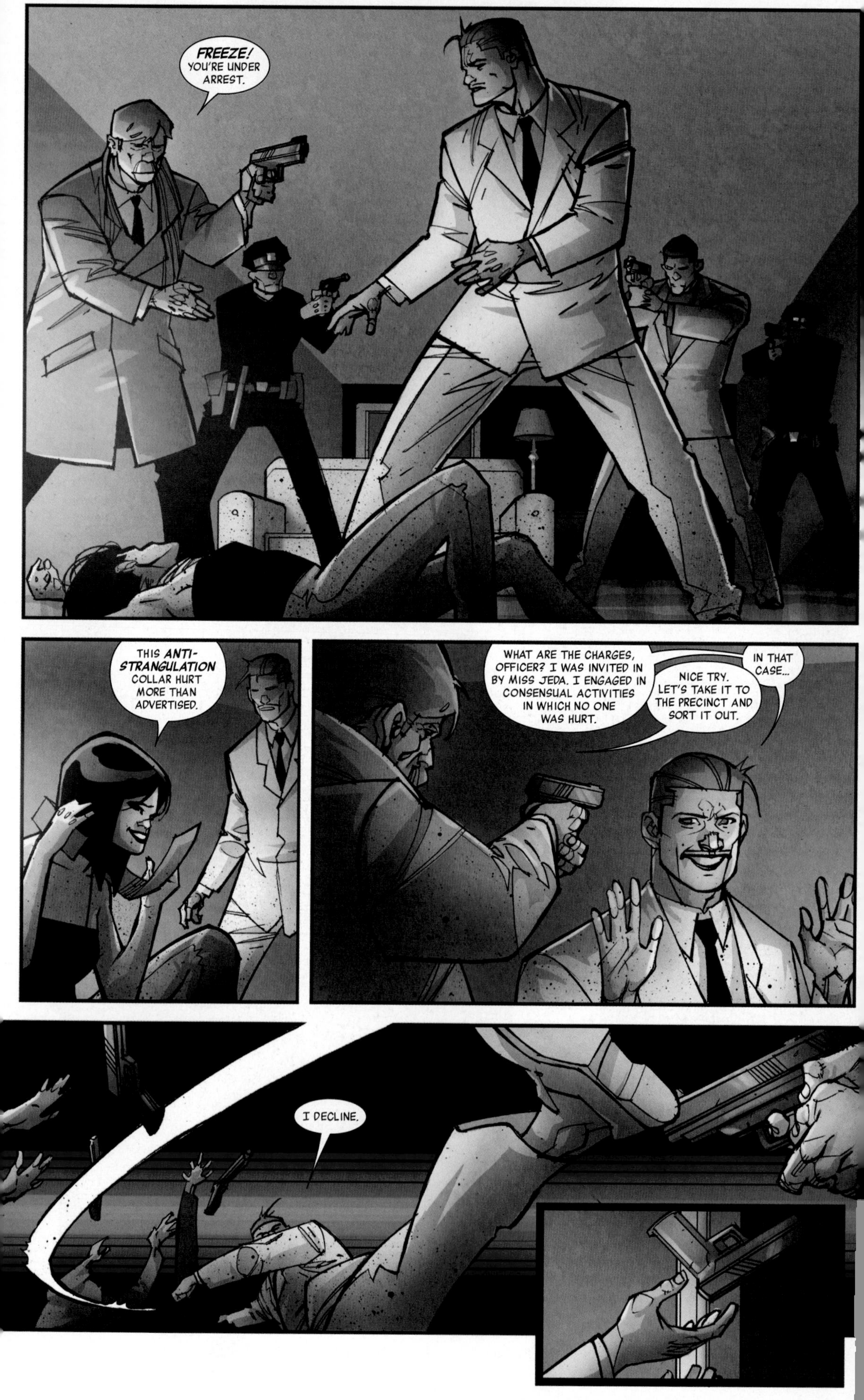
FREEZE! YOU'RE UNDER ARREST.
THIS ANTI-STRANGULATION COLLAR HURT MORE THAN ADVERTISED.
WHAT ARE THE CHARGES, OFFICER? I WAS INVITED IN BY MISS JEDA. I ENGAGED IN CONSENSUAL ACTIVITIES IN WHICH NO ONE WAS HURT.
NICE TRY. LET'S TAKE IT TO THE PRECINCT AND SORT IT OUT.
IN THAT CASE...
I DECLINE.

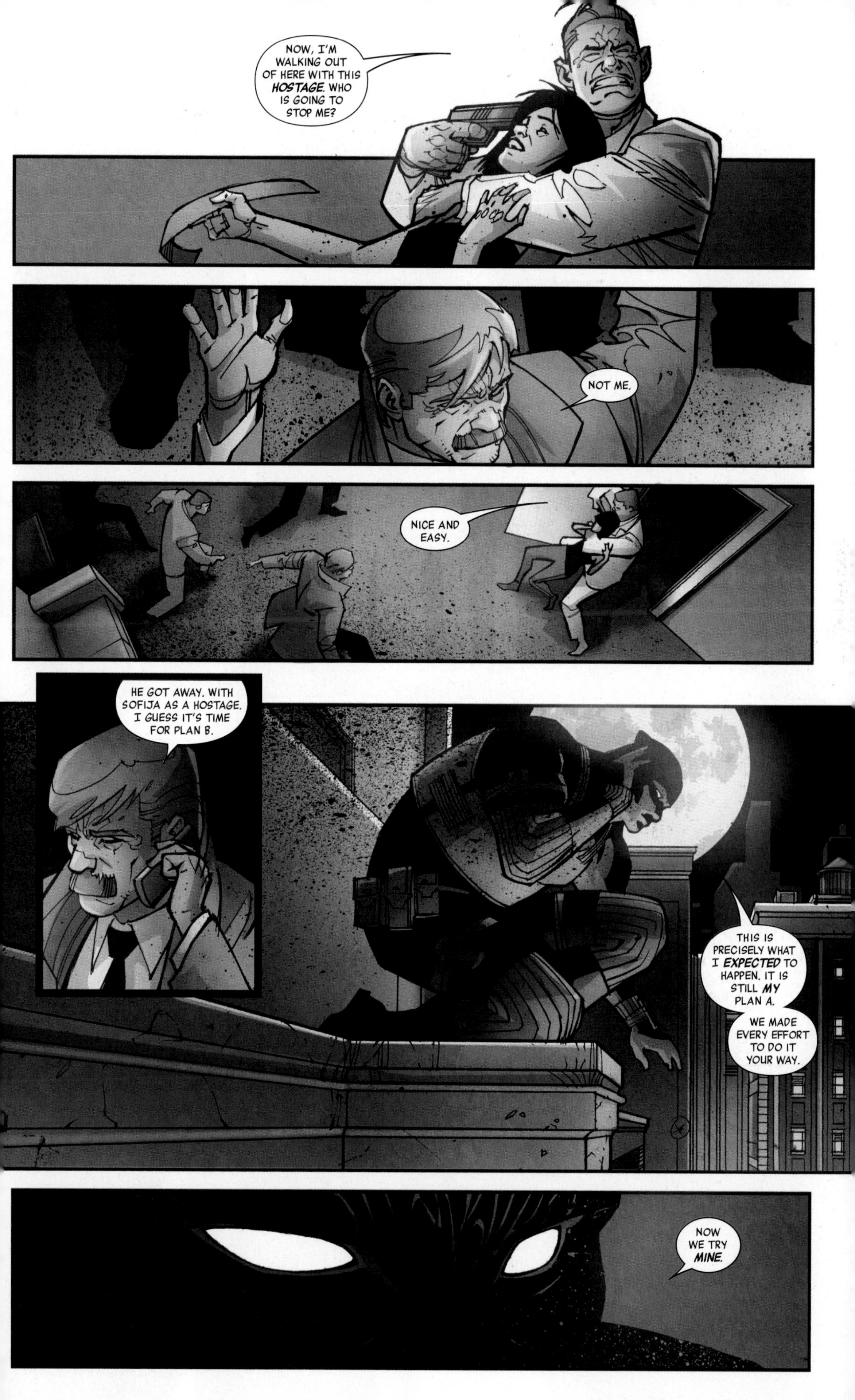

NOW, I'M WALKING OUT OF HERE WITH THIS **HOSTAGE**. WHO IS GOING TO STOP ME?
NOT ME.
NICE AND EASY.
HE GOT AWAY. WITH SOFIJA AS A HOSTAGE. I GUESS IT'S TIME FOR PLAN B.
THIS IS PRECISELY WHAT I **EXPECTED** TO HAPPEN. IT IS STILL **MY** PLAN A.
WE MADE EVERY EFFORT TO DO IT YOUR WAY.
NOW WE TRY **MINE**.

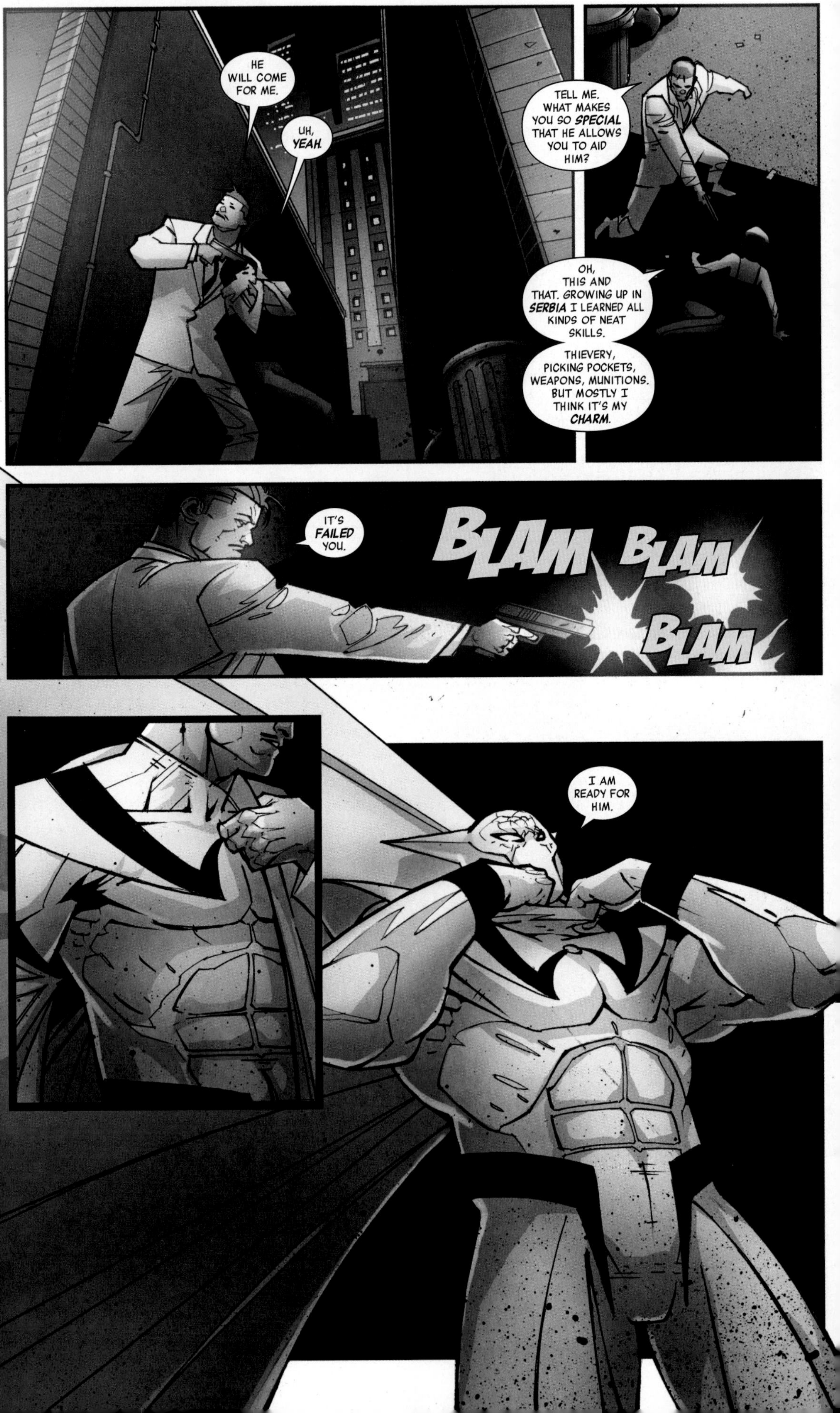
HE WILL COME FOR ME.
UH, YEAH.
TELL ME. WHAT MAKES YOU SO SPECIAL THAT HE ALLOWS YOU TO AID HIM?
OH, THIS AND THAT. GROWING UP IN SERBIA I LEARNED ALL KINDS OF NEAT SKILLS.
THIEVERY, PICKING POCKETS, WEAPONS, MUNITIONS. BUT MOSTLY I THINK IT'S MY CHARM.
IT'S FAILED YOU.
BLAM BLAM
BLAM
I AM READY FOR HIM.

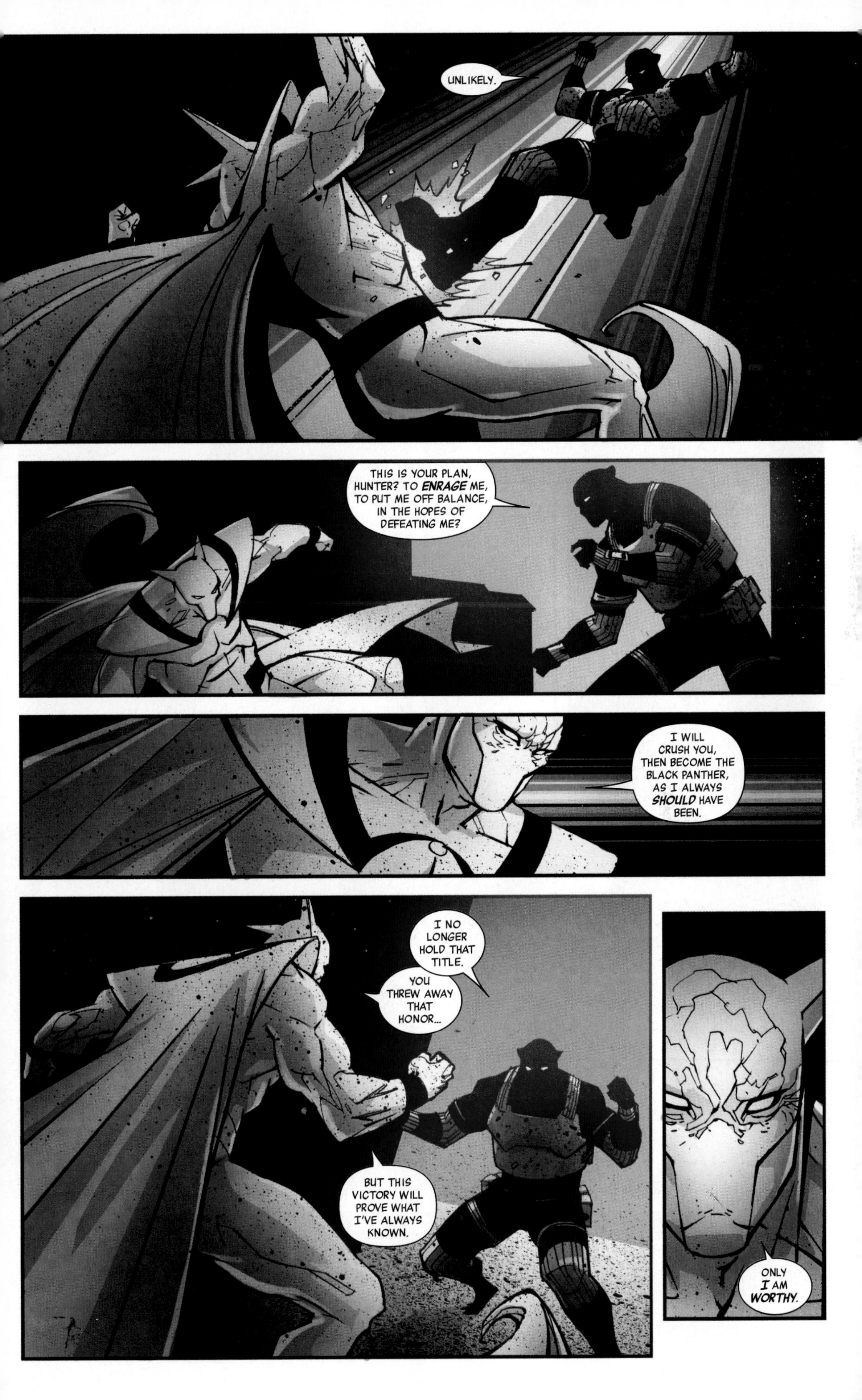
UNLIKELY.
THIS IS YOUR PLAN, HUNTER? TO ENRAGE ME, TO PUT ME OFF BALANCE, IN THE HOPES OF DEFEATING ME?
I WILL CRUSH YOU, THEN BECOME THE BLACK PANTHER, AS I ALWAYS SHOULD HAVE BEEN.
I NO LONGER HOLD THAT TITLE.
YOU THREW AWAY THAT HONOR...
BUT THIS VICTORY WILL PROVE WHAT I'VE ALWAYS KNOWN.
ONLY I AM WORTHY.

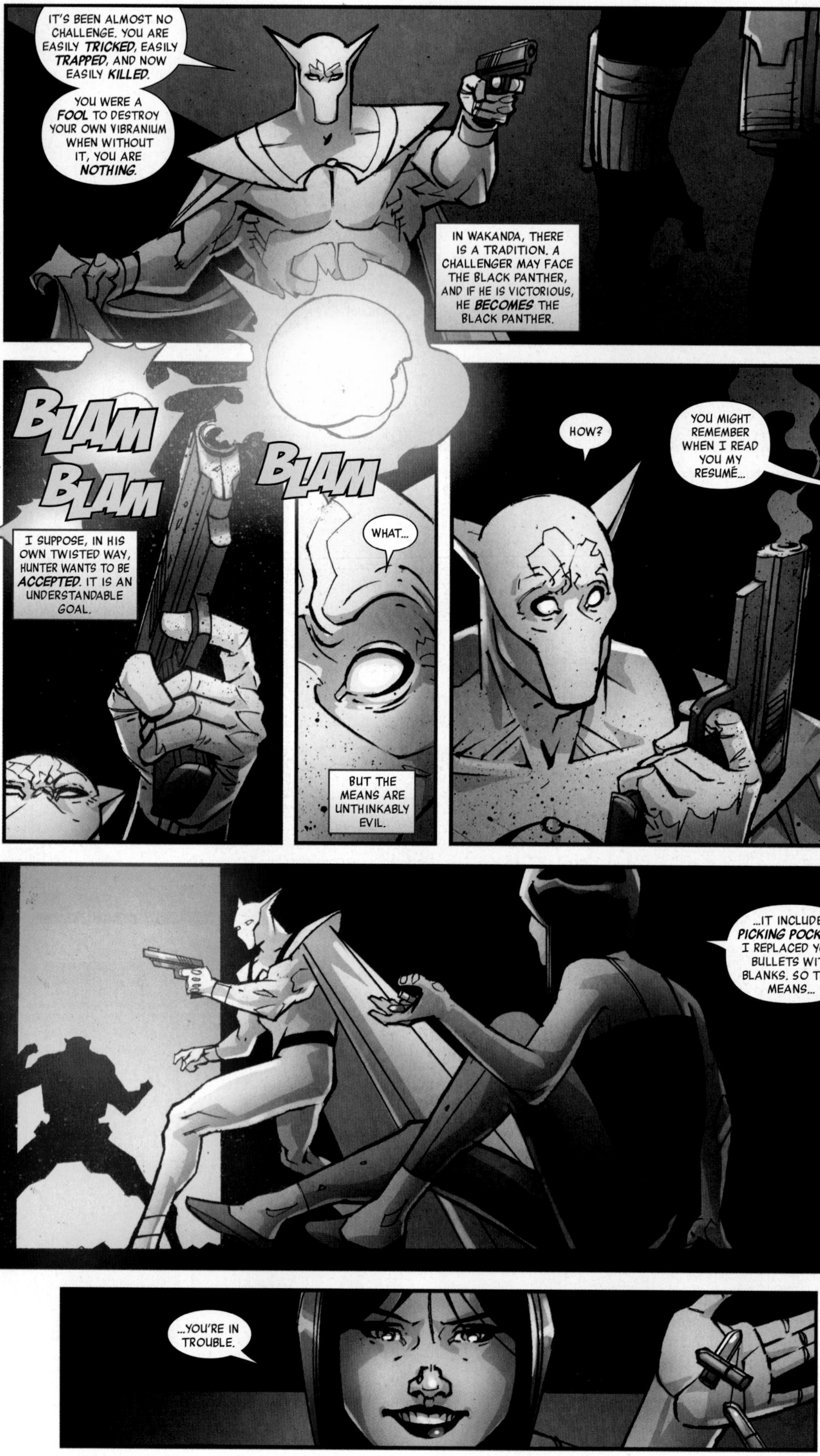
IT'S BEEN ALMOST NO CHALLENGE. YOU ARE EASILY TRICKED, EASILY TRAPPED, AND NOW EASILY KILLED.
YOU WERE A FOOL TO DESTROY YOUR OWN VIBRANIUM WHEN WITHOUT IT, YOU ARE NOTHING.
IN WAKANDA, THERE IS A TRADITION. A CHALLENGER MAY FACE THE BLACK PANTHER, AND IF HE IS VICTORIOUS, HE BECOMES THE BLACK PANTHER.
BLAM
BLAM
BLAM
I SUPPOSE, IN HIS OWN TWISTED WAY, HUNTER WANTS TO BE ACCEPTED. IT IS AN UNDERSTANDABLE GOAL.
WHAT...
BUT THE MEANS ARE UNTHINKABLY EVIL.
HOW?
YOU MIGHT REMEMBER WHEN I READ YOU MY RESUMÉ...
...IT INCLUDED PICKING POCKETS. I REPLACED YOUR BULLETS WITH BLANKS. SO THAT MEANS...
...YOU'RE IN TROUBLE.

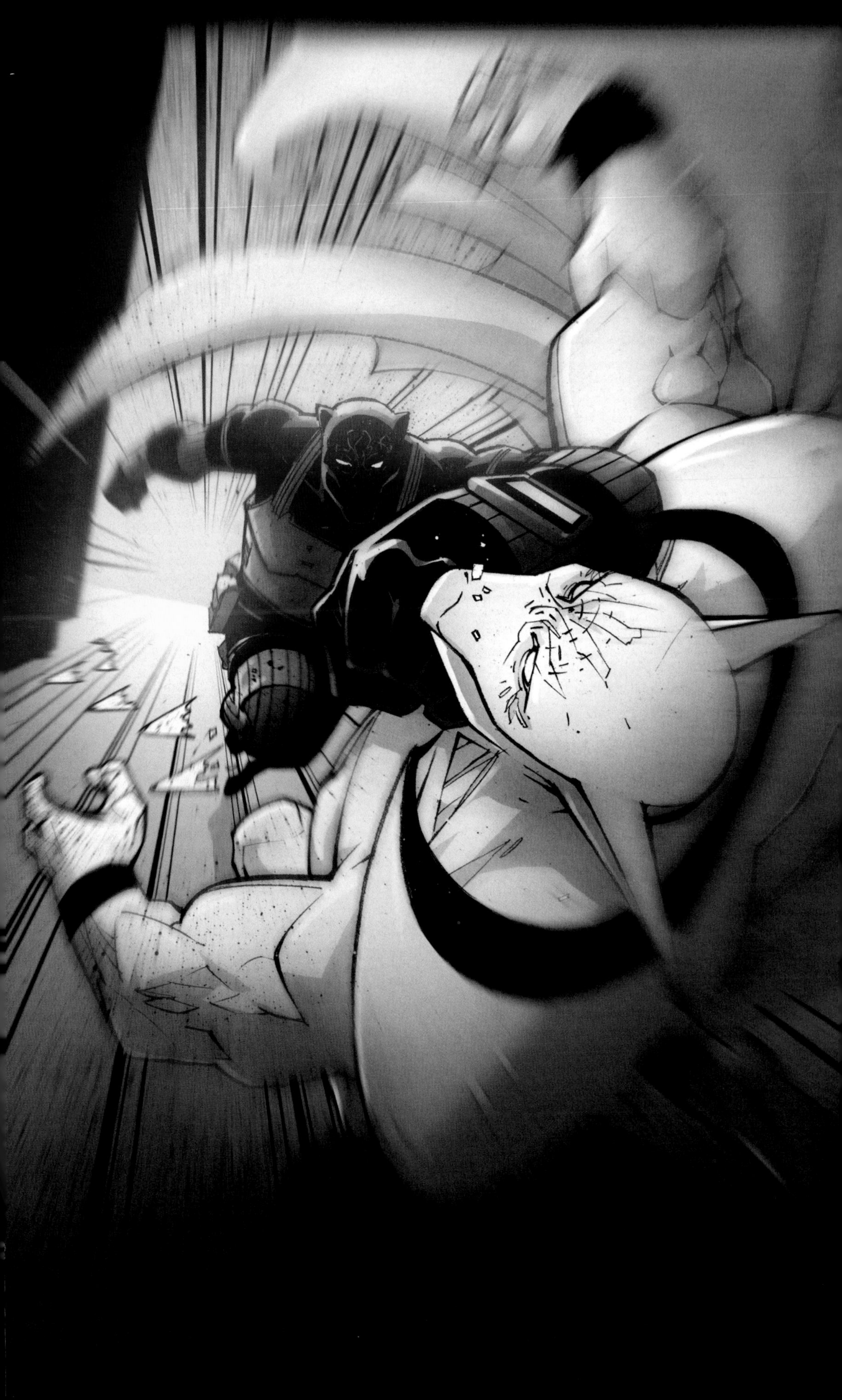

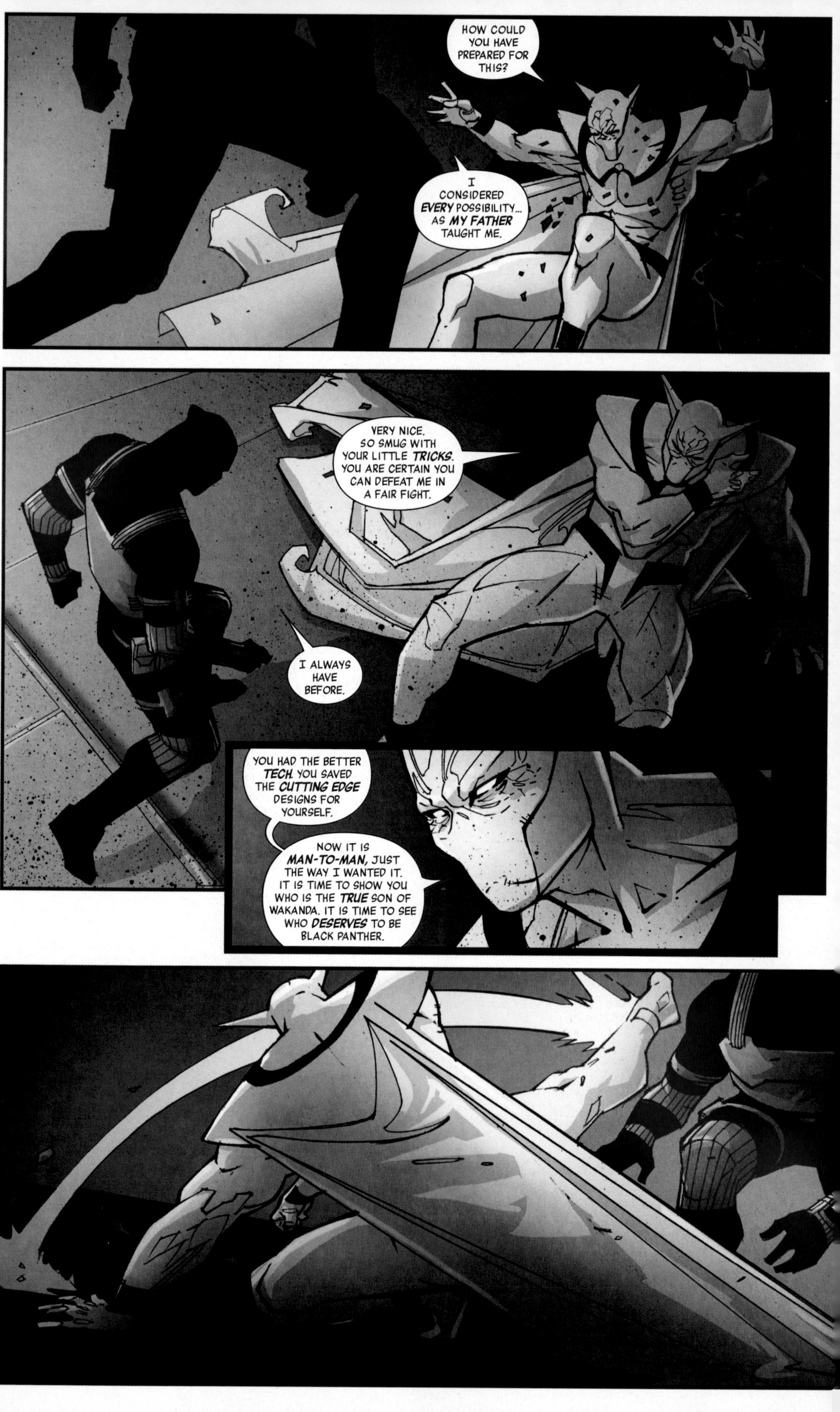
HOW COULD YOU HAVE PREPARED FOR THIS?
I CONSIDERED EVERY POSSIBILITY... AS MY FATHER TAUGHT ME.
VERY NICE. SO SMUG WITH YOUR LITTLE TRICKS. YOU ARE CERTAIN YOU CAN DEFEAT ME IN A FAIR FIGHT.
I ALWAYS HAVE BEFORE.
YOU HAD THE BETTER TECH. YOU SAVED THE CUTTING EDGE DESIGNS FOR YOURSELF.
NOW IT IS MAN-TO-MAN, JUST THE WAY I WANTED IT. IT IS TIME TO SHOW YOU WHO IS THE TRUE SON OF WAKANDA. IT IS TIME TO SEE WHO DESERVES TO BE BLACK PANTHER.

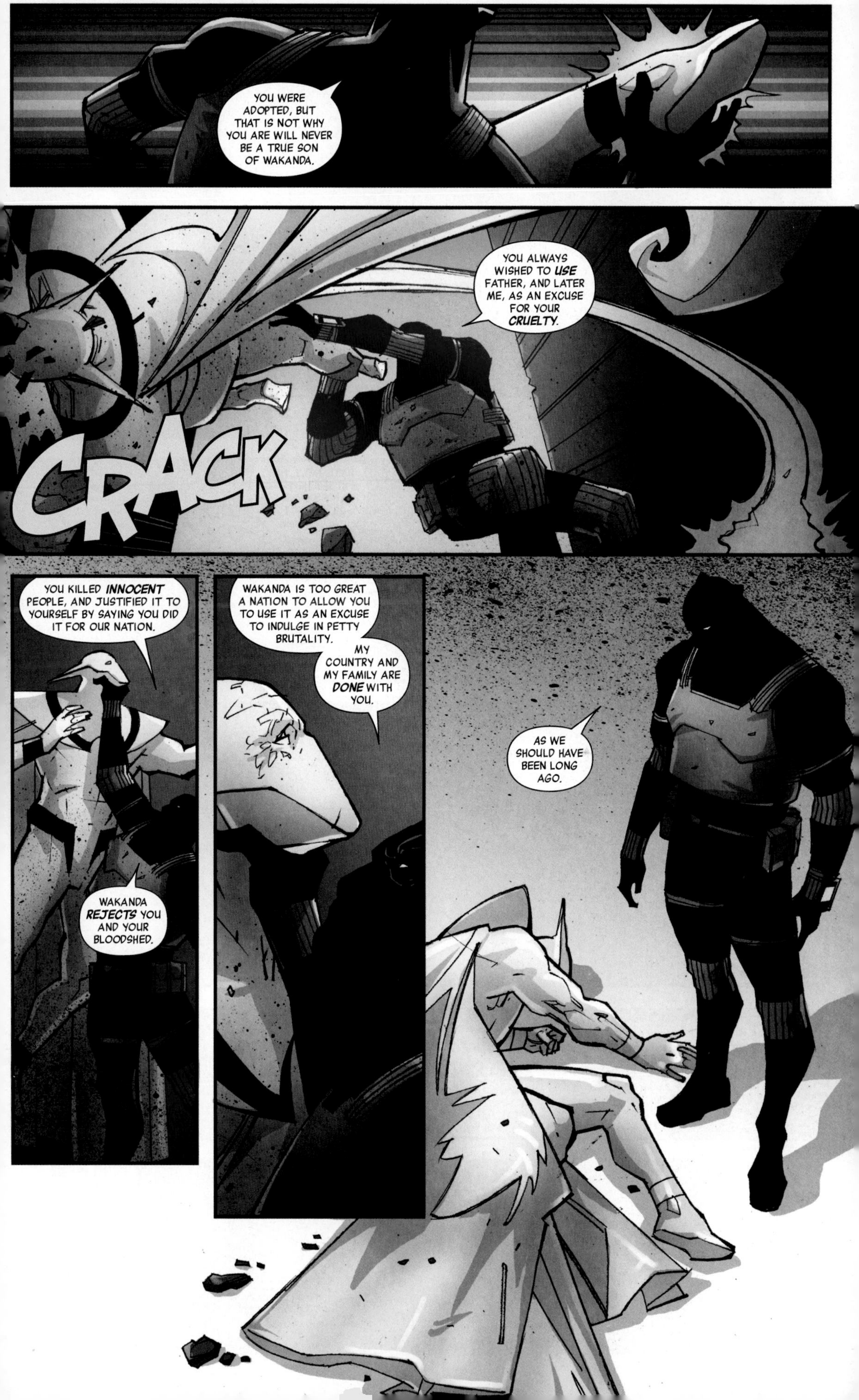
YOU WERE ADOPTED, BUT THAT IS NOT WHY YOU ARE WILL NEVER BE A TRUE SON OF WAKANDA.
YOU ALWAYS WISHED TO USE FATHER, AND LATER ME, AS AN EXCUSE FOR YOUR CRUELTY.
CRACK
YOU KILLED INNOCENT PEOPLE, AND JUSTIFIED IT TO YOURSELF BY SAYING YOU DID IT FOR OUR NATION.
WAKANDA REJECTS YOU AND YOUR BLOODSHED.
WAKANDA IS TOO GREAT A NATION TO ALLOW YOU TO USE IT AS AN EXCUSE TO INDULGE IN PETTY BRUTALITY.
MY COUNTRY AND MY FAMILY ARE DONE WITH YOU.
AS WE SHOULD HAVE BEEN LONG AGO.

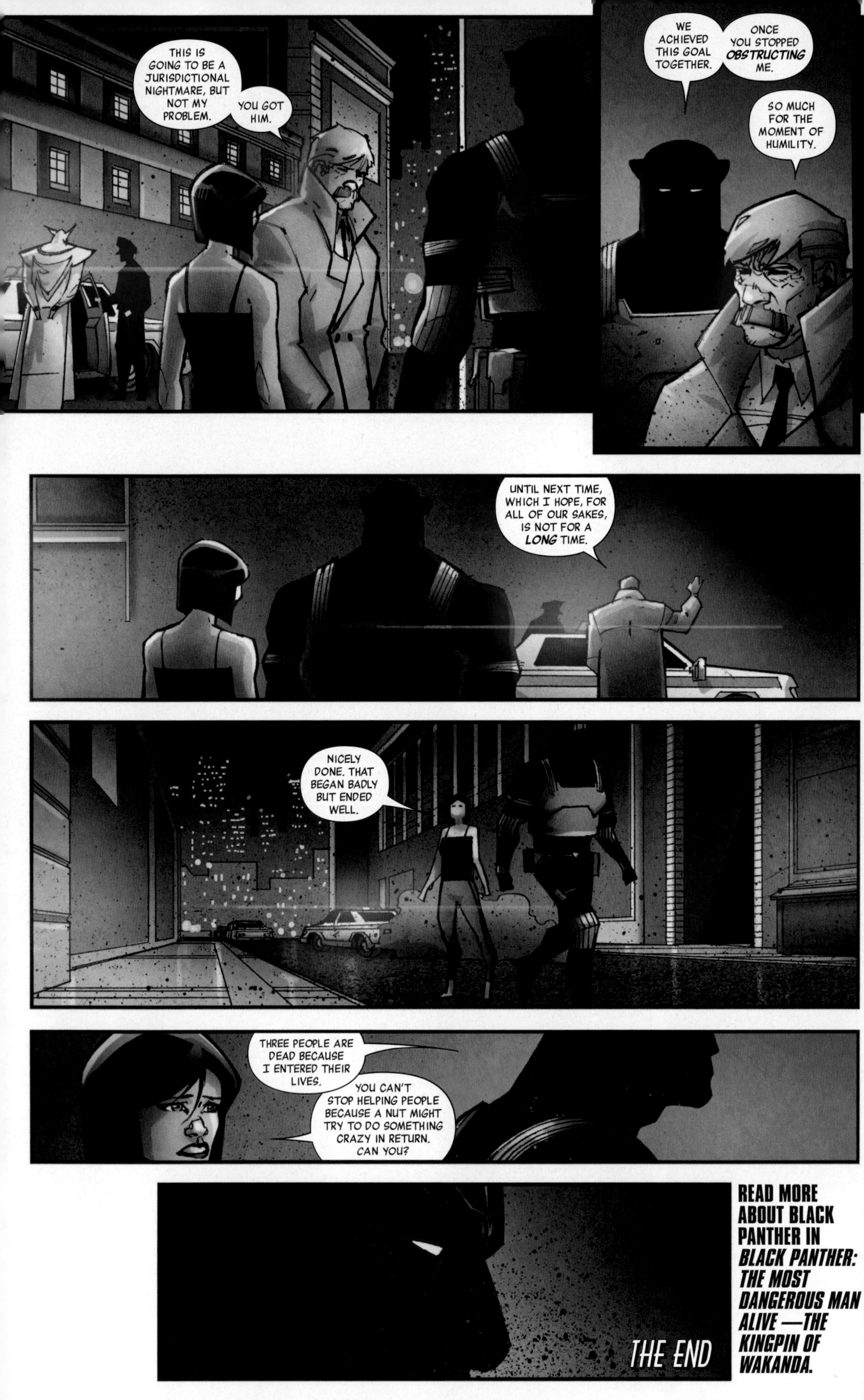
THIS IS GOING TO BE A JURISDICTIONAL NIGHTMARE, BUT NOT MY PROBLEM.
YOU GOT HIM.
WE ACHIEVED THIS GOAL TOGETHER.
ONCE YOU STOPPED OBSTRUCTING ME.
SO MUCH FOR THE MOMENT OF HUMILITY.
UNTIL NEXT TIME, WHICH I HOPE, FOR ALL OF OUR SAKES, IS NOT FOR A LONG TIME.
NICELY DONE. THAT BEGAN BADLY BUT ENDED WELL.
THREE PEOPLE ARE DEAD BECAUSE I ENTERED THEIR LIVES.
YOU CAN'T STOP HELPING PEOPLE BECAUSE A NUT MIGHT TRY TO DO SOMETHING CRAZY IN RETURN. CAN YOU?
THE END

READ MORE ABOUT BLACK PANTHER IN *BLACK PANTHER: THE MOST DANGEROUS MAN ALIVE—THE KINGPIN OF WAKANDA.*

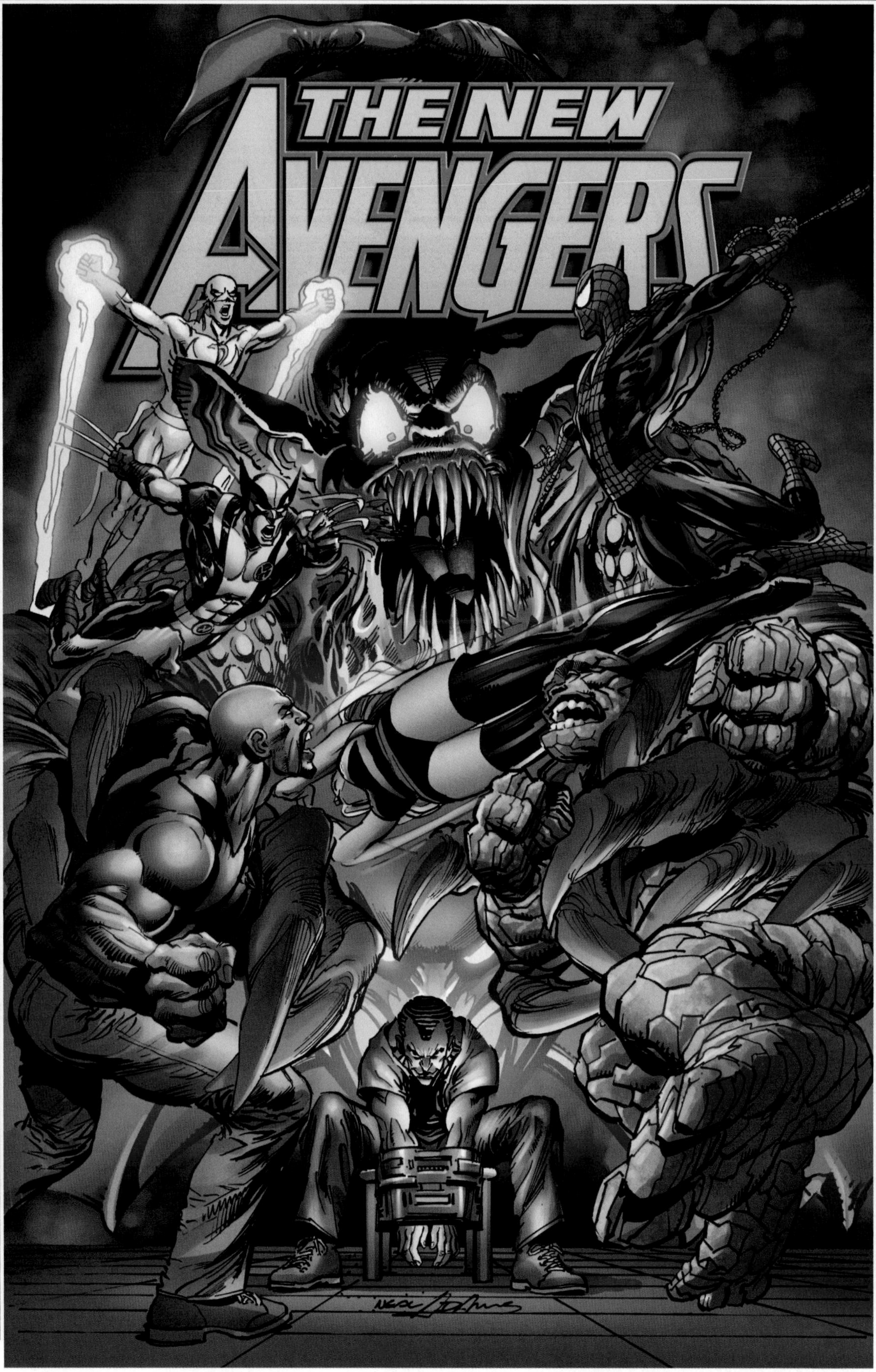
THE NEW AVENGERS

NEW AVENGERS #16.1

EARTH'S MIGHTIEST HEROES, UNITED AGAINST A COMMON THREAT! ON THAT DAY THE AVENGERS WERE BORN, TO FIGHT FOES THAT NO SINGLE HERO COULD WITHSTAND!

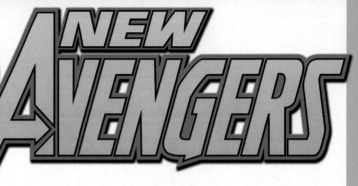

NEW AVENGERS

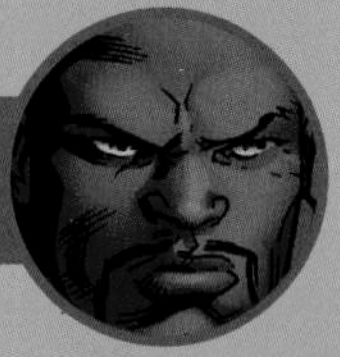
LUKE CAGE

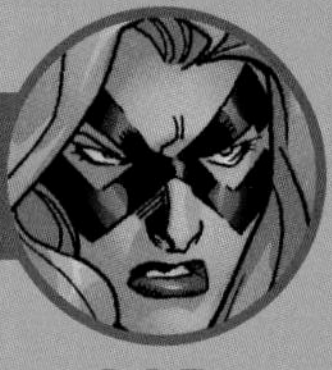
MS. MARVEL

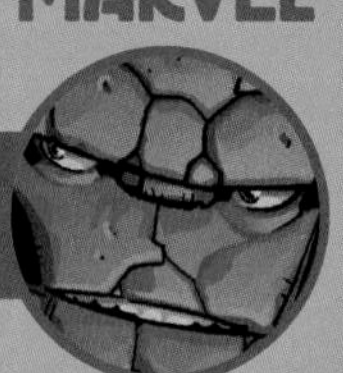
THING

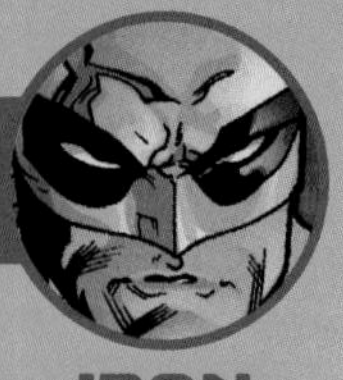
IRON FIST

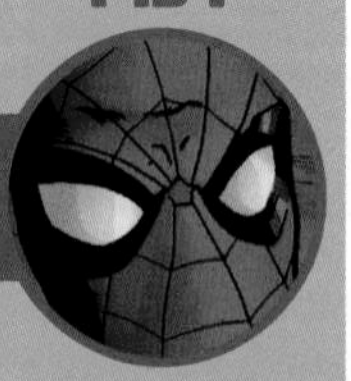
SPIDER-MAN

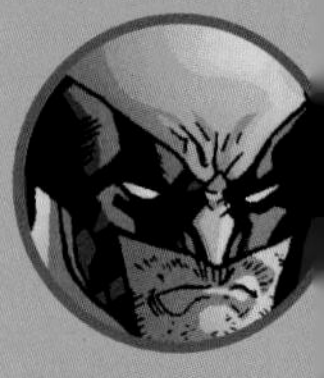
WOLVERINE

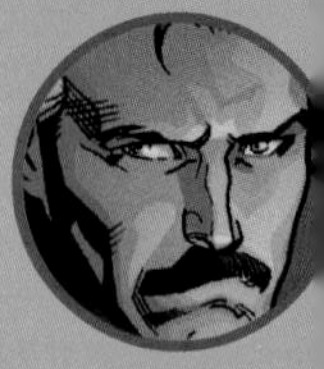
DR. STRANGE

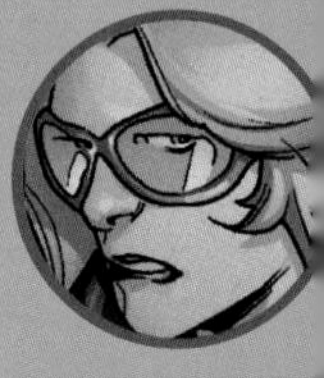
MOCKINGBIRD

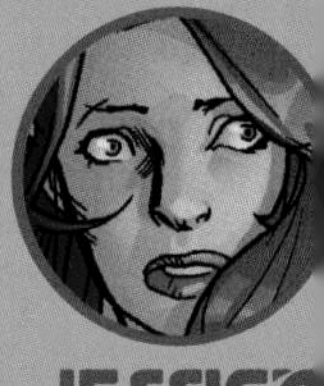
JESSICA JONES

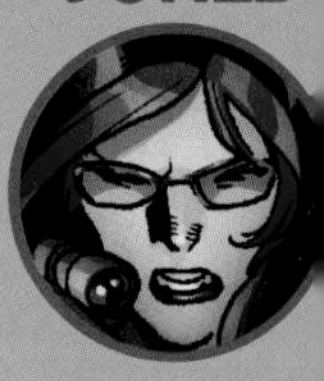
VICTORIA HAND

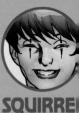

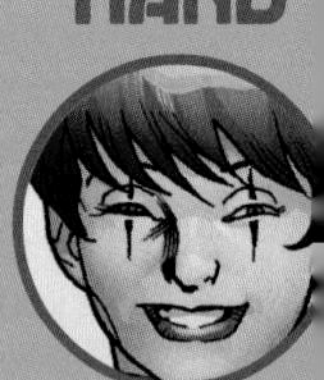
SQUIRREL GIRL

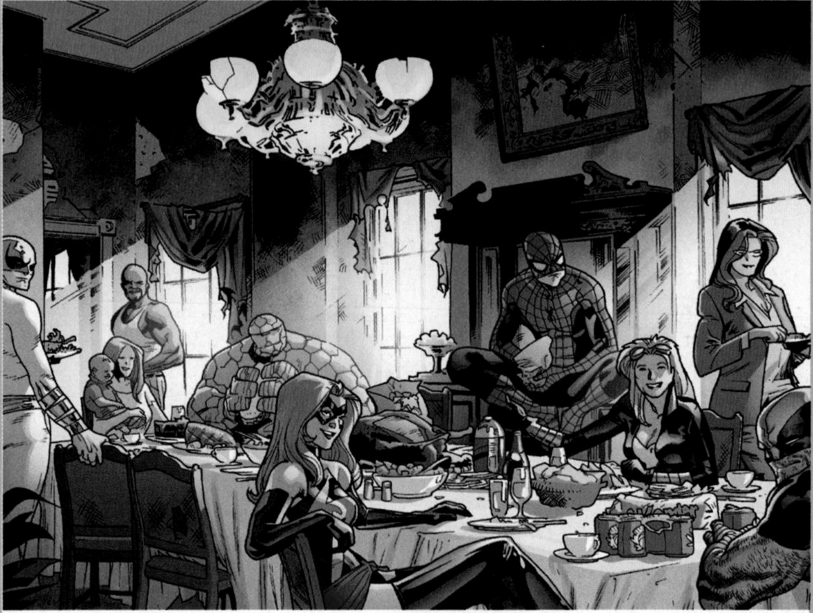

AVENGERS COMMANDER STEVE ROGERS HAS GIVEN LUKE CAGE, JESSICA JONES, MS. MARVEL, MOCKINGBIRD, SPIDER-MAN, WOLVERINE, IRON FIST, DOCTOR STRANGE, AND THE THING THE KEYS TO AVENGERS MANSION, A LIAISON IN THE CONTROVERSIAL FORM OF VICTORIA HAND, AND FREE REIN TO PROTECT THE WORLD ANY WAY THEY SEE FIT.

BRIAN MICHAEL BENDIS
WRITER

NEAL ADAMS
PENCILER

TOM PALMER
INKER

PAUL MOUNTS
COLORIST

VC'S JOE CARAMAGNA
LETTERS & PRODUCTION

NEAL ADAMS & PAUL MOUNTS
COVER ARTISTS

LAUREN SANKOVITCH
ASSOCIATE EDITOR

TOM BREVOORT
EDITOR

AXEL ALONSO
EDITOR IN CHIEF

JOE QUESADA
CHIEF CREATIVE OFFICER

DAN BUCKLEY
PUBLISHER

ALAN FINE
EXEC. PRODUCER

SPECIAL THANKS TO KRIS STONE

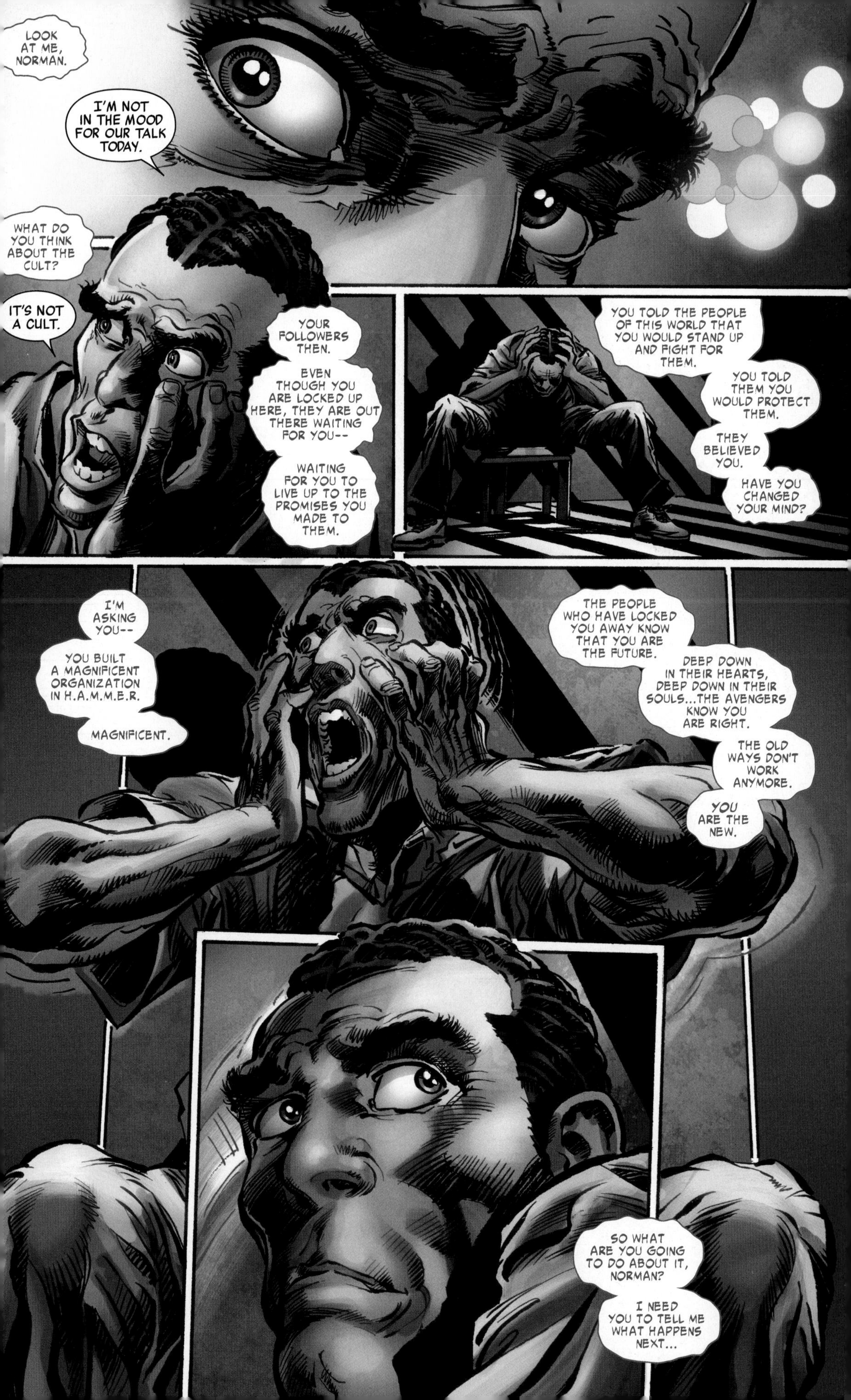
LOOK AT ME, NORMAN.
I'M NOT IN THE MOOD FOR OUR TALK TODAY.
WHAT DO YOU THINK ABOUT THE CULT?
IT'S NOT A CULT.
YOUR FOLLOWERS THEN.
EVEN THOUGH YOU ARE LOCKED UP HERE, THEY ARE OUT THERE WAITING FOR YOU--
WAITING FOR YOU TO LIVE UP TO THE PROMISES YOU MADE TO THEM.
YOU TOLD THE PEOPLE OF THIS WORLD THAT YOU WOULD STAND UP AND FIGHT FOR THEM.
YOU TOLD THEM YOU WOULD PROTECT THEM.
THEY BELIEVED YOU.
HAVE YOU CHANGED YOUR MIND?
I'M ASKING YOU--
YOU BUILT A MAGNIFICENT ORGANIZATION IN H.A.M.M.E.R.
MAGNIFICENT.
THE PEOPLE WHO HAVE LOCKED YOU AWAY KNOW THAT YOU ARE THE FUTURE.
DEEP DOWN IN THEIR HEARTS, DEEP DOWN IN THEIR SOULS...THE AVENGERS KNOW YOU ARE RIGHT.
THE OLD WAYS DON'T WORK ANYMORE.
YOU ARE THE NEW.
SO WHAT ARE YOU GOING TO DO ABOUT IT, NORMAN?
I NEED YOU TO TELL ME WHAT HAPPENS NEXT...

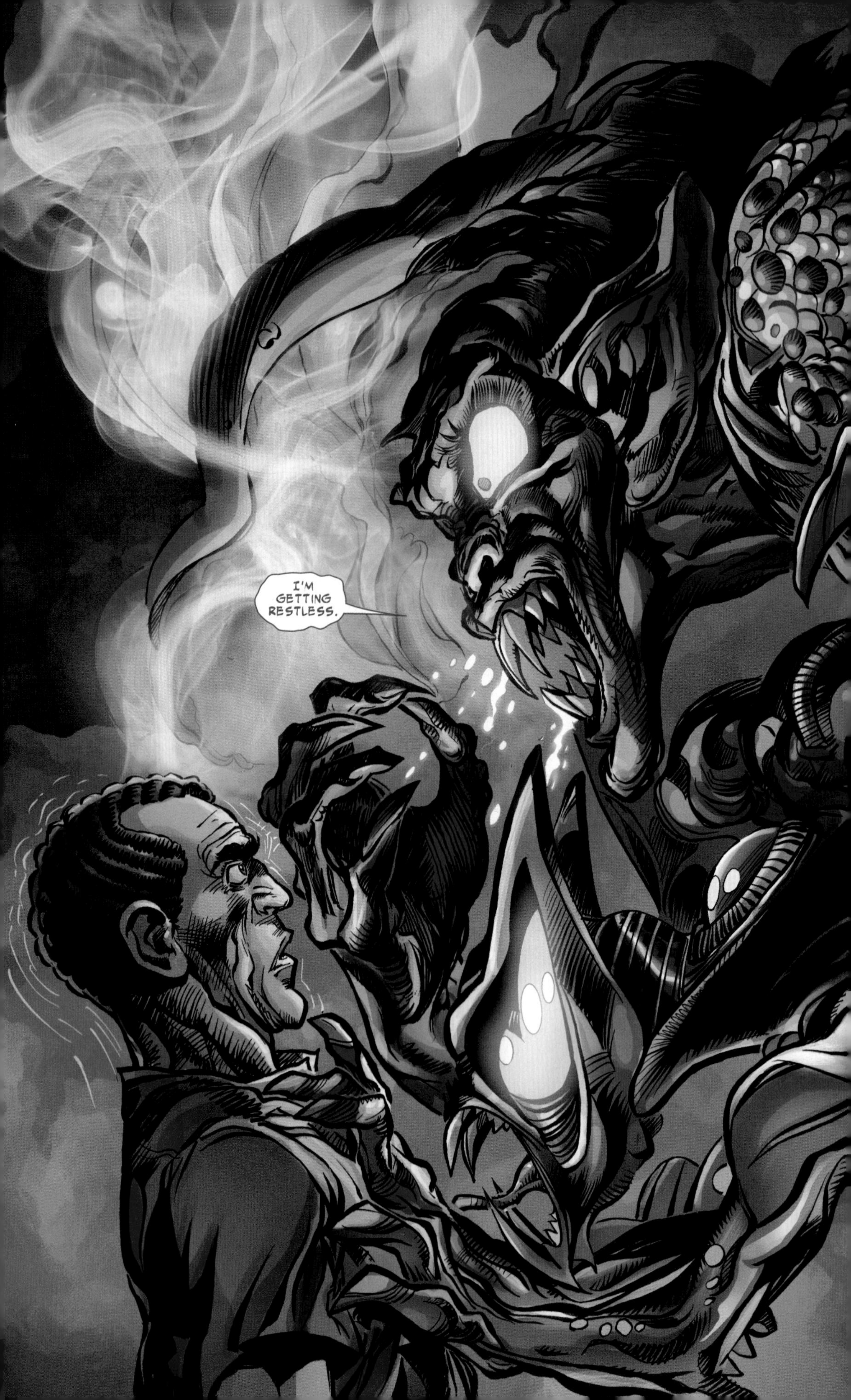
I'M GETTING RESTLESS.

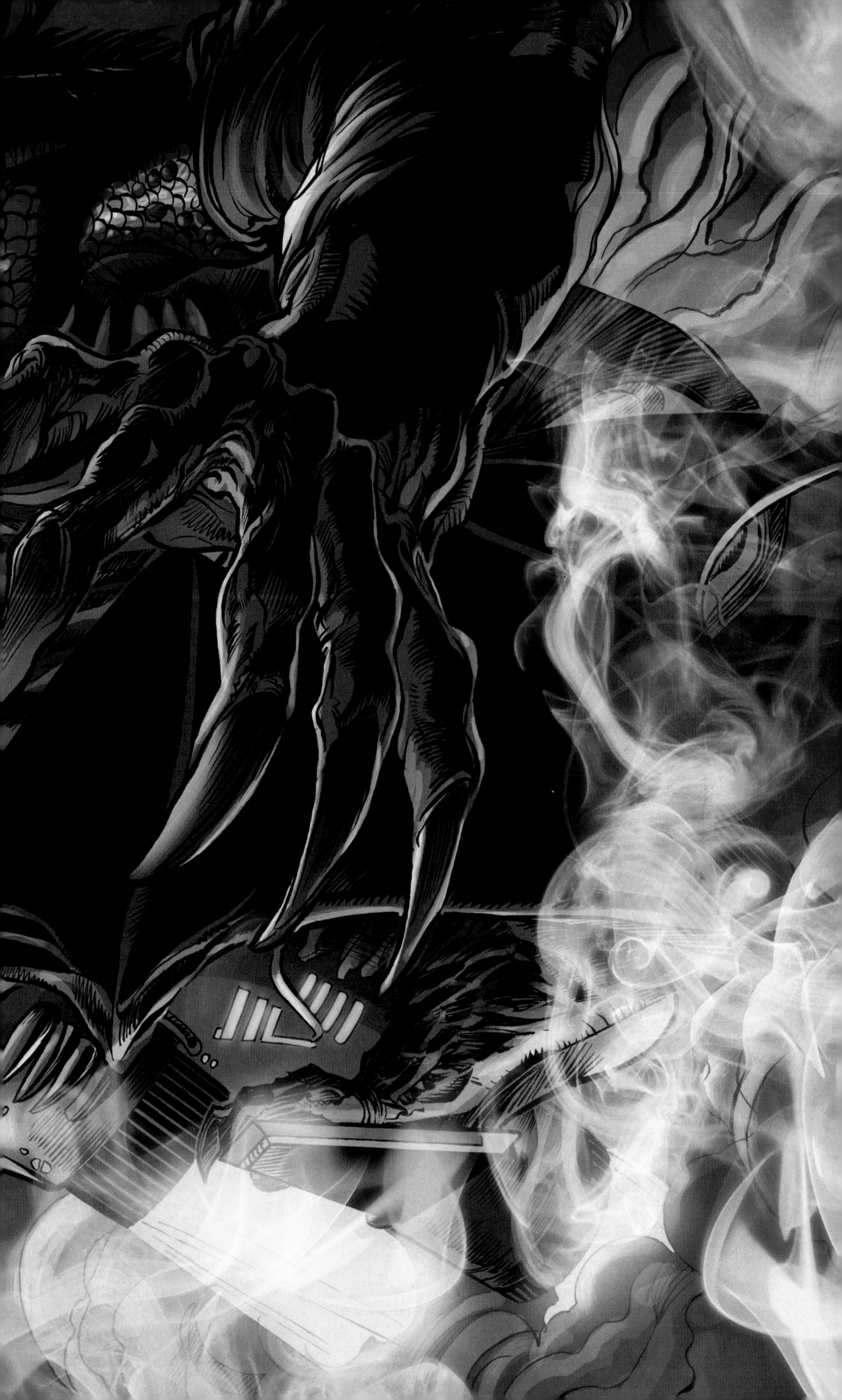

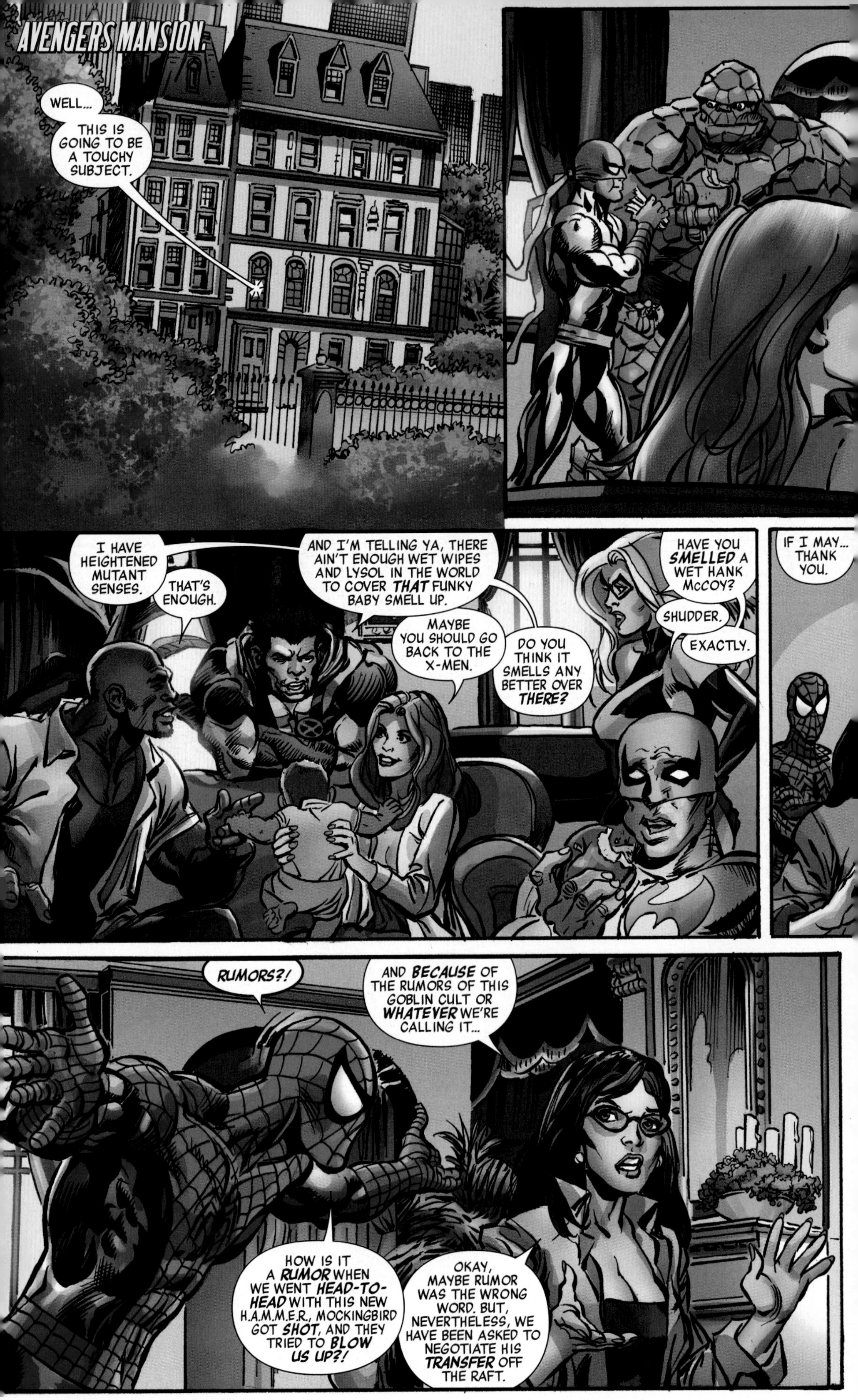

AVENGERS MANSION.
WELL... THIS IS GOING TO BE A TOUCHY SUBJECT.
I HAVE HEIGHTENED MUTANT SENSES.
AND I'M TELLING YA, THERE AIN'T ENOUGH WET WIPES AND LYSOL IN THE WORLD TO COVER THAT FUNKY BABY SMELL UP.
THAT'S ENOUGH.
MAYBE YOU SHOULD GO BACK TO THE X-MEN.
DO YOU THINK IT SMELLS ANY BETTER OVER THERE?
HAVE YOU SMELLED A WET HANK McCOY?
SHUDDER.
EXACTLY.
IF I MAY... THANK YOU.
AND BECAUSE OF THE RUMORS OF THIS GOBLIN CULT OR WHATEVER WE'RE CALLING IT...
RUMORS?!
HOW IS IT A RUMOR WHEN WE WENT HEAD-TO-HEAD WITH THIS NEW H.A.M.M.E.R., MOCKINGBIRD GOT SHOT, AND THEY TRIED TO BLOW US UP?!
OKAY, MAYBE RUMOR WAS THE WRONG WORD. BUT, NEVERTHELESS, WE HAVE BEEN ASKED TO NEGOTIATE HIS TRANSFER OFF THE RAFT.

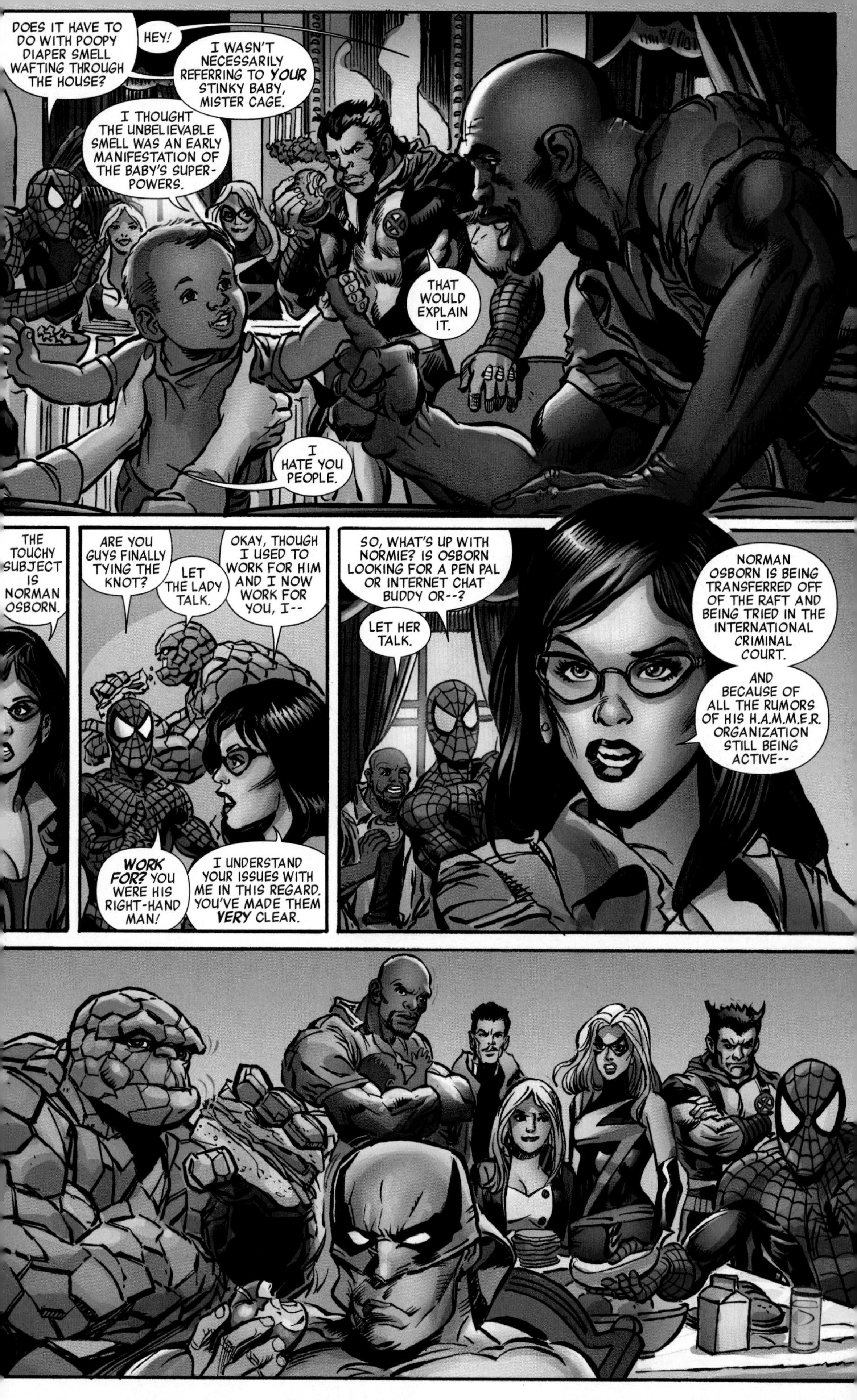
DOES IT HAVE TO DO WITH POOPY DIAPER SMELL WAFTING THROUGH THE HOUSE?
HEY!
I WASN'T NECESSARILY REFERRING TO YOUR STINKY BABY, MISTER CAGE.
I THOUGHT THE UNBELIEVABLE SMELL WAS AN EARLY MANIFESTATION OF THE BABY'S SUPER-POWERS.
THAT WOULD EXPLAIN IT.
I HATE YOU PEOPLE.
THE TOUCHY SUBJECT IS NORMAN OSBORN.
ARE YOU GUYS FINALLY TYING THE KNOT?
LET THE LADY TALK.
OKAY, THOUGH I USED TO WORK FOR HIM AND I NOW WORK FOR YOU, I--
WORK FOR? YOU WERE HIS RIGHT-HAND MAN!
I UNDERSTAND YOUR ISSUES WITH ME IN THIS REGARD. YOU'VE MADE THEM VERY CLEAR.
SO, WHAT'S UP WITH NORMIE? IS OSBORN LOOKING FOR A PEN PAL OR INTERNET CHAT BUDDY OR--?
LET HER TALK.
NORMAN OSBORN IS BEING TRANSFERRED OFF OF THE RAFT AND BEING TRIED IN THE INTERNATIONAL CRIMINAL COURT.
AND BECAUSE OF ALL THE RUMORS OF HIS H.A.M.M.E.R. ORGANIZATION STILL BEING ACTIVE--

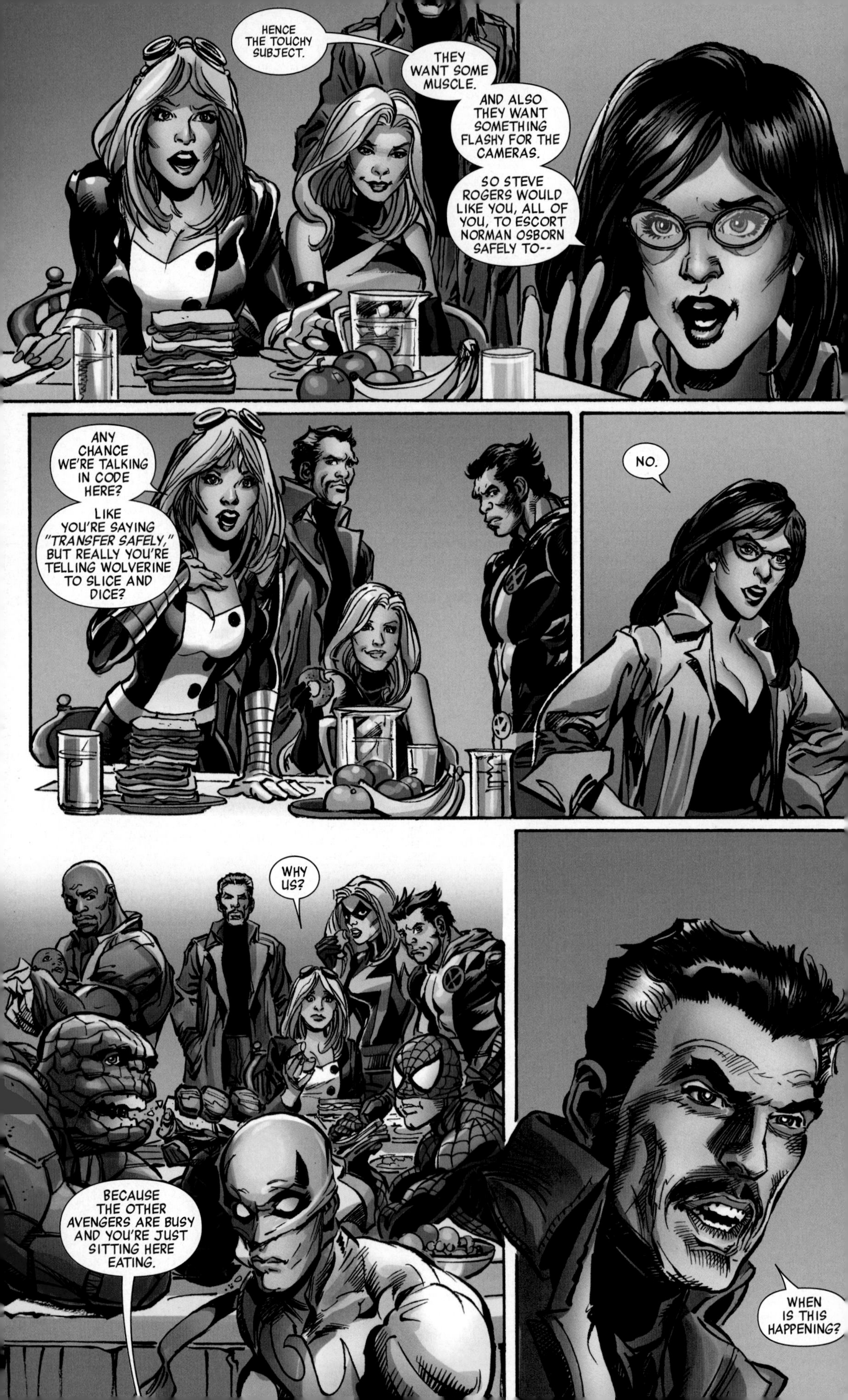
HENCE THE TOUCHY SUBJECT.
THEY WANT SOME MUSCLE.
AND ALSO THEY WANT SOMETHING FLASHY FOR THE CAMERAS.
SO STEVE ROGERS WOULD LIKE YOU, ALL OF YOU, TO ESCORT NORMAN OSBORN SAFELY TO--
ANY CHANCE WE'RE TALKING IN CODE HERE?
LIKE YOU'RE SAYING "TRANSFER SAFELY," BUT REALLY YOU'RE TELLING WOLVERINE TO SLICE AND DICE?
NO.
WHY US?
BECAUSE THE OTHER AVENGERS ARE BUSY AND YOU'RE JUST SITTING HERE EATING.
WHEN IS THIS HAPPENING?

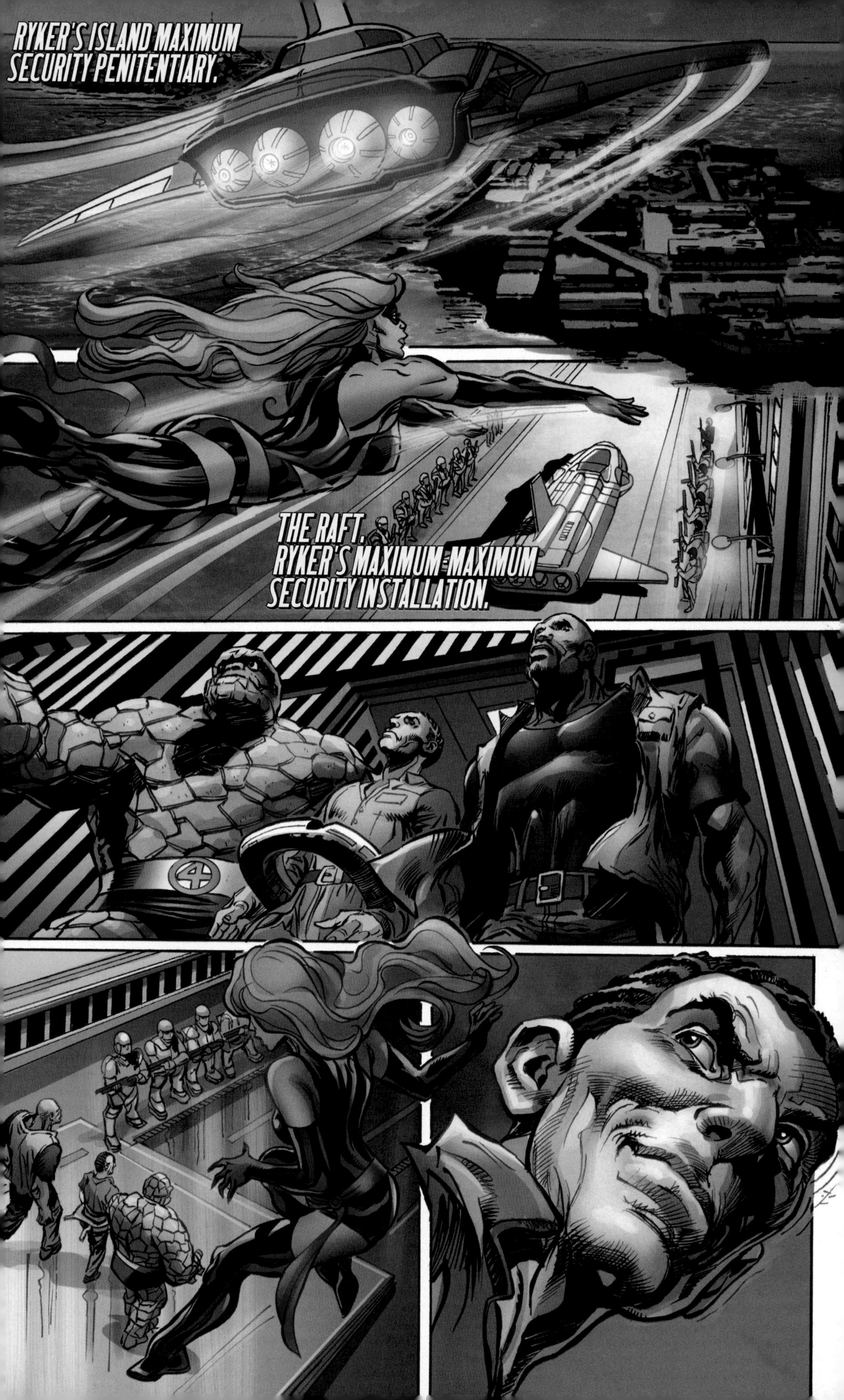
RYKER'S ISLAND MAXIMUM SECURITY PENITENTIARY.
THE RAFT. RYKER'S MAXIMUM-MAXIMUM SECURITY INSTALLATION.

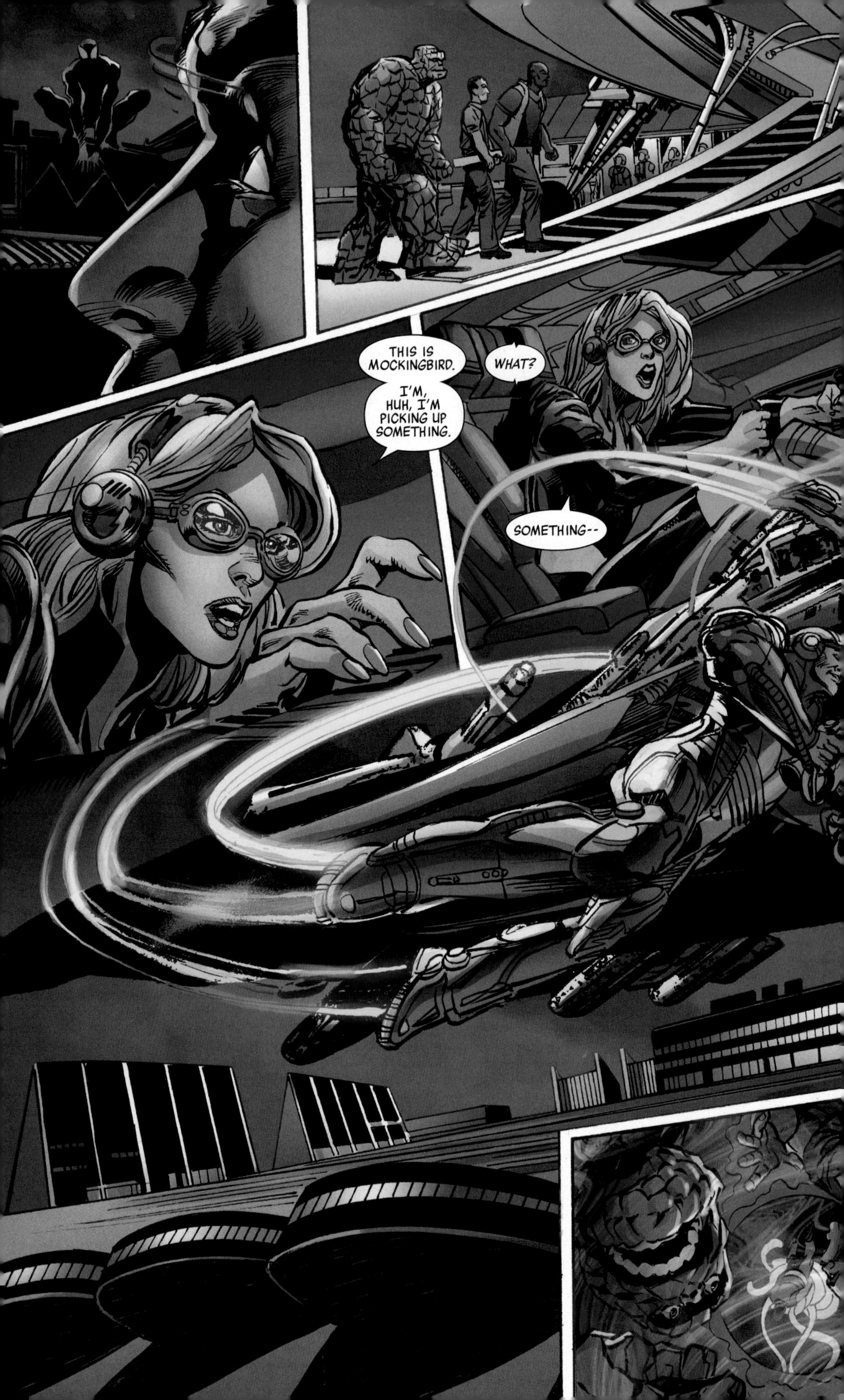
THIS IS MOCKINGBIRD.
I'M, HUH, I'M PICKING UP SOMETHING.
WHAT?
SOMETHING--

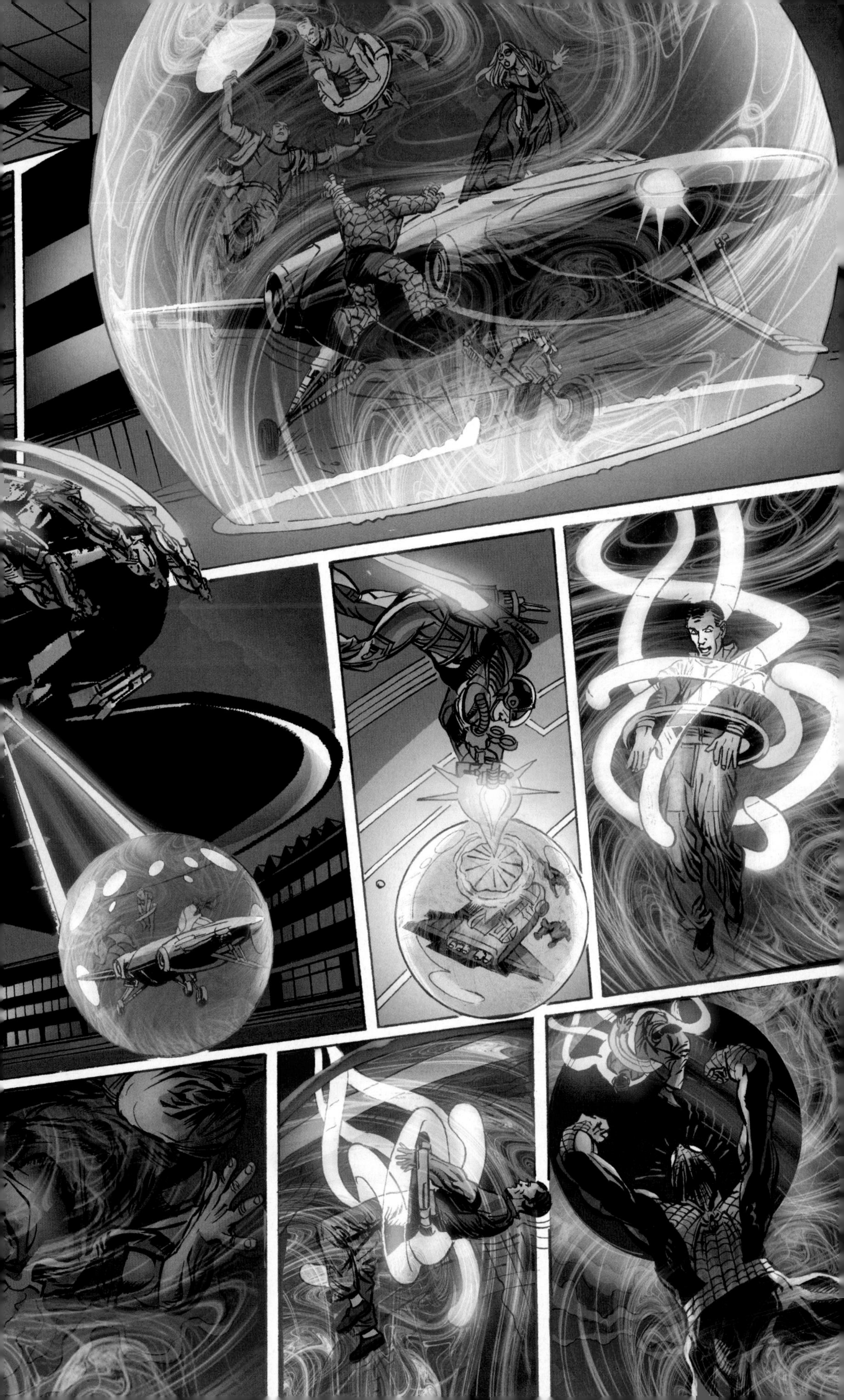

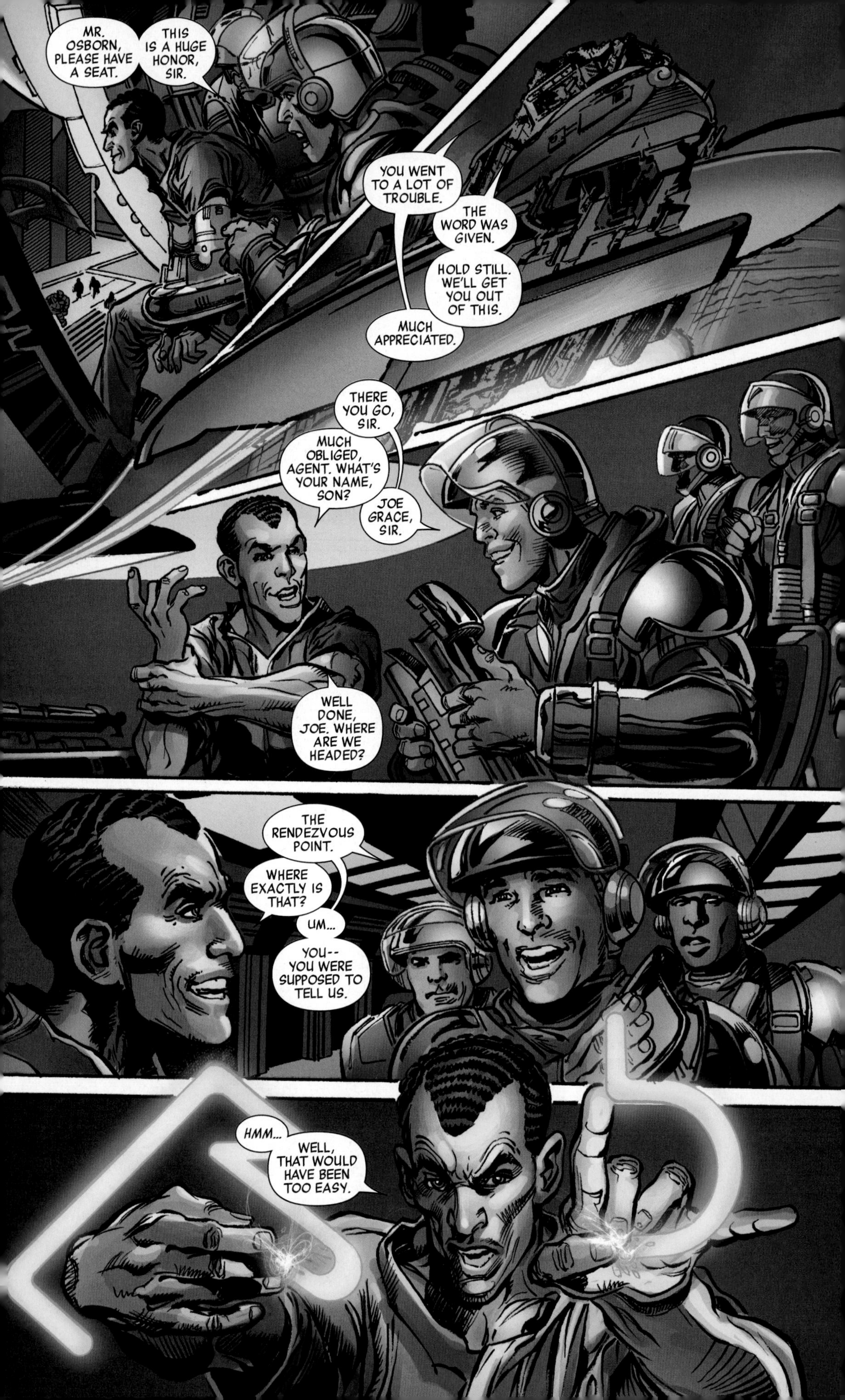

MR. OSBORN, PLEASE HAVE A SEAT.
THIS IS A HUGE HONOR, SIR.
YOU WENT TO A LOT OF TROUBLE.
THE WORD WAS GIVEN.
HOLD STILL. WE'LL GET YOU OUT OF THIS.
MUCH APPRECIATED.
THERE YOU GO, SIR.
MUCH OBLIGED, AGENT. WHAT'S YOUR NAME, SON?
JOE GRACE, SIR.
WELL DONE, JOE. WHERE ARE WE HEADED?
THE RENDEZVOUS POINT.
WHERE EXACTLY IS THAT?
UM...
YOU-- YOU WERE SUPPOSED TO TELL US.
HMM...
WELL, THAT WOULD HAVE BEEN TOO EASY.

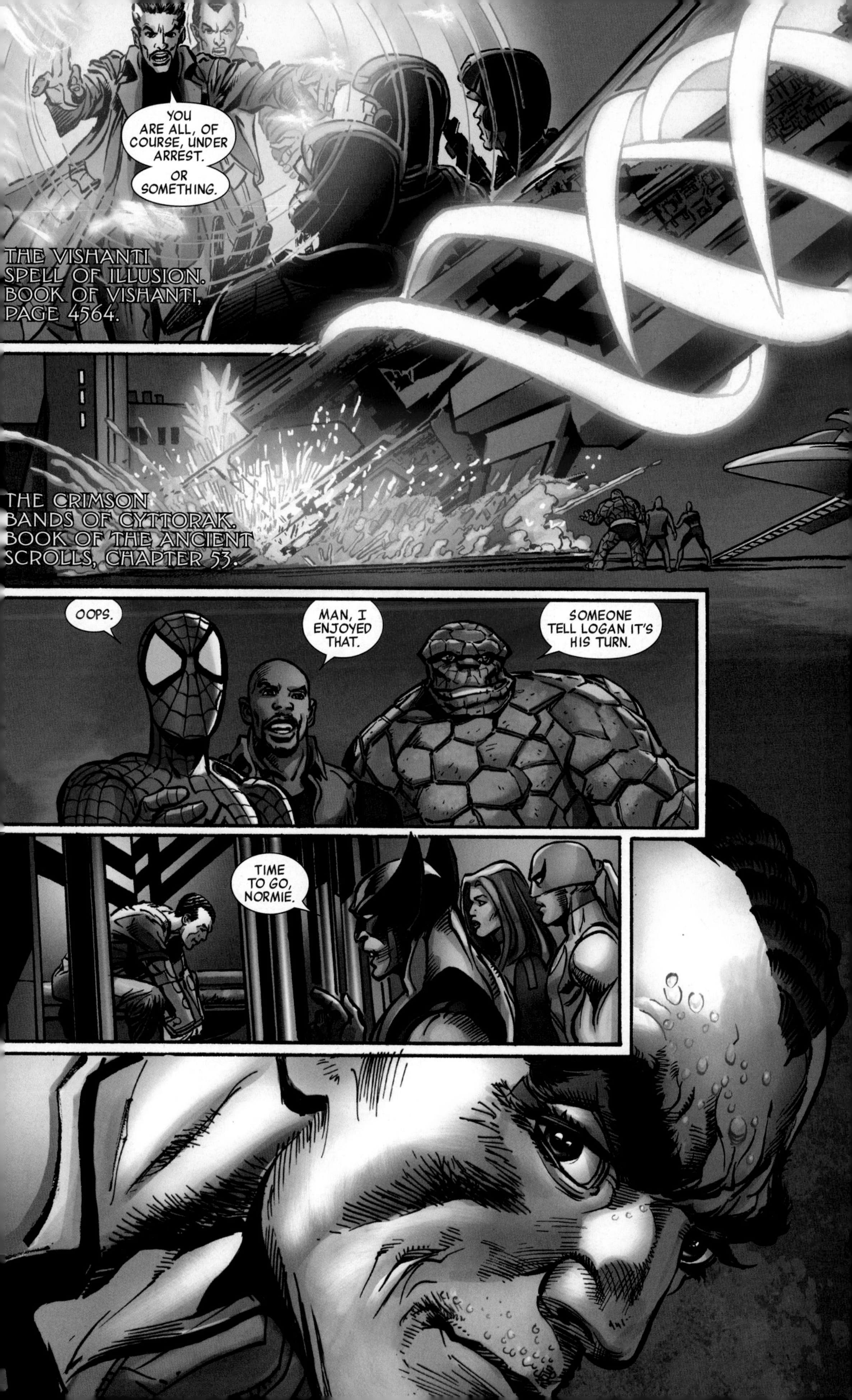
YOU ARE ALL, OF COURSE, UNDER ARREST.
OR SOMETHING.
THE VISHANTI SPELL OF ILLUSION. BOOK OF VISHANTI, PAGE 4564.
THE CRIMSON BANDS OF CYTTORAK. BOOK OF THE ANCIENT SCROLLS, CHAPTER 53.
OOPS.
MAN, I ENJOYED THAT.
SOMEONE TELL LOGAN IT'S HIS TURN.
TIME TO GO, NORMIE.

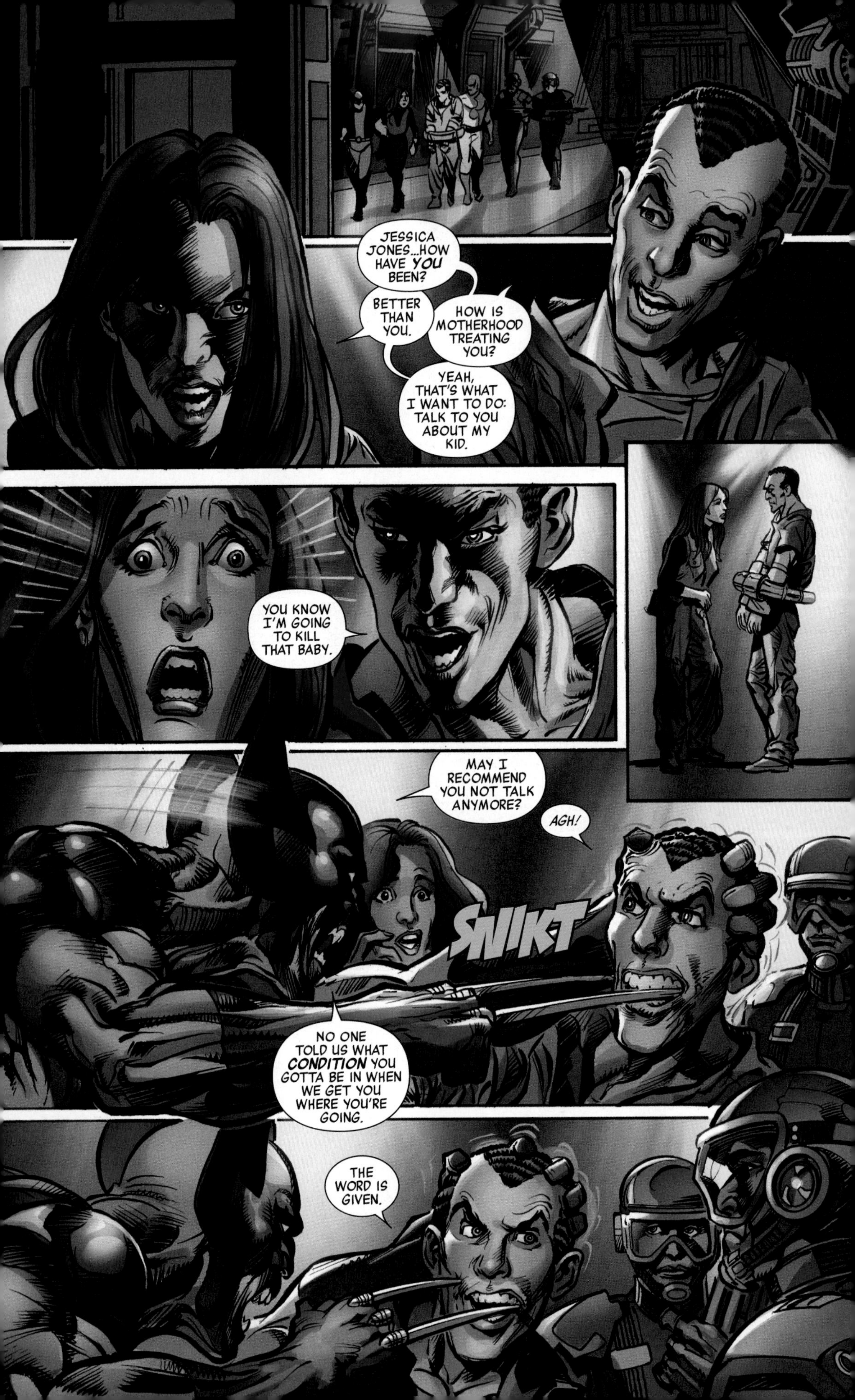
JESSICA JONES...HOW HAVE YOU BEEN?
BETTER THAN YOU.
HOW IS MOTHERHOOD TREATING YOU?
YEAH, THAT'S WHAT I WANT TO DO: TALK TO YOU ABOUT MY KID.
YOU KNOW I'M GOING TO KILL THAT BABY.
MAY I RECOMMEND YOU NOT TALK ANYMORE?
AGH!
SNIKT
NO ONE TOLD US WHAT CONDITION YOU GOTTA BE IN WHEN WE GET YOU WHERE YOU'RE GOING.
THE WORD IS GIVEN.

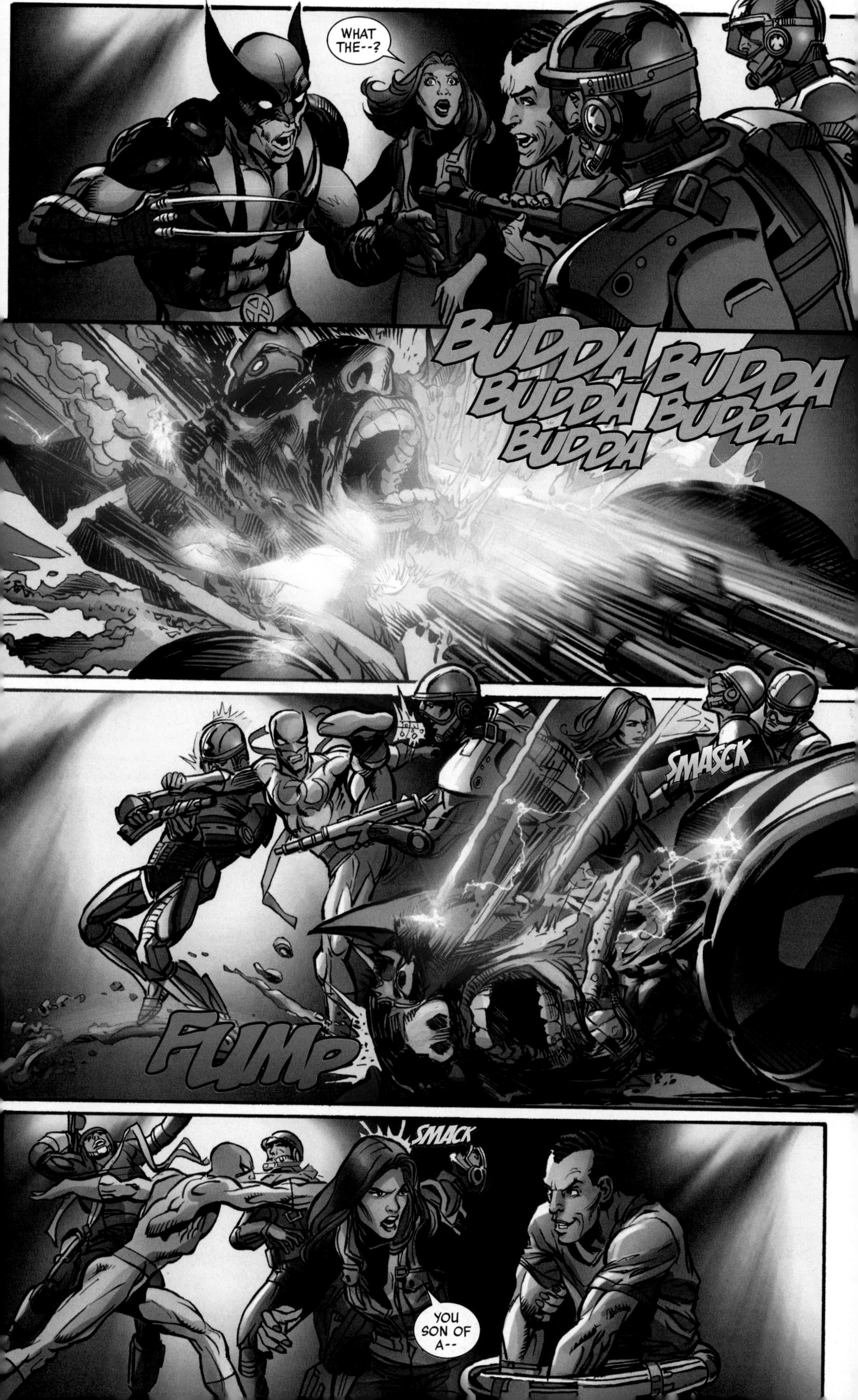
WHAT THE--?
BUDDA BUDDA BUDDA BUDDA BUDDA
SMASCK
FUMP
SMACK
YOU SON OF A--

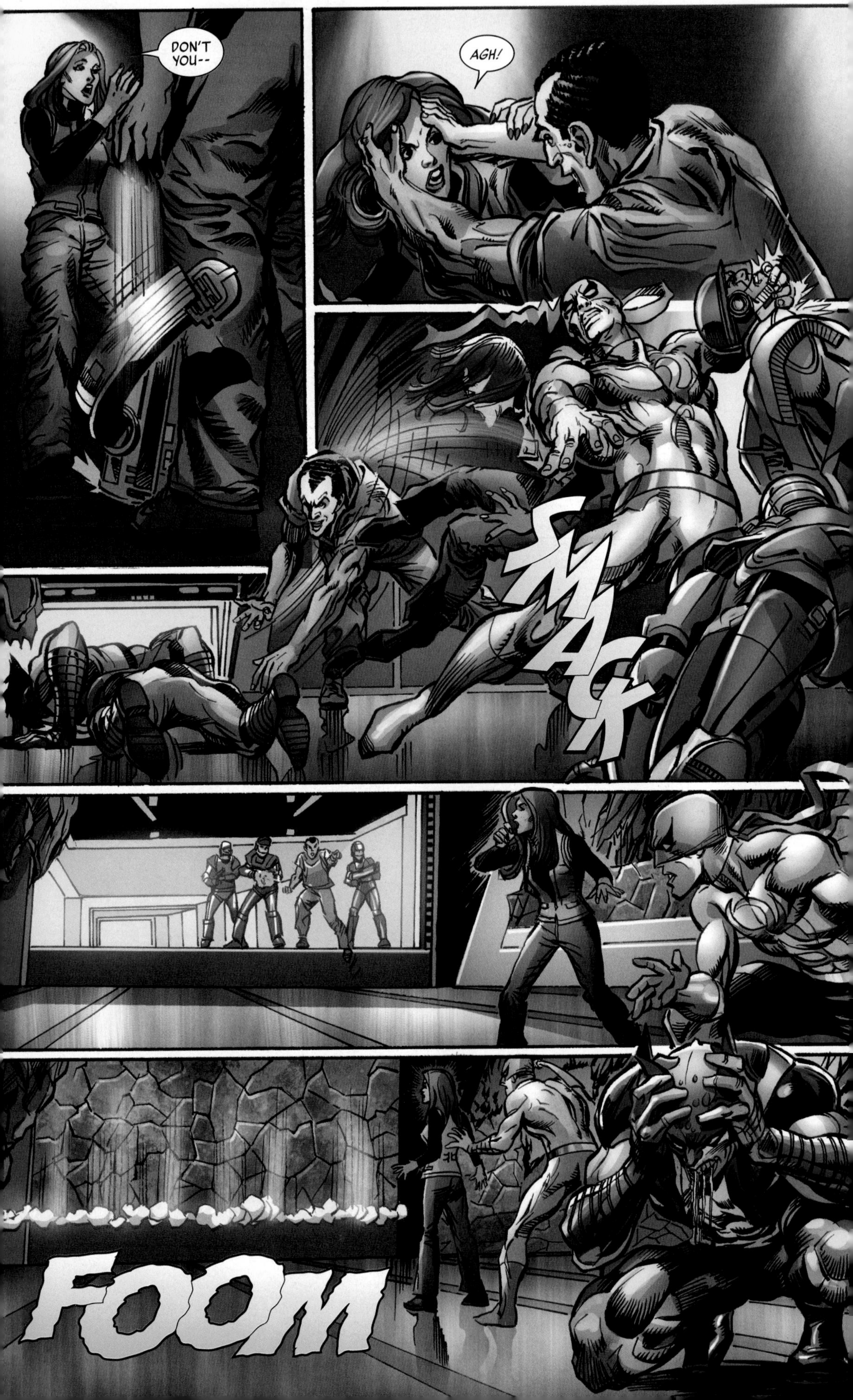
DON'T YOU--
AGH!
SMACK
FOOM

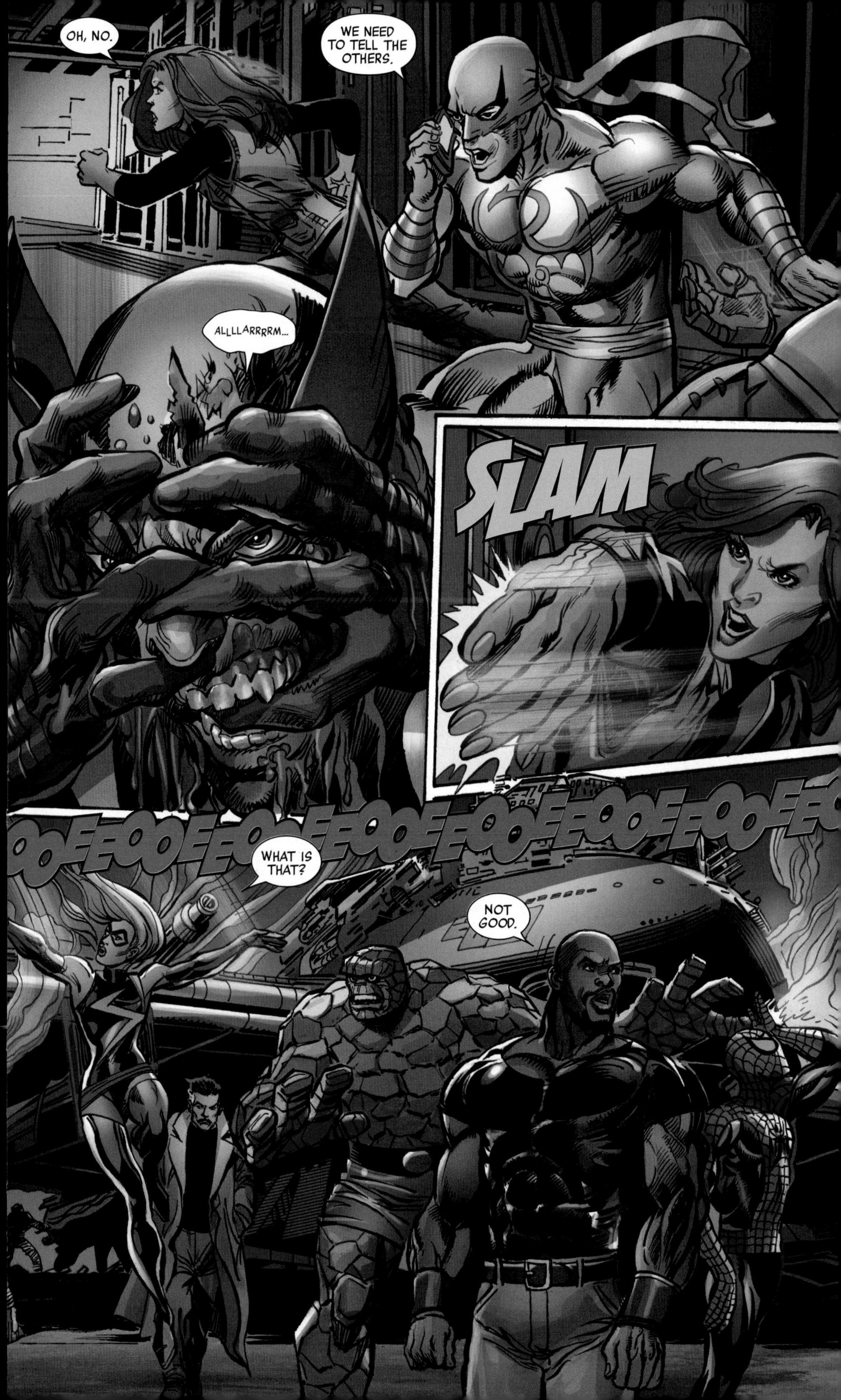
OH, NO.
WE NEED TO TELL THE OTHERS.
ALLLLARRRRM...
SLAM
OOEEOOEEOOEEOOEEOOEEOOEEOOEEOOEEOOEEC
WHAT IS THAT?
NOT GOOD.

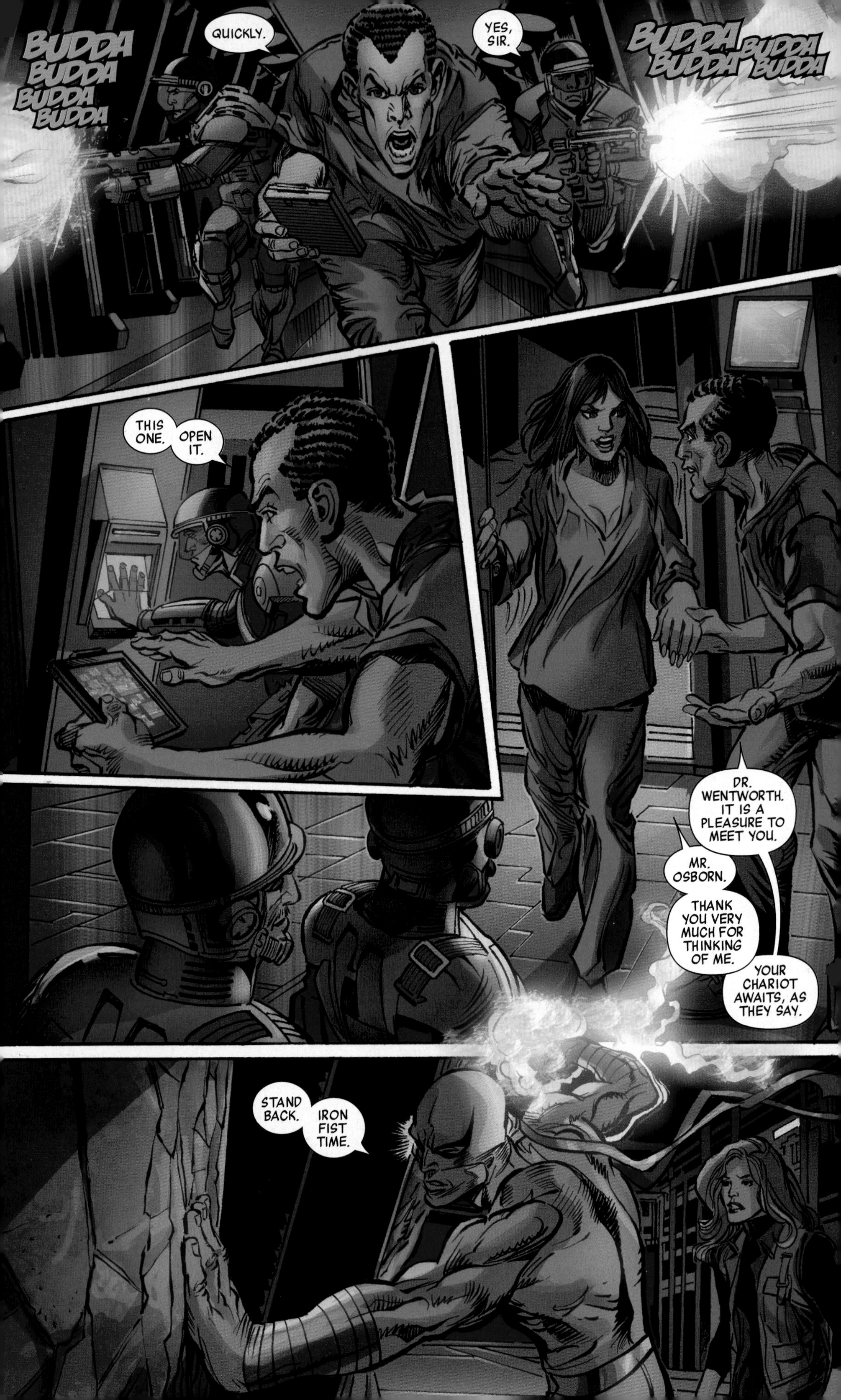
BUDDA BUDDA BUDDA BUDDA
QUICKLY.
YES, SIR.
BUDDA BUDDA BUDDA BUDDA
THIS ONE.
OPEN IT.
DR. WENTWORTH. IT IS A PLEASURE TO MEET YOU.
MR. OSBORN.
THANK YOU VERY MUCH FOR THINKING OF ME.
YOUR CHARIOT AWAITS, AS THEY SAY.
STAND BACK.
IRON FIST TIME.

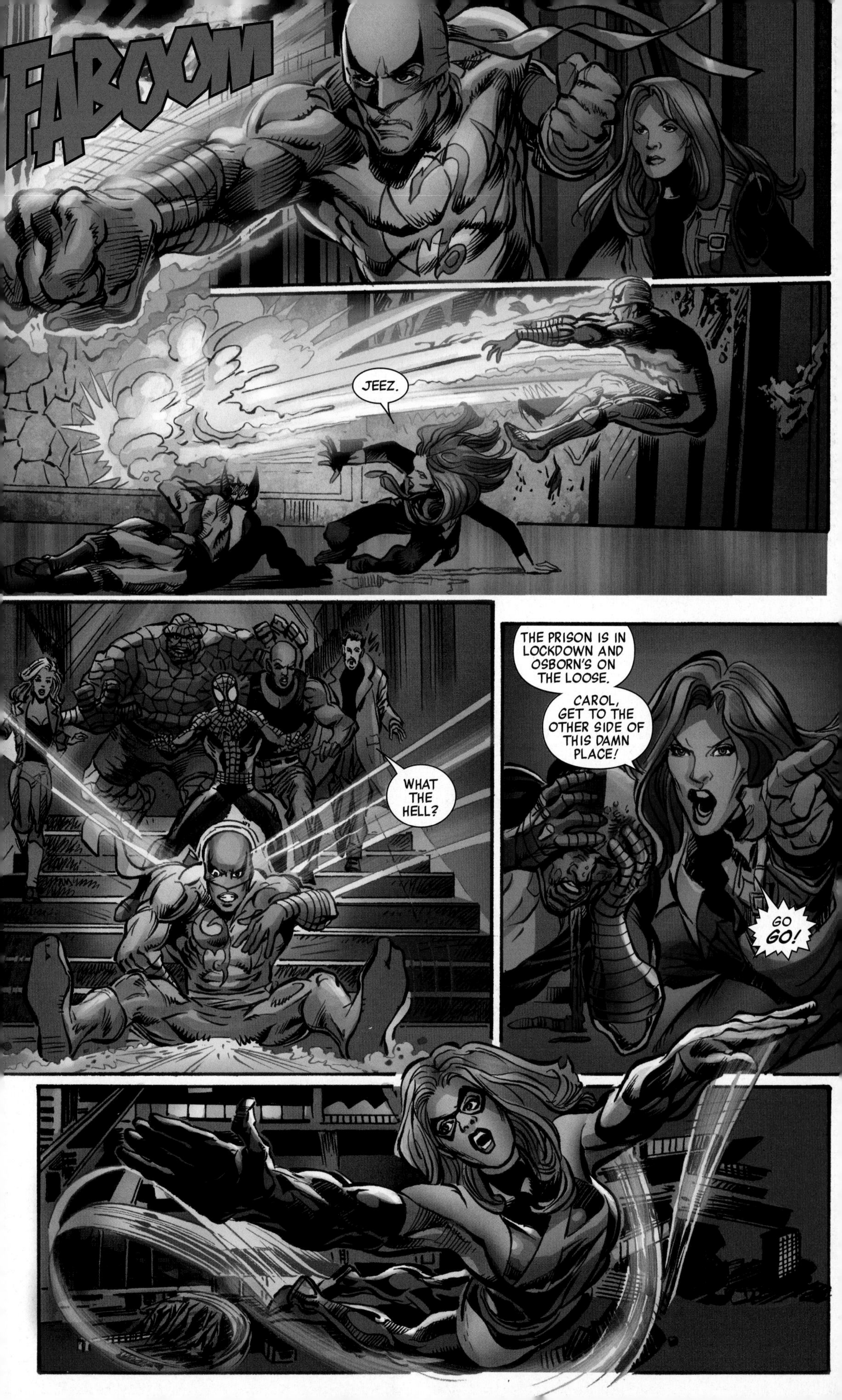
FABOOM
JEEZ.
WHAT THE HELL?
THE PRISON IS IN LOCKDOWN AND OSBORN'S ON THE LOOSE.
CAROL, GET TO THE OTHER SIDE OF THIS DAMN PLACE!
GO GO!

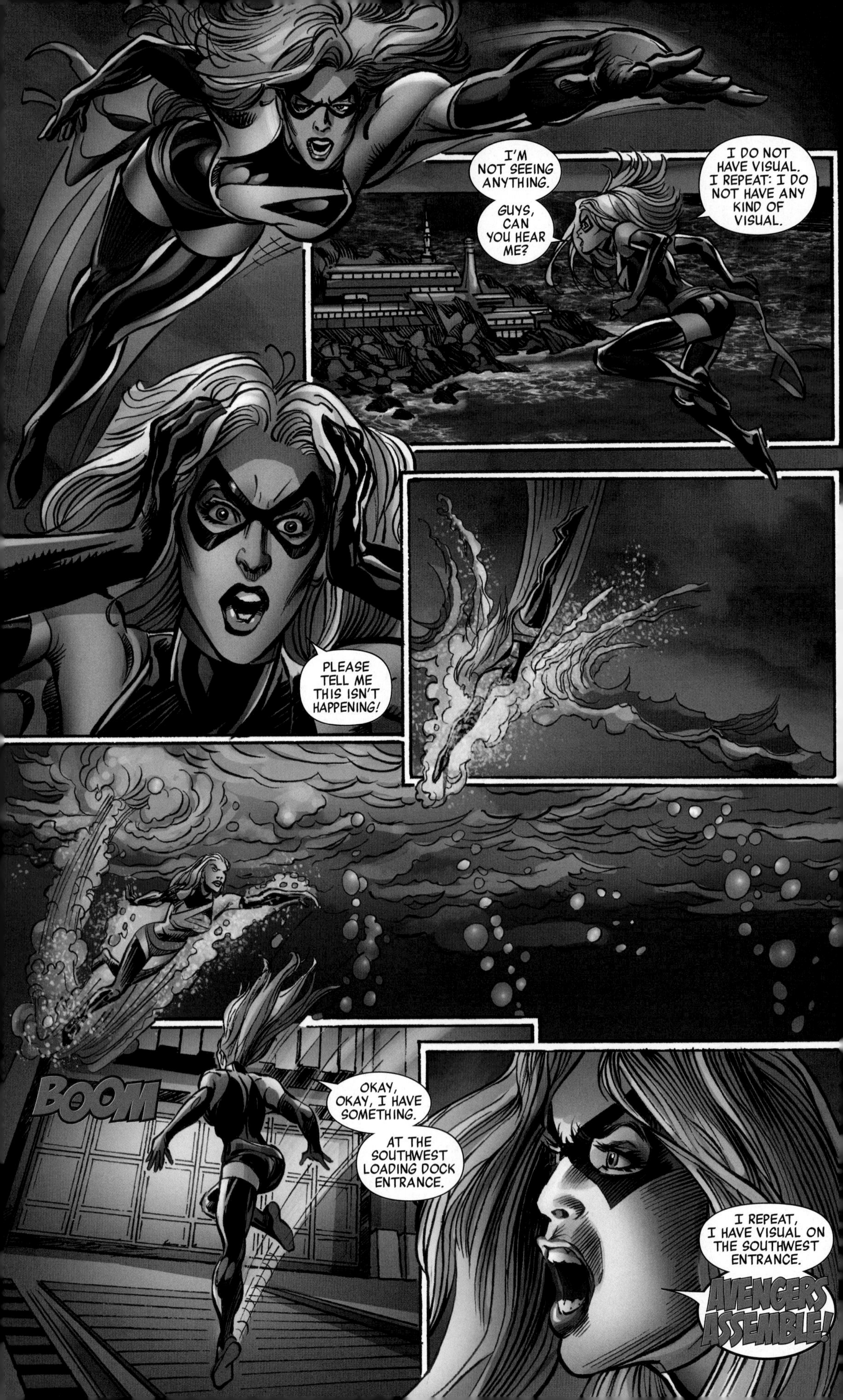
I'M NOT SEEING ANYTHING.
GUYS, CAN YOU HEAR ME?
I DO NOT HAVE VISUAL. I REPEAT: I DO NOT HAVE ANY KIND OF VISUAL.
PLEASE TELL ME THIS ISN'T HAPPENING!
BOOM
OKAY, OKAY, I HAVE SOMETHING.
AT THE SOUTHWEST LOADING DOCK ENTRANCE.
I REPEAT, I HAVE VISUAL ON THE SOUTHWEST ENTRANCE.
AVENGERS ASSEMBLE!

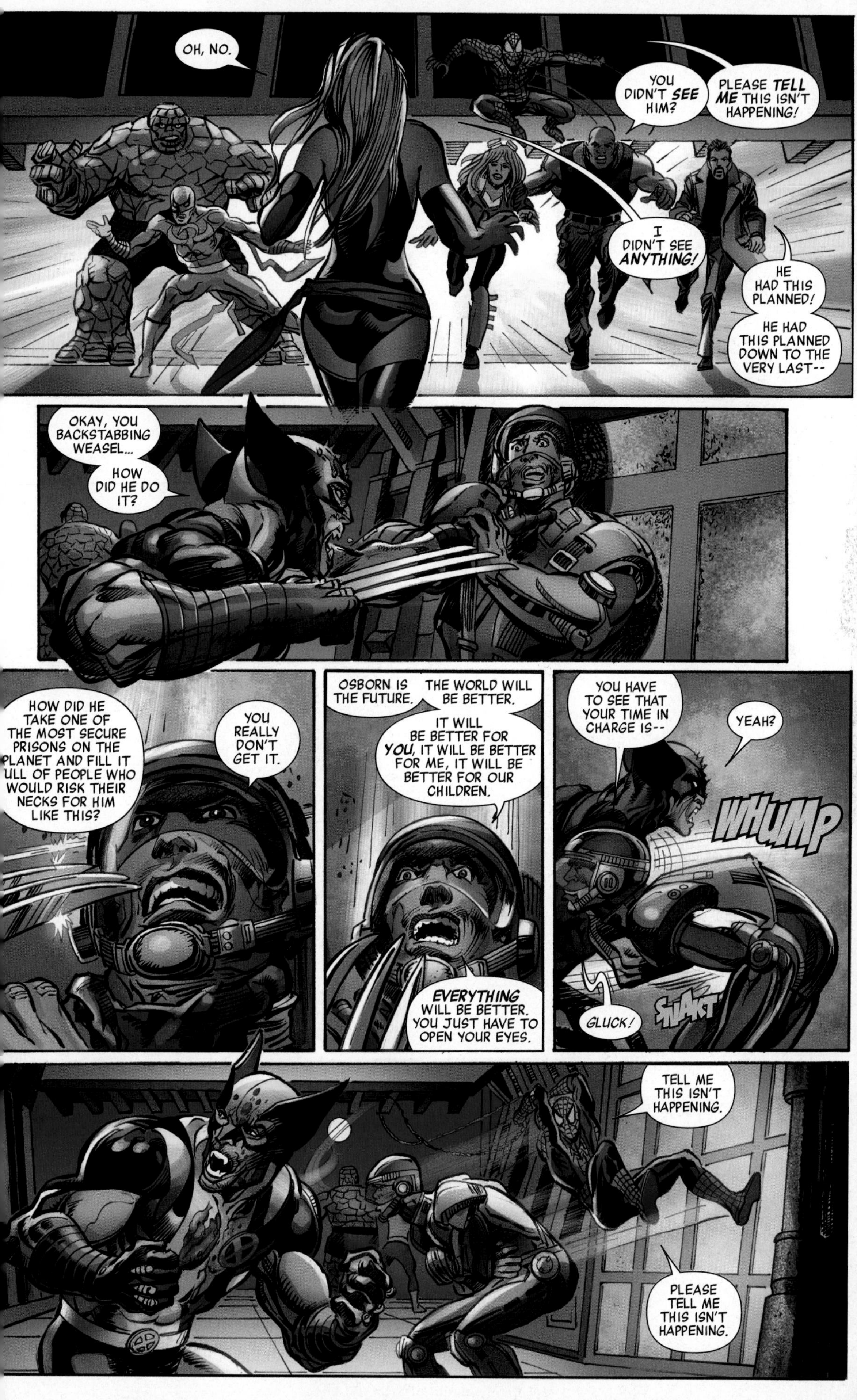
OH, NO.
YOU DIDN'T SEE HIM?
PLEASE TELL ME THIS ISN'T HAPPENING!
I DIDN'T SEE ANYTHING!
HE HAD THIS PLANNED!
HE HAD THIS PLANNED DOWN TO THE VERY LAST--
OKAY, YOU BACKSTABBING WEASEL...
HOW DID HE DO IT?
HOW DID HE TAKE ONE OF THE MOST SECURE PRISONS ON THE PLANET AND FILL IT FULL OF PEOPLE WHO WOULD RISK THEIR NECKS FOR HIM LIKE THIS?
YOU REALLY DON'T GET IT.
OSBORN IS THE FUTURE.
THE WORLD WILL BE BETTER.
IT WILL BE BETTER FOR YOU, IT WILL BE BETTER FOR ME, IT WILL BE BETTER FOR OUR CHILDREN.
EVERYTHING WILL BE BETTER. YOU JUST HAVE TO OPEN YOUR EYES.
YOU HAVE TO SEE THAT YOUR TIME IN CHARGE IS--
YEAH?
WHUMP
SNAKT
GLUCK!
TELL ME THIS ISN'T HAPPENING.
PLEASE TELL ME THIS ISN'T HAPPENING.

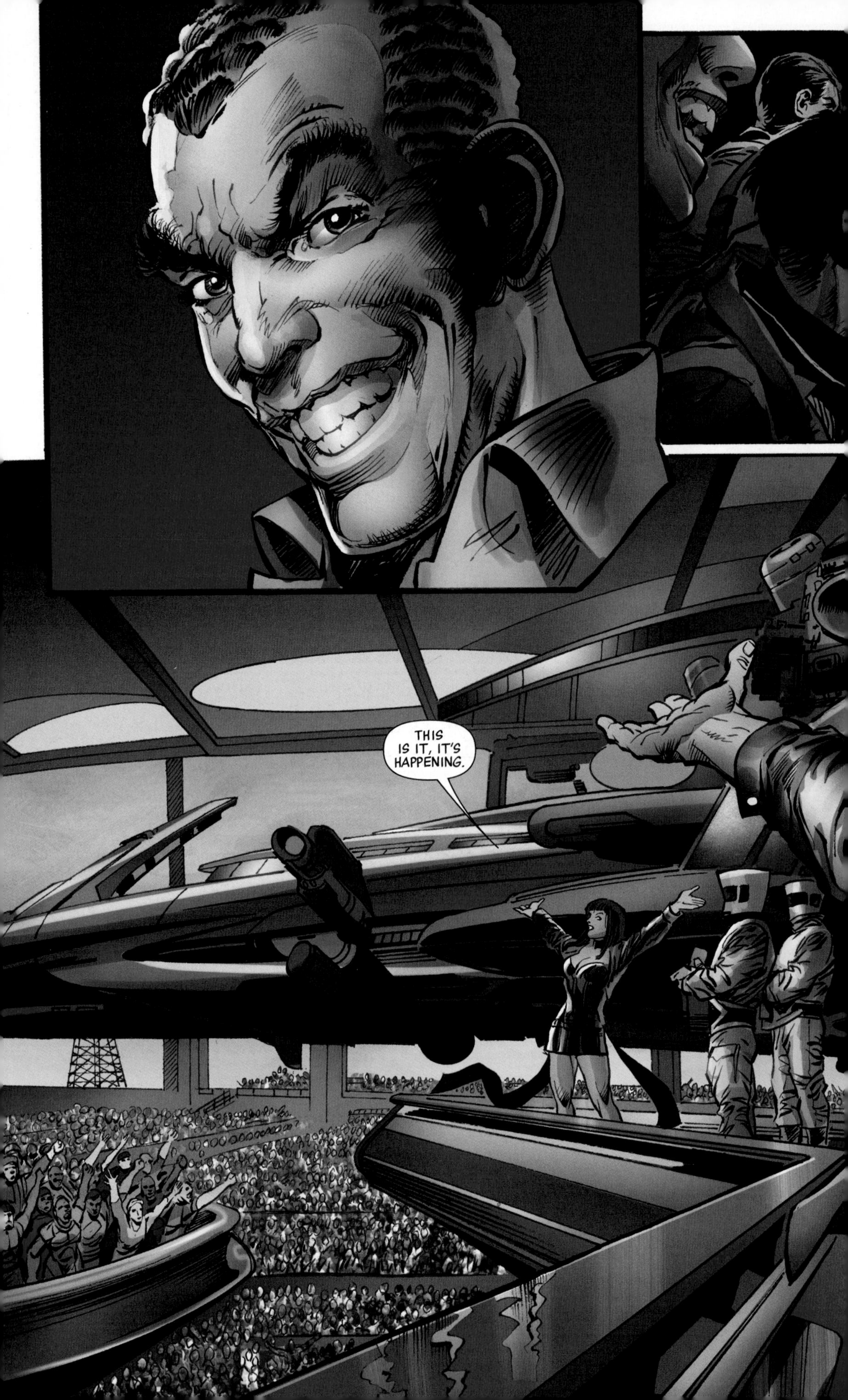
THIS IS IT, IT'S HAPPENING.

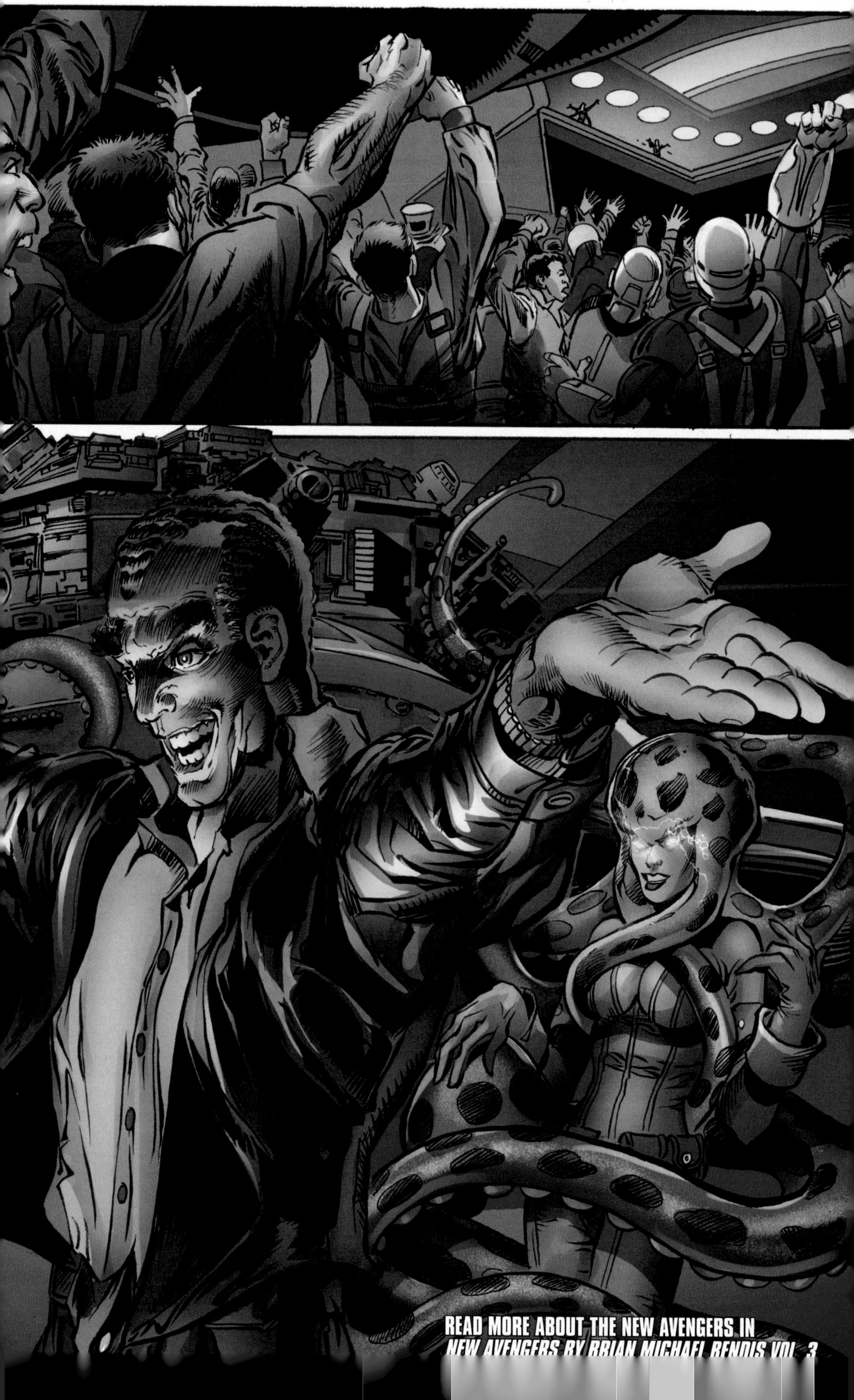
READ MORE ABOUT THE NEW AVENGERS IN
NEW AVENGERS BY BRIAN MICHAEL BENDIS VOL. 3

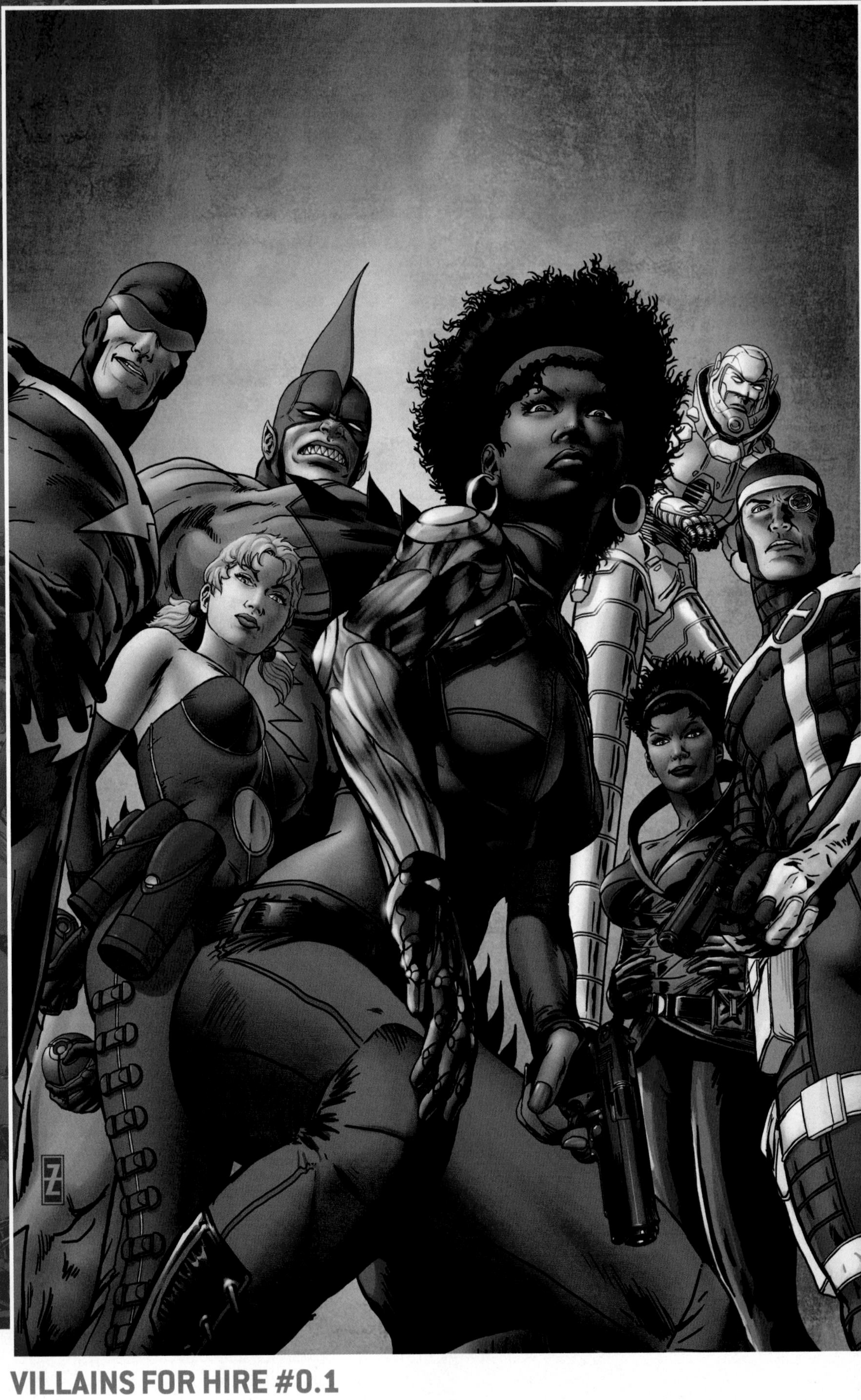

VILLAINS FOR HIRE #0.1

Bringing justice to the city's mean streets, bionic detective **MISTY KNIGHT** has reopened the underground mercenary agency **HEROES FOR HIRE**. From her control room, Knight gets the word out to the right people at the right time so they can do the right thing.

"CONTROL" MISSION LOG.

HERO: SILVER SABLE

International bounty hunter. Exiled. Trying to carve out a new life in America.

HERO: BLACK PANTHER

Former African warrior king. Now pledged to protect his newly adopted home, Hell's Kitchen.

HERO: PALADIN

Cold-blooded mercenary with a hidden heart of gold.

HERO: DAIMON HELLSTROM

Son of Satan. Occult investigator. Looks hot in leather pants.

NEXT MISSION: ACTIVE...

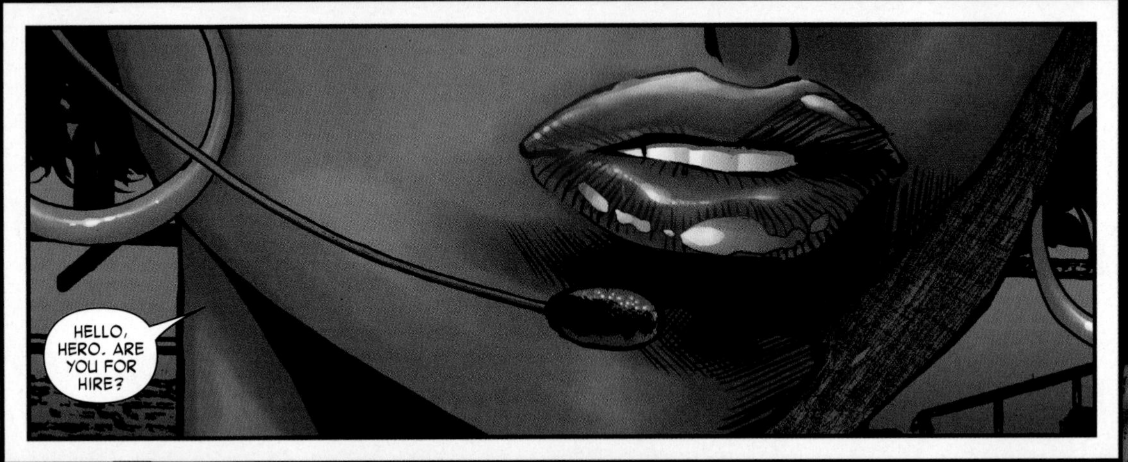
HELLO, HERO. ARE YOU FOR HIRE?

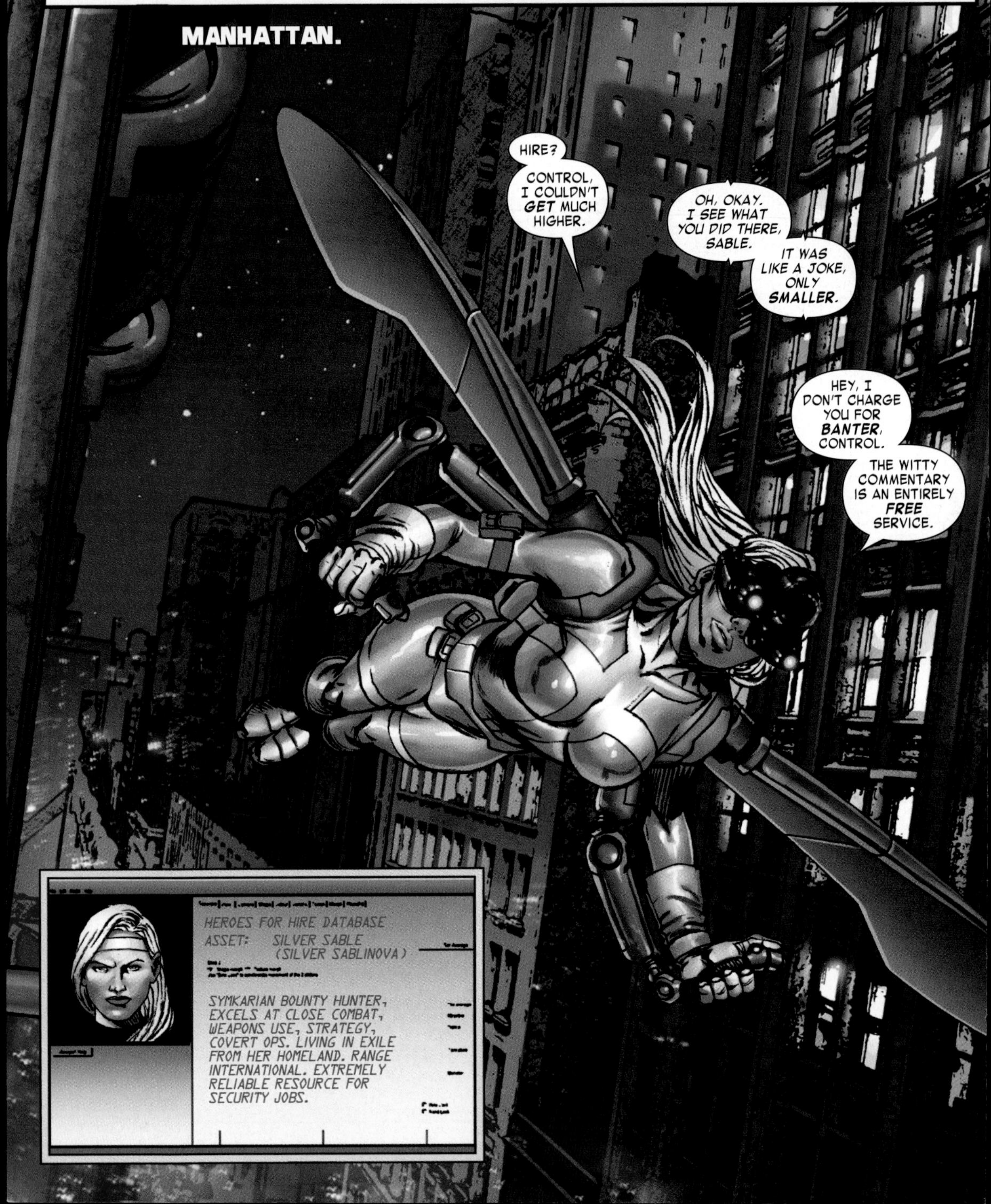
MANHATTAN.
HIRE?
CONTROL, I COULDN'T GET MUCH HIGHER.
OH, OKAY. I SEE WHAT YOU DID THERE, SABLE.
IT WAS LIKE A JOKE, ONLY SMALLER.
HEY, I DON'T CHARGE YOU FOR BANTER, CONTROL.
THE WITTY COMMENTARY IS AN ENTIRELY FREE SERVICE.
HEROES FOR HIRE DATABASE
ASSET: SILVER SABLE (SILVER SABLINOVA)
SYMKARIAN BOUNTY HUNTER, EXCELS AT CLOSE COMBAT, WEAPONS USE, STRATEGY, COVERT OPS. LIVING IN EXILE FROM HER HOMELAND. RANGE INTERNATIONAL. EXTREMELY RELIABLE RESOURCE FOR SECURITY JOBS.

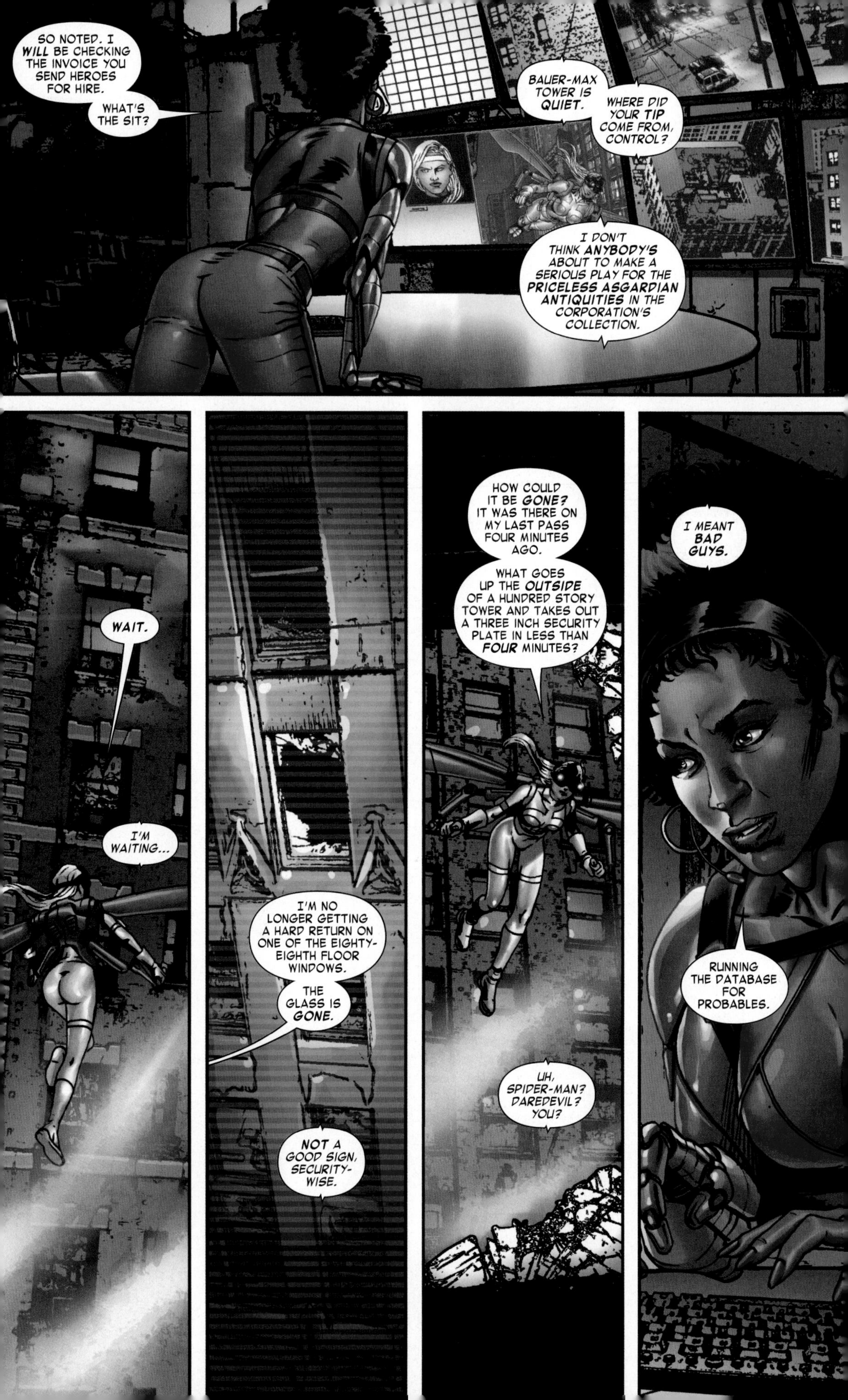

SO NOTED. I WILL BE CHECKING THE INVOICE YOU SEND HEROES FOR HIRE.
WHAT'S THE SIT?
BAUER-MAX TOWER IS QUIET.
WHERE DID YOUR TIP COME FROM, CONTROL?
I DON'T THINK ANYBODY'S ABOUT TO MAKE A SERIOUS PLAY FOR THE PRICELESS ASGARDIAN ANTIQUITIES IN THE CORPORATION'S COLLECTION.
WAIT.
I'M WAITING...
I'M NO LONGER GETTING A HARD RETURN ON ONE OF THE EIGHTY-EIGHTH FLOOR WINDOWS.
THE GLASS IS GONE.
NOT A GOOD SIGN, SECURITY-WISE.
HOW COULD IT BE GONE? IT WAS THERE ON MY LAST PASS FOUR MINUTES AGO.
WHAT GOES UP THE OUTSIDE OF A HUNDRED STORY TOWER AND TAKES OUT A THREE INCH SECURITY PLATE IN LESS THAN FOUR MINUTES?
UH, SPIDER-MAN? DAREDEVIL? YOU?
I MEANT BAD GUYS.
RUNNING THE DATABASE FOR PROBABLES.

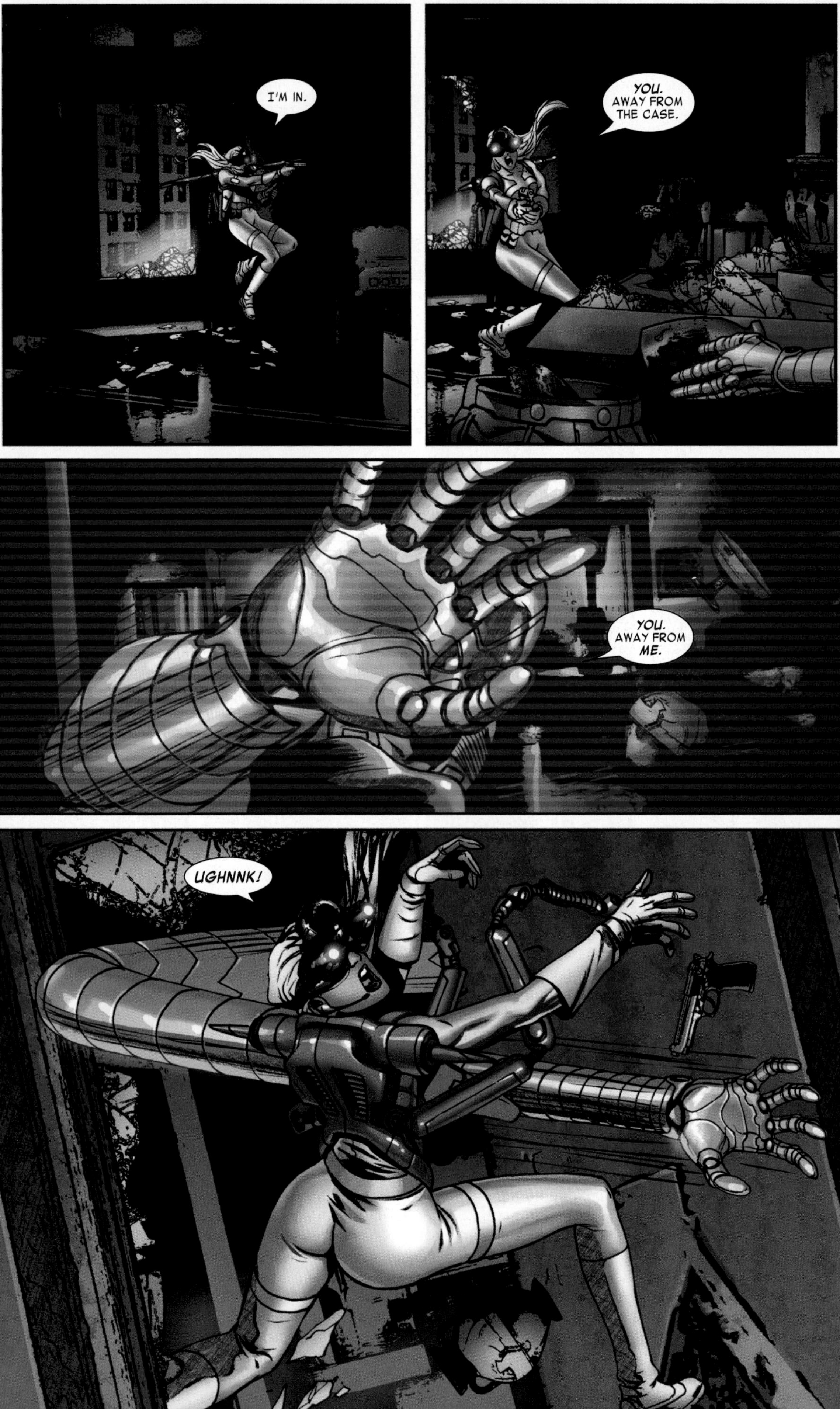
I'M IN.
YOU. AWAY FROM THE CASE.
YOU. AWAY FROM ME.
UGHNNK!

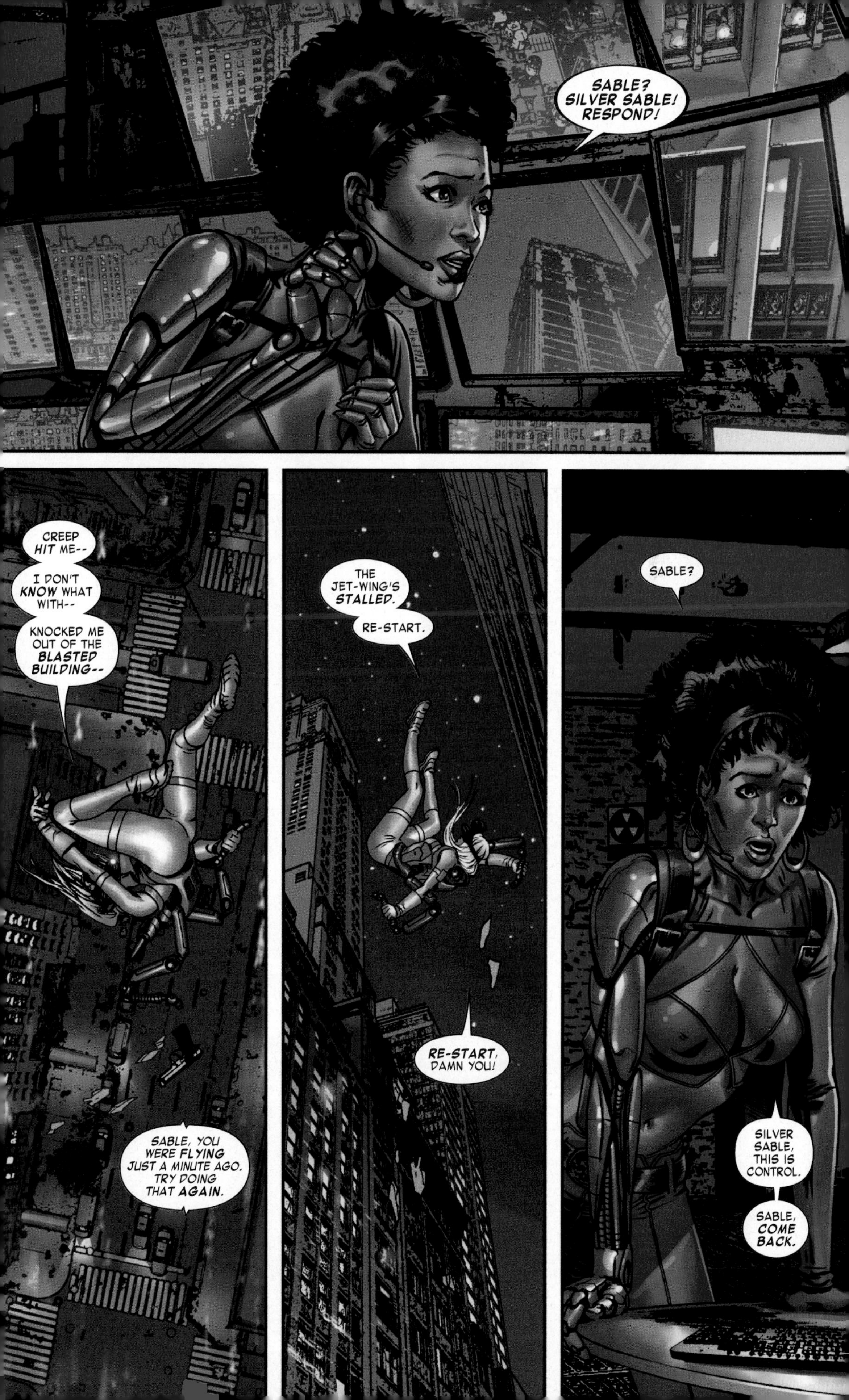
SABLE? SILVER SABLE! RESPOND!
CREEP HIT ME--
I DON'T KNOW WHAT WITH--
KNOCKED ME OUT OF THE BLASTED BUILDING--
SABLE, YOU WERE FLYING JUST A MINUTE AGO. TRY DOING THAT AGAIN.
THE JET-WING'S STALLED.
RE-START.
RE-START, DAMN YOU!
SABLE?
SILVER SABLE, THIS IS CONTROL.
SABLE, COME BACK.

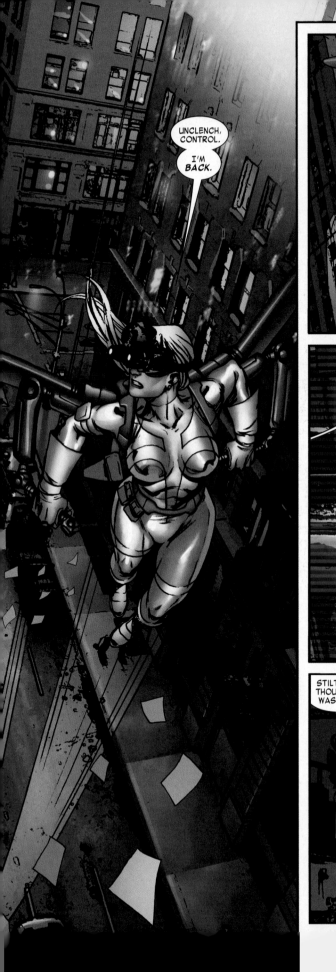

UNCLENCH, CONTROL.

I'M BACK.

THE PERP IS FLEEING THE SCENE.

HE'S GOING TO **OUTRUN** ME.

ZOOMING OPTICS TO GET A CLEAN I.D.

STILT-MAN?

STILT-MAN? THOUGHT HE WAS DEAD.

THIS A NEW ONE?

HOW MANY **ARE** THERE?

SINCE THE ORIGINAL, THREE OR **FOUR**.

YOU'D THINK SOMEONE WOULDA NOTICED IT WAS A DUMB-ASS IDEA THE **FIRST** TIME.

THIS ONE'S GOT SERIOUS TECH UPGRADES.

NOT QUITE THE JOKE HE **USED** TO BE.

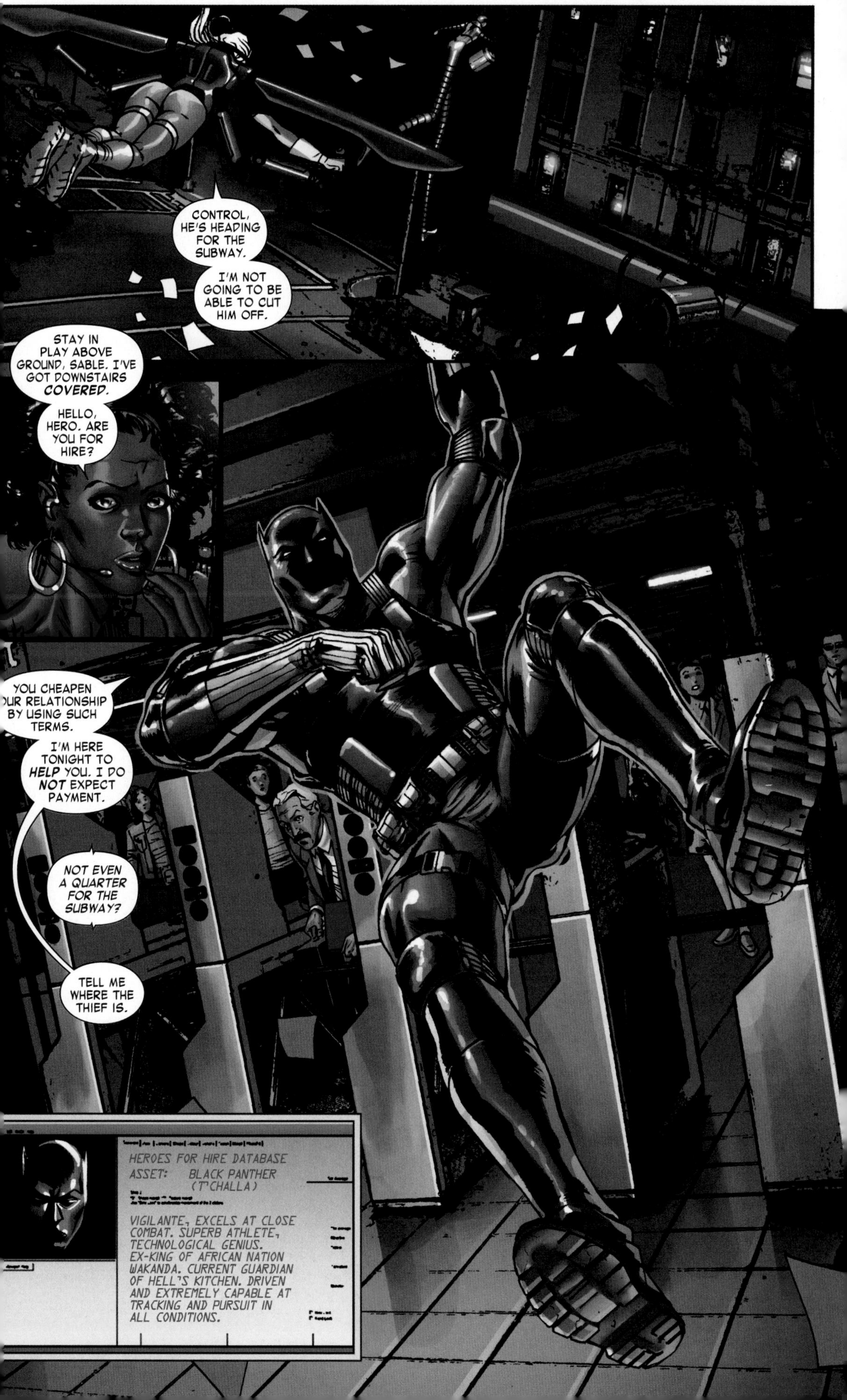
CONTROL, HE'S HEADING FOR THE SUBWAY.
I'M NOT GOING TO BE ABLE TO CUT HIM OFF.
STAY IN PLAY ABOVE GROUND, SABLE. I'VE GOT DOWNSTAIRS **COVERED**.
HELLO, HERO. ARE YOU FOR HIRE?
YOU CHEAPEN OUR RELATIONSHIP BY USING SUCH TERMS.
I'M HERE TONIGHT TO **HELP** YOU. I DO **NOT** EXPECT PAYMENT.
NOT EVEN A QUARTER FOR THE SUBWAY?
TELL ME WHERE THE THIEF IS.
HEROES FOR HIRE DATABASE
ASSET: BLACK PANTHER (T'CHALLA)
VIGILANTE, EXCELS AT CLOSE COMBAT. SUPERB ATHLETE, TECHNOLOGICAL GENIUS. EX-KING OF AFRICAN NATION WAKANDA. CURRENT GUARDIAN OF HELL'S KITCHEN. DRIVEN AND EXTREMELY CAPABLE AT TRACKING AND PURSUIT IN ALL CONDITIONS.

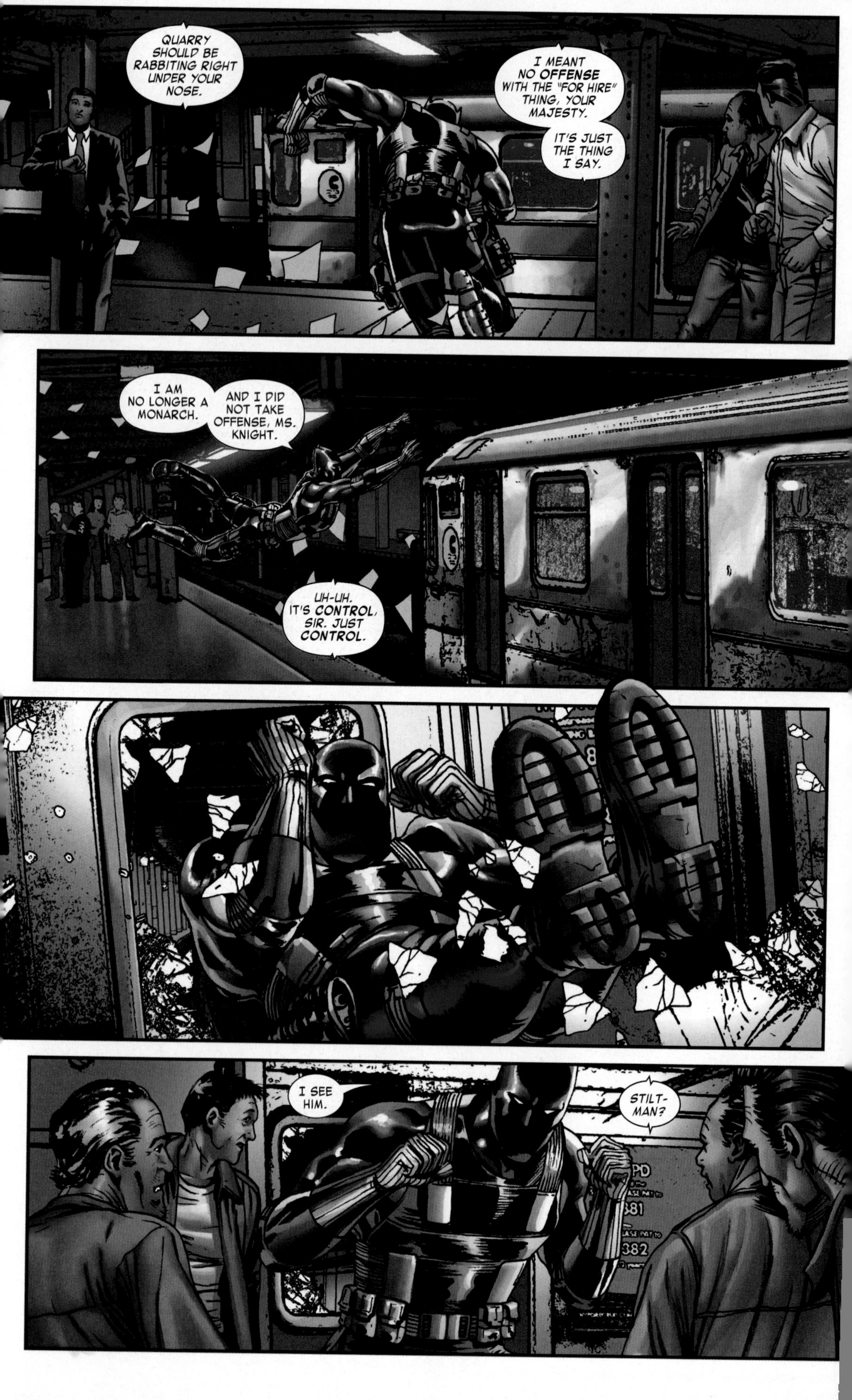
QUARRY SHOULD BE RABBITING RIGHT UNDER YOUR NOSE.
I MEANT NO OFFENSE WITH THE "FOR HIRE" THING, YOUR MAJESTY.
IT'S JUST THE THING I SAY.
I AM NO LONGER A MONARCH.
AND I DID NOT TAKE OFFENSE, MS. KNIGHT.
UH-UH. IT'S CONTROL, SIR. JUST CONTROL.
I SEE HIM.
STILT-MAN?

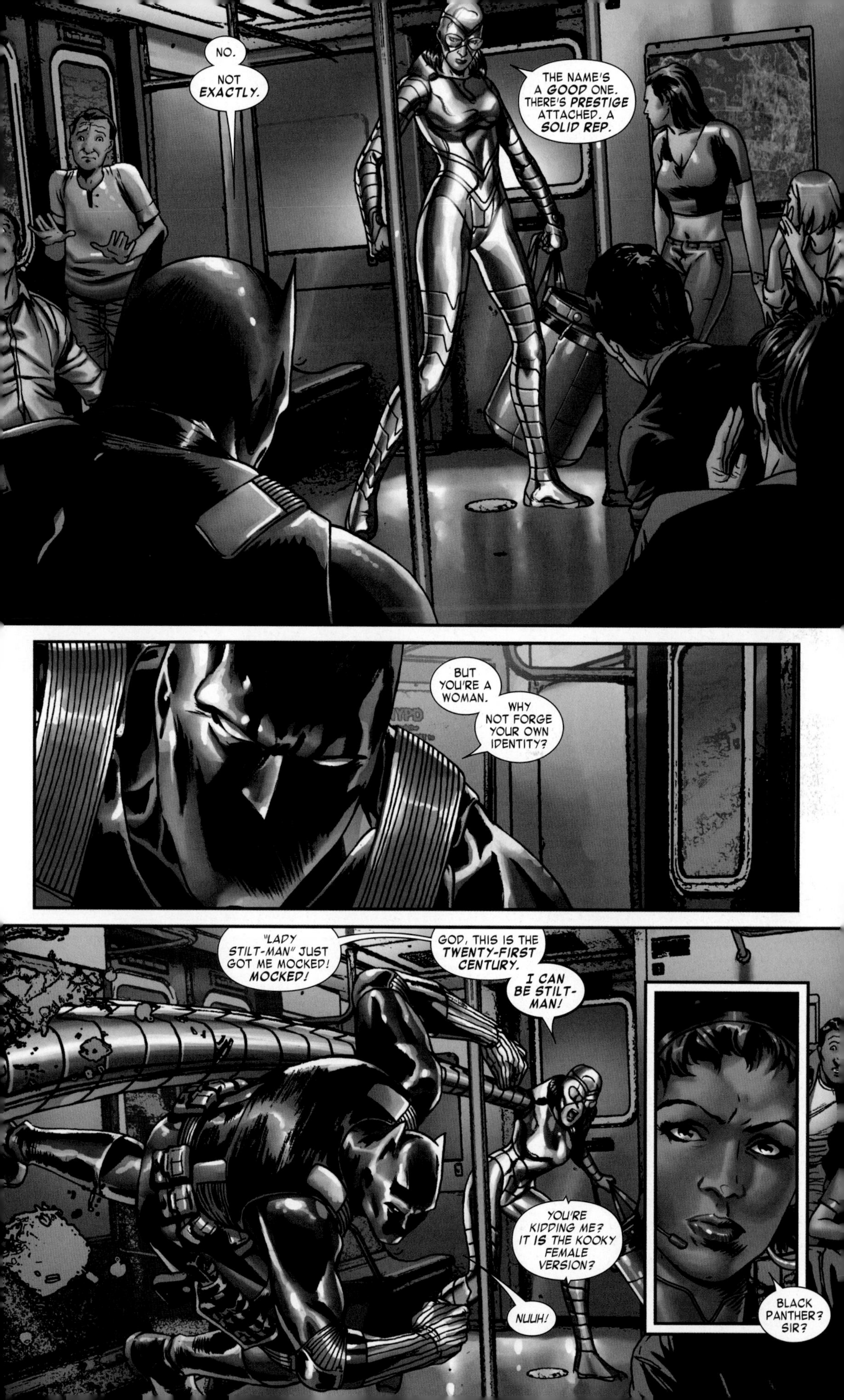
NO.
NOT EXACTLY.
THE NAME'S A GOOD ONE. THERE'S PRESTIGE ATTACHED. A SOLID REP.
BUT YOU'RE A WOMAN.
WHY NOT FORGE YOUR OWN IDENTITY?
GOD, THIS IS THE TWENTY-FIRST CENTURY.
I CAN BE STILT-MAN!
"LADY STILT-MAN" JUST GOT ME MOCKED! MOCKED!
YOU'RE KIDDING ME? IT IS THE KOOKY FEMALE VERSION?
NUUH!
BLACK PANTHER? SIR?

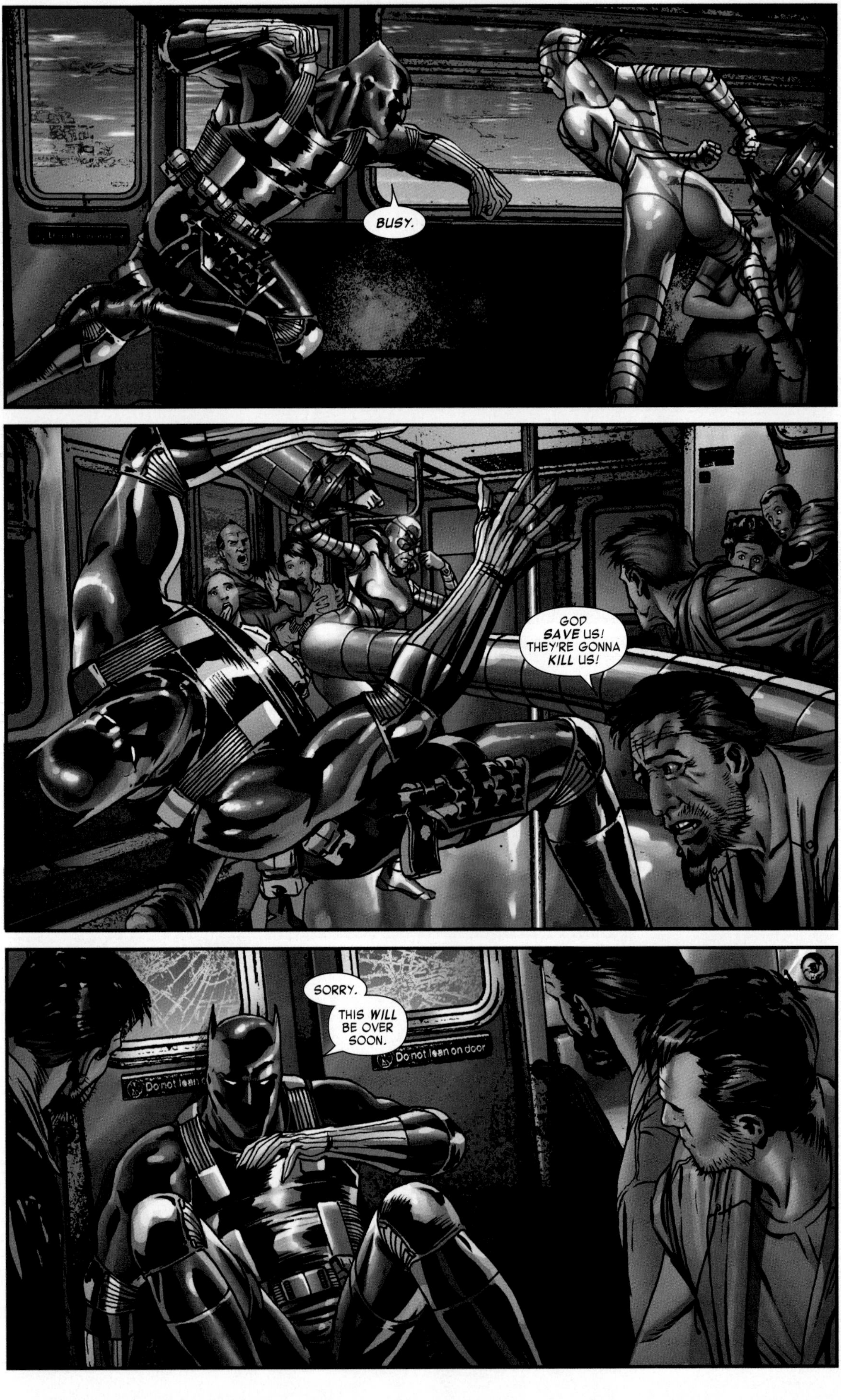
BUSY.
GOD SAVE US! THEY'RE GONNA KILL US!
SORRY.
THIS WILL BE OVER SOON.
Do not lean on door
Do not lean

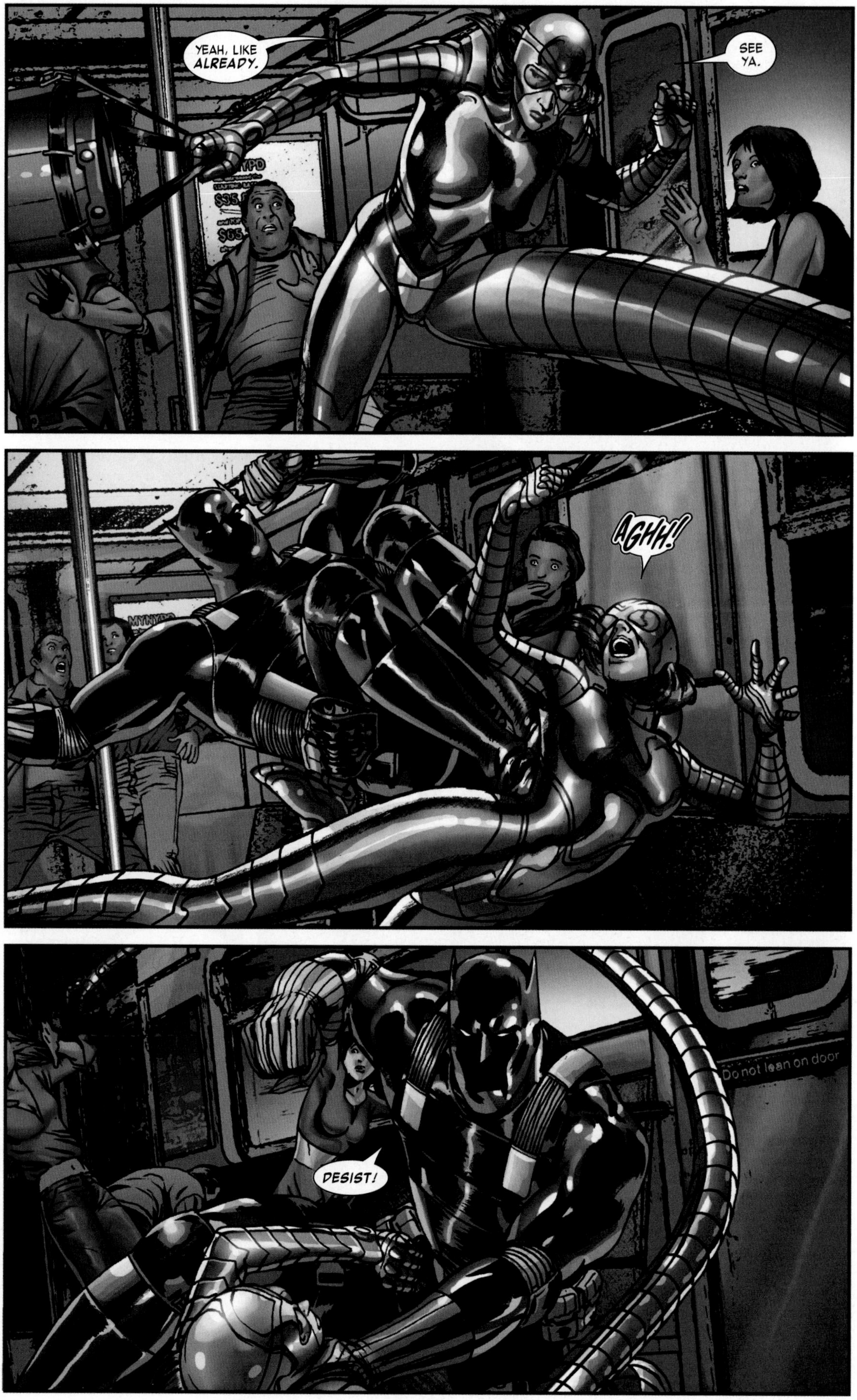
YEAH, LIKE ALREADY.
SEE YA.
AGHH!
Do not lean on door
DESIST!

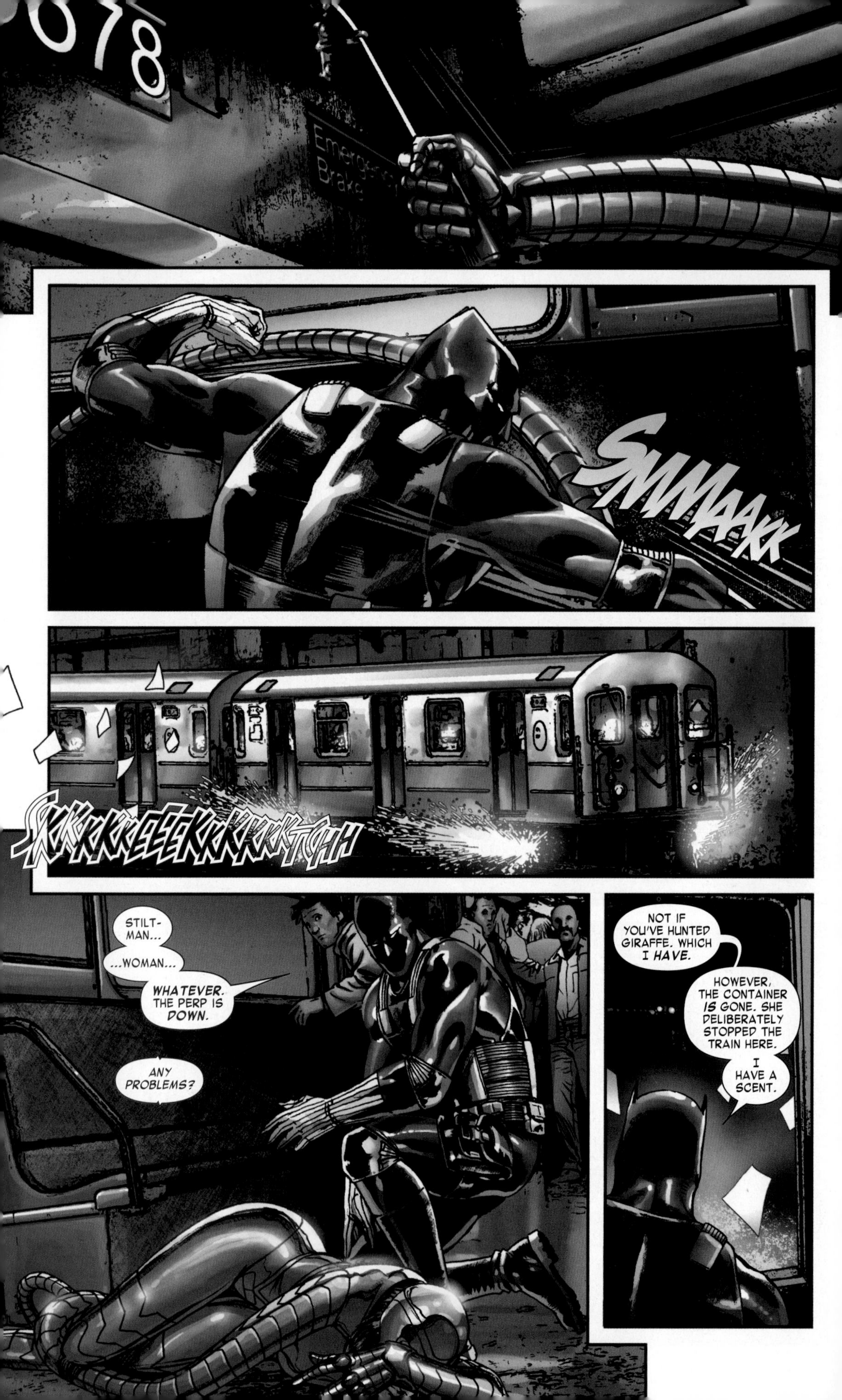

078
Emergency Brake
SMMAAKK
SKKKKKRREEEEKKKKKKKKTCHH
STILT-MAN...
...WOMAN...
WHATEVER. THE PERP IS DOWN.
ANY PROBLEMS?
NOT IF YOU'VE HUNTED GIRAFFE. WHICH I HAVE.
HOWEVER, THE CONTAINER IS GONE. SHE DELIBERATELY STOPPED THE TRAIN HERE.
I HAVE A SCENT.

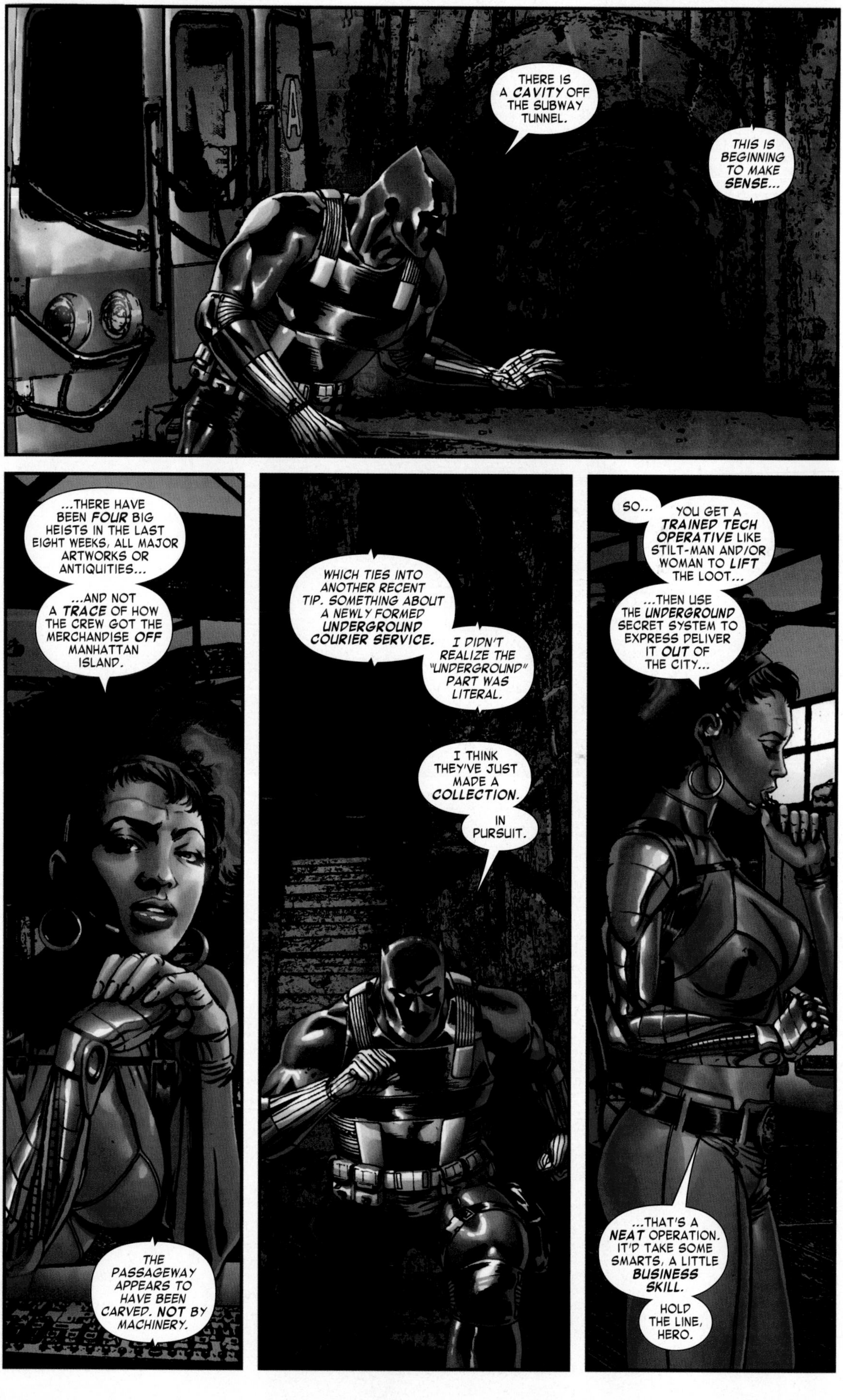

THERE IS A CAVITY OFF THE SUBWAY TUNNEL.
THIS IS BEGINNING TO MAKE SENSE...
...THERE HAVE BEEN FOUR BIG HEISTS IN THE LAST EIGHT WEEKS, ALL MAJOR ARTWORKS OR ANTIQUITIES...
...AND NOT A TRACE OF HOW THE CREW GOT THE MERCHANDISE OFF MANHATTAN ISLAND.
THE PASSAGEWAY APPEARS TO HAVE BEEN CARVED. NOT BY MACHINERY.
WHICH TIES INTO ANOTHER RECENT TIP. SOMETHING ABOUT A NEWLY FORMED UNDERGROUND COURIER SERVICE.
I DIDN'T REALIZE THE "UNDERGROUND" PART WAS LITERAL.
I THINK THEY'VE JUST MADE A COLLECTION.
IN PURSUIT.
SO...
YOU GET A TRAINED TECH OPERATIVE LIKE STILT-MAN AND/OR WOMAN TO LIFT THE LOOT...
...THEN USE THE UNDERGROUND SECRET SYSTEM TO EXPRESS DELIVER IT OUT OF THE CITY...
...THAT'S A NEAT OPERATION. IT'D TAKE SOME SMARTS, A LITTLE BUSINESS SKILL.
HOLD THE LINE, HERO.

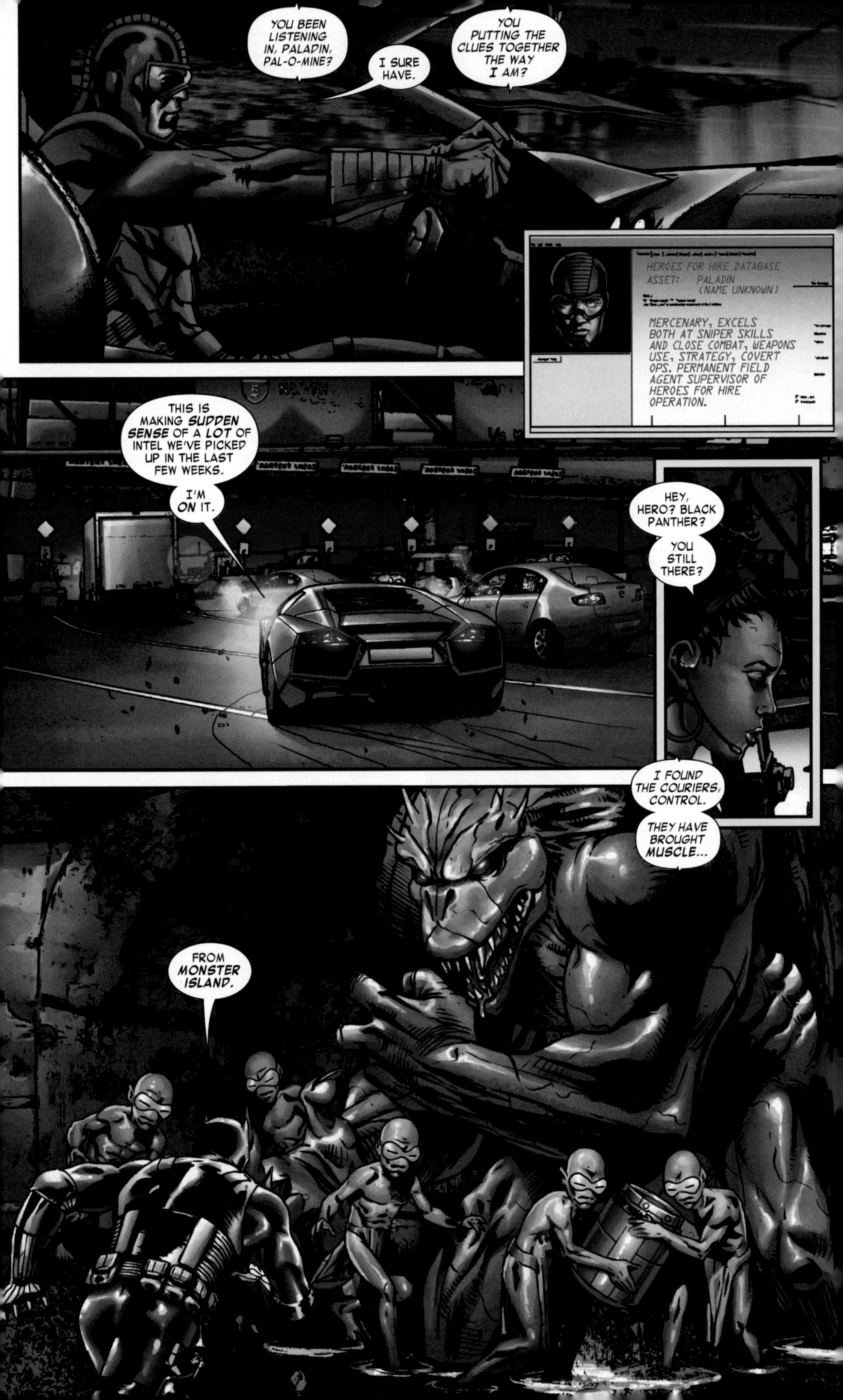
YOU BEEN LISTENING IN, PALADIN, PAL-O-MINE?
I SURE HAVE.
YOU PUTTING THE CLUES TOGETHER THE WAY I AM?
HEROES FOR HIRE DATABASE
ASSET: PALADIN (NAME UNKNOWN)
MERCENARY, EXCELS BOTH AT SNIPER SKILLS AND CLOSE COMBAT, WEAPONS USE, STRATEGY, COVERT OPS. PERMANENT FIELD AGENT SUPERVISOR OF HEROES FOR HIRE OPERATION.
THIS IS MAKING SUDDEN SENSE OF A LOT OF INTEL WE'VE PICKED UP IN THE LAST FEW WEEKS.
I'M ON IT.
HEY, HERO? BLACK PANTHER?
YOU STILL THERE?
I FOUND THE COURIERS, CONTROL.
THEY HAVE BROUGHT MUSCLE...
FROM MONSTER ISLAND.

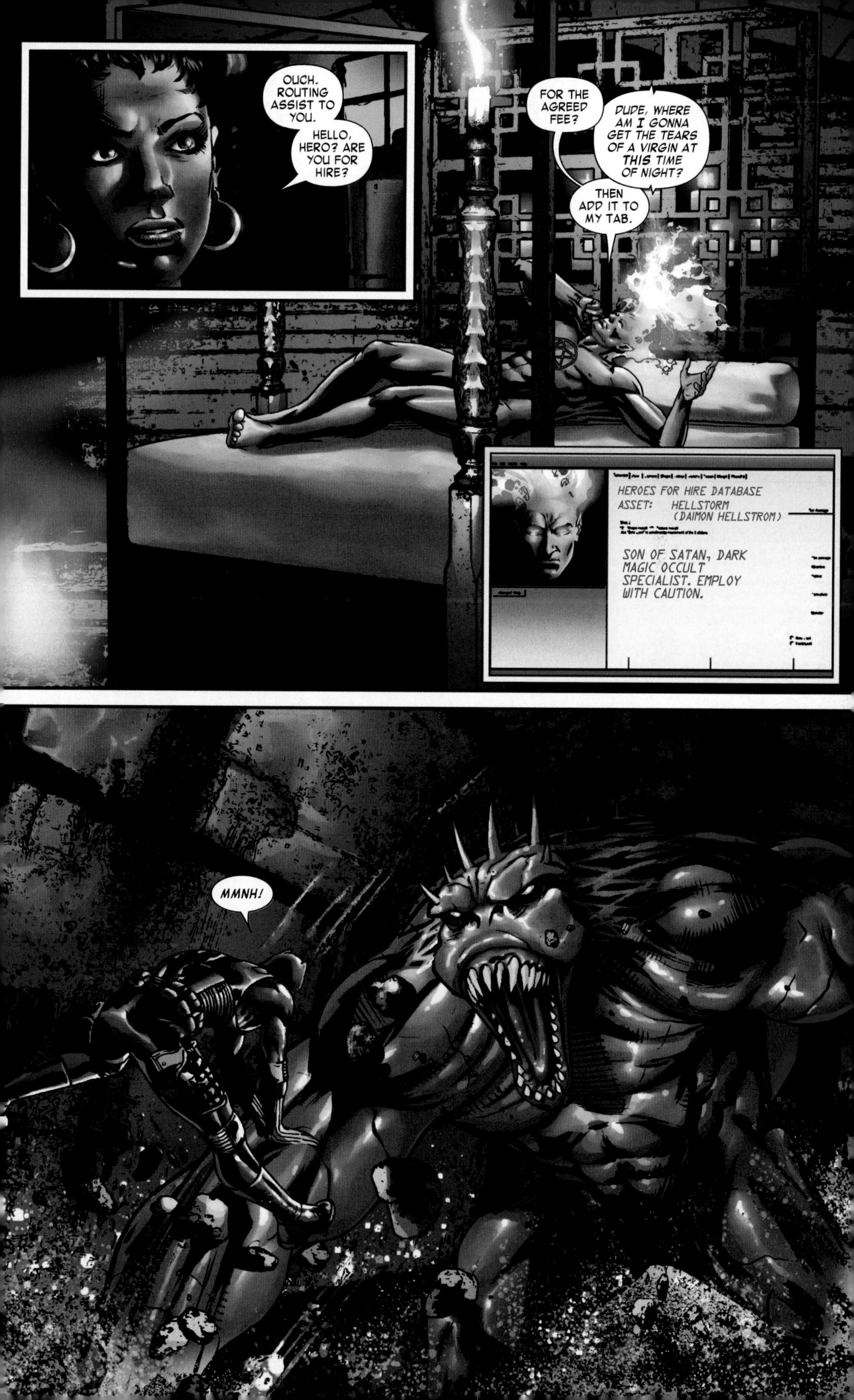
OUCH. ROUTING ASSIST TO YOU.
HELLO, HERO? ARE YOU FOR HIRE?
FOR THE AGREED FEE?
DUDE, WHERE AM I GONNA GET THE TEARS OF A VIRGIN AT THIS TIME OF NIGHT?
THEN ADD IT TO MY TAB.
HEROES FOR HIRE DATABASE
ASSET: HELLSTORM (DAIMON HELLSTROM)
SON OF SATAN, DARK MAGIC OCCULT SPECIALIST. EMPLOY WITH CAUTION.
MMNH!

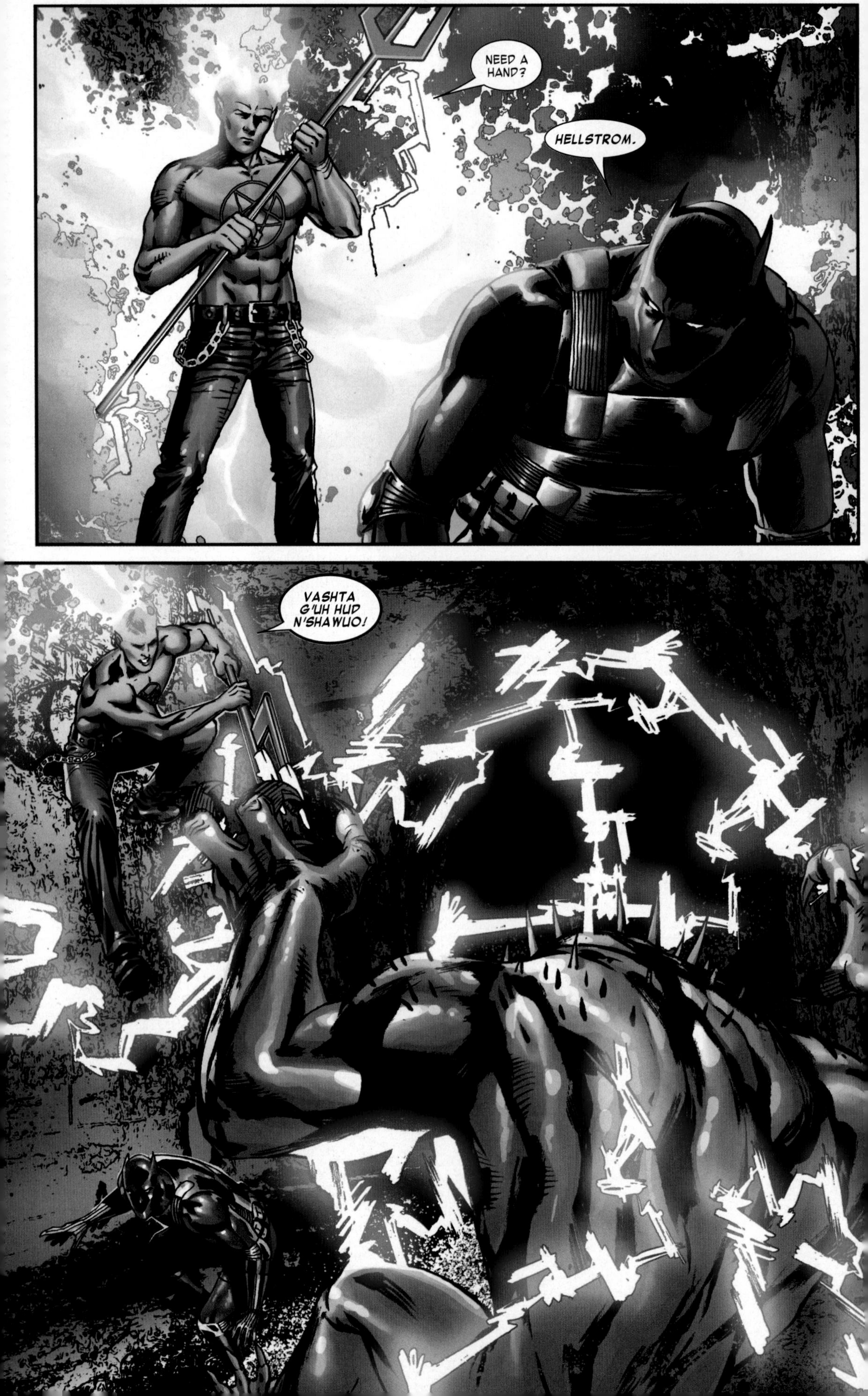
NEED A HAND?
HELLSTROM.
VASHTA G'UH HUD N'SHAWUO!

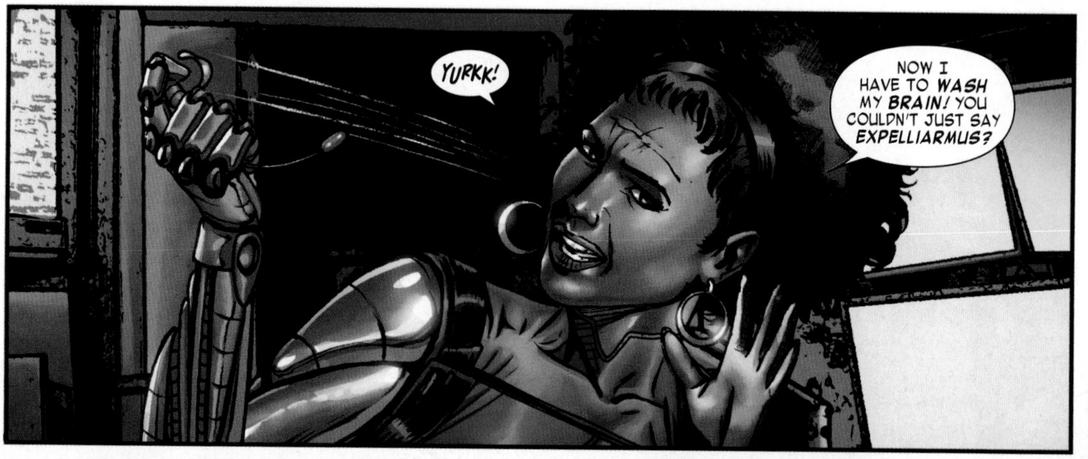
YURKK!
NOW I HAVE TO WASH MY BRAIN! YOU COULDN'T JUST SAY EXPELLIARMUS?

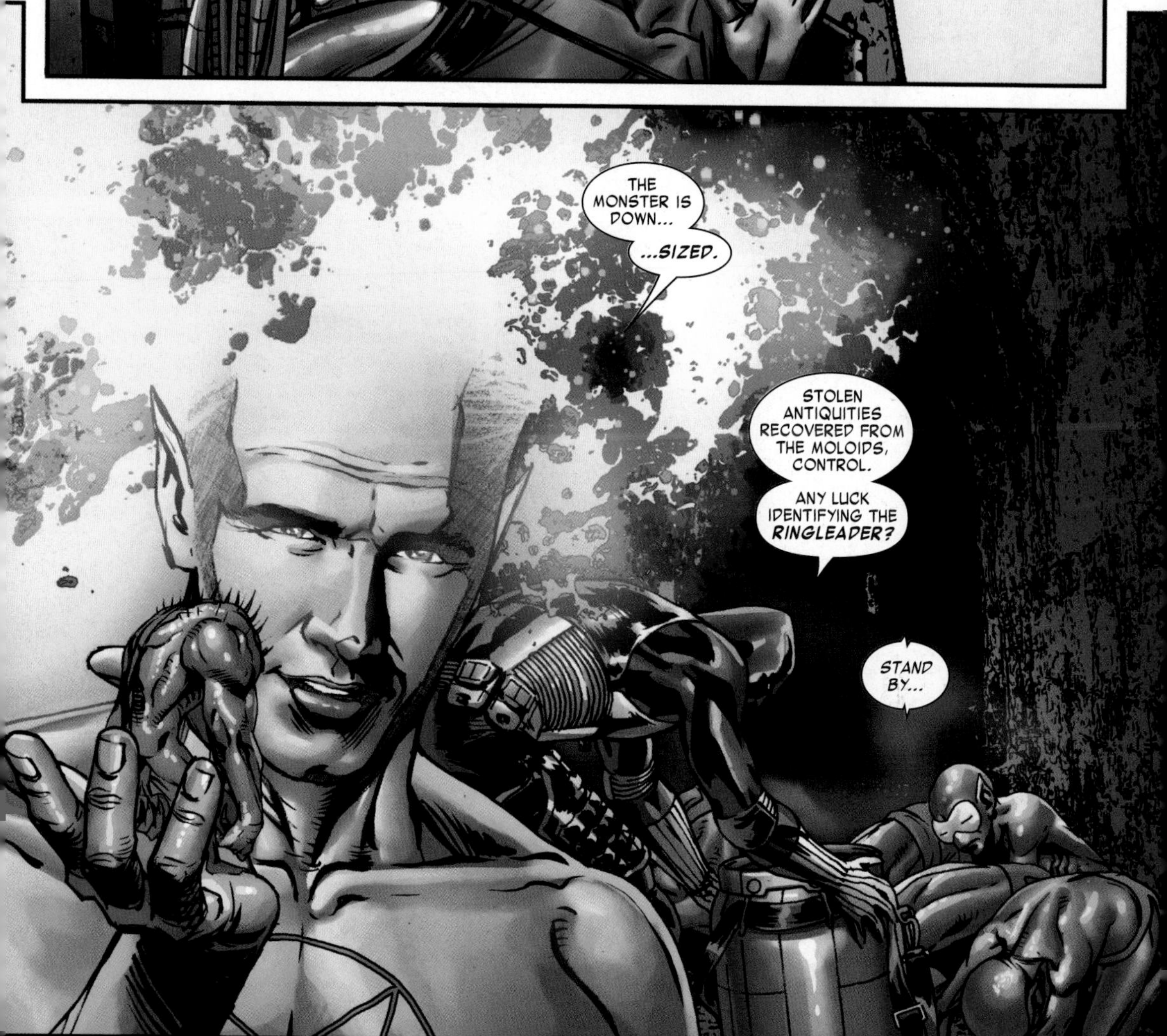
THE MONSTER IS DOWN...
...SIZED.
STOLEN ANTIQUITIES RECOVERED FROM THE MOLOIDS, CONTROL.
ANY LUCK IDENTIFYING THE RINGLEADER?
STAND BY...

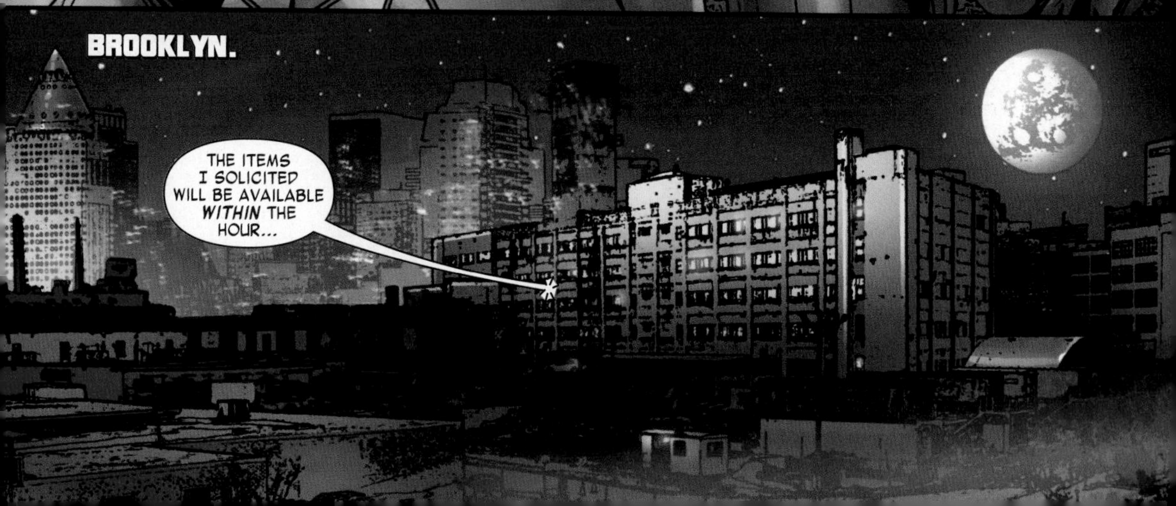
BROOKLYN.
THE ITEMS I SOLICITED WILL BE AVAILABLE WITHIN THE HOUR...

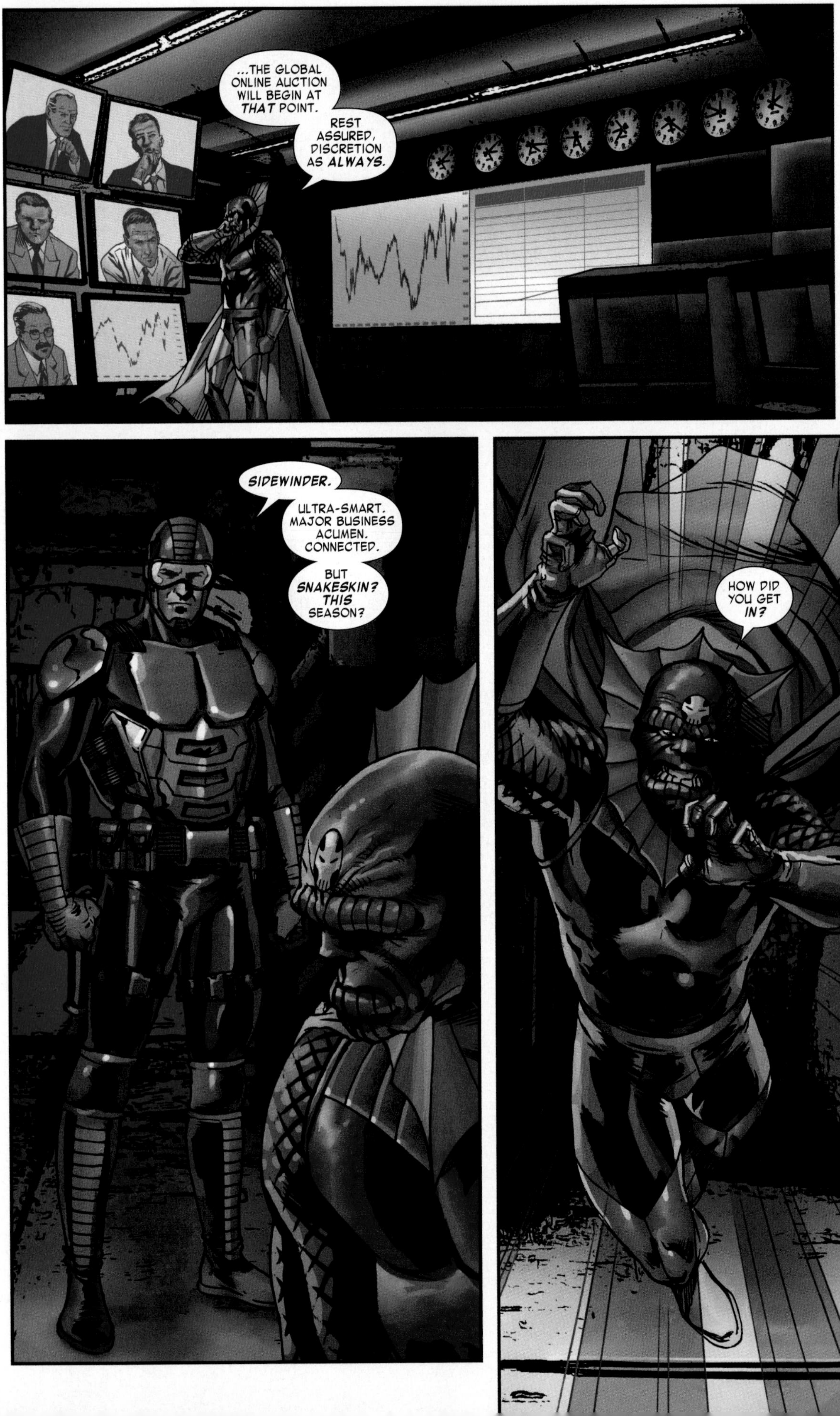
...THE GLOBAL ONLINE AUCTION WILL BEGIN AT THAT POINT.
REST ASSURED, DISCRETION AS ALWAYS.
SIDEWINDER.
ULTRA-SMART. MAJOR BUSINESS ACUMEN. CONNECTED.
BUT SNAKESKIN? THIS SEASON?
HOW DID YOU GET IN?

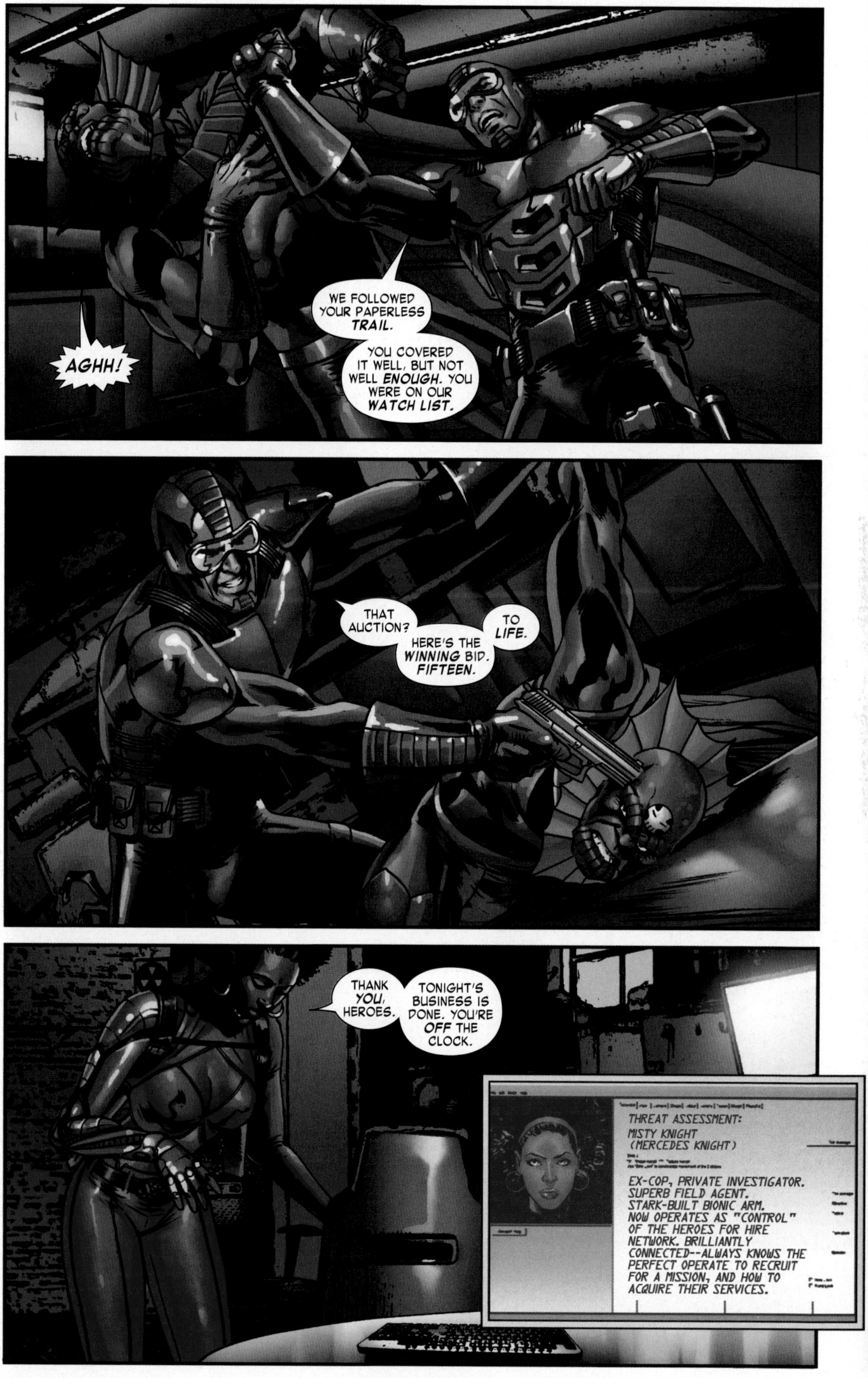

WE FOLLOWED YOUR PAPERLESS TRAIL.
YOU COVERED IT WELL, BUT NOT WELL ENOUGH. YOU WERE ON OUR WATCH LIST.
AGHH!
THAT AUCTION?
HERE'S THE WINNING BID. FIFTEEN.
TO LIFE.
THANK YOU, HEROES.
TONIGHT'S BUSINESS IS DONE. YOU'RE OFF THE CLOCK.
THREAT ASSESSMENT:
MISTY KNIGHT (MERCEDES KNIGHT)
EX-COP, PRIVATE INVESTIGATOR. SUPERB FIELD AGENT. STARK-BUILT BIONIC ARM. NOW OPERATES AS "CONTROL" OF THE HEROES FOR HIRE NETWORK. BRILLIANTLY CONNECTED--ALWAYS KNOWS THE PERFECT OPERATE TO RECRUIT FOR A MISSION, AND HOW TO ACQUIRE THEIR SERVICES.

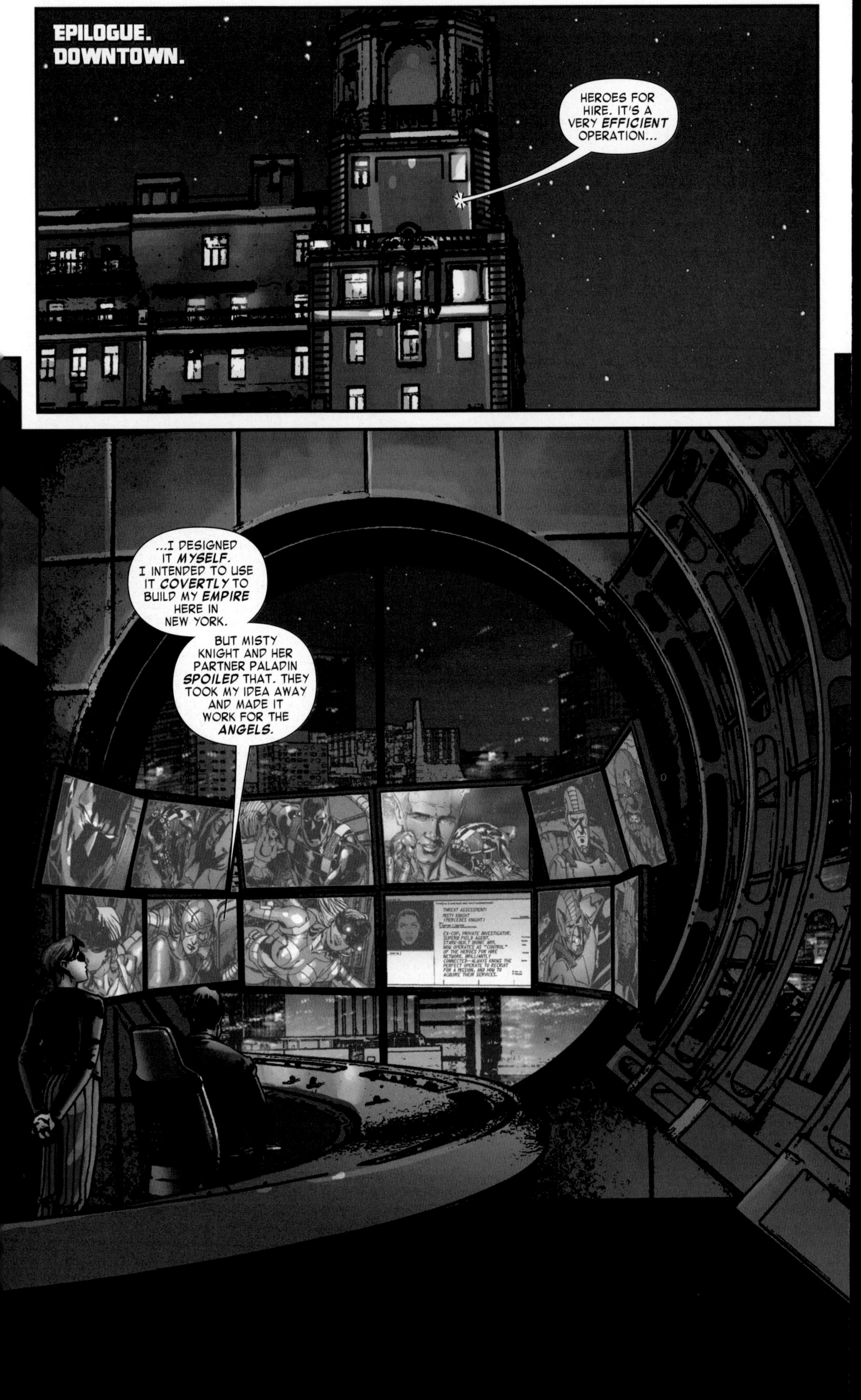
EPILOGUE. DOWNTOWN.
HEROES FOR HIRE. IT'S A VERY EFFICIENT OPERATION...
...I DESIGNED IT MYSELF. I INTENDED TO USE IT COVERTLY TO BUILD MY EMPIRE HERE IN NEW YORK.
BUT MISTY KNIGHT AND HER PARTNER PALADIN SPOILED THAT. THEY TOOK MY IDEA AWAY AND MADE IT WORK FOR THE ANGELS.
THREAT ASSESSMENT:
MISTY KNIGHT (MERCEDES KNIGHT)
EX-COP, PRIVATE INVESTIGATOR. SUPERB FIELD AGENT. STARK-BUILT BIONIC ARM. NOW OPERATES AS "CONTROL" OF THE HEROES FOR HIRE NETWORK. BRILLIANTLY CONNECTED--ALWAYS KNOWS THE PERFECT OPERATE TO RECRUIT FOR A MISSION, AND HOW TO ACQUIRE THEIR SERVICES.

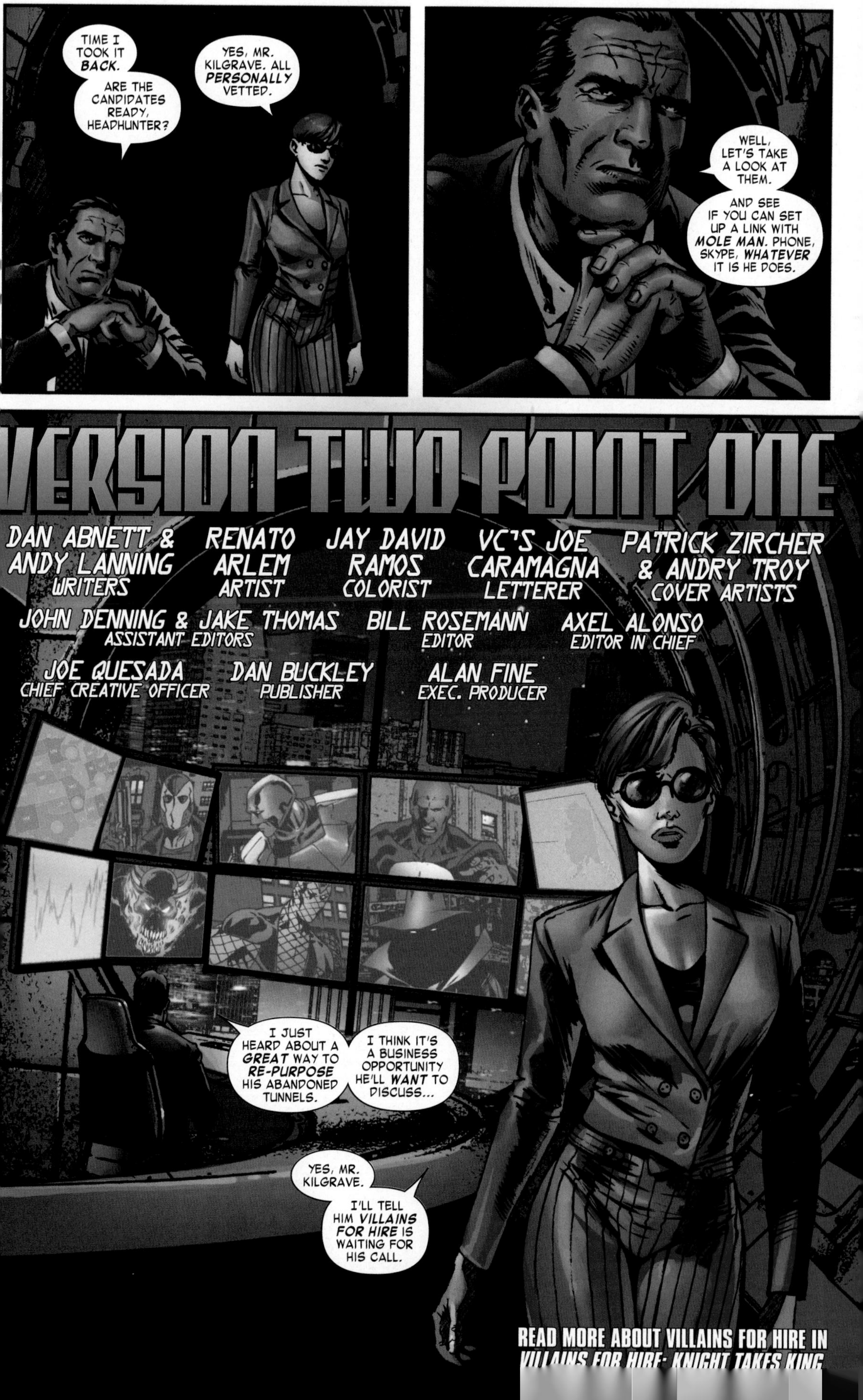

TIME I TOOK IT BACK.
ARE THE CANDIDATES READY, HEADHUNTER?
YES, MR. KILGRAVE. ALL PERSONALLY VETTED.
WELL, LET'S TAKE A LOOK AT THEM.
AND SEE IF YOU CAN SET UP A LINK WITH MOLE MAN. PHONE, SKYPE, WHATEVER IT IS HE DOES.
VERSION TWO POINT ONE
DAN ABNETT & ANDY LANNING WRITERS
RENATO ARLEM ARTIST
JAY DAVID RAMOS COLORIST
VC'S JOE CARAMAGNA LETTERER
PATRICK ZIRCHER & ANDRY TROY COVER ARTISTS
JOHN DENNING & JAKE THOMAS ASSISTANT EDITORS
BILL ROSEMANN EDITOR
AXEL ALONSO EDITOR IN CHIEF
JOE QUESADA CHIEF CREATIVE OFFICER
DAN BUCKLEY PUBLISHER
ALAN FINE EXEC. PRODUCER
I JUST HEARD ABOUT A GREAT WAY TO RE-PURPOSE HIS ABANDONED TUNNELS.
I THINK IT'S A BUSINESS OPPORTUNITY HE'LL WANT TO DISCUSS...
YES, MR. KILGRAVE.
I'LL TELL HIM VILLAINS FOR HIRE IS WAITING FOR HIS CALL.
READ MORE ABOUT VILLAINS FOR HIRE IN
VILLAINS FOR HIRE: KNIGHT TAKES KING

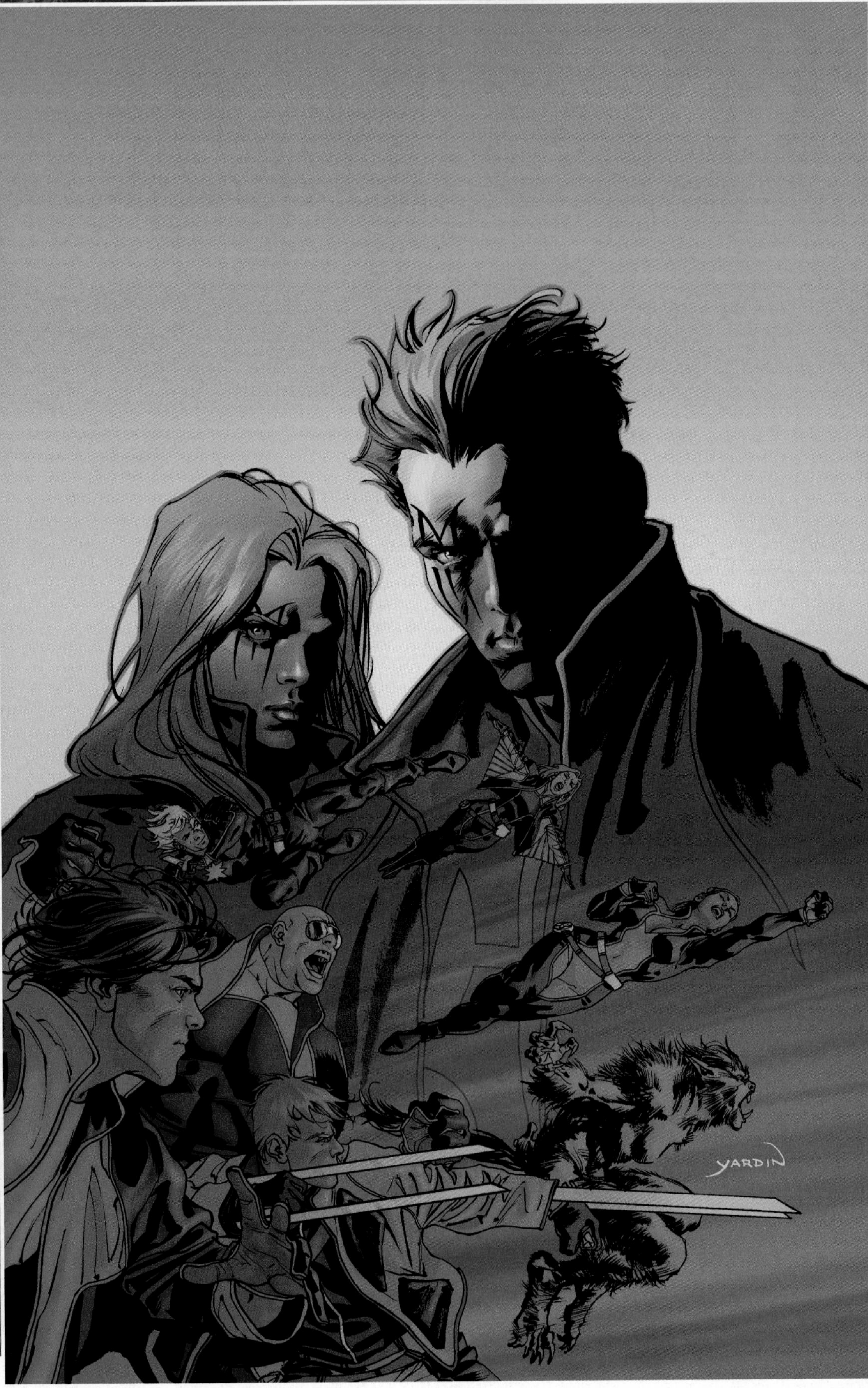
YARDIN

X-FACTOR #224.1

X-FACTOR

PREVIOUSLY...

A DETECTIVE AGENCY THAT SPECIALIZES IN ILLUMINATING THE DARK CORNERS OF
THE WORLD OF SUPER HEROES, JAMIE MADROX AND X-FACTOR INVESTIGATIONS
ARE NO STRANGERS TO THE STRANGE AND UNUSUAL. WHETHER THEY'RE
SEARCHING FOR RENEGADE SUPER-POWERED MERCENARIES, EVADING LUPINE
GODHEADS, OR PROTECTING THEIR CLIENT FROM EVIL DEMONS, THEY NEVER FAIL
TO CLOSE A CASE. THE TEAM HAS BEEN THROUGH THEIR SHARE OF PERSONAL
TRAGEDIES, BUT THROUGH IT ALL, THEY REMAIN A CLOSE-KNIT FAMILY...
ALBEIT ONE WITH ITS SHARE OF SECRETS.

PETER
DAVID
WRITER

VALENTINE
DE LANDRO
PENCILER

PAT
DAVIDSON
INKER

JEREMY
COX
COLORIST

VC'S CORY
PETIT
LETTERER

DAVID YARDIN
COVER ARTIST

JORDAN D. WHITE
ASSISTANT EDITOR

DANIEL KETCHUM
EDITOR

NICK LOWE
X-MEN GROUP EDITOR

AXEL ALONSO
EDITOR IN CHIEF

JOE QUESADA
CHIEF CREATIVE OFFICER

DAN BUCKLEY
PUBLISHER

ALAN FINE
EXEC. PRODUCER

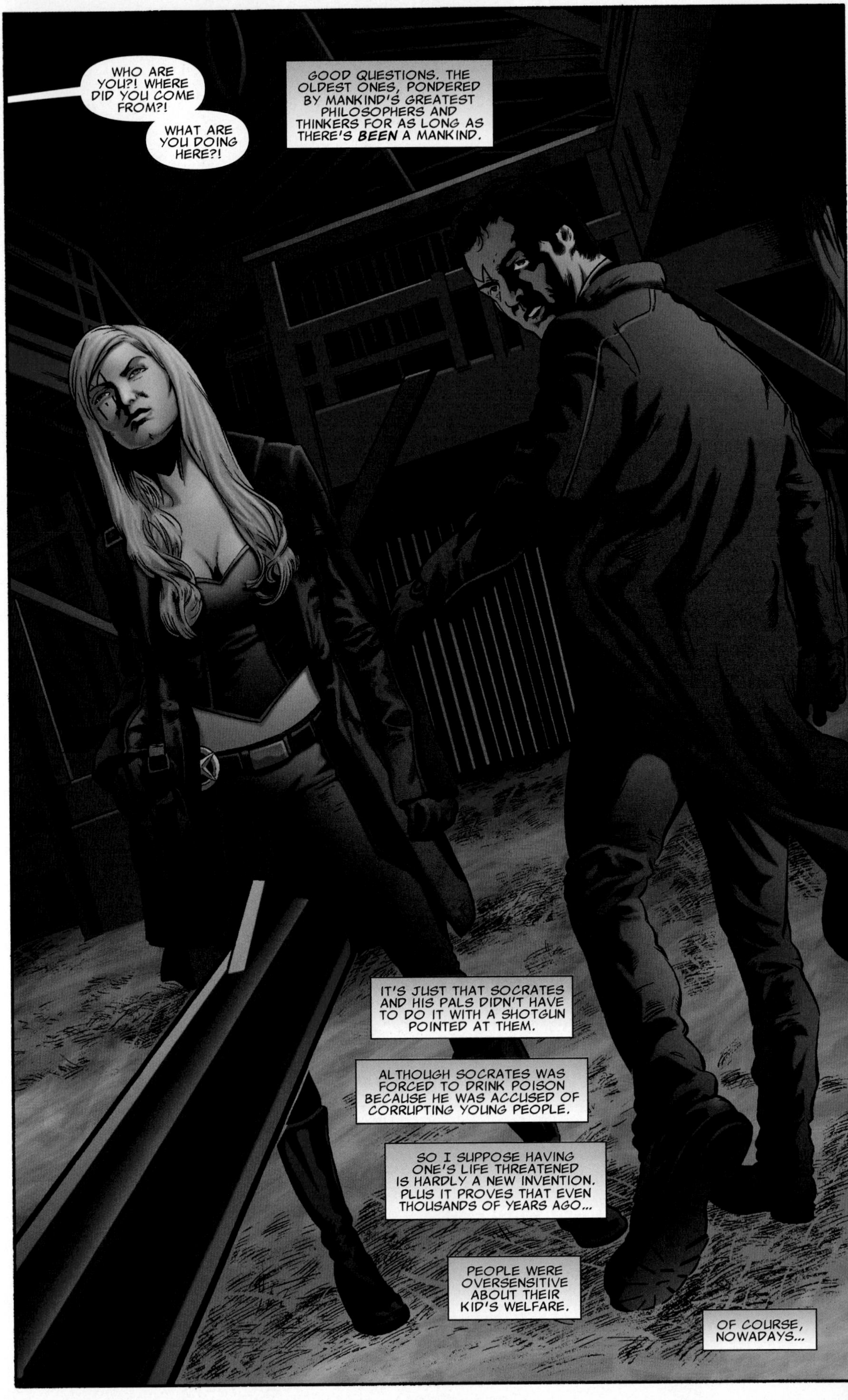
WHO ARE YOU?! WHERE DID YOU COME FROM?!
WHAT ARE YOU DOING HERE?!
GOOD QUESTIONS. THE OLDEST ONES, PONDERED BY MANKIND'S GREATEST PHILOSOPHERS AND THINKERS FOR AS LONG AS THERE'S BEEN A MANKIND.
IT'S JUST THAT SOCRATES AND HIS PALS DIDN'T HAVE TO DO IT WITH A SHOTGUN POINTED AT THEM.
ALTHOUGH SOCRATES WAS FORCED TO DRINK POISON BECAUSE HE WAS ACCUSED OF CORRUPTING YOUNG PEOPLE.
SO I SUPPOSE HAVING ONE'S LIFE THREATENED IS HARDLY A NEW INVENTION. PLUS IT PROVES THAT EVEN THOUSANDS OF YEARS AGO...
PEOPLE WERE OVERSENSITIVE ABOUT THEIR KID'S WELFARE.
OF COURSE, NOWADAYS...

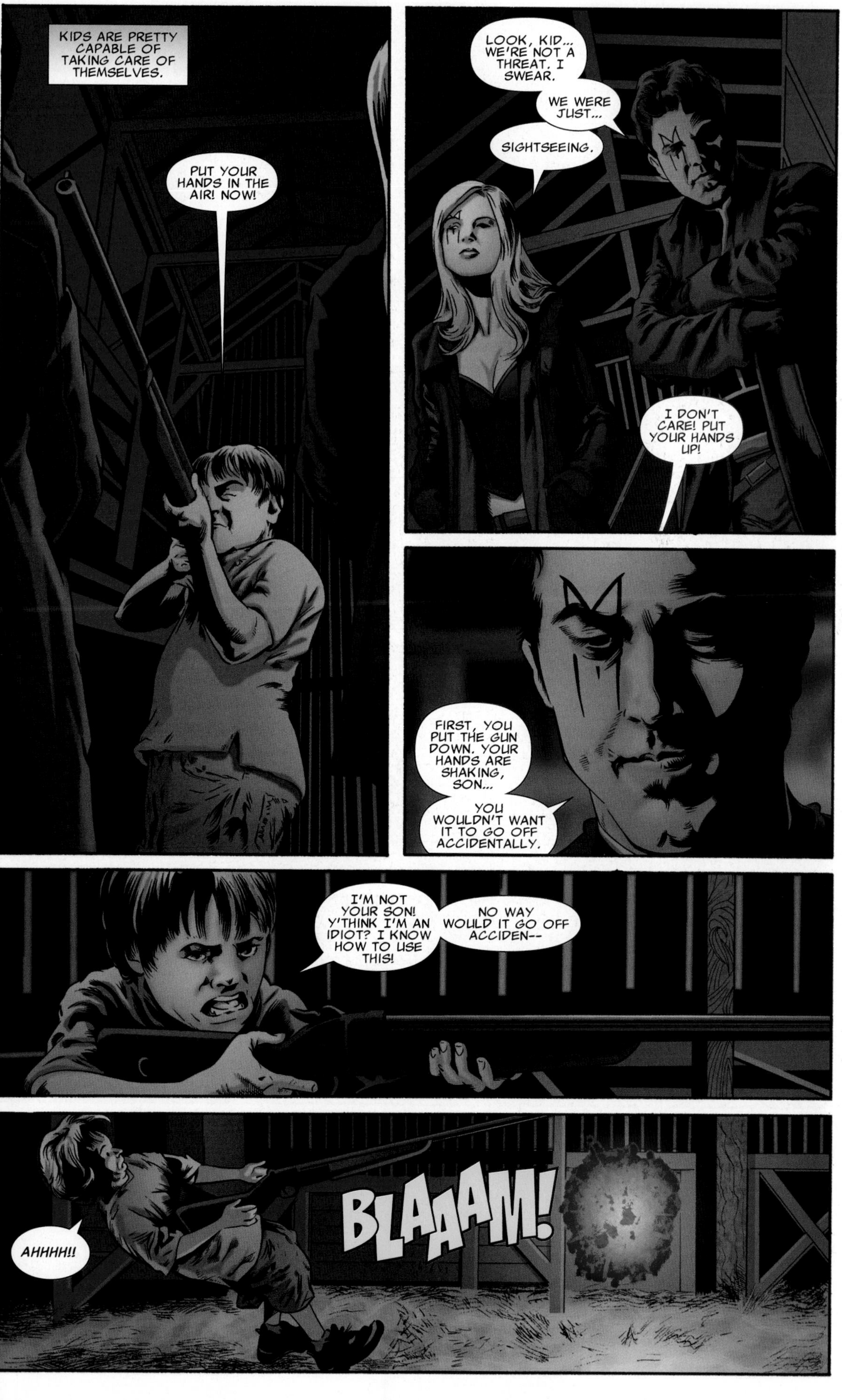
KIDS ARE PRETTY CAPABLE OF TAKING CARE OF THEMSELVES.
PUT YOUR HANDS IN THE AIR! NOW!
LOOK, KID... WE'RE NOT A THREAT. I SWEAR.
WE WERE JUST...
SIGHTSEEING.
I DON'T CARE! PUT YOUR HANDS UP!
FIRST, YOU PUT THE GUN DOWN. YOUR HANDS ARE SHAKING, SON...
YOU WOULDN'T WANT IT TO GO OFF ACCIDENTALLY.
I'M NOT YOUR SON! Y'THINK I'M AN IDIOT? I KNOW HOW TO USE THIS!
NO WAY WOULD IT GO OFF ACCIDEN--
BLAAAM!
AHHHH!!

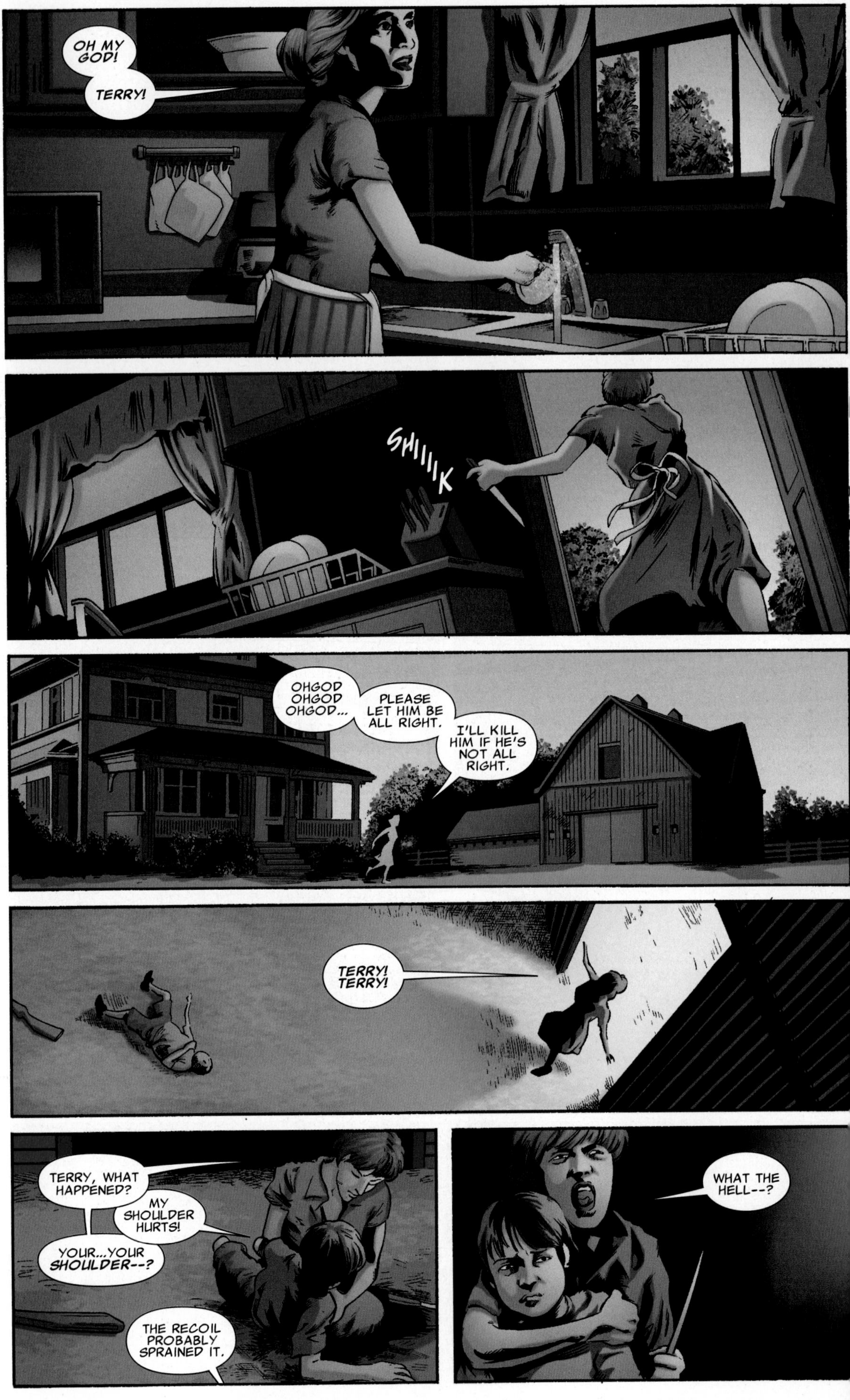
OH MY GOD!
TERRY!
SHIIIIK
OHGOD OHGOD OHGOD...
PLEASE LET HIM BE ALL RIGHT.
I'LL KILL HIM IF HE'S NOT ALL RIGHT.
TERRY! TERRY!
TERRY, WHAT HAPPENED?
MY SHOULDER HURTS!
YOUR...YOUR SHOULDER--?
THE RECOIL PROBABLY SPRAINED IT.
WHAT THE HELL--?

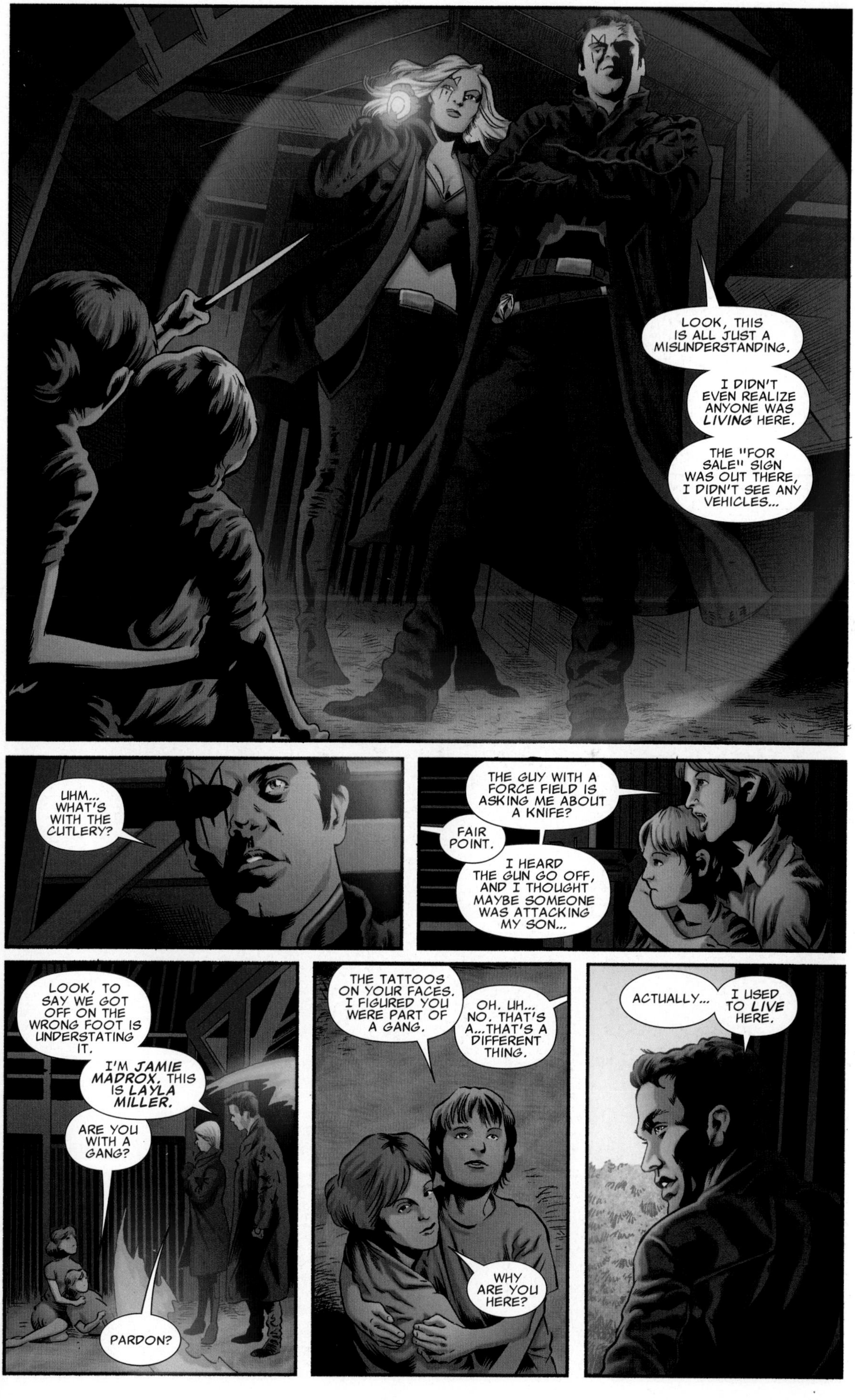
LOOK, THIS IS ALL JUST A MISUNDERSTANDING.
I DIDN'T EVEN REALIZE ANYONE WAS LIVING HERE.
THE "FOR SALE" SIGN WAS OUT THERE, I DIDN'T SEE ANY VEHICLES...
UHM... WHAT'S WITH THE CUTLERY?
THE GUY WITH A FORCE FIELD IS ASKING ME ABOUT A KNIFE?
FAIR POINT.
I HEARD THE GUN GO OFF, AND I THOUGHT MAYBE SOMEONE WAS ATTACKING MY SON...
LOOK, TO SAY WE GOT OFF ON THE WRONG FOOT IS UNDERSTATING IT.
I'M JAMIE MADROX. THIS IS LAYLA MILLER.
ARE YOU WITH A GANG?
PARDON?
THE TATTOOS ON YOUR FACES. I FIGURED YOU WERE PART OF A GANG.
OH. UH... NO. THAT'S A...THAT'S A DIFFERENT THING.
WHY ARE YOU HERE?
ACTUALLY...
I USED TO LIVE HERE.

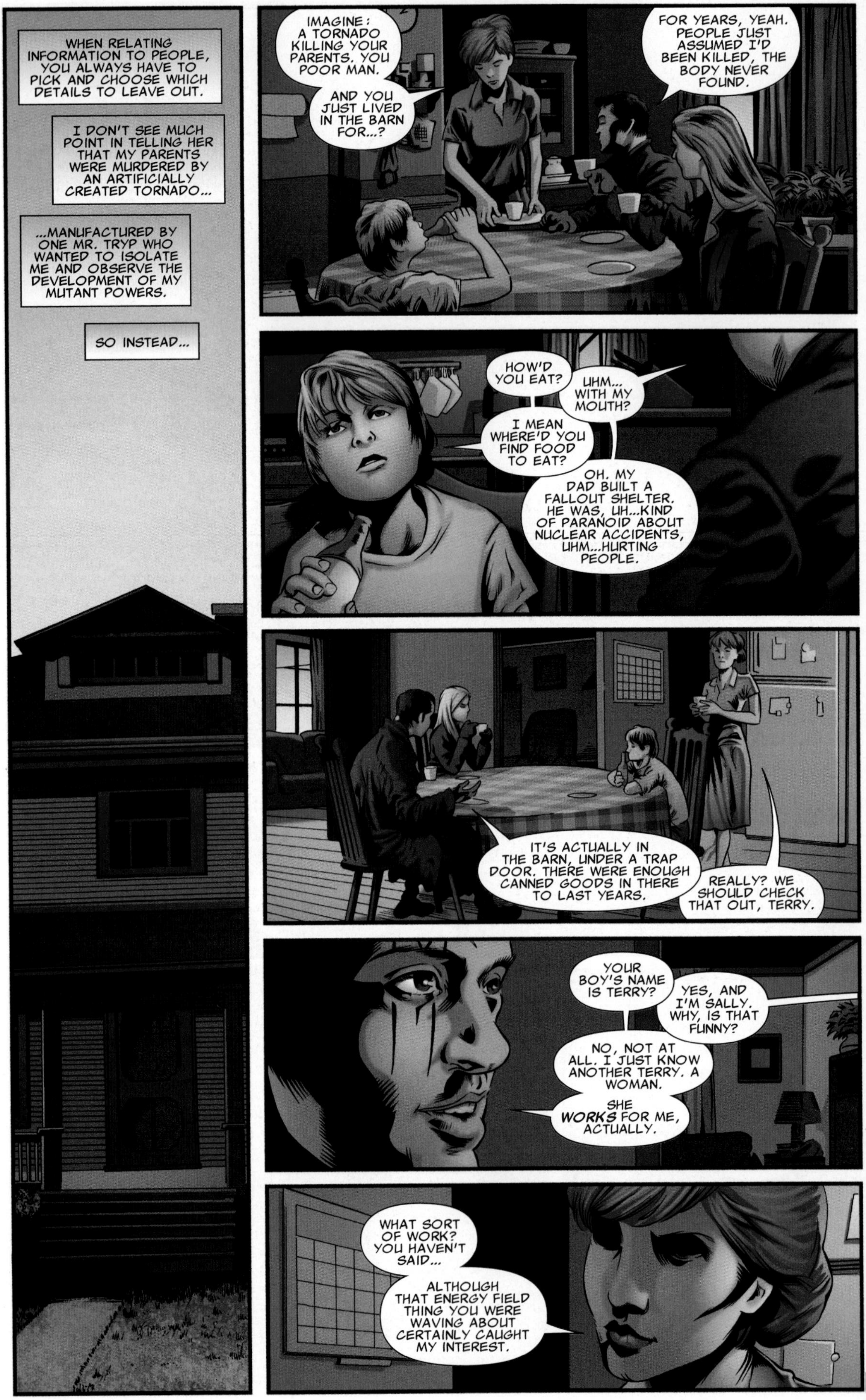
WHEN RELATING INFORMATION TO PEOPLE, YOU ALWAYS HAVE TO PICK AND CHOOSE WHICH DETAILS TO LEAVE OUT.
I DON'T SEE MUCH POINT IN TELLING HER THAT MY PARENTS WERE MURDERED BY AN ARTIFICIALLY CREATED TORNADO...
...MANUFACTURED BY ONE MR. TRYP WHO WANTED TO ISOLATE ME AND OBSERVE THE DEVELOPMENT OF MY MUTANT POWERS.
SO INSTEAD...
IMAGINE: A TORNADO KILLING YOUR PARENTS. YOU POOR MAN.
AND YOU JUST LIVED IN THE BARN FOR...?
FOR YEARS, YEAH. PEOPLE JUST ASSUMED I'D BEEN KILLED, THE BODY NEVER FOUND.
HOW'D YOU EAT?
UHM... WITH MY MOUTH?
I MEAN WHERE'D YOU FIND FOOD TO EAT?
OH. MY DAD BUILT A FALLOUT SHELTER. HE WAS, UH...KIND OF PARANOID ABOUT NUCLEAR ACCIDENTS, UHM...HURTING PEOPLE.
IT'S ACTUALLY IN THE BARN, UNDER A TRAP DOOR. THERE WERE ENOUGH CANNED GOODS IN THERE TO LAST YEARS.
REALLY? WE SHOULD CHECK THAT OUT, TERRY.
YOUR BOY'S NAME IS TERRY?
YES, AND I'M SALLY. WHY, IS THAT FUNNY?
NO, NOT AT ALL. I JUST KNOW ANOTHER TERRY. A WOMAN.
SHE *WORKS* FOR ME, ACTUALLY.
WHAT SORT OF WORK? YOU HAVEN'T SAID...
ALTHOUGH THAT ENERGY FIELD THING YOU WERE WAVING ABOUT CERTAINLY CAUGHT MY INTEREST.

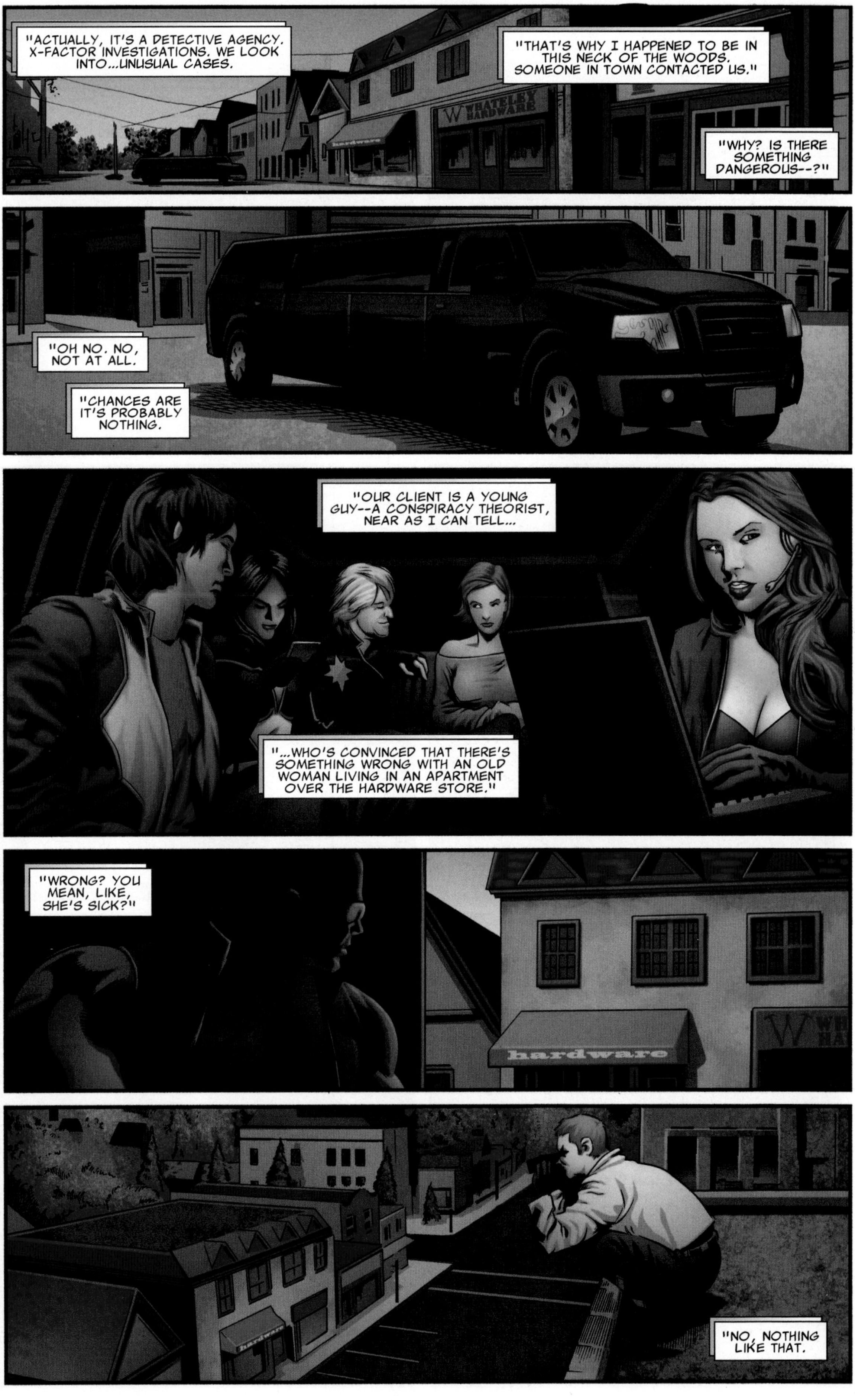
"ACTUALLY, IT'S A DETECTIVE AGENCY. X-FACTOR INVESTIGATIONS. WE LOOK INTO...UNUSUAL CASES.
"THAT'S WHY I HAPPENED TO BE IN THIS NECK OF THE WOODS. SOMEONE IN TOWN CONTACTED US."
WHATELEY HARDWARE
hardware
"WHY? IS THERE SOMETHING DANGEROUS--?"
"OH NO. NO, NOT AT ALL.
"CHANCES ARE IT'S PROBABLY NOTHING.
"OUR CLIENT IS A YOUNG GUY--A CONSPIRACY THEORIST, NEAR AS I CAN TELL...
"...WHO'S CONVINCED THAT THERE'S SOMETHING WRONG WITH AN OLD WOMAN LIVING IN AN APARTMENT OVER THE HARDWARE STORE."
"WRONG? YOU MEAN, LIKE, SHE'S SICK?"
hardware
"NO, NOTHING LIKE THAT.

"BASICALLY, HE SWEARS THAT THIS WOMAN SITS AT HER WINDOW AND JUST STARES OUT, TWENTY-FOUR/SEVEN.

"NEVER BUDGES. NEVER EATS. NEVER GOES TO THE BATHROOM...

"...WHICH WOULD FOLLOW SINCE SHE NEVER EATS, BUT, Y'KNOW...

"ANYWAY, OUR CLIENT'S GONE TO THE COPS, TALKED TO THEM ABOUT IT...

"AND OBVIOUSLY THEY HAVEN'T DONE ANYTHING BECAUSE IT'S NOT ILLEGAL TO STARE OUT A WINDOW.

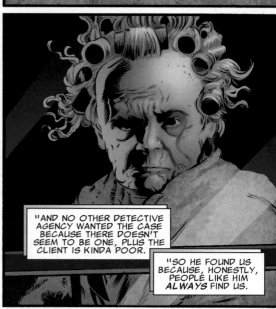

"AND NO OTHER DETECTIVE AGENCY WANTED THE CASE BECAUSE THERE DOESN'T SEEM TO BE ONE, PLUS THE CLIENT IS KINDA POOR.

"SO HE FOUND US BECAUSE, HONESTLY, PEOPLE LIKE HIM ALWAYS FIND US.

"WE'RE WHO PEOPLE GO TO OVER STUFF THAT NOBODY ELSE UNDERSTANDS...

"...OR, FOR THAT MATTER, WANTS TO UNDERSTAND."

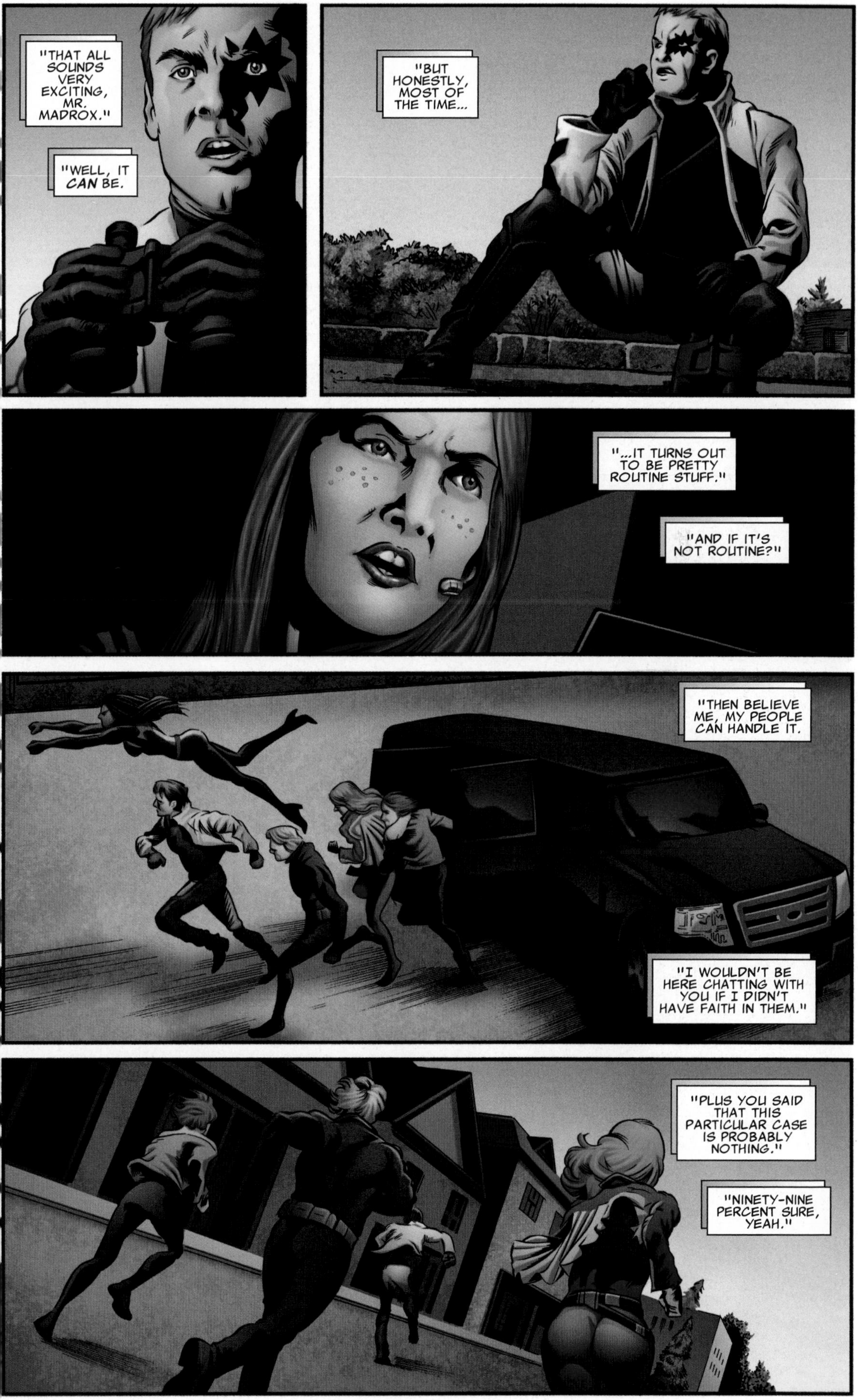
"THAT ALL SOUNDS VERY EXCITING, MR. MADROX."
"WELL, IT CAN BE.
"BUT HONESTLY, MOST OF THE TIME...
"...IT TURNS OUT TO BE PRETTY ROUTINE STUFF."
"AND IF IT'S NOT ROUTINE?"
"THEN BELIEVE ME, MY PEOPLE CAN HANDLE IT.
"I WOULDN'T BE HERE CHATTING WITH YOU IF I DIDN'T HAVE FAITH IN THEM."
"PLUS YOU SAID THAT THIS PARTICULAR CASE IS PROBABLY NOTHING."
"NINETY-NINE PERCENT SURE, YEAH."

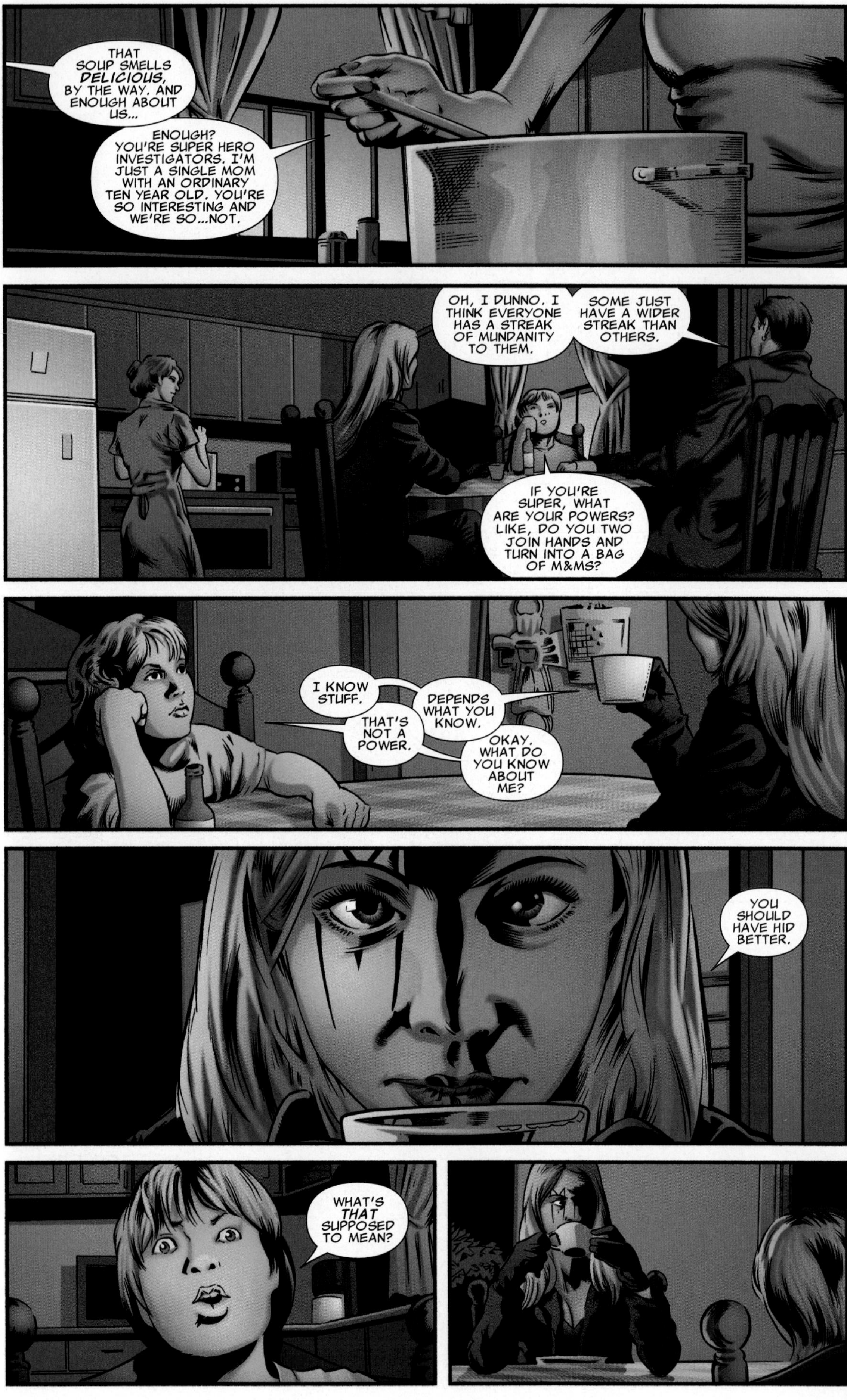
THAT SOUP SMELLS *DELICIOUS*, BY THE WAY. AND ENOUGH ABOUT US...
ENOUGH? YOU'RE SUPER HERO INVESTIGATORS. I'M JUST A SINGLE MOM WITH AN ORDINARY TEN YEAR OLD. YOU'RE SO INTERESTING AND WE'RE SO...NOT.
OH, I DUNNO. I THINK EVERYONE HAS A STREAK OF MUNDANITY TO THEM.
SOME JUST HAVE A WIDER STREAK THAN OTHERS.
IF YOU'RE SUPER, WHAT ARE YOUR POWERS? LIKE, DO YOU TWO JOIN HANDS AND TURN INTO A BAG OF M&MS?
I KNOW STUFF.
DEPENDS WHAT YOU KNOW.
THAT'S NOT A POWER.
OKAY. WHAT DO YOU KNOW ABOUT ME?
YOU SHOULD HAVE HID BETTER.
WHAT'S *THAT* SUPPOSED TO MEAN?

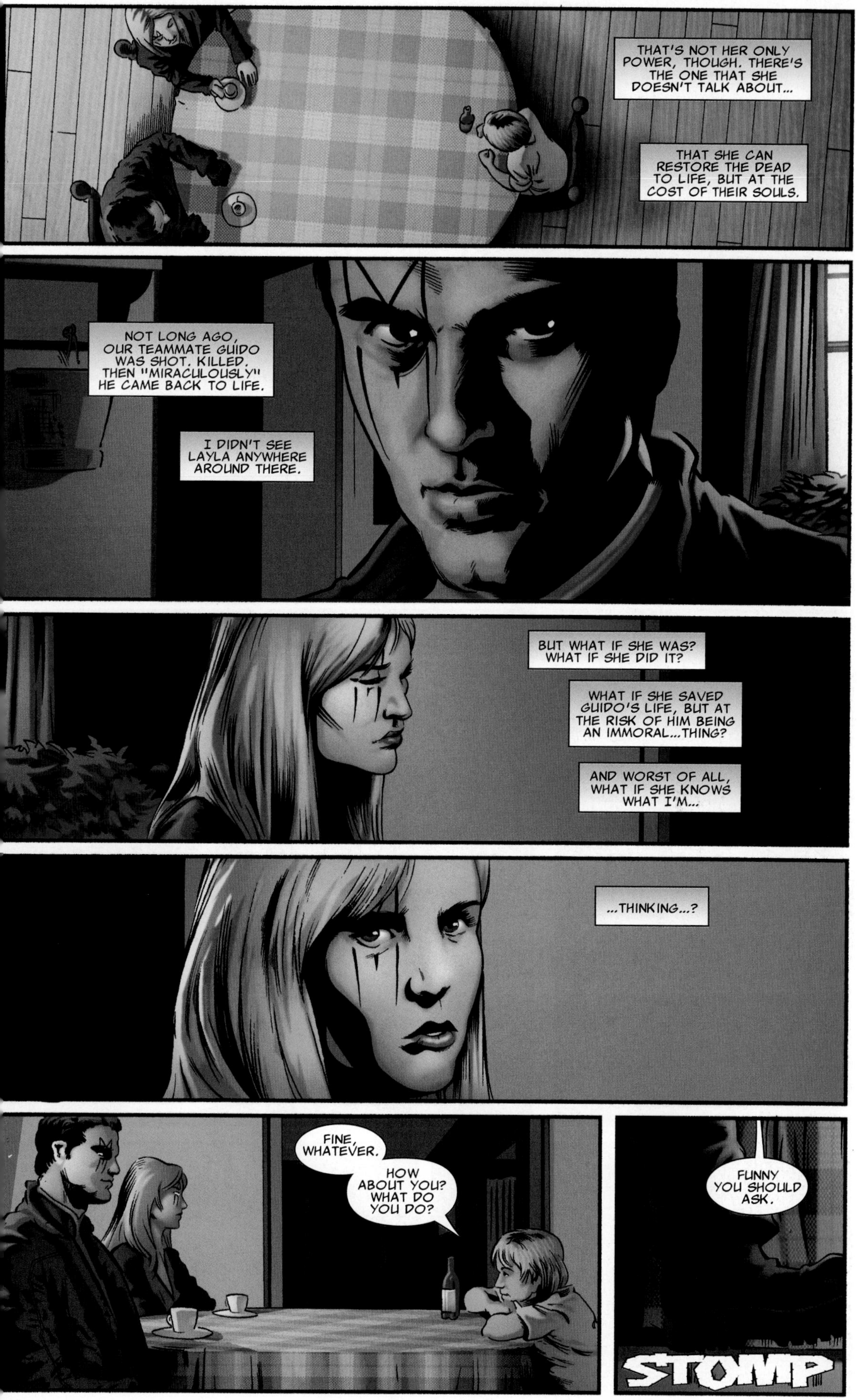
THAT'S NOT HER ONLY POWER, THOUGH. THERE'S THE ONE THAT SHE DOESN'T TALK ABOUT...
THAT SHE CAN RESTORE THE DEAD TO LIFE, BUT AT THE COST OF THEIR SOULS.
NOT LONG AGO, OUR TEAMMATE GUIDO WAS SHOT. KILLED. THEN "MIRACULOUSLY" HE CAME BACK TO LIFE.
I DIDN'T SEE LAYLA ANYWHERE AROUND THERE.
BUT WHAT IF SHE WAS? WHAT IF SHE DID IT?
WHAT IF SHE SAVED GUIDO'S LIFE, BUT AT THE RISK OF HIM BEING AN IMMORAL...THING?
AND WORST OF ALL, WHAT IF SHE KNOWS WHAT I'M...
...THINKING...?
FINE, WHATEVER.
HOW ABOUT YOU? WHAT DO YOU DO?
FUNNY YOU SHOULD ASK.
STOMP

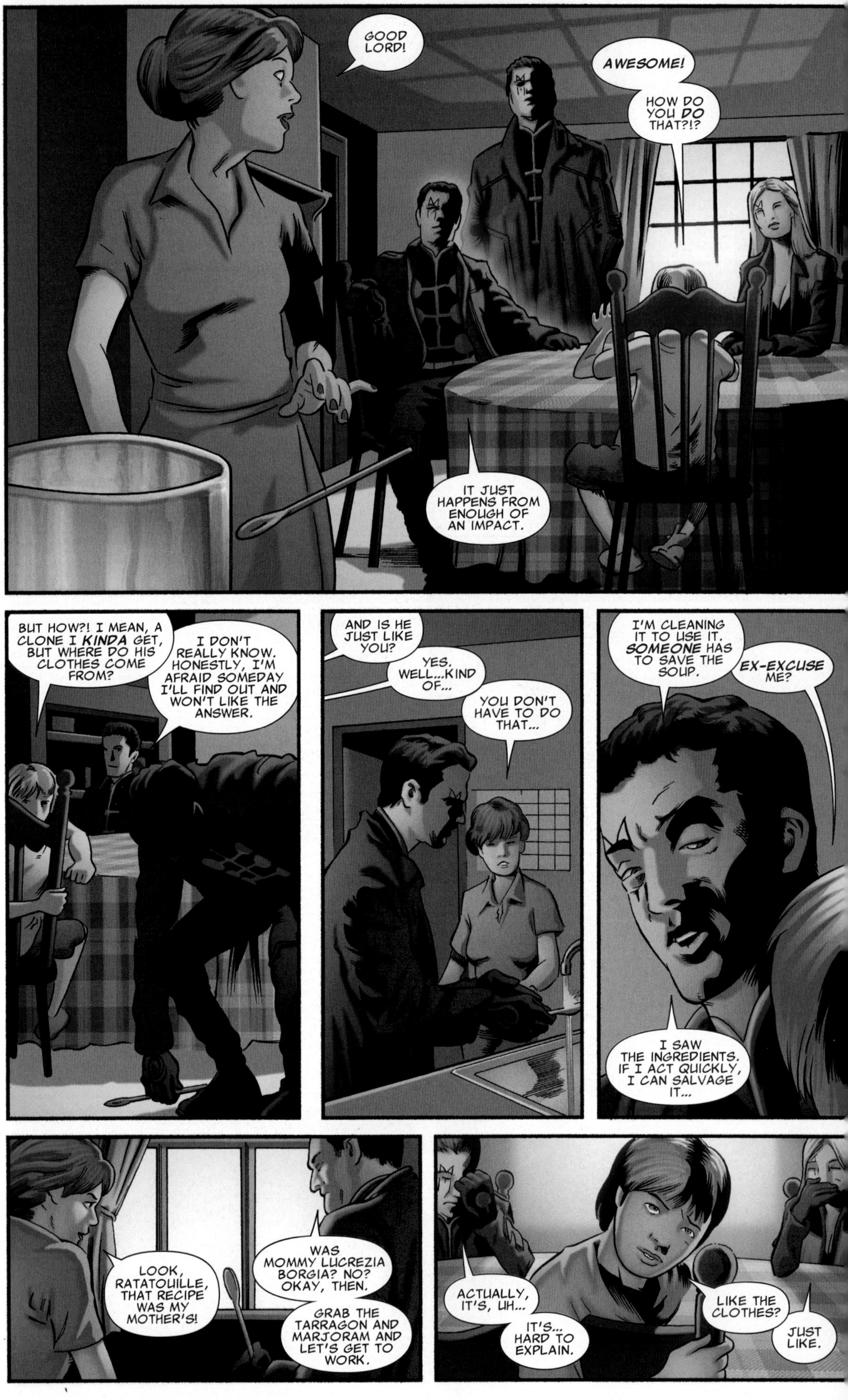
GOOD LORD!
AWESOME!
HOW DO YOU DO THAT?!?
IT JUST HAPPENS FROM ENOUGH OF AN IMPACT.
BUT HOW?! I MEAN, A CLONE I KINDA GET, BUT WHERE DO HIS CLOTHES COME FROM?
I DON'T REALLY KNOW. HONESTLY, I'M AFRAID SOMEDAY I'LL FIND OUT AND WON'T LIKE THE ANSWER.
AND IS HE JUST LIKE YOU?
YES. WELL...KIND OF...
YOU DON'T HAVE TO DO THAT...
I'M CLEANING IT TO USE IT. SOMEONE HAS TO SAVE THE SOUP.
EX-EXCUSE ME?
I SAW THE INGREDIENTS. IF I ACT QUICKLY, I CAN SALVAGE IT...
LOOK, RATATOUILLE, THAT RECIPE WAS MY MOTHER'S!
WAS MOMMY LUCREZIA BORGIA? NO? OKAY, THEN.
GRAB THE TARRAGON AND MARJORAM AND LET'S GET TO WORK.
ACTUALLY, IT'S, UH...
IT'S... HARD TO EXPLAIN.
LIKE THE CLOTHES?
JUST LIKE.

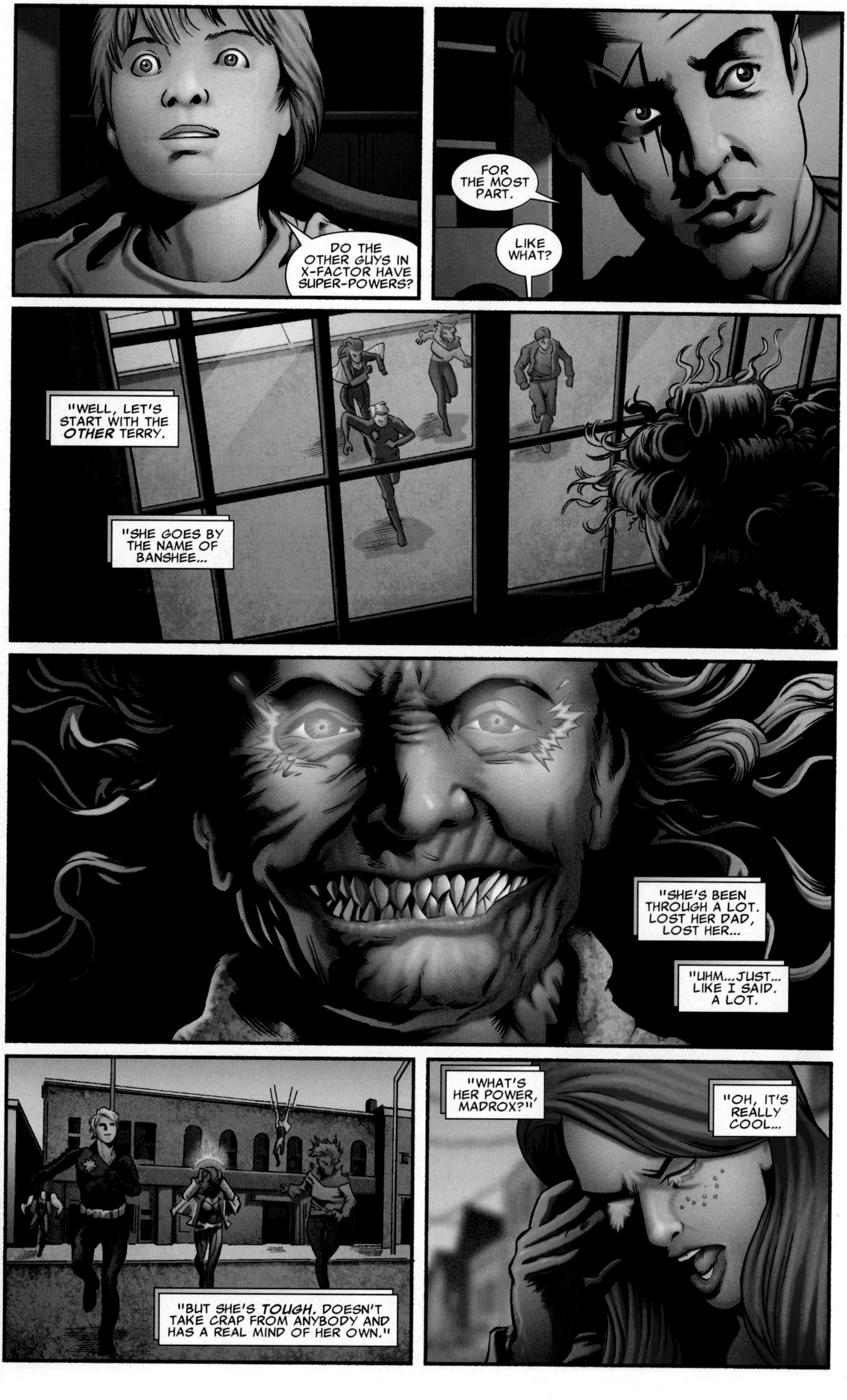
DO THE OTHER GUYS IN X-FACTOR HAVE SUPER-POWERS?
FOR THE MOST PART.
LIKE WHAT?
"WELL, LET'S START WITH THE *OTHER* TERRY.
"SHE GOES BY THE NAME OF BANSHEE...
"SHE'S BEEN THROUGH A LOT. LOST HER DAD, LOST HER...
"UHM...JUST... LIKE I SAID. A LOT.
"BUT SHE'S *TOUGH*. DOESN'T TAKE CRAP FROM ANYBODY AND HAS A REAL MIND OF HER OWN."
"WHAT'S HER POWER, MADROX?"
"OH, IT'S REALLY COOL...

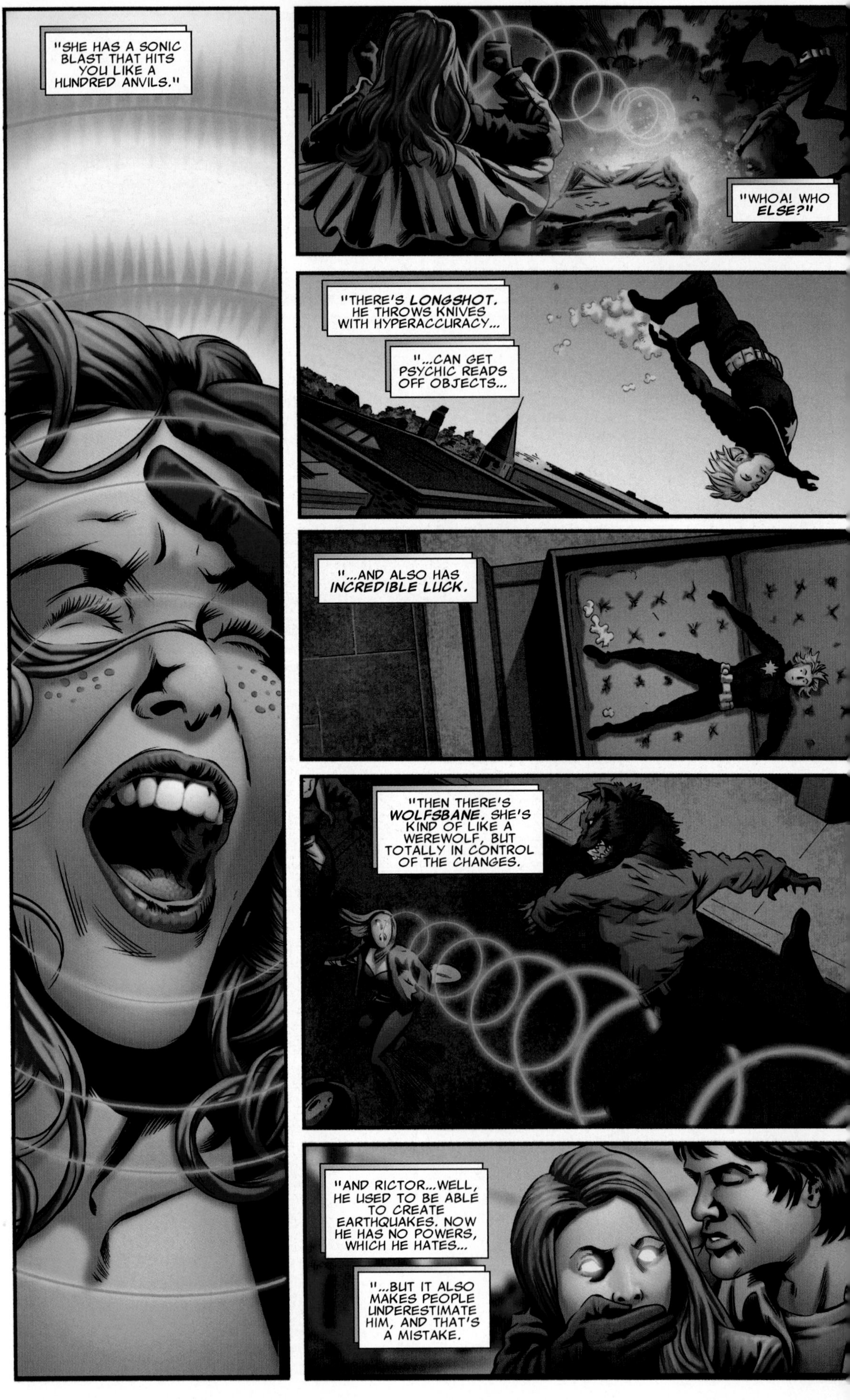
"SHE HAS A SONIC BLAST THAT HITS YOU LIKE A HUNDRED ANVILS."
"WHOA! WHO ELSE?"
"THERE'S LONGSHOT. HE THROWS KNIVES WITH HYPERACCURACY...
"...CAN GET PSYCHIC READS OFF OBJECTS...
"...AND ALSO HAS INCREDIBLE LUCK.
"THEN THERE'S WOLFSBANE. SHE'S KIND OF LIKE A WEREWOLF, BUT TOTALLY IN CONTROL OF THE CHANGES.
"AND RICTOR...WELL, HE USED TO BE ABLE TO CREATE EARTHQUAKES. NOW HE HAS NO POWERS, WHICH HE HATES...
"...BUT IT ALSO MAKES PEOPLE UNDERESTIMATE HIM, AND THAT'S A MISTAKE.

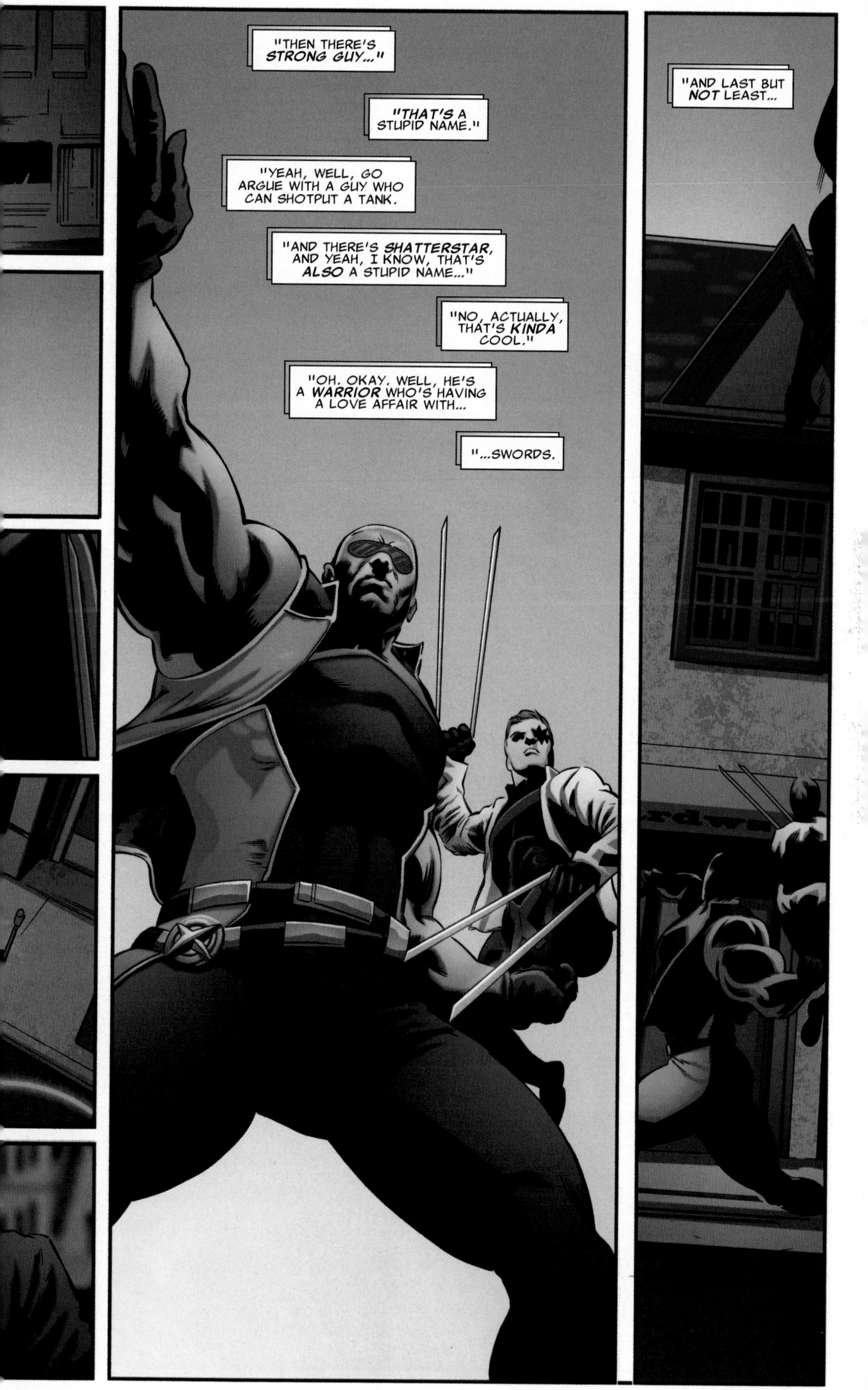
"THEN THERE'S STRONG GUY..."
"THAT'S A STUPID NAME."
"YEAH, WELL, GO ARGUE WITH A GUY WHO CAN SHOTPUT A TANK.
"AND THERE'S SHATTERSTAR, AND YEAH, I KNOW, THAT'S ALSO A STUPID NAME..."
"NO, ACTUALLY, THAT'S KINDA COOL."
"OH. OKAY. WELL, HE'S A WARRIOR WHO'S HAVING A LOVE AFFAIR WITH...
"...SWORDS.
"AND LAST BUT NOT LEAST...

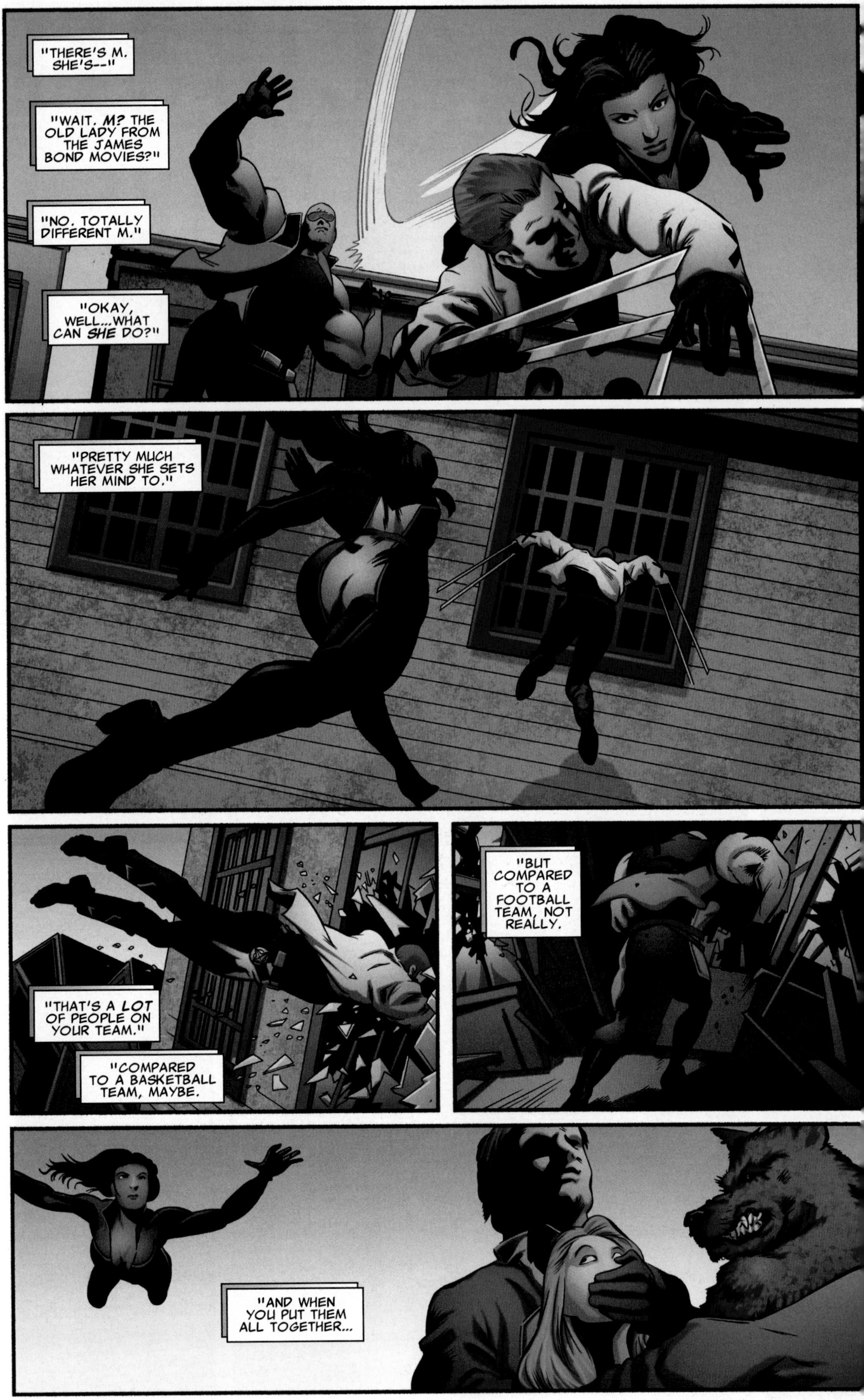
"THERE'S M. SHE'S--"
"WAIT. M? THE OLD LADY FROM THE JAMES BOND MOVIES?"
"NO. TOTALLY DIFFERENT M."
"OKAY, WELL...WHAT CAN SHE DO?"
"PRETTY MUCH WHATEVER SHE SETS HER MIND TO."
"THAT'S A LOT OF PEOPLE ON YOUR TEAM."
"COMPARED TO A BASKETBALL TEAM, MAYBE.
"BUT COMPARED TO A FOOTBALL TEAM, NOT REALLY.
"AND WHEN YOU PUT THEM ALL TOGETHER...

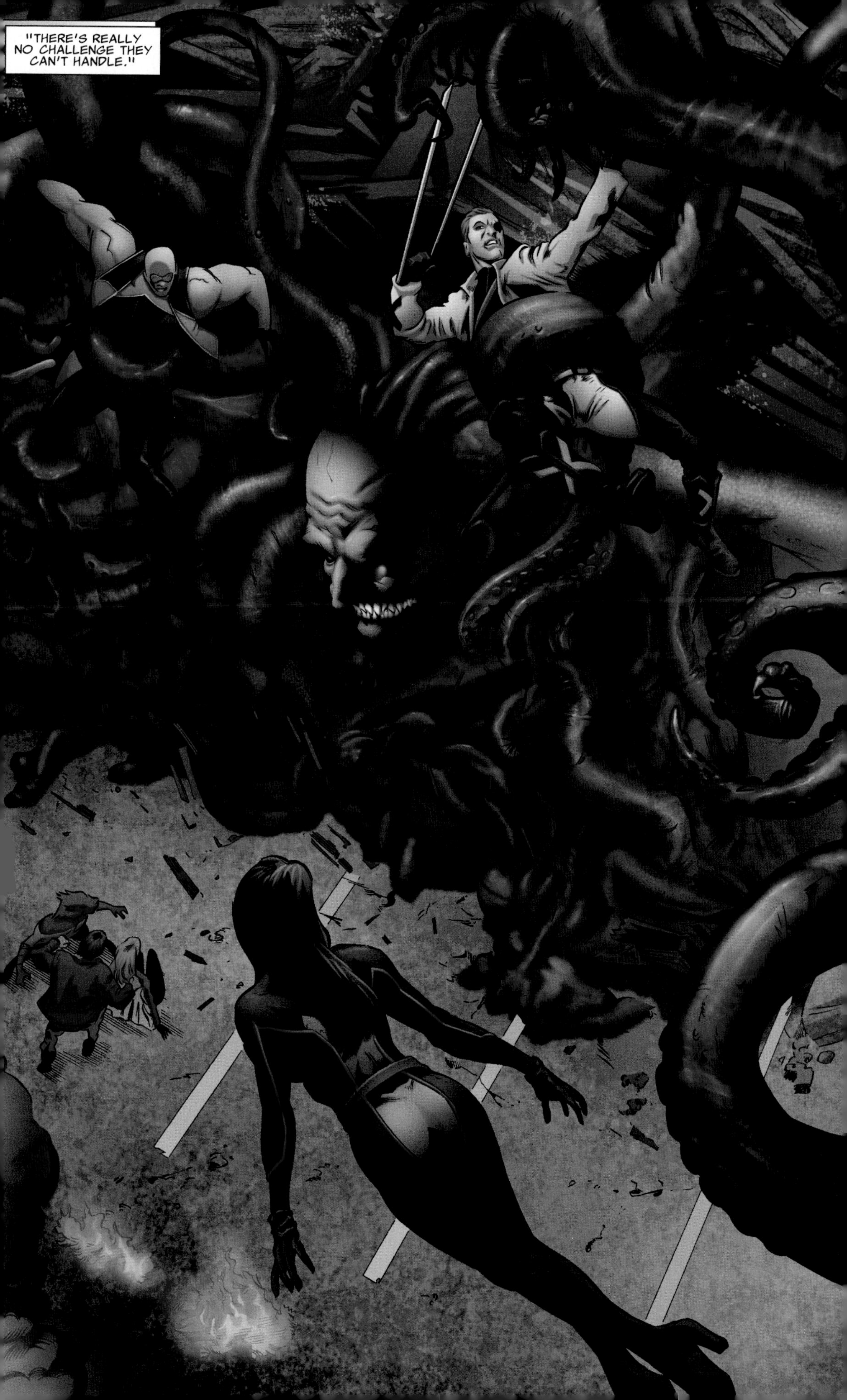
"THERE'S REALLY NO CHALLENGE THEY CAN'T HANDLE."

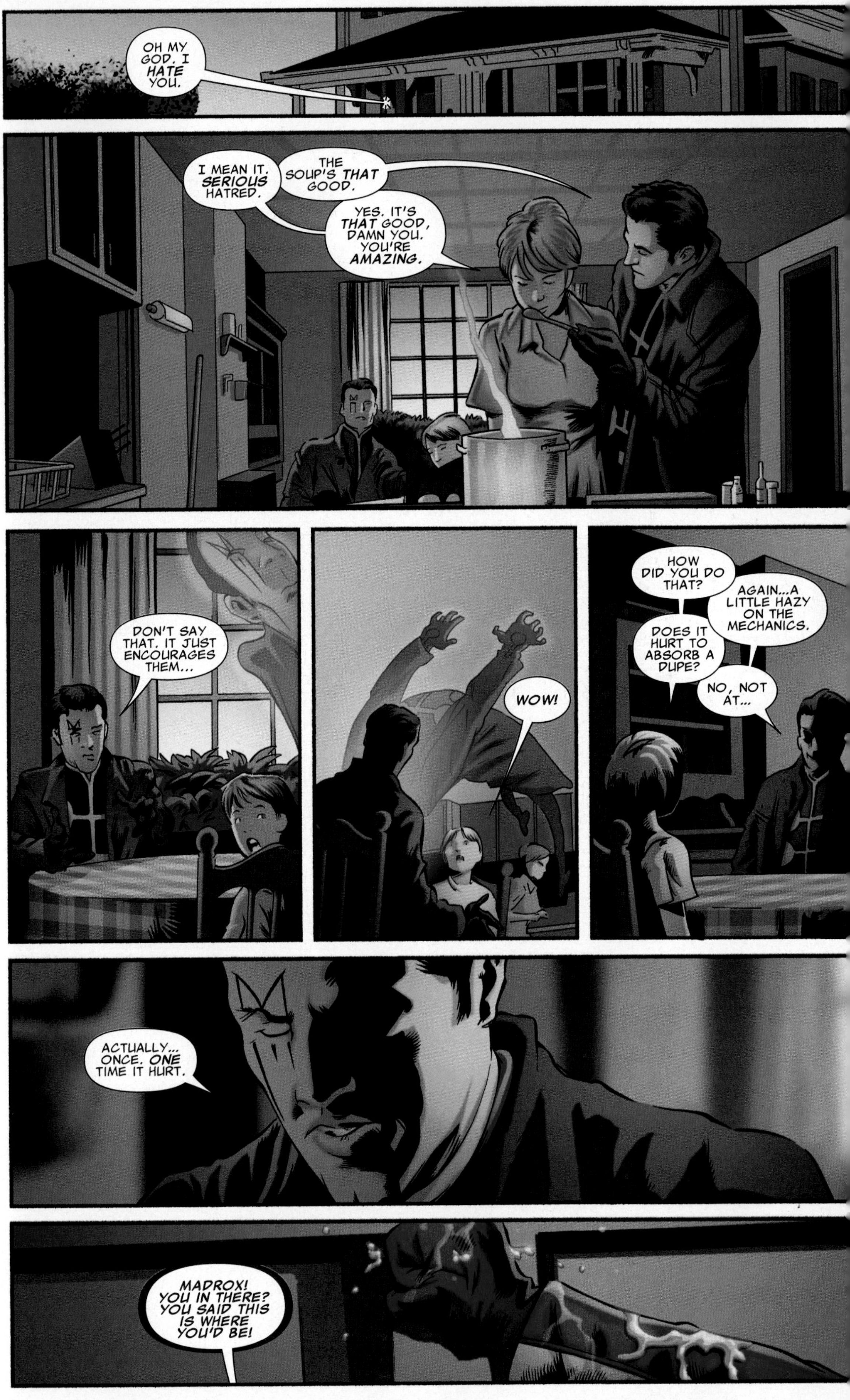
OH MY GOD. I HATE YOU.
I MEAN IT. SERIOUS HATRED.
THE SOUP'S THAT GOOD.
YES. IT'S THAT GOOD, DAMN YOU. YOU'RE AMAZING.
DON'T SAY THAT. IT JUST ENCOURAGES THEM...
WOW!
HOW DID YOU DO THAT?
AGAIN...A LITTLE HAZY ON THE MECHANICS.
DOES IT HURT TO ABSORB A DUPE?
NO, NOT AT...
ACTUALLY... ONCE. ONE TIME IT HURT.
MADROX! YOU IN THERE? YOU SAID THIS IS WHERE YOU'D BE!

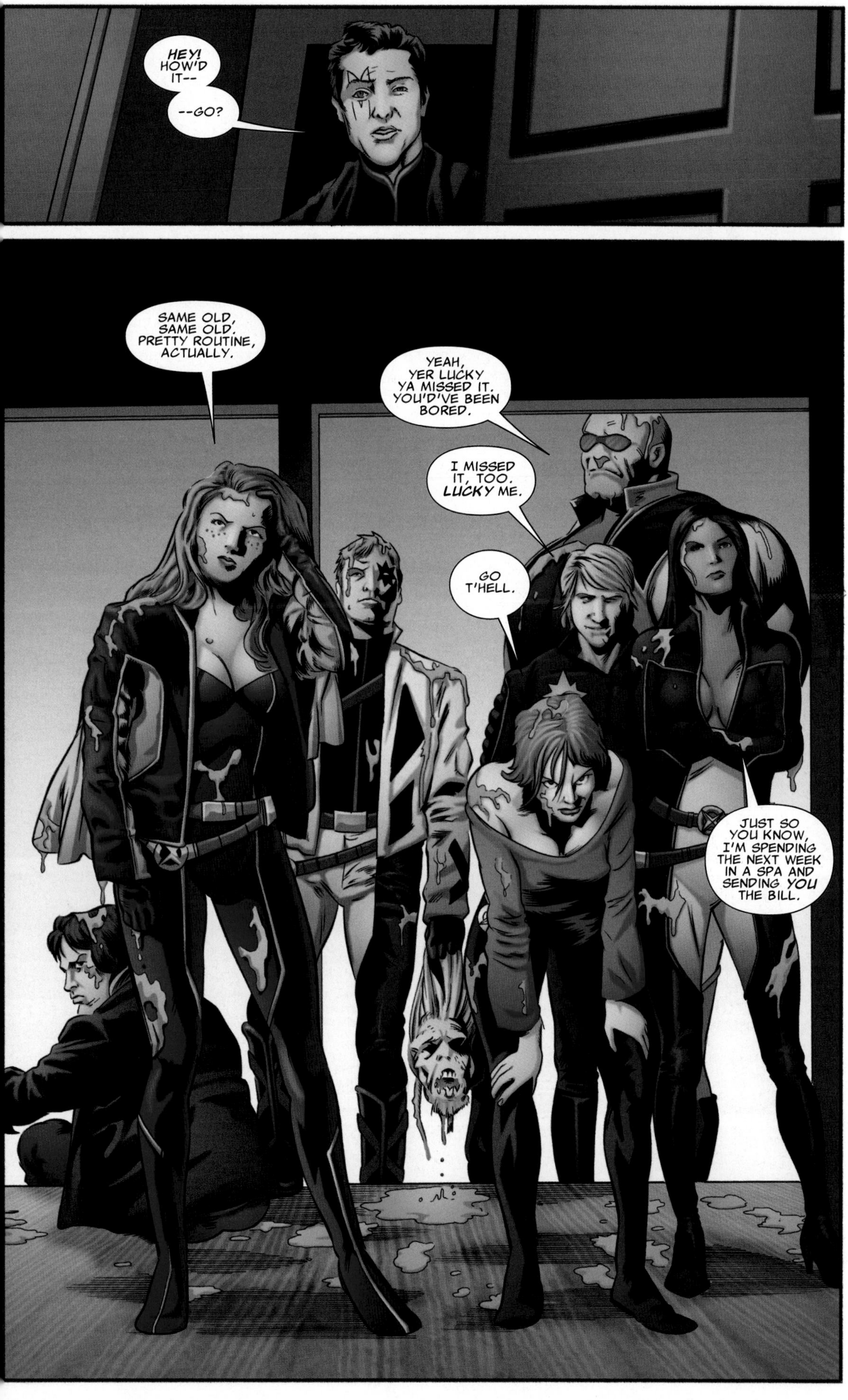
HEY! HOW'D IT--
--GO?
SAME OLD, SAME OLD. PRETTY ROUTINE, ACTUALLY.
YEAH, YER LUCKY YA MISSED IT. YOU'D'VE BEEN BORED.
I MISSED IT, TOO. LUCKY ME.
GO T'HELL.
JUST SO YOU KNOW, I'M SPENDING THE NEXT WEEK IN A SPA AND SENDING YOU THE BILL.

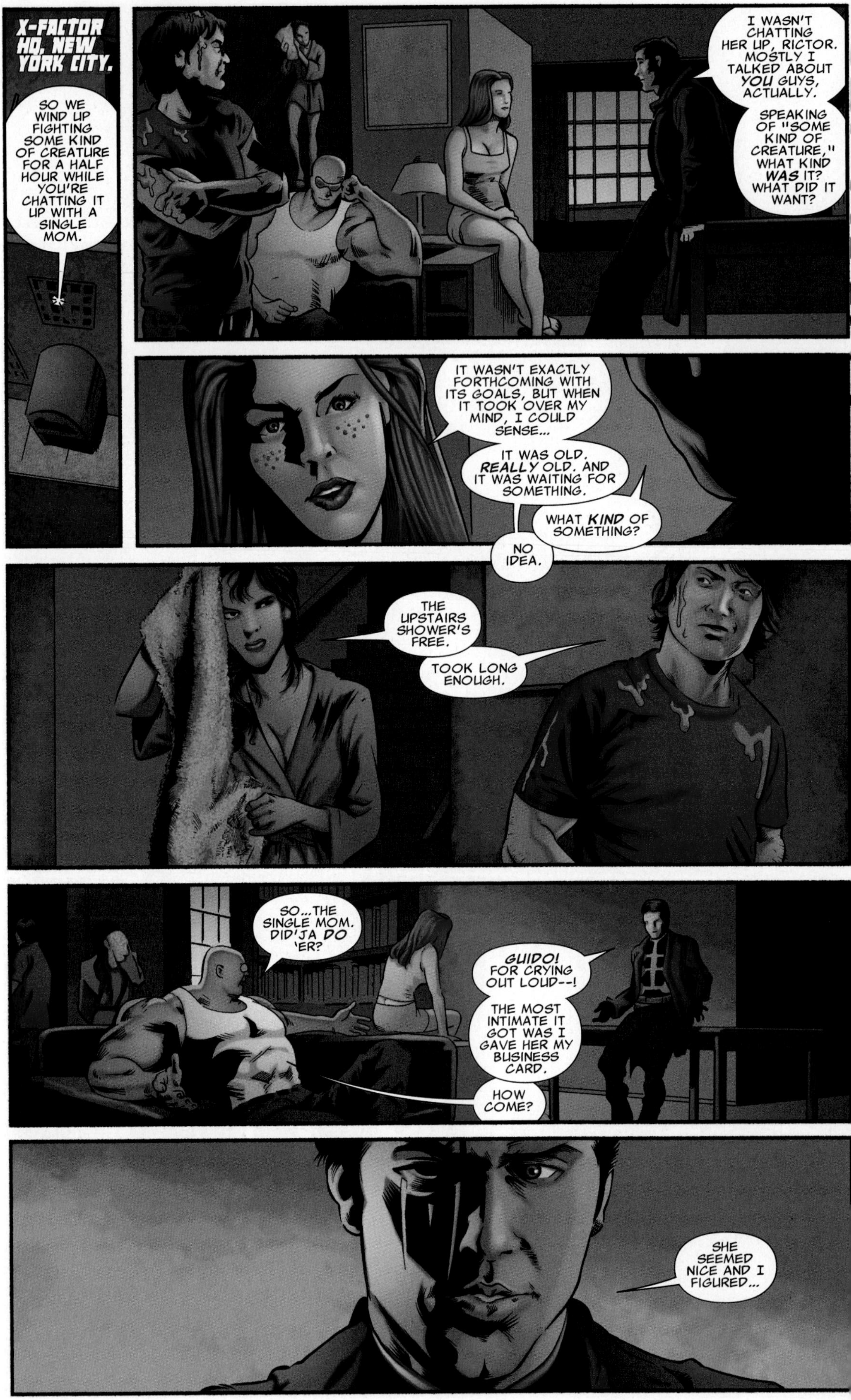

X-FACTOR HQ, NEW YORK CITY.
SO WE WIND UP FIGHTING SOME KIND OF CREATURE FOR A HALF HOUR WHILE YOU'RE CHATTING IT UP WITH A SINGLE MOM.
I WASN'T CHATTING HER UP, RICTOR. MOSTLY I TALKED ABOUT YOU GUYS, ACTUALLY.
SPEAKING OF "SOME KIND OF CREATURE," WHAT KIND WAS IT? WHAT DID IT WANT?
IT WASN'T EXACTLY FORTHCOMING WITH ITS GOALS, BUT WHEN IT TOOK OVER MY MIND, I COULD SENSE...
IT WAS OLD. REALLY OLD. AND IT WAS WAITING FOR SOMETHING.
WHAT KIND OF SOMETHING?
NO IDEA.
THE UPSTAIRS SHOWER'S FREE.
TOOK LONG ENOUGH.
SO...THE SINGLE MOM. DID'JA DO 'ER?
GUIDO! FOR CRYING OUT LOUD--!
THE MOST INTIMATE IT GOT WAS I GAVE HER MY BUSINESS CARD.
HOW COME?
SHE SEEMED NICE AND I FIGURED...

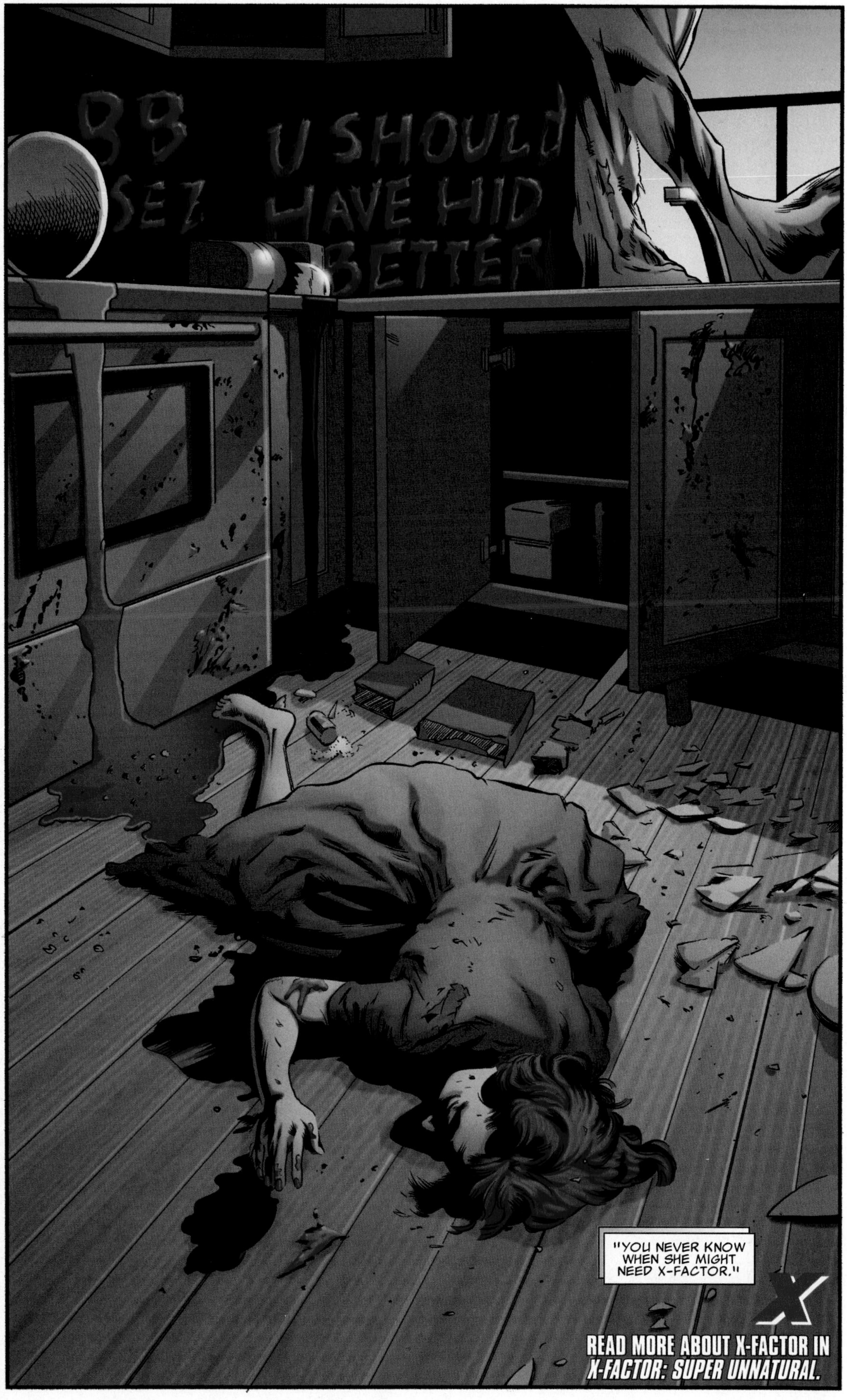
BB SEZ
U SHOULD HAVE HID BETTER
"YOU NEVER KNOW WHEN SHE MIGHT NEED X-FACTOR."
READ MORE ABOUT X-FACTOR IN *X-FACTOR: SUPER UNNATURAL.*

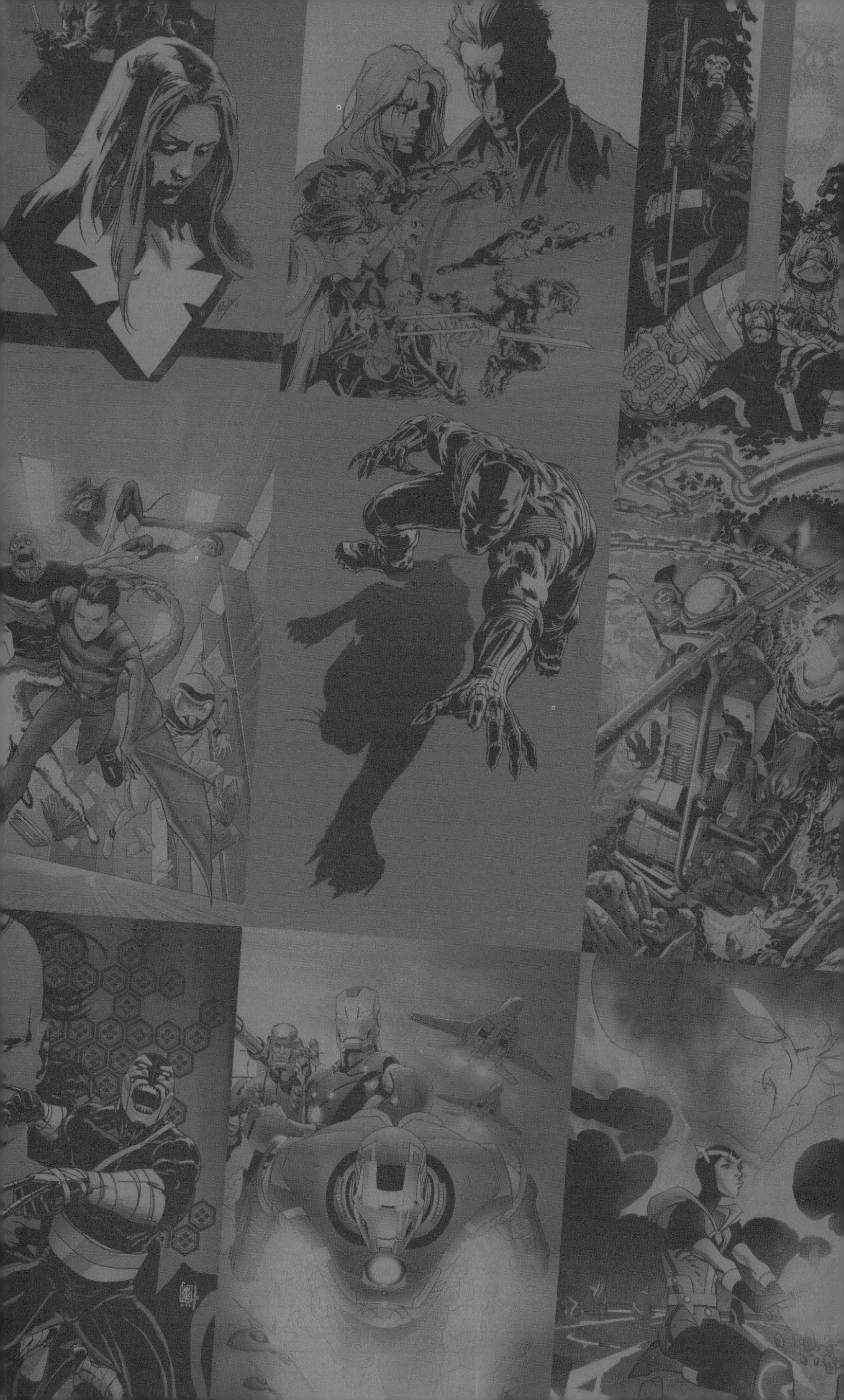

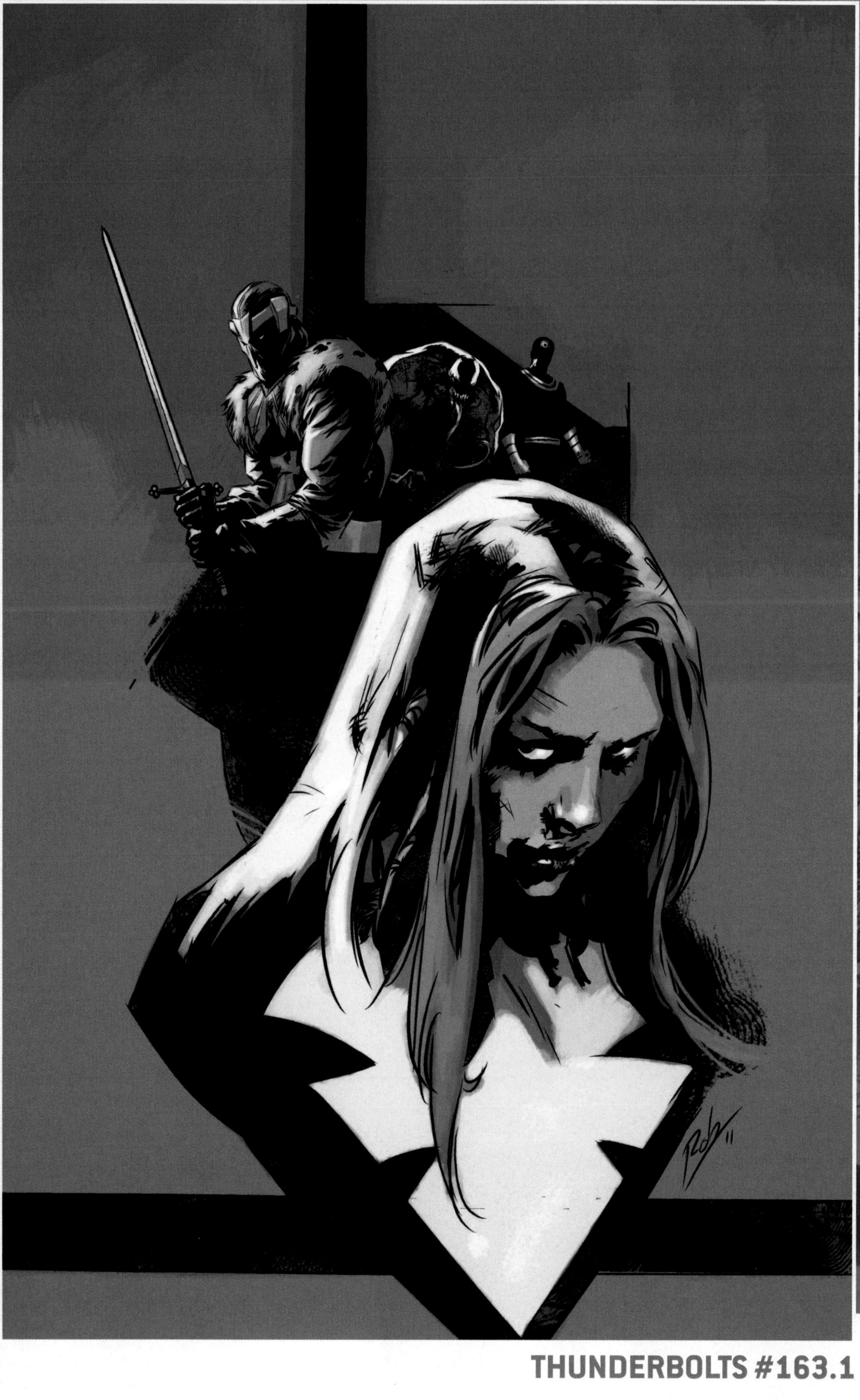

THUNDERBOLTS #163.1

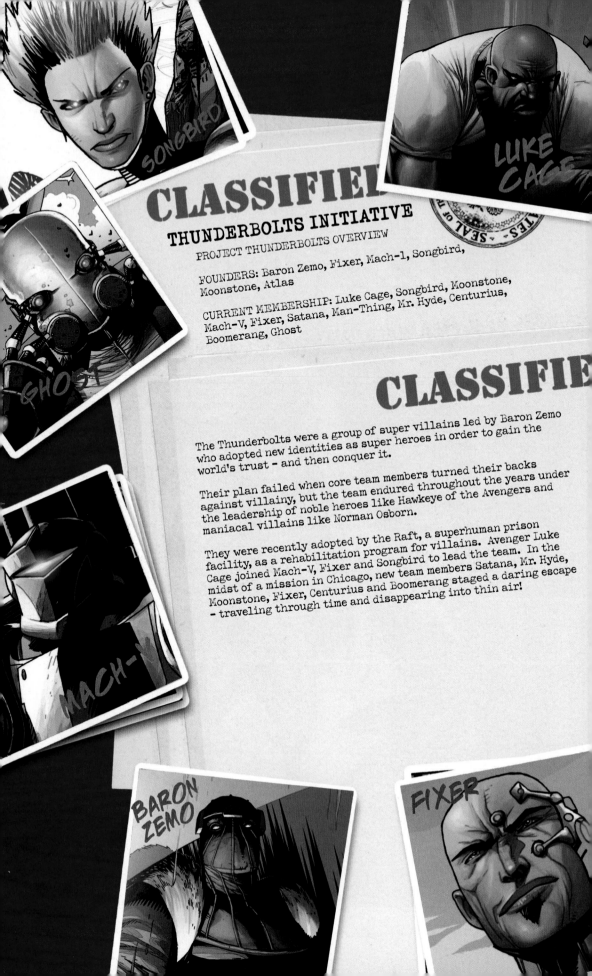

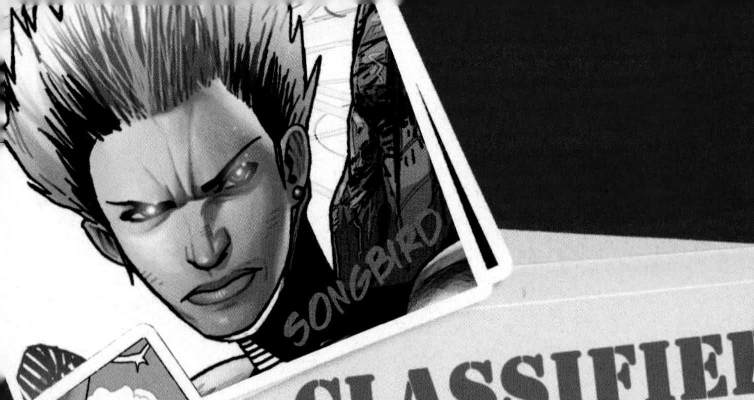
SONGBIRD

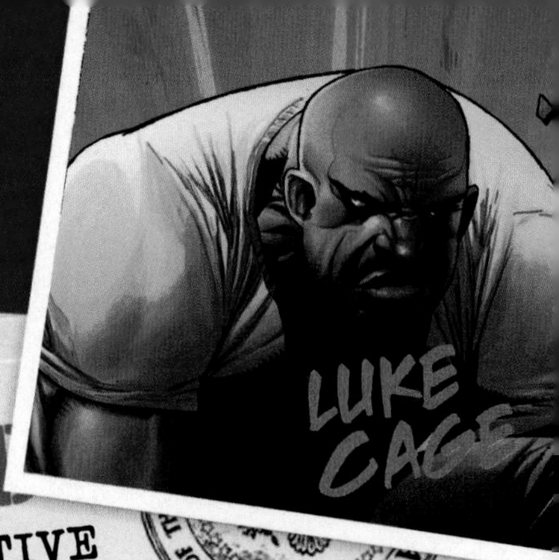
LUKE CAGE

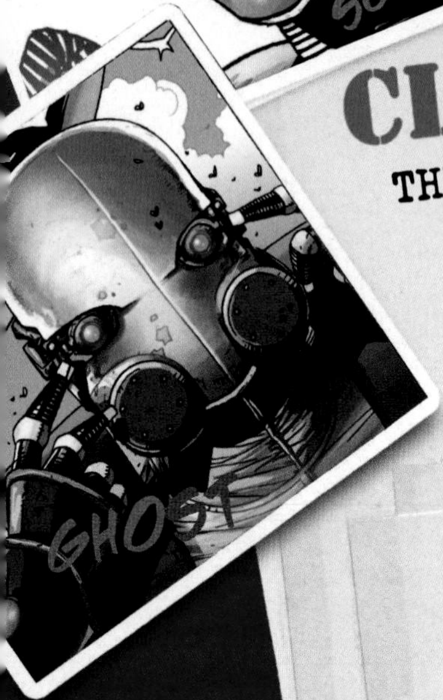
GHOST

CLASSIFIED

THUNDERBOLTS INITIATIVE

PROJECT THUNDERBOLTS OVERVIEW

FOUNDERS: Baron Zemo, Fixer, Mach-1, Songbird, Moonstone, Atlas

CURRENT MEMBERSHIP: Luke Cage, Songbird, Moonstone, Mach-V, Fixer, Satana, Man-Thing, Mr. Hyde, Centurius, Boomerang, Ghost

CLASSIFIE

The Thunderbolts were a group of super villains led by Baron Zemo who adopted new identities as super heroes in order to gain the world's trust - and then conquer it.

Their plan failed when core team members turned their backs against villainy, but the team endured throughout the years under the leadership of noble heroes like Hawkeye of the Avengers and maniacal villains like Norman Osborn.

They were recently adopted by the Raft, a superhuman prison facility, as a rehabilitation program for villains. Avenger Luke Cage joined Mach-V, Fixer and Songbird to lead the team. In the midst of a mission in Chicago, new team members Satana, Mr. Hyde, Moonstone, Fixer, Centurius and Boomerang staged a daring escape - traveling through time and disappearing into thin air!

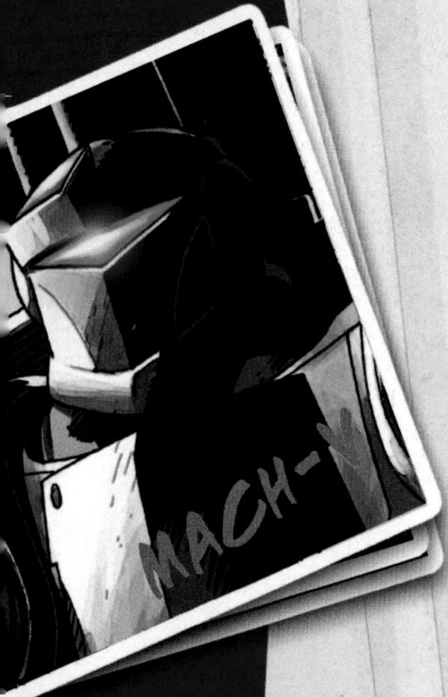
MACH-V

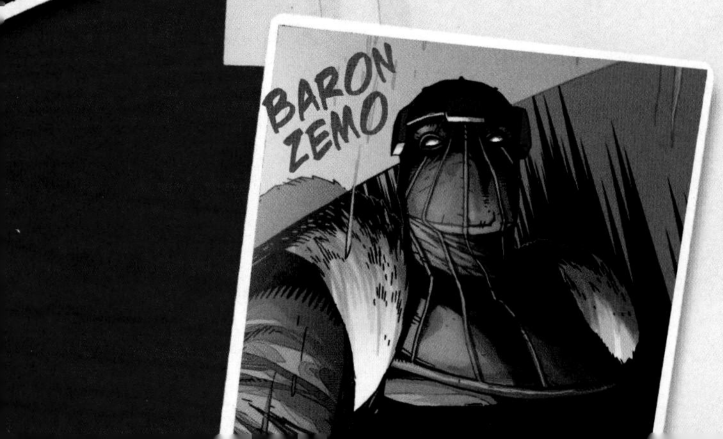
BARON ZEMO

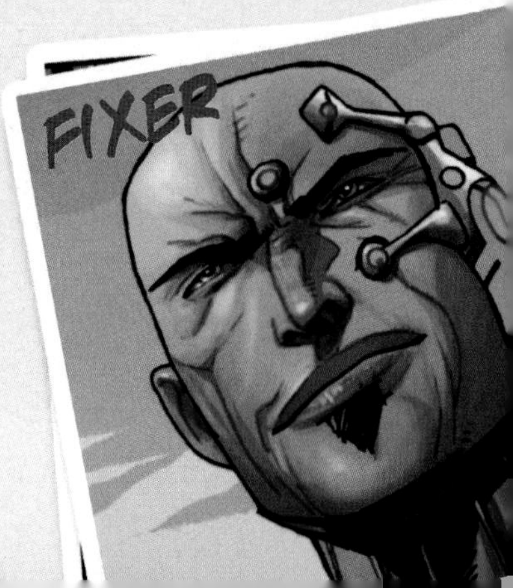
FIXER

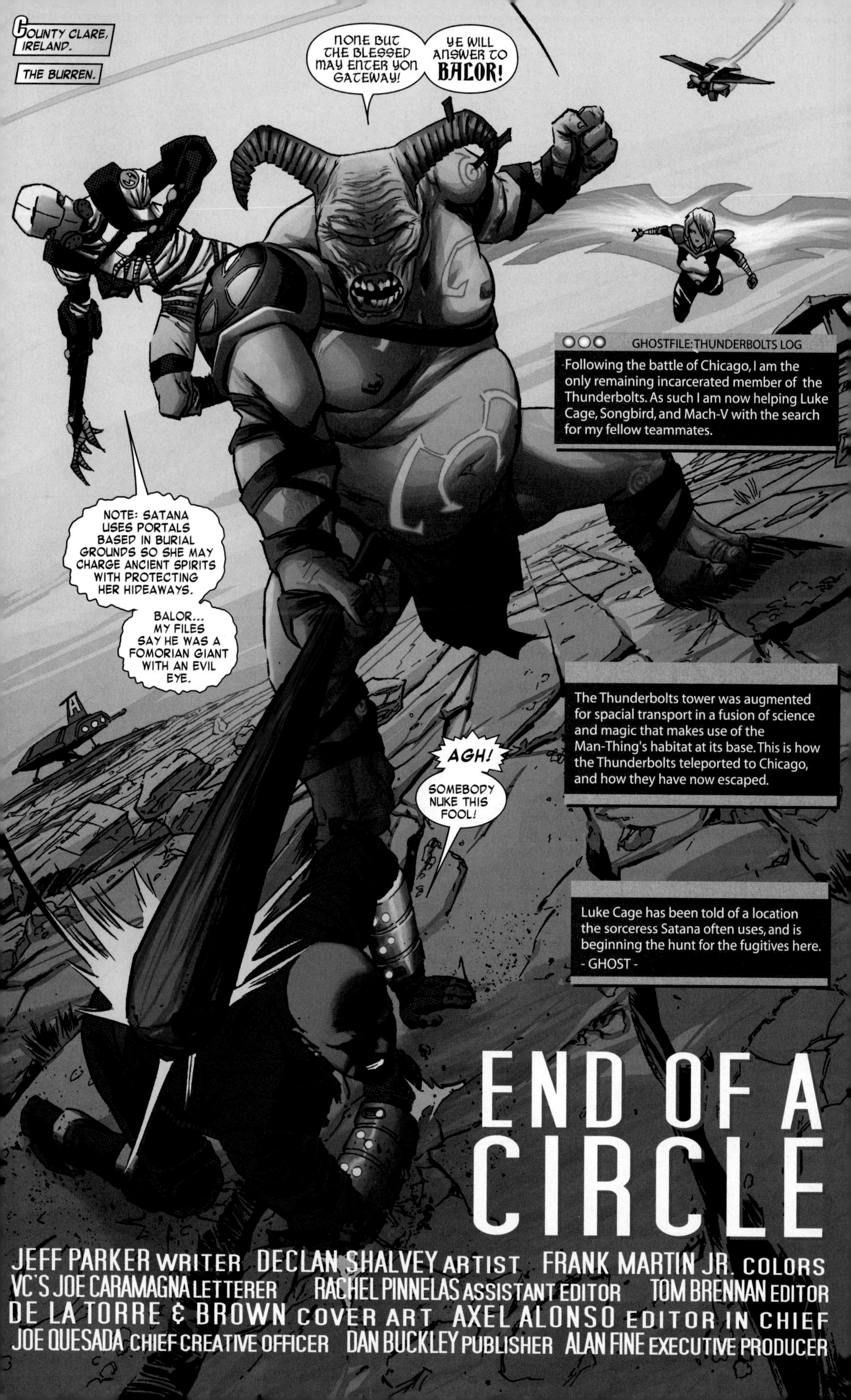
COUNTY CLARE, IRELAND.
THE BURREN.
NONE BUT THE BLESSED MAY ENTER YON GATEWAY!
YE WILL ANSWER TO BALOR!
GHOSTFILE: THUNDERBOLTS LOG
-Following the battle of Chicago, I am the only remaining incarcerated member of the Thunderbolts. As such I am now helping Luke Cage, Songbird, and Mach-V with the search for my fellow teammates.
NOTE: SATANA USES PORTALS BASED IN BURIAL GROUNDS SO SHE MAY CHARGE ANCIENT SPIRITS WITH PROTECTING HER HIDEAWAYS.
BALOR... MY FILES SAY HE WAS A FOMORIAN GIANT WITH AN EVIL EYE.
The Thunderbolts tower was augmented for spacial transport in a fusion of science and magic that makes use of the Man-Thing's habitat at its base. This is how the Thunderbolts teleported to Chicago, and how they have now escaped.
AGH!
SOMEBODY NUKE THIS FOOL!
Luke Cage has been told of a location the sorceress Satana often uses, and is beginning the hunt for the fugitives here.
- GHOST -
END OF A CIRCLE
JEFF PARKER WRITER DECLAN SHALVEY ARTIST FRANK MARTIN JR. COLORS
VC'S JOE CARAMAGNA LETTERER RACHEL PINNELAS ASSISTANT EDITOR TOM BRENNAN EDITOR
DE LA TORRE & BROWN COVER ART AXEL ALONSO EDITOR IN CHIEF
JOE QUESADA CHIEF CREATIVE OFFICER DAN BUCKLEY PUBLISHER ALAN FINE EXECUTIVE PRODUCER

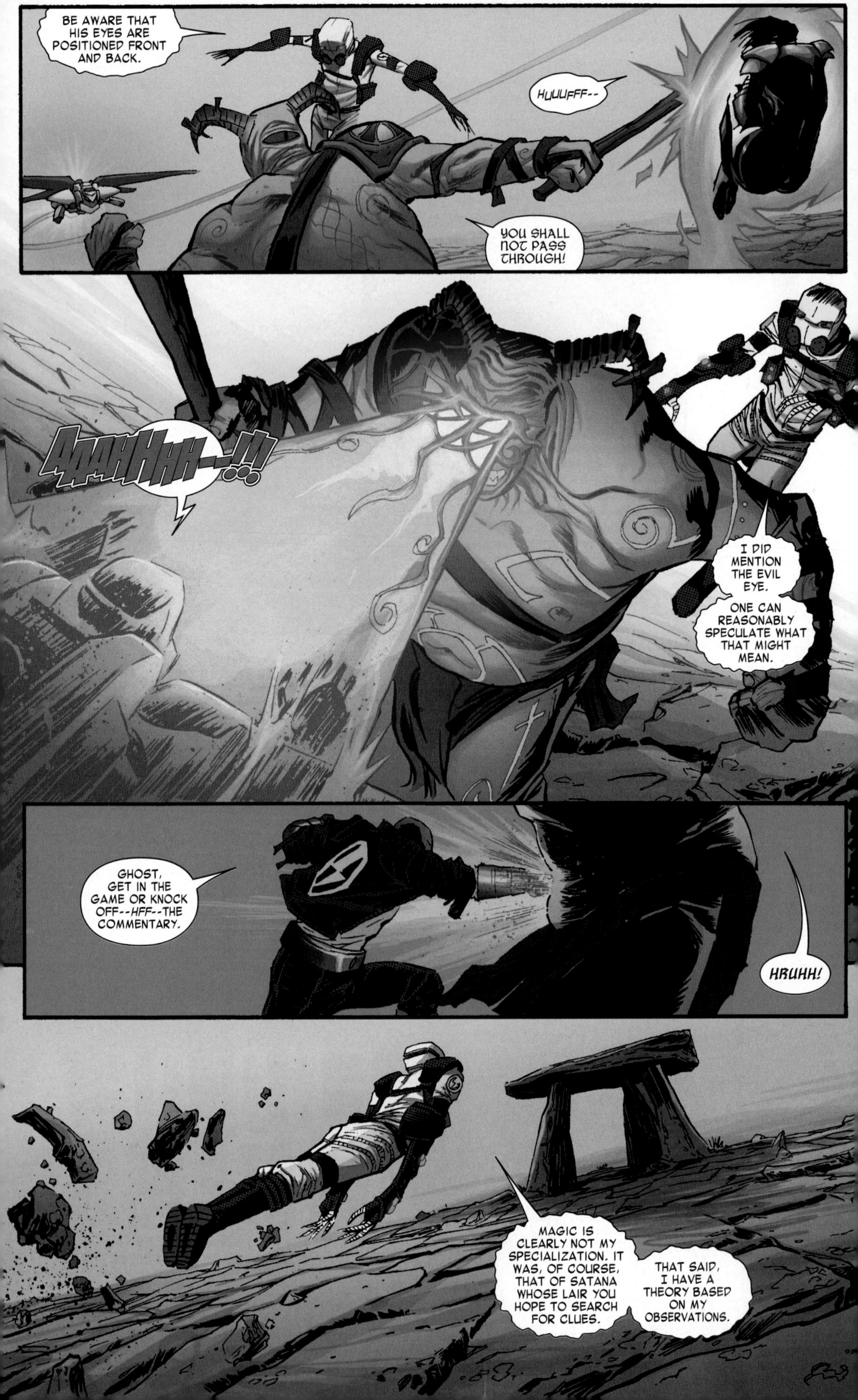
BE AWARE THAT HIS EYES ARE POSITIONED FRONT AND BACK.
HUUUFFF--
YOU SHALL NOT PASS THROUGH!
AAAHHHH--!!!
I DID MENTION THE EVIL EYE.
ONE CAN REASONABLY SPECULATE WHAT THAT MIGHT MEAN.
GHOST, GET IN THE GAME OR KNOCK OFF--HFF--THE COMMENTARY.
HRUHH!
MAGIC IS CLEARLY NOT MY SPECIALIZATION. IT WAS, OF COURSE, THAT OF SATANA WHOSE LAIR YOU HOPE TO SEARCH FOR CLUES.
THAT SAID, I HAVE A THEORY BASED ON MY OBSERVATIONS.

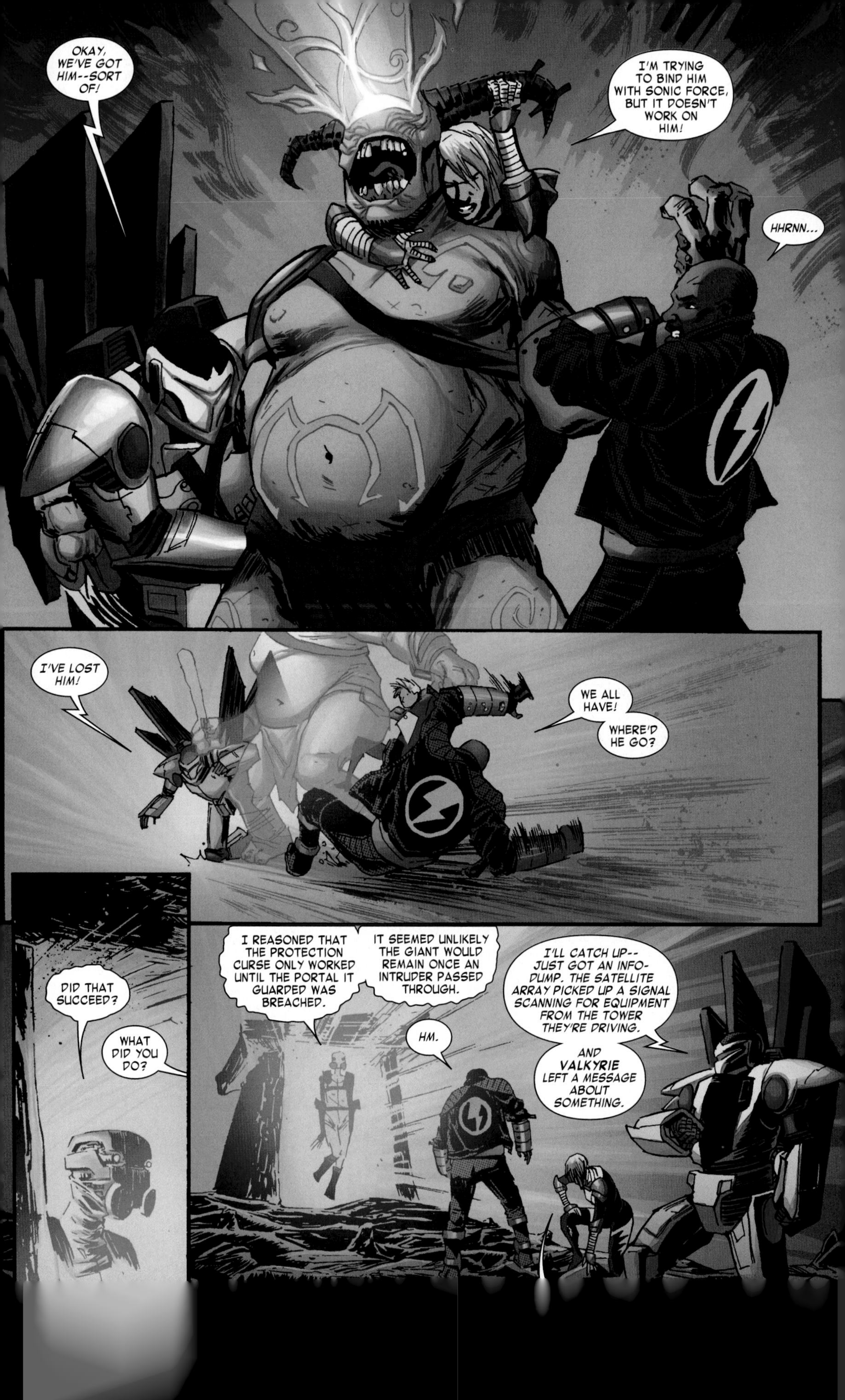
OKAY, WE'VE GOT HIM--SORT OF!
I'M TRYING TO BIND HIM WITH SONIC FORCE, BUT IT DOESN'T WORK ON HIM!
HHRNN...
I'VE LOST HIM!
WE ALL HAVE!
WHERE'D HE GO?
DID THAT SUCCEED?
WHAT DID YOU DO?
I REASONED THAT THE PROTECTION CURSE ONLY WORKED UNTIL THE PORTAL IT GUARDED WAS BREACHED.
IT SEEMED UNLIKELY THE GIANT WOULD REMAIN ONCE AN INTRUDER PASSED THROUGH.
HM.
I'LL CATCH UP-- JUST GOT AN INFO-DUMP. THE SATELLITE ARRAY PICKED UP A SIGNAL SCANNING FOR EQUIPMENT FROM THE TOWER THEY'RE DRIVING.
AND VALKYRIE LEFT A MESSAGE ABOUT SOMETHING.

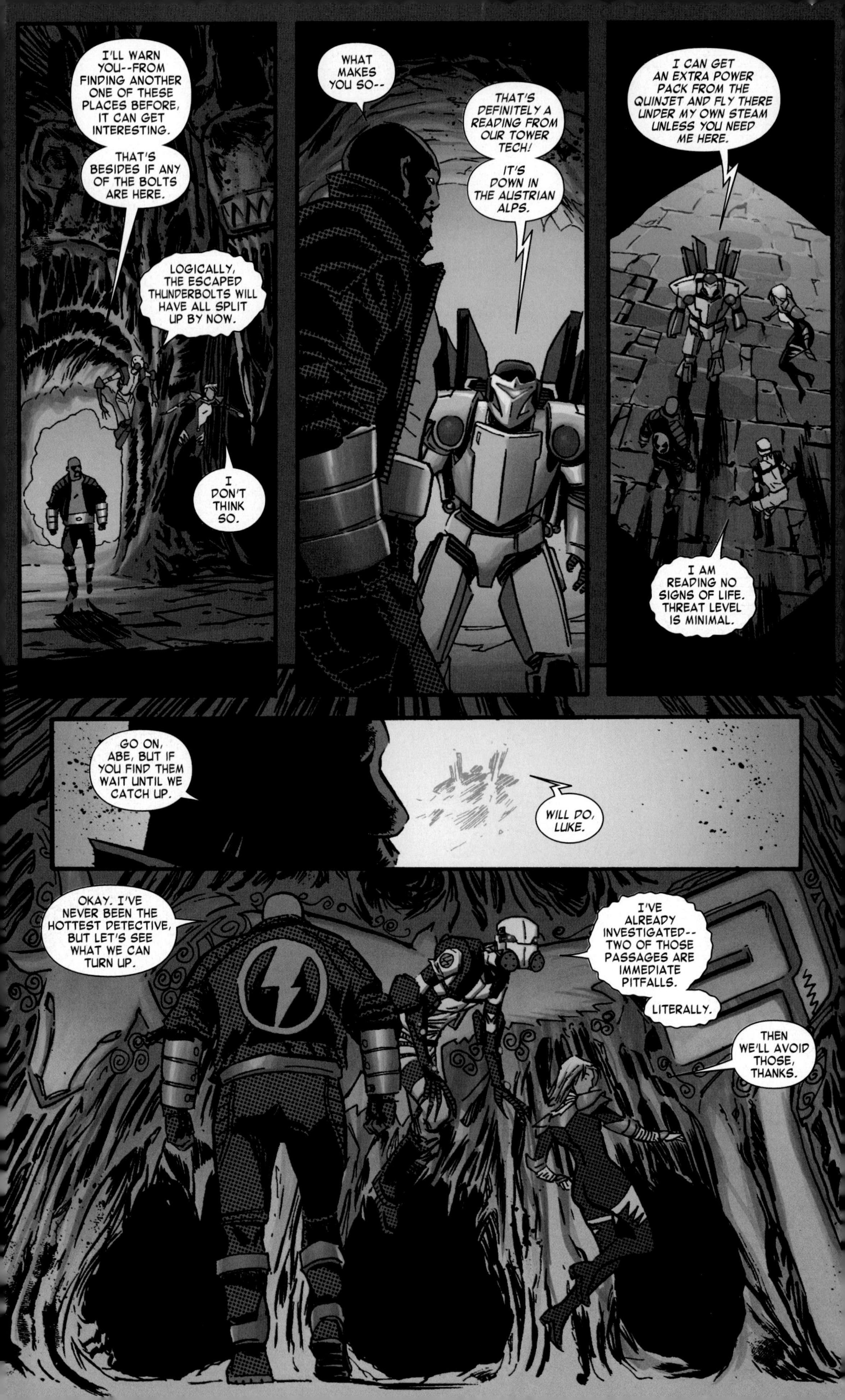
I'LL WARN YOU--FROM FINDING ANOTHER ONE OF THESE PLACES BEFORE, IT CAN GET INTERESTING.
THAT'S BESIDES IF ANY OF THE BOLTS ARE HERE.
LOGICALLY, THE ESCAPED THUNDERBOLTS WILL HAVE ALL SPLIT UP BY NOW.
I DON'T THINK SO.
WHAT MAKES YOU SO--
THAT'S DEFINITELY A READING FROM OUR TOWER TECH!
IT'S DOWN IN THE AUSTRIAN ALPS.
I CAN GET AN EXTRA POWER PACK FROM THE QUINJET AND FLY THERE UNDER MY OWN STEAM UNLESS YOU NEED ME HERE.
I AM READING NO SIGNS OF LIFE. THREAT LEVEL IS MINIMAL.
GO ON, ABE, BUT IF YOU FIND THEM WAIT UNTIL WE CATCH UP.
WILL DO, LUKE.
OKAY. I'VE NEVER BEEN THE HOTTEST DETECTIVE, BUT LET'S SEE WHAT WE CAN TURN UP.
I'VE ALREADY INVESTIGATED--TWO OF THOSE PASSAGES ARE IMMEDIATE PITFALLS.
LITERALLY.
THEN WE'LL AVOID THOSE, THANKS.

SO, LUKE, IF WE HAD FOUND ALL OF THEM, WHAT WAS YOUR PLAN OF ENGAGEMENT?
I WAS GOING TO START HITTIN' 'EM ALL IN THE HEAD UNTIL THEY CRIED.
WE'D BE WAY OUTNUMBERED, AND THEIR NANITE FAILSAFES ARE DISABLED.
I WAS PLANNING ON HITTING PRETTY HARD.
YOU HAVE THE MYSTIC AMULET FOR SATANA, DO YOU NOT?
RIGHT. I CLICK THIS THREE TIMES AND SHE SNAPS OUT OF DAUGHTER OF THE DARK MODE, AND WE GET ANOTHER ON OUR SIDE.
IF WE START TO LOOK LIKE WE MIGHT WIN, THEN MOONSTONE SWITCHES OVER TOO.
HEH, THAT'S FOR SURE.
CENTURIUS IS A SCIENCE GENIUS, BUT GHOST CAN PROBABLY TAKE HIM OUT...
QUITE PROBABLY.
TROLL IS SAVAGE, BUT LOYAL--SHE WAS PULLED ALONG BY ACCIDENT.
MR. HYDE IS THE STRONGEST. BOOMERANG IS FORMIDABLE.
THEN WE ALL GANG UP ON HYDE.
BOOMERANG... WHO'S WORRIED ABOUT HIM?
AY!
SONGBIRD, GIVE ME SOME LIGHT OVER HERE!

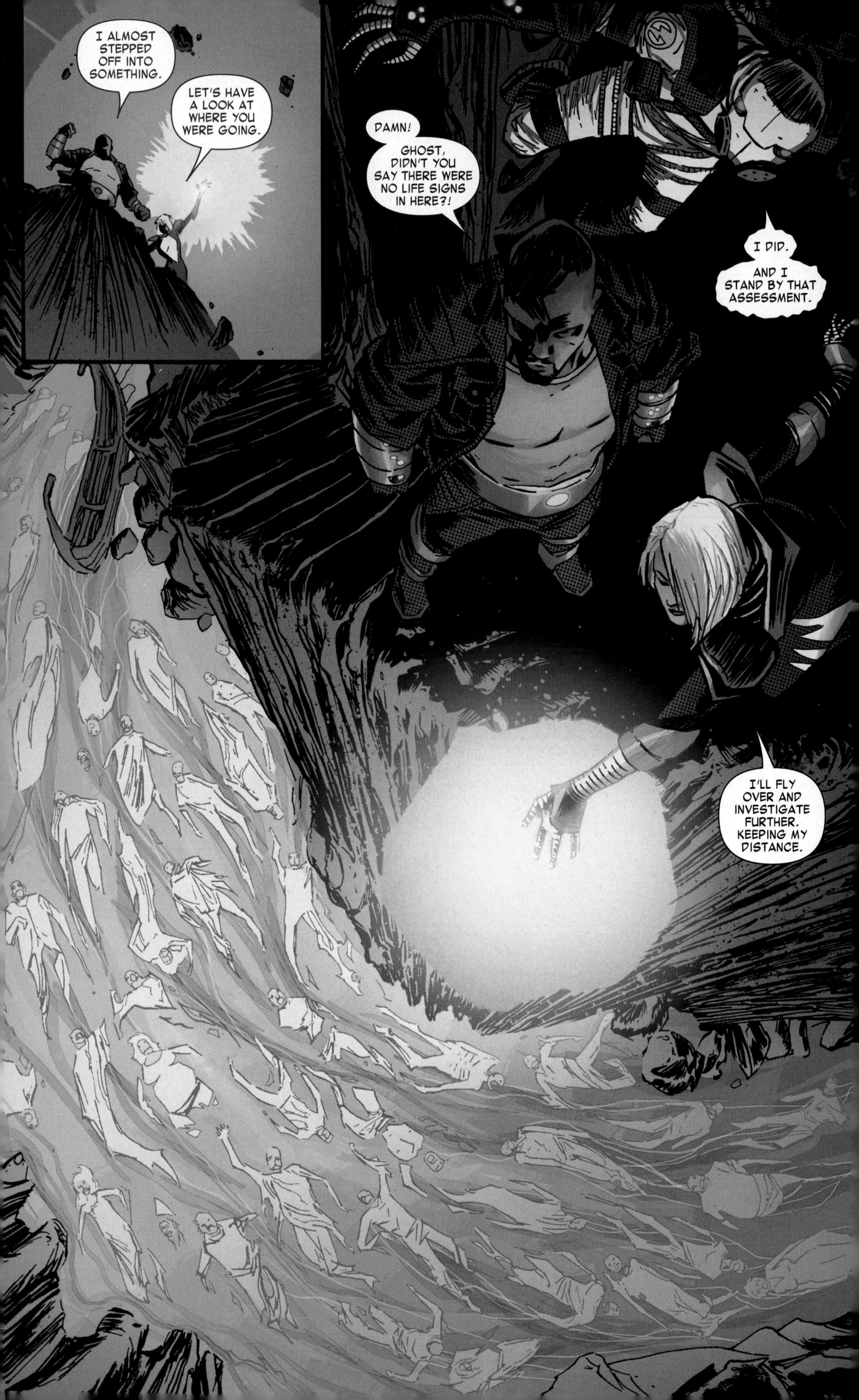
I ALMOST STEPPED OFF INTO SOMETHING.
LET'S HAVE A LOOK AT WHERE YOU WERE GOING.
DAMN!
GHOST, DIDN'T YOU SAY THERE WERE NO LIFE SIGNS IN HERE?!
I DID.
AND I STAND BY THAT ASSESSMENT.
I'LL FLY OVER AND INVESTIGATE FURTHER. KEEPING MY DISTANCE.

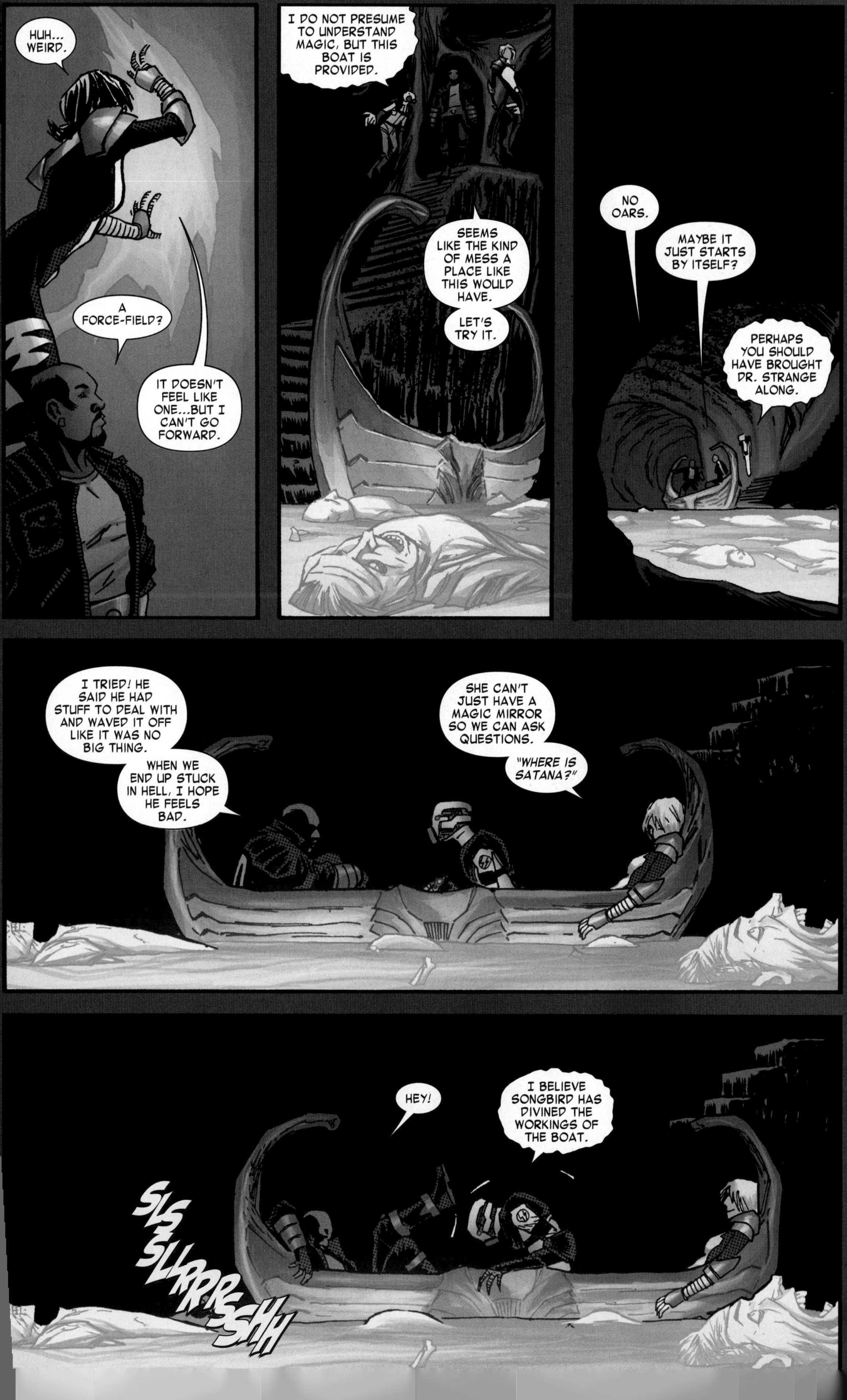
HUH... WEIRD.
A FORCE-FIELD?
IT DOESN'T FEEL LIKE ONE...BUT I CAN'T GO FORWARD.
I DO NOT PRESUME TO UNDERSTAND MAGIC, BUT THIS BOAT IS PROVIDED.
SEEMS LIKE THE KIND OF MESS A PLACE LIKE THIS WOULD HAVE.
LET'S TRY IT.
NO OARS.
MAYBE IT JUST STARTS BY ITSELF?
PERHAPS YOU SHOULD HAVE BROUGHT DR. STRANGE ALONG.
I TRIED! HE SAID HE HAD STUFF TO DEAL WITH AND WAVED IT OFF LIKE IT WAS NO BIG THING.
WHEN WE END UP STUCK IN HELL, I HOPE HE FEELS BAD.
SHE CAN'T JUST HAVE A MAGIC MIRROR SO WE CAN ASK QUESTIONS.
"WHERE IS SATANA?"
HEY!
I BELIEVE SONGBIRD HAS DIVINED THE WORKINGS OF THE BOAT.
SLSSLRRRSSHH

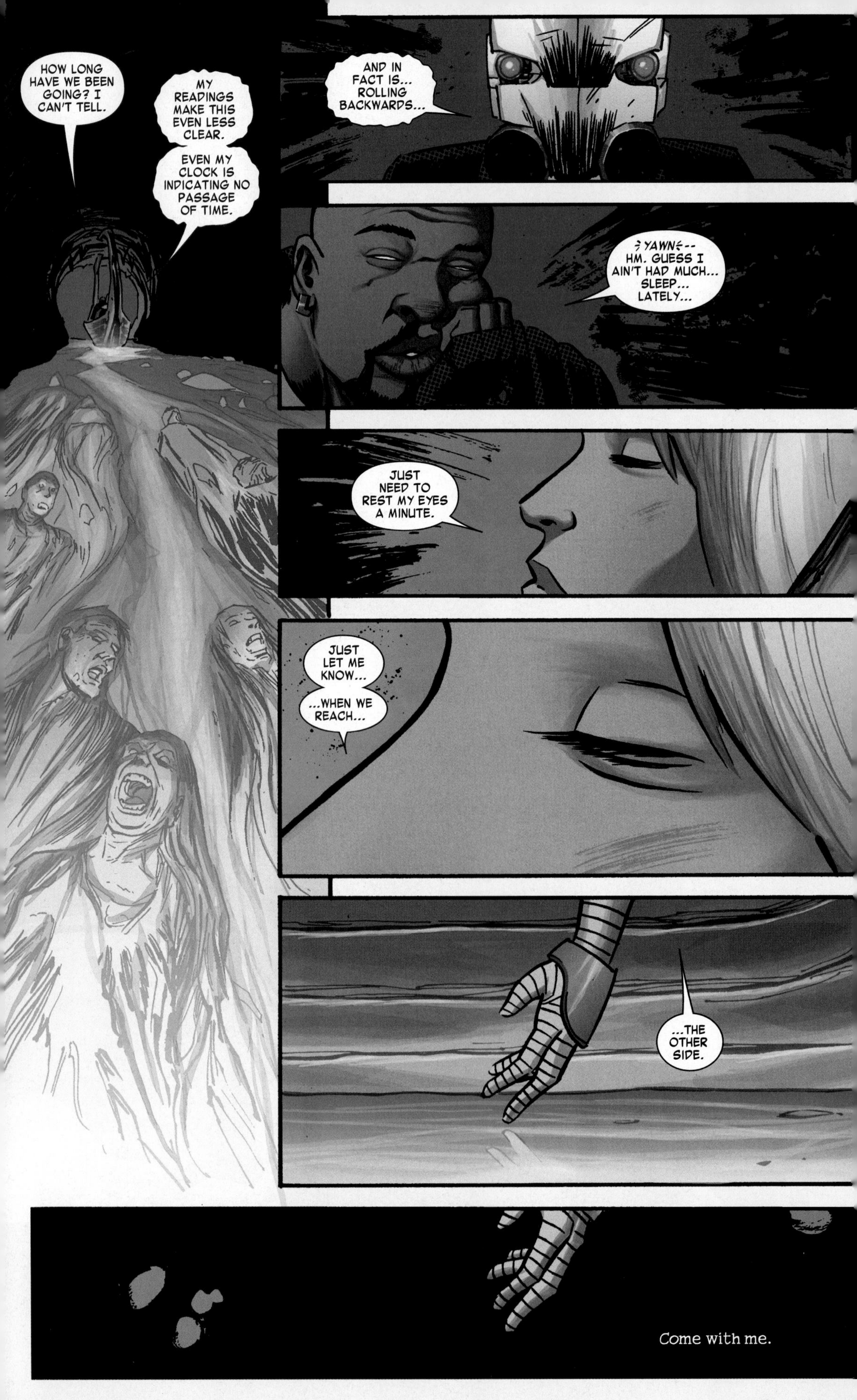
HOW LONG HAVE WE BEEN GOING? I CAN'T TELL.
MY READINGS MAKE THIS EVEN LESS CLEAR.
EVEN MY CLOCK IS INDICATING NO PASSAGE OF TIME.
AND IN FACT IS... ROLLING BACKWARDS...
⸗YAWN⸗-- HM. GUESS I AIN'T HAD MUCH... SLEEP... LATELY...
JUST NEED TO REST MY EYES A MINUTE.
JUST LET ME KNOW...
...WHEN WE REACH...
...THE OTHER SIDE.
Come with me.

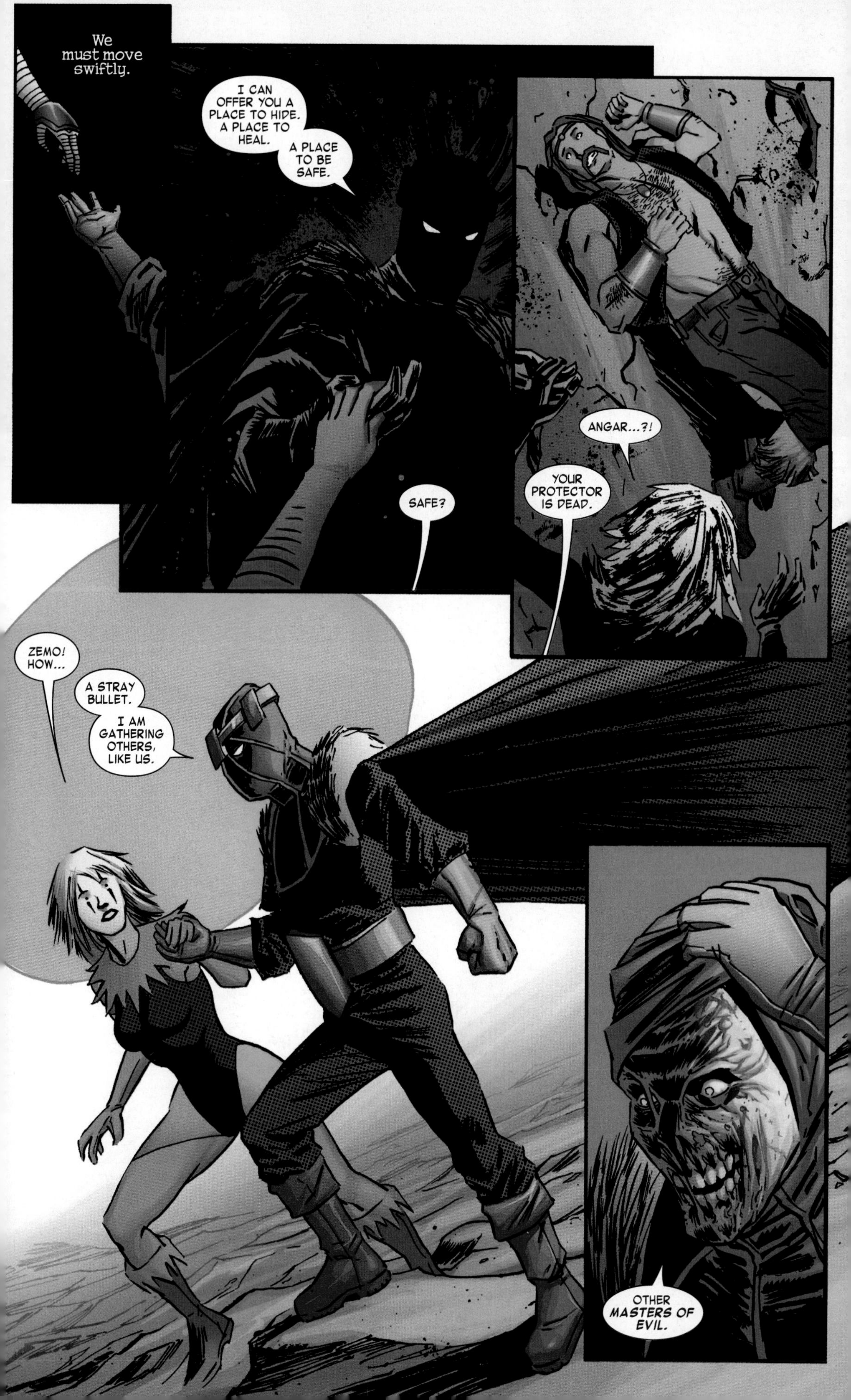

We must move swiftly.
I CAN OFFER YOU A PLACE TO HIDE. A PLACE TO HEAL.
A PLACE TO BE SAFE.
SAFE?
ANGAR...?!
YOUR PROTECTOR IS DEAD.
ZEMO! HOW...
A STRAY BULLET.
I AM GATHERING OTHERS, LIKE US.
OTHER MASTERS OF EVIL.

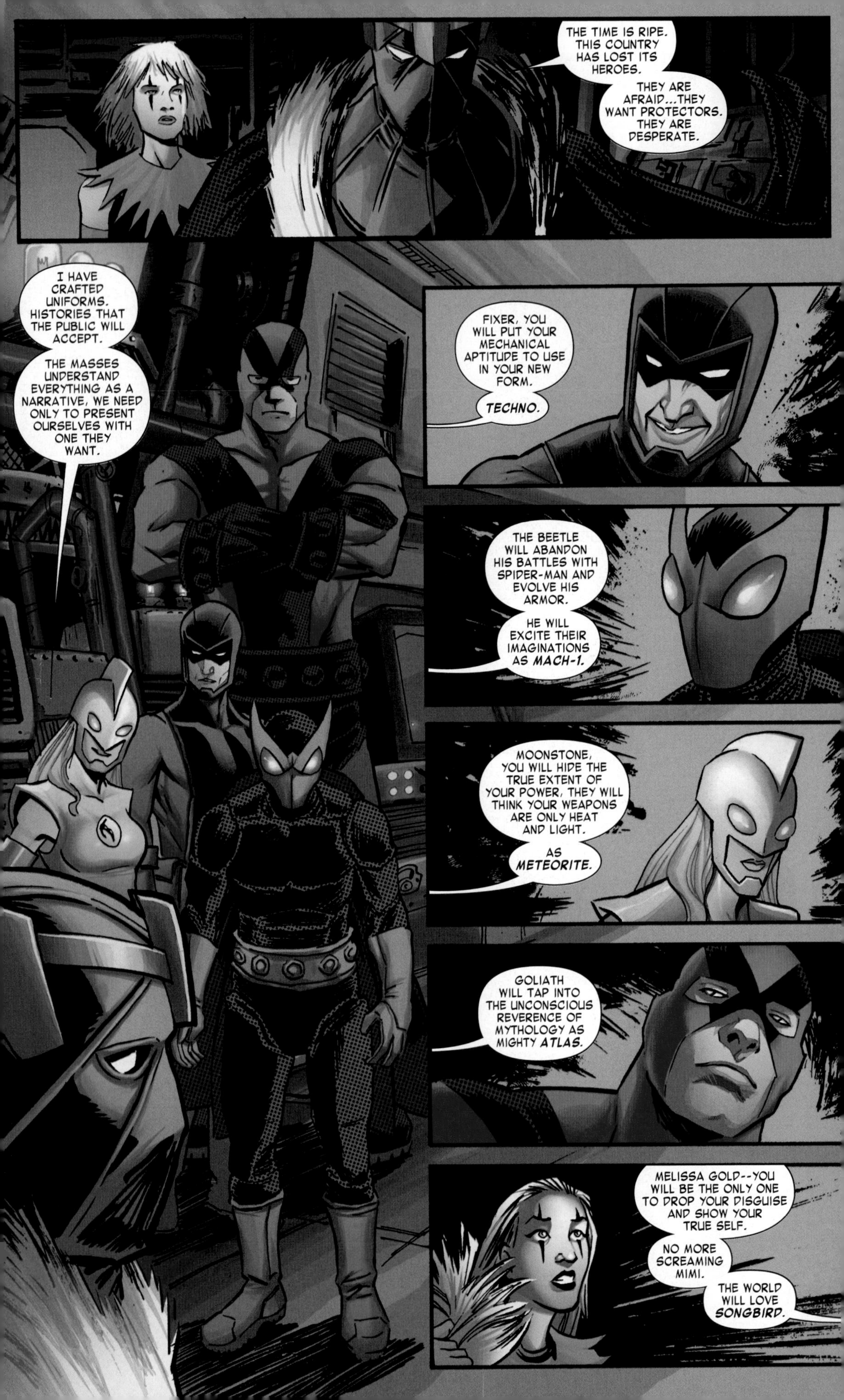
THE TIME IS RIPE. THIS COUNTRY HAS LOST ITS HEROES.
THEY ARE AFRAID...THEY WANT PROTECTORS. THEY ARE DESPERATE.
I HAVE CRAFTED UNIFORMS. HISTORIES THAT THE PUBLIC WILL ACCEPT.
THE MASSES UNDERSTAND EVERYTHING AS A NARRATIVE, WE NEED ONLY TO PRESENT OURSELVES WITH ONE THEY WANT.
FIXER, YOU WILL PUT YOUR MECHANICAL APTITUDE TO USE IN YOUR NEW FORM.
TECHNO.
THE BEETLE WILL ABANDON HIS BATTLES WITH SPIDER-MAN AND EVOLVE HIS ARMOR.
HE WILL EXCITE THEIR IMAGINATIONS AS MACH-1.
MOONSTONE, YOU WILL HIDE THE TRUE EXTENT OF YOUR POWER, THEY WILL THINK YOUR WEAPONS ARE ONLY HEAT AND LIGHT.
AS METEORITE.
GOLIATH WILL TAP INTO THE UNCONSCIOUS REVERENCE OF MYTHOLOGY AS MIGHTY ATLAS.
MELISSA GOLD--YOU WILL BE THE ONLY ONE TO DROP YOUR DISGUISE AND SHOW YOUR TRUE SELF.
NO MORE SCREAMING MIMI.
THE WORLD WILL LOVE SONGBIRD.

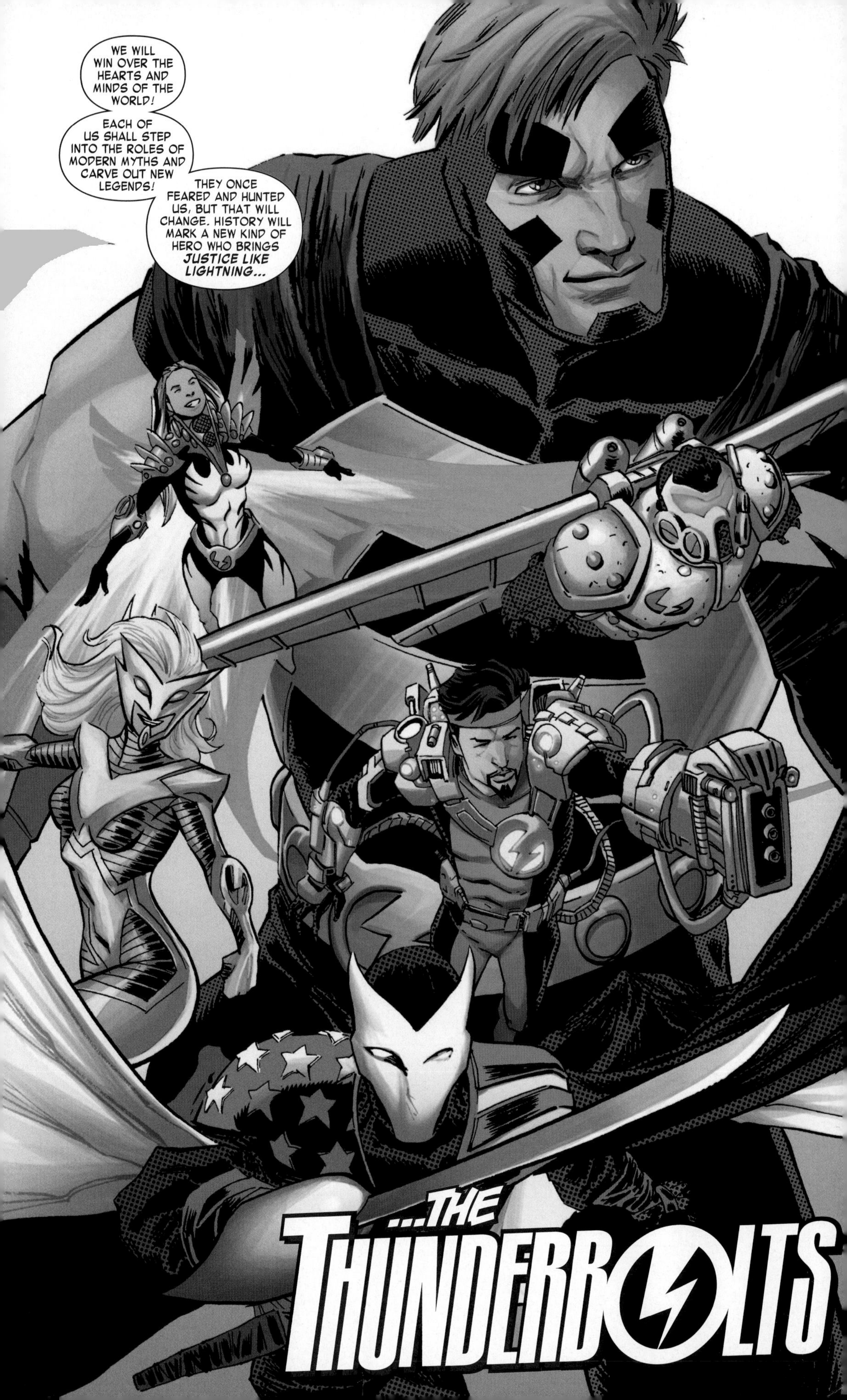
WE WILL WIN OVER THE HEARTS AND MINDS OF THE WORLD!
EACH OF US SHALL STEP INTO THE ROLES OF MODERN MYTHS AND CARVE OUT NEW LEGENDS!
THEY ONCE FEARED AND HUNTED US, BUT THAT WILL CHANGE. HISTORY WILL MARK A NEW KIND OF HERO WHO BRINGS *JUSTICE LIKE LIGHTNING...*
...THE
THUNDERBOLTS

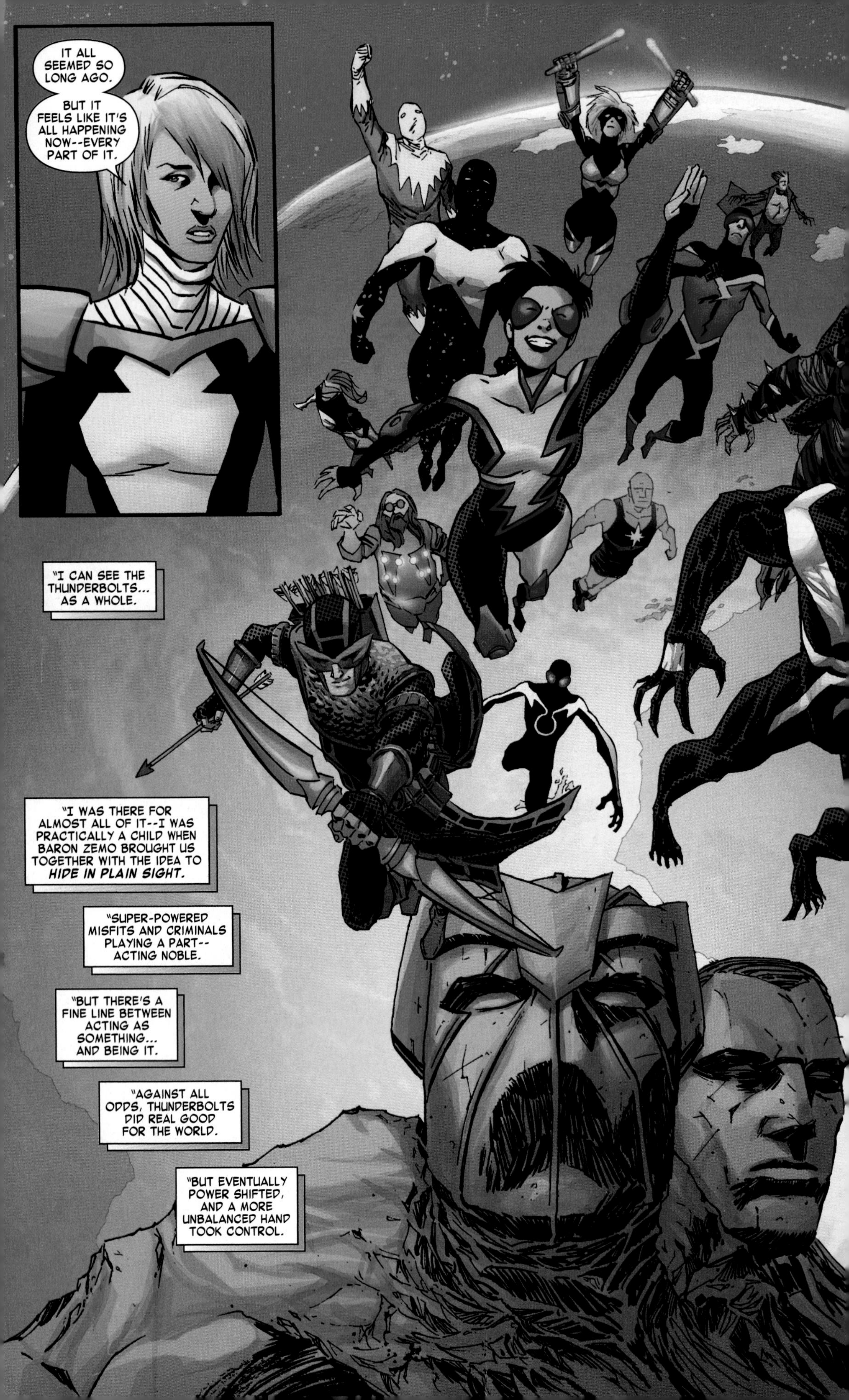

IT ALL SEEMED SO LONG AGO.
BUT IT FEELS LIKE IT'S ALL HAPPENING NOW--EVERY PART OF IT.
"I CAN SEE THE THUNDERBOLTS... AS A WHOLE.
"I WAS THERE FOR ALMOST ALL OF IT--I WAS PRACTICALLY A CHILD WHEN BARON ZEMO BROUGHT US TOGETHER WITH THE IDEA TO *HIDE IN PLAIN SIGHT.*
"SUPER-POWERED MISFITS AND CRIMINALS PLAYING A PART--ACTING NOBLE.
"BUT THERE'S A FINE LINE BETWEEN ACTING AS SOMETHING... AND BEING IT.
"AGAINST ALL ODDS, THUNDERBOLTS DID REAL GOOD FOR THE WORLD.
"BUT EVENTUALLY POWER SHIFTED, AND A MORE UNBALANCED HAND TOOK CONTROL.

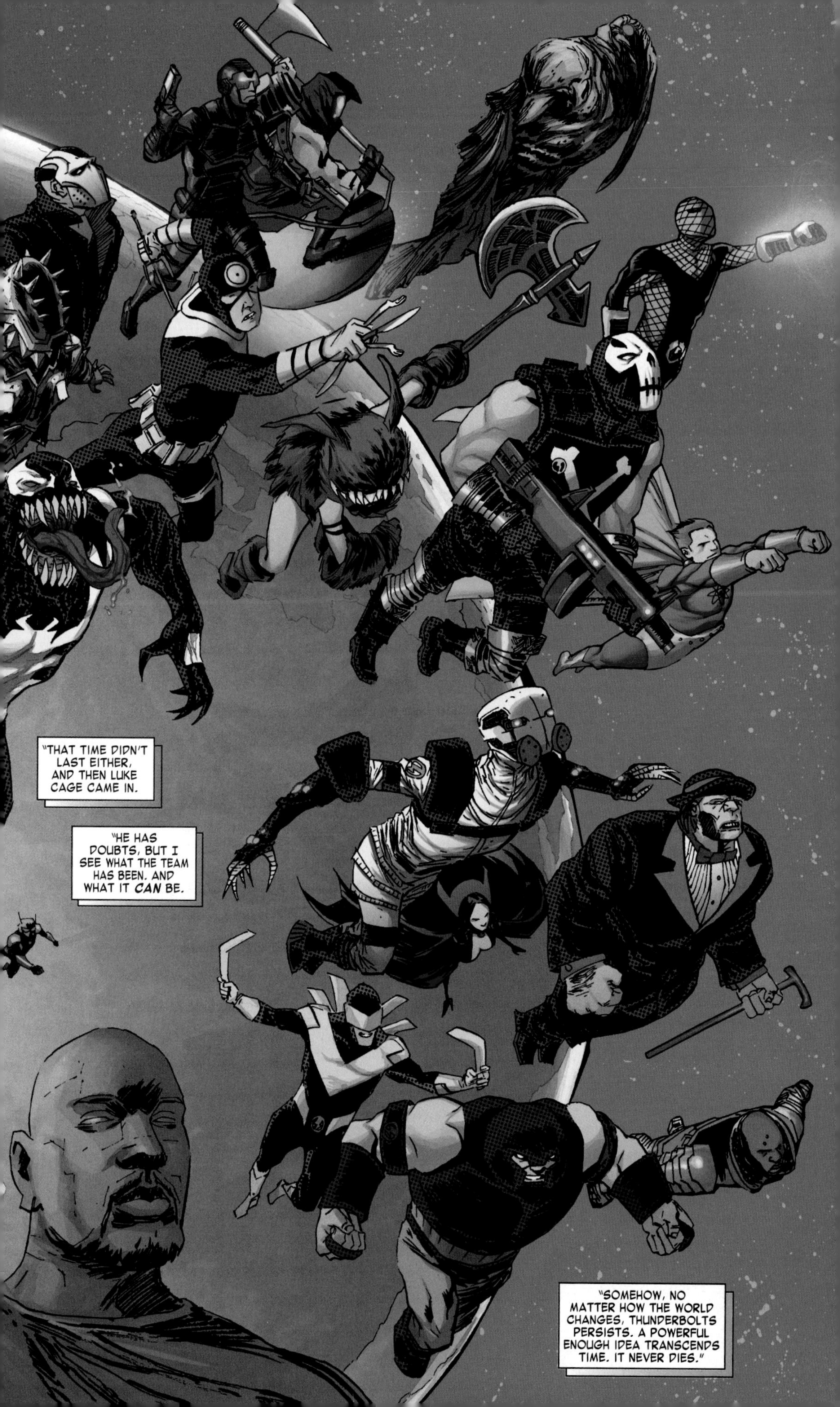

"THAT TIME DIDN'T LAST EITHER, AND THEN LUKE CAGE CAME IN.
"HE HAS DOUBTS, BUT I SEE WHAT THE TEAM HAS BEEN. AND WHAT IT *CAN* BE.
"SOMEHOW, NO MATTER HOW THE WORLD CHANGES, THUNDERBOLTS PERSISTS. A POWERFUL ENOUGH IDEA TRANSCENDS TIME. IT NEVER DIES."

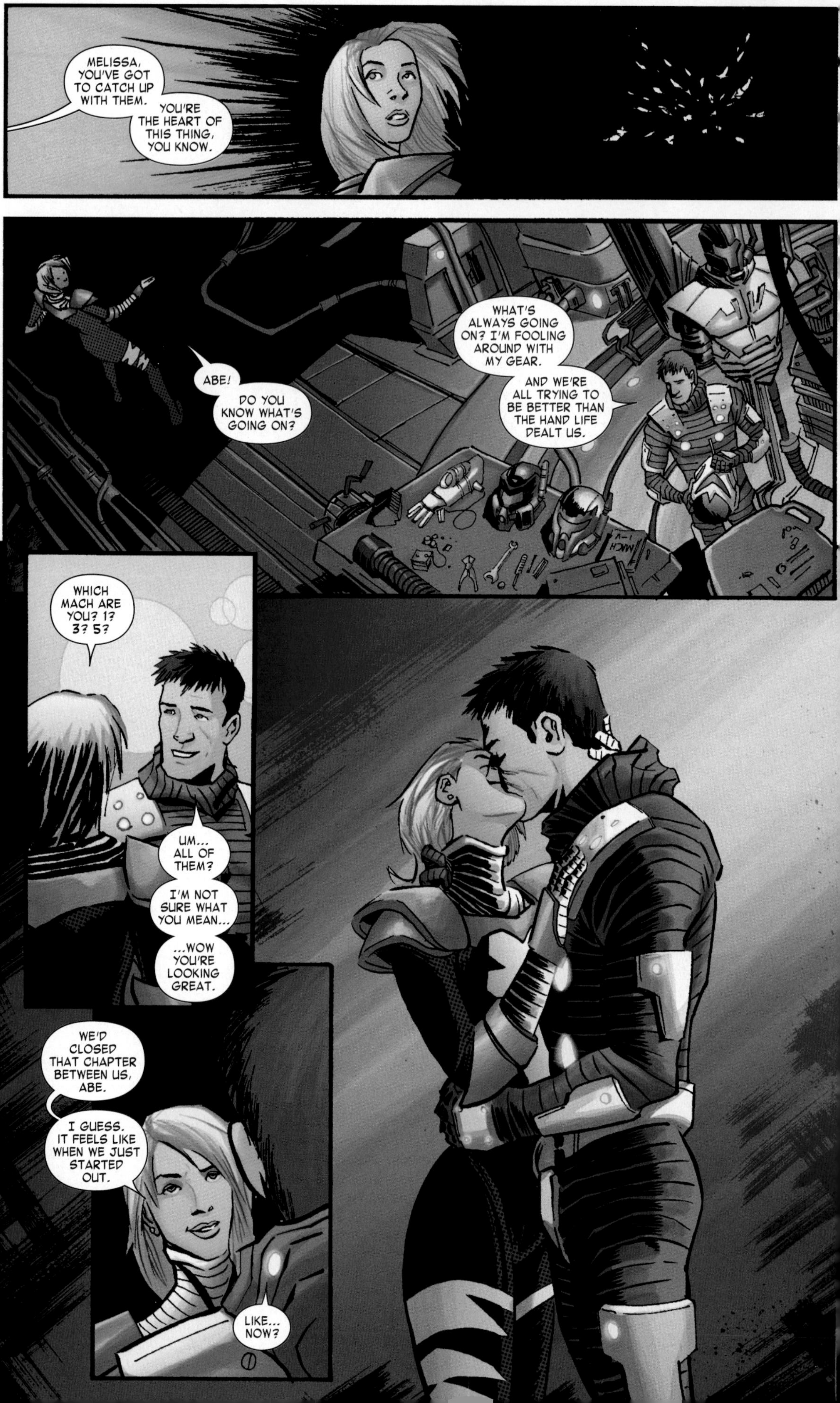
MELISSA, YOU'VE GOT TO CATCH UP WITH THEM.
YOU'RE THE HEART OF THIS THING, YOU KNOW.
ABE!
DO YOU KNOW WHAT'S GOING ON?
WHAT'S ALWAYS GOING ON? I'M FOOLING AROUND WITH MY GEAR.
AND WE'RE ALL TRYING TO BE BETTER THAN THE HAND LIFE DEALT US.
WHICH MACH ARE YOU? 1? 3? 5?
UM... ALL OF THEM?
I'M NOT SURE WHAT YOU MEAN...
...WOW YOU'RE LOOKING GREAT.
WE'D CLOSED THAT CHAPTER BETWEEN US, ABE.
I GUESS. IT FEELS LIKE WHEN WE JUST STARTED OUT.
LIKE... NOW?

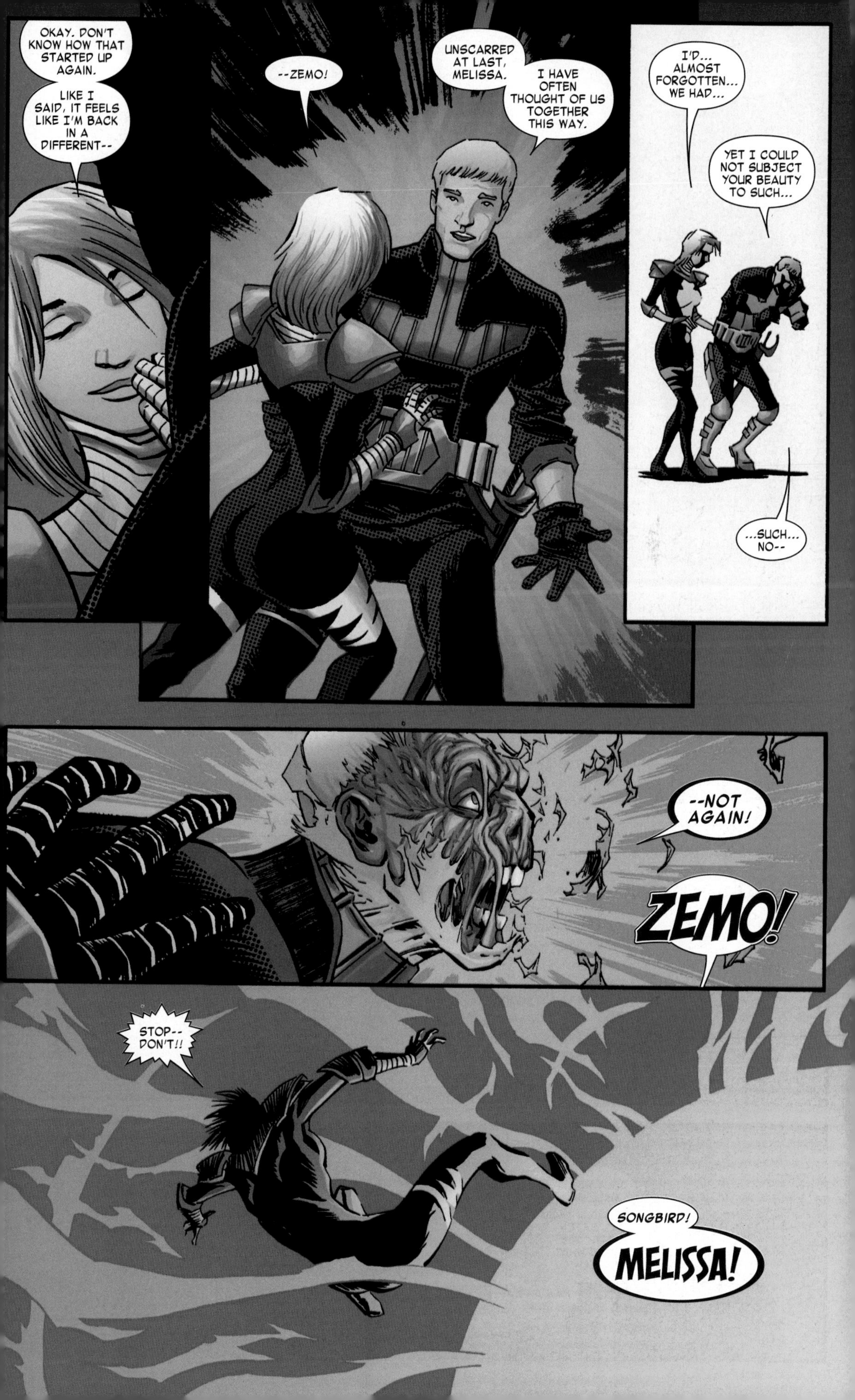
OKAY. DON'T KNOW HOW THAT STARTED UP AGAIN.
LIKE I SAID, IT FEELS LIKE I'M BACK IN A DIFFERENT--
--ZEMO!
UNSCARRED AT LAST, MELISSA.
I HAVE OFTEN THOUGHT OF US TOGETHER THIS WAY.
I'D... ALMOST FORGOTTEN... WE HAD...
YET I COULD NOT SUBJECT YOUR BEAUTY TO SUCH...
...SUCH... NO--
--NOT AGAIN!
ZEMO!
STOP-- DON'T!!
SONGBIRD!
MELISSA!

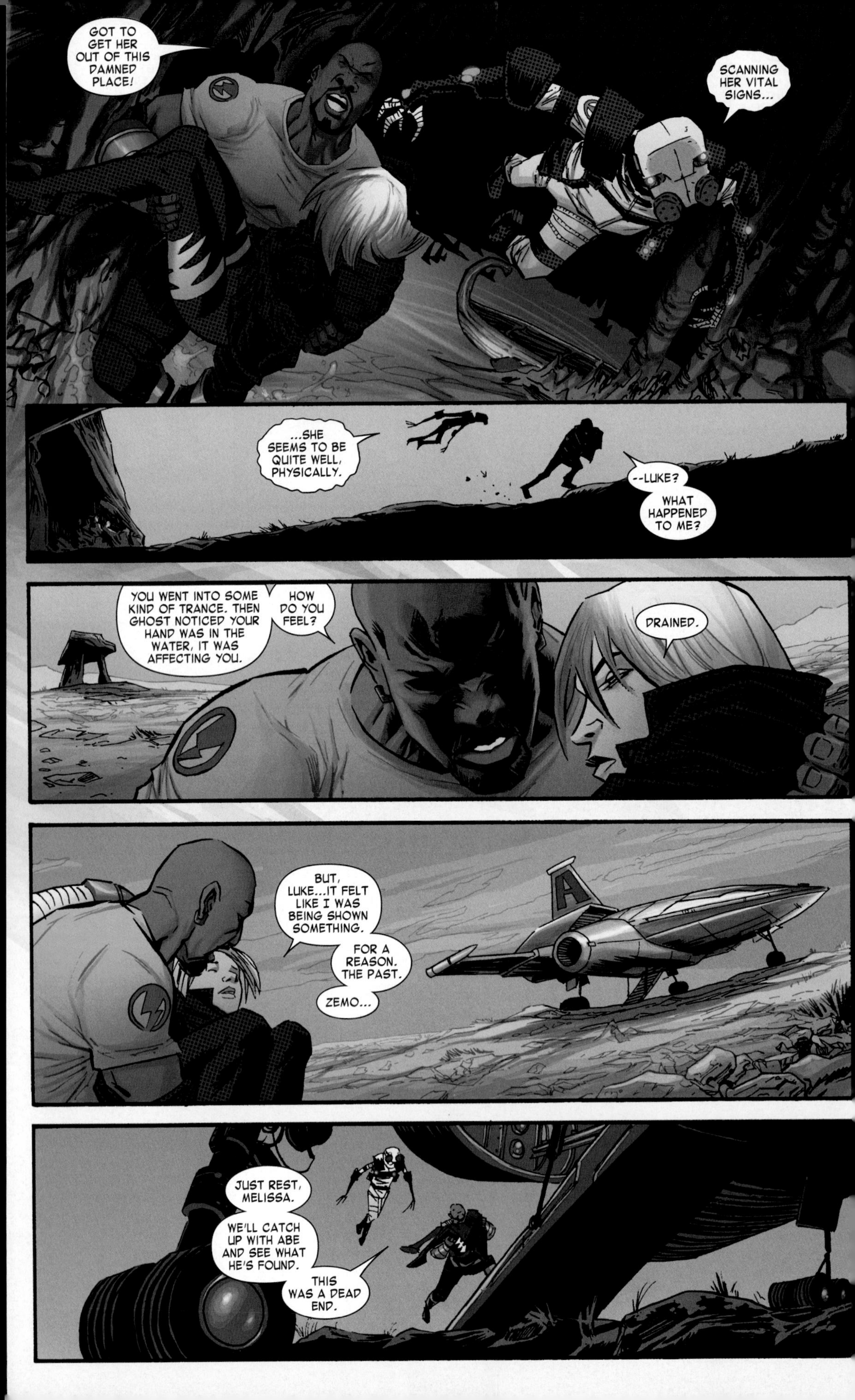
GOT TO GET HER OUT OF THIS DAMNED PLACE!
SCANNING HER VITAL SIGNS...
...SHE SEEMS TO BE QUITE WELL, PHYSICALLY.
--LUKE?
WHAT HAPPENED TO ME?
YOU WENT INTO SOME KIND OF TRANCE. THEN GHOST NOTICED YOUR HAND WAS IN THE WATER, IT WAS AFFECTING YOU.
HOW DO YOU FEEL?
DRAINED.
BUT, LUKE...IT FELT LIKE I WAS BEING SHOWN SOMETHING.
FOR A REASON. THE PAST.
ZEMO...
A
JUST REST, MELISSA.
WE'LL CATCH UP WITH ABE AND SEE WHAT HE'S FOUND.
THIS WAS A DEAD END.

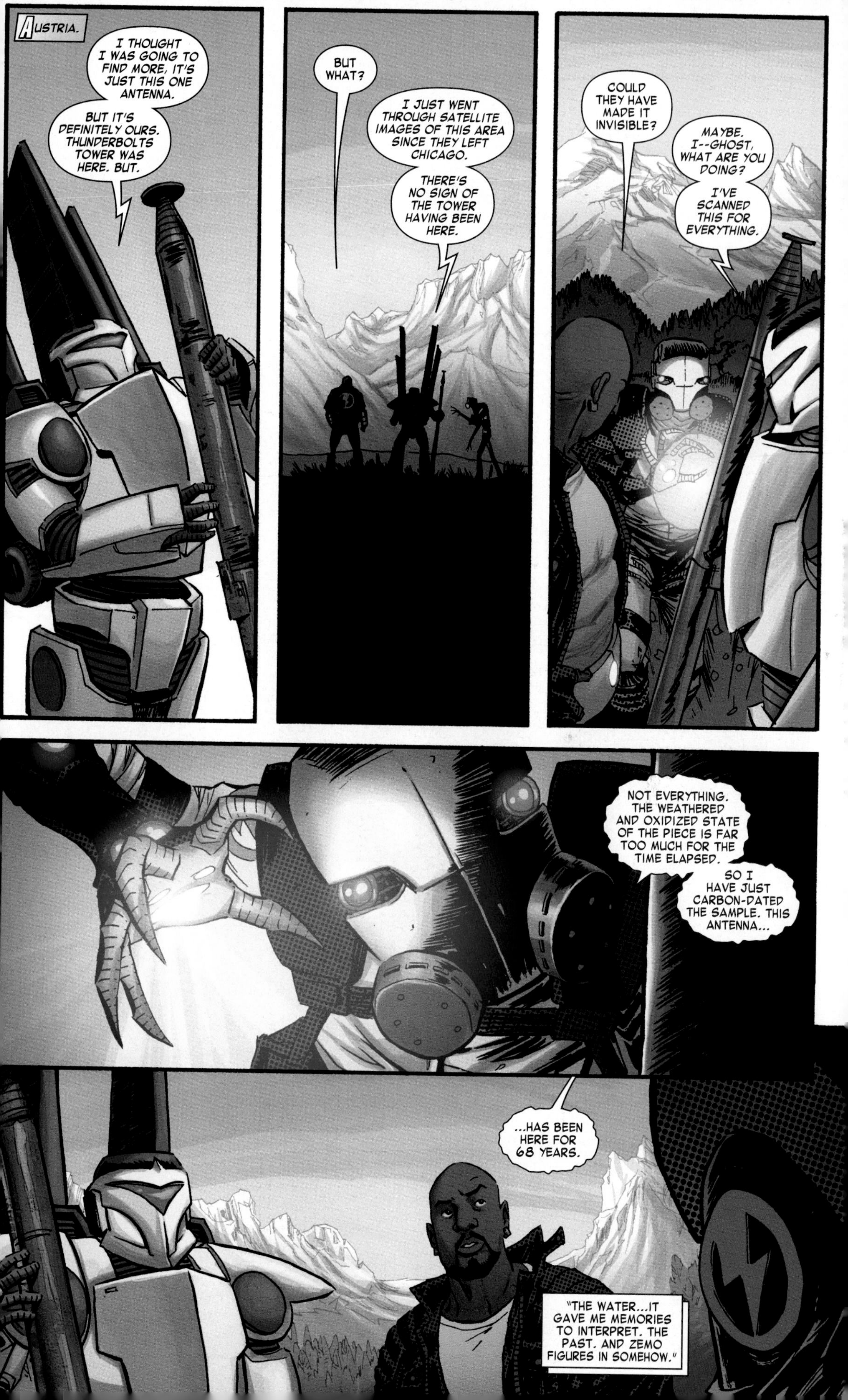
AUSTRIA.
I THOUGHT I WAS GOING TO FIND MORE, IT'S JUST THIS ONE ANTENNA.
BUT IT'S DEFINITELY OURS. THUNDERBOLTS TOWER WAS HERE. BUT.
BUT WHAT?
I JUST WENT THROUGH SATELLITE IMAGES OF THIS AREA SINCE THEY LEFT CHICAGO.
THERE'S NO SIGN OF THE TOWER HAVING BEEN HERE.
COULD THEY HAVE MADE IT INVISIBLE?
MAYBE. I--GHOST, WHAT ARE YOU DOING?
I'VE SCANNED THIS FOR EVERYTHING.
NOT EVERYTHING. THE WEATHERED AND OXIDIZED STATE OF THE PIECE IS FAR TOO MUCH FOR THE TIME ELAPSED.
SO I HAVE JUST CARBON-DATED THE SAMPLE. THIS ANTENNA...
...HAS BEEN HERE FOR 68 YEARS.
"THE WATER...IT GAVE ME MEMORIES TO INTERPRET. THE PAST. AND ZEMO FIGURES IN SOMEHOW."

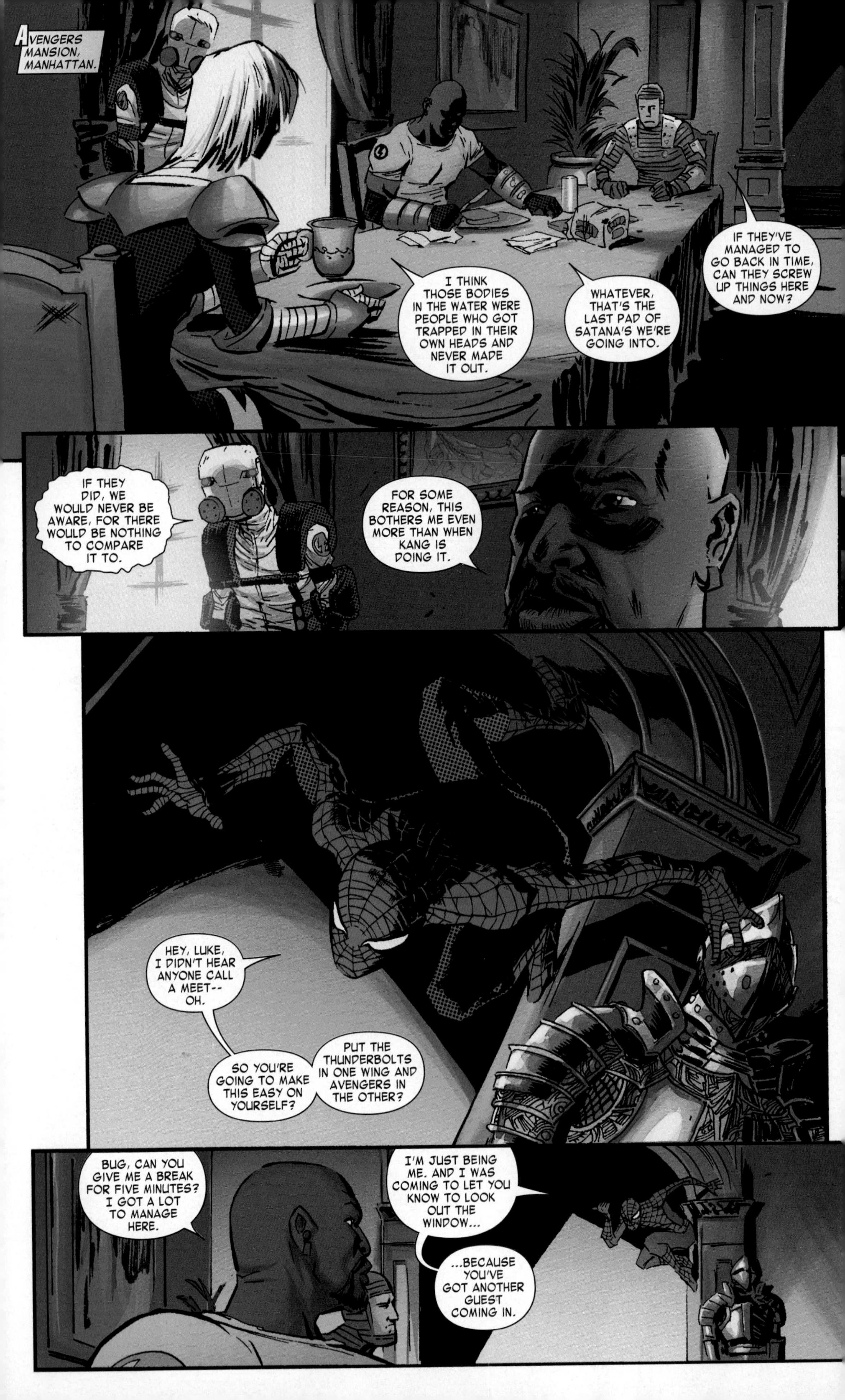
AVENGERS MANSION, MANHATTAN.
I THINK THOSE BODIES IN THE WATER WERE PEOPLE WHO GOT TRAPPED IN THEIR OWN HEADS AND NEVER MADE IT OUT.
WHATEVER, THAT'S THE LAST PAD OF SATANA'S WE'RE GOING INTO.
IF THEY'VE MANAGED TO GO BACK IN TIME, CAN THEY SCREW UP THINGS HERE AND NOW?
IF THEY DID, WE WOULD NEVER BE AWARE, FOR THERE WOULD BE NOTHING TO COMPARE IT TO.
FOR SOME REASON, THIS BOTHERS ME EVEN MORE THAN WHEN KANG IS DOING IT.
HEY, LUKE, I DIDN'T HEAR ANYONE CALL A MEET-- OH.
SO YOU'RE GOING TO MAKE THIS EASY ON YOURSELF?
PUT THE THUNDERBOLTS IN ONE WING AND AVENGERS IN THE OTHER?
BUG, CAN YOU GIVE ME A BREAK FOR FIVE MINUTES? I GOT A LOT TO MANAGE HERE.
I'M JUST BEING ME. AND I WAS COMING TO LET YOU KNOW TO LOOK OUT THE WINDOW...
...BECAUSE YOU'VE GOT ANOTHER GUEST COMING IN.

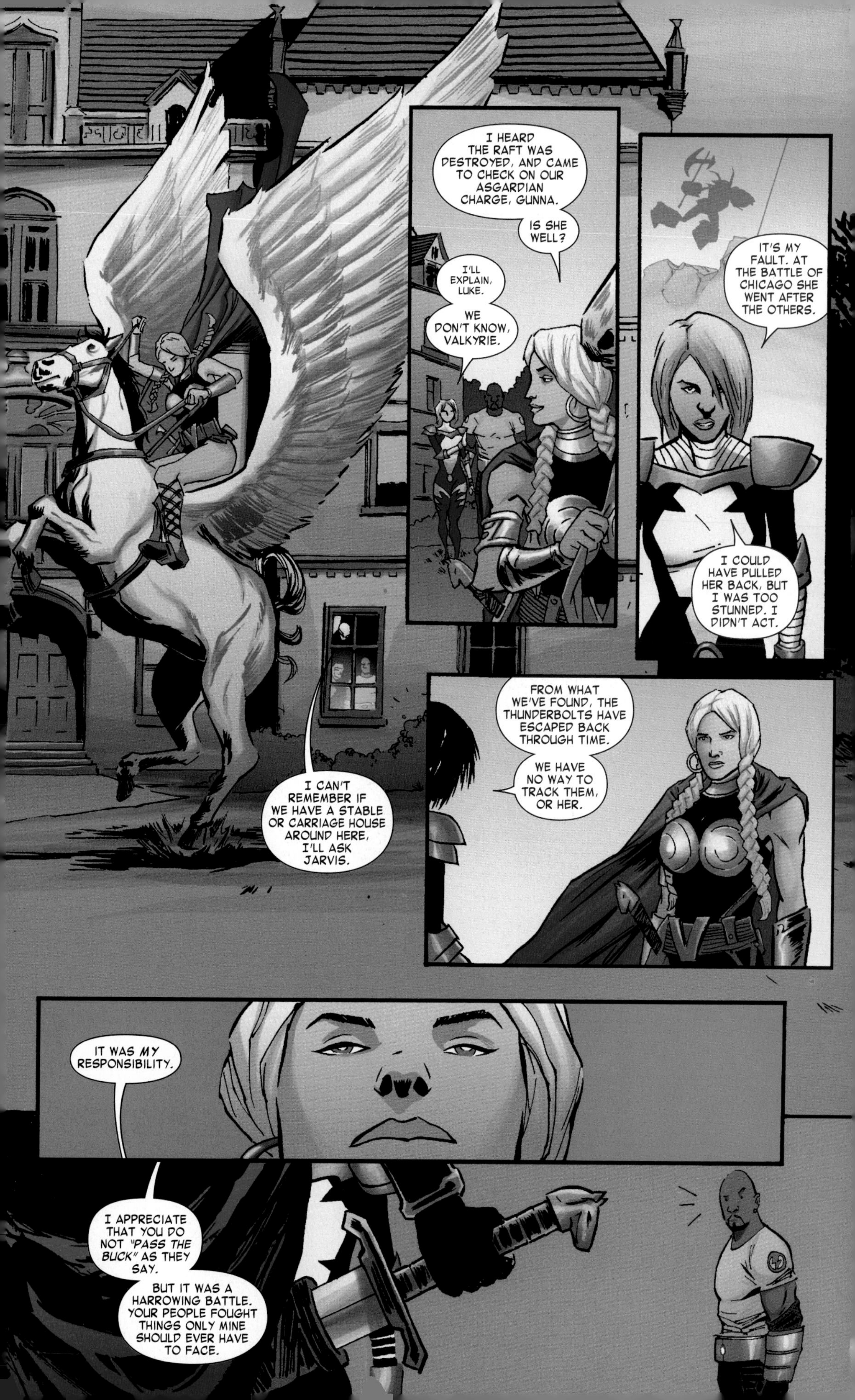
I HEARD THE RAFT WAS DESTROYED, AND CAME TO CHECK ON OUR ASGARDIAN CHARGE, GUNNA.
IS SHE WELL?
I'LL EXPLAIN, LUKE.
WE DON'T KNOW, VALKYRIE.
IT'S MY FAULT. AT THE BATTLE OF CHICAGO SHE WENT AFTER THE OTHERS.
I COULD HAVE PULLED HER BACK, BUT I WAS TOO STUNNED. I DIDN'T ACT.
I CAN'T REMEMBER IF WE HAVE A STABLE OR CARRIAGE HOUSE AROUND HERE, I'LL ASK JARVIS.
FROM WHAT WE'VE FOUND, THE THUNDERBOLTS HAVE ESCAPED BACK THROUGH TIME.
WE HAVE NO WAY TO TRACK THEM, OR HER.
IT WAS *MY* RESPONSIBILITY.
I APPRECIATE THAT YOU DO NOT *"PASS THE BUCK"* AS THEY SAY.
BUT IT WAS A HARROWING BATTLE. YOUR PEOPLE FOUGHT THINGS ONLY MINE SHOULD EVER HAVE TO FACE.

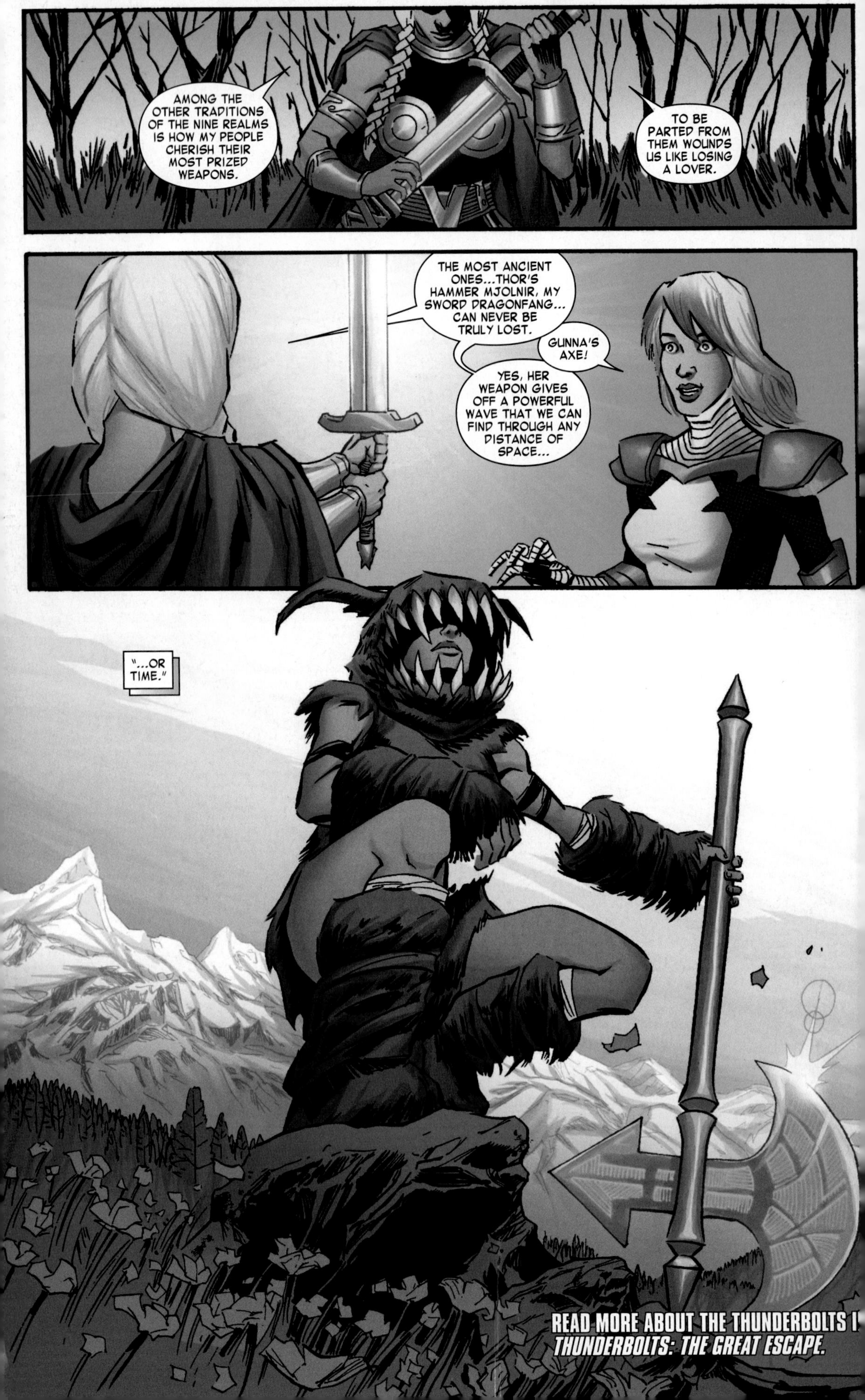
AMONG THE OTHER TRADITIONS OF THE NINE REALMS IS HOW MY PEOPLE CHERISH THEIR MOST PRIZED WEAPONS.
TO BE PARTED FROM THEM WOUNDS US LIKE LOSING A LOVER.
THE MOST ANCIENT ONES...THOR'S HAMMER MJOLNIR, MY SWORD DRAGONFANG... CAN NEVER BE TRULY LOST.
GUNNA'S AXE!
YES, HER WEAPON GIVES OFF A POWERFUL WAVE THAT WE CAN FIND THROUGH ANY DISTANCE OF SPACE...
"...OR TIME."
READ MORE ABOUT THE THUNDERBOLTS I
THUNDERBOLTS: THE GREAT ESCAPE.